P9-AOO-084

1st Edition

Frommer's

Israel

by Robert Ullian

Macmillan • USA

ABOUT THE AUTHOR

Educated at Amherst College and Columbia University, Robert Ullian is a writer whose work has appeared in *Esquire, Mademoiselle,* and *The Boston Phoenix.* A recipient of a National Endowment for the Arts grant in fiction, he has taught art and writing at Hampshire College and the University of Massachusetts in Amherst and is also the author of *Frommer's Walking Tours: Venice.*

MACMILLAN TRAVEL

A Simon & Schuster Macmillan Company
1633 Broadway
New York, NY 10019

Find us online at **http://www.mgr.com/travel** or
on America Online at **Keyword: Frommer's.**

ISBN 0-02860860-7
ISSN 1086-4024

Executive Editor: Alice Fellows
Production Editor: Michael Thomas
Design by Michele Laseau
Digital Cartography by Ortelius Design and Devorah Wilkenfeld
Maps copyright © by Simon & Schuster, Inc.

SPECIAL SALES

Bulk purchases (10+ copies) of Frommer's travel guides are available to corporations at special discounts. The Special Sales Department can produce custom editions to be used as premiums and/or for sales promotion to suit individual needs. Existing editions can be produced with custom cover imprints such as corporate logos. For more information write to: Special Sales, Simon & Schuster, 1633 Broadway, New York, NY 10019.

Manufactured in the United States of America

Contents

4 Getting to Know Jerusalem 77

5 What to See & Do in Jerusalem 132

6 The West Bank 188

List of Maps

This book is dedicated to the hope for better understanding among all the peoples of the Middle East.

ACKNOWLEDGEMENTS

Special gratitude goes to my research assistant **Sadek Shweiki.** Born in Jerusalem and educated at Hampshire College where he majored in psychology and intercultural communication, Sadek brings a careful understanding of Middle Eastern and American societies to this book.

I would like to thank Zahara Schatz of the Jerusalem Artists House and Michael Goldstein of the Israel Museum, who were kind enough to offer encouragement and very valuable logistical help. I would also like to thank Ilana Nadir, Horace Richter, Nader Abu Khalid, Marietta Samuel, Motti Belinco, Wendy Geri, David Perlmutter, Becky Cohen, Ellen Oppenheim, Danielle Conhaim, and Howard Isenberg, all of whom contributed their ideas, enthusiasm and efforts to this book. Finally, I would like to thank my neighbors in Abu Tor, Jerusalem, who made me so welcome while I lived and worked there, and whenever I returned. I hope readers of this book will find such friends in this very special land.

AN INVITATION TO THE READER

In researching this book, we discovered many wonderful places—hotels, restaurants, shops, and more. We're sure you'll find others. Please tell us about them, so we can share the information with your fellow travelers in upcoming editions. If you were disappointed with a recommendation, we'd love to know that, too. Please write to:

Robert Ullian
Frommer's Israel, 1st Edition
Macmillan Travel
1633 Broadway
New York, NY 10019

AN ADDITIONAL NOTE

Please be advised that travel information is subject to change at any time—and this is especially true of prices. We therefore suggest that you write or call ahead for confirmation when making your travel plans. The authors, editors, and publisher cannot be held responsible for the experiences of readers while traveling. Your safety is important to us, however, so we encourage you to stay alert and be aware of your surroundings. Keep a close eye on cameras, purses, and wallets, all favorite targets of thieves and pickpockets.

WHAT THE SYMBOLS MEAN

✪ Frommer's Favorites

Hotels, restaurants, attractions, and entertainment you shouldn't miss.

⑤ Super-Special Values

Hotels and restaurants that offer great value for your money.

The following abbreviations are used for credit cards:

AE	American Express	EU	Eurocard
CB	Carte Blanche	JCB	Japan Credit Bank
DC	Diners Club	MC	MasterCard
ER	enRoute	V	Visa

TELEPHONE NUMBER CHANGES

Israel is in the process of converting from six-digit to seven-digit telephone numbers, to take place during or after the summer of 1996. Where new numbers are available, we have included them in this book. If you dial a number that has been changed, a Hebrew language message will be followed by instructions in English.

In Jerusalem (area code 02) and in the Negev (area code 07) all six-digit numbers that begin with 3, 6, or 8 will become seven-digit numbers by adding an initial 5; numbers beginning with 2, 3, 4, or 7 will add an initial 6. In Tel Aviv (area code 03), numbers that begin with 58 will become seven-digit numbers by adding an initial 6. The Tourist Information Office in each region should be checked for information on additional local telephone number changes.

The Best of Israel

Israel is incredibly dramatic and diverse, the more so when you realize the entire country is the size of New Jersey. You find yourself in the silent, haunting desertscape near the Dead Sea, spotting ibexes on the rims of desolate, sheer cliffs that are dotted with caves like those in which the Dead Sea Scrolls lay hidden for more than 18 centuries. Just 90 minutes away is the 19th-century East European ghetto world of Jerusalem's orthodox Mea Shearim quarter and the labyrinthine medieval Arab bazaars of the Old City. Less than an hour by car to the west, and it's skyscrapers, surfboards, and bikinis on the beach at Tel Aviv; 2 hours to the north, and you're exploring ruined Crusader castles in the green forests of the Galilee mountains.

When I first came to Israel in 1966, it was as a student backpacker fresh from a 2-month odyssey across southern Europe. My student charter flight from Athens had taken a record 47 hours (including an unscheduled landing in Cyprus), a severe *hamsin* (heat wave) had blasted in from the desert the day I arrived, and compared to Provence, Venice, or the Aegean Islands, Tel Aviv was unlovely, hot, and soggy. Worse yet, Jerusalem, the country's crowning jewel, was still divided and the exotic Old City inaccessible to tourists from Israel. It took a few days until I understood that Israel was a different kind of travel experience from the picture-perfect places I had visited. It was new, clearly in the process of building itself, filled with people who could speak English and who wanted to tell their stories; it was a place that challanged you to use vision rather than eyesight to enjoy its powerful beauty. For all its newness and energy, it was a place that at both expected and unexpected moments, could also be mysterious and spiritual.

Over the next two decades I visited Israel nine times, sometimes for an entire summer or a semester of study, sometimes for a conference, and once en route to Iran and India. In 1985, I arranged to work on a 1-year experimental education project in Jerusalem. I stayed for 6 years and came to know the country as my second home.

My experiences in Israel as a visitor and long-term resident have given me the opportunity to see the country from a number of vantage points. Twenty-five years ago, the country was an austere, no-frills society—Israelis lived with few luxuries. Today, the country's economy is booming, the standard of living has skyrocketed, and many surveys rank Israel's per capita income among the top 20 national per capita incomes in the world. Israel is becoming a nation with a lively sense of style and a taste for the good life. Luxury and better-quality hotel accommodations and resorts are going up all over the country, and visitors will find an interesting array of fine restaurants and shopping opportunities that are geared to Israeli society at large rather than to tourists. With the Israeli–Jordanian and Israeli–Egyptian peace treaties, the best of a journey to Israel can also easily include an excursion to the fabulous ancient Nabatean city of Petra in Jordan; a diving or snorkeling odyssey of the coral reefs off the Sinai Peninsula; or a jaunt over to Egypt to see the pyramids and explore Khan-el-Khalili—the legendary bazaar of Cairo.

This book will help direct you, as an independent traveler, to the best and most authentic experiences Israel has to offer. Israel is an easy country to explore and get close to if you know the ropes. We hope to lead you to experiences that will be both personal and rewarding.

1 The Best Travel Experiences

- **Visiting the Dome of the Rock and the Temple Mount** (Jerusalem): Built by the early Islamic rulers of Jerusalem in A.D. 691 on the site of the Temple of Solomon, the Dome of the Rock is one of the most beautiful structures ever created. It is the crown that rests upon a 4,000-year tradition of Western monotheistic belief. One can spend hours on the Temple Mount soaking up the atmosphere and the dazzling views. You might first visit the Temple Mount on a tour, but come back and experience the power of this extraordinary place on your own. See chapter 5.

- **Exploring the Eastern Shore of the Sea of Galilee:** The Sea of Galilee is Israel's greatest natural treasure, and its lyrical shores were the birthplace of Christianity. It is also almost miraculous in its loveliness—a sapphire/turquoise freshwater lake surrounded by the mountains of the Galilee and the Golan. The eastern shore is less developed and gives you a better chance to feel the lake's poetry. There are eucalyptus-shaded beaches where you can have a late afternoon swim and picnic and watch the silver and lavender twilight descend behind the mountains on the western shore of the lake, which sparkles with the delicate lights of farm settlements and kibbutzim. See chapter 10.

- **An Evening Stroll Through Old Jaffa:** The beautifully restored casbah of Old Jaffa is probably the most romantic urban spot in the country, filled with galleries, shops, cafes, restaurants, and vistas of minarets and Crusader ruins against the sunset and the sea. See chapter 7.

- **Sampling the Music Scene:** Israel has an oversupply of magnificent musicians; even suburbs of Tel Aviv and small cities like Beersheva are home to orchestras that would be the envy of many world capitals. You may find the Israel Philharmonic Orchestra performing at Tel Aviv's Mann Auditorium, or the acclaimed Rishon-Le-Zion Symphony Orchestra (filled with new immigrants from the former Soviet Union) giving a visiting concert at the Haifa Auditorium, but you may also find an outdoor performance of *Carmen* in the Valley of the Sultan's Pool, just at the foot of the walls of Jerusalem; a night of Mozart at the 2,000-year-old Roman amphitheater beside the sea at Caesaria; Yemenite wedding singers or Arabic oudists performing at free municipal concerts inside Jerusalem's Jaffa Gate Citadel; African-American blues and jazz musicians from the Hebrew Israelite community of Dimona in the Negev at clubs in Tel Aviv; or you might visit festivals like the Chamber Music Days at Kibbutz Kfar Blum or the Jacob's Ladder Folk Festival on the shores of the Sea of Galilee.

- **Snorkeling in the Red Sea:** The Red Sea, with its coral reefs, is an awe-inspiring natural aquarium, rich with tropical marine life and one of the best places on earth for fabulous scuba diving and snorkeling. At the Coral Beach Nature Reserve just south of Eilat, there's enough to fascinate experts, yet wonders are accessible to all levels of swimmers—dazzling fish abound even in waist-deep water. Experienced divers can scuba dive at the Coral Island, a few miles down the coast from Eilat, or make an excursion into the Egyptian Sinai to the even more extraordinary reefs off Nuweiba, Dahab, and the legendary Ras Mohammed at Sharm-el-Sheik. See chapter 11.
- **Freewheeling in the Galilee:** This is the place to rent a car for a few days and explore Israel's most beautiful countryside—forested mountains, rushing streams, waterfalls, and oceans of wildflowers in late winter and early spring. Among the region's treasures are ruined Roman-era synagogues, Crusader castles, ancient churches, and the walled casbah of Akko beside the Mediterranean. There are also the warm, sparkling waters of the Sea of Galilee to swim in from April to early November. Israel's Kibbutz Bed-and-Breakfast Network, and programs like *Bed and Breakfast with Israeli Arab Families in the Galilee*, make it possible to find affordable, interesting double rooms that will add to the pleasure of your wanderings. Other Galilee options range from country guest ranches and Christian hospices to five-star highrise hotels. See chapter 10.
- **Journeying into the Past at Mea Shearim:** Mea Shearim is the Hassidic Jewish quarter of Jerusalem, little more than a century old, but in the dress and customs of its inhabitants, and in its tangle of courtyards and alleyways, it is a miraculously surviving fragment of the world of East European Jewry that disappeared forever into the Holocaust. A visitor to Mea Shearim must behave almost like an unobtrusive dreamer wandering the past; nothing in the neighborhood can be scrutinized too intensely (residents will not permit you to stare at them or photograph them, nor will they allow anything resembling a tour group to troop their streets). Many visitors will revere the discipline and religious devotion evident in Mea Shearim; others will be troubled by its many constraints. But a walk through these streets will give you insight into the powerful traditions that continue to make Israel unique. See chapter 5.
- **Touching the Desert:** These are not just endless sandy wastes: The deserts of Israel encompass the unworldly and ethereal Dead Sea, the mysterious, abandoned Nabatean cities of Avdat and Shivta, the haunting fortress of Masada, canyon oases, and vast erosion craters that are geological encyclopedias of cataclysms in past eons. These landscapes were the crucible in which monotheism was born. Don't let the desert be just a 45-minute ride on a tour bus from Jerusalem. If you can, spend the night at a guesthouse or hostel near Masada before you make the ascent. Or join an overnight lama trek in the Ramon Crater. Walk alone under the stars; listen to the desert wind in the dark; watch dawn levitate over the Dead Sea; and hear the awesome quiet of sun and rock and time.

2 The Best Luxury Hotels

There was a time when Jerusalem's King David Hotel was the only hotel worth mentioning in all of Israel. The hotel scene is presently in the process of a truly massive change.

- **The King David Hotel** (Jerusalem, ☎ 02/251-111): Built in 1930 during the British Mandate, the King David has outlasted the British Empire and continues to sail on, immaculate, elegant, and up-to-date in every way. The Nubian, fez-adorned lobby attendents of the 1930s are no longer here, but the King David is thick with atmosphere and ambience, and VIPs from Henry Kissinger and Warren Christopher to Barbra Streisand and Bob Dylan seem to pop up here. The gardened swimming pool and views of the walls of the Old City are a real plus. See chapter 4.

- **Eilat Princess Hotel** (Eilat, ☎ 07/365-555): Opened in 1993, this hotel is officially the most expensive in the country (although, as with most Israeli hotels, there are discounts available). Built into a hillside facing the Red Sea a few miles south of downtown Eilat, the Princess is a self-contained world of swimming pools, recreational facilities, restaurants, discos, and desert activities. It also established a new level of style in Israeli hotel design, with guest rooms furnished and decorated in French, tropical Philippine, Chinese, and other motifs that could be worthy of a page in *Architectural Digest*. See chapter 11.

- **American Colony Hotel** (Jerusalem, ☎ 02/279-777): This beautiful, atmospheric, gardened enclave began its existence as a pasha's villa in the 19th century. As an international meeting place between the worlds of East and West Jerusalem, it attracts journalists, writers, archeologists, and all sorts of VIPs, and is probably the most savvy, romantic spot in the Middle East with the possible exception of Rick's Cafe in *Casablanca*. Some of the suites, furnished with antiques and traditional crafts, are as splendid as anything you'll find in the region, yet prices are comparatively reasonable (standard rooms are not exceptional). The hotel's Saturday afternoon luncheon buffet is famous throughout the country. See chapter 4.

- **Tel Aviv Sheraton Hotel & Towers** (☎ 03/528-6222): This is the most fun of Tel Aviv's five-star hotels—right on the beach, but also just steps away from the city's restaurant and gallery district, so you have the unusual feel of being in an urban resort. Restaurant services here are probably the best of any hotel in the country, topped off with the Twelve Tribes Restaurant, serving an elegant, luxurious menu that is both inventive and kosher. The direct Mediterranean views from many of the guest rooms, complete with dazzling sunsets, are a plus, as is the very efficient business center and its services. See chapter 7.

- **Dan Carmel Hotel** (Haifa, ☎ 04/306-211): With sweeping views from its site at the top of the Carmel Range, as well as a careful staff and a relaxing, gardened pool enclave for guests to enjoy, this hotel, built in the 1950s, has aged gracefully. The better category of guest rooms, newly renovated and with views of the bay, are beautifully decorated and well worth the extra money. Lower-category rooms are still furnished and decorated in a style that recalls the Eisenhower era. See chapter 9.

- **Isrotel Royal Beach Hotel** (Eilat, ☎ 800/368-888 in the U.S.): Brand new and Isrotel's masterpiece property, this hotel is set on a palm tree–dotted bathing beach in Eilat itself, within strolling range of much of the city. Architecturally, the Royal Beach is a pleasure, with open public areas and glass corridors in its upper stories that are designed to access spectacular vistas of the city and the surrounding countryside you might not normally see. Guest rooms are beautiful, stylish, and each faces directly onto the Red Sea. See chapter 11.

- **Hyatt Regency Jerusalem** (Jerusalem, ☎ 02/331-234): At the moment, this stands as the best and most architecturally interesting of the newer mega hotels in Jerusalem; it was designed by David Resnick, whose other creations include the Mormon Center on the Mount of Olives, and many of Hebrew University's more famous structures. Beautiful vistas of the city, excellent fitness and recreation facilities, a thoughtful, energetic staff, and good in-house restaurants are big advantages. See chapter 4.

- **Tel Aviv Hilton** (☎ 03/520-2222): With an unequaled staff, business center, and guest services, the Hilton, built in the 1950s and well maintained, is the doyenne of Tel Aviv's beachfront hotels. Suites and better-category rooms are beautifully furnished and decorated; the sheltered beach offers a resort atmosphere, but the kosher sushi bar (the only one in Tel Aviv) and the availability of Japanese breakfasts hint at the Hilton's role as a center for business as well as tourism exchanges between Asia and the Middle East. See chapter 7.
- **Radisson Moriah Plaza Dead Sea** (☎ 07/584-221): Currently the most complete of the Dead Sea spa hotels, the Radisson Moriah Plaza is also the most luxurious available at this remote location. Although it will soon be overtaken in terms of size and luxury by the new Hyatt Hotel at Ein Bokek, the Radisson Moriah's location right on the Dead Sea, with its own spacious private beach, cannot be matched by the Hyatt, which is not directly on the beach. The atmosphere is quiet and oriented toward desert activities and therapeutic health programs. See chapter 11.

3 The Best Value Hotels

This selection of hotel choices runs from splurges to economy strategies; each establishment offers something special.

- **Three Arches Hotel at the YMCA** (Jerusalem, ☎ 02/257-111): This is in no way your average YMCA; instead, Jerusalem's YMCA is a respected hotel frequented by many savvy travelers. For $110 you end up in a well-appointed double in an atmospheric landmark (designed by the same architect who designed New York's Empire State Building), right across the street from the famed King David Hotel. Remember, you'd pay three or four times as much across the street! See chapter 4.
- **Vered Ha Galil Guest Farm** (Galilee, ☎ 06/935-785): Set in the hills a few miles north of the Sea of Galilee, with sweeping vistas of the countryside, this intimate, family-run place began as a simple horseback riding lodge and over four decades has slowly been turned into a small garden of Eden. It offers a variety of rustic, charming accommodations and well-informed, personal attention; you don't have to come here for riding, but if you do, the programs are probably the best in the country. See chapter 10.
- **Jerusalem Inn Guest House** (Jerusalem, ☎ 02/252-757): Just a short walk from the Old City, and a block and a half from Zion Square and the bustling Ben Yehuda and Yoel Salomon malls, this small hotel offers tidy, no-frills doubles (with a touch of style as well as excellent beds!) for $50–$68 depending on the time of year. Bathless doubles go for less, and you can arrange breakfast downstairs at Eucalyptus, one of Jerusalem's best restaurants. See chapter 4.
- **Gordon Inn** (Tel Aviv, ☎ 03/523-8239): Another of the new breed of simple, well-located, clean and bright little hotels, the Gordon Inn Guest House is a long block inland from the beach in the heart of a neighborhood filled with smart shops and art galleries that's a world away from the sleaze surrounding many other frugal Tel Aviv hostelries. See chapter 7.
- **Isaac Taylor Youth Hostel** (☎ 07/584-349): Right at the base of Masada, overlooking the Dead Sea, this large, modern Israel Youth Hostel Association establishment allows you to overnight in the desert and make the ascent to Masada at dawn. Mobbed in summer and Jewish holidays, midweek during off-season, you can often arrange a private double with bath for $45. See chapter 11.

- **Church of Scotland Center Guest House** (Tiberias, ☎ 06/723-769): With its 19th-century buildings, beautiful terraces, and overgrown gardens looking out on the Sea of Galilee, this well-run guesthouse seems almost like a villa on the Italian coast, and welcomes visitors of all faiths. Rooms have recently been redone; doubles rent for $70. See chapter 10.

- **Rimon Inn** (Safed, ☎ 06/920-665): In a country with few really romantic, atmospheric hotels, this upper-moderate-range inn, synthesized from an ensemble of beautiful buidings from Ottoman times, is a real winner and an example of what might be done elsewhere in the country. A stay here helps make the often elusive magic of Safed more tangible. See chapter 10.

- **Radisson Moriah Plaza** (Tel Aviv, ☎ 03/527-1515): This five-star hotel is right on the beach, with newly renovated interiors, and if you buy the Radisson Moriah Hotels 9-Night Package, you can book a double for $95 to $140 a night, depending on the season. A luxury hotel on the beach can turn Tel Aviv into a truly wonderful city, and the Radisson Moriah Hotels Packages (see chapter 3), which let you plan an itinerary around Radisson Moriah Hotels in Jerusalem, Tiberias, Tel Aviv, Eilat, and the Dead Sea, are the cheapest possible way to have five-star accommodations in Israel. See chapter 7.

- **Ein Gev Holiday Village** (Sea of Galilee, ☎ 06/758-027): At the Ein Gev Kibbutz, with bungalows, caravans, and basic doubles set in eucalyptus and date palm groves right on the shores of the Sea of Galilee, this is a paradisical place to unwind and swim the warm waters of the lake. The kibbutz runs an excellent fish restaurant a mile down the road. See chapter 10.

- **Riviera Apartment Hotel** (Eilat, ☎ 800/552-0141 in the U.S.): A block from the beach, built around a pool, units here can accommodate two to four people, and are equipped with kitchenettes, TVs, and other useful amenities. Although not a kibbutz guesthouse, a double here can be booked as part of the Kibbutz Guest House 7-Night Package Plan, the most affordable way to have accommodations in costly Eilat. See chapter 11.

- **St. Mark's Lutheran Guest House** (Jerusalem, ☎ 02/285-107): Beautiful, atmospheric, and immaculate, with gardens above the main Arab bazaar, this is the best possible place to stay in the Old City, and one of the most remarkable hotels in the country. Depending on the value of the German mark, a double could run from $70 to $75. See chapter 4.

- **Jerusalem Hotel** (East Jerusalem, ☎ 02/271-356): A small place run by a well-informed, attentive family, the Jerusalem Hotel offers a pleasant garden restaurant with live music a number of times a week, and a general atmosphere that makes it seem like a more affordable version of the renowned American Colony Hotel. See chapter 4.

- **Jerusalem Tower Hotel** (Jerusalem, ☎ 02/252-161): A well-run four-star hotel located on the upper floors of a highrise. You are right in the center of everything here—restaurants, cafes, window shopping—but you're high above the street noise, and with luck, you'll have a dazzling view. It's $40–$60 for a double (5-night maximum stay) on El Al's Sunsational Package. See chapter 4.

- **St. Andrew's Hospice** (Jerusalem, ☎ 02/732-401): One of the most dramatic and atmospheric sites in West Jerusalem, on a vista-sweeping hilltop overlooking the Old City, this Church of Scotland guesthouse offers simple rooms in an interesting 1930s-style building, and a hearty, welcoming staff. See chapter 4.

- **Bed-and-Breakfast in Jerusalem:** Israel Hotel Reservations Center (☎ 800/552-0141 in the U.S.) can reserve a small flat from North America (minimum stay of 1 week) for $55 a night double occupancy, and will try to zero in on your preferred neighborhood. Your host will bring in your breakfast from nearby. Flats are often in lovely neighborhoods like Yemin Moshe, the German Colony, or Rehavia. In Israel, you can rent directly from Good Morning Jerusalem, the agency represented by Israel Hotel Reservations Center. See chapter 4.

- **Bed-and-Breakfast in a Galilee Arab Village** (☎ 04/901-555): This program introduces both foreign tourists and Jewish Israelis to the many Arab Israeli communities of the Galilee countryside. You can make a special request to stay with a family in residence, or you can choose a guest flat where breakfast will be brought in by the owner from his or her own house. In either event, your room will be immaculate, and filled with amenities and personal touches that convey a real sense of hospitality. See chapter 10.

4 The Best Luxury Dining

Until the 1980s, it was almost considered anti-Zionist to spend money and effort on gourmet cuisine. Israel was a practical, egalitarian society, and good, healthy fresh food was all that was necessary to create a sturdy population. Man does not live by bread alone, however, and Israel has developed a group of truly fine, personal restaurants rooted in French tradition, but also exploring the traditions of the Mediterranean Rim.

- **Ocean** (Jerusalem): Although Jerusalem is a mountain city, this is Israel's masterpiece restaurant for fish and seafood. Service is formal, but the menu takes light, natural preparation to levels of perfection that are sublime. See chapter 4.
- **American Colony Hotel** (Jerusalem): At $28 plus VAT, the Saturday luncheon buffet in the Arabesque Room is a Jerusalem tradition, with real atmosphere as well as a vast, all-you-can-eat buffet of excellent Middle Eastern and continental choices. Sadly, this treat is only for lunch, and only a once-a-week affair. See chapter 4.
- **Cow On The Roof** (Jerusalem): *Gourmet* magazine has dubbed Shalom Kadosh "the high priest of glatt kosher," and this decorous restaurant in the Jerusalem Sheraton Plaza Hotel is his sanctuary, with an unequaled standard of French cuisine prepared within the bounds of kashrut. See chapter 4.
- **Voila** (Haifa): A small, intimate place that specializes in French/Swiss cuisine, the atmosphere here is romantic; the food is rich, rustic, and expertly prepared. See chapter 9.
- **Capot Tmarim** (Tel Aviv): A carefully re-created enclave of 1930s Tel Aviv architecture and decor is the setting for Ofer Gal's menu of brilliant Mediterranean Rim creations presented with such attention to detail that even the slices of watermelon sorbet are flecked with chocolate seeds. Along with Keren and the Golden Apple (see below) this is at the very apex of Tel Aviv's luxury restaurants. See chapter 7.
- **Keren** (Jaffa): Set in a wooden house brought to Jaffa by ship from America over 100 years ago, Keren abounds in romantic charm; the elegant, always interesting French menu with touches of Mediterranean Rim is a constant joy. See chapter 7.
- **Golden Apple** (Tel Aviv): This French restaurant is the brainchild of Israel Aharoni, a vibrant perfectionist who set standards unheard of in Israel by ordering Limoges china for the Golden Apple's opening. With a respected background in Asian cooking already to his credit, Aharoni has developed a formal but lively menu that sits well in Tel Aviv's most elegant eatery. See chapter 7.

- **Twelve Tribes** (Tel Aviv): Long admired for its innovative menu of nouvelle cuisine, prepared within the rules of kashrut under executive chef Hans Lelie, the restaurant has moved toward a slightly rustic, earthy style that doesn't try to disguise the basic elements of the foods being presented. Probably the most interesting hotel restaurant in the country. See chapter 7.
- **Lilith** (Tel Aviv): A breath of easy elegance, Lilith's decor has been chosen with an eye for natural shapes and textures. One of Lilith's co-owners is the author of a famous book on the art of grilling, and her gourmet menu is filled with light touches that almost magically bring out the best natural qualities of everything served. See chapter 7.
- **Taboon** (Jaffa Port): Affiliated with Lilith, Taboon does inventive but understated things with fish and seafood, all designed to let flavor and freshness speak for themselves. Everything is memorable; in good weather you can dine outdoors beside Jaffa's harbor. See chapter 7.
- **Au Bistro** (Eilat): This gem in the French/Belgian tradition is presided over by chef Michel Torjiman, who turns out nightly miracles of expertise. Au Bistro is heavenly, reasonably priced, and runs circles around its competition in Eilat's big hotels. See chapter 11.

5 The Best Moderate Dining

Israel is filled with interesting, affordable restaurants ranging from authentic ethnic to natural Mediterranean Rim, and from kosher Indian or kosher Mexican to gracefully inventive French. In order to be accessible to kosher diners, who cannot eat at restaurants that serve both milk and meat products, many Israeli restaurants (far more than in most countries) offer only vegetarian menus. They're healthy, good for hot weather, imaginative, and affordable. The following is a selection of unusual choices for atmosphere, good food, and good value, but you'll find many other fabulous restaurants throughout this book.

- **Abu Christo** (Old Akko): Fresh fish and a covered dining terrace right beside the sea give this restaurant a delightful Greek Island harborside ambience. You can put together a feast here, complete with Middle Eastern appetizers, for $15 to $20. See chapter 8.
- **Eucalyptus** (Jerusalem): This is a must stop for sampling genuine Israeli food so beautifully prepared some critics call it the nucleus of an actual Israeli cuisine. Chef Moshe Basson blends traditional recipes, local herbs and spices, and seasonal vegetables and fruits into works of art, and also serves the best Arabic-style chicken Mahlouba and homemade Middle Eastern salads. See chapter 4.
- **Eddie's Hideaway** (Eilat): In a tourist town at the end of the earth, where most restaurants plan for customers they'll never see again, Eddie puts his heart into every meal and keeps coming up with menus that are delicious and inventive. See chapter 11.
- **Kohinoor** (Tiberias and Jerusalem): These two kosher Indian restaurants provide a rare opportunity for kosher visitors to sample this cuisine at a high level of perfection. The nonkosher **Tandoori Restaurants** (Tel Aviv, Eilat, and Herzlia) of the same chain are equally excellent, elegant, and a good value. The all-you-can-eat luncheon buffets served at Jerusalem's Kohinoor and Tel Aviv's Tandoori are very affordable. See chapters 4 and 11.
- **Margaret Tayar's** (Jaffa): A small, authentic place a short walk from trendy Old Jaffa, with a covered terrace overlooking the sweeping Tel Aviv shoreline, and a master cook who loves to see people enjoying her creations. Jaffa's fishermen adore

Margaret—she gets first choice of the catch. This is a one-woman *tour de force*. Always call to confirm hours. Among the best restaurants in the country at any price. See chapter 7, section 4.

- **Misadonet** (Jerusalem): A Kurdish restaurant, and one of the best homestyle kitchens in the country, the dish to die for here is Mama Nomi's *giri-giri*, a rich creation of lamb hearts stuffed with rice, meat, raisins, walnuts, and pine nuts, all served in a curried apricot sauce. Kubbeh soups, each with its own special flavor, are also quite special. See chapter 4.

- **Pepperoni's** (Jerusalem): With its bountiful first-course buffet, ever-changing main-course selections, atmospheric building, and bargain fixed-price meals, this is always a great choice for an interesting meal in the relaxed, Mediterranean style. See chapter 4.

- **Pagoda/The House** (Tiberias): Perhaps the best Chinese restaurant in the country, with beautiful vistas of the Sea of Galilee from its lakeside terraces, the Pagoda's staff trained at one of the most famous hotels in Bangkok. The Pagoda is kosher, and when it closes for Shabbat, **The House,** its nonkosher affiliate across the road, opens and serves up almost the same excellent but nonkosher menu. See chapter 10.

- **Spaghettim** (Jerusalem and Tel Aviv): These fabulous restaurants offer a vast array of spaghettis in absolutely fantastic sauces that are bountiful with fresh ingredients. The Jerusalem branch, set in an old Ottoman-era mansion with a delightful dining garden, is an especially romantic location. See chapters 4 and 7.

- **Yemenite Step** (Jerusalem): Here you can sample *mellawach* (flaky Yemenite phyllo crepes) filled with spiced meats, chicken, or vegetables. Yemenite garnishes, soups, and vegetables are especially worthwhile. Always popular with both Jerusalemites and visitors. See chapter 4.

- **Cacao at the Cinémathèque** (Jerusalem): The view of the Old City walls from the terrace here is breathtaking, the crowd is intelligent and stylish, and the menu is very affordable, including salads, peasant sandwiches, and an excellent but reasonably priced fish menu designed by the owners of **Ocean,** Jerusalem's most elysian and expensive restaurant. In good weather, a meal, or at least dessert on the terrace, is a must. See chapter 4.

6   The Best Inexpensive Restaurants & Street Food

Israel has truly become a food festival, and you'll be tempted by inexpensive, exotic, and healthy snacks and tidbits as you walk the streets of almost every urban center.

- **Moshiko's Shwarma and Felafel** (Jerusalem): This tiny, busy, stand-up counter sells the best shwarma I've had in Israel; don't hesitate to ask them to pack as much of your favorite salads as you want into your sandwich. In good weather, you may be able to grab a table out on the mall. See chapter 4.

- **Abu Shukri's Hummus Restaurant** (Old City, Jerusalem): This simple Formica-tabled place serves the most famous hummus in the world—written up in publications ranging from the *New York Times* to (amazingly) *Playboy*. In the late 1980s during the Intifada, the local joke was that Abu Shukri's is the only hummus worth risking your life for. A minor feast can be bought for $5 or $6; bring your own napkins. See chapter 4.

- **Family Restaurant** (West Jerusalem): The best no-frills all-around restaurant in town, this tiny place offers a hot counter filled with delicious, unusual European and Sephardic homestyle dishes. Portions are large, prices are low, and specialties change every day. The menu is designed by a genuine Israeli matriarch. See chapter 4.

- **Families Restaurant** (Old City, Jerusalem): The best authentic Arabic restaurant in the Old City, with a roomy dining area and everything done with special care. Very reasonable prices. See chapter 4.
- **Village Green** (Jerusalem): A vegetarian landmark, where you can eat elephantine portions of very tasty food and still pay well under $10. Self-service, with two downtown Jerusalem locations, this should be a mainstay for those who want to eat inexpensively, as well as those who like healthy eating. See chapter 4.
- **Eternity** (Tel Aviv): This tiny vegetarian restaurant was created for members of the Hebrew Israelite community, an African-American group whose rules of kashrut are so strict that all meat or milk products are totally forbidden. They've designed a menu of interesting creations that are healthy, cheap, and loved by many Tel Avivians. See chapter 7.

7 The Most Evocative Ancient Sites

People come to Israel to touch the past. The events that occurred here in ancient times and the stories and legends that arose in Israel are firmly planted in the minds of more than a billion people throughout the world.

- **Masada:** Above the shores of the Dead Sea, Masada was an almost inaccessible palace fortress built by Herod; 75 years after his death, in A.D. 73, it became the last stronghold of the First Revolt against Rome. The meaning of the mass suicide of Masada's defenders is fiercely debated by Israelis today. Even without the drama of Masada's last stand, the site is one of haunting, audacious magnificence. See chapter 11.
- **City of David:** Now the Arab village of Silwan (in the Bible, Siloam), this is the oldest part of Jerusalem, located on a ridge that slopes downhill just south of the present Old City. David, Solomon, and the prophets walked here. By late Roman times, warfare had advanced to the point where this area was too low to be easily defended and it was left outside the walls of Jerusalem. The ancient gardens of Siloam inspired the Song of Songs; an overgrown orchard of fig and pomegranate trees, watered by the same Gihon Spring that was used by the prophets to anoint the kings of Judah, still stands at the foot of modern-day Silwan. Silwan is best visited on an organized tour or with a guide. See chapter 4.
- **Northwest Shore of the Sea of Galilee:** This enchantingly lovely corner of the lake, in many ways the birthplace of one of the world's great religions, was the landscape of Jesus's ministry. Centering on the ruins of **Capernaum** (once a fishing town, and the site of St. Peter's house), and **Tabga,** where the multitudes were fed with the Miracle of the Loaves and the Fishes, the shoreline is dominated by the **Mount of Beatitudes.** Churches and archeological excavations mark the locations of New Testament events. See chapter 10.
- **Bar Am Synagogue:** In the northern Galilee, near the Lebanese border, this is the best preserved and perhaps most beautiful of the many ruined synagogues of antiquity. Built in the 4th century A.D., it was once the centerpiece of a small town in the breathtaking wooded mountains of this northern region. See chapter 10.

8 The Most Important Holy Places

The great sacred sites all possess extraordinary power, mystery, and beauty, at least partly conveyed upon them by centuries, if not millennia, of reverence. The ownership and histories of Israel's holy places are often a matter of contention and debate, not only among the three great monotheistic religions, but also among sects within these religions. This list is chronological, according to the period in which each site was first venerated.

- **Dome of the Rock** (Jerusalem): A gloriously beautiful Islamic shrine, built in A.D. 691, covers the rock believed to have been the altar or foundation stone of the First and Second Temples. According to Jewish tradition, the rock was the altar upon which Abraham prepared to sacrifice Isaac; Islamic tradition holds that it was Abraham's first son, Ishmael, the father of the Arabic people, whom Abraham was called upon to sacrifice, either at this rock, or at Mecca. The rock is also believed to have been the point from which the Prophet Mohammed ascended to glimpse heaven during the miraculous night journey described in the 17th Sura of the Koran. Most religious Jews today do not enter the Temple Mount, upon which the Dome of the Rock is located, because of the sacredness of the place. See chapter 5.

- **Tomb of the Patriarchs** (Hebron, on the West Bank): This is the burial place of Abraham, Isaac, and Jacob, as well as their wives, Sarah, Rebecca, and Leah (Rachel, the second wife of Jacob, is buried in Bethlehem). Surrounded by massive walls built by King Herod, and venerated by both Jews and Muslims, rights to this place are a point of bitter contention between the Islamic and Jewish worlds. See chapter 6.

- **Mount Sinai** (Sinai Peninsula, Egypt): Controversy still rages over which of the Sinai's mountains is the true site where the Ten Commandments were given to Moses, but the traditional identification of Mount Sinai is very ancient. An isolated Byzantine monastery at the foot of the mountain adds to the mysterious aura. See chapter 12.

- **Church of the Nativity** (Bethlehem): This church marks the site of the birthplace of Jesus. It is the oldest surviving church in the Holy Land; the Persians spared it during their invasion in A.D. 614 because, according to legend, they were impressed by a representation of the Magi (fellow Persians) that decorated the building. See chapter 6.

- **Church of the Holy Sepulcher** (Jerusalem): Christianity's holiest place, this church covers the traditional sites of the crucifixion, entombment, and resurrection of Jesus. Built about A.D. 330, the complex is carefully divided among the Greek Orthodox, Roman Catholic, Armenian Orthodox, Coptic, Syrian, and Ethiopian churches. See chapter 5.

- **Western Wall:** Part of a massive retaining wall built by Herod around the Temple Mount in Jerusalem, this is the sole visible structure remaining from the Second Temple complex. Because of the sanctity of the Temple Mount itself, the Western Wall is the place closest to the site of the original temple where observant Jews are permitted to approach and pray. See chapter 5.

- **Mount of Olives:** Overlooking the Old City of Jerusalem from the east, the mount offers a sweeping vista of the entire city. Here, Jesus wept at a prophetic vision of Jerusalem lying in ruins; in the Garden of Gethsemane, on the lower slope of the mount, Jesus was arrested; the ridge of the Mount of Olives is the place from which, according to tradition, Jesus ascended to heaven. An encampment site for Jewish pilgrims in ancient times, the Mount of Olives contains Judaism's most important graveyard. See chapter 5.

- **El Aksa Mosque** (Jerusalem): On the southernmost side of the Temple Mount, built in A.D. 720, this is the third most important Muslim place of prayer after Mecca and Medina. See chapter 5.

- **Baha'i Gardens** (Akko): At the northern edge of Akko, this site marks the tomb of the founder and prophet of the Baha'i faith, Baha'u'llah. As such, it is the holiest place for members of the Baha'i faith. See chapter 8.
- **Baha'i Gardens and Shrine** (Haifa): The shrine was built to memorialize the remains of one of the Baha'i faith's martyrs, Bab Mirza Ali Muhammad, who was executed by Persian authorities in 1850. See chapter 9.

9 The Best Ancient Cities

Israel and neighboring Jordan are filled with ruins of lost, ancient cities from every part of their long history. In Herodian–Roman times, the population of Judea and the Galilee may have been around 3 million. Almost 2 millennia of wars, religious rivalries, persecutions, and misgovernment drove the population down to less than half a million by the start of the 19th century. Even knowledge of the location of many ancient sites was forgotten. Now pieces of the past are being recovered at a rapid pace, dazzling physical monuments to the past.

- **Caesaria** (on the coast between Tel Aviv and Haifa): Built by Herod as the great harbor and seaport of his kingdom, this was the splendid administrative capital of Palestine after the fall of Jerusalem in A.D. 70. There are impressive, vast ruins of the Roman city (including two theaters), as well as of the Crusader-era city, made all the more romantic by the waves lapping at the ancient stones. Caesaria was an important Byzantine Christian city, but it is not a biblical site. See chapter 8.
- **Petra** (Jordan): The legendary 2,000-year-old Nabatean capital carved from the walls of a desert canyon is now the highlight of excursion tours into Jordan from Israel. The entire Petra experience, including the trek into the canyon, has the air of adventure and mystery—especially if you plan 1 or 2 nights at Petra and give yourself time to get a feel for the place early in the morning and in the evening, before the hordes of tourists arrive. See chapter 12.
- **Gamla** (Golan Heights): Once a small Roman-era Jewish city located on a ridge in the Golan Heights, the site has a story chillingly similar to that of Masada, but the number of dead was far greater. In A.D. 67, at the beginning of the First Jewish Rebellion against Rome, Gamla was overrun by Roman soldiers, and as many as 9,000 townspeople flung themselves from the cliff, choosing death over subjugation. This dramatic site is especially beautiful amid late winter wildflowers and waterfalls. A ruined synagogue, one of the few that can be dated to the Second Temple period, is here. See chapter 10, section 4.
- **Korazim** (Galilee): A Roman-Byzantine–era Jewish town in the hills just north-east of the Sea of Galilee, this is a beautiful place, with sweeping views of the lake. Portions of ruins still stand. A black basalt synagogue, with beautifully carved detailing, and some surrounding houses, also of local black basalt, give a good idea of what the more than 100 towns once in this area must have been like. Jesus visited Korazim, but developed little following there. See chapter 10, section 3.
- **Megiddo** (Armageddon, about 20 miles southeast of Haifa): This town stood in the path of invading armies from ancient until modern times. It is an encyclopedia of Near Eastern archeology with more than 20 levels of habitation from 4,000 B.C. to A.D. 400 having been discovered here. The water tunnel dug from inside the fortified town to the source of water outside the walls in the 9th century B.C. is a miracle of ancient engineering. See chapter 10, section 1.
- **Bet Shean** (Jordan Valley): This place has been continuously inhabited for the past 6,000 years. A vast, Roman–Byzantine city with colonaded streets and a theater

that could house 5,000 people once stood here, although by the 19th century, Bet Shean was a small village. Remnants of earlier civilizations can be seen on the ancient tel above the Roman ruins. See chapter 10, section 5.

- **Zippori** (Sepphoris, near Nazareth): A cosmopolitan Jewish–Hellenistic city, it was the capital of the Galilee in Roman and Talmudic times. Especially interesting because it may have been familiar to Jesus, Zippori's highlights include a colonaded street; a mosaic synagogue floor depicting the zodiac; and the beautiful mosaic portrait of a woman dubbed "the Mona Lisa of the Galilee," recently discovered in a late Roman–era villa. See chapter 6, section 1.

10 The Best Beaches

Israel has four seas (the Mediterranean, the Sea of Galilee, the Dead Sea, and the Red Sea), connections to two oceans (the Atlantic and the Indian), and offers an amazing variety of swimming experiences. The beaches of Israel look beautiful, but be careful about going in the water. Unusually strong riptides, whirlpools, and undertows along the Mediterranean coast can claim the strongest swimmer. Never swim in unguarded areas. Along much of the coast, especially north of Tel Aviv, the beaches seem sandy, but a few steps into the surf, and you're standing on a rocky shelf—not a good place to be when waves come crashing down on you. Pollution is also a serious problem, as it is throughout the Mediterranean. Israel's standards for allowing beaches to open for swimming are much higher than those of most Mediterranean countries, but many days, garbage from other countries swirls along the coast. At Nahariya, Akko, and the Poleg Nature Reserve (8km south of Netanya), which have no sewage treatment plants, I would hesitate to put my head in the water. Israelis play compulsive paddleball on any stretch of beach they're on, regardless of sleeping sunbathers in the line of fire. Expect beaches to be lively, watch out for sea urchins and stinging coral in the Red Sea, and the burning medusas (jellyfish) that attack the Mediterranean beaches in July, and your beach experiences will be much happier.

- **Gordon Beach** (Tel Aviv): Perhaps the most accessible place to sample the Mediterranean, this free municipal beach has showers, and a friendly mix of Israelis, new Russian immigrants, and tourists from luxury hotels; there are nearby places to take a break for a snack or meal; the sand is passably clean, and when the tide is clear, the beach is a pleasure. See chapter 7.
- **Mikmoret Beach** (between Netanya and Caesaria): If you have a car, this is a lifeguarded, slightly sheltered out-of-the-way beach with a restaurant, showers, and changing rooms. To the south, the beach goes on straight for miles, and is good for long walks. In-season entrance is $2.40 per person, deducted from your restaurant bill if you have a full meal. See chapter 8.
- **Aqueduct Beach** (just north of Caesaria): An ancient Roman aqueduct gives this beach its name and travel-poster ambience. There are no showers or amenities or crowds except on summer weekends, when vendors sell drinks and snacks. Not good for swimming if the water is rough, but on calm days, as you float in the Mediterranean and gaze at the romantic ruins, you know it's not the Jersey Shore. Currently the beach is free, with an impromptu parking area. See chapter 8.
- **Kibbutz Ein Gev Holiday Village Beach** (Sea of Galilee): The freshwater Sea of Galilee is warm and cleansing, spiritually as well as physically. You have to be a guest at the Ein Gev Holiday Village to be allowed to use the beach here, but it's the prettiest one on the lake, with a date palm grove and thick lawns stretching down to the water, which is relatively free of foot-stubbing rocks. Just to the south

are several miles of eucalyptus-shaded beaches along the road (in summer there's a $3 parking fee); they're rockier underwater, but very pleasant when not crowded with weekenders. Late afternoon often brings real breakers to the eastern shore of the lake; twilight here is soft and magical. See chapter 10, section 3.

- **Ein Gedi Beach** (Dead Sea): Everyone should experience swimming in the Dead Sea, the strangest body of water and the lowest point on the face of the earth. The extremely high salt content of the Dead Sea makes you feel like a cork; if you float, it's impossible to keep much of yourself underwater. The salt and minerals in the water are believed to be therapeutic, but the water will sting any cuts on your skin, and if you stay in too long, you'll be pickled. There are freshwater showers as well as a restaurant. High daytime temperatures so far below sea level mean that even in winter a dip may be possible. See chapter 11.

- **Coral Beach Nature Reserve** (Eilat): The Nature Reserve has staked out a strip of beach alongside Eilat's best reefs. Here you can snorkel among dazzling fish and coral formations, and even take interesting scuba expeditions. Snorkeling gear is for rent, and there are showers, changing areas, and snack facilities. Admission and all-day rental of snorkel equipment (which can be shared) will come to $12. This beach is not good for recreational swimming—unless you wear a face mask and foot protection, you can easily step on the quills of a sea urchin, or be cut and burned by stinging coral. See chapter 11.

- **Dolphin Reef Beach** (Eilat): A good choice for everyday swimming in the Red Sea, Dolphin Reef is the most picturesque beach in Eilat, with palapas, a shady garden cafeteria, and a thatched-roof, sand-floor pub/restaurant for when you want to be out of the sun. It also has a resident dolphin population in the water, separated from the human swimming area by a net fence. You can swim under supervision in the dolphin zone for $30 a half hour; or better yet, stay in the roomy people's zone (with a sandy, nearly sea-urchin-free bottom) and enjoy watching the dolphins' leaps and frolics. See chapter 11.

- **Nuweiba Hilton Coral Resort** (Sinai Peninsula, Egypt): If you want to really beach out for a few days at a luxury resort that has lowrise desert architectural style, and a quiet, distant end-of-the-earth ambience, with the mountains of Arabia facing you across the water, this Hilton Hotel is a splurge, but at $140 per night for a double room, it's a bargain by most world standards. Contact a good travel discounter in Eilat at off-season or when business is slow, and you might find a double room for as low as $70! There's a pool as well as beaches for swimming and snorkeling. See chapter 12.

11 The Best Museums

Israel's museums are relatively new, innovative, and interactive with the discoveries of the past, of the self, and of nationhood that are happening so intensively every day in Israeli society. The most interesting museums are those that could only be found in Israel.

- **Israel Museum** (Jerusalem): Although it only opened in 1965, in three decades the Israel Museum has made its place on the world museum map. Its greatest treasures, beautifully exhibited, include a number of the Dead Sea Scrolls; a dazzling, all-encompassing collection of archeological finds from Israel; a vast treasury of world Judaica and costumes, including reconstructions of the interiors of synagogues brought to Israel from Italy, Germany, and Cochin, India; and excellent collections of primitive, pre-Colombian, European, and Modern Art, including the exciting Billy Rose Sculpture Garden. There's also an enticing Children's Wing. See chapter 5.

- **Yad VaShem Holocaust Museum** (Jerusalem): This large complex is a memorial to the 6 million Jews killed by the Nazis during World War II. Part of the museum is a teaching experience, with films, photographs, and documents pertaining to the Holocaust; part is an archive in which information about each individual victim will be gathered and kept. A third part of the complex consists of memorial structures, gardens, and installations such as the Avenue of the Righteous, in memory of those who risked their lives to shelter Jews; the darkened, terrifying interior of the Children's Memorial; the tragic sculpture of the Valley of Destroyed Communities. No visitor can leave unaffected. See chapter 5.
- **Eretz Israel Museum** (Tel Aviv): This museum covers many aspects of the land of Israel, including its natural history, flora and fauna, archeology, folklore, and traditional crafts. Highlights include a bazaar filled with craftspeople demonstrating such skills from antiquity as glass blowing, olive pressing, weaving, and pottery-making; an extraordinary collection of ancient glass; and excavations of a tel located on the grounds of the museum. See chapter 7.
- **Tel Aviv Museum of Art** (Tel Aviv): Notable for strong collections of Israeli art, and contemporary European (including Russian) art, the museum has just begun to exibit its newest gift—the Jaglom Collection of Impressionist and Post-Impressionist Art. There is a lively program of public events, performances, and special exhibitions. See chapter 7.
- **Bet Hatfutsot, The Diaspora Museum** (Tel Aviv): Not a museum in terms of displaying actual genuine artifacts, Bet Hatfutsot is rather a state-of-the-art multimedia exhibit that illustrates the histories of Jewish communities through-out the world. It's fascinating, fun, and the special visiting exhibitions are always worthwhile. See chapter 7.
- **Wolfson Collection of Judaica** (Jerusalem): Right in the heart of Jerusalem, this little-known gem consists of a large but intimate private collection of Judaica from all over the world. It is exhibited on the fourth floor of Hechal Shlomo, the Great Synagogue complex on King George Street. See chapter 5.
- **Mayer Islamic Museum** (Jerusalem): Another undervisited treasure, with an excellent collection of Islamic and Middle Eastern art, and well-chosen special and visiting exhibitions. See chapter 5.

12 The Best Nature & Outdoor Experiences

Israel's diverse landscapes and unusual natural phenomena provide opportunities for unusual outdoor activities, many of which you might never have thought of in connection with a trip here.

- **Snorkeling and Diving the Reefs of Eilat:** The Red Sea coral reefs are among the most interesting and easily accessible in the world; anyone who can swim even moderately well can snorkel and enjoy the underwater scene. If you want to scuba dive, you must bring your certification from abroad or obtain a license in Israel. Eilat is home to a number of diving schools with short- and longer-term programs for tourists, as well as programs in underwater photography. Once you've graduated from the coral reef just off the shores of southern Eilat, you can graduate to a dive cruise to the more extensive reefs of the Coral Island. You can snorkel in the Coral Beach Nature Preserve for less than $20, including rental of gear, or you can join diving cruises that begin at $40 for a dive. Diving instruction programs and major diving trips to the Sinai coast can run from $140 to thousands of dollars. See chapter 11.

• **Diving at Dahab** (Sinai Peninsula): From Eilat, you are just across the border from the Sinai Peninsula, with its extraordinary reefs and clear, light-filled water. Reefs teeming with exotic marine life extend all the way down the coast; perhaps the most famous is the suicidal Blue Hole, off the town of Dahab (but *not* recommended by this book). At the southernmost tip of Sinai (you'll need a standard visa to Egypt rather than the Sinai Only visa to travel there) is the **Egyptian National Park at Ras Mohammed,** which is a diver's super paradise (the diving metropolis of Sharm-el-Sheik is your base for Ras Mohammed). Diving schools in Eilat and good Eilat travel agents and discounters can arrange diving-package excursions to the Sinai. See chapter 12.

• **Lama Trekking in the Ramon Crater** (Negev): In the Negev Highlands, near Mitzpe Ramon, this geological encyclopedia can be visited on a speedy, bone-dismantling jeep tour, or on a rather arduous hike, or you can experience the mysterious quiet of the desert as you explore the crater accompanied by a guide, with a lama to carry your water and equipment. This novel approach can be arranged for a variety of itineraries, including half- and full-day treks, as well as longer excursions with overnight camping and Bedouin-style cookouts. The Alpaca Farm and travel agencies in Mitzpe Ramon can set it up for you at reasonable prices. See chapter 11.

• **Birding in Eilat:** The Jordan Valley, far below sea level and extending through the Red Sea to the Great Rift Valley of Africa, is the great highway for bird migration between Europe and Africa. Spring and fall are the migration seasons, when sightings are truly spectacular. Write to the **International Birdwatching Center,** P.O. Box 774, Eilat, 88106, for information on birdwatching festivals, activities, tours, and hotel and car rental packages available to birdwatchers. The Society for Protection of Nature in Israel (SPNI) will also direct you to birdwatching activities in the northern Hula Valley region. See chapter 11.

• **Hiking to Gamla:** A beautiful trail throughout the year, in late winter, this 1- to 2-hour hike in the Golan takes you past wildflowers, streams, and waterfalls. The reward at the end of the trail is the dramatic ruined city of Gamla (see "The Best Ancient Cities" above). The countryside is also dotted with prehistoric dolmens and Stone Age tombs. This walk brings you into contact with nature, archeology, and a very moving piece of Israeli history. Plan additional time for the return walk, although a shorter trail is available. See chapter 10.

• **Hiking Down Wadi Kelt:** This hike, manageable for most walkers, takes you down one of the extraordinary canyons leading from the Judean mountains to the Jordan Valley and the Dead Sea. On the route, you pass the ancient and almost inaccessible Monastery of Saint George, built into the walls of the canyon above the stream of Wadi Kelt. This dramatic canyon may soon be under the control of the Palestinian Authority. At present, it should only be visited by organized group tour. See chapter 6, section 1.

• **Digging for a Day:** Joining an archeological dig as a volunteer requires a definite commitment of time, money, and backbreaking labor. However, you can often arrange to dig for a day and get a close-up look at the hard work and thrills involved in bringing so much of Israel's history to light. Contact the Municipal Tourist Information Office in Jerusalem for current options. The digging season is during the dry summer months.

Getting to Know Israel 2

To millions of Jews, Christians, and Muslims, Israel is the Holy Land where Solomon reigned in all his glory, where Jesus died on the cross, and where Muhammad visited during a miraculous journey.

Religion is the basis of Israel's political importance. Were it not for its sacred character, few people would choose to live on this narrow strip of land between the sea and desert. Jews have been living here since the time of Abraham, almost 4,000 years ago; Christianity began in the Galilee two millennia later. During the very early days of Islam in the 7th century A.D., before Mecca became a sacred city, Muslims prayed in the direction of Jerusalem.

All three religions have battled to capture and hold the holy territory: Israelites fought Canaanites, Jews fought Romans, and Muslim armies fought Crusaders. In the 20th century, Muslim Turks were driven out by the British, and the British in turn were driven out by groups of Zionists and Palestinian Arabs.

Israel looms large in the great political happenings of our times. Realizing the ancient Jewish dream of a homeland has meant the displacement of many Palestinians, which, in turn, has meant alienating the surrounding Arab countries in the already unstable Middle East. The problem of finding a truly fair solution to the many valid and conflicting claims on the Holy Land is one of the great challenges facing the Christian, Jewish, and Muslim communities in Israel today.

1 The Natural Environment

Israel is a surprisingly small country. Starting from Jerusalem, you can drive down to Jericho, along the Dead Sea to Masada, inland to Beersheva at the edge of the Negev, north to Tel Aviv, then all the way up to the Lebanese border, the Golan Heights, around the Sea of Galilee, and back to Jerusalem—and the distance would be only about 600 miles.

The land itself is remarkably varied. Depending on your itinerary, you are likely to find anything from beaches to lush valleys and mountainsides, rambling foothills, flat plains, snowcapped peaks, the hot wilderness that surrounds the mineral-saturated waters of the Dead Sea, desert regions, and the multicolored crags and crevices of the Negev.

In ancient times, this land was looked upon as a corridor between the richer, lusher lands of Egypt and Mesopotamia. When drought threatened, people were forced to go north or south to reach the fertile lands fed by rivers. But that's not to say Israel is all desert—far from it. According to the Bible, the land lured the Israelites from the deserts of Sinai. Moses sent spies into Canaan to report on the land, and they returned with figs, pomegranates, and a single bunch of grapes so huge that two men were needed to carry it. The Israel Ministry of Tourism has adopted this as its symbol: two men, each bearing one end of a pole, with an immense bunch of grapes suspended from its middle.

2 Israel Past & Present

Dateline

- **600,000** B.C. Early human habitation of caves in Carmel Mountains near Haifa.
- **15,000** B.C. Appearance of farming settlements in the Galilee and Jordan Valley.
- **7000** B.C. Defensive wall built around Jericho in Jordan Valley. Early domestication of animals. Evidence of early centers for cult and fertility worship.
- **4500–3100** B.C. Cities develop at Bet Shean, Ein Gedi, Megiddo, and Beersheva.
- **3100** B.C. Start of Early Canaanite era; development of cities.
- **1850–1800** B.C. Era of Abraham. Migration of Semitic tribes into Egypt.
- **1600** B.C. Hebrews enslaved in Egypt.
- **1250** B.C. Exodus of Hebrews under Moses. Early Canaanite–Hebrew alphabet appears.
- **1100** B.C. Israelite tribes settle in much of Canaanite highlands. Philistine people occupy Canaanite coast. Deborah judges loose confederation of Israelite tribes.
- **1025** B.C. Saul anointed first Israelite king by the prophet Samuel.

continues

A LOOK AT THE PAST

Recorded Jewish history goes back to the time of Abraham, between 2000 and 1800 B.C. Many elements of the patriarchal chronicles have been confirmed as accurate by recent archeological discoveries. Modern scientific methods reveal that human beings have lived in the Holy Land since the Old Stone Age, some 600,000 years ago. But a history so deep and full of universal significance is almost impossible to grasp in its entirety, so I've provided an outline of the major periods before 1917 as well as a supplemental dateline.

HISTORICAL PERIODS

In Israel's museums, and at Israel's archeological sites, you will encounter the terms used to define the many time periods in Israel's long history.

Old Stone Age (600,000–12,000 B.C.): Cavemen, hand axes, hunting, fire.

Middle Stone Age (12,000–7500 B.C.): Cultivation of grain, more sophisticated tools.

Late Stone Age (7500–4000 B.C.): First villages appear, including Jericho; animal husbandry, irrigation, and pottery begin.

Chalcolithic (Copper) Age (4000–3200 B.C.): Copper used in tools; towns grow; designs show on pottery; a culture develops at Beersheva.

Early Bronze (Canaanite) Age (3200–2200 B.C.): Towns are fortified, temples and palaces built.

Middle Bronze (Canaanite) Age (2200–1550 B.C.): The Age of the Patriarchs; Abraham's travels; trade develops; the Hyksos invade Canaan and Egypt.

Late Bronze (Canaanite) Age (1550–1200 B.C.): Israel captive in Egypt; the alphabet develops; the Exodus from Egypt; Ten Commandments delivered on Mount Sinai; Israel conquers the Promised Land.

Early Iron Age (1200–1020 B.C.): Period of the Judges; Philistine invasion.

Middle Iron Age (1020–842 B.C.): The united monarchy under King Saul and King David (1000 B.C.); Jerusalem is capital of kingdom; in 961 King Solomon builds First Temple; golden age of Israelite culture and power.

Late Iron Age (842–587 B.C.): Period of the later kings and prophets; in 587, destruction of First Temple.

Babylonian and Persian Periods (587–332 B.C.): Israel captive in Babylon, followed by Persian domination; the Second Temple is built; times of Ezra and Nehemiah.

Hellenistic and Maccabean Periods (332–37 B.C.): Domination by Alexander the Great, by the Ptolomies and Seleucids; the Maccabean struggle; Hasmonean Dynasty.

Roman Period (37 B.C.–A.D. 324): Herodian Dynasty; birth of Jesus, his ministry and crucifixion; wars against Rome; Second Temple and Jerusalem destroyed (A.D. 70); fall of Masada (73); Talmud and Mishnah compiled; Bar Kokhba's revolt against Rome (132–35).

Byzantine Period (324–640): Jewish revolt, Byzantine domination; Jerusalem Talmud completed; Persian invasion and sack of Jerusalem (614); birth and rise of Islam in the Middle East.

Arab Period (640–1096): Jerusalem conquered by Islamic armies (638); Arab Empire capital first at Damascus, later Baghdad; joint Christian–Muslim protectorate of holy places; Christian pilgrimage rights curtailed.

The Crusades (1096–1291): First Crusade (1096–99), sack of Jerusalem, Crusader kingdom under Godfrey of Bouillon. Second Crusade (1147–49): Saladin captures Jerusalem for Islam (1187). Third Crusade (1189–92); Fourth Crusade (1202–04).

Mameluke and Ottoman Turkish Period (1291–1917): Mongols and Seljuks replace Arabs and Byzantines as overlords of the Holy Land; Ottomans conquer Palestine; Suleiman the Magnificent rebuilds Jerusalem; Jews, expelled from Spain and Italy, welcomed into the Ottoman Empire; Napoleon's campaign in Egypt and Palestine (1799); movement to re-create a Jewish homeland led by Theodor Herzl (1860–1904), published *The Jewish State;* the first Zionist Congress in Basel (1897).

- **1004–1000** B.C. David, second king of Israelites, makes Jerusalem his capital; begins conquest of territories from southern Syria to Eilat.
- **950** B.C. King Solomon builds First Temple of Jerusalem.
- **928** B.C. After death of Solomon, David's kingdom divided into Israel in the north, and Judah, with its capital at Jerusalem.
- **870–722** B.C. Pagan religions flourish. Assyria conquers Kingdom of Israel.
- **701** B.C. Judah devastated by Assyrian invasion. Jerusalem, led by King Hezekiah and inspired by the prophet Isaiah, remains unconquered.
- **627–586** B.C. Prophet Jeremiah in Jerusalem.
- **586** B.C. Nebuchadnezzar destroys Jerusalem and Temple of Solomon. End of First Temple period. Jews exiled to Babylon.
- **540** B.C. Babylon defeated by Persians. Jews allowed to return to Jerusalem.
- **515** B.C. Second Temple built upon ruins of Solomon's Temple in Jerusalem.
- **445** B.C. Ezra the Scribe begins public reading of Torah in Jerusalem.
- **332** B.C. Alexander the Great conquers Judea. Hellenistic era begins.
- **167** B.C. Antiochus IV desecrates Jerusalem temple; outlaws Jewish religion.
- **164** B.C. Judah Maccabee captures Jerusalem; temple rededicated. Judea independent under Maccabee (Hasmonean) Dynasty; borders greatly expanded.
- **63** B.C. Judea incorporated into Roman Empire.
- **37** B.C. Romans proclaim Herod the Idumaean king of Judea.

continues

History of Israel

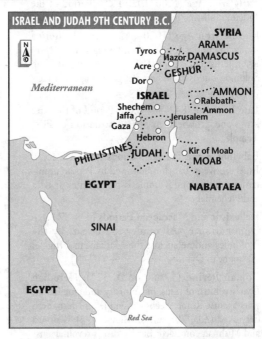

ISRAEL AND JUDAH 9TH CENTURY B.C.

Mediterranean

Tyros
Acre
Dor
SYRIA
ARAM-DAMASCUS
Hazor
GESHUR

ISRAEL
Shechem
Jaffa
Gaza
Hebron
Jerusalem
AMMON
Rabbath-Ammon

PHILLISTINES
JUDAH
Kir of Moab
MOAB

EGYPT
NABATAEA

SINAI

EGYPT

Red Sea

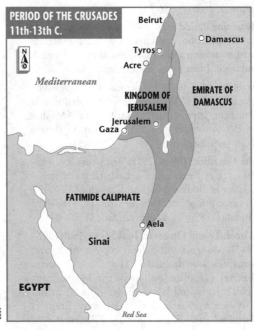

PERIOD OF THE CRUSADES 11th-13th C.

Beirut
Damascus

Mediterranean

Tyros
Acre

KINGDOM OF JERUSALEM
EMIRATE OF DAMASCUS

Jerusalem
Gaza

FATIMIDE CALIPHATE

Aela

Sinai

EGYPT

Red Sea

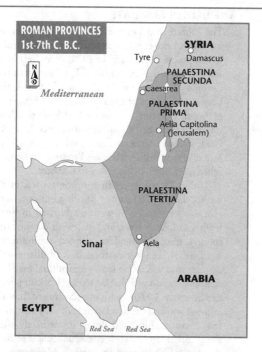

ROMAN PROVINCES 1st–7th C. B.C.

N

Mediterranean

Tyre

SYRIA
Damascus

PALAESTINA SECUNDA

Caesarea

PALAESTINA PRIMA

Aelia Capitolina (Jerusalem)

PALAESTINA TERTIA

Sinai

Aela

ARABIA

EGYPT

Red Sea   Red Sea

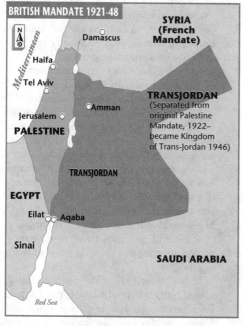

BRITISH MANDATE 1921-48

N

Mediterranean

Damascus

SYRIA (French Mandate)

Haifa

Tel Aviv

Jerusalem

Amman

PALESTINE

TRANSJORDAN
(Separated from original Palestine Mandate, 1922– became Kingdom of Trans-Jordan 1946)

TRANSJORDAN

EGYPT

Eilat   Aqaba

Sinai

SAUDI ARABIA

Red Sea

21

- **18** B.C. Herod begins vast renovation of Second Temple.
- **8–4** B.C. Jesus born in Bethlehem.
- A.D. **62** Completion of Herodian renovation of Second Temple.
- **66–73** Jewish revolt against Rome. Jerusalem and Second Temple captured by Rome and razed; Masada falls.
- **132** Second Revolt against Rome led by Bar Kokhba; ruins of Jerusalem freed; temple service resumed.
- **135** Bar Kokhba defeated. Hadrian orders Jerusalem rebuilt as Aelia Capitolina, a Roman city forbidden to Jews.
- **160–300** Early Talmudic era. Classical synagogues built throughout Holy Land; Galilee center of Jewish population.
- **313–326** Emperor Constantine recognizes Christianity as new religion of Roman Empire. His mother, Queen Helena, visits Holy Land to identify sites of Jesus' life and ministry.
- **326–614** Hundreds of Byzantine churches and monastic communities built. Restrictions against Jews.
- **351** Jews of Galilee rebel against Byzantine/Christians.
- **400** Codification of Palestinian Talmud.
- **614–629** Jerusalem conquered by Persians, recaptured by Byzantines.
- **638** Islamic conquest of Palestine. Omar Ibn El Khattab conquers Jerusalem.
- **691** Dome of the Rock built on Temple Mount.
- **720** El Aksa Mosque built on Temple Mount.
- **1008** Caliph Al Hakim destroys churches and prevents Christian pilgrimage.

continues

THE BRITISH MANDATE

The Balfour Declaration in 1917 announced British support for the creation of a national home for the Jewish people in Palestine. In 1920, after Great Britain had captured the region of Palestine from the Ottoman Empire at the end of World War I, the League of Nations granted the British a "mandate" to govern Palestine, and Sir Herbert Samuel, a Jew, was named first British high commissioner. In 1922, Great Britain separated Trans-Jordan (present-day Jordan) from British Mandate Palestine and established a separate Arab country in that area.

Within Palestine, enormous progress was made during the first 20 years of British administration. Hospitals and schools were established in both Jewish and Arab areas, and in Jewish areas of the country, dazzlingly modern, planned communities, both urban and agricultural, were built; much desolate land was reclaimed for agricultural use. The Arab population of Palestine resented British policy in the early 1920s, which encouraged Jewish immigration and the development of the Palestinian Jewish community, and almost immediately after the British Mandate took effect, political disorders developed. The era of the British Mandate was characterized by three-way disputes between British, Jewish, and Arab factions and by Arab attacks on Jewish communities, especially in 1921 and 1929. Jewish immigration increased during the early Hitler years. An Arab insurrection from 1936 to 1939 led the British, in 1939, to severely limit Jewish immigration before cutting it off entirely. Thus, during World War II, Jews seeking to escape the Nazi Holocaust in Europe were denied refuge in Palestine. After the outbreak of World War II, political tensions within Palestine diminished somewhat, and the area became an important Allied military base for the Middle East. However, the coming conflict was inevitable. In 1946, Arab and Jewish terrorism against the British increased, the King David Hotel was blown up by a Jewish underground group at odds with Ben-Gurion's more mainstream Zionist organization, and the cycle of violence rose to new heights.

In November 1947, with Britain abstaining, the United Nations General Assembly voted to partition Palestine into two separate states, one Arab and one Jewish. On May 14, 1948, with the Jewish parts of Jerusalem under Arab siege, with fighting widespread across Palestine, and with 400,000 Arab Palestinian civilians fleeing their homes, the British

Mandate ended in shambles, and the state of Israel was proclaimed. The Palestinian state proposed for those areas that remained under Arab control did not come into being. The West Bank and East Jerusalem, including the Old City, were annexed to the Kingdom of Jordan. Although most of the international community did not recognize this act, Jordan granted citizenship to all Palestinians under its control, the only Arab nation to do so. Egypt occupied but did not annex the Gaza Strip. Its inhabitants were declared stateless.

TOWARD THE PRESENT
AN INDEPENDENT STATE

In the beginning of the state of Israel's history there was enormous exhilaration, but also a grim determination. The double weight of the horrors of World War II and the enormous casualties suffered in the 1948–49 War of Independence prodded the country to hang on, to protect every sand dune, to force life out of the desert, and to create a haven for any Jews who might ever find themselves in danger. Life was austere in the newly won state. For years, food, clothing, razor blades, and paint were severely rationed as the country struggled to survive as well as to feed and shelter the thousands of new immigrants who arrived each month. In less than a decade, the nation's population quadrupled as hundreds of thousands of Holocaust survivors from Europe and Jewish refugees from the Middle East arrived and were absorbed. Hundreds of thousands more were added in the 1960s as the Jewish communities of North Africa fled to safer havens in France and Israel.

Slowly, with enormous effort, conditions grew more stable. Basic housing was built, uprooted people began to develop new identities, and although life was still Spartan (Ben-Gurion and the founding fathers refused to allow television stations to be established in Israel, claiming that the nation had more important things to attend to), the country began to flourish. Modern farming and irrigation, along with dedication, made the desert bloom, and the long season ensured by the Mediterranean sun made marginal land wonderfully fruitful. Jaffa oranges and Israeli tomatoes and avocados and the wines of Mount Carmel became famous. But even more important than its agriculture were Israel's developing industries. Today the country manufactures its own tools and machinery, arms and airplanes, and is becoming an important center for

- **1099** Crusaders conquer Jerusalem. Muslims and Jews massacred.
- **1187** Saladin recaptures Jerusalem from Crusaders.
- **1189–91** Third Crusade. Crusader Kingdom along coast with Akko as capital.
- **1240** Turkish armies plunder Jerusalem.
- **1261** Mongols devastate countryside.
- **1267** Post-Crusader Jewish community reestablished in Jerusalem.
- **1291** Mameluke conquest. Akko falls; end of Crusader Kingdom.
- **1517** Ottoman Turkish conquest of Jerusalem.
- **1538** Ottoman Sultan Suleiman the Magnificent orders walls of Jerusalem rebuilt.
- **1550** Safed becomes center of Jewish scholarship and mysticism.
- **1569** Recodification of normative Judaism (Shulkan Aruckh) in Safed.
- **1776** Jezzar Pasha rebuilds Akko.
- **1799** Napoleon attacks but fails to win Akko.
- **1841** First Protestant mission in Jerusalem.
- **1863** First Hebrew newspaper in Jerusalem.
- **1870** Mikvah Yisrael, first agricultural school, founded.
- **1878** Petah Tikva, near Jaffa and Rosh Pinna, in Galilee, first Jewish farming settlements, founded.
- **1882** First aliyah from Europe and Jewish immigration from Yemen.
- **1897** First Zionist Congress in Basel.
- **1898** Herzl meets German kaiser in Jerusalem.
- **1909** Tel Aviv founded.
- **1911** First kibbutz founded at Degania in the Galilee.

continues

Israel

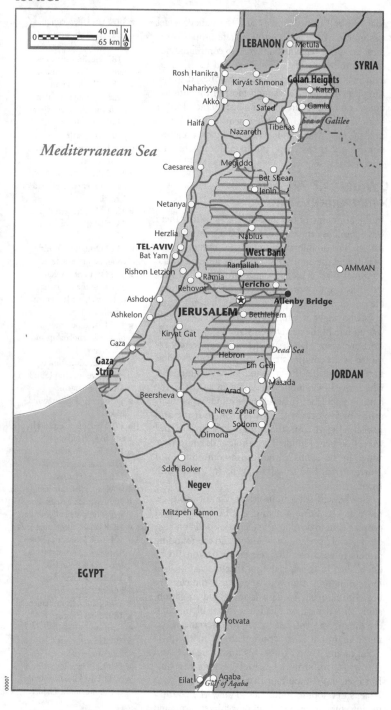

high-tech electronics. It also supports a burgeoning diamond and fashion industry—Israeli designs are highly regarded throughout the world. The Dead Sea, heavily saturated with minerals, has only begun to be exploited. Oil, however, must be imported. Israel's brilliant medical community, scientific establishment, and computer industries may one day benefit the entire region.

WAR & THE SEARCH FOR PEACE

During the Suez War of November 1956, Great Britain and France invaded Egypt in order to secure the Suez Canal, which Egypt had nationalized, and Israel, in coordination with Great Britain and France, conquered Egypt's Sinai Peninsula and the Gaza Strip hoping to put an end to 9 years of Egyptian terrorist attacks on southern Israel. In exchange for the stationing of a United Nations peacekeeping force on the Egyptian side of the Israeli–Sinai border, and with promises of freedom to send its shipping through the Red Sea and the Suez Canal, Israel withdrew entirely from the Sinai Peninsula and Gaza in early 1957. Ten years of relative peace and consolidation followed, punctuated by periodic Syrian sniping attacks on the Galilee from Syrian batteries on the Golan Heights.

Then, in May 1967, the United Nations peacekeeping force that had maintained security on the Israeli–Egyptian border for 10 years was unilaterally ordered out by Egypt's President Gamal Abdel Nasser, in violation of international guarantees. At the same time, Nasser blockaded the port of Eilat on the Red Sea, economically strangling Israel, while from the Golan Heights, Syria stood ready to attack the Galilee. The pace of Arab propaganda against Israel reached new pitches of frenzy and Arab armies mobilized to deliver what was claimed would be a crushing blow. For Israelis, only too aware that the nation was less than 10 miles wide at Tel Aviv, and that the Jordanian Army in East Jerusalem was aimed point blank at Jewish West Jerusalem, the agony of these weeks was unbearable. On June 5, 1967, Israel made a preemptive strike against the air forces of Egypt and Syria; Jordan, despite diplomatic pleas that it stay out of the conflict, began to shell West Jerusalem. In the Six-Day War that followed, Israel swept to an unimaginable victory, occupying the Sinai Peninsula, the Gaza Strip, the Golan Heights, East Jerusalem, and the entire West Bank. The Egyptian blockade of Eilat was broken. The Arab world was left in a state of shock. Suddenly

- **1914** Jews from Russia and Allied countries expelled by Ottoman Turks.
- **1917** Balfour Declaration supporting Jewish national home in Palestine. British free Jerusalem from Turks.
- **1920** Official start of British Mandate.
- **1922** British create Trans-Jordan (now Jordan) from Palestinian lands east of Jordan River.
- **1925** Hebrew University founded in Jerusalem.
- **1929** Arab–Jewish riots. Jews massacred at Hebron.
- **1936–39** Arab strikes and uprisings.
- **1939** British White Paper curtails Jewish immigration on eve of World War II.
- **1939–45** Six million Jews killed by Nazis in Europe.
- **1947** United Nations votes partition of Palestine into Jewish and Arab states. First Dead Sea Scrolls found.
- **1948** State of Israel declared. Five Arab countries attack.
- **1949–56** Cease-fire. Terrorist attacks on Negev from Egypt.
- **1956** Israel joins Anglo–French attack on Egypt. Conquers Sinai Peninsula.
- **1957** Israel returns Sinai. United Nations peacekeeping force installed in Egypt.
- **1967** Egypt expels peacekeeping force. Israel wins Six-Day War, occupies Sinai, Golan, West Bank, and Gaza.
- **1972** Palestinian terrorists massacre Israeli athletes at Munich Olympics.
- **1973** Egypt and Syria attack. Yom Kippur War.
- **1976** Israelis rescue Jewish hostages at Entebbe Airport.
- **1977** Likud wins elections. Sadat of Egypt comes to Jerusalem.
- **1979** Camp David peace treaty with Egypt.

continues

- 1981 Israel bombs atomic reactor in Iraq.
- 1982 Israel invades Lebanon.
- 1984 Labor–Likud Coalition. Withdrawal from most of Lebanon. Aliyah of Ethiopian Jews.
- 1987 Intifada begins.
- 1989 Great Soviet aliyah begins.
- 1991 Iraq attacks with Scud missiles. First peace talks with Arab states in Madrid.
- 1992 Labor Coalition government headed by Yitzhak Rabin elected. Rabin pledges new peace effort.
- 1993 Rabin and Arafat sign Declaration of Principles at White House.
- 1994 Israel withdraws from Jericho and Gaza as first step toward peace with Palestinians.
- 1995 Further Israeli withdrawals from West Bank. Prime Minister Rabin assassinated; world leaders attend his funeral in Jerusalem.

Israel was no longer a struggling state hanging on tenaciously to its hard-won independence. Land areas had more than trebled. Infusions of new immigrants swelled the country's Jewish population. The economy was burgeoning and tourism was increasing at a rate greater than ever before.

For travelers, Israel, with its artifacts, excavations, and kibbutzim, always had a lot to offer. After the 1967 war, it had more. Most important of all, there was united Jerusalem, the Western (Wailing) Wall, the Levantine veneer of the Old City. For Christians, Israel became a synonym for the entire Holy Land. Both sides of Jerusalem were joined together. Barbed-wire fences and the Mandelbaum Gate border post became things of the past. In the early days of what most hoped would be a short and benign occupation, Israelis and tourists enjoyed the exotic bazaars and holy sites of East Jerusalem and the West Bank. Bethlehem, once virtually inaccessible from Israel, was only minutes away from Jerusalem. Jericho, believed to be the oldest city in the world, and Hebron, where the ancient Hebrew patriarchs were buried, were open to visits. In the north, the Golan Heights provided a double meaning: tranquillity in Galilee and a new area for tourist inspection.

In the south, there was a new accessibility to the great historic wilderness called Sinai. Eilat, once considered by Israelis as the end of the earth, awoke one morning with a deep and dependable hinterland. The craggy isolation of the Santa Katerina Monastery, at the base of Mount Sinai where Moses was believed to have received the Ten Commandments, provided an unforgettable experience. Command cars, Jeeps, buses, and airplanes began penetrating the desert that had once sustained the ancient Israelites during their 40-year odyssey from Egypt to the Promised Land.

In those days the mood was optimistic. No one any longer questioned the premise that Israel was on the map for good. World economies were booming, and there was a tremendous quantity of expendable wealth. For tourists, the major concerns were hotel accommodations and airline space, and an empty hotel room in July was as rare as summer rain in the desert.

As the years passed, the Arab world continued to refuse to recognize Israel diplomatically, and the plight of the Palestinian refugees scattered throughout the Middle East continued to be ignored by the world at large. In the absence of a peace settlement that would trade most land captured in 1967 for peace, the occupation of the West Bank and the Gaza Strip began to seem less temporary. The small political movement for Jewish settlement of the Occupied Territories began to grow, although initially opposed by the Israeli government. Resentment among the Palestinians under occupation quietly rose.

The country experienced a sharp change in fortune in October 1973. The completely unexpected Yom Kippur War had a sobering effect on the entire nation. The price was steep. More than 2,500 young men were killed in 1 month, losses proportionately higher than the casualties the United States sustained during the entire Vietnam War. Egyptian and Syrian casualties were enormous. While the war ended with Israel closer to Cairo and Damascus than ever before, the initial setbacks and the high cost in lives shook the nation's confidence, and tarnished the image of national heroes. In a backlash, voters turned against the Labor Party, which had led the state since its foundation, and elected a new government dominated by the right-of-center Likud.

A few weeks after he assumed office in 1977, Prime Minister Menachem Begin quietly asked neutral intermediaries to arrange a meeting with Egypt's President Sadat anywhere in the world. This set in motion a series of events highlighted by President Sadat's dramatic visit to Jerusalem, the conclusion of a framework for the Middle East peace agreement in Camp David, and the treaty with Egypt in March 1979 terminating 30 years of war between the two countries. Accordingly, Israel withdrew from the Sinai, and Mount Sinai with the Santa Katerina Monastery reverted to Egypt. With the state of peace it remains open to tourists from Israel.

The hopes for a regional peace settlement, which the Egyptian–Israeli settlement raised, were not quickly realized. No additional Arab countries came forward to negotiate. The 1982 invasion of southern Lebanon put further strains on Israel's relations with its neighbors, and provoked a great deal of debate in every sector of Israeli society. Triple-digit inflation and deteriorating relations with Palestinians in the Occupied Territories, as more land was appropriated for Jewish settlements, marked the early 1980s. The withdrawal from Lebanon and the economic stability achieved under Shimon Peres's brief tenure as prime minister from 1984 to 1986 promised better times, but in late 1987, the Palestinian population of the West Bank and Gaza, under military occupation since 1967, decided it could no longer allow its land and future to be endlessly controlled by Israel. The *Intifada*, a grass-roots program of daily commercial strikes and demonstrations (both violent and nonviolent) against the military authorities, began. The Israeli people suddenly had to face long-postponed decisions about the nature of their democracy, and about how much of their tiny margin of security they dared to trade for promises of peace. Polls indicated a majority of the Israeli public did not support unlimited settlement of the West Bank and Gaza, but the Likud government, led by Yitzhak Shamir, continued to pursue a policy of developing Israeli settlements in those areas.

The year 1990 brought unexpected challenges to Israel, initially with a massive wave of 350,000 immigrants from the dissolving Soviet system, and in the summer of 1990, with the Kuwait crisis. Israel was not a direct participant in the Allied coalition against Iraq; however, in an attempt to win support for his policies throughout the Arab World, Saddam Hussein threatened to "incinerate half of Israel" with missile-born chemical attacks should the Allied coalition move against him. The United States asked Israel to refrain from retaliating if it came under attack and pledged that any threat to Israel from Iraqi missiles would be destroyed by American bombing within the first hours of the war. Nevertheless, Israelis found themselves sitting in sealed rooms, experiencing Scud missile attacks almost nightly for the entire 6 weeks of the Gulf War. Although in the end the missiles were not armed with chemical weaponry, the ordeal of the Scuds and their threat of chemical annihilation has left its mark on the Israeli mind. Faced with the prospect of more terrible chemical, bacteriological, and nuclear weapons in the future, many Israelis have come to believe it is worth taking extraordinary risks to try to achieve peace and create stability in the Middle East now. Other Israelis are more determined than ever to avoid any further concessions.

Negotiating directly with Palestinians and with moderate Arab governments, Israel began a planned withdrawal from the West Bank and Gaza in 1994. In the same year, a peace treaty was signed with the Kingdom of Jordan. The assassination of Prime Minister Rabin by a Jewish opponent of the peace process in November 1995 was a blow for those who hope to create a new Middle East. The extraordinary gathering of world leaders for Rabin's funeral in Jerusalem indicates the depth of concern throughout the world for the future of the peoples who live in the Holy Land.

3 Israel's Famous People

Menachem Begin (1913–92)   Polish-born Zionist leader, he was rescued from a Stalinist prison in Russia in 1942 through international efforts spearheaded by his wife, Aliza. Begin arrived in Palestine during World War II, having lost much of his family in the Holocaust, and assumed command of an underground organization responsible for attacks against the British presence in Palestine. Condemned by Ben-Gurion and the Israeli provisional government for these tactics, and for reported killing of Arab civilians, Begin led the opposition to the Labor governments of 1948–77. He became prime minister in 1977, and presided over the Camp David negotiations and peace treaty with Egypt in 1979. Though he approved the invasion of Lebanon in 1982, he resigned as prime minister in 1983 in despair over the course of the Lebanese War and the death of his wife. With Anwar Sadat, he was the recipient of the Nobel Prize for Peace.

David Ben-Gurion (1886–1973)   Polish-born Zionist leader, he immigrated to Ottoman-ruled Palestine in 1906. Exiled by Ottoman Turks during World War I, he fled to the United States, where he met his wife, Paula. Ceaseless architect of the emerging Jewish state in the 1920s and 1930s, he became Israel's first prime minister and led the country in the 1948 War of Independence. Deeply committed to the land, a visionary who believed Israel's future lay in the development of the desert, he retired to the Negev kibbutz of Sde Boker after his final term in office. In the euphoria after the 1967 war, Ben-Gurion urged magnanimous terms for a peace settlement, including the return of conquered lands. He lived just long enough to see his country survive the onslaught of the Yom Kippur War in 1973.

Abba Eban (1915–)   A South African–born, Cambridge-educated author, diplomat, and former foreign minister, he is noted for an eloquence and wit unrivaled among Western leaders since Winston Churchill. (Asked by reporters to comment on the division between hawks and doves in the Israeli government during the tense days before the outbreak of the Six-Day War in 1967, he solemnly replied, "The government of Israel is hardly an aviary.") Known for his PBS television series, *Civilization and the Jews,* Eban is also an Arabic scholar and a supporter of more moderate policies regarding the West Bank and Gaza.

Teddy Kollek (1910–)   Indefatigable mayor of Jerusalem for 28 years, Kollek was raised in Vienna, arrived in Palestine during the rise of the Nazis in the 1930s, and was originally a member of Kibbutz Ein Gev. Leader of the One Jerusalem Coalition, his commitment to maintaining peace among the many ethnic and religious groups in the city has been matched by his determination to adorn Jerusalem with every kind of artistic, cultural, and civic treasure possible. Incredibly accessible to the people of Jerusalem, during his long tenure Teddy often answered the municipality office phones himself in the early morning hours before his staff arrived.

Golda Meir (1898–1978)   Born in Russia, she emigrated to the United States as a child. As a young Milwaukee schoolteacher and ardent Zionist, she decided to emigrate to British Mandate Palestine in 1921. She held many posts in the Labor Party and was famous for personal courage: In 1948, on the eve of Israeli independence, she traveled to Jordan at great risk, disguised as an Arab woman, to plead with King Abdullah not to make war on the new Jewish nation. Prime minister from 1969 to 1974, her government was criticized for failing to detect the Egyptian and Syrian Yom Kippur surprise attack in 1973, and bore responsibility for heavy casualties. Named by Ben-Gurion as "the only real man in the government," Meir projected a grandmotherly image, often doing business with Israeli and foreign leaders in her kitchen. In 1977, when Anwar Sadat made his electrifying journey to Jerusalem to address the Knesset, Meir, at the climax of the assembly, spoke in the practical down-to-earth style for which she is best remembered: "It's late. Go home. Go to sleep. There's a lot of work to be done in the morning."

Yitzhak Rabin (1922–1995)   Rabin was the first Israeli prime minister to be born in the land that was to become Israel. Originally a student of agronomy, he joined Palmach, the elite Haganah strike force, and served with Allied forces fighting in the Middle East during World War II. A brilliant strategist, as commander in chief of Israel's armed forces during the Six-Day War in 1967, he led the country to its greatest military triumph. Rabin's first term as prime minister, from 1974 to 1977, was distinguished by the successful raid on Entebbe Airport in Uganda, which rescued almost 100 Jewish and Israeli hostages. As defense minister in a Likud–Labor Coalition government at the start of the Intifada in 1987, he supported a hard line against Palestinian demonstrators, but came to be increasingly committed to creating a world in which Israelis and Palestinians could live side by side—"In dignity. In empathy. As human beings." A modest, noncharasmatic leader, public faith in Rabin's caution and judgment enabled him to make concessions and territorial withdrawals in the search for peace. He was the recipient of the Nobel Peace Prize. Rabin was assassinated by an Israeli opponent to his policies in November 1995.

Boris Schatz (1866–1932)   Lithuanian-born court sculptor to Prince Ferdinand of Bulgaria, and ardent follower of Theodor Herzl, Schatz arrived in Jerusalem in 1906 and founded the Bezalel Academy of Arts and Crafts with the purpose of developing an indigenous artistic tradition for the nation he believed would one day be reborn. The Bezalel Academy planted the seeds for a modern cultural scene in Jerusalem, which had previously been a remote, religiously oriented community. Israel's extraordinary commitment to the arts is in no small part due to Schatz's vision of art as a necessary component of Zionism, as well as to his legendary struggle to keep the Bezalel School alive despite overwhelming odds.

Abraham Ticho (1883–1960)   Born in Moravia, Dr. Ticho arrived in Jerusalem in 1912 determined to battle against trachoma and other endemic eye diseases that caused thousands of cases of blindness among the local population. As founder and head of Jerusalem's first ophthalmic hospital, he became a modern Jerusalem legend, at times brusquely dragging off both Jewish and Arab children he spotted on the streets for treatment at his clinic, and working devotedly to save the eyesight of all who approached him, including Emir Abdullah (later King Abdullah) of Jordan. When he was stabbed and left for dead during the political unrest of 1929, thousands in Jerusalem's Jewish, Christian, and Muslim communities prayed for Dr. Ticho's recovery. As one whose life's work was bringing light to others, Dr. Ticho was fascinated by Hanukkah menorahs used to celebrate the Jewish festival of lights, sometimes accepting Hanukkah lamps in exchange for treatment. His remarkable collection of menorahs is now in the Israel Museum. The 19th-century mansion he shared with his wife, the artist Anna Ticho, is now a downtown branch of the Israel Museum, as well as a popular cafe and meeting place.

Yigael Yadin (1917–84)   The son of the legendary Professor E. L. Sukenik of Hebrew University (who first identified the Dead Sea Scrolls, and who, at the risk of his life, managed to obtain a number of the first-discovered scrolls for Israel on the eve of the War of Independence in 1947), Yigael Yadin was a leading member of the Haganah during the 1940s and was responsible for drawing up and implementing Haganah's operations during the War of Independence. After serving as chief of staff of the Israel Defense Forces until 1952, Yadin devoted himself to archeology, leading and writing about excavations at Hazor, Masada, and in the caves of the Judean Desert, and publishing extensively on the Dead Sea Scrolls. As a brilliant teacher and lecturer, his ability to explain archeological artifacts in their cultural context, and to use these finds to cast new light on basic questions about the biblical, Second Temple, and Talmudic periods, made archeology so thrilling and accessible to the Israeli people that Yadin was virtually a national hero. (Once, when Yadin rushed into a grocery shop, and without introducing himself or explaining why, asked for empty containers that were needed to pack an unexpected archeological find, the grocer tore his shop apart to supply the proper-size boxes. No explanations were necessary.) In the late 1970s, Yadin led an unsuccessful movement to reform the Israeli political system.

4 Architecture

Casting a shadow over all other structures in Israel are two that long ago vanished: the legendary First Temple, built by King Solomon in approximately 960 B.C. and destroyed by the Babylonians, and the Second Temple, originally put together on the ruins of the First Temple, then reconstructed into a vast Hellenistic-style pilgrimage complex by order of the Roman-installed King Herod in 18 B.C. (the final touches of this ceremonial center were not completed until A.D. 64, almost 70 years after Herod's death). In front of the First Temple, a Canaanite-style sanctuary building embellished with decorations of cedar, ivory, and gold, King Solomon is recorded in the Bible to have prayed: "The heavens, even the heaven of heavens, cannot contain Thee; how much less this house that I have built." Of the Second Temple, the Roman historian Tacitus records that on the eve of the destruction of Jerusalem by Roman armies in A.D. 70, the Roman General Titus called a council to decide whether, in victory, Rome should destroy "the Temple, one of man's consummate building achievements." The fact that the Romans would hesitate to destroy the temple of a stubbornly rebellious subject nation is an indication of the Herodian structure's grandeur and charisma. The Western Wall is part of the retaining-wall system that holds up the vast artificially created ceremonial plaza that surrounded the Herodian temple. A few architectural details found in archeological excavations since 1967 have been identified with the structures that formed part of the Herodian complex, but no fragment of the actual Second Temple building has yet been found.

Of all the still-standing buildings you will see in Israel, nothing is more incredible than the Dome of the Rock, built on the site of the First and Second Temples by the early Islamic rulers of Jerusalem in A.D. 691. The Byzantine architects who were commissioned to design the Dome of the Rock may have been inspired by the legends of the two vanished structures. One of the world's most beautiful buildings, adorned in the 16th century with Persian tiles by Sultan Suleiman the Magnificent, this shrine acts as a crown to a site that is both physically and spiritually sublime. With its golden dome, like a gilded balloon against the skies, offering intimations of ascension to the heavens (as Koranic tradition records Muhammad did from this very spot), it is difficult to believe that any other building could have combined such simplicity with such intricacy and done equal justice to the unadorned monotheistic concept and complex traditions associated with the site.

Two remarkable Frankish Romanesque churches remain from the Crusader period: the heavily restored Church of Saint Anne in Jerusalem, and the church in Abu Ghosh, near Jerusalem, which is more in its original state. Both, designed using Eastern and Western techniques to create marvelous acoustics, are musical instruments to be played by the human voice: a single soprano will sound like a choir of angels. The Street of the Chain and the Temple Mount in Jerusalem offer many examples of architecture from the Mameluke period. The labyrinthine Old City of Akko, with its medieval khans and Ottoman Al-Jazzar mosque, should be considered a national treasure. Unfortunately, the bazaars and residential quarters of Old Akko, while still fascinating to visitors, have been deliberately left in ill repair due to local political considerations.

The International Style of the 1930s and 1940s was brought to British Mandate Palestine by refugee architects who had studied at the Bauhaus and worked in the studios of Le Corbusier, Gropius, and Mies van der Rohe. Tel Aviv has one of the world's largest urban concentrations of such buildings, with their crisp white concrete curvilinear and blocklike shapes. These buildings were recorded in international architectural publications of their times as visionary gems, but a combination of civic unconcern and the fact that the sand-laden bricks used for construction did not weather well, has left many of these structures in a state of near ruin.

The British Mandate period also left an architectural legacy in Jerusalem, where the high commissioner issued an ordinance that all construction must be faced with Jerusalem stone. Both the YMCA Building on King David Street (designed by the same American firm that did New York City's Empire State Building) and the Rockefeller Museum, designed by the noted British architect Austin S. B. Harrison, exhibit an interesting mixture of art deco, Byzantine, and Islamic themes.

The vast neighborhoods constructed after 1948 in Israel's main cities and development towns were built quickly, according to European concepts of practicality. Most Israelis detest these postindependence apartment blocks, locally known as egg boxes, but they have come to dominate the landscapes of cities and towns.

Renovation and restoration have become important factors in saving the architectural heritage Israel still possesses. The reconstructions of the old quarter of Jaffa, and of the Jewish Quarter in Jerusalem's Old City, as well as the gentrified 19th-century Jerusalem neighborhoods like Yemin Moshe, Ein Kerem, and the German Colony, are places of real charm and sense of community; but other urban planning projects, like the expanded routing of a major road system alongside the walls of Jerusalem's Old City, complete with pedestrian under- and overpasses to the Jaffa Gate, and the piecemeal destruction of West Jerusalem's 19th-century Ha-Nevi'im Street neighborhood, may prove to be repetitions of mistakes already made in Western cities.

5 Language

The *lingua franca* of modern Israel is Hebrew—the resurrected language of biblical times. Hebrew has only come to life again as a language of day-to-day speech during the past 100 years. Although Hebrew ("the tongue of Canaan," according to the Prophet Isaiah) was the language of much of the time period of the Old Testament, it was gradually supplanted after the Babylonian Captivity (586 B.C.) by Aramaic, another Semitic language that became the *lingua franca* of the region for the next 500 years. As Jewish history moved into the Diaspora, Jewish communities spoke Greek and Greek *koine,* Judeo-Persian, Latin and Arabic, Ladino (the late medieval Spanish of the Jewish community expelled from Spain in 1492 and spoken by many of their descendants to this day), and expressive, irony-prone Yiddish, a medieval Rhine Valley German written with Hebrew letters, which the Jewish communities of northern Europe maintained and developed as they wandered deeper and deeper into Eastern Europe over the centuries.

When Eliezer Ben-Yehuda (1858–1922), a Polish-born linguist, came to Jerusalem in 1881, he believed that ancient Hebrew, used mainly as a liturgical language since the 5th century B.C., should be the language of the reborn Zionist vision. He codified Hebrew grammar, wrote the first modern dictionary, and coined words necessary for a modern vocabulary. Ben-Yehuda and his wife, also a linguist, spoke only Hebrew to their son, Itamar, who became the first primarily Hebrew-speaking person in the modern world.

From their initial determination, the Hebrew language, with its uniqueness and vitality, was brought back to life, changing and growing each day—the Israeli people's great communal work of art. Modern Hebrew (by no means an artificial language) is being stretched by the hour by its Israeli speakers as they take the language of a laconic, pastoral Iron Age civilization and reshape it to the needs of an enormously cosmopolitan, gregarious, heterogeneous society of the late 20th century.

Written in its own alphabet, Hebrew must be transliterated into the Latin alphabet for non-Hebrew speakers. The varying ways in which Hebrew names are transliterated is sure to confuse you—most places seem to have several different names and spellings. Is it Jaffa, Joppa, or Yafo? Safed, Safad, Zfat, or Zefat? Lake Tiberias, the Sea of Galilee, or Kinneret Lake?

The confusion stems partly from Israel's long history, partly from myriad cultures and languages, and partly from Hebrew itself. Vowels are not normally written in

❓ Did You Know?

- Half of all Israeli Jews emigrated from or are descendants of immigrants from countries in the Middle East.

- Approximately 70,000 American and Canadian Jews have emigrated to Israel since 1948. This represents 1% of the total Jewish population of North America from 1948 to 1991.

- The former Soviet Union has ranked first among countries of origin for immigrants to Israel since 1948. Other nations that have provided the greatest number of immigrants to Israel are (in order) Romania, Morocco, Poland, Iraq, and Iran.

- One out of every six Israeli citizens living inside the pre-1967 borders of Israel is Arab, Druze, or Bedouin.

- The 1.7 million Palestinians under Israeli administration in the Occupied Territories are not Israeli citizens.

- Whether or not they are Israeli citizens, Palestinians in East Jerusalem are permitted to vote in municipal elections.

Hebrew (this is also true of Arabic), and so in transliteration you get such un pronounceable words as Sde (for Sede) and Sderot (Sederot). Further confusions are added by sounds like the guttural "kh" sound, a rasping in the back of the throat usually rendered as "ch," but pronounced very differently from the "ch" in "church." You might come across "Hen" and "Chen," which are the same Hebrew word, pronounced more like "khen." How does one cope? The only way is to pronounce the word you want and compare it to the one you've found. If it sounds the same, it probably is: Mikveh Israel, Miqwe Yisra'el, Elot-Elat-Eilat, Tiberias-Teverya . . .

Arabic is the second official language of Israel, and English is Israel's major inter national language, so you will find that street and road signs are in Hebrew, Arabic, and English. English will work in virtually every shop, restaurant, and hotel in the three major cities, as well as most other places. If, however, you chance to encoun ter a storekeeper who speaks only Russian, Hebrew, Arabic, or one of the 17 or so other relatively common languages, just look for his 12-year-old son, who's study ing English in school.

If you find yourself groping for another language, try French, German, or Yiddish. Many Israelis of Romanian origin know French, and most of the Israelis of North African birth, who come from Morocco, Algeria, and Tunisia, also speak fluent French.

You can use the Hebrew and Arabic glossaries at the back of this book as a crutch— you'll find that your stabs at speaking the native tongues will be warmly appreciated.

6 Religion

Israel is special, if not sacred, to more faiths than is any other country in the world. Today for at least 15 different Jewish sects, several Christian sects, Muslims, Druze, Baha'is, Samaritans, Circassians, Karaites, Bedouin, and still others, Israel is holy, and although many of the groups claim the land as "their own," the differing faiths are practiced side by side, and within these faiths there are often further differences from group to group. This calls for daily tolerance. For instance, there are Jews who visit Israel and return home shaking their heads in woe because it isn't "Jewish" in the way they personally practice or understand Judaism. Christians traveling in Israel are often perplexed by certain Israeli Christian groups—those that charge entrance fees at holy shrines, or those that subdivide famous churches (with actual lines of demar cation on walls and floors) among different sects of Christianity. Protestants are often amazed to find most holy places tended by Catholics; Catholics are surprised to find their Israeli counterparts functioning as they did hundreds of years ago, instead of following the modern practices that have spread to most parts of the Catholic world.

To Muslims, the patriarchs were holy men and Jesus was a prophet, though not the final one. Islam, in some ways, is closer to Judaism and the nomadic-type culture of the patriarchs than to the Greek-influenced culture of Christianity. Muslims are dedicatedly monotheistic: There is but one God, Allah, and the only way is submission to his will. Muslims pray five times a day, fast in daylight hours during the month of Ramadan, make a pilgrimage to Mecca, and give alms. Thursday's sunset to sunset on Friday is the Muslim Sabbath. Like Jews, Muslims are enjoined from eating pork. Gambling and drinking alcohol are also prohibited to Muslims, and they may not make paintings or sculptures of human beings or animals. The men may marry up to four wives, although this tradition is practiced very rarely.

7 Cuisine & Customs

THE SABBATH   You will need to know a few things about Sabbath dining. On Friday afternoons and afternoons before holidays, shops, offices, and kosher restaurants close around 2pm in preparation for the Sabbath, which begins at sunset. Most restaurants don't reopen until Saturday evening after dark. In summer, the Saturday evening reopening can be quite late. Depending on the volume of business, some restaurants may stay open beyond normal closing hours on Saturday night. In most cities an increasing number of nonkosher restaurants remain open on the Sabbath.

Saturday's breakfast is usually provided by your hotel, and by Saturday's dinnertime, restaurants will be open again. That leaves Friday's dinner and Saturday's lunch. If you're kosher, eat a hearty lunch on Friday, and buy snacks or picnic supplies for Friday evening and Saturday's lunch.

KOSHER FOOD   Those unfamiliar with kosher food may find a few surprises as well. To outsiders, the kosher prohibitions against eating pork and serving meat and milk products at the same meal are the most noticeable laws of *kashrut*.

According to the rigorous regulations of kashrut, only peaceful animals that chew their cuds and have cleft hooves and birds that do not eat carrion may be used for food, but only if they have been killed instantly according to methods supervised by religious authorities. If there is reason to believe that an animal may have died in pain, or of disease, it cannot be considered kosher (which means no hunted animals). Only fish with fins and scales can be eaten, which means no shellfish or dolphins.

A restaurant may maintain a kosher menu, but if it prepares and cooks food or does business on Shabbat, it will generally not be able to receive a kashrut certificate. Many hotels prepare meals before Shabbat for their anticipated guests, and either serve cold Saturday meals, or meals that have been kept warm on fires that were started before Shabbat.

Kosher restaurants that serve milk will not serve any food containing meat or poultry, although they are permitted to serve fish. This means that cheese lasagne must be meatless. In restaurants serving meat, your coffee will be served with milk substitute.

In many cases, kosher restaurants may be 5% to 10% more expensive than comparable nonkosher restaurants. If kashrut is not a concern, you can save a bit by seeking out nonkosher places. Glatt kosher almost always means a higher price. Most kosher restaurants have adapted so skillfully to their constraints that you will notice nothing very unusual in your dining experiences.

THE CUISINE   For the first half of Israel's existence the restaurant scene was almost as Spartan and no-nonsense as the State of Israel itself. Kibbutz cuisine was king, starting with hotel breakfasts, where you could have your fill of bland but healthy chopped tomato and cucumber salad, hard-boiled egg, heavy, government-subsidized white bread, soft cheese, olives, and orange juice or punch. A typical tourist lunch was felafel, hummus, or shwarma in pita bread with chopped salad, and for dinner, there was no lack of places with Formica tables where you could get turkey schnitzel or a chicken thigh with french fries and that ubiquitous, healthy chopped salad. Anyone looking for a bagel and lox with cream cheese or corned beef on rye would be directed to New York (*beigele* still means a pretzel in Israel to this day) and the one consolation was that most tourists returned home from 2 weeks in Israel able to fit comfortably into clothes that had previously been tight.

Israeli Street Food

Felafel and shwarma tucked into a pita bread with chopped salad and eaten on the run have become the national fast foods of Israel.

1. A quality felafel (spiced chickpea fritter) sandwich should contain at least four felafels and include your choice of a number of fresh salads.

2. Buy from places with a big turnover and fresh, hot felafels. You should be able to see felafels being fried; if the oil is dirty or idle and not constantly boiling, move on.

3. A good, fresh salad bar is an indication of fresh felafel and shwarma.

4. A sandwich made with giant napkin-size Iraqi pita bread (available at stands in Jerusalem's Mahane Yehuda and Tel Aviv's Hatikvah) costs half a shekel more and fills you up for most of the day.

5. Shwarma (spiced turkey or lamb on a spit) should be freshly sliced from the spit. If the proprietor must turn on the flame and heat the spit of shwarma for you, move on.

6. Many stands offer hummus (spiced chickpea paste) either as a separate sandwich choice or with felafel. Avoid it after 11am on a hot summer day.

7. Felafel sandwiches, especially with lots of essential tchina sauce, tend to be messy. Grab tons of napkins. Pay extra for a place where you can sit.

Gone are those days! After 1967 things began to change. Israeli restaurants began to offer a wide variety of main and side dishes done in real Middle Eastern tradition. Israeli fish farming began to thrive, and with it, choices such as St. Peter's fish from the Galilee, trout from the Dan, and even homegrown salmon, which over the years has been refined to a high level of excellence. A new fast food, the boureka, a flaky, salty cheese pie of Greek origin, swept the nation. People began to envision possibilities beyond hummus and felafel. Pizza hit the streets of every downtown district. Israelis from Asian and North African countries—Yemenites with their *melawach* dishes, Iraqis with their spicy *kubbehs*, Moroccans with their exotic sauces—all began to challenge the notion that East European borscht, blintzes, and chicken soup were the only true Jewish cuisine. In the 1970s, Israel began to admit boat people as well as other Asians. Chinese and Thai restaurants cautiously opened and many Asians found jobs in traditional Israeli restaurants, where they began to make interesting suggestions. Israelis, hitherto hampered by a heavy travel tax, suddenly found themselves free to visit other lands when the tax was removed in 1977. Exotic tastes began to develop.

Israeli cuisine simmered for a decade and finally burst forth in the late 1980s with a new generation of restaurants offering inventive, intelligent menus that find their roots in the country's remarkably international character. Israeli restaurant owners are falling in love with elegant sauces and exotic seasonings, and customers are responding to quality meals. The country has become the vanguard of a new approach to cooking that mixes the informal rustic cuisines of countries around the Mediterranean Rim with a touch of Hungarian and East European traditions.

You can find interesting food at all prices. In the budget range, I especially like Sheba, an Ethiopian restaurant in Jerusalem, and the Yemenite Step in Jerusalem, with its exotic spices and melawach dishes.

At the other end of the price scale, Israel now offers many worthwhile luxury restaurants. Where else but in Israel can you find such an array of elegant nouvelle cuisine restaurants that are kosher! The Tel Aviv Sheraton's Twelve Tribes restaurant is perhaps the most exciting of these choices, with an exquisite and endlessly inventive kosher menu. Jerusalem's nonkosher seafood restaurant, Ocean, is a superb example of the new Mediterranean Rim cuisine at its very best.

In the moderate price range, there are memorable finds, like Niss in Jerusalem, where you can order homemade Kurdish *angesia* in apricot-raisin sweet-and-sour sauce, or the Pagoda in Tiberias, where you can dine on world-class Thai cuisine (kosher) while enjoying vistas of the Sea of Galilee. For those who are not kosher, pleasures expand logarithmically, from the baklavaries and hummus parlors of Jerusalem's Old City (Abu Shukri, long a master of hummus, has recently been immortalized in the pages of *Playboy* magazine) to the inventiveness and gusto of places like Victor and Margaret Tayar's Fish Restaurant in Jaffa, Voilà (Swiss–French) in Haifa, Retavim in Tel Aviv with its kaleidoscope of sauces, or the unexpected exoticism of Tandoori in Eilat, where classical Indian musicians and dancers perform during your meal.

Israel in the 1990s is a genuine food festival that's nothing like what grandma used to make. Enjoy! Eat and be well! *Betayavon!*

8 Recommended Books & Recordings

BOOKS
GENERAL BACKGROUND

A History of the Holyland, edited by Michael Avi-Yonah, is a helpful book. Josephus's *The Jewish Wars* is on every English-speaking Israeli's bookshelf. A Jewish general in the Galilee during the revolt against Rome in A.D. 66—and an eventual traitor—Josephus was also a historian who provided volumes of historical commentaries and anecdotes about almost every area you'll see in Israel. *The Earthly Jerusalem,* by Norman Kotker (Scribners, 1972), is a graceful, wryly intelligent history of Jerusalem from earliest to modern times. *Jerusalem on Earth,* by Abraham Rabinovich (Macmillan, New York and London, 1988), contains wonderful real-life stories about people in contemporary Jerusalem by one of the *Jerusalem Post*'s finest human-interest writers. *Jerusalem, Rebirth of a City,* by Martin Gilbert, the official biographer of Winston Churchill (Viking, New York, 1985; Butler and Tanner, Great Britain), is an absolutely fascinating, illustrated, year-by-year survey of Jerusalem in the 19th century. *Sinai, The Great and Terrible Wilderness,* by Burton Bernstein (Viking, 1979), originally published in the *New Yorker,* is an amazing account of the natural wonders, people, and history of this wilderness so crucial to the spiritual origins of Judaism. *Summer in Galilee,* by Juliette de Bairacli-Levy (Shocken Press, New York; Faber & Faber, London, 1959), is a noted British herbalist's reminiscences of two summers beside the Sea of Galilee, told with a fine eye for the plants, animals, and legends of the countryside.

POLITICS & RECENT HISTORY

Among the most readable books in this field are *The Yellow Wind,* by David Grossman (Farrar Straus & Giroux, 1989), in which interviews and anecdotes collected by a talented Israeli novelist reveal the passion and despair of the Palestinian people; *From Beirut to Jerusalem,* by Thomas L. Friedman (Farrar Straus & Giroux, 1989), an analysis of the current Arab–Israeli problem, filled with fascinating personal stories and background material by the *New York Times* Middle East correspondent; *They Must Go,* by Meir Kahane (Grosset & Dunlap, 1981), a delineation of the case for believing no peace will come to the region until Arabs are expelled from Israel and the lands under Israeli control; *My Enemy My Self,* by Yoram Binur (Doubleday, 1989), an Israeli journalist's revealing and powerful report of his experiences disguised as a Palestinian laborer inside Israel. *Zealots for Zion,* by Robert I. Friedman (Random House, 1992), is a fascinating survey of the West Bank settlement movement. An unusual book is *Blood Brothers,* by Father Elias Chakour (Chosen Books, 1984), the decades-long odyssey of Father Chakour's own Israeli Christian Arab village, exiled and dispersed throughout the Galilee by Israeli authorities for what at first promised to be a short period of time during the 1948 War of Independence. Father Chakour's account of Israeli politics and history may seem sometimes naive, but the book documents his personal attempt, as an Israeli Arab, to come to terms with the suffering of his people, and to bring about reconciliation between Arabs and Jews.

ARCHEOLOGY

Yigael Yadin, the Israeli archeologist whose father, Professor E. L. Sukenik of Hebrew University, identified the first fragments of the Dead Sea Scrolls in 1947, has written a beautifully photographed, thrilling book about the final archeological search of the Dead Sea Caves in the early 1960s. The book, *Bar-Kokhba* (Harper & Row, 1971), which almost reads like a novel, is available in bookstores throughout Israel and most American libraries. Perhaps no other book lets you share the excitement of each amazing discovery, and lets you understand what archeology means to those who love Israel. Yigael Yadin is also the author of books on the Masada and Hazor archeological projects.

Other recommended books about archeology include *Judaism in Stone,* by Hershel Shanks (Harper & Row, New York and London, 1979), a heavily illustrated survey of ancient synagogues in Israel and the Middle East; and *In the Shadow of the Temple,* by Meir Ben-Dov (Harper & Row, New York, 1985), a lavishly illustrated and photographed volume detailing recent archeological discoveries in the Jewish Quarter of Jerusalem.

FICTION & POETRY

Israeli writers face the problem of creating a literature in a language that has mainly been used for prayer and religious study for over 2,000 years. Working in a tradition so long interrupted, writers face many problems. Young Israeli readers often find the work of Tchernichovsky and Bialik, leading figures in Hebrew literature from the early decades of this century, to be stilted and distant from current Hebrew-speaking style and society, and often blanch at flowery, romantic sensibility and at rhymes that depend on what is now considered to be a graceless East European distortion of true Hebrew pronunciation. On the other hand, English-speaking readers may find much of the new-generation Israeli writing to be deliberately ponderous and philosophical, lacking the sense of humor and feeling for the ridiculous that often characterizes the work of Jewish writers outside Israel.

Among the Israeli writers most accessible to English-speaking readers are Amos Oz, whose early novel, *My Michael,* with its delicate narrative voice, has been beautifully translated into English; Yehuda Amichai, whose poetry is personal, yet filled with evocative Israeli locales, imagery, and a graceful, visionary wit; and Aharon Appelfeld, who writes in the surreal, European tradition of Kafka. The revered S. Y. Agnon, Israel's first Nobel Prize–winning writer, worked in a disciplined Hebrew that drew intensively on a knowledge of East European legends and Jewish intellectual and religious history. Try his novel, *The Bridal Canopy.* Emile Habiby is an award-winning writer from Israel's Arabic community; his wry approach can be sampled in *The Secret Life of Saeed, the Ill-fated Pessoptimist: A Palestinian Who Became a Citizen of Israel.* Anton Shamas displays an interesting blend of both Hebrew and Arabic style and sensibility. His novel, *Arabesques,* points to rich, new directions in which Israeli writing may develop. Among other outstanding modern novels are *The Smile of the Lamb,* by David Grossman, and *A Late Divorce,* by A. B. Yehoshua.

For a sampling of Israeli poetry, read *The Modern Hebrew Poem Itself,* anthology edited by Stanley Burnshaw (Holt Rinehart & Winston, 1965); *Poems of Jerusalem,* by Yehuda Amichai (Harper & Row, 1988); and *Even a Fist Was Once an Open Palm with Fingers,* by Yehuda Amichai (Harper Books, 1991).

OTHER BOOKS

Footloose in Jerusalem, by Sarah Fox Kaminker (a former American who held a seat on the Jerusalem City Council and led a movement for neighborhood preservation), and *Jerusalemwalks,* by Nitza Rosovsky, are two books filled with interesting guided walking tours in Jerusalem.

RECORDINGS

The **Oranim Zabar Troup** featuring **Geula Gill** orchestrated and performed many of the classic 1950s Israeli songs that are known to Israeli folk dancers around the world. Look for "Shalom!" "Hora," and "On the Road to Eilat" (Electra Records).

The noted ethnomusicologist Deben Bhattacharya has compiled a wonderful four-record collection of traditional Israeli musicians from Morocco, Uzbekistan, Bukhara, Yemen, and other lands, called *In Israel Today* (Westminster Recordings).

Israeli popular music reflects a lively, unusual blend of Western and Middle Eastern styles and sensibilities. Among the current favorites to look for are **Ethnix,** a group that does orientalized versions of Western dance rock; **Zehava Ben,** a wildly popular songstress of Jewish–Moroccan ancestry (her song, "Ketourne Massala," in collaboration with Ethnix, was one of Israel's biggest hits in recent years); **Ofra Haza,** one of the few Israeli singers to break into the international market, with a repertoire that includes both traditional Yemenite songs and rearrangements of these pieces into disco (*Shadai* is her most popular album; *Desert Wind* is geared to the dance market); and **Yehuda Poliker,** the son of a Holocaust survivor from the Greek community of Salonika, whose 1985 best-selling album *Enayim Sheli (My Eyes)* opened the door to Hebrew interpretation and rendition of Greek music. Finally, of special interest to Westerners is **Ahinoam Nini** (in America, she's known as "Noa"), who grew up in the United States and has returned to dazzle her homeland. Her original songs and renditions of classics range from witty to dramatic and reflect a lively New York, English-language, Yemenite–Israeli sensibility that's absolute dynamite! **Bustan Avraham** (The Gardens of Abraham), a group that does lovely interpretations of traditional Middle Eastern music, is also currently popular.

Planning a Trip to Israel 3

In this chapter, the where, when, and how of your trip are discussed—
the advanced planning that gets your trip together and takes it on
the road.

1 Visitor Information & Entry Requirements

VISITOR INFORMATION

The Ministry of Tourism maintains information offices overseas,
known as the Israel Government Tourist Office (IGTO). Offices are
located in each of the following cities:

Australia: Australia–Israel Chamber of Commerce, 395 New
South Head Rd., Double Bay NSW 2028, Sydney (☎ 2/326-1700).

Canada: 180 Bloor St. West, Suite 700, Toronto, ON M5S 2V6
(☎ 800/669-2369; fax 416/964-2420).

South Africa: Nedbank Gardens, 5th Floor, 33 Bath Ave.
Rosebank, Johannesburg (☎ 11/788-1703).

United Kingdom: 18 Great Marlborough St., London W1V 1AF
(☎ 071/434-3651).

United States: 5 S. Wabash Ave., Chicago, IL 60603 (☎ 800/
782-4306/8); 6380 Wilshire Blvd., Suite 1718, Los Angeles, CA
90048 (☎ 213/658-7462/3); 5151 Belt Line Road, Dallas, TX
75240 (☎ 800/472-6364); 800 Second Ave., New York, NY 10117
(☎ 212/499-5645).

Within Israel, branches of the Municipal Tourist Information
Offices are found in almost all Israeli cities and near most major
sightseeing destinations. The following listing gives addresses, area
codes, and telephone numbers of the main local offices in Israel and
the West Bank:

Allenby Bridge: Jordan–West Bank Border near Jericho
(☎ 02/941-038).

Arad: Visitors' Center, 28 Ben-Yair St. (☎ 07/954-4409).

Ashkelon: Afridar Commercial Center (☎ 07/732-412).

Bat Yam: 43 Ben-Gurion Blvd. (☎ 03/507-2777).

Beersheva: 6A Ben-Zvi St. (☎ 07/236-001/3).

Ben-Gurion Airport: Arrivals Hall (☎ 03/971-1485).

Bethlehem: Manger Square (☎ 02/741-581).

Eilat: Tourist Center, corner Arava Road and Yotam Road (☎ 07/372-111).
Haifa: 20 Herzl St. (☎ 04/666-521, 666-522, or 645-692).
Jerusalem: 17 Jaffa Rd. (☎ 02/258-844), and Jaffa Gate (☎ 02/282-295/6 or 280-382).
Jordan River Crossing Jordan: Israel Border Near Beit Shean (☎ 06/586-410).
Nahariya: Municipal Square, Ga'aton Boulevard (☎ 04/879-800).
Nazareth: Casa Nova Street (☎ 06/573-003).
Safed: 50 Yerushalayim St. (☎ 06/920-961/3).
Tel Aviv: New Central Bus Terminal, 6th Floor, Shop 6108, South Tel Aviv at the terminus of Bus Routes 4 and 5 (☎ 03/639-5660).
Tiberias: Archeological Garden (in front of Radisson Moriah Hotel) (☎ 06/725-666).

ENTRY REQUIREMENTS

Visas are given free to U.S., U.K., and Canadian citizens, without prior application, when they enter Israel and show passports that are valid for at least 9 months beyond the time of arrival. Good for 3 months, the tourist visa can be extended for another 3 consecutive months at any office of the Ministry of the Interior (you may be asked to prove you have adequate funding for your extended stay). To work, study, or settle in Israel, you need the proper permit before arrival. If you plan to visit Arab countries, ask for your visa stamp to be placed on a piece of paper separate from your passport (if your passport is stamped by the Israelis, that stamp will close most Arab-world doors). Israeli passport control is quite used to this request and will cooperate.

2 Money

The basic unit of currency is the New Israel Shekel (NIS), which we estimate during the time span of this edition to range from NIS 3 to NIS 3.3 to $1. This means 1 shekel is approximately 30 cents. Over the past 5 years the general value of the New Israeli Shekel has fallen slowly in relation to the American dollar. During the time span of this edition, you may even find the rate of exchange moving closer to NIS 3.5 to the dollar, but uncertainties in the Israeli economy could alter this trend. British travelers will find the rate of exchange to be approximately NIS 5 to 1 pound; 1 shekel is about 20 new pence.

The shekel is divided into 100 agorot, and the smallest denomination you will encounter is a copper-colored 5-agorot coin. There are 10-agorot copper-colored coins, and larger, copper 50-agorot (half shekel) coins, all of which are useful to make up busfare. The 1-shekel coin (worth approximately 30 to 33 cents) is a tiny silver buttonlike object that is extremely easy to lose. Hang onto a few 1-shekel coins: pay phones in restaurants and hotels often only take 1-shekel coins instead of the cheaper per call telephone cards. There is a larger, silver-colored 5-shekel coin ($1.50), as well as a smaller, thinner 10-shekel coin composed of both copper- and silver-colored metals. There are also 10-, 20-, 50-, and 100-shekel notes. The small 10-shekel ($3) coins are not popular; they coexist with 10-shekel notes, which may be phased out during the time span of this edition.

Warning: Black-market street dealers sometimes try to pass off pre-1985 Old Shekel notes in denominations of 500 and 1,000. These notes have no value and are not in circulation, although their design is exactly like current notes of lower

What Things Cost in Israel	U.S. $
Taxi from Ben-Gurion Airport to Jerusalem	30.00–35.00
Sherut (shared taxi) from Ben-Gurion Airport to any address in Jerusalem (per person)	10.00
Bus fare from Ben-Gurion Airport to Jerusalem	4.00
Bus fare from Ben-Gurion Airport to Tel Aviv	3.00
Local phone call from public phone	.25–.30
Double room at Radisson Moriah Hotel (expensive)	165.00–230.00
Double room at Jerusalem YMCA, King David Street (upper moderate)	110.00
Double room at Saint Andrew's Hospice (moderate)	70.00
Double room at Jerusalem Hotel (budget)	45.00–50.00
Meal for one at Ocean (luxury)	40.00–65.00
Meal for one at Cezanne (expensive)	18.00–35.00
Meal for one at Gilly's (moderate)	14.00–20.00
Meal for one at Shanty (budget)	8.00–12.00
Shwarma at Moshiko's (budget)	3.00
Beer	2.00
Coca-Cola	1.10
Cup of coffee	1.40
Admission to Israel Museum	6.60
Ticket to attraction in Jerusalem Festival	30.00 and up
Ticket to small folk or classical concert	10.00–13.00
Municipal bus fare	1.20

denominations. Be certain that all currency notes you accept are clearly marked "New Sheqels" in English.

TRAVELER'S CHECKS Traveler's checks in major hard currencies are accepted at all banks and money changers. Always take your passport when changing traveler's checks. In addition to your traveler's check receipts, it is a good idea to make a few photocopies of your check packet receipts: keep one with you, leave one at home or with a trusted friend you can contact in case you are totally wiped out by thieves or other disasters. (One bathing-suit-attired Frommer's reader saw his daypack with all his money, identification, and traveler's check receipts wash overboard on a rough boat ride in the Red Sea!) Personal checks are sometimes accepted, but you can never depend on it. Ask the merchant before you assume you can pay with a personal check.

CREDIT CARDS The major credit cards—American Express, MasterCard, Visa, Access, Eurocard, etc.—are accepted at most hotels, at many restaurants and shops, and for cash advances at banks. Some banks accept one card, but not others: try the local branch of Bank Leumi le-Israel and the Israel Discount Bank for Visa; for MasterCard, try a Bank Ha-Poalim or United Mizrachi branch.

ATM CARDS Automated teller machines at *some* Bank Ha-Poalim and Mizrachi Bank branches are now connected to the CIRRUS-NYCE systems. Your American

The Shekel & the Dollar

At this writing NIS 1 equals approximately 30¢, or NIS 3.3 to $1, and this was the rate of exchange used to calculate the dollar values given in this guide. NIS 1 equals about 20 pence, or NIS 5 to £1. This rate fluctuates from time to time and may not be the same when you travel to Israel. Therefore, the following table should be used only as a guide:

NIS	U.S.$	U.K.£	NIS	U.S.$	U.K.£
1	.30	.20	20	6.00	4.00
2	.60	.40	25	7.50	5.00
3	.90	.60	30	9.00	6.00
4	1.20	.80	40	12.00	8.00
5	1.50	1.00	50	15.00	10.00
6	1.80	1.20	100	30.00	20.00
7	2.10	1.40	125	37.50	25.00
8	2.40	1.60	150	45.00	30.00
9	2.70	1.80	200	60.00	50.00
10	3.00	2.00	500	150.00	100.00
15	4.50	3.00	1,000	300.00	200.00

account will be debited and you will receive shekels from the machine. Check with your home bank about service charges for withdrawals from overseas ATM machines.

3 When to Go

CLIMATE The Israeli seasons are somewhat different from those in the United States and Western Europe. To start with, the Israeli winter doesn't normally involve snow—although there are occasional flurries every couple of years in Jerusalem and Upper Galilee, and Mount Hermon on the Golan Heights is snow-covered. Winter in Israel starts with showers in October and continues through periodic heavy rainfalls from November to March. Swimming is out in the Mediterranean during this time, except during occasional heat waves, although you can usually swim in Eilat and the Dead Sea in the winter.

From late March to September, it seldom rains at all. You can count on constant sunshine during the summer months. In late February and the beginning of March the entire country seems to turn green from the winter rains, and wildflower displays in the Galilee and the Golan regions are truly spectacular. In the months that follow, the heat gathers intensity, reaching its peak in July and August, when the only relatively cool spots are Jerusalem and the high mountains around Safed. The landscape is dry and parched by May, but by September temperatures are falling off a bit.

Generally, Israel's Mediterranean climate is somewhat like that of southern California: intense summer heat and sunshine, breezy nights, the coastal winds of winter. In addition, Israel also experiences hot and dry desert winds at the beginning and end of the summer, usually May and September, although a *hamseen* can occur anytime from March to November. These south and eastern winds are named from the Arabic word meaning "fifty," since the wind was traditionally believed to blow for 50 days a year. Thankfully, it doesn't.

In winter (November through March) cold rain systems move in from the north. Because they are prevented from continuing south by the constant tropical weather systems of Africa, these storms can stall over Israel for days until they rain themselves out. If you find a few days of your trip hampered by constant rain, your reward will be the chance to visit pine forests near Jerusalem and in the Galilee as fragrant and misty as those of the Pacific Northwest, and the chance to see the countryside carpeted with wildflowers and a rare, fragile veil of greenery.

Israel's Average Temperatures in Fahrenheit Degrees

		Jan	Mar	May	July	Sept	Nov
Jerusalem	Temp. (°F)	39–57	52–66	61–80	67–83	66–82	50–66
Tel Aviv	Temp. (°F)	48–66	55–71	60–79	71–87	70–83	55–75
Haifa	Temp. (°F)	50–62	55–70	62–76	71–83	72–83	59–70
Tiberias	Temp. (°F)	54–69	57–79	68–92	77–98	72–96	62–77
Eilat	Temp. (°F)	52–72	67–75	73–97	80–105	80–100	59–82

ISRAEL'S CALENDAR(S)   If awards were given for "daily" confusion, or for having the maximum number of holidays a year, Israel would probably win them all. Israel "officially" operates on two separate systems for determining day, month, and year: the Jewish calendar with its roots in ancient Canaanite and Babylonian tradition, dating from some 5,750-odd years ago, and the Gregorian calendar, used in most countries, including the United States. Recognized, but "unofficial," are even more calendars—such as the Julian (Julius Caesar) calendar, which runs 13 days behind the Gregorian; or the Muslim era, dating from A.D. 622, when the Prophet Muhammad led the *hejira* from Mecca to Medina. Not only do these calendars disagree about dates, but also about whether time is measured by sun, moon, or a combination of the two, and when the year should start and end. (I've never calculated how many New Year celebrations occur each year in Israel, but I do know of at least three Christmases.)

HOLIDAYS   Israeli holidays and events will affect your visit in several important ways. First, hotels and campsites will fill to capacity and rates will rise by as much as 20%. Next, transportation and restaurant service may be curtailed or completely suspended, and places of entertainment may be closed. On the other hand, a holiday is a special occasion, and you won't want to miss the special events that may take place.

Israel is also a most confusing place when it comes to the weekly holiday schedule. Jews stop work at midafternoon on Friday; some Muslims at sundown on Thursday (although many shops remain open on Friday); most Christians all day on Sunday. In Tel Aviv, no buses run from late Friday afternoon until Saturday after sundown, although small private minibuses cover the main routes. In Jerusalem, buses run only in the Arab neighborhoods on Saturday; in Haifa, there's partial bus service on Saturday. In nonreligious Eilat, there is no public transport on Shabbat.

Some shops open just as others are closing for a holiday. Lots of religious holidays change dates each year. The entire Muslim religious calendar starts 11 days earlier each year—it's a lunar calendar. This means the Islamic holy month of Ramadan, when Muslims may not eat or drink during daylight hours, slowly migrates across the year. How to keep your wits amid all these openings and closings? Read the following information carefully.

JEWISH SABBATH   The Bible states that the seventh day is one of rest—a time when no work can be done. For Orthodox Jews, this means no fires are lit, no human beings or animals can be made to work, no machines can be operated, no traveling can be done, no money handled, no business transacted. So officially that's the way it is in most of Israel, where the Sabbath, or Shabbat, is celebrated on Saturday. By 2 or 3 o'clock on a Friday afternoon, depending on whether it's winter or summer (Shabbat begins at sundown), most shops have closed for the day. Buses and trains stop running at least an hour before Shabbat, and the movie houses are closed at night. There is a growing list of exceptions: in central Tel Aviv, many restaurants, cafes, discos, and theaters close on Friday afternoon for a few hours, but reopen on Friday night; Haifa has always had a quiet alternative Friday night-life; and in Jerusalem a number of cinemas and restaurants (nonkosher) remain open; recently the pub area around Jerusalem's Russian Compound has begun to boom.

On Saturday almost all shops throughout the country are closed (except for a few cafes and Arab or Christian establishments) and nearly all transportation stops (only Haifa has limited municipal bus service at this time, and only taxis or small sherut companies ply in or between cities). Gas stations are mostly open on Shabbat; few are located in religious neighborhoods. Most admission-free museums are ordinarily open for part of Shabbat; entrance tickets, when required, must some-times be bought from private-duty guards outside the museum entrance. A few strictly kosher restaurants follow this same no-money-handling rule, accepting only advanced prepaid orders for Shabbat meals, which will often be cooked in advance and served tepid or cold; 99% of kosher restaurants, however, will be closed. Also, do watch for signs in restaurants or hotel dining rooms asking you not to smoke, so as not to offend Orthodox guests. (Lighting a cigarette or turning on a light switch are considered forms of starting a fire, which is an act of work forbidden on the Sabbath.)

Precise hours of the duration of Shabbat, which vary according to the time of sun-set, are listed in the Friday *Jerusalem Post*. The restarting of buses and reopening of cinemas and restaurants can be quite late in summer, as Shabbat does not end until you can see three stars in the sky at one glance.

Most Israelis are not Sabbath observant and love to travel on their day off, so if you want to drive on Saturday, you'll find the roads to beaches and parks quite busy. About the only people who'll try to stop you are the ultrareligious Jews, such as those in Jerusalem's Mea Shearim section. There they tend to get rather heated about people who ignore their interpretation of Sabbath restrictions. Many streets in reli-gious areas will be blocked with boulders; most ultraorthodox neighborhoods in Jerusalem and Bnei Brak, near Tel Aviv, have official permission to close their streets to traffic. Don't even think of trying to drive in or up to such areas. You can be stoned, and you will have little or no help from the police.

Israelis work 6 days a week, and as almost everything is shut down on Friday nights, they make Saturday nights their stay-up-late-and-have-a-party time. By night-fall, transportation services resume, and movie houses begin selling tickets for evening shows. By dark, all entertainment places are usually packed full, including the many sidewalk cafes in cities. Restaurants need about an hour after the end of Shabbat to assemble their staffs and prepare things before they open their doors to the public. You won't get the best possible meal at a restaurant on Saturday night: conditions are crowded, staffs are harried, and many items will have been prepared on Thursday or Friday.

ISRAEL CALENDAR OF EVENTS

Here's a general guide to when holidays and festivals occur. Keep in mind that a Jewish holiday that generally falls in March, say, may some years fall on a late date in February. Note also that not all Jewish holidays are subject to Sabbath-like prohibitions and closings. Holidays on which things do close down are indicated by an asterisk (*). Celebration of each holiday commences at sundown on the evening before the date listed.

January–February

- **Israeli Arbor Day (Tu b'Shevat):** Thousands of schoolchildren singing, dancing, and traipsing off to plant trees all over the country. February 5, 1996; January 23, 1997.

March

- **Purim (Feast of Lots):** Recalling how Queen Esther saved her people in Persia (5th century B.C.), this is an exciting time (so too the food) when folks, especially children, dress up in fancy or zany (or sometimes irreligious) costumes, have parties, parade in the streets, give gifts, spray shaving cream at passersby, and generally make merry. In Jerusalem and Safed, which are considered walled cities, Purim is celebrated 1 day later than in the rest of the country. March 5, 1996; March 23, 1997.

April

- **Pesach (Passover):*** No bread, beer, or other foods containing leavening are obtainable for 7 days (8 days outside Israel), and hotel and restaurant meals may cost more because of the culinary complexities. Many restaurants simply shut down for this period of time. During the days just before the holidays, housewives furiously clean their kitchens, and houses in general, to render them spotless and free of any stray bits of leavening. The first night of the holiday is devoted to a seder, a family meal and ritual recalling the exodus of the ancient Israelites from Egypt. (Unlike the Diaspora, where the seder is held on both the first and second nights of Passover, inside Israel the seder meal is only celebrated on the first night.) Many hotels and restaurants have special seders for tourists. The first and last days of this holiday are Sabbath-like affairs, which means the country more or less closes down. April 22, 1997.

April–May

- **Holocaust Memorial Day (Yom Ha-Shoah):*** Marking the time of the year in 1945 when the last of the concentration camps in Europe were liberated, and the Holocaust came to an end. All places of entertainment are closed. As the day begins (like all Jewish days, at nightfall) most restaurants are closed, although public transportation continues and most shops and businesses are open. At 11am on Yom Ha-Shoah, a siren sounds throughout the nation, and a period of silence is observed in memory of the 6 million who perished. A special memorial ceremony is held at Yad VaShem in Jerusalem. Some places for simple meals and snacks are open during the day.
- **Memorial Day:*** One week after Yom Ha-Shoah, the nation remembers its war dead. Restaurants and places of public entertainment are closed, but transportation operates and most shops are open. Again, at 11am, a siren sounds, and a period of silence is observed. Throughout the country, memorial services are held.
- **Independence Day:** The day after Memorial Day, commemorating on the Jewish lunar calendar, the day in 1948 when the British Mandate ended, and the

State of Israel was proclaimed. It is celebrated with house parties and municipal fireworks at night. April 24, 1996; May 12, 1997.

May–June

- **Lag b'Omer:** Ending 33 days of mourning, this is the chief happy celebration for the Hasidim, who leave Jerusalem and other cities at this time to sing and dance around bonfires at the Meiron tomb of the mystical Rabbi Shimon Bar Yochai, in Galilee. There are also Sephardic pilgrimages to the tombs of great rabbis. Children around the country also sing, dance, and light evening bonfires.
- **Shavuot (Pentecost):*** The early summer harvest celebration is a joyous time, a special favorite of agricultural settlements. It is often marked by plays, entertainment, and children dressed in white, wearing floral crowns. Since it also recalls the receipt of the Ten Commandments, as well as the bringing of the "first fruits" to the temple, it is observed as a religious holiday. Dairy foods such as blintzes and cheesecakes are traditionally prepared for the holiday, and at synagogues throughout the country, as well as at the Western Wall, the Torah is read throughout the night. May 24, 1996; June 11, 1997.
- **Jerusalem Festival of the Performing Arts:** In late spring, music groups and theater and dance companies come from all over the world to perform.

July–August

- **Tisha b'Av:** The fast day on the ninth day of the month of Av is a time set aside to remember the destruction of the First and Second Temples, which by ominous coincidence were destroyed on the same calendar day in the years 586 B.C. and A.D. 70, respectively. Entertainment facilities are closed. Many restaurants are closed. July 25, 1996; August 12, 1997.
- **Israeli Folkdance Festival:** Jewish ethnic dancers come from around the world. The festival is held in Karmiel, in the Galilee, early in July.
- **Jerusalem International Film Festival:** At the Jerusalem Cinémathèque, it takes place the first week in July.
- **Hebrew Song Festival:** This event takes place at Arad, in the Negev, in late July. Because of a stampede that resulted in a number of deaths and injuries during the 1995 festival, the future of this event is in doubt.
- **Jacob's Ladder Country, Folk, and Blues Festival:** An important event, it is held in the Galilee each year, varying from May to late August. For information call 06/945-633.
- **Red Sea Jazz Festival:** The jazz festival is held in Eilat in July or August. For information ☎ 07/334-353.

September–October

- **Rosh Hashanah (Jewish New Year):*** The start of the High Holy Days. Since the Jewish calendar starts in September or October, that's when the new year falls. It is a 2-day religious festival, not an occasion for revels but rather for solemn contemplation and prayer. Almost everything in the Jewish sector of the country is closed. September 14–15, 1996; October 2–3, 1997.
- **Yom Kippur (Day of Atonement):***Ten days after the Jewish year begins, the High Holy Days culminate in the most solemn of Jewish holidays. Observant Jews spend nearly the whole day in synagogue. Places of worship are crowded, but the large synagogues reserve seats for tourists, and some of the larger hotels organize their own services. Yom Kippur is a fast day, but hotel dining rooms serve guests who wish to eat. Everything comes to a standstill; even television and radio stations suspend broadcasting. September 23, 1996; October 10, 1997.

- **Sukkot (Feast of Tabernacles):*** Beginning 5 days after Yom Kippur, this 7-day holiday recalls how Moses and the Children of Israel dwelled in "booths" (or "sukkot") as they left Egypt to wander in the desert. Observant families have meals and services in specially built, highly decorated yet simple huts, located outside in gardens or on balconies. Sukkot is also a harvest festival and thus an agricultural and kibbutz favorite. In ancient times, the harvest of Sukkot was the most important of the annual pilgrimage festivals to Jerusalem. On the first day of Sukkot, Sabbath-like restrictions are observed. September 28, 1996; October 16, 1997.
- **Simhat Torah:*** As Sukkot ends, Jews rejoice that they have the Torah (the Law); street festivities in Jerusalem and Tel Aviv mark this day. On Simhat Torah, cantors read the final verses of the Torah (the first five books of the Bible), and then start again at its beginning. October 5, 1996; October 23, 1997.

December

- **Hanukkah:** Celebrates the victory of the Maccabees over Syrian–Greeks and the consequent rededication of the Temple in 164 B.C. For 8 days this history-based holiday is marked by the nightly lighting of the Hanukkiah, or eight-branch menorah (as opposed to the traditional seven-branch menorah, which is a more ancient symbol of the Jewish people). December 6, 1996; December 24, 1997.
- **International Choir Concerts:** These take place in Bethlehem on December 24.
- **Liturgica:** A week of choral music organized by the Jerusalem Symphony Orchestra in Jerusalem in late December.

4 The Active Vacation Planner

CAMPING

Beautiful, interesting sites, and serviceable facilities mark Israel's camping sites. You can live in a hut or caravan, complete with electricity. Modern showers and conveniences are always nearby, and kiosks supplement or provide all your food needs. Some camping sites offer mobile homes—fully furnished units with a living room, two bedrooms, kitchen, bath, and toilet. These can accommodate up to six people. Bed linens are supplied, as well as kitchen utensils. There's usually good transportation to each location.

You can avoid paying VAT if you pay in foreign currency. There's a minimum 3-day charge on Rosh Hashanah and Shavuot Passover, Sukkot, and other Jewish holidays, when the rates are highest.

Package deals including airport transfers, auto rentals, etc., are available. Contact the **Israel "Chalets" and Camping Union,** P.O. Box 53, Nahariya 22100 (☎ 04/925-392), for rates, literature, and further information.

Here's an example of costs per night: A campsite for adults with their own tent costs $20 to $35; children are charged between $3 and $5. A bed in a campground dormitory bungalow, sheets and electricity included, costs $15 to $18. To rent a small mobile home or cabin sleeping four costs $60 to $130 total, depending on the campground, the services provided, the season, etc. Remember that fees skyrocket on weekends, Jewish holidays, and during summer school vacation.

By the way, you'll be glad to know that containers of propane and butane gas are readily available in Israel, and many of them have American-style fittings, so you can use your stateside stove or lantern in Israel. French "camping gaz" tanks are also available.

CYCLING

The **Israel Cyclists Touring Club** (☎ 03/685-6262) promotes guided tours between March and October. Generally, the tours are 8, 9, or 14 days, and packages include accommodations, meals, a guide, bus transportation when necessary, entrance fees to sights on the itinerary, and insurance. Contact the ICTC for further information.

Also check with the **Jerusalem Cyclists Club** (☎ 02/816-062). They rent out bicycles by the day, and organize low-price tours with hostel accommodations.

Beyond Biking, 7 Pinsker St., 52713 Haifa (☎ 04/679-796; fax 04/227-335), is a private company, the creation of Alan Lutzker, a young American immigrant to Israel, that does beautifully planned and executed bicycle trips throughout the country for groups of about 10 to 20 people. Quality mountain bikes and equipment are used, and support vans or Jeeps can be arranged to carry personal effects and equipment. Most important is Alan Lutzker's expertise in planning imaginative routes, and his eloquent explanations of nature, history, geology, and archeology along the way. The price for a 2-day trip is about $120, which includes bicycle rentals, all meals, entrance fees to parks and historical sites, and overnight accommodations (usually at youth hostels). The en route meals, prepared by the support team, are fabulous. For a small additional fee, private room and bath in hostels can be arranged. One-day trips and trips for Sabbath and kashrut-observant travelers are also offered, as are 10% student discounts. It is best to write ahead of time for information and reservations.

HIKING & NATURE WALKS

The **Society for Protection of Nature in Israel (SPNI)** offers overnight treks, detailed hiking trips, and active package tours throughout Israel. They also offer excellent nature walks of a few hours through the wadis and deserts near Jerusalem and tours of the Jerusalem Old and New Cities. Call 212/755-9150 or 800/726-8687 in the U.S. for information, brochures, and reservations.

5 Learning Vacations, Volunteer & Special Programs

LANGUAGE SCHOOLS

In order to absorb enormous numbers of new immigrants over the past 5 decades, Israel has developed an expertise in intensive Hebrew language programs, centered around an institution called an *ulpan.* If you plan an extended visit to Israel, you should know that a good many kibbutzim operate *ulpanim* that are based on the principle of working for your education, room, and board. In exchange for half a day of Hebrew-language classroom instruction, you work the other half day in a job assigned by the kibbutz—in the fields, kitchen, or wherever you are needed.

The Jewish Agency—in the United States, abroad, and in Israel—makes the arrangements for you to do work/study at a specific kibbutz. In the U.S., send requests for information to the **Jewish Agency,** Kibbutz Aliyah Desk, 110 E. 59th St., New York, NY 10022 (☎ 212/318-6130). In Israel, apply to the **Kibbutz Volunteer Office,** 124 Ha Yarkon St., Tel Aviv (☎ 03/522-1325). In most cases, you must be between 18 and 35, and you must make a commitment for at least 2 months. Classes are mixed, and your classmates may be Argentinean, Polish, Romanian, Moroccan, Iranian, and Russian.

Study at ulpanim in Israel not affiliated with kibbutzim may be accepted for credit or fulfillment of language requirements at a number of American universities.

The three big cities have ulpanim where you pay a fee. There are 3-, 8-, 12-, and 20-week courses, very reasonably priced. If you're interested, apply to the **World Zionist Organization Ulpan Center,** 4 E. 34th St., 4th Floor, New York, NY 10016 (☎ 212/532-4176).

The well-established **Ulpan Akiva,** P.O. Box 6086, Netanya 42160, Israel (☎ 09/352-312/3; fax 09/652-919), offers intensive, live-in programs in both Hebrew and Arabic for varying periods of time in a pleasant seaside community. Ulpan Akiva supplements its language programs with a full range of tours, social and cultural activities. Courses at Ulpan Akiva are accepted for credit at a number of American universities.

As far as students are concerned, the **Israel University Center,** 110 E. 59th St., New York, NY 10022 (☎ 212/339-6941 or 800/27-ISRAEL), is a clearinghouse for information on kibbutz programs, ulpanim, and language programs, university study (undergraduate and graduate), summer study, tours, archeological digs, internships, yeshivas, and volunteer programs. You can call or write for a current, detailed listing of programs and tours.

ARCHEOLOGICAL DIGS

You can volunteer to work at an archeological dig if you are 18 or older, prepared to stay for at least 2 weeks, and capable of doing strenuous work in a hot climate. You will have to pay your own fare to and from Israel. Most excavations take place between June and October, but there are off-season digs. Lectures are given at some sites, and some offer academic credits for the work. If you'd like to join a dig, contact the **Israel Antiquities Authority,** Rockefeller Museum, P.O. Box 586, Jerusalem 91911 (☎ 02/292-607 or 292-627; fax 02/292-628). It's best to inquire as far in advance as possible. The best summary of current digs you can work in—or just visit as you tour the country—is found each year in the January/February issue of the magazine *Biblical Archeology Review,* P.O. Box 7026, Red Oak, IA 51591, available at many libraries and newsdealers.

KIBBUTZIM

You can volunteer for work in most of Israel's 250 kibbutzim or communal settlements. The work can be difficult, and can range from agricultural labor to kitchen, laundry, or factory work 6 hours a day, 6 days a week. Many volunteers find the experience rewarding, but a major complaint is that the lifelong kibbutz members remain aloof and isolated from the constantly changing temporary volunteers, and high expectations of becoming a true part of kibbutz life are not generally achieved. Also, be aware that there are different groups of kibbutzim based on various ideologies. All kibbutzim share a great commitment to developing the land; most are opposed to settlements in the Occupied Territories. The Hashomer Hatzair Kibbutz Movement is the most actively committed to civil rights and liberal social issues throughout the country; the mainstream United Kibbutz Movement (the largest in Israel) is more middle-of-the-road. There is also a religious kibbutz movement. Most kibbutzim accept volunteers of any nationality or religion.

In kibbutzim that have an *ulpan* program, you can often study Hebrew intensively while you work.

The **Kibbutz Aliyah Desk,** 110 E. 59th St., New York, NY 10022 (☎ 212/318-6130), offers information and will help you complete your plans.

Jerusalem 3,000—Trimillennium

The year 1996 is the 3,000th anniversary of King David's conquest of Jerusalem in 1004 B.C. To commemorate the anniversary, the city of Jerusalem is hosting a vast array of cultural and performing arts events. To obtain information on the schedule of the trimillennium events, call the Israel Tourism Information Center in the U.S. at 800/596-1199, and in New York City, 212/560-0600, extension 245.

SPECIAL PROGRAMS

Each year the Ministry of Tourism comes up with new and exciting events and plans and also repeats some favorite events each season.

JERUSALEM TRI-MILLENNIUM CELEBRATIONS   To take place in 1996, this year-long program of special events concerts, performances, and exhibitions was conceived by Teddy Kollek to mark the 3,000-year anniversary of King David's conquest of Jerusalem in 1004 B.C., and the establishment of Jerusalem as the spiritual and political capital of the Jewish people.

MEET THE ISRAELIS   The tourist information offices throughout the country can put you in touch with a program whereby you can meet Israelis in their homes and share a cup of tea with the family. The idea is to bring together people of similar interests and backgrounds. If, for example, you're an architect and want to talk shop with an Israeli architect, you need only apply to the Meet the Israelis Program, which will set it up for you.

PLANT A TREE   Once in Israel, you can plant a tree with your own hands and feel some connection with the physical development and beauty of the country. This emotional outlet for sightseers was established by the Jewish National Fund. It costs $10 a tree, and the JNF will tell you how it's done. Check with the **Keren Kayemet** directly: in Jerusalem, 02/241-781 or 707-433; in Tel Aviv, 03/523-4449 or 523-4367. All tourism information offices will have current infor-mation on tree planting in their localities.

6 Organized Tours & Package Tours

TOURS & PACKAGES

Most major airlines serving Israel offer a variety of land-package arrangements that include discounts on accommodations throughout the country, as well as organized and escorted tours and itineraries. El Al and Tower Air, specializing in travel to Israel, have the widest variety of choices in all price ranges. El Al, for example, offers tours such as "The Holyland Experience," with emphasis on Christian sites in Israel. For more information on these tours and packages, call **El Al** at 800/El Al SUN in the U.S. For **Tower Air**'s Smart Vacations, call 800/34 TOWER. Airlines and private travel agencies also offer escorted tours of Jordan and Egypt that originate from Israel.

You'll find a wide choice of escorted day trips (usually by bus) inside Israel offered by the **United** and **Egged** agencies. These tours originate from every major city and can generally be booked with a few days notice. The Society for Protection of Nature in Israel (see "Hiking & Nature Walks," above) arranges tours and packages with an emphasis on nature and outdoor activities.

TOURS TO CAIRO, THE SINAI & OTHER DESTINATIONS **By Plane** If you plan to go by air to Cairo or the Sinai, a tour package can offer lower rates to counter the high cost of flying. El Al has four flights a week between Cairo and Tel Aviv, and similar service is operated by Air Sinai. Cost is $136 one way, $272 round-trip, and the flight takes about 45 minutes. Excursion fare is $170 round-trip if bought together with El Al round-trip flight from the United States to Israel.

By Bus You can easily get from Tel Aviv to Cairo and back by signing up for one of the daily (except Saturday) bus tours offered by every travel agency. Buses leave from Jerusalem, pick up more passengers in Tel Aviv (if not already full), and then head off for Cairo. The trip takes 10 to 12 hours. Sign up just for the one-way bus ($17 to $25), the round-trip bus ($30 to $40), or a tour that gives you hotel, or hotel and sightseeing, or the works: a full-blown guided tour of all the Nile's treasures. Students get good discounts.

By Car You cannot drive an Israeli rental car into Egypt, and that includes Sinai. If you make the trip in your own vehicle you must obtain a permit to take a vehicle into Egypt from the **Consular Section, Ministry for Foreign Affairs,** Hakirya, Romema, Jerusalem (☎ 02/235-111).

OTHER DESTINATIONS El Al offers direct air service fares between Israel and exotic destinations such as Kenya, Thailand, and Turkey in case you'd like to extend your vacation to areas that are difficult and expensive to reach by direct flight from the United States. Local Israeli travel agents and discounters often offer spectacular discount packages to these destinations.

PRIVATE GUIDES

Israel is an easy country for English speakers to explore on their own, but if you are considering hiring a private guide for part of your visit, it will be necessary to plan well in advance. The county has a system of licensing guides who have completed an extensive program of preparatory training. A private guide will arrange all the logistics of travel during the times he or she is under hire, and can take you to major sites as well as out-of-the-way places efficiently. For those with little time, this can be a restful way to get a great deal done in depth. The government licensing program has helped to raise the general quality of guides in Israel, but you still may find yourself engaging a guide whose personality or politics don't exactly mesh well with yours. Or, despite English-language requirements, you may encounter a guide who is not especially articulate. (There are also the guides who are on their cellular phones taking other bookings and making arrangements as they drive you through pristine deserts in their Land Rovers, which can destroy the atmosphere of a tour.) It is a good idea to ask friends who have visited Israel for personal recommendations, and to discuss plans with a prospective private guide by phone, in order to get a feel for his or her approach before making a commitment. Most good professional guides have put together a brochure or video that will give you an indication of their styles and approach.

Approximate rates for a private guide are $150 per day for a Jerusalem tour by foot and taxi; $300–$400 a day party rate within Israel for up to 10 people with vehicle included; $240 per day for two to four people, and $100 per day extra for off-road trips and use of off-road vehicle. If your guide accompanies you overnight, the fee should include the cost of his or her hotel room. If you engage an Israeli guide to arrange excursions into Jordan and to accompany you on these trips, the rate could be $660 to $700 per day, including a vehicle and hotel accommodations.

Following are some guides with unusual background qualifications and specialities in nature and active tours. If they are not able to meet your time specifications or interests, they may be able to refer you to other guides that will better match your needs.

David Perlmutter, 5 Ben Tabai St., P.O. Box 8015, Jerusalem 91080 (☎ 02/787-765 or car phone 50/201-353; fax 02/795-118). American-born Mr. Perlmutter was a guide for the Society for Protection of Nature in Israel and helped design that organization's hikes and tours. He specializes in off-road tours in a comfortable four-wheel-drive vehicle.

Judy Stacey Goldman, 265 Dizengoff, Tel Aviv (☎ 03/546-6885). The co-author of *The Underground Guide to Jerusalem* and *The Underground Guide to Tel Aviv,* two lively, insider books on the country's two major metropolitan areas. Ms. Goldman was born in Canada.

Izat Abu Rabia, Kibbutz Shefayim, Israel (☎ 09/574-234 or car phone 050/262-465; fax 09/523-411). Another licensed guide with an off-road vehicle who has worked with the Society for Protection of Nature in Israel, Mr. Abu Rabia is an Israeli Bedouin who guides in English, Hebrew, and Arabic, and is recommended for his energy and knowledge of the countryside.

Laura Nelson-Levy (☎ 02/434-602) is a young former American and an avid specialist in bicycling. **Miriam Feinberg Vamoosh** (☎ 02/345-071) is an especially articulate guide, and writes for *Eretz Magazine,* a publication about history, travel, and nature in Israel.

7 Tips on Accommodations

Rates quoted for hotel rooms in this book are in dollars only. The Israel Ministry of Tourism, the Israel Hotel Association, and hotels themselves have for years quoted their room rates in U.S. currency rather than in shekels, although this policy may change if Israel's current economic miracle continues, and the shekel's value against the dollar begins to rise. As of now, only a few small hotels and pensions will quote you room or bed rates in shekels.

Almost all Israeli and most West Bank hotels add a 15% service charge to your hotel bill. Unless otherwise noted, the 15% has already been included in the room prices I quote. These prices are per room, single or double, and not per person. The hotel may quote prices differently: "Double room for $15 per person plus 15% service."

If you are not Israeli and pay your hotel bill in hard currency (dollars, marks, francs, etc.) in the form of notes, traveler's checks, or credit card, you won't be subject to Israel's additional 17% value-added tax (VAT), a tax that is normally added onto the price of any shekel purchase. Thus, it's a good idea to put hotel restaurant meals and drinks and such on the hotel bill rather than paying for them on the spot with cash shekels. Every time you pay in shekels, you're paying that tax, whether it's shown as a separate charge or hidden in the total price.

Virtually every hotel will provide a large breakfast to guests for no additional charge. Often the breakfast is a kosher buffet—long tables packed with salads, eggs, breads and rolls, fruits and vegetables, cheeses, dips, cereals, juices, even pickled fish.

Children up to the age of 6 years are usually allowed a 50% reduction on the extra-person rate if they stay in the same room with their parents. Policies vary for children under 18 at different hotels.

HOTEL RESERVATIONS

If you write for hotel reservations, be certain to print or type both your letter of inquiry and the address on the outer envelope. Israeli post office and hotel personnel often have difficulty reading English handwriting.

Zip codes in Israel are similar to American zip codes; it is advisable to write them in front of the name of the Israeli city or town in order to avoid confusing unwary American postal workers. Zip codes are not widely used, especially in Jerusalem. Zip codes have been noted only where essential, mainly for smaller towns.

I can't stress enough that you should start the reservations process very early. Fax or phone are the quickest ways to confirm your plans. It can take 3 weeks for a letter to cross the seas and continents to Israel (by air!), and another 3 weeks for the reply. Assume 2 weeks of turnaround time (for the hotel to go through its paperwork), and you've logged 2 months—and the answer you get might be "full up"! Also, if you wish a confirmation, enclose International Reply Coupons (on sale at any post office) to pay the return postage. Hotels, which can run up huge postage bills, look very favorably upon requests that include IRCs.

If you choose to make arrangements by telephone, remember that when it's 7am EST in New York, it's 2pm in Israel. Also, many Israelis will not answer the telephone during the Sabbath (Friday evening to Saturday evening).

If you plan to travel through the countryside and stay at kibbutz holiday villages and guesthouses, contact the **Israel Hotel Reservation Center (IHRC),** 20 S. Van Brunt St., Englewood, NJ (☎ **201/816-0830** or 800/552-0141 in the U.S.; 800/526-5343, fax 201/816-0633 in Canada).

This office represents the Kibbutz Hotel Chain, as well as Israel's Isrotel and Sheraton Hotel chains. With a minimum of effort on your part, the Israel Hotel Reservation Center will send you current brochures and information about discount packages available through these chains, make and confirm reservations, and arrange prepaid Avis car rental packages that will match up with your hotel plans if you'll be traveling through the countryside. In most cases, the car rental arrangements you can make at IHRC will be less expensive than those you'll find through other channels. The IHRC can also expand the Kibbutz Guest House packages to include a range of moderate and luxury nonkibbutz choices in Eilat, Jerusalem, and Mitspe Ramon. The IHRC can also make bed-and-breakfast arrangements, and represents a new organization of inexpensive Moshav and Kibbutz Bed-and-Breakfast Country Lodgings throughout the country (see below). IHRC can also arrange a car rental package to coordinate with your travels in Israel. The IHRC is recommended by the Israel Ministry of Tourism.

HOTEL SEASONS   Israel's hotels fill up during certain seasons and holidays, and you should be prepared with advanced reservations, secured by a deposit. Generally speaking, hotels are busiest during July and August, and on the major Jewish and Christian holidays such as Passover, Easter, Rosh Hashanah and Yom Kippur, Hanukkah and Christmas. For detailed information, and a full list of holiday dates, see the "Israel Calendar of Events."

Off-season is generally November through February (except for Hanukkah–Christmas–New Year's). It is, however, the busiest season in Eilat, which has almost perfect, sunny weather when it's chilly up north.

Some of the best bargains in Israeli hotel accommodations are offered by El Al, which, as the national carrier of Israel, has a special commitment to the nation's economy and tourism industry, and a real stake in making your trip a success. In a truly extraordinary package, El Al is offering 5 nights in a four-star or superior three-star hotel in Jerusalem or Tel Aviv (or any combination of the two cities) and the cost is $30 a night per person, breakfast included, double occupancy! Not only that, but you also get a Hertz rental car for as many of the 5 days as you like, 35¢ per kilometer for a car with manual transmission, 66¢ per kilometer for automatic. There is no daily-rate charge, and in many cases, your credit card will cover the insurance. Rental cars in Israel are very expensive by American standards. When you realize that a youth hostel dorm bed plus breakfast costs $18 per person per night, the beauty of this package becomes apparent. Almost all airlines serving Israel offer discount land-package arrangements: El Al and Tower Air (in that order) offer the best and widest range of choices. El Al and Tower passengers will find their airline tickets entitle them to buy packages that save on hotel rates in all price ranges.

THE RADISSON MORIAH HOTELS PACKAGES

The Israeli Moriah hotel chain has recently been linked with Radisson Hotels Worldwide. The chain's five-star hotels in Jerusalem, Tel Aviv, and Tiberias are currently offering a 9-night minimum stay "As-You-Please" room-only package for $120 in winter and $160 in summer (service tax included). The Radisson Moriah Plaza Dead Sea Spa offers a 7-night "Beauty and Relaxation" package for $1,275 per person in a double. Rheumatic-treatment packages are also available; the 7-night package is $2,220 per person, based on double occupancy. Ask about expanding your package to the Radisson Moriah Plaza in Eilat, the most luxurious downtown hotel in that city. For information and reservations, call the **Radisson Moriah Hotels** at 800/333-3333 in the U.S. and Canada or 0800/374-411 in the U.K.

KIBBUTZ PACKAGES

The Kibbutz Hotel Chain Fly and Drive Package is especially enticing; it lets you explore the real Israeli countryside while overnighting at comfortable kibbutz holiday villages and guesthouses, the equivalent of three-star hotels, that have swimming pools or beaches, and invariably lovely settings. There are minimum 7-night deals in which you get a double room and breakfast for $33 to $35 per person per night, double occupancy, most of the year, and a middle-grade Avis rental car beginning at $230 per week (with unlimited mileage and manual transmission), or $294 a week (with unlimited mileage and automatic transmission). For $9 per person per night more, you can book into a package that gives you a choice of more luxurious kibbutz accommodations.

Although all accommodations in the kibbutz guesthouse and holiday village network are the equivalent of three- or four-star hotels, you'll find great variety in the general setup and character of each facility. You'll be amazed at the loveliness and sheer drama of many of the kibbutz sites, from such desert retreats as Ein Gedi, dramatically perched above the Dead Sea near the fortress of Masada, to places like Ye'elim, adjacent to the Negev's Hai Bar Wildlife Reserve. There are semiluxury resorts such as the lovely Kfar Blum, or the hotel at the orthodox Kibbutz Lavi; there are also more simple holiday villages such as Nasholim, on the shores of the Mediterranean; or Ein Gev, with its private beach shaded by a grove of date palms, on the Sea of Galilee; or Nes Ammim, a Christian kibbutz near the northern Mediterranean coast, which you reach by a road that winds through an enchanting avocado forest. Not only do you get to explore the countryside and stay in some of the miraculous paradises the kibbutz-movement members have created for tourists as well as themselves, but many of the kibbutzim in the program are just a few minutes' drive from Jerusalem or within easy distance of Tel Aviv. You can start off each

Kibbutz Accommodations

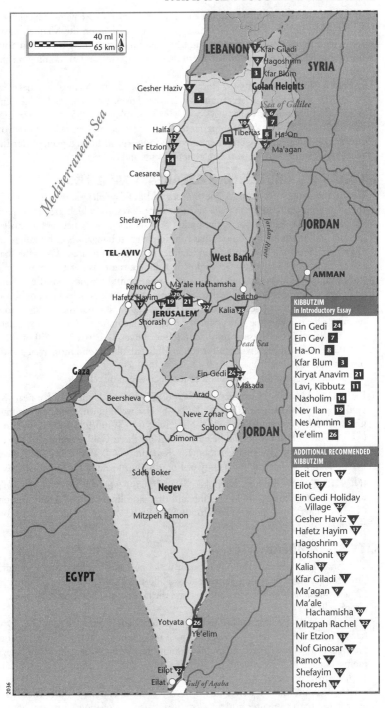

55

day beside the pool in rustic country guesthouses like Kiryat Anavim or Neve Ilan, set amid the forests of the Judean hills, or Shefayim, right on the Mediterranean coast, with its own isolated beaches and busy water-park swimming pool, then drive into Jerusalem or Tel Aviv for an afternoon of sightseeing and an evening on the town.

You can arrange for a kibbutz land package independently of any airline ticket by calling the Israel Hotel Reservation Center (see above). Reservations for **Kibbutz Association Fly and Drive** packages can be made by calling 800/552-0141. You may add additional days to the Kibbutz Hotel Chain Plan at rates far below those you could book independently and then move on to independent arrangements for the rest of your trip. There are also single supplements and children's rates.

MOSHAV & KIBBUTZ BED & BREAKFAST FACILITIES

Unlike the network of kibbutz guesthouses and holiday villages, which are really three- or four-star country hotels, and the kibbutz resorts, which are often quite separate from the actual kibbutz, this option consists of a growing network of smaller kibbutz and moshav communities that run simple guest bungalows or buildings, or kibbutz families who have guestroom facilities in their own houses. With rates that can be as low as $45 to $60 per night for a double room, you get a comfortable bedroom, usually with private bath, in interesting countryside locations. Best of all, you have a chance to see how real Israelis live. This is an especially good option if you want to keep your accommodation expenses down and put the savings into a rental car for freewheeling independent travel. For a commission of approximately $25, the Israel Hotel Reservation Center (see above; ☎ 201/816-0830 or 800/ 221-0203) will make reservations for you at affiliated kibbutz and moshav bed-and-breakfast places.

The following are some of the best tourist facilities in this class.

IN THE GALILEE   Kibbutz Snir (☎ 06/952-500) in Upper Galilee near the Banias Springs; Moshav Amirim (☎ 06/989-571), a well-known vegetarian community between Safed and Karmiel; Kibbutzim Sasa (☎ 06/988-699) and Yiron (☎ 06/988-311), both in the beautiful wild northern Galilee countryside near the ancient Baram Synagogue; Kibbutzim Kedarim (☎ 06/987-222) and Amiad (☎ 06/933-929), both in the vicinity of Korazim, northwest of the Sea of Galilee.

IN THE NEGEV   Kibbutz Sde Boker (☎ 057/565-079 or 565-933), Ben-Gurion's verdant desert kibbutz; the interesting and dramatically located Maktesh Ramon (Ramon Crater) Art Colony (☎ 057/889-50 or 889-33), with 2-bedroom 4-person apartments costing only $40 per night.

CITY BED & BREAKFAST

The Israel Hotel Reservation Center can make bed-and-breakfast arrangements through the **Good Morning Jerusalem** bed-and-breakfast rental office. There is a $25 commission for this service, but you save the expense and bother of international phone calls and faxes.

For bed-and-breakfast accommodations in Jerusalem (chapter 4) and Tel Aviv (chapter 7), there are rental services that will make note of your requirements and preferences and try to match them to a room in their listings. Reservations for these rooms, ranging in price from about $41 for a single, to $54 to $66 for a double, can be made from overseas.

At tourist information offices in Tel Aviv, Jerusalem, and many other Israeli cities, you can use a computer bank to access lists of accommodations in private homes for any area in the country. The information disbursed by these computers is rather lean: just a list of names, addresses, and phone numbers, but with a little courage and a few phone calls, you can usually come up with something. If you're looking at local listings, the staff at the Municipal Tourist Information Office may be willing to direct you to places they know to be especially good. Summers, weekends, and holidays, it is always best to reserve ahead.

YOUTH HOSTELS

The concept of youth hostels is right at home with the traditional Israeli preference for functional, practical lifestyle and congenial atmosphere in which travelers can meet freely and easily. Youth hostels often offer the only available accommodations in remote areas of the country, or in areas along hiking routes.

In the past few years, the Israel Youth Hostel Association (IYHA) has been busy upgrading its network of facilities. Many hostels are set up with a maximum of four to six beds per room; a large percentage of these rooms now have private shower/baths and can easily be converted into doubles or family rooms. Dining facilities now offer meals far superior to the once Spartan youth hostel fare. The upgraded menus are a special pleasure in remote areas where there are no dining facilities nearby.

Age is no barrier, nor is membership. Hostels offer rock-bottom prices and a friendly welcome to all. Only hostels bearing the triangular sign are authorized by the Israel Youth Hostels Association. It is advisable to book in advance.

Having a youth hostel membership card does give you certain advantages—such as better rates at the hostels, plus discounts at some restaurants, national parks, historical sites, museums, and on buses and trains. In Jerusalem the **Israel Youth Hostels Association** is located at 3 Dorot Rishonim St. (P.O. Box 1075), Jerusalem 91009 (☎ 02/252-706; fax 02/235-220), where you can obtain information on present offerings of the Youth Travel Bureau.

Note: Not all youth hostels take foreign currency, and it's a good idea to check availability of space (especially in summer months) before arriving. The Israel Youth Hostels Association also has 14-, 21-, and 28-day bargain-price tours and car rental packages. Fax, write, or inquire at the Jerusalem office for further information.

8 Health & Insurance

HEALTH

You do not need to take any special precautions for traveling to Israel. Vaccinations are not necessary unless you have spent the preceding 14 days in a country where there is an epidemic of a disease such as cholera or smallpox. Take along an adequate supply of any prescription drugs you need as well as a prescription that uses the generic name of the drug you are using.

INSURANCE

HEALTH & ACCIDENT   Many credit card companies insure their users in case of a travel accident, providing the ticket was purchased with their card. Sometimes fraternal organizations have policies that protect members in case of sickness or accident abroad. Don't forget that Medicare does not cover U.S. citizens in Israel. Canadians, however, are generally protected by the health insurance plans in their individual provinces.

LOST LUGGAGE   Many homeowners' insurance policies cover theft of luggage during foreign travel and loss of documents—your passport or your airline ticket, for instance. Coverage is usually limited to about $500 U.S. To submit a claim on your insurance, remember that you'll need police reports or a statement from a medical authority that you did in fact suffer the loss or experience the illness for which you are seeking compensation.

Some policies (and this is the type you should have) provide advances in cash or else transferrals of funds so that you won't have to dip into your precious travel funds to settle medical bills.

TRIP CANCELLATION If you've booked an economy, discount, or charter fare, you will probably have to pay a cancellation fee if you cancel a trip suddenly, even if it is due to an unforeseen crisis. It's possible to get insurance against such a possibility. Some travel agencies provide such coverage, and often flight insurance against a canceled trip is written into tickets paid for by credit cards from such companies as Visa or American Express. Many tour operators or insurance agents provide this type of insurance.

Among the companies offering such policies are:

Travel Guard International, 1145 Clark St., Stevens Point, WI 54481 (☎ 800/826-1300; 800/634-0644 in Wisconsin), offers a comprehensive policy that covers basically everything, including lost luggage.

Access America, Inc. (an affiliate of Blue Cross–Blue Shield), 6600 W. Broad St., Richmond, VA 23230 (☎ 800/284-8300), writes coverage for single travelers or families, providing medical, trip cancellation, and lost-luggage policies.

Health Care Abroad, MEDEX, c/o Wallach & Co, 107 W. Federal St., Middleberg, VA 22117-0480 (☎ 703/687-3166 or 800/237-6615), offers accident and sickness coverage on trips lasting 10 to 90 days, charging $3 per day for $100,000 coverage.

9 Tips for Special Travelers

FOR PEOPLE WITH DISABILITIES

A handy and detailed guide entitled *Access in Israel, A Guide for the Disabled and Those with Problems Getting Around,* is published by Pauline Hephaistos Survey Projects, 39 Bradley Gardens, West Ealing, London W13 18HE, England. The charitable organization that publishes the guide does not charge a set price, and in fact will send you a copy for free. But each copy actually costs them about £4, and they ask that you make a contribution in a similar amount, if you can, to cover publishing, research, and (in addition) postage and handling.

The 122-page guide includes useful maps of easily traversed routes, including Jerusalem's Old City; a handy guide to hotels, kibbutz inns, youth hostels, and their conditions of access. It even covers access and transportation situations at the major airports such as New York's JFK, Chicago's O'Hare, London's Heathrow, and Lod's Ben-Gurion. This guide can often be obtained in the United States through the **Travel Information Service** (☎ 215/456-9603), Moss Rehabilitation Hospital, 1200 W. Tabor Rd., Philadelphia, PA 19141. The cost is $7 plus postage. Telephone for assistance before ordering this guide.

The **Information Center for Individuals with Disabilities,** Fort Point Place, 27-43 Wormwood St., Boston, MA 02210 (☎ 617/727-5540), offers lists of travel agents specializing in tours for the disabled.

The **American Foundation for the Blind,** 15 W. 16th St., New York, NY 10011 (☎ 212/620-2147 or 800/232-5463), offers information on travel and various requirements for the transport and border formalities for seeing-eye dogs.

You can obtain a copy of "Air Transportation of Handicapped Persons," published by the **U.S. Department of Transportation.** A copy will be sent to you without charge by writing for Free Advisory Circular No. AC12032, Distribution Unit, U.S. Department of Transportation, Public Division, M-4332, Washington, DC 20590.

Yad Sarah Institute (☎ 02/242-242), 43 Ha-Nevi'im St. (P.O. Box 6992), Jerusalem 91609, lends canes, crutches, walkers, wheelchairs, and other medical equipment, and offers advice on transportation and other special problems. Most services are free.

FOR SENIORS

The **Association of Americans and Canadians in Israel (AACI)** sponsors many social activities and support groups. The offices in Jerusalem, 6 Mane St. (☎ 02/667-151), and in Netanya, 28 Shmuel Ha-Naziv St. (☎ 09/330-950), are especially active. Check for their list of activities.

Elderhostel (☎ 617/426-7788), 75 Federal St., 3rd Floor, Boston, MA 02110, is a highly recommended organization that arranges short-term residental/education programs throughout the world. Residential arrangements are usually simple but adequate, often in off-season university dormitories, and study programs are lively and unusual. In Israel, Elderhostel programs include tours and other group activities. Elderhostel is mainly for people over 55. For a free catalog, write to: Elderhostel, P.O. Box 1959, Dept. XH, Wakefield, MA 01880-5959.

FOR SINGLE TRAVELERS

Budget hotels and hostels, such as the Jerusalem Inn Guest House in Jerusalem (see chapter 4) or Tel Aviv's Gordon Inn (see chapter 7), offer a welcome atmosphere of camaraderie. The **Society for Protection of Nature in Israel (SPNI)** in Jerusalem, 13 Helena Ha-Malka St. (☎ 02/244-605; fax 02/254-953), in Tel Aviv, 4 Ha-Shfela St. (☎ 03/369-0644), and in Haifa, 8 Menachem St. (☎ 04/664-135), offers intelligent and unusual tours, ranging from walks, treks, hikes, and field trips of a few hours to package tours throughout Israel and into Jordan and Egypt. You can obtain a current brochure of SPNI offerings and make reservations from North America by contacting SPNI's American representative, **Excursions Unlimited Tours,** 545 Madison Ave., New York, NY 10022 (☎ 212/755-9150 or 800/726-8786). A very small, local Israeli company, **Off the Beaten Track** (☎ 03/641-4586), which is run by former Americans, does unusual day trips that often attract English-speaking Israelis and tourists on their second and third trips to Israel who are looking for something different. Groups are usually interesting, younger, and energetic. Israel is an easy place to strike up conversations with other travelers that you meet at tourist sites, concerts, tours, and on public transportation.

FOR FAMILIES

Israel is a young country with a young population. After a week in the country, you get used to the surprising number of babies, baby carriages, and playgrounds.

The better hotels, and even most of the smaller ones, will know who to call for babysitting services, so the front desk is your first resort. Car seats are available from rental firms, but you must reserve one as early as possible. Disposable diapers, called *tafnukim,* are sold at some drugstores, but they are relatively expensive. Baby food is not available in the variety that exists in the U.S.

FOR STUDENTS

The discounts offered to students traveling in Israel are unequaled anywhere else in the world. Students are treated royally, via an elaborate program of reductions that lower the tab in youth hostels and hotels, on buses and trains, even in swimming pools, restaurants, and sundry places of entertainment.

Your passport to all these savings is one of the following student I.D. cards.

The **International Student Identity Card** is available in the United States from **Council Travel Services,** the travel division of the Council on International Educational Exchange, 205 E. 42nd St., New York, NY 10017 (☎ 212/661-1450 or 800/223-7402); you must present proof of full-time student status. The office is open Monday to Friday from 9am to 5pm. Information and assistance on student, youth, and budget travel to Israel (and other destinations, for that matter) are available from any Council Travel Services office. There are 37 other offices in the U.S., including Boston, Chicago, Dallas, Los Angeles, San Francisco, and Seattle. Be sure to ask for the council's free Student Travel Catalog.

In the U.K., similar services for the International Student Identification Card and discount student travel are offered at **STA Travel,** 86 Old Brompton Rd., London SW7 3LQ (☎ 0171/937-1733 for travel to Israel). In Canada these services are handled by **Travel CUTS** (Canadian Universities Travel Services Ltd.), 187 College St., Toronto, ON M5T 1P7 (☎ 416/798-CUTS).

International Youth Hostel Cards are available in the United States from **American Youth Hostels, Inc.,** 733 15th St. NW, Room 840, Washington, DC 20005 (☎ 202/783-6161; fax 202/783-6171); in the U.K., from **Hosteling International,** 9 Guessens Rd., Welwyn Garden City, Hertfordshire AL8 6QW, England (☎ 01707/332-487).

If you arrive in Israel equipped with student and hostel cards, then you can go directly to the central train and bus stations in any of the three major cities to receive discounts on their routes throughout the country. Your student card gives you discounts on Mano Seaways ferries between Israel and Greece, as well as discounts on Neot Ha Kikar tours, and entrance fees to museums, parks, and nature reserves. Always keep your school identification card or a letter from your school handy as an extra verification of your student status.

ISRAEL STUDENTS TRAVEL ASSOCIATION (ISSTA)   When you arrive in Israel, make your first stop ISSTA, which does an excellent job of looking after visiting young people. ISSTA offices in Israel are at 109 Ben-Yehuda St., Tel Aviv (☎ 03/527-0111; fax 03/523-0698); 31 Ha-Nevi'im St. (☎ 02/257-257); and 2 Balfour St., Haifa (☎ 04/669-139). Hours are usually 9am to 1pm and 3 to 6pm; offices close on Wednesday and Friday at 1pm, and all day Saturday. With proof of student status, you can buy an International Student Identification Card from ISSTA for NIS 33 ($10).

ISSTA's staff is composed of young people, specialists in the field of student and youth travel. Here the student is treated as a first-class client and is offered a wide variety of special services, planned and developed by people who fully understand the student's needs and problems.

Tours of Israel   ISSTA operates tours within Israel ranging from 4 to 7 days; they're open to individual as well as group bookings. The tour price includes bed-and-breakfast accommodations, entrance fees, a tour bus, and a government-licensed guide.

Charter Flights   ISSTA operates on a year-round basis special charter flights between many destinations in Europe and Israel for students and scholars. The seat you buy is confirmed—you are not a standby. These flights are jointly operated with various national student travel bureaus in Europe and form an extensive network of flights between Israel and Europe, often on carriers such as Arkia and Dan-Air. These flights are priced specially for students and offer discounts of 40% to 70% off the regular fare. ISSTA also offers charter flights to the Far East and Africa.

Members of students' families—husband or wife and children—are now allowed to fly to and from Israel on student charter flights, at the same rates and subject to the same conditions as the student in the family. Remember that penalties for canceling out of a charter can be severe, baggage allowances can be far less than on normal flights, and charter carriers to Israel can be draconian about charges for overweight baggage.

10 Getting There

BY PLANE

The airline you choose can have a major effect on what your trip to Israel will be like. Some airlines offer a wide variety of gateway cities with direct flights that can make the very long flight to Tel Aviv considerably easier. You'll find that some flights have New York transfers or European layovers (sometimes an hour or two, sometimes for a full day or overnight); a day in London or an evening in Prague or Bucharest might be a welcome addition for some, but for others it might be just one more tiring obstacle. Some European airline flights with long stopovers even include a free overnight hotel, which travelers with unlimited time and little patience for long flights may find attractive.

An airline that will honor frequent flier points or coupons can save you money or enable you to upgrade your seat, which can be a worthwhile investment—a comfortable, restful flight in Business Class can do wonders toward helping you fight 8 hours of jet lag: if you're on a 10-day or 2-week visit, you don't want to spend a week as a walking zombie.

Check the time of your flight departure from Israel. Many flights to North America leave at 6 or 7am, which means you must be at the airport by 3 or 4am. For many, this is ideal: you have maximum use of your last day in Israel, and you can skip having a hotel room for the final night. For others who prefer to get a good night's sleep, an early afternoon flight that gets you back to North America just in time for bed the same day can make your reentry into Western Hemisphere time, and adjustment to your normal schedule, much easier.

Check into youth fares, senior discounts, and family plans. Some airlines offer them; others only at limited times or not at all. If you're eligible, the savings can be substantial. Remember, you must shop around. The rules constantly change, and your travel agent may not take the time to dig up the best buy for you.

Finally, for religious reasons, some airlines cannot fly to or from Israel from Friday afternoon through Saturday night. If time is short, and you need to begin your trip right after work on Friday, this can be an overriding consideration. On the other hand, a flight that leaves Friday at 8pm but has poor connections may not get you to Tel Aviv that much earlier.

El Al (☎ 212/768-9200; 800/223-6700 in the U.S, or 800/EL Al Sun for information about packages; 0345/125725 in the U.K.; 800/361-6174 in Canada), Israel's national carrier, has the largest schedule of nonstop and direct flights between Israel and New York, Boston, Chicago, Miami, Baltimore/Washington, DC, and Los Angeles. There is also nonstop service from Newark to Tel Aviv as well as via London. El Al offers a very flexible free stopover policy in Europe on its Newark–Tel Aviv flights. A reciprocal arrangement with Royal Jordanian Airlines permits El Al passengers from North America to do one leg of their flight either to or from Amman.

El Al also provides many special services to help make the trip to Israel as convenient as possible from any point in the United States. For example, for Philadelphia area passengers, El Al has round-trip shuttle service for $15 per person from several locations to the El Al terminals at either JFK or Newark, timed to efficiently connect with your flight. There are also special night-before check-in services for El Al passengers in Boro Park (Brooklyn), Jerusalem, Haifa, and Tel Aviv. El Al is the only airline to employ new state-of-the-art Boeing 747-400 aircraft on its nonstop United States–Israel routes. An additional consideration, especially for flights outside the United States, is the fact that El Al's security is extremely thorough. El Al does not fly from Friday afternoon until Saturday evening after the end of the Jewish Sabbath.

As the airline of a country in which tourism is a major part of the economy, El Al has developed the best-priced land-package arrangements in the business, starting with the remarkable "Sunsational Israel" package that includes 5 nights at upper moderate hotels in Jerusalem or Tel Aviv for $30 a day (or less) per person, double occupancy, and a rental car (there is a 35¢ per kilometer charge plus insurance). If you are not in need of a hotel room, but would like a car, El Al has a "Sunsational" car package. El Al's "Dantastic" packages include accommodations at the luxury Dan Hotel chain at considerable savings. See section 7, "Tips on Accommodations," above.

El Al has a program of add-on fares that can only be purchased in conjunction with a round-trip El Al ticket to Israel from the United States. An add-on fare of approximately $326 allows you to fly to any two of the following three cities: Cairo, Athens, or Istanbul. El Al passengers from North America may also purchase an excursion ticket from Tel Aviv to Cairo for $170, a considerable saving over the regular fare.

Tower Air (☎ 800/34-TOWER), is a small airline that for the past decade has specialized in the New York–Israel route. It offers daily nonstop service (except Friday) between JFK Airport in New York and Tel Aviv. For the past 2 years, more U.S. passengers have flown to Israel on Tower Air than on any other American airline, making Tower the number-one U.S. carrier to Israel. Tower offers a number of useful bargains. I especially like the Premiere Economy Class ticket, which, for $150 one way, upgrades you to a seat with a guaranteed empty seat beside you, so that you can stretch out on the long flight; many times the Premiere Economy section is empty enough so that you can recline across three adjacent seats. This ticket also includes an excellent upgraded meal and personal service, all of which help you to feel more human when you arrive at your destination. You are not required to purchase the upgrade on a round-trip basis: you pay only for the part of your trip you choose to upgrade. You can also upgrade to Business Class for only $250 each way. Tower Air offers long-term tickets, good for 6 months, as well as youth fares (valid for 1 year) and special promotional fares that are excellent bargains. In 1995, Tower Air began to offer land-package arrangements including hotels and car rentals. A Tower Air ticket also entitles independent travelers to discounts at a long list of three- to five-star-equivalent hotels (ask Tower to send you their land arrangement brochure). Tower has a reciprocal agreement with Royal Jordanian Airlines in which Tower passengers from North America can land at Ben-Gurion Airport, but return via Amman. Because Tower, like El Al, specializes in travel to Israel, these packages are often a bit better than those offered with other airline tickets.

Other American carriers, such as **TWA** and **World Airways,** offer the opportunity for frequent flyer bonuses, land-package arrangements, and stopover plans, and they do fly on Friday and Saturday. **British Airways** led the field in promotional fares from Britain to Israel during 1995. The airlines of Romania, the Czech Republic, Poland, and Hungary sometimes offer fares to Israel at slightly bargain rates. These, and other European airlines, can provide unique stopover possibilities and packages. Refunds from some European airlines can be unusually difficult to obtain.

Royal Jordanian Airlines (☎ 800/RJ-TOURS-8) now has a reciprocal arrangement with El Al and Tower Air: Passengers from North America can land at Ben-Gurion Airport in Jerusalem, travel overland to Jordan, and return home from Amman on Royal Jordanian. During 1996, Royal Jordanian Airlines will initiate service between Amman and Ben-Gurion.

AIRFARES   Airfares are in a constant state of flux. The following El Al fares, therefore, are guidelines that were correct at presstime.

The year is divided into low season, high season, and shoulder season, and each type of ticket has different fare periods. Thus, you may find that if you buy a 6- to 90-day excursion ticket, you might only be able to fly at the low winter rate up to April 3; but if you buy a 6- to 60-day APEX super-saver fare (for several hundred dollars less), you can fly at the winter rate only until March 23. You'll have to check with your travel agent for exact dates. Do it early. You can save up to $200 by flying on the last day of the winter fare period rather than 24 hours later when the new fare period begins.

Super Apex 6- to 30-Day Fare, New York–Tel Aviv   Special fares on selected flights are priced from $890 in low season to $1,258 in high season. You must stay at least 6 days and complete your travel within 30 days, and your ticket must be bought at least 14 days in advance. There are charges and penalties for changes in reservations or if you cancel your trip. Stopovers are only possible on the Newark–Tel Aviv–Newark route. Super Apex Fares for London–Tel Aviv–London run from £339 in low season to approximately £409 in high season. Super Apex Fares are also available on routes between Montreal or Toronto and Israel.

Apex 6 to 60-Day Fare, New York–Tel Aviv   Somewhat higher than the Super Apex Fare, ranging in price from about $1,066 in low season to $1,460 in high season, this ticket offers greater flexibility. You can travel for a longer period of time and you are allowed one free stopover en route either to or from Tel Aviv from any gateway city in the United States. If you must cancel within 14 days of your flight, there is a $50 fee, but the ticket is refundable. The London–Tel Aviv–London Apex Fare ranges from £379 in low season to £449 in high season.

Special Short-Term Promotional Fares   These fares are extraordinary bargains, usually offered without advance notice and for only limited periods of time. For example, in the summer of 1995, El Al offered a round-trip London–Tel Aviv fare on its Tuesday night flight of £270, and round-trip fare on other days of the week for £370. Unlike many airlines, which offer promotional fares only for a very limited number of seats on each flight, El Al's promotional fares are valid for all seats of the class and flights advertised. El Al and Tower Air, both closely tied to the Israeli tourism industry, often do promotionals when the country seems short on tourists. It is always a good idea to call the airlines directly in order to learn exactly what promotional fares may be available, then check with a good travel agent or an agent that specializes in travel to Israel. Promotional fares are sometimes unadvertised and only available through agents.

Fares Between Tel Aviv and Cairo   With many travelers adding excursions to Egypt onto their Israeli vacations, this short hour-and-a-half flight route has become increasingly important. Visitors with limited time may especially want to avoid the full day of arduous overland travel each way between Israel and Egypt. Normal coach fare from Tel Aviv to Cairo is $136 each way; $272 round-trip. El Al offers a special round-trip rate of $170 if purchased in conjunction with a round-trip El Al ticket from the United States to Israel. If you plan to stay in Israel for some amount of time, you may be able to find local Israeli travel discounters offering slightly lower fares on local Egyptian and Israeli airlines.

CHARTER FLIGHTS   Chartering a whole plane or a section of one and filling it with budget-minded travelers is still one of the best ways to save money on a flight.

The disadvantages are these: The flight may be canceled due to insufficient demand; it may be delayed on departure, sometimes for several hours; you are committed to fly on specific flights, and it may be impossible to switch to other flights. If you miss the flight, you may lose your money.

BUCKET SHOPS   Travelers from London to Israel can easily locate bargains on one-way and round-trip flights (usually charters) to Israel, advertised in bucket shops throughout the city. Note that on many of these charters, baggage-weight restrictions are mercilessly enforced (handbags and hand luggage are often weighed in with the allowance, and there are steep penalties for excess weight). The bucket shop scene from New York is less freewheeling, and occurs mostly in the form of discounters buying up blocks of seats on scheduled flights. At the present time, standby fares to Israel have been phased out, although, if you have no special time constraints, and don't mind a long airport stakeout in addition to the lengthy flight to Israel, it can't hurt to check out this possibility.

Because of security considerations, traveling to Israel as a courier for an overnight air freight firm (an option many budget-conscious travelers like to explore) is unusually difficult.

ARRIVING

Ben-Gurion International Airport, at Lod on the outskirts of Tel Aviv, serves the whole country. Other, smaller airports exist in Jerusalem, Tel Aviv, Haifa, Rosh Pinna, and Eilat, but most points within Israel are so easily accessible by bus and sherut that few people spend the relatively large amount to fly.

After landing and passing through Immigration and Security, you'll be in the Arrivals Hall waiting for your baggage. There are lots of people on hand to help you here, including a fully staffed tourist office, a hotel reservations desk, car rental desks, and a desk for the helpful Voluntary Tourist Service representatives. From the Arrivals Hall you pass through Customs, then you're outside, in Israel.

AIRPORT TRANSPORTATION   By Bus   Egged operates buses more or less every half hour from the airport to Jerusalem at a price of NIS 14 ($4.70). The trip takes about 45 minutes. Schedules are posted by the bus ticket window that is in the low building amid the bus stops. Going by bus, you can be at your hotel in Jerusalem within 2 hours after your plane has landed.

To get to Tel Aviv from the airport, take the **United Tours Airport Shuttle Service** bus no. 222 that departs at least once every hour, usually more frequently, between 4am and midnight (on Saturday, noon to midnight). It leaves the airport, stops at the El Al Air Terminal at the Central Railway Station, then stops near the Bnei Dan Youth Hostel, and then travels all along the waterfront boulevard, Ha-Yarkon Street, stopping at each cluster of hotels. The trip from the airport to your hotel should take a half hour; the fare is NIS10 ($3). There are also buses to Haifa and several other points directly from the airport. Check the schedules next to the bus ticket window.

By Sherut A *sherut* is a shared Mercedes limousine or a van. The sherut service is to the right as soon as you exit from the terminal. Sherut service from the airport to Jerusalem is highly regulated, with a fixed fare (about $10) for the trip from Ben-Gurion to almost any address point within Jerusalem. The price posted on the sign by the parked sheruts may be out of date—shekel prices rise frequently although the dollar equivalent stays the same. Notice what the other passengers are paying, and then pay exactly the same, not a penny more, for the trip right to your hotel door. There is no charge for normal baggage, although if you have a trunk, the driver will expect a tip.

DEPARTING

EL AL CHECK-IN SERVICE Passengers on El Al flights who are leaving from Jerusalem, Tel Aviv, Haifa, or Eilat can use El Al's in-city check-in service. The Jerusalem office, at **Center One,** 49 Yermiyahu St. (☎ 02/383-166), opens especially for this purpose Sunday to Thursday from 4 to 10pm. The check-in service also operates on Saturday and holidays from 1 hour after sunset until 11pm. In Tel Aviv, **El Al's in-town terminal** (☎ 03/691-7198), near the Central Railway Station on Arlozerov Street, is open from 1 to 11pm every day except Friday (on Saturday it opens after the end of the Sabbath). In Haifa, early check-in is at the **El Al office,** 6 Ha-Namel St. (☎ 04/677-036), in the port area only a block from the Paris Square Carmelit station, open each evening except Friday from 6:30 to 10pm (after the end of Shabbat on Saturday). In Eilat, advance check-in is available at the Eilat Airport (☎ 07/331-515) every evening except Friday from 6 to 8pm.

Some details you should know about early check-in: You can check in only the night before your flight is scheduled to depart; early check-in is not applicable to all flights (you can't check in early for some night flights, for example); you must have your ticket, passport, and payment receipt for the airport departure tax when you check in, just as though you were at the airport. Your bags will be inspected right there in the El Al office, and then sent directly to the aircraft. The next day, you need arrive at the airport only in time for passport control, security check, and boarding, for which you must figure 1 hour and 15 minutes. Without early check-in, you're required to be at the airport $2^1/_4$ hours before flight time. For instance, if your flight were scheduled to leave at 8am, you'd be required to get to Ben-Gurion Airport at least 3 hours before flight time, or at 5am. This is no idle deadline, by the way. You could miss your flight if you ignore this time limit.

BY SHIP

FROM ITALY, GREECE & CYPRUS Several car-ferries make the journey to Haifa from Venice, Piraeus (Athens), Heraklion (Crete), Rhodes, and Limassol (Cyprus). Ships include the **Stability Line**'s *Vergina* and the **Sol Maritime Services'** *Sol Phryne,* which are either Greek- or Cypriot-flag vessels.

The usual route is Piraeus, Rhodes, Limassol, Haifa, with each port being reached on a different day. Standard itinerary calls for departure from Piraeus (Athens) on Thursday, arriving in Haifa on Sunday. The route and departure days are the same for the ships when they leave Haifa; that is, departures are on Sunday. These schedules can change according to the seasons, so use them as a general indication only; get the latest details in Piraeus or Haifa.

While several of these ships have good accommodations and service, others are not so hot. Conditions can change from season to season, so check out the ship in advance, if possible. It's also a good idea to pack some food along, even if you intend to buy your meals on board. Sometimes the dining rooms run out of food before everyone has dined. Don't depend on buying food in the ports of call either, as arrival and departure might be in the middle of the night.

Prices are higher from June to September. Prices may range from $80 for a deck chair to $250 for a berth in a cabin with shower and toilet, including three meals. Cars and motorcycles are charged a separate fee.

For bookings and exact prices, go to any major travel agent in Athens, Crete, Limassol, Rhodes, or Israel. There are connections to Turkey via Rhodes.

11 Getting Around

BY PLANE

If you can afford it, and if traveling overland on hot days just isn't your cup of tea, then by all means use **Arkia,** Israel's inland air service. There are no flights on the Sabbath, but otherwise daily flights connect Tel Aviv with Eilat and Rosh Pinna (Safed/Tiberias), Jerusalem with Eilat and Rosh Pinna, and Haifa with Eilat. Other flights are scheduled according to demand, as the seasons change. A round-trip flight from Tel Aviv to Eilat, for example, costs $140.

Arkia also sponsors very popular air tours, including journeys from Tel Aviv and Jerusalem to Eilat. Or you can design your own tour, gather a group of people, and charter an Arkia aircraft, from nine-seaters to Boeing 737s.

You can book tickets and check flight schedules at any travel agency or at the following Arkia offices: Tel Aviv, Sde Dov, Tel Aviv Municipal Airport (☎ 03/541-2222); Jerusalem, Clal Center, 97 Jaffa Rd. (☎ 02/255-888); Haifa, 84-Atzma'ut St. (☎ 04/643-371); Eilat, Downtown Airport (☎ 07/373-141), or Shalom Center (☎ 07/376-102). Information is also available at GTIO throughout the world.

BY TRAIN

Trains are even cheaper than buses, but Israel Railways trains don't run nearly as often, and link only six cities—Jerusalem, Beersheva, Dimona, Tel Aviv, Haifa, and Nahariya (with local stops made along the way). Although some of the trains are ancient, they are usually roomy, and the routes run through some of central Israel's most beautiful areas. Just as you should experience the overland to Eilat, in order to get a sense of the whole country, so too you really should make the trip from Tel Aviv to Jerusalem by train. Unlike the Tel Aviv–Jerusalem highway route, the final portion of the train route runs through the beautiful Judean Hills, a winding, mountain-clinging ride through a magical and rugged landscape.

By the way, you may notice unused railroad tracks, seemingly running to nowhere, when you're traveling by bus or sherut. These abandoned tracks are a throwback to British Mandate times, when these railway lines connected Israel with Jordan, Egypt, Syria, and Lebanon.

Note: The International Student Identity Card holder obtains a 25% to 50% train discount.

Excepting the Sabbath and religious holidays, trains run daily. Operations close earlier on Friday and prior to holidays. For train information call 03/693-7515. In Tel Aviv, the Central Train Station (sometimes called North Station) is on Arlosoroff Street near Haifa Road. Trains for Jerusalem leave only twice a day; there is more frequent service northward along the coast to Nahariya.

BY BUS

Most city and intercity bus routes are operated by two cooperative-shareholder companies, Dan and Egged. Their equipment varies widely. Depending on the whim of fortune, you'll take your intercity bus ride in either spanking-new buses with red upholstery and efficient air conditioning or in a run-down, torn-upholstered, dirty-windowed, breathlessly hot bus.

Buses run from about 5:30am until late evening. In major cities, most routes operate until midnight. If possible, you should avoid bus travel at rush hours (7 to 8am and 4 to 6pm). On Friday and the eves of Jewish holidays buses run only until about 2 or 3 hours before sunset. East Jerusalem and the West Bank have partial bus service on Friday evening and Saturday, and Haifa has partial service on Saturday, but otherwise there is no bus service throughout the country from Friday afternoon until Saturday evening.

Both Dan and Egged have discount fare plans for both city and intercity buses. For instance, if you get to Jerusalem, Tel Aviv, or Haifa, and plan to stay long enough for 25 rides, the first time you climb on a city (municipal) bus don't just buy a single-fare ticket. Instead, ask for a *kartisiya,* one of the multifare cards that are right at the driver's fingertips next to the single-fare tickets. The kartisiya gives you one or two free rides, and frees you from having to fumble for change. If you are a senior citizen or a student, show your identification. The driver will sell you a multifare card at a regular, senior, or student discount. The color of the card is different for each category. Each time you get on a bus, the driver will punch your card. At 90¢, city bus tickets are not all that expensive, but why pay even that when you can pay less? The kartisiya is not supposed to be transferable, but there is rarely a problem if two people together present it as a fare. Just say *pa-mai-yim* and the driver will punch the kartisiya twice.

As for intercity travel, Egged offers 14-, 21-, and 30-day passes good for unlimited travel throughout the country. Ask at any **Egged Tours** office for details. Egged offices are open Sunday through Thursday from 7am to 8pm, on Friday from 7am to 2pm; closed Saturday. Students can apply for discounts here. For further information, in Jerusalem call 02/304-704; in Tel Aviv call 03/537-5555; in Haifa call 04/549-555. For Egged bus route toll-free information, call 177/022-5555. The **Dan Bus Company** runs some interurban routes from Tel Aviv along the coast. Dan interurban information is 03/639-444.

BY SHERUT & TAXI

SHERUTS The Israeli sherut ("service" in Hebrew) is a shared taxi that goes from city to city or point to point within a city. They supplement city and intercity bus routes and often go where the bus doesn't go. On Saturday in many parts of the country they are the only transportation available. Sheruts usually make regular stops close to the central bus stations of the cities they service, but by and large they'll let you off at any bus stop in or out of the city along their routes. These days they're mostly limousinelike Mercedes-Benz cars or eight-passenger vans. Sheruts won't depart for intercity runs until each seven-passenger car is full (or almost so).

Sherut fares can be a shekel or so higher than the bus; in times of heavy competition, sheruts will match the fares on Egged. Service is often faster and more comfortable. Sheruts from Jerusalem to Tel Aviv leave from Rav Kook Street, just across Jaffa Road from Zion Square. If you are staying in the center of town, this is much more convenient than taking a bus to Jerusalem's Central Bus Station and waiting on line for the bus to Tel Aviv. There is no charge for a child under 5 traveling on the lap of an adult. Sometimes two children under 5 pay one adult fare. For each additional child under 5, the full fare is required. Smoking is supposed to be forbidden inside sheruts.

Note: When looking for a sherut, always ask before climbing in to see that it truly is a sherut. Otherwise, a gloating driver may whisk you to your destination at taxi rates.

TAXIS Each municipality sets taxi fares and issues a chart quoting current fares. But in all cases, it's good to agree on an amount before you get in the cab, as many cabbies ignore the meters. That avoids any unpleasantness at the end—and there is often unpleasantness. Having trouble finding a taxi on the Sabbath? Go to a big hotel entrance. They're there!

BY CAR

CAR RENTALS Rent-a-car agencies, both the international ones such as Avis, Hertz, Budget, and National (Europcar), as well as local agencies, rent small cars at about $35 to $45 a day, depending on the season, the company, and the size of the car. These rates are for such cars as Fiats and Autobianchis. The best bargains are often on packages purchased with your flight.

Driving is one of the best ways to see Israel. And should you feel that renting is too great a luxury, remember that with your newfound mobility you can stay at independent and kibbutz bed-and-breakfast places or even out-of-the-way youth hostels throughout the countryside, and thus recoup in low-cost hotel accommodations your car rental splurge.

Even so, car rental can turn out to be extraordinarily expensive if you don't realize what's involved. Let's run down the costs, item by item.

The very cheapest cars are often not available, even though their rental prices are widely publicized by agencies. So let's assume you end up renting the "B" group of economy cars, such as Ford Fiesta, Peugeot 104, Daihatsu Charade, or Talbot Samba. Your best deal will be on a weekly, unlimited kilometer basis. As the deductible on the agency-provided collision insurance is a staggering $750 to $1,000, you'll want to protect yourself against that much liability for damage to the car. So you must initial the little block that shows you want the collision damage waiver insurance, which will cost $10 to $12 per day. Thus, a balance sheet of what you'll actually end up paying for a week's vehicular liberation may look like this:

Basic weekly charge, unlimited kilometers	=	$275
Collision damage waiver, 7 days at $10 per day	=	$70
Gasoline, 100 liters at 60¢ per liter	=	$60
Total	=	**$405**

This works out to $57.50 per day for one of the cheapest cars available at the best rates offered by the big companies. Remember that your credit card company may cover insurance on rental cars, which can mean a pleasant saving.

These figures are an average of going rates. You'll save significant sums by shopping around. Be sure to ask in advance what the collision damage waiver will cost, because—as you can see from the figures above—it ends up being a significant sum. If one firm offers a weekly rate of $250, but with an enormous collision damage waiver fee, you may be better off going with another company that charges $260, but only $20 for a week's collision damage waiver.

By the way, you should not be misled by firms offering extremely low daily rental rates such as $6 or $8. The daily rental rate is only a small portion of the total rental bill. If the daily rental rate is $8, but the collision damage waiver is also $8 and the kilometer charge is 30¢, a day's rental for a 175-kilometer (78-mile) trip from, say, Tel Aviv to Jerusalem and back will still end up costing a whopping $68.50! You could do the trip by taxi for about the same price.

Among the international car rental companies doing business in Israel, Avis usually clocks in with the best prices. El Al's "Sunsational" car package, starting at $3 per day with unlimited mileage (available only for El Al passengers), is generally unbeatable. Reserving and prepaying from the United States through the Israel Hotel Reservation Center or a travel discounter can also cut costs.

Some smaller Israeli companies offer no rental charge for Shabbat, although you do have to pay Saturday insurance. Others offer free transportation from the airport to your hotel if you have a reservation but desire to rest a few days before starting your car rental period. Companies offering such services are often more expensive, but you may find these extras worthwhile. **Eldan** is a solid Israeli firm with reasonable rates and a good service record.

Be aware—tourists are cautioned to deal only with reputable rental companies, not to sign a contract without reading it thoroughly in a language completely understood, and to make sure of proper and full insurance coverage.

Age minimums for rentals vary from company to company, but usually you must be 21 years old to rent or drive a rental car in Israel. Seniors over 70 may have a difficult time finding an agency that will rent to them. Check American companies in the United States for their rental policies in Israel. You may pay more for insurance if you're under a certain age.

Car rental offices are everywhrere in Israel. If you don't happen to pass the one you want, your hotel or any travel agent will be glad to arrange the rental. It's a good idea to reserve a car as far in advance as possible. Except in holiday periods, a day in advance should be enough time to secure some kind of vehicle, but keep in mind that cars with automatic transmission are often in short supply. You should not expect to walk into a rental office and drive away a half hour later in the car of your choice. The earlier you reserve, the more certain you can be of getting the car you want, when you want it.

There are no toll roads or bridges in Israel, so this is not an expense. Parking is usually on the street, and in cities you must purchase timed parking cards from news stands if you want to park in central areas.

GASOLINE Gasoline comes as 91 octane at about 50¢ per liter, and 96 octane at about 60¢ per liter. Rental cars are often "required" to have the higher-octane gas. These gas prices work out to about $1.90 to $2.30 per U.S. gallon. When you return the car, the rental company will estimate—to their advantage—the amount of gas needed to fill the tank.

Gas stations are plentiful enough on main roads, except that on Saturday some of them are closed. And on Saturday and Jewish holidays it's virtually impossible to have a flat tire repaired in the Jewish sections of Israel.

DRIVING RULES Although Israel honors American, Canadian, and U.K. driver's licenses, if you plan to drive in other countries you might want to have an International Driver's License, which should be obtained in advance in your hometown.

The local automobile club, called **MEMSI** (☎ 03/564-1122), has its main office in Tel Aviv at 20 Rehov Ha-Rakevet, Tel Aviv 65117; office hours are 9am to 5pm, until noon on Friday; closed Saturday. The Jerusalem office of MEMSI (☎ 02/259-711) is on Bezalel Street, two blocks west of King George Street. It offers AAA members the following services: information on touring, hotels, car hire, etc.;

emergency assistance on the roads, patrolled by radio-controlled yellow vans with MEMSI's name and emblem; and good road maps of Israel.

Provided a tourist's foreign car registration is valid and the driver is in possession of a valid driver's license, a car may be brought into Israel for a period of up to 1 year. No Customs document or Customs duty deposit is required.

But before you decide to bring in a car or even drive in Israel, you should understand that this is a tough country for autos. Auxiliary roads are rarely wide and straight, and once you're off the main highways, you're faced with winding, narrow mountain roads—particularly in the Golan Heights and the Negev.

Besides the roads themselves, there are many other problems confronting a driver in Israel. The main problem is the Israeli drivers themselves; brashness on the road is the national sport. The Israelis' driving habits, especially those of taxi drivers, directly reflect two main personality components: aggressiveness and impatience. You will see cars taking daredevil chances and passing regularly on blind curves, and without any sensible regard for oncoming traffic, narrowly squeezing back into their lanes only by a hair's breadth. Such foolishness (or should I say recklessness?) has caused tragedy and death on Israel's roads to an extent way out of proportion to the number of cars in the country.

Other hazards? First, rains bring up loose gravel and dirt and make for unstable, slippery conditions. Flash floods occur in the desert during the rainy season, often gutting low sections of the highway.

The number of cars in Israel has quadrupled during the past few years, so Israel now has real, honest-to-goodness traffic jams, and a parking problem in the big cities. In Jerusalem, Tel Aviv, Tiberias, and other cities, when you park on streets in downtown areas during daylight hours, you must display a parking card in the passenger window. This is a strip of paper with punched tabs for the hours of the day. You tear a tab to designate the month, day, and hour when you parked. Cards can be purchased at news stands or from lottery ticket vendors. Parking on many residential streets in Jerusalem and Tel Aviv will soon be by residential sticker only.

BREAKDOWNS/ASSISTANCE   Your car rental agency will supply you with numbers to call in case of emergencies. Bigger companies usually have better service.

SUGGESTED ITINERARIES

Without doubt, Jerusalem is the most fascinating place in Israel. If you have very limited time, plan to spend most of it based there. Distances are not great in Israel, and it is possible to get a quick taste of the desert, the Mediterranean coast, and even the Sea of Galilee by doing a day excursion from Jerusalem. If you plan to visit Eilat, or get a real feel for the Galilee, then overnight trips become necessary.

If You Have 1 Week

Day 1   You might do well to make Tel Aviv your first stop, where from May to October you can recover from jet lag by beaching and swimming in the sparkling, warm Mediterranean.

Day 2   Take in the ambience of Israel's beachside metropolis. Spend at least a few hours at the unique Diaspora Museum. Visit Old Jaffa for outdoor seaside dining and a stroll.

Day 3   Move on to Jerusalem. Stroll through the restored Jewish Quarter of the Old City in the late afternoon or at twilight; include a visit to the Western Wall, which is fascinating at any hour. Dine in the New City.

Day 4   Explore the Old City. Do the Arab bazaars from 9am to noon (they currently close by midday to demonstrate Palestinian solidarity). Then see the Dome of the Rock and the El Aksa Mosque, which close by 3pm. (These two sites are closed all day Friday). The Holy Sepulcher Church is best scheduled for last because it remains open until early evening.

Day 5   Take in more of the Old City and the view from the Mount of Olives or do the highlights of the New City: the Israel Museum, Yad VaShem Holocaust Memorial and Museum, Hadassah (Ein Kerem) Hospital, the Knesset, or any of the city's smaller museums.

Day 6   Rental car or package tour to the fortress of Masada in the Judean Desert; swim in the Dead Sea at Ein Gedi. Or take a rental car to the Dead Sea, take a fast superbuoyant swim, drive up the Jordan Valley to the Sea of Galilee, visit Nazareth or the ancient, ruined synagogues around the lake, overnight, swim in the lake, and return to Jerusalem the next morning.

Day 7   Free day in Jerusalem; optional morning trip to Bethlehem, 5 miles south of Jerusalem.

If You Have 2 Weeks

Days 1 and 2   Head for Tel Aviv and overcome jet lag at the beach. Kibbutz guesthouses along the coast are a relaxing alternative if you have a car; swim at Caesarea's Roman Aqueduct Beach. Dine at Caesarea's port amid Crusader ruins.

Day 3   Go north along the coast. Make Haifa, Nahariya, or a kibbutz guesthouse your base. Explore the walled Arabic port city of Akko, Lohamei Ha-Getaot Holocaust Museum, and the cliffs at Rosh Ha-Niqra on the Lebanese border.

Day 4   Move inland across the northern Galilee. Base in Safed, Metulla, or a kibbutz guesthouse. Visit the ancient ruined synagogue at Baram (perhaps the loveliest in Israel) and the nature reserves and springs at Baniyas and Tel Dan.

Day 5   Spend the day at the Sea of Galilee. Circle the shoreline of this mysterious and lovely lake with its New Testament sites at Tabgha, Capernaum, and the Mount of Beatitudes. Swim at the Ein Gev Holiday Village (worth the fee). Overnight at Tiberias, a kibbutz holiday village, or guesthouse along the lake.

Day 6   Use your accommodations at the Sea of Galilee as a base. Explore the Golan Heights or Nazareth and the central Galilee. Have a late swim in the lake and dinner in Tiberias.

Day 7   Travel south through the Jordan Valley visiting the archeological park at Bet Shean or the Bet Alpha Byzantine mosaic synagogue floor at Kibbutz Hefzibah. Overnight at Kibbutz Kalia or Kibbutz Ein Gedi guesthouse along the dramatic coast of the Dead Sea.

Day 8   Explore the Herodian fortress of Masada; try to sink in the unearthly Dead Sea. Then head south through the Negev to Eilat, stopping at the national park at Timna for an off-the-main-highway view of the real Negev. Dine and overnight in Eilat.

Day 9   Snorkel the coral reef with its exotic Indian Ocean fish or view the fish at the aquarium or from a glass-bottom boat. Enjoy Eilat's busy restaurant scene and nightlife.

Day 10   Head to Jerusalem. Take an evening walk to the Jewish Quarter of the Old City and the Western Wall. Dine in the New City.

Days 11, 12, 13, and 14   Explore both the Old and New Cities; include a morning trip to Bethlehem, 5 miles south of Jerusalem.

If You Have 3 Weeks

Day 1   Arrive in Israel. Overnight in Jerusalem, or, in warm weather, at a rustic kibbutz guesthouse such as Kiryat Anavim near Jerusalem, while you overcome jet lag.

Day 2   Visit Jerusalem's Old City and wander the bazaars. Choose one or two historical sites to enjoy, rest in the afternoon, and dine at a restaurant with special Jerusalem atmosphere.

Day 3   Spend the day exploring the Old City or the New City (or both). Scout up something interesting from Jerusalem's evening entertainment scene.

Day 4   Drive down to the Dead Sea, 1 hour from Jerusalem. Explore Masada; overnight at Kibbutz Ein Gedi near the Dead Sea. Try swimming in the Dead Sea.

Day 5   Head toward Eilat via the desert kibbutz Sde Boker, where Ben-Gurion retired. Take in the nature reserve at the Ramon crater or the ruins of the ancient Negev city of Avdat. Arrive in Eilat in time for a late dinner, or overnight at desert kibbutz facilities at Ye'elim or Sde Boker, from which you can visit the Hai Bar Wildlife Park or the Timna National Park before arriving at Eilat on Day 6.

Day 6   Swim, snorkel, or dive the coral reef at Eilat. Enjoy Eilat's interesting restaurant and evening scene.

Days 7 and 8   Take a day or overnight excursion to Mount Sinai and the Santa Katerina Monastery in Egypt's Sinai Peninsula. Or cruise Eilat's reef, and beach-out for the day.

Day 9   Move on to Tel Aviv via Beersheva. Visit the remarkable Museum of Bedouin Culture near Kibbutz Lahav en route. Arrive in Tel Aviv in time for a late afternoon or evening swim after the desert drive (if you took an early morning dip in Eilat, you will have touched base with the Indian Ocean's Red Sea and the Atlantic/Mediterranean in 1 day!). Overnight in Tel Aviv.

Day 10   Spend the day in Tel Aviv feeling the pace of the city. Visit the Diaspora Museum. Spend the evening in Old Jaffa.

Day 11   Check out the Eretz Israel Museum complex or the Tel Aviv Museum of Art; shop trendy Tel Aviv or browse the Jaffa Flea Market. Dine in Tel Aviv.

Day 12   Move up the coast toward Haifa. Visit the ruins at Caesarea and the lovely Roman Aqueduct Beach. Overnight at a kibbutz holiday village along the coast such as Nasholim or at Netanya. Consider dining at a restaurant among the ruins of Caesarea.

Days 13 and 14   Visit Haifa and the surrounding area.

Days 15, 16, and 17   Tour Akko, the Sea of Galilee, and the north.

Day 18   Travel south from the Sea of Galilee to Jerusalem, via the Jordan Valley and Jericho. Arrive in Jerusalem by evening.

Days 19, 20, and 21   Spend this time getting to know Jerusalem better. Consider a morning excursion to Bethlehem during this time.

FAST FACTS: Israel

American Express   The toll-free information and refund number is 177/440-8694. There are representatives in Jerusalem, Tel Aviv, Haifa, and Amman in Jordan.

Business Hours   Israel does not have a standard set of business hours. For local business hours, see "Fast Facts" for the destination. Government offices are open on weekdays, usually from 7:30 or 8am. Some are closed to the public on Friday, and all are closed on Saturday; in summer they are open until 1 or 3pm; in winter they remain open until 2 or 4pm.

Camera/Film   Although film is cheaper in the United States, it can be bought almost anywhere in the country. Since the sun's so bright, and reflections tend to get glaring, many "pro" photographers use special filters to soften such effects. If you're really a photography fanatic, I suggest you investigate this and other special photographic conditions in Israel before leaving home. There are three restrictions on picture taking in Israel: certain military areas, which are plainly marked in several languages as no-photo territories; aerial photography over inland routes without special permission; and certain people, who use their own sign language (usually hands over their face, or in your face) to let you know they don't want to be photographed, for religious or other reasons.

Customs   You can bring $150 worth of tax-free gifts into the country. You can also bring in 250 cigarettes, 1 bottle (four-fifths quart) of liquor, and a reasonable amount of film. When you leave you can convert up to $3,000 back into foreign currency at the airport, so keep your bank receipts.

Dentists   See "Doctors," below.

Doctors   Embassies and consulates keep lists of English-speaking doctors and dentists who have been used successfully by staffers and visitors in the past. Remember also that on weekends and holidays the consulate always has a duty officer on call if a real emergency arises.

Drug Laws   Drug laws are enforced in Israel. Travelers should never attempt to buy illegal drugs.

Drugstores   If you need or want something for sunburn or minor physical discomforts, look for one of the many pharmacies, or chemist shops, in all towns and cities. In Israel pharmacists are allowed to advise about medicines and medications, and can sell you many items that would require a prescription in the United States. In fact, unless the medicine you require is in the addictive-drug category, you can buy it by simply asking in most pharmacies.

  If you need a medication at night, on Friday afternoon, or on Saturday, when drugstores are closed, check the *Jerusalem Post* for a list of pharmacies on round-the-clock emergency duty in your area.

Electricity   The electric current used in Israel is 220 volts AC, 50 cycles. If you bring an electric shaver, iron, or radio, you can buy an inexpensive transformer in Israel to convert the current to the American voltage cycle. Or you can buy 220-volt equipment at special shops that can be directly used in Israel. Sockets (or power points) usually take special Israeli three-prong plugs or sockets designed for round plugs. If your appliance has two prongs on its plug, you can buy a plug adapter in Israel quite easily for 2 or 3 shekels.

Embassies/Consulates   Israel's official capital is Jerusalem, but most countries do not recognize this position, so many embassies remain in Tel Aviv and operate consulates in Jerusalem. Embassies normally operate on the Monday to Friday work-week with a 1pm closing on Friday; closed Saturday and Sunday; closed for lunch from 1 to 2pm. The Canadian Embassy is in Tel Aviv at 220 Ha-Yarkon St. (☎ 03/527-2929). The consular, visa, and passport offices are at 7 Havakok St. (☎ 03/546-2878). The embassy for the United Kingdom is in Tel Aviv at 192 Ha Yarkon St. (☎ 03/693-1313); the consulate-general in East Jerusalem is at 19 Nashishibi St. (☎ 02/282-281). The U.S. Embassy is in Tel Aviv at 71 Ha-Yarkon St. (☎ 03/517-4338); in West Jerusalem at 18 Agron St. (☎ 02/253-288; offers few services); in East Jerusalem at the intersection of Nablus Road

(Derekh Shechem) and Pikud Ha-Merkaz Street (☎ 02/895-118). The East Jerusalem post has the consular section (same phone number).

Emergencies   Magen David Adom (Red Shield of David) is the Jewish equivalent of the Red Cross. They provide ambulance and first-aid service in virtually every city and town. At their clinics in major cities, you can get emergency medical or dental treatment on the Sabbath or at other times when normal practitioners are unavailable. For Magen David Adom emergency service in Jerusalem, Haifa, Tel Aviv, and most other parts of the country, dial 101. For emergencies requiring hospitalization, dial 102. The Magen David Adom clinic in Jerusalem is in Romema, near the Central Bus Station.

Mail   Post offices and mailboxes in Israel are identified by a red sign bearing a white leaping deer. English-style red-letter boxes are also used. Special yellow intracity mailboxes are found in Tel Aviv and Jerusalem. You can buy stamps at shops and news stands bearing a similar sign.

The main post offices in the large cities are usually open from 7am to 7pm on Sunday to Thursday; hours for branch post offices are 8am to 12:30pm and 3:30 to 6pm. All post offices are open on Friday and eves of holidays from 7am to 1pm. All are closed on Saturday.

Post offices have current postal-rate schedules, printed in English and Hebrew, on their bulletin boards. By the way, post offices in Israel are also the points from which you send telegrams or telexes, and the post office also operates overseas telephone calling centers. Zip codes are not necessary for sending letters.

You should know that it can take 2 weeks or more for a letter to travel between Israel and the North American continent, and that's airmail.

Newspapers/Magazines   Your indispensable source of news, entertainment, and information in Israel is the daily English-language newspaper, the *Jerusalem Post.* The *Post* will tell you about concerts in Haifa, movies in Tel Aviv, and entertainment events throughout the country. If you can't find it in the business section of the town you're in, or at a newspaper kiosk, try the big tourist hotel early in the morning before it sells out.

The Friday morning edition of the *Post* carries the weekly magazine section filled with features, entertainment notices, and radio and television listings. You pay a bit more for this larger edition. On Monday, the *Post* includes an insert bearing "The Week in Review" section from the *New York Times's* Sunday edition. The *Post* does not appear on Saturday. The big hotels also stock various foreign newspapers and periodicals.

A relatively new English-language news magazine, the *Jerusalem Report,* offers excellent coverage of Israel, and is published every 2 weeks. *Eretz* magazine is a beautifully photographed journal of Israeli nature, travel, and history and is widely available.

Police   Each city and town has its own municipal force, and the army keeps a vigil throughout the country. In the major cities, in an emergency, dial 100.

Radio/Television   Radio signals come in from all eastern Mediterranean countries, and often from Europe as well. The Voice of America, with a relay station on the Greek island of Rhodes, and the BBC's World Service are both accessible on the AM (middle-wave) dial.

Kol Israel (The Voice of Israel) broadcasts news bulletins in English on 576 or 1170 kHz at 7am, 1pm, and 5pm. News in French follows these English programs. There's even a schedule of bulletins in easy Hebrew for those learning the language.

Also, you can hear news broadcasts in English from Cairo and Amman at various times throughout the day.

Jordanian television broadcasting from Amman is easily picked up in Jerusalem and some other cities. There's always an evening news broadcast in English at either 9 or 10pm, depending on the time of year, and many familiar American or European programs.

Restrooms   Israeli cities and tourist sights are well provided with public toilets. Look for signs to the "WC," or "OO," or look for the various male–female symbols: pipe and fan, man and woman silhouettes, etc.

Safety   In general, Israel is a pretty safe place, but this doesn't mean you can ignore simple, commonsense precautions. Remember that whenever you're traveling in an unfamiliar city or country, stay alert. Be aware of your immediate surroundings, and don't leave valuables on view in a rental car. Watch out for pickpockets, especially in crowds, markets, in the crushes at bus stops, or in the narrow streets of Jerusalem's Old City bazaar. Muggings are rare, but they do occur.

Warning: Get away from and report any unattended objects in public places.

Taxes   A 17% value-added tax (VAT) is included in the price of everything paid for in shekels. When hotel bills are paid by foreigners in dollars, however, VAT is not applicable. Everything charged to the hotel bill—meals, room, telephone receive the VAT exemption, but meals paid for separately from the hotel bill do not.

In most tourist-oriented shops, the VAT on single-item purchases of more than $50 can be refunded at the airport. You should be warned that claiming this refund may be a lengthy business, so get to the airport early if you intend to do so.

Telegraph   Most hotels will accept them; big-city post offices often have late-hour counters from which you can send a wire. In Jerusalem, the counter at the main post office at 23 Jaffa Rd. stays open 24 hours a day. In Tel Aviv, a similar service is provided at the Telegraph Office on Mikveh Israel (Miqwe Yisra'el) Street: go down Allenby Road to Yehuda Ha-Levi Street, turn left, and immediately bear right onto Mikveh Israel Street. You can send a telegram by phone by calling 171.

Telephones   Public pay telephones accept magnetic phone cards, good for 10, 20, or 50 units. Magnetic phone cards cost a bit less if you buy them at the post office. A local call is generally 1 unit and permits you to speak for 3 minutes. There are also more expensive pay phones that accept shekels. Phone cards can be bought at news stands, post offices, stationers, and at many hotel desks. Pay phones that use cards do not accept coins.

Dialing 144 will get you directory assistance. Operators speak English. The overseas operator is 188.

Each city in Israel has an area code: Tel Aviv and the airport are 03; Jerusalem is 02; Haifa, 04; and Netanya, 09; Eilat and most of the Negev, 07; Tiberias, Nazareth, Safed, and most of the northeastern Galilee is 06. Look in the phone book for others.

When you call from another country to a number in Israel, you do not dial that initial "0" (zero). Dial Israel's country code (972), Jerusalem's area (or city) code (2), then the local number (241-281). If you're calling within Israel, say from Jerusalem to a number in Haifa, you must use the initial zero of the area code.

Telex   The post office will send a telex, which is cheaper than a telegram, from most of its major post offices. Unlike the recipient of a telegram, the addressee must have telex service (a telex machine in the office). Telex offices have telex directories.

Time   Israel has daylight saving time in summer but only from late March to early September. The basic time difference between New York and Jerusalem is 7 hours: When it's 5am in New York, it's already noon in Jerusalem. When daylight saving times don't match, the time difference comes down to 6 hours: When it's 6am in New York, it's noon in Jerusalem. For the time, dial 155.

Tipping   It used to be that no one tipped in Israel. The social consciousness and idealism of the early days has worn off somewhat now, however. In tourist spots and better-quality hotels, restaurants, and clubs, tip 10%, unless the menu states that a service charge is included. In more modest restaurants, do as the Israelis do: leave small change in the 5% to 10% range. The person waiting on you may pick up your offering with indifference. That's probably because he or she didn't really expect a tip, rather than because the tip was too small.

You needn't tip taxi or sherut drivers unless they've performed some special service. But you should always offer a tip to a guide or caretaker (self-appointed or otherwise) who actually does help you to see some holy site or ancient ruin. If there is no admission fee, and if a man or boy comes running to unlock the gate for you, he deserves a small tip. But when he offers you a guided tour, or simply begins to guide you, you can say no. By saying nothing, you encourage misunderstanding. By saying yes, you've made a contract, and you should proceed to agree on a price.

Tip about 10% at the barber's or hairdresser's, part to the person who washes your hair, part to the one who cuts it. Cinema or theater ushers don't expect tips. But a hat or coat checker and a lavatory attendant do—a few coins will do unless a price is posted. When staying in a hotel room for the better part of a week or more, the housekeeping staff deserves a tip. When you first go to your room, the bellhop should get a tip.

Useful Telephone Numbers   For the time, dial 155; for weather, dial 03/625-231. Dialing 100 reaches the police, and 101 gets first aid. Airport arrivals can be checked by dialing 03/973-1122; departures are 03/972-2333.

Water   Drink lots and lots of it to prevent dehydration during the hot, dry Israeli summer. Tap water is drinkable throughout Israel, although in some areas local minerals may cause short-term upset stomach. You may prefer to be extra safe and buy the bottled water available in grocery stores. In a cafe, ask for "soda" and you'll receive a club soda.

Getting to Know Jerusalem

4

No one will ever be able to pinpoint what makes Jerusalem so special. The mountains, the wind, the extraordinary light may be part of it. The physical grandeur of Herodian Jerusalem was long ago lost to the ravages of warfare and time. Only in the late 19th century did the city begin to come alive and emerge from behind its walls. During the years of the British Mandate (1918–1948) the current incarnation of Jerusalem developed as a quiet religious center, tourist attraction, and university town in a remarkably beautiful mountain setting. Nineteen years of the city's division by war, barbed wire, and minefields from 1948 to 1967 brought Jerusalem's gentle renaissance to a temporary halt. With the city's reunification in 1967, however, Teddy Kollek, the city's world-renowned mayor, began a 25-year crusade to make sure Jerusalem would not merely exist or even thrive but would absolutely shine!

1 Jerusalem Past & Present

JERUSALEM TODAY

Jerusalem today is a vibrant place. Against all odds, the Israeli–Palestinian conflict seems to be moving toward a settlement, and Jerusalem, always at the heart of the conflict, has suddenly become a magnet for optimists. New construction is going on everywhere, bringing new industry, new highways, and, in the next few years, a whole new hotel scene. The constant stream of civic delights—museums, concerts, performances—developed by Teddy Kollek helped turn an austere outpost in the Judean hills into a lively, Mediterranean city with cafes, pubs, and restaurants packed to the brim with activity. The newly created pedestrian streets of the downtown center are flooded with strollers and, especially in summer, you'll find a nightly air of festive celebration.

A walled city is always a small town at heart, and for the past century, as Jerusalem expanded beyond its walls and across the surrounding hills, it remained in spirit a small town: inward looking, personal, always in touch with local gossip and also with its thundering history. Now, for good or for ill, Jerusalem stands on the verge of becoming a true metropolis rather than the small city of exotic neighborhoods and communities the world has known for the past 60 years. What Jerusalem will be like as the decade leads to a new century is a point of international interest and concern. To be Jerusalem, a place that makes hearts thump throughout the world, you have to be unique. For 3,000 years, through splendor and desolation, glory and poverty, despite all imperfections, the earthly Jerusalem has always managed to live up to its extraordinary legend. Will the New Jerusalem be able to maintain its mystique? With a major highway system routed just 30 feet from the walls of the Old City, so that visitors have to climb a pedestrian overpass in order to enter the Jaffa Gate? With many of the eccentric, small-scale 19th-century courtyards and neighborhoods of the New City (underappreciated in a town with Herodian, Byzantine, and Omayyid treasures to preserve) slated to be demolished and replaced with office blocks? With a new wave of skyscrapers and the arrival of such worldly establishments as Pizza Hut, McDonald's, Tower Records, and Toys Я Us? At what point will Jerusalem begin to seem like anywhere else?

The city is at a crossroads politically and socially as well as physically. Will it become a capital for the Palestinian as well as the Israeli people? Will the religious Jewish community become the demographic and ruling majority in West Jerusalem and, if so, what will happen to the museums, parks, entertainment, and cultural institutions created by the city's secular community over the past 30 years? Should developers be allowed a free hand or should limits be placed on the future growth of the city? What would happen to Jerusalem or any city forced to exist under severe growth restrictions?

Optimists believe Jerusalem's extraordinary power has never merely come from what can be seen and that city planners will find a way to turn a mysterious walled holy city into a fast-paced holy megalopolis. For now, the city still manages to walk a tightrope between its legend and the encroaching world of the late 20th century.

A LOOK AT JERUSALEM'S PAST

Jerusalem ranks among the cities of the world that have the longest record of continual habitation. Few cities have such a special aura about them. Not only has Jerusalem been a holy city for 3,000 years, far eclipsing the length of time that any other place has borne such a title, but it has been a holy city for the three great religions of the Western world: Judaism, Christianity, and Islam. It is the most exotic of Israel's three principal cities as well as its seat of government. Old-time residents take an uncommon pride in living there.

In Genesis it is recorded that Abraham visited Melchizedek, "king of Salem," one of the first known references to Jerusalem. However, for the next 800 years the city played no part in biblical or Jewish history. Then, in 1004 B.C., King David, the charismatic poet–warrior, captured Jerusalem, which was a small Jebusite/Canaanite city perched on a narrow hill just to the south of the present Old City walls. The city was considered neutral territory, situated on land not controlled by any of the 12 tribes of Israel, and seemed an ideal choice for a capital that would not exacerbate tribal rivalries. David brought the Ark of the Covenant to Jerusalem from his former capital, Hebron. On the Ophel, a stretch of ascending land between the settlement of Jerusalem and the high place that was to become the Temple Mount, David built his palace and declared that henceforth Jerusalem would be the capital.

Under the reign of David's son Solomon, Jerusalem grew in importance. It was the center of a brief-lived empire that stretched from southern Syria to the Gulf of Eilat. African ivory and gold, cedarwood from Lebanon, spices, textiles, and pottery from distant lands adorned its houses and were bargained for in its markets. Solomon built the great Temple (960 B.C.) and constructed a more magnificent palace (although the Bible records the grandeur of Solomonic Jerusalem with awe, it would

Historic Jerusalem

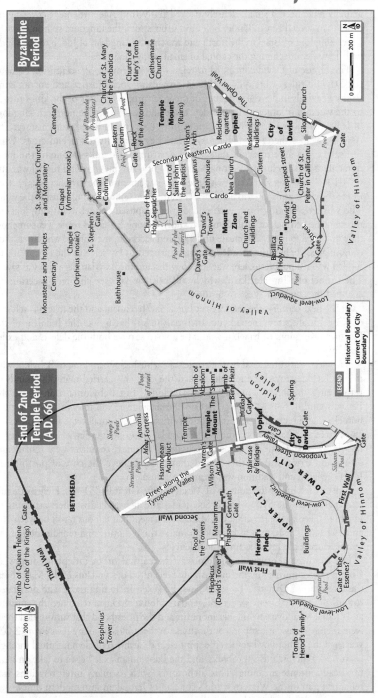

Byzantine Period

Monasteries and hospices
Cemetery

St. Stephen's Church and Monastery
Chapel (Armenian mosaic)
Chapel (Orpheus mosaic)
St. Stephen's Gate
Bathhouse

Cemetery
Roman Column
Pool of Bethsada (Probatica?)
Church of St. Mary of the Probatica
Church of Mary's Tomb
Gethsemane Church
Pool
Pool
Eastern Forum
Gate
Rock
Church of the Antonia
Temple Mount (Ruins)
Wilson's Arch
The Ophel Wall
Residential quarter
Ophel
Residential buildings
City of David
Siloam Church
Gate

Church of the Holy Sepulcher
Forum
"David's Tower"
David's Gate
Decumanus
Church of Saint John the Baptist
Bathhouse
Secondary (eastern) Cardo
Nea Church
Cistern
Cardo
Mount Zion
Church and buildings
"David's Tomb"
Basilica of Holy Zion
Stepped street
Church of St. Peter in Gallicantu
N Street
N Gate
Pool
Gate

Pool of the Patriarch
Valley of Hinnom
Low-level aqueduct
Valley of Hinnom

0   200 m
N

End of 2nd Temple Period (A.D. 66)

0   200 m
N

Tomb of Queen Helene (Tomb of the Kings)
Gate
Third Wall
BETHESDA
Pesphinus' Tower

Pool of Israel
Sheep's Pools
Antonia Fortress
Moat
Struthion Pool
Hasmolean Aqueduct
Street along the Tyropoeon Valley
Warren's Gate
Wilson's Arch
Second Wall
Pool of the Towers
Mariamme
Phasael
Gennath Gate
Hippicus (David's Tower)
First Wall
Herod's Place
Buildings

Temple
Temple Mount
"Tomb of Absalom"
Tomb of Bene Hezir
Huldah Gates
Ophel
Gate
Gate
City of David
LOWER CITY
UPPER CITY
Staircase & Bridge
Low-level aqueduct
Tyropoeon Street Valley
Spring
Cate
Kidron Valley
The "Isam"
First Wall
Siloam Pool
Gate

Serpents' Pool
Gate of the Essenes?
Low-level aqueduct
"Tomb of Herod's family"
Valley of Hinnom

LEGEND
Historical Boundary
Current Old City Boundary

79

actually have been a small, densely packed Early Iron Age settlement covering no more than several acres). Under Solomon's successors, the kingdom split in two: the larger kingdom of Israel to the north and the smaller kingdom of Judah to the south, with Jerusalem becoming the capital of small, struggling Judah.

The House of David continued to reign in Jerusalem for 3^1/$_2$ centuries. Some of the Davidic rulers were quite noble in dispensing social justice and encouraging relgious revivals under the influence of the great prophets; some of the kings turned to the worship of other gods. Invaders came and retreated. The northern kingdom of Israel fell to Assyria in the late 8th century B.C. and vanished from history. The Assyrian armies then stormed across Judah, destroying its towns and cities. Only Jerusalem was able to avoid defeat and destruction, thanks to one of the most miraculous and fateful engineering feats in history. An underground tunnel was dug in 701 B.C. by King Hezikiah (with the encouragement of the Prophet Isaiah) from inside the city's walls to Jerusalem's water source, the Gihon Spring, outside the walls. The workers, digging from each end of the proposed tunnel, frantically hacked through the bedrock of Jerusalem in a wildly curving S-shaped route, yet somehow they managed to meet, and create underground access to, the Gihon (which was then camouflaged) before the dreaded Assyrians arrived to lay seige to the city. With its hidden water supply Jerusalem was able to withstand the Assyrian siege and was saved. The tunnel of King Hezikiah, which still exists today (see chapter 5, section 4), changed the course of Western history.

In the next century, the messages of Isaiah and Jeremiah, and the religious reforms of King Josiah, strengthened Judean Judaism, so that unlike the Judaism of the Northern Kingdom of Israel, it would be able to survive both the defeats and exiles that lay ahead.

Jerusalem was conquered by the armies of Nebuchadnezzar, king of Babylon, who in 586 B.C. destroyed the temple, sacked the city, and carried many thousands of Jerusalem's inhabitants into exile in Babylonia. But Babylonia soon fell to the Persians, and in 540 B.C. King Cyrus of Persia allowed the Jews to return to their homeland and rebuild a modest Second Temple. Only a small remnant of the exiles chose to leave what had become a comfortable, cosmopolitan Jewish community in Babylonia and resettle the ruins of Jerusalem. The next centuries were remarkably quiet, and it was during this period that many believe the core of postbiblical Jewish religion and tradition was created in Jerusalem.

The city fell under the domain of Alexander the Great in 331 B.C. Hellenistic rule later passed to the Syrian-based Seleucids, and it was against their attempts to forcibly Hellenize the Jews that the Maccabees staged their famous revolt between 167 and 141 B.C. The festival of Hanukkah marks the recapture and rededication of the temple during the revolt against the Seleucids.

For the next century, Jerusalem was the capital of an independent Jewish Commonwealth ruled by the increasingly Hellenized descendants of the Maccabees, the Hasmonean Dynasty. To some Jews, however, including those who gravitated toward the ascetic Essene sect, the legendary House of David remained the spiritual and eternal royal dynasty; the Hasmoneans and the priesthood that surrounded them were merely transient temporal authorities. In the minds of many Jews living 2,000 years ago the dichotomy between the spiritual and earthly Jerusalem nurtured through centuries of the psalmists, prophets, and the Babylonian exile began to take on new, mystically intense meaning. This dichotomy, with its many interpretations, has remained part of the Western world's concept of Jerusalem into modern times.

Pompey claimed Jerusalem for Rome in 63 B.C., and in 37 B.C. Herod (whose Idumaean father converted to Judaism) was appointed king of Judea by the Romans.

Perhaps in an effort to make himself loved by his reluctant and resentful subjects, perhaps in an effort to impress his Roman overseers with his industry, Herod rebuilt Jerusalem and designed a palatial temple area that dwarfed the original Temple of Solomon.

Herod died in 4 B.C. The city that he built, with its fortress, towers, aqueducts, and vast temple complex, was the Jerusalem that Jesus knew. Herod's great temple complex, initially opposed by many Jews who felt it was too Roman in its grandeur, became a symbol of Jewish national and religious aspiration and a constant flashpoint in Jewish opposition to Roman rule. As never before, the temple became a center for Jewish pilgrimage from Judea, the Galilee, Babylonia, Persia, and all parts of the Roman Empire; 100,000 pilgrims could be accommodated in Jerusalem during the great festivals of Passover and Sukkot. To a greater extent than ever, religion was Jerusalem's major industry, and it was increasingly big business. During this period, rabbinical Judaism was also developing, grounded in study, prayer, synagogue, and careful analysis of ethical and ritual rules governing Jews everywhere. This component of Judaism flourished alongside the priestly cult, which was centered on the temple at Jerusalem.

It was to the city that was a magnet for the ancient Jewish world that Jesus came to celebrate Passover, and it was in Jerusalem that under Pontius Pilate, the Roman procurator, Jesus was imprisoned and crucified. According to most Christian traditions the Church of the Holy Sepulcher marks the site of the crucifixion and burial of Jesus, and the Via Dolorosa is the way Jesus trod, carrying the cross, from prison to Golgotha.

The Jewish rebellion against Roman rule in A.D. 66 drove the Roman occupiers from Jerusalem, and brought the Roman armies of Titus and Vespasian to reconquer Jerusalem. In A.D. 70, Rome starved out the population of Jerusalem, destroyed the city and its temple, and killed or sold into slavery most of its surviving inhabitants. The Roman Tenth Legion was stationed beside the ruins of the Jaffa Gate for more than 60 years to prevent Jews from filtering back and reestablishing their city.

There is evidence that Jews and early Christians (who were considered to be a Jewish sect) were permitted to visit Jerusalem during these years and were still able to identify the exact locations of specific holy sites among the ruins. Talmudic lore records that a group of rabbis walking on the Temple Mount noticed that a fox had made its lair in the wreckage of the Holy of Holies. Aging witnesses to Jesus's last days in Jerusalem would have been able to pass on their memories of where those events took place to a younger generation. Although the city was now desolate, the powerful charisma of Jerusalem continued to grow.

Bar Kokhba's revolt in A.D. 132, triggered by the decision of the Emperor Hadrian to rebuild Jerusalem as a non-Jewish Roman outpost, returned the ruined city to the Jews for 3 short years. The temple site was rededicated, though probably not rebuilt, and daily sacrifice was reinstated. The revolt ended in A.D. 135 with even greater military disaster for the Jews than the revolt of A.D. 70. According to some estimates,

Impressions

Jerusalem: the city which miraculously transforms man into pilgrim; no one can enter it and remain unchanged.

—Elie Wiesel

Jerusalem of gold, of copper, of light . . . To all your songs, I am the harp.

—Popular Israeli Song

Two Great Conquerors

Jerusalem has been conquered by Islamic forces twice: in A.D. 638, and again in 1187, when it was recaptured after 88 years of Crusader rule. Both times, the warriors who won Jerusalem were among the most extraordinary men Islamic civilization has ever produced. In each case, Jerusalem was captured without resort to a final military onslaught, and in each case, these leaders, who only stayed in Jerusalem briefly, left an enduring touch on the city.

Omar ibn el Khattab (d. 644), the second successor to the Prophet Mohammed, was a warrior of great saintliness who eschewed all luxuries and dressed in a simple roughspun cloak. According to legend, when the Byzantine ambassador came to Medina to seek an audience with Caliph Omar, he was directed to a hill outside the city. There he found only a man alone, asleep on the ground under a palm tree, using his dusty sandals for a pillow. When the ambassador was told that this was the caliph, he responded, "Great Omar, you are truly a ruler of peace and justice unequaled to be able to go unprotected among your people in such a way."

Accepting the peaceful submission of Jerusalem from the Byzantine patriarch Sophronius in A.D. 638, Omar declined an invitation to pray in the Church of the Holy Sepulcher for fear that in future times, any place in which he had prayed would be turned into a mosque. According to tradition, the tolerant and visionary Omar permitted Jews to reside in Jerusalem again, initiated the cleaning of the Temple Mount, which had been used as a garbage dump for 300 years, and ordered the transformation of Jerusalem into an Islamic as well as a Jewish and Christian holy city. The Dome of the Rock is a lasting monument to Omar's brief, radiant encounter with Jerusalem.

Saladin (1137–1193), of Kurdish origin, was the Sultan of Egypt, Syria, Yemen, and Palestine, founder of the Ayyubid Dynasty, and the most romantically heroic

half a million civilians died in each of the revolts against Rome, numbers unheard of in ancient warfare. Hadrian leveled the ruins of Jerusalem, sowed the land with salt, and, with an entirely different city plan and arrangement of streets, built a Roman city called "Aelia Capitolina" in honor of the imperial family and the Roman god Jupiter Capitolina. Hadrian filled Aelia Capitolina with pagan temples and barred Jews from the city for all time. Herod's great Temple Mount platform, too massive and still too politically sensitive to demolish, was one of the few features from Herodian Jerusalem that remained. According to some historians, a Roman temple may have been installed on the site of the Jerusalem temple itself. Jews were generally allowed into the city only to visit the ruins of the Temple Mount and only on the ninth day of the month of Av, the anniversary of the temple's destruction.

Today, little from this alien interlude in Jerusalem's history remains to be seen, except for a fragment of the colonnaded Cardo, Aelia Capitolina's main north–south thoroughfare, which was uncovered by archeologists in the 1970s. The basic layout of the Old City, divided into quadrants by perpendicular intersecting market streets leading from the Damascus and Jaffa Gates, is inherited from this time, as is the Arabic name for Damascus Gate (Bab-el-Amud, or Gate of the Column), recalling a towering, long-lost column that once stood inside the gate to serve, in traditional Roman fashion, as a distance marker.

The Emperor Constantine, who converted the Roman empire to Christianity, turned Jerusalem into a Christian holy city. He built the Church of the Holy Sepulcher in of all Islamic generals. Saladin's moral leadership and passion, rather than overwhelming tactical advantage, brought many disparate forces to victory over the Crusaders at the Horns of Hittin, near Tiberias, on July 4, 1187. Three months later, Jerusalem surrendered under Saladin's siege. In contrast to the massacre of Muslims and Jews that had accompanied the Crusader conquest of Jerusalem in 1099, Saladin's victory was marked by chivalry and compassion. Native Christians were allowed to remain as before in the city; those of Crusader origin were offered safe passage with their goods out of the country via Akko on payment of a ransom of 10 dinars a piece. As Saladin and his brother watched the wealthy, including the Crusader patriarch and his retinue, depart with wagons filled with treasure, leaving thousands of unransomed poor to be sold into slavery, they announced a donation to ransom 7,000 poor Christians, thus shaming the patriarch into matching their generosity. In one of the many historical coincidences fraught with meaning to Jerusalemites, Saladin conquered the city on October 2, 1187, the anniversary of the Prophet Muhammed's Miraculous Night Journey from Mecca to Jerusalem, and his ascension from the Temple Mount to the heavens for a glimpse of Paradise. The selfless Saladin, in the great tradition of early Islamic leaders such as Omar ibn el Khattab, died without even enough money to pay for his grave. The extraordinary stair pulpit of the El Aksa Mosque, one of Islam's great artistic treasures for more than 7 centuries, was commissioned by Saladin for the rededication of El Aksa as a mosque after the Crusader occupation. It was destroyed when a mentally disturbed Australian tourist set fire to the El Aksa in 1969, and is being painstakingly reconstructed by craftspeople trained in techniques that have not been used for hundreds of years.

approximately A.D. 330, and the Byzantine emperor, Justinian, 200 years later, rebuilt and enlarged it. Jerusalem regained its ancient name, and again became an extraordinary destination for religious pilgrimage from all over the ancient world—this time by members of a new religion. The city was filled with churches, monasteries, and convents, and daily religious processions. Jews were forbidden to reside in Byzantine Jerusalem and often allowed only to view the city from the Mount of Olives.

Caliph Omar, in A.D. 638, began the Muslim occupation—and shortly thereafter (A.D. 687–691), on the Temple Mount, Caliph Abd el-Malik built the masterpiece Dome of the Rock, marking the spot from which the Prophet Muhammad, in his miraculous night journey, rose from the earth to glimpse Paradise. Under the tolerant rule of the early Muslims, Jews were allowed again to reside in Jerusalem and the Christian community continued to flourish, but around the year A.D. 1000, Caliph Al Hakim began a wave of anti-Christian persecution that culminated in the burning of the Church of the Holy Sepulcher. Feudal Europe responded with the Crusades, and in the wars that followed, the mystical concept of Jerusalem was burned more strongly than ever into the traditions of both Christianity and Islam. After the intitial success of the First Crusade in 1099, Jerusalem changed hands several times between Crusaders and Muslims (most notably under Saladin). The Crusader Church of Saint Anne (A.D. 1147), with its near miraculous acoustics, is Jerusalem's great architectural treasure from this era. Hundreds of architectural fragments from Crusader buildings, in secondary use adorning Mameluke and Ottoman period buildings throughout the Old City, attest to the massive destruction inflicted on the city during these centuries. The entire Jewish population of Jerusalem was massacred by Crusader armies in 1099.

Four centuries later in 1517 the Ottoman Turks, also Muslims, conquered Jerusalem. In an esthetic stroke of genius, the 16th-century Ottoman rulers faced the deteriorating exterior of the Dome of the Rock with dramatic cobalt blue and turquoise ceramic tiles from Persia and Anatolia. The Ottomans also rebuilt the magnificent walls around Jerusalem in 1538, but these largely ceremonial fortifications (gunpowder and cannon had made such defensive structures obsolete) surrounded a depopulated community devastated by centuries of Crusader wars and struggling to survive. By the early 19th century, the city's population, estimated to have been close to 100,000 in Herodian times, had shrunk to under 15,000. Only in the second half of the 19th century did the city begin to come alive again, with its Jewish, Christian, and Muslim communities spreading into neighborhoods beyond the walls of the Old City.

In the last decades of the the 19th century, as the European powers vied for influence in this strategic portion of the floundering Ottoman Empire, each government planted its flag in Jerusalem under the guise of vast church-related construction projects. The number of monuments to European nationalism that date from this brief era is amazing. Germany's massively Romanesque Dormition Church and Monastery on Mount Zion recalls Worms Cathedral, overlooking the Rhine; the delicate, Renaissance-inspired Holy Trinity Church in the Russian Compound echoes the late 15th-century Cathedral of the Assumption in the Kremlin; St. George's Cathedral in East Jerusalem, completed in 1912, is an enclave of neogothic Britain built from Jerusalem stone, with a Jerusalem-stone bell tower and cloister reminiscent of Magdalene College at Oxford. The exotically medieval Russian Church of Saint Mary Magdalene with its guilded onion-shaped domes transformed the vista of the Mount of Olives. Florentine, Ethiopian, and French architecture sprang up across the city in the form of hospitals, churches, convents, and pilgrimage facilities.

Turkish rule lasted exactly 400 years, until General Allenby marched through Jerusalem's Jaffa Gate at the head of a British regiment in the final year of World War I. The New City blossomed under the British Mandate era (1918–48), and much of downtown West Jerusalem took on its basic shape. Landmarks such as the YMCA, the King David Hotel, the Rockefeller Museum in East Jerusalem, the original Hadassah Hospital and Hebrew University on Mount Scopus, the art-moderne Central Post Office on Jaffa Road, Saint Andrew's Church near Abu Tor, and West Jerusalem's King George Street all stand as monuments to that era. The Rehavia neighborhood, with its streamlined, curved balcony buildings designed in the International Style by refugee architects from Germany, and the exotic mansions built for the leading Arabic families in the adjacent neighborhood of Talbeyeh, are also part of Jerusalem's British Mandate era heritage.

TO THE PRESENT DAY

In November 1947, the United Nations voted to establish two states in Palestine: one Jewish, the other Arab. Jerusalem was to remain a united, international city. In spite of this decision, by early 1948 the Jewish sector of Jerusalem found itself under siege by Arab forces and suffered shelling and bombardment for many weeks. Eventually, Israeli forces secured a narrow strip of mountainous land (the Burma Road), which connected the Jewish part of Jerusalem to the rest of Israel, and the siege was broken. The State of Israel was established in the 1948 War of Independence, but Jerusalem was split down the middle from north to south by a wall of concrete, barbed wire, and minefields. The modern western section of the city remained in Israeli hands, but the Old City, including the Jewish Quarter (from which all Jews had been expelled) and the modern Arab neighborhoods north of the Old City (along with the rest of West Bank), were annexed by the Kingdom of Jordan.

In the Six-Day War of 1967, East Jerusalem came under Israeli control and the city was reunited once again. But the distinctions of two decades still remain: downtown East Jerusalem and the Old City are predominantly Palestinian (Christian and Muslim Arabs) and West Jerusalem is predominantly Israeli.

2 Orientation

ARRIVING

BY PLANE   The best way to get to Jerusalem from Ben-Gurion Airport is by sherut, which is a shared stretch limousine or van with a fixed per-person rate. The driver must—without charging an extra agora—take you from the airport to the hotel or residential address of your choice anywhere in United Jerusalem. The driver is not allowed to charge for each hotel drop. If you're lucky, you'll be the first in your group to be dropped off at your destination in Jerusalem. If not, you'll get to see a bit of the city as other passengers are dropped off, and you'll still get to your hotel in good time and at a reasonable price without the hassle of dragging your luggage on and off public transportation, or the expense of a private taxi. The current fare is NIS 33 ($10) per person. The sherut stand is to the far right as you exit the terminal building. The rate for a private taxi from Ben Gurion to Jerusalem is about $30 to $35.

For the return trip to the airport, your hotel will be glad to call in advance and make an appointment for a sherut to pick you up. If you'd rather do it in person, at the intersection of Ben-Yehuda Street and King George V Avenue in West Jerusalem, right across from the City Tower, you'll find the office of Nesher Sheruts (☎ 02/257-227), known for its extremely reliable airport service.

All major car rental companies have offices at Ben-Gurion Airport.

BY TRAIN   One or two trains a day from Tel Aviv arrive at the old Ottoman Railroad Station. The scenery as the train approaches Jerusalem is quite beautiful, but the scanty schedule can be a hassle. Municipal buses to all parts of Jerusalem leave from outside the Jerusalem Train Station. Downtown buses are across the street.

BY BUS   Most buses arrive and depart from the Central Bus Station, which is at the western entrance to the city, right on Jaffa Road not far past the intersection with Herzl/Yirmiyahu Boulevard, and virtually across the street from Binyane Ha-Uma, Jerusalem's large convention center. *Note:* After depositing most passengers, Egged intercity buses from Tel Aviv and Haifa arriving in Jerusalem after 7 or 8pm generally continue down Jaffa Road to the center of town, and make additional request stops along the way. The buses then stop at the corner of Agron Street and the beginning of King David Street, and at the corner of Agron Street and King George Street. Check with your bus driver: If you're going to the center of town, this is a convenient free option.

However, if you are traveling by bus to Jerusalem from the south or east (Bethlehem, Hebron, or Jericho), your bus may arrive at the East Jerusalem Bus Station on Sultan Suleiman Street near the Damascus Gate, between Nablus Road and Saladin Street. Buses from this station arrive and depart mainly from West Bank towns.

Above the doors as you leave the Central Bus Station, you'll see a large sign that tells you which city bus to catch for each general destination inside Jerusalem, and also where to catch it. The system works like this: The board shows a bus number, and then (in English) the high points of its route. Bus no. 9, for example, goes to Hebrew University's Givat Ram campus, the Israel Museum, and the Knesset. Right beside this information is a symbol that indicates where you can catch the bus. There are four boarding areas, each bearing a letter and a symbol. To get to Area A, symbolized by a square, you simply head out the bus station door and you're there. To get to Area B (a triangle), Area C (a circle), and Area D (an octagon), you go out the bus station doors and down the stairs into an underpass beneath Jaffa Road. Go up the stairs at the opposite end of the underpass for Area B; for C and D, keep walking straight along the path and follow the signs. If you're going toward the center of town, just cross the street for your bus stop. Outbound buses stop on the bus station's side of the street. Remember, however, that you must take a cab or sherut from 1 hour before sundown on Friday until Saturday evening, as local buses do not run on the Sabbath.

When you come out to Jaffa Road from the Central Bus Station, look left up Jaffa Road and you'll be looking east toward the center of the city. See "Getting Around: By Bus," below, for more information on how to use Jerusalem's bus system.

BY CAR   There are many ways to enter Jerusalem, or to "go up" to the city, as expressed by the Hebrew word, implying a physical and spiritual ascension. From the north, you can either take the Jordan Valley way, passing through Tiberias, Bet Shean, and Jericho, and enter Jerusalem from the east, or alternatively (not recommended at this time due to West Bank political problems), a beautiful way between mountains, passing Jenin, Nablus, and Ramallah. The third and longest way is via Afula, Hadera, and the coastal plain to Tel Aviv, reaching the city from the west. The southern entry is Beersheva through Hebron and Bethlehem—but because of problems and uncertainties in the West Bank, drivers from Beersheva to Jerusalem are advised to detour to the Israeli town of Kiryat Gat and continue from there to Jerusalem rather than take the more direct route (see also chapter 6, "The West Bank").

From Tel Aviv, take the newer road—a 57-kilometer (34-mile) four-lane highway finished in 1979. It passes by beautiful countryside and the Ben-Gurion Airport, en route to the Latrun area that bisects a wide natural pass between the Judean Hills and the coastal region. In the Latrun area, you will see the former police station (Fortress Latrun) and the Latrun Monastery. Tourists seldom stop at the fortress, but they do enter the road to the Trappist Monastery, where the monks—many of whom have taken a vow of silence—sell wine from the monastery's vineyards.

Directly past the monastery, the road to Jerusalem continues straight, past the interchange for the highway to Ramallah. A gas station on the left and an old ruined travelers' lodge to the right mark the entrance to Sha'ar Ha Gai, The Gate of the Valley (Bab El Wad in Arabic), the pass that for thousands of years has led travelers through the western Judean mountains to Jerusalem. From here on, you'll be climbing through steep but lovely terraced hills. For almost half a century, the reforestation plantings of evergreen trees along this road have been the pride of the nation. The greenery seems even more a symbol of the rebirth of Israel when contrasted with the stony barren hills in the distance. Sadly, in the summer of 1995, the Jerusalem Corridor was swept by a devastating forest fire. Only a few of the hillsides were saved and continue to look like pieces of Switzerland or Norway. During the next few years, the area will probably be replanted with trees and vegetation more native to the region and more resistant to the danger of forest fire.

The last leg of the way is a steep ascent up a corridor strewn with wrecked military vehicles that serve as memorials to the 1948 War of Independence and the struggle to break the siege of Jerusalem.

VISITOR INFORMATION

There's a Ministry of Tourism information desk (☎ 03/971-1145) in the Arrivals Hall of Ben-Gurion International Airport. The staff will provide city maps, brochures, and the answers to your questions. A hotel reservations desk nearby can also help you find a room for the night.

A Tourist Information computer is located at 24 King George V Ave. (the Ministry of Tourism Building) in downtown West Jerusalem, just a few blocks off Jaffa Road near the intersection of King George V Avenue and Hillel Street. (*Note:* That's Hillel Street, not to be confused with the nearby Ben-Hillel Street.) The computer can answer some of your questions and give you printouts of reasonably up-to-date information, but it is not a good substitute for dealing with a well-informed, carefully trained person. The Ministry of Tourism no longer maintains an actual information office at this crucial downtown location, and advises tourists to get information from their hotels and from Municipal Tourism Offices. You will not be allowed inside the Ministry of Tourism Building unless you have official business. There is always a chance that the ministry may reestablish an information office during the time span of this edition.

In the Old City there's a Municipal Tourist Information Office just inside Jaffa Gate, a few steps down on the left (☎ 02/745-910), open on Saturday from 10am to 2pm; other days it's open from 9am to 5pm (until 12:30pm on Friday). There is a second Municipal Tourist Office at 17 Jaffa Rd. in West Jerusalem (☎ 02/258-844), one block from the walls of the Old City, across the street from the large, modern Municipal Government Center and a bit down Jaffa Road in the direction of the Old City. It is often closed for lunch, but as the Municipality takes over responsibility for Tourist Information from the Ministry of Tourism, this may develop into a more active center.

MAPS & PUBLICATIONS   The *Jerusalem Post* has a daily section on city events, but the Friday edition is your best bet, with an exhaustive list of the week's activities throughout Israel.

Another excellent source of information is the free weekly *Events in the Jerusalem Region,* prepared by the Tourist Office and available at the Municipal Tourism Information Offices and in hotel lobbies.

Excellent free maps can be obtained at both tourist information offices. The free tourist newspaper *Your Jerusalem* contains the best bus directions in town. There are many small bookletlike free publications for tourists, ranging from *Hello Israel* to *Jerusalem Menus,* filled with current information and discount dining coupons, but keep in mind that the shopping and restaurant information in these magazines is paid advertising.

CITY LAYOUT

To get around Jerusalem easily, you must understand how the city grew. In the early 1800s, Jerusalem was still a walled medieval city—a tortuous maze with sewage running down the streets. After the mid-19th century, Christian pilgrims and Zionist settlers began to create neighborhoods outside the city walls. From 1948 to 1967, Jerusalem was further divided when modern West Jerusalem remained under Israeli jurisdiction while the Old City became part of the Kingdom of Jordan. Although the city has been united under Israeli control since 1967, Jerusalem is still three different cities in one: the Old City, the Israeli new city of West Jerusalem, and the Arab new city of East Jerusalem.

Due east of the Old City the Kidron Valley lies between ancient Jerusalem and the Mount of Olives (Et-Tur in Arabic). On the slopes of the mount, facing the Old

City, is the Garden of Gethsemane. Farther down the valley, south of the Old City walls, is the Arabic town of Silwan, where the earliest settlement of Jerusalem developed more than 5,000 years ago. This is where the Jerusalem of King David and King Solomon was located.

NEIGHBORHOODS IN BRIEF

The Old City   The Old City is easily defined: It is the area still enclosed within the grand walls built by the Ottoman Turkish sultan, Suleiman the Magnificent, in 1538. The Old City is divided into four quarters: the Muslim Quarter, the Christian Quarter, the Armenian Quarter, and the Jewish Quarter. Seven gates provide access through the massive walls; two of these are important for the tourist. The Jaffa Gate (Sha'ar Yafo in Hebrew, Bab el-Khalil in Arabic), at the end of the Jaffa Road (Derekh Yafo), is the main access to the Old City from West Jerusalem. Damascus Gate (Sha'ar Shechem in Hebrew, Bab el-Amud in Arabic) is the main access from East Jerusalem (if you get lost in the Old City's labyrinthine alleys, just ask for either gate).

Except in the Jewish Quarter, the dominating motif here is Arab: food is Arabic, the language is Arabic, and customs are Eastern.

West Jeruselum   To the west and south of the Old City, this modern Israeli city is a huge area of residential, commercial, and industrial development punctuated by highrise hotels and office towers. Extending far to the south and west, and encroaching on the east, the "New City" (as it's sometimes called) includes the Knesset and the government precinct on the western edge of town, one of Hebrew University's two large campuses, the Israel Museum, and—on a distant hilltop—the Hadassah Medical Center. Broad avenues twist and turn along the tops of the Judean Hills to connect West Jerusalem's outlying quarters with the century-old downtown area.

Downtown West Jerusalem is centered on Zion Square (Kikar Ziyon), where Jaffa Road intersects with Ben-Yehuda Street. A few short blocks west of Zion Square is King George V Avenue (known as King George Street or Rehov Ha-Melekh George), which joins Ben-Yehuda and Jaffa Road to form a triangle. Many of the hotels, restaurants, and businesses you'll want to know about are in or near this triangle. Ben-Yehuda Street is now a bustling pedestrian mall filled with souvenir, jewelry, and Judaica shops, cafes, and places to grab a quick snack. Evenings, especially in good weather, Ben-Yehuda becomes a mecca for younger travelers and young Israelis. A quainter pedestrian mall network, centering on Yoel Salomon Street, runs off Zion Square at the foot of Ben-Yehuda Street. This area is known as Nahalat Shiva. The renovation of this area has transformed Jerusalem's evening ambience from that of a quiet mountain town to a lively, gregarious Mediterranean-style city where people like to stroll and rendezvous in cafes. This small enclave of old West Jerusalem is being preserved, but other such 19th-century neighborhoods in West Jerusalem are slated for demolition and will be replaced by large office blocks.

East Jeruselum   Not as modern and sprawling as the western part, East Jerusalem is nevertheless a bustling 20th-century cityscape lying north of the Old City. Its compact business, commercial, and hotel district starts right along the Old City's north wall on Sultan Suleiman Street, which runs from Damascus Gate to Herod's Gate, and then downhill to the Rockefeller Museum. Nablus Road (Derekh Shechem in Hebrew) runs northeast from Damascus Gate to the American Colony Hotel and Saladin Street (Salah ad-Din in Arabic), the area's chief shopping thoroughfare, starts at Herod's Gate and meets Saladin Street near the American Colony Hotel. The triangle formed by these streets encloses the heart of downtown East Jerusalem. This area is quiet at night, and is only beginning to recover economically from the years of the Intifada. The best bets for a pleasant evening in this part of town are the courtyard cafe or the cellar bar at the beautiful American Colony Hotel, the musical evenings and special buffet dinners at the less pricey Jerusalem Hotel, and the solid Philadelphia restaurant.

During the years when East Jerusalem was part of Jordan, much effort was made to develop Amman, the nation's capital. Under Israeli administration, East Jerusalem received little of the attention lavished on the western part of the city. As a result, there are still lots of stony fields and open land between downtown East Jerusalem and Mount Scopus, topped by Hebrew University's hilltop campus.

3 Getting Around

BY BUS Here are some of the most important destinations, and the buses that take you there:

Abu Tor (and Railroad Station):	5, 6, 7, 8, 21, 30, 48
American Colony (East Jerusalem):	23, 27
Bet Ha-Karem:	5, 6, 14, 17, 18, 20, 21, 24, 27
Damascus Gate (Old City):	27
East Jerusalem:	23, 27, 99
Ein Kerem:	17
German Colony (South Jerusalem):	4, 14, 18, 24
Ge'ula Quarter:	3, 9, 39
Hadassah Hospital:	27
Israel Museum:	9, 17, 24
Jaffa Gate (Old City):	3, 19, 20, 30, 80, 99
Jewish Quarter (Old City):	1, 38
King George V Avenue:	4, 7, 8, 9, 14, 31, 48
Mount Scopus:	9, 23, 26, 28
Mount Zion:	38
Railroad Station:	5, 7, 8, 21, 30
Yad VaShem:	13, 17, 18, 20, 23, 24, 27, 39, 40, 99
Zion Square:	5, 6, 13, 15, 18, 20

A full-fare city bus ticket costs NIS 3.50 ($1.15). But if you ask the driver for a kartisiya (that's "kahr-tee-see-yah"), he'll sell you a pass good for 20 trips, plus one extra trip for free. You'll be amazed at how quickly you can use up a kartisiya. The pass is punched each time you board a bus. If two of you are traveling together, just tell the bus driver, "pamayim" (twice) as you hand him the kartisiyah, and he'll punch two fares. Students pay reduced fares and can buy special discount kartisiya as well.

There is a city bus station near Damascus Gate on Nablus Road for destinations in East Jerusalem and surrounding Arabic communities.

BY TAXI OR SHERUT Sheruts travel the main bus route from Sederot Herzl to Jaffa Road and Zion Square on the Sabbath; they charge a shekel per person more than standard bus fare. The trick is finding one with room and flagging it down. Private taxis will take you throughout the city and charge higher night and Shabbat rates. The standard initial drop is approximately NIS 6 ($1.80), but this rate is always rising. You have a right to ask that the meter (ha-sha-on) be turned on, or you can agree on a price before starting. Taxi drivers do not expect tips; at most, if your driver claims to have no change, round off the fare to the nearest shekel. Your driver may charge extra if he assists you with heavy baggage. If he doesn't charge you, a tip of a few shekels may be warranted. Whether or not the meter is used, you may request a receipt (ka-ba-lah).

FAST FACTS: Jerusalem

American Express   American Express International's new office is at 40 Jaffa Rd. (☎ 02/231-710; fax 02/231-520). Exchange rates here, especially for American Express traveler's checks, are relatively good and there is no commission charge. Lost or stolen American Express traveler's checks can be reported by calling toll free 177/440-8694.

Area Code   The area code is 02.

Babysitters   Ask at the front desk of your hotel.

Bookstores/Newsstands   Most are within two blocks of Zion Square. Look for the following stores: Librairie Française Alcheh, 30 Jaffa Rd., between Zion Square and the central post office; the well-stocked Steimatzky chain, with its large main branch at 39 Jaffa Rd. and smaller branches at 9 King George V Ave. and on the Ben-Yehuda Pedestrian Mall. Steimatzky's maintains very small branches in many major hotels and sells a good selection of English- and foreign-language periodicals. Steimatzky's holds a virtual monopoly on imported books, and although it maintains a good selection in English, prices can be steep. For used books try Sefer Ve Sefel Bookshop, 4 Yavetz St., where you'll generally find a vast selection of fiction and used but current guidebooks; Clal Center Bookstore, 97 Jaffa Rd.; or Yalkut Bookstore, in the rear plaza of the Redjwan Building on King George V Avenue. Tmol Shilshom Bookstore Cafe in a courtyard off 5 Yoel Salomon St., has an eclectic collection of new and used books and magazines, and remains open until midnight on Sunday through Thursday. All other bookstores in West Jerusalem are open Sunday through Thursday from 9am to 7pm, closing early on Friday and all day on Shabbat. The Bookshelf, 2 Jewish Quarter Rd., in the Jewish Quarter of the Old City, has an especially helpful management. It also offers fax service and does photocopying. It is open from Sunday through Thursday from 10am to 6pm, closing at 1pm on Friday for Shabbat.

Crime   See "Safety," below.

Currency Exchange   Banking hours are 8:30am to noon or 12:30pm; on Sunday, Tuesday, and Thursday from 4 to 5pm. There are many banks on Ben-Yehuda Street, Jaffa Road, and King George V Avenue. Money changers, which are legal and offer slightly better rates than banks, will change money in less time with no commission. In East Jerusalem, a number of money-changer offices are on Saladin Street; in the Old City these offices can be found around Damascus and Jaffa gates; they are generally open daily from 9am to 5 or 6pm. In West Jerusalem, Change Point, a convenient money-changing office, has branches on the Ben-Yehuda Mall near Zion Square and in the Beit Yoel Building at the corner of Jaffa Road and Rivlin Street, open Sunday through Thursday from 9am to 8pm and on Friday from 9am to 1pm.

Bank Ha-Poalim ATM machines connected to the CIRRUS/NYCE system can be found at the intersection of Shlomzion Ha-Malka Street and Jaffa Road, just east of Zion Square, and at the City Tower, corner of Ben-Yehuda Street and King George V Avenue.

Dentists/Doctors   You can get a list of English-speaking doctors and dentists from your consulate and often from your hotel's front desk. For a centrally located, American-trained and -certified dentist try Dr. Mat Weiner, 16 Straus St. (☎ 02/384-577), two blocks north of Jaffa Road. For Dental First Aid, call 254-740. Open daily.

Drugstores   The *Jerusalem Post* lists under "General Assistance" the names and addresses of duty pharmacies that stay open nights and on the Sabbath.

Embassies/Consulates   The U.S. consulate in East Jerusalem is at the intersection of Nablus Road (Derekh Shechem) and Pikud Ha-Merkaz Street (☎ 02/234-271; 253-288, or 895-118). The West Jerusalem consulate building is at 18 Agron St. (same phones), just down the hill from the Jerusalem Plaza Hotel. The British consulate is near East Jerusalem's Sheikh Jarrah Quarter at 19 Nashashibi St. (☎ 02/282-481). Canadians should contact the consular section of their embassy in Tel Aviv at 7 Havakuk St. (☎ 03/546-2878).

Emergencies   To call the police, dial 100. Dial 101 for Magen David Adom (Red Shield of David), Israel's emergency first-aid service. For medical emergencies requiring hospitalization, dial 102. Magen David Adom has a clinic in Romema, near the Central Bus Station, and also a mobile intensive-care unit (☎ 02/523-133) on call 24 hours a day.

Hospitals   Holders of Blue Cross–Blue Shield are eligible for prepaid hospitalization at Hadassah Hospital in Ein Kerem and on Mount Scopus (☎ 02/776-040).

Hotlines   You can call the Jerusalem Rape Crisis Center at 02/514-455 daily, 24 hours. The Mental Health Hotline (Eran) can be reached at 610-303; if this office is closed, call 03/523-4819 in Tel Aviv. The women's Emotional First Aid Hotline (☎ 02/257-171 or 610-603) may be reached daily from 8am to 11pm; English is spoken, and tourists are welcome to call.

Libraries   The American Cultural Center Library is on Keren Hayesod Street on the block between Agron Street and the Radisson Moriah Hotel, open Sunday through Thursday from 10am to 4pm.

Liquor Laws   East Jerusalem is largely Muslim; Islamic law forbids the use of alcohol. Drinks are served in hotels that cater to Western visitors, but unless an East Jerusalem or Old City restaurant offers a wine list with its menu, assume that alcohol is not available. Do not attempt to drink outdoors or in public places in East Jerusalem or the Old City.

Lost Property   Unattended objects stand a good chance of being zapped by the bomb squad. Check with the local police, and try to retrace your steps.

Luggage/Storage Lockers   Bags are best stored at your hotel. Be prepared for a security check before storing.

Newspapers/Magazines   The *Jerusalem Post* is the major local English-language daily newspaper. A weekend edition with arts and entertainment information comes out on Friday. Many of the *Post*'s best writers have moved to the twice monthly *Jerusalem Report* magazine, which has become Israel's English-language answer to *Time* and *Newsweek*. *Eretz* magazine, beautifully written and photographed, focuses on nature, history, and travel in Israel.

Photographic Needs   The downtown King George Street/Ben-Yehuda area abounds with 1-hour photo-developing shops. Prices are comparable to nondiscount developing in the United States. To avoid X-ray problems at the airport, it's a good idea to develop film before leaving Israel. Photo Prisma at 44 Jaffa Rd. (☎ 02/234-796), just across from Zion Square, is one of many shops with an English-speaking staff. It has a good reputation for stocking fresh film.

Police   Dial 100. Border police in military uniforms, carrying highly visible weaponry, patrol Ben-Yehuda Mall and other central areas. (They fine jaywalkers.)

Post Office   Jerusalem's Central Post Office is at 23 Jaffa Rd., near the intersection with Shlomzion Ha-Malka Street. General hours for all services are Sunday to Thursday from 7am to 7pm; limited services (telephone and telegraph) are open nights and on the Sabbath. East Jerusalem had its own main post office, which is now a branch, opposite Herod's Gate at the corner of Saladin Ibn Sina and Sultan Suleiman streets.

In the Old City, the post office is a few steps from Jaffa Gate, up past the Citadel of David and next to the gate of the Christ Church Anglican Hospice. A branch in West Jerusalem is on Keren Kayemet Street half a block from the corner with King George V and the Jewish Agency.

Radio   News in English is on Israel Radio at 7am, 1pm, 5pm, and on AM 575, 1170, and 1458 kHz.

Religious Services   The Christian Information Center (P.O. Box 14308; ☎ 02/272-692), inside Jaffa Gate on Omar Ibn El-Khattab Square near the Christ Church Hospice and opposite the entrance to the Tower of David, has a list of all Christian services. The center is open Monday through Saturday from 8:30am to 1pm; closed Sunday and holidays. *This Week in Jerusalem*, available free at major hotels and tourist offices, will list Reform, Conservative, and Orthodox Jewish synagogues.

Restrooms   Municipal facilities are everywhere: near Zion Square, walk up Rav Kook Street; at the Western Wall in the Old City, go to the north side of the square; near Saint Anne's Church and Saint Stephen's Gate. Signs read "WC" or "OO."

Safety   Jerusalem is a low-crime city, but beware of pickpockets in the crowd crushes of the Old City and avoid the deserted bazaars after dark. While political demonstrations in West Jerusalem are passionate but usually safe, it is advisable to avoid demonstrations in East Jerusalem or in the Old City. Keep alert at all times. Get away from and report any unattended or suspicious object immediately.

Telegrams/Telex/Fax   There are telex and fax services at the Central Post Office, 23 Jaffa Rd. Inside the Old City, the Bookshelf, Jewish Quarter Road (☎ 02/273-889), offers very conscientious fax service and will even notify you after hours about any fax responses you may receive. For telegrams, dial 171.

Television   Check the Friday *Jerusalem Post* for the week's schedule. Jordan's channel 2 broadcasts an English-language evening schedule from Amman at 8:30 or 9pm, with news in English at 10pm. Jordan TV's scheduling is often an hour earlier in summer, when it does not always coordinate with Israel on daylight saving time. Israel television's channels 1 and 2 offer many British and American programs. CNN news is available at many hotels. For the first time, a number of international cable and commercial channels are also available. Israel's noncable state-operated Channel 1 broadcasts international and local news in English at 6:15pm.

Useful Telephone Numbers   For nightlife information, call 02/241-197.

4 Where to Stay

Israel has been building five-star hotels at an almost breakneck pace, but inexpensive and moderately priced hotels are in short supply, especially in Jerusalem. There are a few hotels with atmosphere and ambience in every price category, but most choices are internationally generic and bland. However, the endless fascination of Jerusalem tends to make up for the lack of personality in the city's hotels.

There are plans afoot to renovate the beautiful 19th-century Russian pilgrimage compound in the center of downtown West Jerusalem and turn it into a group of three-, four-, and five-star hotels. If this plan takes off quickly, they may be ready for tourists during the time span of this edition. A new Hilton Hotel and a new Dan Hotel, both five-star properties and both located in West Jerusalem just outside the walls of the Old City, are scheduled to open in late 1996 or 1997.

A number of the four- and five-star hotels listed here can often be booked as part of El Al, Tower Air, or other packages, or through discounters, at substantially lower prices. Especially in off-seasons, there are spectacular discounts to be found in all price categories if you plan ahead through a good travel agent. Jerusalem's hotels are busiest at Passover and Easter, in September or October during the Jewish High Holidays (Rosh Hashanah, Yom Kippur, Sukkot, Simchat Torah), and at Christmas. Many hotels consider July and August regular season.

An interesting alternative to a stay in a hotel is a bed-and-breakfast accommodation in a private home or apartment. Prices are considerably lower than hotels, and you have the chance to experience the lifestyle of one of the city's many unusual neighborhoods. Hosts are often senior citizens with lovely, spacious (by Israeli standards) homes, and a genuine interest in working with visitors from abroad.

A room in an apartment that has its own private bath should be about $34 for a single and $50 for a double, with breakfast and service included. A small studio or private flat would be about $41 for a single and $56 for two people, and really unusual places, with private entrances, gardens, views, or especially nice decor could be about $50 for a single and $68 for two.

Good Morning Jerusalem (☎ 02/651-1270; fax 02/511-272) is a new bed-and-breakfast clearinghouse with its office in the main foyer of Binyanei Ha'ooma, the Jerusalem Convention Center opposite the Central Bus Station on Jaffa Road. Working in cooperation with the Jerusalem Development Authority and the Ministry of Tourism, Good Morning Jerusalem will reserve accommodations for you and try to match your requirements regarding noise, neighborhood, kashrut, etc., to the listings available in its files. (The office cannot vouch for the kashrut standards of any particular household, and accepts the claims of its participating hosts.) The office is open Sunday to Thursday from 9am to 7pm, and Friday from 9am to 1:30pm. It is often possible for a tourist arriving at Ben-Gurion Airport to call and arrange for accommodations that night, but obviously, it is best to reserve ahead of time. With advance notice, the office can make arrangements to meet nighttime arrivals.

Jerusalem Inns (☎ 02/611-745; fax 02/618-541), a private agency, provides a similar service and is run by Anita Ellis, originally from Philadelphia, who carefully works at matching rooms and visitors with a special awareness of what Americans, Canadians, and Britons require. Advanced booking is almost always necessary and minimum stays of 2 or 3 nights are generally required. The mailing address for Jerusalem Inns is P.O. Box 4233, Jerusalem 91044.

If you are interested in renting an apartment, keep an eye out for posters in store windows and read the classified section of the *Jerusalem Post*. You can also reserve an entire flat for yourself (rate is according to number of people; 1-week minimum stay) from Good Morning Jerusalem through the Israel Hotel Reservation Center (☎ 201/816-0830 or toll free in the U.S. ☎ 800/552-0140; in Canada ☎ 800/ 526-5343). There is a $25–$35 fee for this service, but you save on overseas phone bills and can discuss the neighborhood and kind of flat you would like to try for.

Other alternatives are to stay in a Christian hospice or a YMCA. Originally built to accommodate the pilgrims and tourists that began to arrive in great numbers in the 1880s, many hospices are housed in atmospheric 19th-century buildings with evocative Jerusalem architecture and style. They are open to travelers of all faiths, and offer comfortable private rooms with baths. Many hostels also offer private rooms and good services in interesting surroundings.

THE OLD CITY

The advantage to staying in the Old City is that you feel the rhythms and hear the sounds of this extraordinary (largely car-free) place—the calls to prayer from the minarets, the medley of bells from the city's ancient churches. You'll watch the bazaars come to life in the morning and slowly close down for night; you'll catch glimpses of streetlife that a visitor based in the New City would never see. You won't come across any highrise (or even lowrise) luxury palaces in the Old City, just a few inexpensive to moderately priced hotels, hospices, and hostels. The crime rate in the Old City, as in all of Jerusalem, is low, but the streets of the Old City (except for parts of the Jewish Quarter) are deserted at night and can seem intimidating. You'll need a spirit of adventure and an enjoyment of labyrinths and casbah-like alleyways in order for this to be the right part of town for your base.

Jaffa Gate is the place to start your search for Old City accommodations. Most are only a few minutes' walk from the gate. See the Old City map in chapter 5 for exact locations of those described below.

INEXPENSIVE

Christ Church Guest House. Jaffa Gate (P.O. Box 14037), Jerusalem 91140. ☎ **02/277-727.** Fax 02/277-730. $32–$40 per person, single or double; $20–$26 per person triple or quadruple; 50% discount for children. Rates include breakfast and service.

This is one of the best-located hospices, situated just inside the Jaffa Gate, next to the post office and across from the entrance to Tower of David. Through the big iron gates you'll find a flagstone courtyard with trees and benches, a century-old English-style church that now houses a Protestant/Messianic congregation, and single, double, and triple rooms in a series of beautifully maintained 19th-century buildings. The gates to Christ Church Guest House close at 11pm, and stay locked until 6am, except by special arrangement. As with most good guesthouses, this one is heavily booked during the summer months and at Christian holidays—best to reserve in advance for those times. Meals cost $10 extra for lunch and dinner. This establishment also runs the nearby inexpensive Coffee Shop and organizes tours and lectures oriented toward the Protestant Messianic movement. A protected parking area is an added feature, although the management cannot take responsibility for cars parked there.

Gloria Hotel. Latin Patriarchate Street (P.O. Box 14070), Jerusalem. ☎ **02/282-431** or 282-432. Fax 02/282-401. 64 rms (all with bath or shower). $40 single; $60 double. Discounts in off-season. Add $10 per person for Christmas and Easter. Rates include breakfast and service. No credit cards.

The three-star-equivalent Gloria is moderately priced, considering its location and modern facilities. The entrance is up a flight of steps; from there an elevator takes you up one more level to the hotel desk, where an English-speaking clerk awaits you. The lobby is spacious, with lots of Jerusalem stone and a scattering of local crafts as decorative touches. The rooms, which were renovated in 1987, are relatively large and quiet and have either twin or double beds, and central heating. The dining room, where you'll find the breakfast buffet, overlooks the Tower of David and West Jerusalem. Small amenities may not be available, but the Old City ambience, good management, and excellent location are big pluses.

About 20 paces inside Jaffa Gate, turn left on Latin Patriarchate Street; hotel is on the right.

⊙ **Saint Mark's Lutheran Guest House.** Saint Mark's Road (P.O. Box 14051), Old City, Jerusalem. ☎ **02/285-107.** Fax 02/282-120. 23 rms (all with bath or shower). TEL. High season (Easter, fall, and Christmas) $45 single; $73 double. Regular season (June 16–Sept 14 and winter except Christmas) $41 single; $69 double. Prices depend on rate of exchange between U.S dollar and German mark. Rates include breakfast. No credit cards. Bus: 20 to Jaffa Gate.

The most beautiful, atmospheric, and well-run hotel in the Old City (and perhaps all Jerusalem), this German Lutheran Guest House occupies a series of lovely restored stone buildings and terraced gardens overlooking the main bazaar, just a 5-minute walk from Jaffa Gate. The location, close to the heart of the Old City, allows guests to experience the atmosphere and rhythms of life inside the Old City walls, yet the guesthouse itself is a secluded oasis. Rooms are simply furnished but comfortable; bathrooms are modern. The site is shared by, but separated from, the Evangelical Lutheran Hostel. Although this part of the Old City, bordering the restored Jewish Quarter and the Jaffa Gate, is quite safe, a slight drawback for the less adventurous might be the idea of walking to the guesthouse at night. The staff of Saint Mark's is very welcoming to visitors from all countries and backgrounds. Call before going for directions or to arrange for a porter to meet you.

WEST JERUSALEM

This is the place to stay if you want to be close to the city's lively restaurants, cafes, and bars, and in an area where you can stroll, shop, and people watch in the evenings. There are a few moderate and inexpensive hotels right in the center of things, in the Zion Square/Ben-Yehuda Mall area. A number of hotel choices are a few blocks further south, in the King George Street/King David Street triangle; these hotels are within walking distance or a short bus ride of Zion Square. Farther south you'll find a number of pleasant hotels in the interesting neighborhoods of Abu Tor and the German Colony (you'll need a bus or taxi to get to Zion Square); the outlying Bus Station/Sderot Herzl area on the western side of town is the fourth major West Jerusalem hotel area. It can be a 20-minute or more bus ride into Zion Square from this area, and you'll need a taxi on the Sabbath. The better hotels in this area offer shuttle service into town.

ZION SQUARE, JAFFA ROAD & BEN-YEHUDA MALL

Hotels in this neighborhood are right in the heart of the downtown shopping and restaurant district; step out of your hotel, and you have a great variety of eateries, cafes, window-shopping, and people-watching possibilities. The area is noisy, and in summer, discos add to the roar of traffic. There are no luxury hotels here; only moderate and inexpensive choices.

Moderate

⊙ **Jerusalem Tower Hotel.** 33 Hillel St., Jerusalem. ☎ **02/252-161.** Fax 02/252-167. 120 rms (all with bath). A/C TEL TV. $87–$103 single; $114–$143 double; $40–$60 double on El Al Sunsational 5-Night Package. Rates include breakfast. AE, DC, MC, V. Parking available for charge.

This modern upper moderate–range hotel is the most comfortable place to stay if you want to be in the heart of downtown West Jerusalem, just steps from the shopping and restaurants of the Zion Square/Ben-Yehuda triangle. You enter through a small lobby on the ground floor of an office tower two short blocks from Zion Square; rooms are on the upper floors of the building and many offer sweeping views (try to get a room facing the Old City). Rooms are compact but modern and well planned, equipped with radios as well as TVs, and newly decorated with a colorful wall of patchwork design that frames an arabesque arch above the beds; best of all, the upper floors are buffered against the city's street noise. Babysitting, laundry, and room service are offered. The staff is good for this category of hotel. The 5-night El Al Sunsational Package makes this great location affordable for almost everyone; specify that you want this downtown location rather than other choices in the package.

Lev Yerushalayim Suite Hotel. 18 King George St., Jerusalem. ☎ **02/250-033.** Fax 02/232-432. 50 suites. A/C TEL TV. $115–$240 double plus 15% service. Rates include breakfast. AE, DC, MC, V.

"Lev Yerushalayim" means "heart of Jerusalem," and this glistening, relatively new tower complex is indeed located in the heart of West Jerusalem, right across the street from the intersection of King George Street and the Ben-Yehuda Mall. The pleasant suites consist of a contemporary living room/kitchenette and bedroom decorated in soft colors and buffered against the roar of downtown traffic by elevation as well as thick windows. Rates are for two people, but the suites are a good choice for families. Extra sleeping space is available on convertible living-room sofas, with a surcharge of $15 per night for each additional guest. Fully equipped kitchenettes include a microwave oven. A self-service laundromat and fitness center in the complex are available to hotel guests. During most of the year, double occupancy rates are in the $130–$165 range; rates increase greatly for Jewish holidays.

✪ **Notre Dame Guest House.** P.O. Box 20531, Jerusalem. ☎ **02/279-111.** 50 rms (all with bath or shower). A/C TEL. $68 single; $86 double. Rates include breakfast. No credit cards.

Located in a beautifully restored landmark just steps away from both sides of the city, convenient to Israeli as well as Arab municipal bus routes, the massive Notre Dame complex is a center for Roman Catholic institutions and pilgrim groups, but all travelers seeking a tranquil atmosphere with expertly managed three-star accommodations are welcome. Public areas are spacious, with Jerusalem stone architecture; rooms are simple but comfortable, and many share a terrace balcony. A coffee shop, open daily from 9am to 11pm, serves light meals in the $3.50 to $12 range. In summer, the Guest House's restaurant offers a very nice Sunday evening all-you-can-eat buffet-barbecue on the fountain terrace for $15. La Rotisserie, a luxury restaurant patronized by savvy Jerusalemites, is also on the premises. There are slight discounts in the winter season and surcharges during holidays.

The hotel is best reached initially by taxi; it's a half block downhill from the Municipality Building at the end of Jaffa Road, opposite the New Gate of the Old City.

Zion Square Hotel. 25 Shammai St., Jerusalem. ☎ **02/244-644.** Fax 02/244-136. 120 rms (all with bath). A/C TEL TV. $115 single; $161 double; 20% to 30% discount Jan 10–Feb 28, June–Sept., Nov 1–Dec 7. AE, DC, MC, V.

Housed on the upper floors of a massive 1980s stone office tower, this hotel is literally built over Zion Square, at the intersection of Jaffa Road and the Ben-Yehuda Mall. The modern, rather plain guest rooms have double-glazed windows that keep street noise to a minimum and many are equipped with small refrigerators; TVs receive CNN. Some rooms are extra large, although when rented as doubles there is no extra charge; try for these more spacious accommodations. The hotel caters largely to European groups; use of a health club in the building with an exercise room, sauna, and indoor heated swimming pool is available to hotel guests for $5 per day. Manager Rafi Stub offers Frommer's readers who book independently and stay 7 nights a special discount in which they only pay for 6 nights.

Accommodations in Downtown West Jerusalem

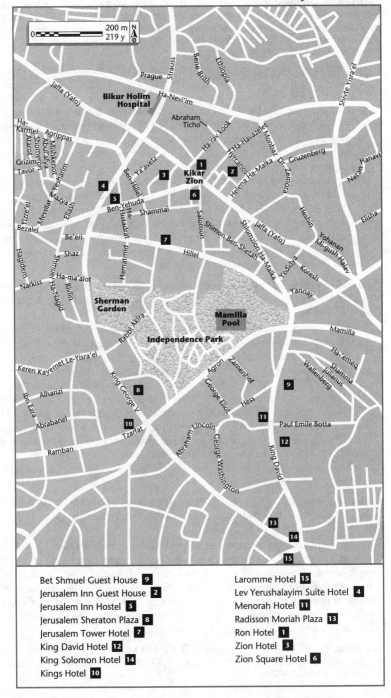

Bet Shmuel Guest House **9**
Jerusalem Inn Guest House **2**
Jerusalem Inn Hostel **5**
Jerusalem Sheraton Plaza **8**
Jerusalem Tower Hotel **7**
King David Hotel **12**
King Solomon Hotel **14**
Kings Hotel **10**

Laromme Hotel **15**
Lev Yerushalayim Suite Hotel **4**
Menorah Hotel **11**
Radisson Moriah Plaza **13**
Ron Hotel **1**
Zion Hotel **3**
Zion Square Hotel **6**

Inexpensive

✪ Jerusalem Inn Guest House. 5 Hyrcanos St., Jerusalem. ☎ **02/252-757.** 20 rms (most with shower). CEILING FAN TV. $33–$50 single; $36–$40 double without bath, $50–$62 double with bath. 10%–30% higher at holidays and during high season, which includes July and August. Breakfast $5 extra. MC, V. On Jaffa Road, coming from Zion Square, turn left on Helena Ha-Malka Street, then left on Hyrcanos.

The location of this new, nondormitory affiliate of the excellent Jerusalem Inn Hostel (see below) is perfection: on a relatively quiet street a lengthy block from Jaffa Road. You'll find simple, bright rooms (many with small balconies) decorated with framed art posters and furnished with comfortably firm beds (high-density foam mattresses on heavy wooden slat frames especially designed by the hotel's owner) as well as a careful management that nourishes a friendly atmosphere. Good for both family groups and single travelers, larger rooms can be arranged for up to four or even five people. Some bathrooms are shared, but well kept. Newly refurbished rooms with private bathrooms that have sliding-door-enclosed stall showers (in this price category, most other hotels offer only shower sprays that flood your entire bathroom) are at the higher end of the price range. For a surcharge, you can arrange breakfast (not included in the price of the room) at the excellent Eucalyptus Restaurant, which is separate from the hotel, but on the premises. Each room has a television, and during 1996, phones will be installed in most rooms. Small refrigerators will be available on request. Guest rooms are reached by stairway.

✪ Jerusalem Inn Hostel. 6 Ha-Histadrut St., Jerusalem. ☎ **02/251-294.** Fax. 02/251-297. 60 beds in dormitory rms, singles, and doubles. $10 dormitory; $36–$44 double room. High-season holidays, up to 30% increase. MC, V.

Centrally located on a quiet street just off both King George Street and the Ben-Yehuda Mall, this is one of the few private hostels recommended by the Ministry of Tourism, and its reputation is well deserved. Spotlessly clean and efficiently run, the Jerusalem Inn also manages to maintain a friendly ambience, with a bar and lounge that are great for meeting fellow travelers (mostly English-speaking or Scandinavian), exchanging stories, and making plans. You'll find discounts for IYHA and student IDs, key arrangements for those out after the midnight closing, and an atmosphere both lively and considerate, which is important for family groups and those who need sleep. The 24-hour security, free storage, washing machine, hot meals ($2 to $4), and helpful staff make this the best of West Jerusalem's hostels.

The entrance to Ha-Histadrut Street is off King George Street across from Hamashbir department store.

Ron Hotel. 42A Jaffa Rd., Jerusalem 94222. ☎ **02/253-471.** Fax 02/250-707. 22 rms (21 with shower, 1 with bath). TEL TV. $65 single; $75 double. AE, MC, V. Bus: 5, 6, 13, 20, or 21 to Zion Square.

Set virtually in Zion Square, the entrance to this hotel provides a touch of old-fashioned elegance. Through its gracious portal is a tiny registration booth; up a long flight of steps are modern rooms with thick comforters on the beds. The sound of traffic on Jaffa Road can be a problem for some travelers, despite the installation of windows that help shut out the noise. For much of 1996–97, construction of a new office block just behind the Ron may be an additional problem. The public areas are filled with mirrors, marble floors, and vaulted ceilings.

Zion Hotel. 10 Dorot Rishonim St., Jerusalem. ☎ **02/259-511.** Fax 02/257-585. 26 rms (all with bath or shower). Low, regular, high seasons $50, $53, $69 single; $67, $72, $80 double. Rates include breakfast. MC, V.

Half a block from Zion Square and Jaffa Road, set among the cafe- and restaurant-lined pedestrian streets of the Ben-Yehuda Mall, the veteran Zion Hotel has recently been completely renovated. The result is a small centrally located hotel choice with public areas and guest rooms that show a bit of atmospheric old Jerusalem architecture. Rooms are small, but newly furnished, with completely remodeled bathrooms; service is friendly, but, as with most moderately priced hotels, laid-back. Street noise from the all-day-and-late-into-the-night Ben-Yehuda Mall may be something to consider.

KING GEORGE STREET & KING DAVID STREET

A few blocks away from the Ben-Yehuda/Zion Square triangle is a group of hotels spread out along the southern reaches of King George Street, which becomes Keren Hayesod Street. About half a mile from Zion Square, Keren Heyesod runs into King David Street, and another cluster of hotels. The distance to Zion Square from most of these hotels is walkable, but in the hot sun or after a hard day's touring, many will want to take a bus or taxi to the Zion Square area. Nearby are Liberty Bell Park, Yemin Moshe, and the Cinémathèque, with its hillside of neighboring cafes and restaurants.

Very Expensive

✪ **King David Hotel.** 23 King David St., Jerusalem 94101. ☎ **02/251-111.** Fax 02/232-303. 255 rms including 76 deluxe rooms and 39 suites. A/C MINIBAR TEL TV. Low season $184–$350 single; $204–$400 double. High season $318–$440 single; $340–$470 double. 15% service charge. AE, DC, MC, V. Bus: 5, 6, 18, or 21.

The luxurious five-star King David is Jerusalem's status address, built in 1930 as a regional companion to the legendary Shephard's Hotel in Cairo (Shephard's was destroyed during anticolonialist riots in the early 1950s). The massive King David is a perfectly maintained symbol of a bygone era (including a rather formal staff), but its reputation and list of diplomatic and celebrity guests continues to grow. The lofty Egyptianesque/Canaanite art deco public rooms always impress; the view from the gardens and the terrace (where Paul Newman and Eva Marie Saint had a rendezvous in the 1960 film *Exodus*), with vistas toward the walls of the Old City, are filled with atmosphere. The gardened, country club–style swimming pool is a plus in summer. Higher-priced suites and superior rooms, with views of the Old City, are definitely special; views from rooms facing King David Street are less interesting. Most private rooms are not really exceptional; you pay for ambience. The gigantic breakfast buffet is famous, but the hotel's food services are average and definitely surpassed by the choice of interesting restaurants in town. The hotel is the raison d'etre for a surrounding colony of expensive tourist, Judaica, and jewelry shops, which provide window-shopping possibilities. The Zion Square/Ben-Yehuda Mall area is several rather lonely uphill blocks away. Discounters and package tours can get you into the King David for considerably less than the prices above.

Dining/Entertainment: Seven restaurants and cafes, plus an indoor and terrace bar.

Facilities: Outdoor swimming pool, fitness and massage center, sauna, tennis court, shopping arcade.

Expensive

Jerusalem Sheraton Plaza. 47 King George St., Jerusalem. ☎ **02/298-666.** Fax 02/231-667. 300 rms (all with bath or shower). A/C, REF or MINIBAR, TEL, TV. $135–$250 single; $168–$292 double. Club Floor rooms $25–$60 per person extra. 15% service charge. Rates include breakfast. AE, DC, MC, V.

This 1970s 22-story tower is the luxury hotel closest to the Ben-Yehuda Mall area, though it's still a 10-minute walk. Always bustling, the public areas are what is expected of a hotel in this class, but not unusual. Guest rooms are moderately spacious and have balconies; those facing south offer spectacular views of the Old City. Among the Sheraton's dining facilities, the Cow on the Roof (see restaurant listings) is the outstanding kosher French restaurant in Jerusalem, with its kitchen under the direction of the world's preeminent kosher chef, Shalom Kadosh; menus throughout the Sheraton's other restaurants reflect Kadosh's advice and influence. Club Floor rooms contain minibars, fax machines, P.C. outlets, and receive special staff service. The hotel's entrance plaza is below street level; to leave by foot entails climbing a hill or stairway.

Dining/Entertainment: Four restaurants and a bar/lounge.

Facilities: Outdoor in-season pool, massage room, sauna, shopping arcade, hairdresser.

King Solomon Hotel. 32 King David St., Jerusalem. ☎ **02/695-555.** Fax 02/241-774. 148 rms (all with bath). A/C MINIBAR TEL TV. $100–$185 single; $130–$240 double. Rates include breakfast. AE, DC, MC, V. Bus: 5, 18, or 21.

Although situated at the fork of busy King David and Keren Hayesod streets, the design of this modern hotel, built in the 1980s, manages to keep street noise to tolerable levels. The main entrance is on a service driveway between the two major thoroughfares and opens to an airy, pleasant multilevel stone-floor lobby. Guest room furnishings are blandly modern but superior rooms are spacious and many offer excellent views. The large rooftop pool, with a view of the Old City walls in the distance, is quite spectacular. Dining facilities in the Queen of Sheba (Middle Eastern/Continental restaurant) and the Lobby Lounge are glatt kosher. The hotel is within walking distance of Yemin Moshe, the German Colony, and the Cinémathèque, but you'll probably want to take a bus to the downtown Ben-Yehuda Mall area. In off-seasons, special packages offer double rooms in the $100 range.

✪ Laromme Hotel. 3 Jabotinsky St., Jerusalem. ☎ **02/756-666.** Fax 02/756-777. 294 rms (all with bath); 8 rms for disabled; 14 suites. A/C MINIBAR TEL TV. Single $130–$230; double $145–$245. Rates include breakfast. AE, DC, MC, V.

Originally slated to be a skyscraper, the initial plan for the Laromme was redesigned into a lowrise that would not clash with the city's skyline. The result is an interesting structure set at the edge of Liberty Bell Park (a plus for guests with children) and built around a gardened, balconied atrium lobby. The Laromme's reputation for service is good. Guest rooms come in two sizes: the larger (Maximum) rooms are spacious, with luxurious baths, and range about $30 additional for a double room. Both categories of rooms are light, airy, and contain well-designed contemporary furnishings of natural grain wood and wrought iron. The location is close to the quaint Yemin Moshe neighborhood, but a 15-minute uphill walk to the Ben-Yehuda Mall downtown area (downtown buses stop around the corner in front of the Radisson Moriah Plaza Hotel). A roomy, heated outdoor swimming pool and Jacuzzi (covered by an air balloon in winter) provides the best year-round swimming in the center of the city. The Bistro Restaurant is one of the best in-hotel dining facilities in the city.

Dining/Entertainment: Three kosher restaurants, including separate meat and dairy/vegetarian facilities, and a lounge/piano bar in the evening.

Facilities: Fitness room, sauna, indoor/outdoor heated year-round swimming pool, shopping gallery, hairdresser, free parking.

⭕ **Radisson Moriah Plaza Jerusalem Hotel.** 39 Keren Hayesod St., Jerusalem 94188. ☎ **02/ 232-232;** 212/541-5009 in New York, or 800/221-0203 in the U.S. 292 rms (all with bath). A/C TEL TV. $85 per person double, low season; $115 per person double, high season. Rates include breakfast. 9-Day Radisson Moriah Hotels Package (without breakfast): $43 per person double, low season; $64 per person double, high season. 15% service charge extra. Radisson Moriah Plaza Jerusalem only, two children under 18 free. AE, DC, MC, V. Bus: 4, 7, 8, 14, or 48.

Located around the corner from the King David Hotel, close to Liberty Bell Park, Yemin Moshe, and the Cinémathèque, a walk or quick bus ride to the downtown Ben-Yehuda Mall area (the bus stop is at the hotel's front door), the carefully run Radisson Moriah Plaza offers the most economical prices in the five-star range. It is less fancy than, say, the Hilton, but it's centrally located, with elegant public areas that glisten and guest rooms that are pleasant and very comfortable. The staff is friendly and efficient; in-house food services are better than average. The Radisson Moriah Plaza becomes a great bargain if you stay here on the special package that commits you to 9 nights at your choice of Radisson Moriah Hotels in Jerusalem, Tel Aviv, Tiberias, the Radisson Moriah Dead Sea Spa, or the luxurious Radisson Moriah Hotel in Eilat. A 6-night minimum stay in Radisson Moriah Hotels is $5 per person more; a current El Al/Radisson Moriah Package starts at $30 per person double occupancy.

Facilities: Rooftop swimming pool.

Services: Free transfer service to the Radisson Moriah Plaza Hotel in Tel Aviv, children's activities weekday afternoons in summer, optional minibar.

Moderate

Kings Hotel. 60 King George St., Jerusalem. ☎ **02/201-201.** Fax **02/201-211.** 187 rms (all with bath). A/C TEL TV. $110–$140 single; $133–$172 double; $20 supplement for renovated room. Rates include breakfast. AE, DC, MC, V. Bus: 4, 8, 9, or 48.

Right at the entrance to the prestigious Rehavia neighborhood, and a 10-minute walk to the Ben-Yehuda area, location is the big plus for this hotel (it's also next door to Hechal Shlomo, the Great Synagogue, and two short blocks from the Prime Minister's house). A good supermarket is half a block away. The lobby and lounge areas were renovated in the late 1980s, and have a light, gardenlike feel. Guest rooms, whether renovated or not, are functional rather than gracious, and rather small. The hotel is often used by tour groups and is available at discounts through package consolidators. You enter the hotel on Ramban Street; note that this busy intersection suffers from a high level of traffic noise. Service is marked by small economies; guest-room air conditioning may be turned off at midday, when most guests are out. The hotel contains two restaurants and a lounge/bar.

⭕ **YMCA Three Arches Hotel.** 26 King David St., P.O. Box 294, Jerusalem 91002. ☎ **02/ 257-111, 253-438.** Fax 02/253-438. 68 rms (all with bath or shower). A/C TEL TV. $90 single; $110 double; $160 suite. Rates include continental breakfast and service. AE, MC, V. Bus: 5, 18, or 21 to King David Street.

This historic landmark, across the street from the King David Hotel, opened in 1933 and was designed in an art deco Byzantine–Islamic style by Arthur Loomis Harmon, who also did New York's Empire State Building. It is a center for lectures, performances, and classes as well as an excellent hotel. Public areas are lovely and atmospheric; all guest rooms have recently been totally reconstructed and now sport modern bathrooms and an intelligent decor designed around kelim motifs that is the envy of five-star hotels. Beds are medium firm. The atmosphere, facilities, and location make this the best value for the money in Jerusalem.

The YMCA houses a good cafe, in addition to the Tsriff Restaurant, where the elegant terrace is one of the most popular fair-weather dining places in town. Guests may use the 1930s-style indoor swimming pool on the premises and also have free use of tennis and squash courts, jogging track, and a fitness room.

Inexpensive

✪ **Beit Shmuel Guest House.** 13 King David St., Jerusalem (entrance around corner at 3 Shamia St.). ☎ 02/203-466. Fax 02/203-446. 40 rms (all with bath). A/C. $45–$55 single; $66–$80 double; $84–$108 triple; $96–$120 quad; dormitory beds $18. Rates include breakfast. No credit cards. Closed June 15–Aug 15 (to individual travelers). Bus: 5, 6, 18, or 21 to first stop on King David Street.

Affiliated with the IYHA, and opened in the 1980s, this guesthouse and cultural center, sponsored by the World Union for Progressive Judaism, has attracted tourists of every age and faith from all over the world. The large, modern complex, designed by Moshe Safdie (who also designed Montreal's Habitat), offers views of the Old City, a network of terraces, gardens, and courtyards, and a full schedule of lectures, concerts, and cultural activities on the premises. Rooms can be set up as dorms, family facilities for up to six people, private doubles, or even as singles. Despite the architecturally impressive building, the place can seem somewhat institutional, and with heavy use, decor in rooms is wearing thin. Dining hall meals run $10. From December 12 to January 4, visitors are charged summer rates. Early reservations are recommended. Call ahead for information on wheelchair access. Groups only are booked in summer.

Rosary Convent Guest House and Hostel. 14 Agron St. (P.O. Box 54), Jerusalem. ☎ 02/228-529. Fax 02/235-581. 23 rms (shower facilities available). $30 single; $46 double; $66 triple. Rates include breakfast. No credit cards.

For spotless, simple but pleasant accommodations, you can't beat the Rosary Convent, set back from the road in a quiet garden located around the corner from the Jerusalem Plaza Hotel and across the street from the Supersol supermarket. The gate to the complex closes at 10pm; if you plan to be out later, you must try to make arrangements with the management ahead of time.

Menorah Hotel. 24 King David St., Jerusalem. ☎ 02/253-311. Fax 02/242-860. 64 rms (all with bath). TEL. $57 single; $76 double. Add 20% for Jewish holidays. Rates include breakfast. MC, V. 3% surcharge for credit cards. Bus: 5, 18, or 21.

This is a fabulous location on King David Street, just beside the YMCA and across the street from the King David Hotel. The building is from the 1970s; rooms are simply furnished and in most cases spacious; decor is basic gray and functional; beds are medium firm. There are a number of room sizes, and some can manage four or even five people quite comfortably, which makes the Menorah a good choice for families or small groups. Optional extras are $3 per day for a TV, $3 for a refrigerator; half the rooms are air-conditioned. Housekeeping may not be a strong point here but the management is friendly. Discounts often available.

SOUTH JERUSALEM

South of the King George Street/King David Street area, you'll likely use buses or taxis to get to the center of town, although many will find the half-hour walk interesting. Two atmospheric hospices are located in the Abu Tor and German Colony neighborhoods. Hebron Road, with views of the Old City, also offers two hotel choices. A half-hour municipal bus ride from the center of town, you'll find a large kibbutz hotel in the Judean mountains on the edge of the desert.

MODERATE

Ariel Hotel. 31 Hebron Rd., Jerusalem. ☎ 02/719-222. Fax 02/734-066. 126 rms (all with bath or shower). A/C TEL TV. $81, $92, $125 single; $100, $115, $142 double. Rates include breakfast. MC, V.

Originally planned as a residential hotel, the modern, relatively highrise Ariel offers a variety of room sizes (some quite large) and arrangements, which makes this a good choice for families or those traveling in small groups. Many rooms have fine views of the Old City. Public areas have been recently redone. Decor in private rooms is utilitarian, but there may be renovations during this edition's time span. The hotel is not far from Liberty Bell Park, which has children's facilities; the Cinémathèque; and the beautiful Yemin Moshe neighborhood, with its gardens and marvelous vistas. A block away, across from the railroad station, you'll find buses to every part of town.

Mitzpeh Ramat Rachel. Kibbutz Ramat Rachel, M. P. North Judea. ☎ **02/702-555.** Fax 02/733-155. 93 rooms (all with bath or shower). A/C TEL TV. $80–110 single; $100–$135 double. Jewish holidays 15% extra. Rates include breakfast. AE, DC, MC, V. Bus: 7.

More like a resort than a hotel, Mitzpeh Ramat Rachel is the only kibbutz guest facility within the reach of Jerusalem's municipal bus routes. Historically, the kibbutz is famous for holding out against overwhelming odds during the 1948 war, thus preserving West Jerusalem's southern defense line. Today, Ramat Rachel offers its visitors a vast swimming pool with a huge water slide (heavily patronized by Jerusalemites in summer), tennis and basketball courts, a playground, fitness center, and vistas of Bethlehem and the Judean desert. For those who want to relax as well as sightsee, or for families with children, this is a unique choice. The grounds are landscaped with pieces of contemporary Israeli sculpture, and rooms are brightened with colorful soft art textile creations by the noted artist Calman Shemi. Service is above average for a kibbutz establishment, and there is airport shuttle service to Ben-Gurion for guests.

Mount Zion Hotel. 17 Hebron Rd., Jerusalem 94356. ☎ **02/724-222.** 80 rms (all with bath). A/C TEL. June–Sept, $80–$145 single; $90–$160 double, $220 suite; Apr–May, Oct–mid-Nov, Christmas, Passover, and Sukkot $15–$25 per person extra. 15% service charge. Breakfast $9 extra. AE, MC, V. Bus: 5, 6, 7, 8, 21, or 48.

One of Jerusalem's newest and architecturally most interesting hotels, the Mount Zion is partly composed of renovated 19th- and early 20th-century Jerusalem stone buildings that have been carefully blended into a modern complex giving the whole structure an old-world charm, yet offering modern conveniences. The hotel is built on a cliff facing the Old City's walls, and on a hillside shared by Jerusalem's fashionable Cinémathèque. The hotel's terraces, sprawling wings, hidden gardens, and swimming pool offer views of the Old City that rival those of the King David Hotel. There are standard and superior rooms as well as suites. Superior rooms have better views and polished stone bathrooms. Suites, with wonderful vistas, are spacious and have minibars. TVs are available for a fee on request. Don't expect to find a hotel with five-star service; people choose the Mount Zion for its vistas and beauty.

Manager Michael Cohen has offered that guests who book independently and present this book will be upgraded (subject to availability) to one of the hotel's superior rooms at no additional charge. Under the same policy, readers who book superior rooms will be upgraded to one of the hotel's truly magnificent suites and Frommer's readers who book independently will receive a 10% reduction for stays of more than 3 days. The Mount Zion Hotel also offers a family plan (one child up to age 12, sharing the parents' room, is free) that could make the chance for an upgrade to a suite an extremely good value. In winter season (mid-November to March 1, excluding Christmas), rates go down $10 per person.

INEXPENSIVE

✪ **Saint Andrew's Hospice.** Church of Scotland, P.O. Box 8696, Jerusalem. ☎ **02/732-401.** Fax 02/731-711. $48 single; $70 double. $5 per person lower Nov 1–Dec 14 and

Jan 11–Feb 28. Rates include breakfast. Bus: No. 4, 8, or 48 along King George V Avenue or Keren Hayesod Street, or 5, 6, 18, or 21 on Jaffa Road; railroad station or Khan Theater stop.

Situated on a small hill, the banner of St. Andrew waving from its tower, and surrounded by a garden with panoramic views of Mount Zion and the Old City, this hospice is only a few steps from the railroad station and the Khan Theater. Rooms are simple but spotless; the building is adorned with beautiful examples of Armenian ceramic tiles, created by Jerusalem's famous Palestinian Pottery Workshop in 1930. The efficient and friendly Scottish staff offers a hearty $10 dinner. Craftaid, a nonprofit shop selling fine Palestinian embroidery and local crafts, is also on the premises. Excellent value.

WESTERN EDGE OF CITY/SDEROT HERZL

Stretching from the area of Jaffa Road near the Central Bus Station to the area of Sderot Herzl that runs toward the residential neighborhood of Beit Ha-Kerem, this area offers modern, comfortable, expensive, and moderate choices. There's not much interesting within immediate walking distance of most of these hotels, but they are all close to major bus routes into the center of town; the better, more distant hotels offer free shuttle service to various points in the city. This area is not far from the Knesset and Government Center, the Hebrew University's Givat Ram Campus, and the Israel Museum; however, the highway system in the area does not lend itself to excursions by foot.

EXPENSIVE

Holiday Inn Crowne Plaza. Givat Ram, Jerusalem. ☎ **02/581-414.** Fax 02/514-555. 397 rms and suites. A/C MINIBAR TEL TV. $150–$250 single; $175–$275 double. 15% service charge. Two children up to age 19 in parents' room free, except during high season and in Club Level rooms. Rates include breakfast. AE, DC, MC, V. Bus: 5, 6, 20, 21, 48, or any bus to Central Bus Station.

For over 20 years, this landmark tower on a hill at the western edge of the city was the Jerusalem Hilton, and many locals still refer to it as such (the Hilton has opted for a new more central location near the Jaffa Gate). Strong points include an outdoor swimming pool in a pleasantly sheltered garden, and the in-house Kohinoor Restaurant, serving splendid kosher Indian food. Hotel restaurant services are above average, with a dairy/vegetarian luncheon buffet offered in the lounge. Public areas, though spacious, are a bit jumbled. Vistas from the guest rooms, all of which have small balconies, are a plus here; rooms themselves are unremarkable. The location is perfect for conventions at the neighboring Binyinei Ha-Oma Convention Center. Special services are available for business travelers and for Club guests.

Dining/Entertainment: Two restaurants, bar/lounge.

Services: Free downtown shuttle service.

Facilities: Outdoor pool, tennis courts, miniature golf, playground; health club (at extra charge) with sauna and Jacuzzi; parking for fee; quality shopping arcade; no-smoking rooms and rooms for those with disabilities.

Jerusalem Renaissance Hotel. 6 Wolfson St., Jerusalem. ☎ **02/528-111.** Fax 02/511-824. 625 rms (all with bath). A/C TEL TV. $112–$165 single; $125–$195 double. 15% service charge. Rates include breakfast. AE, DC, MC, V. Free parking. Bus: 5, 6, 14, 18, 20, 21, or 48.

There are two separate highrise towers in this well-equipped 14-year-old Ramada International complex; the less expensive section is sometimes closed during off-season, and everyone is moved into the attractive deluxe rooms. Public areas are spacious and serve as a conduit between the two sections, with hundreds of tiny starlights creating a romantic, almost sculptural effect at night.

Large indoor and outdoor swimming pools, a tennis court, and use of the excellent health club are major strong points. Restaurant facilities are glatt kosher. Except in high season, you'll often find a discount policy: stay 7 nights and pay only for 6. This is the farthest hotel from the center of town on Sderot Herzl; from here you can walk to Mount Herzl and Yad VaShem.

Dining and Entertainment: Three restaurants, lounge/bar.

Services: Free downtown shuttle service.

Facilities: Fitness center, Jacuzzi, wet and dry saunas, indoor and outdoor swimming pools, tennis court, shops.

Paradise Jerusalem Hotel. 4 Wolfson St., Jerusalem. ☎ **02/558-888.** Fax 02/512-266. 198 rms (all with bath). A/C TEL TV. $122–$180 single; $152–$223 double. $40–$60 double on El Al Sunsational 5-Night Package. Rates include breakfast. AE, DC, MC, V. Free parking. Bus: 5, 6, 18, 20, 21, or any bus on Jaffa Road to Sderot Herzl.

A 15- to 25-minute bus ride into the center of town, this hotel is a moderate choice for El Al passengers who book it as part of an El Al Sunsational Package. Located in a major hotel strip near the Binyanei Ha-Uma Convention Center, this is a highrise built for business travelers and tourists in the 1980s. Rooms are comfortable but small and standard in decor. The big draws here are the indoor and outdoor swimming pools and excellent free sports facilities. Specify if you want this location when you purchase the El Al Sunsational Package.

Services: Room service, babysitting, business services, laundry.

Facilities: Indoor and outdoor swimming pools, health club, tennis courts, Jacuzzi, poolside lawn and playground, children's activities in summer.

MODERATE

Park Plaza Hotel. 2 Wolfson St., Jerusalem. ☎ **02/652-8221.** Fax 02/652-8423. 217 rms. A/C TEL TV. $75–$150 single; $87–$172 double. Rates include breakfast. AE, DC, MC, V. Bus: 5, 6, 18, 20, or 48.

Formerly the Sonesta Jerusalem, this modern hotel built in the 1980s is wrapped around a light-filled atrium which, unfortunately, is only used for private functions. Public areas and facilities are skimpy, but the rooms are pleasant for this category, and equipped with small-screen TVs. The lack of a pool is a shortcoming; facilities include a restaurant and a lounge/bar as well as free parking.

FARTHER WEST: EIN KEREM
INEXPENSIVE

Sisters of Sion Convent. Ezor "D," Ein Kerem, Jerusalem. ☎ **02/415-738.** Fax 02/437-739. 34 rms (most with bath). $40 single; 60–$65 double. No credit cards. Bus: 17 to Ein Kerem.

Located in the village of Ein Kerem, this hospice is a quiet, atmospheric retreat a half hour or so by municipal bus from downtown Jerusalem. Not all guests are religious; some travelers come for the tranquillity and charm of Ein Kerem, which was the birthplace of John the Baptist. Rates are slightly higher on weekends; reservations are essential. Meals are always beautifully prepared and a full pension plan can be arranged.

NORTH JERUSALEM
EXPENSIVE

✪ **Hyatt Regency Jerusalem.** 32 Lehi St., Jerusalem. ☎ **02/331-234.** Fax 02/815-947. 503 rms and suites. A/C MINIBAR TEL TV. $125–$235 single; $147–$250 double. 15% service charge added. Rates include breakfast. AE, DC, MC, V. Bus: 4. Free shuttle to downtown Jerusalem.

Designed by David Resnik, one of Israel's foremost architects, the Hyatt Regency opened in 1987 and has gained a reputation as one of the city's finest hotels. Set on

Jerusalem Accommodations and Dining

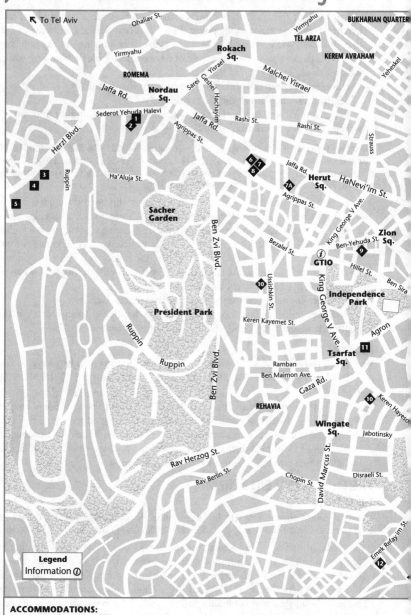

ACCOMMODATIONS:

American Colony Hotel **32**
Ariel Hotel **15**
Holiday Inn Crowne Plaza **1**
Holyland East Hotel **26**
Hyatt Regency Jerusalem **33**
Jerusalem Hotel **27**

Jerusalem Renaissance Hotel **5**
Mount of Olives Hotel **34**
Mount Zion Hotel **19**
National Palace Hotel **28**
Notre Dame Guest House **24**
Paradise Jerusalem Hotel **4**

Park Plaza Hotel **3**
Pilgrims Palace Hotel **25**
Rosary Convent & Guest House
Saint Andrew's Hospice **20**
St. George Hotel **30**
St. George's Hostel **31**

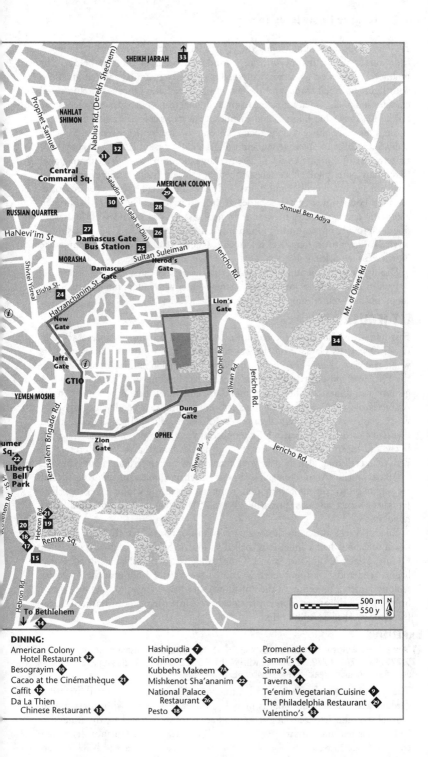

SHEIKH JARRAH 33

NAHLAT SHIMON

Prophet Samuel

Nablus Rd. (Derekh Shechem)

Central Command Sq.

31 32

RUSSIAN QUARTER

AMERICAN COLONY 29

Saladin St. (Salah el-Din)

30 28

HaNevi'im St.

27

Damascus Gate Bus Station 25

26

Shmuel Ben Adiya

MORASHA

Damascus Gate

Sultan Suleiman

Herod's Gate

Shivtei Yisrael

Elisha St.

24

Hatzanchanim St.

New Gate

Jericho Rd.

Lion's Gate

ⓘ

Ophel Rd.

Silwan Rd.

Jericho Rd.

Mt. of Olives Rd.

Jaffa Gate

ⓘ

GTIO

34

YEMEN MOSHE

Jerusalem Brigade Rd.

Dung Gate

Zion Gate

OPHEL

Silwan Rd.

Jericho Rd.

umer Sq. 22

Liberty Bell Park

Hebron Rd.

21

20 19

18

17

Remez Sq.

15

Hebron Rd.

To Bethlehem

14

0   500 m / 550 y   N

DINING:

American Colony Hotel Restaurant 32
Besograyim 10
Cacao at the Cinémathèque 21
Caffit 12
Da La Thien Chinese Restaurant 13
Hashipudia 7
Kohinoor 2
Kubbehs Makeem 7A
Mishkenot Sha'ananim 22
National Palace Restaurant 26
Pesto 18
Promenade 17
Sammi's 8
Sima's 6
Taverna 14
Te'enim Vegetarian Cuisine 9
The Philadelphia Restaurant 29
Valentino's 33

107

the lower slopes of Mount Scopus, the Hyatt's seven arcaded courtyards settle gracefully across the landscape, offering wonderful vistas of the city below. The multilevel public areas are almost sculptural spaces laid out around a vast atrium filled with light, polished stone, and the sound of water falling through architectural cascades and pools. Guest rooms are less institutional than in most Israeli hotels; those on the Regency Club floors include many special staff services. Among the Hyatt's strong points are above average food services, crowned by the inventive, top-class Valentino's Restaurant (see restaurant listings) and theme buffets (Tex-Mex; Middle Eastern; Asian) 3 nights a week. There is a large, beautiful outdoor swimming pool (like many hotel pools, it's often mobbed with locals during summer and school holidays) and two floodlit tennis courts, and guests are offered discounts or free passes to the in-house fitness center, regarded as the best in town. The hotel's location, in a rather isolated, open area between residential districts of East and West Jerusalem, doesn't provide opportunities for an interesting evening stroll, but free shuttle service to downtown Jerusalem is available. There are often special discounts like 5 nights for the price of 4.

Dining/Entertainment: Four restaurants plus a choice of cafes, bars, and disco/pubs.

Facilities: Outdoor swimming pool; fitness center with indoor pool; sauna, steam room, business center, shopping arcade, hairdresser.

EAST JERUSALEM

East Jerusalem's hotels are located downtown, within walking distance of the Old City's Damascus Gate, or on the way to, and on the Mount of Olives, with its wonderful views. There has been no new hotel construction in this part of town since the 1967 war; most of East Jerusalem's hotels were built in the 1950s and 1960s. A genuine helpfulness and hospitality found in many hotels here is very much in the Arabic tradition. As a rule, East Jerusalem hotels offer very good value, especially when compared to West Jerusalem prices. As of 1996, the daily commercial strikes that had closed East Jerusalem for a number of years are over, and the area is again lively and interesting for tourists, though not as bustling as West Jerusalem's Ben-Yehuda district. Plan to make your initial arrival to East Jerusalem hotels by taxi.

All rates include your room and a 15% service charge, unless otherwise noted, and are current during the summer months (rooms are cheaper in winter). Also, most East Jerusalem hotels raise their prices by 20% to 25% during the Christmas and Easter holidays.

Saladin Street, the main thoroughfare, begins opposite Herod's Gate and runs north for about half a mile. It is spelled variously: Saladin, Salah ad-Din, Salah Eddine, Salach A'Din, and Salah E-Din. It roughly parallels Nablus Road, which begins at Herod's Gate and meets Saladin at the crest of a hill near the American Colony Hotel. The center of the downtown area is a triangle, formed by Saladin Street, Port Said Street (frequently called Az-Zahra Street), and Rasheed Street (sometimes called Rachidya Street).

EXPENSIVE

✪ **American Colony Hotel.** Nablus Road (P.O. Box 19215), Jerusalem 97200. ☎ **02/ 279-777.** Fax 02/279-779. 92 rms (all with bath). AC TEL TV. $75–$120 single; $114–$200 double. Rates include breakfast and service. AE, DC, MC, V.

The former home of a Turkish pasha, this romantic four-star hotel with beautiful gardens and a swimming pool is in a class by itself. Popular with international journalists, scholars, archeologists, diplomats, and savvy travelers, the American Colony has become almost as legendary as Rick's Cafe in Casablanca. Its walled courtyards are just past the top of the hill where Saladin Street and Nablus Road meet. Public areas are decorated with splendid Armenian ceramics, intricately painted antique wooden ceilings, and other authentic old Jerusalem touches; in the cloisterlike lobby above the garden, local archeological finds are displayed in glass cases. In the rooms, too, you'll find antiques juxtaposed with modern bathrooms; some rooms are decorated with mother-of-pearl cocktail tables, copper trays, feenjons, and ornate gold-and-blue ceilings. Many accommodations are in less august buildings across the courtyard. Suites and luxury rooms are atmospheric and worth the extra money; the standard rooms are often quite ordinary. Some rooms are air-conditioned. Even if you decide you can't afford this kind of luxury and ambience, you might want to treat yourself to the elegant Saturday afternoon buffet or the charming garden cafe for a light meal or dessert.

Dining/Entertainment: Three restaurants, including the French/Continental Arabesque Room; excellent, atmospheric bar; pianist and live music many nights.

Services: Room service, babysitting, laundry, dry cleaning.

Facilities: Outdoor pool, children's pool, free parking.

MODERATE

Holyland East Hotel. 6 Harun er-Rasheed St. (P.O. Box 19700), Jerusalem 91196. ☎ **02/ 272-888.** Fax 02/280-265. 105 rms (all with bath). A/C TEL. $53–$69 single; $70–$99 double. Rates include breakfast. AE, DC, MC, V. Bus: 27.

Be sure to check out the roof—this hotel, built in the 1950s, offers stunning rooftop views that include the Old City, the Dome of the Rock, the Mount of Olives, and the New City. The lobby is decorated with 1960s modern furnishings, and most bedrooms have a balcony and new, firm mattresses. Try for a room with a view toward the Old City. Rates are reduced when business is slow.

National Palace Hotel. 4 Az-Zahra St., Jerusalem. ☎ **02/273-273.** Fax 02/282-139. 105 rms (all with bath). A/C TEL TV. $75–$93 single; $81–$114 double; 15% service charge. Rates include breakfast. Discounts for groups. MC, V. Bus: 27.

Built in the 1960s and located on a relatively quiet street off Saladin Street, this hotel is a center for tour groups and for social gatherings and business activity in East Jerusalem. The large lounge is dotted with groupings of chairs around small oriental rugs. Rooms are standard but comfortable. The rooftop restaurant is one of the best dining choices in this part of town.

Pilgrims Palace Hotel. Sultan Suleiman Street, Jerusalem 97200. ☎ **02/272-418.** Fax 02/ 894-658. 87 rms (all with bath). A/C TEL TV. $50–$80 single; $65–$120 double. 10% student discount. AE, DC, MC, V.

This conveniently located three-star hotel is on the western side of the East Jerusalem bus station—which means that rooms on that side tend to be noisier. The two-story, limestone building has views of the Old City walls (across the street). It's not an opulent place, but it does have immaculate rooms, and a bar and souvenir shop. Lower prices are for low season, which includes June 10 to August 10, but excludes Easter and Christmas. Rates are sometimes negotiable.

✪ **Saint George Hotel.** Saladin Street, Jerusalem 91194. ☎ **02-277-232.** Fax 02/282-575. 144 rms. A/C TEL TV. $87 single; $120 double. Lower group rates available. Rates include breakfast. AE, V.

Right on Saladin Street, a short walk to the Old City, this is one of the best East Jerusalem hotels, and was awarded five stars under the now defunct system of hotel ratings. The building is 1960s modern and set right in the center of a business district, but the public rooms sport Middle Eastern design flourishes that add a touch of ambience. The hotel is being slowly redecorated, bathrooms are being modernized (request one of the renovated rooms), and although guest rooms are not unusual, they are comfortable, and many have balconies and good views. There is a small outdoor swimming pool, and the housekeeping staff is one of the best in the city.

INEXPENSIVE

✪ **Jerusalem Hotel.** Nablus Road (entrance at 4 Antara Ben-Shadad St.), Jerusalem. ☎ **02/ 271-356.** ☎ and fax 02/283-282. 15 rms (all with shower). $34 single; $46 double. Rates include breakfast. AE, DC, MC, V.

This increasingly popular hotel, run by the very hospitable, well-informed Saadeh family, is a real winner, housed in an old stone mansion with thick walls, high ceilings, and a cafe garden. Rooms are simple but comfortable with central heating. The restaurant, run by Mrs. Waded Saadeh, offers good Middle Eastern dishes in a traditional dining room with low tables and pillow-covered divans. Often on Friday evenings from 8 to 11, there is live classical music to accompany your meal; Saturday evenings the hotel serves an excellent Lebanese buffet ($11) with salads, vegetarian dishes, and six hot dishes, plus traditional Middle Eastern oud (lute) music. During much of the year, Thursday night features an international buffet ($12), and some of the city's most interesting pianists entertain. Extremely good value.

The entrance at 4 Antara Ben-Shadad Street is off Nablus Road, on a side street facing the north side of the Egged East Nablus Road Bus Station.

✪ **St. George's Hostel.** 20 Nablus Rd. (P.O. Box 19018), Jerusalem. ☎ **02/283-302.** Fax 02/282-253. 22 rms (most with private bath). $41 single; $60 double. No credit cards. Bus: 27.

This Anglican/Episcopal establishment is really a guesthouse with private rooms housed in a cloister around an English garden. Accommodations are simple but newly redecorated and the ambience is both atmospheric and comfortable. The entire very British enclave seems like the setting for a chapter of *The Jewel in the Crown.* There is a knowledgeable, helpful staff.

To find it, walk up Nablus Road from Aelia Capitolina, and you'll be approaching Saint George's Cathedral on the right. The hotel is in cathedral compound, where Nablus Road and Saladin Street meet. Bus no. 27 comes right to the door of Saint George's (bus noise may be a problem for some).

OUTSIDE THE CITY

Kiryat Anavim Kibbutz Hotel. Kiryat Anavim 90833. ☎ **02/348-999.** Fax 02/348-848. 85 rms (all with bath or shower). A/C TEL. $55–$80 single; $74–$115 double. Rates include breakfast. AE, DC, MC, V. Bus: to Kiryat Anavim and Abu Ghosh from Central Bus Station.

This three-star establishment combines the services of a comfortable hotel with a country atmosphere. Several of the rooms can be arranged to lodge a family of three or four. The hotel offers such facilities as a swimming pool, restaurant, TV room. snack bar, and cocktail bar. The hotel's rustic site, among the forests and orchards of the Judean mountains, is especially lovely. The location, so close to Jerusalem, lets you combine a tranquil resort experience with major sightseeing. Discounts are available on Kibbutz Hotel Package plans.

The hotel is near the village of Abu Ghosh, 12km (7¹/₂ miles) west of Jerusalem, just north of the highway to the airport and Tel Aviv.

INEXPENSIVE

✪ **Neve Shalom-Wahat al Salaam Guest House and Hostel.** Doar Na Shimshon 99761. ☎ **02/917-160.** Fax 02/917-412. $50–$60 single; $60–$80 double. Passover and August 10% higher; 10% lower Nov 1–Feb 28. Rates include breakfast. No credit cards.

Located in the countryside near the Latrun Monastery, between Tel Aviv and Jerusalem just where the plain of Ayalon begins to rise into the mountains of Judea (the ancient borderland between the Israelites and the Philistines), the joint name of this community means "oasis of peace" in both Hebrew and Arabic. The village of Neve Shalom-Wahat al Salaam was founded as a place where Israeli Jews and Israeli Arabs could live together in friendship and understanding. Neve Shalom-Wahat al Salaam is admittedly an uncharted experiment, but over the years its inhabitants have made their community effort into a national center for learning and dialogue. The guesthouse and hostel, originally built for visiting groups and study seminars, are now open to the public, and tourists are welcome to spend a night or two here within a 25-minute drive of Jerusalem and Tel Aviv, enjoying the lovely countryside and getting a feel for this unusual project. The simple but comfortable guesthouse rooms all have private bathrooms, radios, and use of a TV room. Bed and breakfast in the hostel is $16 per person, with a $2 additional charge during high season. Lunch or dinner is $12, and if groups are scheduled, you can join a lecture (if offered in your language) for about $5. Although not a kibbutz, Neve Shalom-Wahat al Salaam can be included as an overnight choice in the Kibbutz Hotel Chain packages, which can be reserved through the Israel Hotel Reservation Center in the United States by calling 800/552-0141; in Canada 800/526-5343.

Buses and sheruts between Tel Aviv and Jerusalem will let you off at the Latrun Junction. You must prearrange with Neve Shalom for a pickup near the junction.

5 Where to Dine

Jerusalem has a huge selection of restaurants, dairy bars, lunch counters, snack shops, delicatessens, and cafes. In the Old City and East Jerusalem you'll find mostly Middle Eastern cuisine. Shellfish and pork are prohibited to Muslims, as they are to Jews, but you will find these dishes in restaurants catering to Christian Arabs. Almost no kosher restaurants exist in the Old City (except in the Jewish Quarter) or in East Jerusalem.

In West Jerusalem the dining scene is quite different. Downtown West Jerusalem has become something of a food festival. You'll find some streets that are virtually wall-to-wall restaurants and cafes. There are pizza parlors, hamburger stands, and Viennese-style cafes (often called "conditory," an anglicization of the German Konditorei). Restaurants in West Jerusalem serve American, Indian, Spanish, Italian, Central European, and Middle Eastern cuisine, and most of them are kosher. But don't assume that the Jewish cuisine you know from home will be served in every West Jerusalem restaurant.

SABBATH DINING   Restaurants usually close by 2 or 3pm on Friday. The following nonkosher restaurants, described in detail later in this chapter, have Friday evening or Saturday afternoon hours and provide a good variety of choices. Downtown Jerusalem: Cezanne, Kamin, Pie House (Le Tsriff) Restaurant, Pepperoni's, Niss, Ocean, Spaghettim, Gilly's, Pie House (Le Tsriff) at the YMCA, YMCA Café. German Colony and Baka: Da La Thien. East Jerusalem: Philadelphia, American Colony Hotel, National Palace Hotel Restaurant.

The Old City has plenty of snack stands and inexpensive Arab restaurants. Most Old City eating places are open daily from 9am to 5 or 6pm.

THE OLD CITY
NEAR JAFFA GATE
Inexpensive

✪ **Armenian Tavern.** 79 Armenian Orthodox Patriarchate Rd. ☎ **273-854.** Reservations recommended Friday and Saturday evenings. Appetizers and light meals NIS 6–22 ($1.80–$6.60); main courses NIS 25–40 ($7.50–$12). AE, DC, MC, V. Daily noon–11pm. ARMENIAN.

This is the prettiest restaurant in the Old City, in a newly restored room with exposed stone walls, Crusader-era arched ceilings, an indoor fountain, rustic wooden tables, and panels of hand-painted Armenian tiles that are a feast for the eye. The food is done with special Armenian herbs and seasonings that give each dish a slightly novel taste. There are delicate homestyle meat pizzas (small and pricey, but delicious) and a range of cold salads, soups, and stuffed vegetables. Main courses are only mildly unusual, but on Friday nights, special traditional dishes are brought in from the kitchen of the owner's house. Background music is Armenian and Greek; wine and beer, a rarity in Old City restaurants, is an added attraction.

After entering Jaffa Gate, turn right at the Tower of David (Citadel). Continue straight; restaurant is on the right, down a flight of stairs.

Coffee Shop. Jaffa Gate. ☎ **286-812.** Soup NIS 9 ($2.70); salad NIS 10 ($3); soup and salad bar NIS 18 ($5.40). No credit cards. Mon–Sat 10am–6pm. SOUP/SALAD.

Spotless, wholesome, and brightly decorated with contemporary tiles designed by the Jerusalem Pottery Workshop, the Coffee Shop is one of the best bets in the Old City. It serves a thick homemade soup of the day (as much as you want) plus a fresh all-you-can-eat salad bar. Tasty homestyle bread and butter comes with your meal. The Coffee Shop is occasionally closed at odd times for religious services.

When you enter Jaffa Gate, turn right just after David Citadel; it's on the left.

NEAR DAMASCUS GATE

While there are not many restaurants in this area, you can find many Arabic pastry shops, places grilling whole chickens (which can be carved and packed for takeout), and fresh juice bars. Wander from Damascus Gate along Suq Khan es-Zeit Street, which bears to the right at the fork.

Abu Assab Refreshments. Suq Khan es-Zeit Bazaar. No phone. NIS 3.5–6 ($1.20–$1.80). Daily 9am–5pm. FRESH JUICES.

The best place in the Old City for fresh orange, grapefruit, and carrot juice (often as sweet as cantaloupe juice), Abu Assab always purchases the best of the crop. Have yours at the juice bar, or follow the tiny staircase upstairs for table service. It's located three-quarters of the way from Damascus Gate to the Cardo, on the right side.

✪ **Abu Shukri.** 63 Al Wad Rd. ☎ **271-538.** Main courses NIS 7–10 ($2–$3). No credit cards. Daily 8am–5pm. HUMMUS.

This restaurant, one of the best and cheapest in Jerusalem, can be found at the fifth station of the cross (look for a large, red Coca-Cola sign), just where Via Dolorosa and Al Wad Road meet. The tables are Formica and the napkins are scraps of paper (if possible, bring your own), but the hummus (mashed, seasoned chickpeas eaten with pita bread) is so spectacular that people in Jordan used to send out for it, and in better times, lines of Israelis waited for tables on Saturday afternoons. Try your hummus with whole chickpeas in olive oil, or black beans, or with roasted pine nuts (about $3 for a serving), and be sure to ask for hot pita bread (included in the price), which you use to scoop up the hummus. Mint tea is a good beverage choice here.

☻ **Families Restaurant.** Suq Khan es-Zeit Bazaar. No phone. Appetizers and light meals NIS 7–18 ($2.10–$5.40); main courses NIS 15–36 ($4.50–$11). No credit cards. Daily 8am–7pm. MIDDLE EASTERN.

For decades, this restaurant, owned by the Abdulatif family, has been the best in the bazaar, and the energetic current owner, Musa Abdulatif, with awards from his years with the Sheraton Hotels in Los Angeles, runs his family business according to exacting standards. Everything from the shwarma to the soups and traditional oven dishes like hummus and meat casserole (siniyah) is excellent. From outside, you'll see a spit of shwarma and a counter where felafel is sold, but inside, you'll find a spacious dining room. Salads here are especially worthwhile; if you order something simple like shwarma or felafel, see if you can pay 2 or 3 shekels extra for a bit of tabbouleh or eggplant in addition to the standard salads that are included. Light, home-made fruit ice creams, available at the take-out counter, are a specialty of the house.

Coming from direction of Jaffa Gate, it will be on the right about 100 feet after the turning for Via Dolorosa.

Jaffar and Sons Pastry Cafe. Suq Khan es-Zeit Bazaar. No phone. NIS 5 ($1.50). Daily 9am–5pm. ARABIC PASTRY.

People flock to Jaffar for a wonderful Middle Eastern dessert called kanafeh, which you will see being cut from large pizzalike trays. A recipe probably from ancient times, kanafeh is mildly sweet cheese, grains, and pistachios baked in a very light honey syrup and served (optionally) with a bit more honey syrup on top. Buy a ticket at the cashier's counter for an order of kanafeh and take a table (drinking glasses are communal—you'll probably prefer a soft drink straight from the bottle) in the newly renovated polished gray marble cafe that has unfortunately replaced the old domed-ceiling rooms, or ask to have your order boxed for takeout (bring your own napkins and plastic forks). Absolutely delicious when warm!

From Damascus Gate, bear right at the fork in the road, and continue into the narrow bazaar. Jaffar is the second large pastry shop with glass windows on the right.

THE JEWISH QUARTER

This part of the Old City is home to a number of kosher but bland fast-food spots. On Jewish Quarter Road are two wonderful old-fashioned Arabic-style bread bakeries where you can buy warm, freshly baked pita and big sesame bread rolls, which are tasty to snack on as you make your way around the Old City. Ask for a tiny package of *zatar* (local spices) to flavor the bread in the traditional Middle Eastern style.

Moderate

Keshet. 2 Tiferet Israel St. ☎ **02/287-515.** Appetizers and light meals NIS 15–22 ($4.50–$6.60); main courses NIS 22–60 ($6.60–$18). AE, DC, MC. V. Sun–Thurs 9am–7pm; Fri 10am–3pm. Closed Sat. DAIRY/VEGETARIAN.

Tucked away in the corner of Tiferet Israel Square, with a few outdoor tables in a shaded area in good weather, this is the Jewish Quarter's best choice for a comfortable sit-down meal. Step inside and you'll find a pleasant white-walled dining room with terracotta tile floors and wooden tables. The menu offers omelets, crêpes, pastas, cheese blintzes, soups, and a variety of hefty salads in the $8–$12 range as well as pastas and bagel sandwiches. A daily fish platter, at the top of the price range, is a consideration for a major meal.

WEST JERUSALEM
NEAR ZION SQUARE
Expensive

Katy's. 2 Ha-Soreg St. ☎ **02/279-777.** Reservations recommended. Appetizers NIS 28–48 ($8.60–$14.30); main courses NIS 72–90 ($21.60–$27). AE, DC, MC, V. Daily 12:30pm–4pm and 6:30pm–midnight. FRENCH.

Long a favorite with Jerusalemites for an intimate, special night out, this is the very personal restaurant of Katy Ohana, who draws on French, North African, and local traditions to create her cuisine. Katy *is* the menu; what her restaurant offers can be very different each day. Her eggplant and goat cheese with basil and her mushrooms, salmon, and seafood with caviar sauce are among well-known first courses you may find. Duckling with black currant sauce and her wonderful goose liver and fish creations may be main course selections. Servings are usually bountiful, and many take the large first courses for a complete meal.

Moderate

Wild Bull. 3 Ya'avetz St. ☎ **02/244-395.** Reservations weekends. Appetizers and light meals NIS 14–30 ($4.20–$9); main courses NIS 30–60 ($9–$18). No credit cards. Sun–Thurs noon–11pm; Sat after Sabbath. Closed Fri. SOUTH AFRICAN STEAKS.

The once heavily vegetarian Israeli eating public is developing a distinct taste for beef and the Wild Bull is the South African immigrant community's delicious contribution to rising cholesterol levels in the Middle East. All meat is fresh and aged and no frozen meat is used; the cuts are tender and imbued with wonderful barbecue flavor that's a bit different from Argentinian- or American-style steak. Appetizers include maken, a kind of kosher South African beef bacon; and Boerewors sausage rolls. Traditional garlic and monkey gland sauce is available.

Yo Si Peking. 5 Shimon Ben-Shetah St. ☎ **02/250-817.** Reservations recommended on weekends. Appetizers NIS 10–22 ($3–$6.60); main courses NIS 21–40 ($6.30–$12). MC, V. Lunch Sun–Thurs noon–midnight; Sat 1 hour after Shabbat–midnight. Closed Fri. GLATT KOSHER CHINESE.

Set in a 19th-century building on a side street near Zion Square, this glatt kosher restaurant has a devoted following and offers a variety of vegetarian, chicken, and meat dishes. The food is tasty, though not strongly authentic. Downstairs (entrance is from a separate door on the street) Yo Si Peking's Express section offers great value with complete set meals (including excellent, filling soups) for $6 to $8 from noon to 7pm.

Inexpensive

✪ **Alumah.** 8 Ya'avetz St. ☎ **02/255-014.** Appetizers NIS 7–18 ($2.10–$5.40); main courses NIS 13–33 ($4–$10). MC, V. Sun–Thurs 10am–10pm; Fri 10am–2pm; Sat after Shabbat. NATURAL FOOD.

No other natural-food restaurant in Israel compares to Alumah; housed in an Ottoman Turkish mansion in the heart of Jerusalem, Alumah is filled with dried wildflowers and herbs, a soft background of classical and folk music, and devoted customers enjoying the array of hearty tofu casseroles and pastas, vegetable pies and quiches, as well as fabulous nonsugar dessert cakes, all made from Alumah's fresh daily stone-ground wheat flour. In summer and during Sukkot, customers can enjoy full meals or dessert and tea in the garden. Fish, tempe, soya-fruit milkshakes, and sweet dessert wine made without sugar are the latest menu additions. Kosher lemehedrin; takeout available.

✪ **Angelo.** 9 Hyrcanos (Horkanos) St. ☎ **02/236-095.** Reservations recommended. Appetizers NIS 9–18 ($2.70–$5.40); pasta courses NIS 22–38 ($6.60–$11.30); fresh fish NIS 50 ($15). MC, V. Sun–Thurs noon–4pm and 6:30–midnight; Sat after Shabbat–midnight. Closed Fri. KOSHER ITALIAN.

The most superb pasta in the country is served at this little place run by Angelo, a new immigrant from Rome, and his wife Lori, a new immigrant from the United States. The ravioli is light as a cloud; the gnocchi is elegantly tender and the risotto (a rarity in Israel) is excellent. Angelo's sauces are alive with flavor, and he does special homestyle favorites of the Roman Jewish community, like spaghetti cacio e pepe (with cheese and black pepper). If you arrange ahead of time, Angelo can prepare other Roman Jewish dishes. Focaccia and thin crust one-person pizzas are

Dining in Downtown West Jerusalem

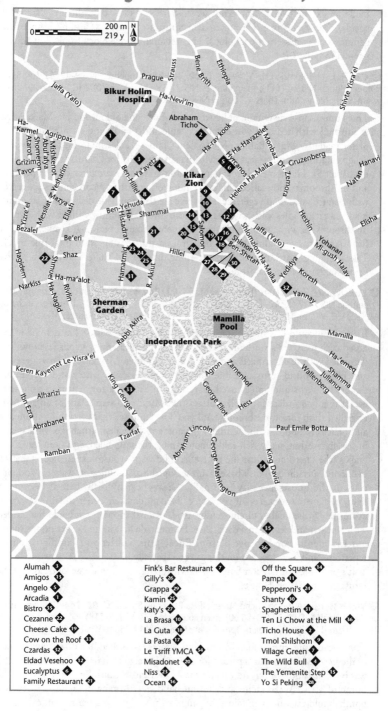

Alumah 3	Fink's Bar Restaurant 7	Off the Square 14
Amigos 13	Gilly's 26	Pampa 11
Angelo 5	Grappa 29	Pepperoni's 24
Arcadia 1	Kamin 25	Shanty 30
Bistro 35	Katy's 27	Spaghettim 31
Cezanne 22	La Brasa 10	Ten Li Chow at the Mill 36
Cheese Cake 19	La Guta 18	Ticho House 2
Cow on the Roof 33	La Pasta 17	Tmol Shilshom 9
Czardas 32	Le Tsriff YMCA 34	Village Green 7
Eldad Vesehoo 12	Misadonet 20	The Wild Bull 4
Eucalyptus 6	Niss 23	The Yemenite Step 15
Family Restaurant 21	Ocean 16	Yo Si Peking 28

made in a stone oven. Meat is not served here, but most days there is a fresh fish special that varies in price, up to a maximum of about $15. The homemade, genuine Italian desserts are fabulous. The restaurant is one block from Zion Square, parallel to Jaffa Road.

✪ Czardas. 11 Shlomzion Ha-Malka St. ☎ 02/243-186. Appetizers NIS 9–12 ($2.70–$3.60); 3-course lunch NIS 36 ($11); main courses NIS 21–29 ($6.30–$8.70). MC, V. Lunch Sun–Fri 10am–3pm; dinner Sun–Thurs 6–10pm. HUNGARIAN.

This Hungarian-style restaurant between Jaffa Road and Shlomzion Ha-Malka Street is adorned with red and white damask tablecloths and hand-painted decorative plates made by Marie Balian of Jerusalem's famous Palestinian Pottery as well as delightful folk paintings created by Mrs. Balian especially for Czardas (see "Shopping" in chapter 5). The homestyle menu includes a traditional roast goose dinner, pot roast and mushrooms, and stuffed chicken, among other dishes. Main courses are served with potato, salad, and vegetable, and there are delicious side dishes, such as home-made sweet noodles with walnuts. You can also have blintzes filled with liver or mushrooms, or with apple and banana; homemade kugel pudding, kishke, or gefilte fish. The soft gypsy and classical background music is an additional fine touch. Takeaway (a good choice for Friday evening dinner) is 15% less. You must reserve Friday takeaways ahead of time.

✪ Eucalyptus. 7 Hyrcanos (Horkanos) St. ☎ 02/244-331. Reservations recommended. Appetizers NIS 7–17 ($2.10–$5.10); main courses NIS 22–33 ($6.60–$10); 10% service charge. AE, DC, MC, V. Sun–Thurs 11am–11pm; Fri 11am–2pm; Sat after Shabbat. ISRAELI.

If anything could be called "Israeli cuisine," chef Moshe Basson has defined it and raised each recipe to a work of art. The walls of this pleasant, spacious restaurant are decorated with rustic artifacts and antique farming tools. Mr. Basson knows the fields and farms around Jerusalem like the shelves of his own pantry and the vibrant flavors of herbs and spices used in Jerusalem kitchens for centuries appear in everything you order. Try a plate of assorted Middle Eastern salads or an appetizer of grilled fresh forest mushrooms, and you'll begin to see that everything is unusual and delicious. Soups include sorrel, eggplant, and Jerusalem artichoke, with special in-season creations like a rich cold almond and garlic soup filled with mint leaves and grapes (the chef knows just the taste effects he wants you to experience). Chicken mahlooba, a traditional dish baked with seasoned rice, cauliflower, walnuts, and pine nuts, is the house specialty (normally a heavy, earthy dish, here it becomes a light, elegant masterpiece—if you don't like dark chicken, order it with skewers of exquisitely grilled cubes of chicken breast). Seasonal specialties include figs stuffed with chicken and served in a date sauce. Homemade liquors and other tidbits round out the menu. For $25 per person, Eucalyptus will let you sample its entire repertoire, and have seconds on things you especially like.

It's one block from Zion Square parallel to Jaffa Road on the second floor of the Jerusalem Inn Guest House.

✪ Ticho House. Abraham Ticho Street off Ha Rav Kook Street. ☎ 02/244-186. Appetizers and light meals NIS 10–22 ($3–$6.60); main courses NIS 27–60 ($8–$18). No credit cards. Sun–Thurs 10am–11:45pm; Fri 10am–3pm; Sat after Sabbath–11:45pm. VEGETARIAN.

This terrace cafe, surrounded by beautiful gardens, is located in a downtown branch of the Israel Museum and is perfect for a light leisurely lunch or dinner. Ticho House was built in 1880 as a private villa for the Aga Rashid Nashishibi; later it became the home of artist Anna Ticho and her husband, Dr. Abraham Ticho, a legendary ophthalmologist who maintained his surgery there. There's a permanent exhibition of Anna Ticho's drawings, and another holding Dr. Ticho's international collection of antique Hanukkah lamps. In the cafe, either indoors or outdoors, you can order crêpes, soups, sandwiches (hot cheese and herbs is a favorite), or vegetable pies and casseroles. Service is friendly, and the kitchen is kosher.

SALOMON STREET MALL & VICINITY

Expensive

La Guta. 16 Rivlin St., ☎ **02/232-322.** Reservations advised. Appetizers NIS 30–50 ($9–$15); main courses NIS 55–80 ($16.50–$24); luncheon specials NIS 66 ($20). AE, MC, V. Sun–Thurs noon–midnight; Fri noon–3pm; Sat after Shabbat–after midnight. FRENCH/MOROCCAN (KOSHER).

This is one of the most interesting quality kosher choices in the city, serving rustic and classic French dishes in an intimate 19th-century Jerusalem building. First courses include mushrooms stuffed with veal brain; the house special, stuffed dried fruit with veal, or pasta with kosher "shrimp" done in a number of interesting sauces. Main courses range from classics like duckling à l'orange, fillet of beef Wellington, or tournedos Rossini to more inventive creations, like veal cutlet in a mushroom lime sauce. There's a touch of Moroccan tradition to the menu, with a special interest in the use of dried fruits (such as you'll find in *tajinnes*) and North African spices. Desserts are very worthwhile, with crêpes Suzette and crème caramel prepared within the rules of *kashrut.*

✪ **Ocean.** 7 Rivlin St. ☎ **02/247-501** or **233-899.** Reservations required. Appetizers NIS 39–79 ($12–$24); main courses NIS 90–130 ($27–$39). Fixed-price lunch NIS 75 ($22.50); fixed-price dinner NIS 130 ($39). AE, DC, V. Daily 1–4pm and 7pm–1am. SEAFOOD MEDITERRANEAN STYLE.

Set in the small, intimate stone rooms of a century-old building one block from the Yoel Salomon Mall, this is one of Israel's masterpiece restaurants, with an international reputation for excellence. Ocean's creator and chef, Eyal Shani, lets nothing come from his kitchen that is less than perfection, be it the freshest giant prawns grilled on citrus charcoals; a grouper baked with fresh herbs in a clay oven; a heavenly focaccia (rustic Italian bread) served with herbed olive oil, rosemary, and antipasti; or a simple grilled tomato garnishing a plate of paradisical seafood pasta. Everything is done within a framework of simplicity and lack of pretension that lets the freshest, finest ingredients speak for themselves, yet the elegance and uniqueness of each dish is very clear.

The wine list and desserts are equal to the rest of the menu. I especially recommend a medley of inventive sorbets. The main arched-ceiling dining room does not quite have the right acoustics for a quiet conversation, but like everything else in the restaurant, it has understated charm. Carefully chosen flowers and extra attentive service are part of the Ocean experience.

Moderate

✪ **Eldad Vesehoo.** Jerusalem Courtyard. ☎ **02/254-007.** Appetizers NIS 15–33 ($4.50–$10); main courses NIS 33–56 ($10–$17). Complete luncheon specials NIS 33 ($10). Complete fixed-price dinner NIS 63 ($19). AE, DC, MC, V. Daily noon–1am or later. FRENCH/MEDITERRANEAN.

Tucked away in a lane leading into the restaurant-filled Jerusalem Courtyard, this little restaurant with a few extra tables outside in summer has the feel of a place in southern France. The food, too, can vie with French standards. The filet mignon is superb and only a shekel or so more than at Gilly's bustling, cut-rate steak house over on Hillel Street; the difference is that here you can enjoy a leisurely pace and a selection of fine first courses and wines to accompany your steak. Appetizers include goose liver done to perfection in a number of styles, shrimp soup, and salads. Main courses, aside from the much admired filet mignon, range from tarragon chicken and grilled fish to lobster (which I've never tried—both wallet and intuition tell me that Israel may not be the best place to invest in a lobster). The name of this restaurant means "Eldad by Himself," and although Eldad has helpers, this is a small, personal place where everything is done carefully under his supervision.

The Courtyard can be reached through the gate at 31 Jaffa Rd. or via the lane to the side of the Ocean Restaurant on Rivlin Street.

✪ **Gilly's.** 33 Hillel St. ☎ **02/255-955.** Reservations not accepted. Appetizers NIS 12–NIS 30 ($3.60–$9); main courses NIS 30–NIS 60 ($9–$18). No credit cards. Mon–Thurs noon–4pm; dinner Mon–Thurs 6–11pm; Fri–Sat noon–4pm, 7–11pm. Closed Sun. STEAK.

One of Jerusalem's biggest success stories, Gilly's offers the thickest, most delicious cuts of meat in town (salad and potatoes au gratin included) at prices that, by Israeli standards, are unbelievably low. As a result, Gilly's arched-ceilinged 19th-century dining room is almost always filled with the hubbub of happy customers. Especially recommended are the beef sirloin ($13.50) or the more expensive filet, served with a choice of sauces, the spareribs (a meal in itself), and the massive hamburger plate. Turnover is fast, but for lunch or dinner plan to come either early or late if you don't want to wait for a table. It's located in the last building on Yoel Salomon Street Mall, at the corner of Hillel Street.

Grappa. 7 Ben Shetach St. ☎ **02/234-470.** Reservations necessary. Appetizers NIS 20–40 ($6–$12); main courses NIS 30–66 ($9–$20). AE, MC, V. Daily noon–3am. FRENCH/CONTINENTAL.

With its eye-catching logo and walls painted a hot 1950s coral, this small, bustling place is packing customers in and has become *the* restaurant in which to see and be seen. Tourists may find the lively scene interesting; the upper range of the menu contains ambitious dishes that sometimes turn out well; at times, in the crush of a busy night, they may disappoint a bit. The Grappa Steak is a landmark here—a tower of meat consisting of filet mignon, goose breast, and foie gras. A popular selection of pastas and salads (hot mushroom salad with garlic, butter, and wine; grilled salad with smoked goose breast and ham) are good choices in the under $10 end of the menu.

La Pasta. 16 Rivlin St. ☎ **02/257-687.** Reservations recommended. Appetizers NIS 16–30 ($4.80–$9); main courses NIS 33–65 ($10–$19.70). AE, MC, V. Sun–Thurs noon–3:30pm and 6:30pm–11:30pm; Fri noon–1 hour before Sabbath. Sat after Shabbat–midnight. KOSHER ITALIAN.

Located upstairs in a 19th-century building in the Yoel Salomon–Rivlin Mall, La Pasta does every dish with an especially enjoyable touch, and has become a favorite among Jerusalem's kosher diners. Among first courses, you'll find eggplant parmesan or mushrooms marinara. Main dishes include homemade pizza and pastas in a variety of sauces; there's also a selection of fish, elegantly but simply prepared, trout in butter and pine nuts, or St. Peter's fish grilled with herbs. This is a relaxed, cozy place for a pleasant meal and dessert.

Ⓢ **Pampa.** 3 Rivlin St. ☎ **02/231-455.** Appetizers NIS 8–30 ($2.40–$9); main courses NIS 16–70 ($4.80–$21). AE, DC, MC, V. Sun–Thurs noon–midnight; Fri noon–2pm; Sat after Sabbath. SOUTH AMERICAN.

With a special grill imported from Argentina, this new restaurant turns out tasty, barbecue meats, starting with reasonably priced takeaway steak, chicken or Argentinean sausage sandwiches on large rolls, and moving up market to main meals of barbecue chicken, salmon, delicious asado (order it with bones for more flavor), and filet mignon. You can add a skewer of grilled vegetables to balance the large portions of meat. The place is cozy, and in good weather there are outdoor tables on the mall (the nearby El Gaucho, which also does delicious South American–style steaks, has maddening accoustics in winter, when the indoor dining room is packed). The banana tortilla with rum is expensive at $6, but very delicious.

Sakura Japanese Restaurant. 31 Jaffa Rd., in the Feingold Courtyard. ☎ **02/235-464.** Appetizers NIS 9–22 ($2.70–$6.60); main courses NIS 36–50 ($11–$15); business lunches from NIS 28 ($8.50). AE, DC, MC, V. Mon–Thurs noon–4pm, 6:30pm–11:30pm; Fri noon–3pm; Sat after Sabbath. Closed Sun. KOSHER JAPANESE.

Designed to suggest a typical, small-town restaurant in Japan, Sakura is a pleasant new addition to the local restaurant choices, and a rare opportunity for kosher diners to experience Japanese cuisine. There are traditional first courses like miso soup and wakame salad, and a selection of main courses that includes tempura and soba noodle dishes, a sushi platter for one for $14.50, salmon teriyaki, and mixed sashimi.

It's in a courtyard reached by an alley to the left of Ocean restaurant on Rivlin Street, or from 31 Jaffa Rd.

Inexpensive

⑤ Amigos. 19 Yoel Salomon Mall. ☎ **02/234-177.** Reservations recommended for dinner. Appetizers NIS 12–20 ($3.60–$6); main courses NIS 30–42 ($9–$13). AE, MC, V. Sun–Thurs noon–midnight; Fri noon–3pm; Sat after Shabbat. KOSHER MEXICAN.

Kosher and Mexican cuisines may seem mutually exclusive, but Amigos serves up excellent versions of classics like tortilla soup, chili, tacos, and burritos, as well as margaritas that are works of iced sculpture. Filled with Israelis making excursions into the world of kosher quesadillas and Americans yearning for the taste of home, by late evening Amigos evolves into a Mexican-style bar. Salads and nonmeat fajitas make this a good place for vegetarians as well as omnivores. Complete luncheon specials, including the excellent fajitas, are $10.

✪ Cheese Cake. 23 Yoel Salomon Mall. ☎ **02/245-082.** Desserts NIS 14–24 ($4.20–$7.20); appetizers NIS 9–15 ($2.70–$4.50); main courses NIS 18–44 ($5.40–$13.20). AE, DC, MC, V; $10 minimum for credit cards. Sun–Thurs 9am–midnight; Fri 10:30am–2pm; Sat after Shabbat–1am. DESSERTS/VEGETARIAN MEALS.

Inside this 19th-century Jerusalem stone building, you'll find some of Israel's greatest cheesecakes (in 20 flavors), elaborate ice cream dishes, apple pies, and lavish brownies. A selection of hefty salads, quiches, and soups, and lasagne makes this an ideal spot for an afternoon or evening meal as well as for dessert. Enter through the restaurant's garden.

La Brasa. 7 Yoel Salomon Mall. ☎ **02/231-456** or **235-025.** Appetizers NIS 8–12 ($2.40–$3.60); main courses NIS 18–42 ($5.40–$13). No credit cards. Sun–Thurs 11am–1am; Fri 11am–1 hour before Shabbat; Sat after Shabbat–1am. SOUTH AMERICAN CHICKEN.

This bustling place offers the most delicious barbecued chicken in town, exquisitely seasoned and grilled to perfection over an open fire. A quarter of a chicken fresh off the fire with french fries and salad comes to just under $8; for the same price before 5:30pm, you'll get a soft drink as well. Other choices include quality hamburgers (the "extra" comes with a slab of smoked goose breast), sandwiches, and tasty empanadas, all served with your choice of Peruvian or chimichurri sauces. A whole chicken to take away is $13, and far fresher and more delicious than any take-out chicken you'd find in a local supermarket or delicatessen. There's a delivery service, including to hotels.

✪ **Misadonet.** 12 Yoel Salomon St. ☎ **02/248-396.** Appetizers NIS 12–20 ($3.60–$6); main courses NIS 28–40 ($8.60–$12). AE, DC, MC, V. Sun–Thurs 11am–11pm; Fri 11am–3pm; Sat after Sabbath. KURDISH.

This is one of the best ethnic restaurants in the country, located in a quaint 19th-century building, with its kitchen supervised by a wonderful Kurdish–Israeli matriarch who truly knows her stuff. Kubbeh, a kind of dumpling often made with a cracked wheat crust and stuffed with meat or vegetables, is the heart of Kurdish cuisine. Here a number of varieties are served as appetizers and in homemade soups that are delicate blends of many tastes. A specialty of the house is *anjesia*, a large meat kubbeh in an apricot-raisin sauce; the dish to die for is giri-giri, a rich creation of lamb hearts stuffed with rice, pine nuts, walnuts, and meat, served in a slightly curried sauce of apricot, walnuts, and raisins.

Look for the sign midway down Yoel Salomon Mall; Misadonet is in a courtyard off the mall.

✪ **Off the Square.** 6 Salomon St. ☎ **02/242-549.** Appetizers NIS 8–12 ($2.40–$3.60); main courses NIS 20–42 ($6–$12.60). AE, DC, MC, V. Sun–Thurs 9am–11pm; Fri 11am–3pm; Sat after Shabbat–midnight. GLATT KOSHER DAIRY.

A short block off Zion Square and down a passage on the right, this restaurant has become a Jerusalem institution, with an ever expanding menu of vegetarian, dairy, and fish choices all prepared within the bounds of strict glatt kosher standards. There are many other reasons for this place's popularity: great food, a friendly atmosphere, beautiful landmark building (one of the oldest outside the walls of the Old City) with many rustic dining rooms and a shaded patio for summer and Sukkot dining. The desserts are wonderful, including apple and pecan pies. You can have a vegetarian casserole or soup and salad for a modest price or you can have soup, fish, dessert, and wine, and spend two or three times as much. Whichever way, you will get your money's worth. There are special low-cholesterol dishes, and absolutely wonderful faux meat vegetarian creations including schnitzel and Middle Eastern kubbeh. No MSG is used. Beer and wine are served as well as herbal teas and milkshakes.

Shanty. 4 Nahalat Shiva. ☎ **02/243-434.** Appetizers and light meals NIS 14–30 ($4.20–$9); main courses NIS 25–45 ($7.50–$13.50). No credit cards. Sun–Thurs 7:30pm–after midnight; Fri 11am–3pm and 9:30pm–after midnight; Sat after Shabbat to after midnight. INTERNATIONAL/VEGETARIAN.

Located in the heart of the city's restored 19th-century restaurant district, the popular and trendy Shanty is a pub restaurant that keeps unusual hours and serves fresh, interesting food. You can have a simple Jerusalem-style country plate of toasted pita, zatar, fresh vegetables, and labaneh, or you can try Southeast Asian beef, chicken, or veggie patai; designer broccoli blintzes in a béchamel, garlic, and walnut sauce; spectacular salads filled with chunks of hot chicken or marinated livers; or South American beef asado in brandy and rosemary sauce. In good weather, when tables are set in the courtyard, this is a favorite spot for a salad, soup, and conversation. There is a full bar and good wine list.

Tmol Shilshom Bookstore Cafe. 5 Solomon St. ☎ **02/232-758.** Light meals NIS 12–25 ($3.60–$7.50); main courses NIS 22–36 ($6.60–$11). Sun–Thurs 8:30am–after midnight; Fri 8:30am–3pm. Closed Sat. VEGETARIAN/CAFE.

The bookshelved walls of this atmospheric retreat are lined with an eclectic collection of new and used books and magazines for sale, and Tmol Shilshom ("Yesterday and the Day Before") invites its patrons to read and browse, write letters, or just linger over coffee, soup, or salad. The background music is soft classical, folk, or jazz, and the place has become so popular that during meal times, customers may be asked to order something substantial. You can choose vegetarian chili, curry, quiches, or salmon as well as bagel and cream cheese with lox, or try the NIS 20-starving-artist deal of soup, salad, and a roll. Dishes are beautifully prepared, though portions are not generous. There are cakes, and a large array of wines, beers, and hot and cold drinks including such American treats as hot cider with cloves and cinnamon, and hot chocolate with a touch (or more) of brandy. Owner David Erlich, who modeled this bookstore after those he came to love in America, arranges a marvelous calendar of evening concerts, and readings in Hebrew, English, and other languages: Ask for a copy of the bookstore's monthly events.

From Jaffa Road, walk down the Yoel Solomon Mall; turn left into a covered alleyway beside the 8 Together Ceramics Gallery. Once in the courtyard, the cafe is at the far left and up a flight of outdoor stairs.

✪ **Yemenite Step.** 10 Salomon St. ☎ **02/240-477.** Reservations recommended for dinner. Appetizers NIS 8–20 ($2.40–$6); main courses NIS 20–31 ($6–$9.30). MC, V. Sun–Thurs noon–1am; Fri noon–3pm; Sat after Shabbat–1am. YEMENITE.

This place, which I consider the most special of the many interesting choices on Salomon Street, offers a chance to sample homestyle Yemenite cooking. The decor is unexotic, but there's a smattering of Yemenite artifacts and photographs. You can order Yemenite meat soup—a meal in itself—with homemade Yemenite bread ($5.30), or large, flaky, fried melawach pancake-like dishes served with spiced beef, chicken, or vegetables for $10 to $13. The spicy meat shaweeya, made partly with organ meats, is fabulous. There are also vegetable dishes and special, delicious Yemenite teas and coffees to try with dessert.

On & Off The Ben-Yehuda Street Mall

Along the Ben-Yehuda Street Mall, **Cafe Chagall** and the **Riveria Cafe** are the best spots for people-watching as well as pastry and coffee. A great cup of coffee, one of the best in town, can also be found two blocks away, at **Aroma**, on the corner of Hillel Street and Rabbi Akiva Street. It's a counter and a few tables, but in a short time it has become a Jerusalem institution. It is open daily from 7am to well after midnight, and may open round the clock as its reputation soars.

Moderate

Niss. 6 Hillel St. ☎ **02/233-880.** Appetizers NIS 14–33 ($4.20–$10); main courses NIS 36–63 ($11–$19). AE, DC, MC, V. Daily noon–midnight. CONTINENTAL/KURDISH.

This place started out as a Kurdish restaurant, but has slowly expanded into a continental restaurant as well, and has upgraded its decor accordingly to a sleek international look, with polished stone floors and elegant wrought-iron decorative touches. You can still order Kurdish first courses, like stuffed grape leaves with lemon juice and yogurt, but now you can go on to main courses such as grilled fish stuffed with pine nuts and garlic, as well as pasta, shrimp, and steak dishes, and of course, Kurdish specialties. There is a good selection of wines.

Inexpensive

✪ **Family Restaurant.** 23 Hillel St. ☎ **02/231-590.** In the arcade passageway that connects Hillel Street and Shammai Street, alongside the Orion Cinema. Appetizers NIS 6–11 ($1.80–$3.30); main dishes NIS 12–20 ($3.60–$6.60). MC, V. Sun–Thurs 8am–8pm; Fri 8am–2pm. Closed Sat. ISRAELI HOMESTYLE.

From the outside this looks like another hole-in-the-wall selling shashliks and mixed grill at its front window, but inside, you'll find a hot counter filled with a wonderful array of homestyle dishes that are a mixture of both East European and North African Jewish traditions. The best choices include fabulous fluffy potato-vegetable latkes; artichoke hearts stuffed with meat and served in a creamy lemon sauce; schnitzel stuffed with mushrooms; and house rice with raisins, pine nuts, and walnuts. Busiest at lunchtime when it may be hard to grab a table, you may find many items sold out by evening. Come at off-hours, ask for Itzik, and he'll let you put together a full meal with whatever seems most interesting to you for $9, coffee or tea included. The reasonably priced grilled meats are also quite good. Takeaway is 20% less.

✪ **Pepperoni's.** 4 Rabbi Akiva St. ☎ **02/257-829.** Antipasto buffet NIS 22 ($6.60); buffet plus full meal starting at NIS 38 ($12); lunch special NIS 33 ($10). AE, DC MC, V. Daily noon–midnight. ITALIAN/MEDITERRANEAN.

As you enter this rustic 19th-century Jerusalem stone building, you are greeted with a bountiful selection of more than 20 wonderful appetizers and salads that are brought to your table (as much as you like) by your waitress, along with a cutting board filled with sausages, cheeses, breads, and fresh vegetables, all included in the fixed price of your meal. The ever-changing choices are done with a fine touch and lots of fresh herbs: potato salad in a cold yogurt and dill dressing; spicy Sephardic-style carrot salad; roasted pepper with hummus beans, parsley, and onion; or baked and smoked eggplant casserole. After grazing on these robust country starters, it's hard to believe the main course is yet to come. You choose from at least a dozen interesting daily specials, or, for a small surcharge, select from some extra special choices. An apéritif on the house starts out your feast! Though it's often busy, this is a great place for a leisurely meal.

✪ **Spaghettim.** 8 Rabbi Akiva St. ☎ **02/235-547.** Appetizers NIS 10–15 ($3–$4.50); spaghetti NIS 18–38 ($5.20–$12). AE, DC, MC, V. Daily noon–1am. ITALIAN.

This bustling new restaurant hit (one of my favorites) holds forth in the spacious arched-ceiling rooms of one of the city's great 19th-century mansions. Antipasto, salad, and soups here are hefty and filled with fresh herbs. The spaghetti is al dente and served with your choice of more than 50 sauces, also filled with fresh herbs and vegetables, and divided into three categories based on tomatoes, olive oil, or cream. My favorites are pollo zingara (sliced breast of chicken, peppers, fresh mushrooms, garlic, hot chili, and red wine), and bianco (peas, lemon, dill, garlic, and hot chili). Ostrich meat in a red wine hunter's sauce of fresh mushrooms and cream and the frutti di mare are among the more unusual choices. For dessert, or as a meal in itself, you might want to try one of the sweet spaghettis, ranging from arancio (fresh orange, butter, cream, and liqueur) to chocolate or poppyseed. Imported and Israeli wines are available, there is a garden terrace for dining in good weather, a no-smoking section, and on Friday afternoon until 6pm there is music, dancing, and an all-you-can-eat buffet with wine for $11.

☉ **Village Green.** 10 Ben-Yehuda Mall. ☎ **02/252-007.** Full meals NIS 20–30 ($6–$8). MC, V. Sun–Thurs 11:30am–10pm; Fri 11:30am–3pm. Closed Sat. VEGETARIAN CAFETERIA.

Managers Barry and Kobi have put their hearts and talents into making this one of Israel's best vegetarian choices, with big portions and absolutely delicious food. Grab a tray, and proceed to the counter, where English-speaking staff will explain the changing array of freshly baked vegetable pies in whole-wheat crusts, quiches, lasagnes, buckwheat burgers, and grilled tofu served with herbs or with spicy peanut sauce. Full meals come with your choice of a custom-designed salad, steamed vegetables, and brown rice or soup, and a selection of great breads and dressings. Fridays at lunchtime the bread counter often includes a special salad or pasta you are welcome to sample for free! Some macrobiotic foods are offered, but this is not mainly a health/natural foods restaurant. Microwave ovens are used.

There is a quieter branch of Village Green in the Old Bezalel Art School building at 1 Bezalel St. (☎ 251-464). Prices and menus are the same. Excellent homemade cakes at both places are NIS 10 ($3).

To find the restaurant, enter the garden to the Kamin Restaurant, bear right, and follow the signs to the back of the building.

Kamin. 4 Rabbi Akiva St. ☎ **02/256-428.** Appetizers NIS 12–30 ($3.60–$9); main courses NIS 24–46 ($7.20–$13.80). DC, MC, V. Sun–Fri 10am–midnight; Sat 1pm–midnight. CONTINENTAL.

In summer especially, this old stone house and candlelit garden terrace is the perfect spot for a relaxed, romantic meal with wine. Here you can get a steak as well as good fish dishes and special creations like boneless breast of chicken in honey sauce, or vegetarian pies and pastas. Main courses include potato, vegetable, and salad, and there are interesting appetizers.

To get there from Hillel Street, roughly parallel to Ben-Yehuda Street, you'll come to Ron Cinema, on the corner of Rabbi Akiva Street. Turn here; it's about 100 feet on the right, behind a garden hedge.

ON & OFF KING GEORGE V AVENUE

Expensive

✪ **Arcadia.** 10 Agrippas St. ☎ **02/249-138.** Reservations recommended. Appetizers NIS 25–36 ($7.50–$11); main courses NIS 65–80 ($19.70–$24); luncheon specials and fixed-price menus. AE, MC, V. Mon–Sat noon–3pm and 7pm–10:30pm. Closed Sun. In the lane between 63 Jaffa Rd. and 8 Agrippas St. FRENCH/MEDITERRANEAN RIM.

This new little hideaway has atmosphere, charm, and delicious food, and it offers the chance to have a light meal (such as a fabulous quiche and salad) as well as the usual major meal one orders at a top-quality restaurant. There are two sections to Arcadia: the first for simpler meals, the other for more formal dining. Arcadia has become a favorite of young professionals with expensive tastes but moderate budgets, as well as those looking for an exquisite but not overwhelming meal. The French/Mediterranean Rim menu is done with a light, inventive touch. Among the cold first courses, you'll find a heavenly terrine of salmon served with a dill sauce based on fragrant, home-pressed olive oil (the terrine of eggplant with goat cheese is also fine), or calamari with virgin olive oil and fresh herbs; goose liver sautéed in balsamic vinegar and onion jam is one of the warm first courses. Fish is done simply and beautifully here: Look for red snapper with beet vinaigrette and ginger oil, or grilled shrimp in saffron sauce. Meat dishes include interpretations of classics, as well as robust creations like sautéed veal with shrimps, peppers, and risotto. The pastry chef does wonderful things, from shrimp tarts to quiche and onward to the desserts. The wine list is especially good. Arcadia is set in 19th-century arched-ceiling rooms beside a courtyard garden, away from the bustle of the downtown restaurant district, and is reached through an offbeat little lane.

Cezanne. In the Jerusalem Artists' House, 12 Shmuel Ha-Nagid St. ☎ **02/259-459.** Appetizers NIS 18–48 ($5.30–$14.40); main courses NIS 42–65 ($11.70–19.50). AE, DC, MC, V. Daily noon–4pm and 6pm–midnight. FRENCH.

Praised by many Frommer's readers, Cezanne is famous for its filet mignon, which you can order in a number of styles, ranging from the simplest to a filet with mushroom and pigeon stuffing served in a horseradish and lime sauce. Main courses are so large that you may want to share or forgo an appetizer, and lightness of preparation is not part of Cezanne's style. Goose liver in calvados sauce, breast of quail and goose livers in port wine, and Jordan mushrooms with cream and roquefort cheese are among the first-course choices; in addition to steaks, second courses range from grilled shrimp with smoked goose breast en brochette to a simple breast of chicken cooked in cider. Be warned that the kitchen at times seems a bit heavy on salt. Without being pretentious or glitzy, this is a place where you can enjoy good food in a leisurely atmosphere. There are often $20 fixed-price dinners, making Cezanne a relatively moderate splurge.

✪ **Cow on the Roof Restaurant.** In the Sheraton Jerusalem Plaza Hotel, 47 King George V Ave. ☎ **02/259-111.** Reservations required. Appetizers $5.50–$20; main courses $22–$32; special fixed-price dinners offered. All prices in U.S. dollars only. Add 15% VAT; service charge included. AE, DC, MC, V. Sun–Thurs 7–11pm. FRENCH.

Shalom Kadosh, the world's most renowned kosher chef, is the moving spirit behind this elegant establishment, where service matches the high standards of the extraordinary menu. Kadosh (who is observant, and eats only kosher food) spends several weeks each year visiting the kitchens of the greatest French chefs outside Israel, and has devised ways to translate the creations he finds on his travels into dishes that can be prepared within the bounds of glatt kosher restrictions. As if this were not a tour de force in itself, Kadosh has also created a repertoire of his own elegant creations, all in the classic French tradition, but often with a touch of Mediterranean Rim and Israeli elements as well. Presentation is another element of Kadosh's style: Each plate is served with visual imagination and grace. This is a rare opportunity for even those with glatt kosher requirements to experience French cuisine at a high level of excellence.

Fink's Bar Restaurant. 2 Ha-Histadrut St. ☎ **02/234-523.** Reservations recommended evenings. Appetizers NIS 15–170 ($4.50–$51); main courses NIS 45–140 ($13.50–$42). AE, V. Sat–Thurs 6pm–after midnight; closed Fri. CONTINENTAL.

This is a Jerusalem legend, and the oldest of all West Jerusalem's restaurants. A quick early-evening visit may make you wonder what all the fuss is about; however, what appears to be a small middle-class American bar with a few tables on the side offers an amazingly lengthy, beautifully prepared menu and knowledgeable service that has kept its clientele of political leaders, statesmen, artists, writers, and travelers-in-the-know coming back for over half a century. A recent addition to Fink's legend was Peter Arnett and the CNN news team, who decided to celebrate the end of the Gulf War here, and phoned in by satellite from Baghdad to make the reservation. You can order Russian caviar, a sliced avocado salad, or chateaubriand for two; whatever you want, Fink's will provide. The bar (with a range of offerings beyond belief) is the best stocked in the country, and can be an interesting spot for evening encounters. It's located off King George V Avenue near Ben-Yehuda.

Mishkenot Sha'ananim Restaurant. Yemin Moshe (below the Windmill). ☎ **02/251-043** or **254-469.** Reservations recommended. Appetizers NIS 50–80 ($15–$24); main courses from NIS 66 ($20); business lunch $29. AE, DC, MC, V. Daily 11am–1am. Bus: No. 5, 18, or 21 to Liberty Bell/Bloomfield Garden; take staircase street from the Yemin Moshe Windmill. FRENCH/CONTINENTAL.

Located in the beautifully restored 19th-century Yemin Moshe neighborhood, with vistas of the walls of the Old City from its windows, this restaurant is on the itinerary of most VIP visitors. Moise Peer has created a classic French restaurant that derives extra pomp from its inspiring views, formal service, museumlike wine cellar, and culinary standards. Duckling and foie gras are mainstays; in addition to duck à l'orange, the duckling Paradise with figs is recommended, as are the tournedos Rossini (cuts of filet steak on a bed of artichoke hearts covered with truffles and a Madeira-based sauce) and the exotically flavored salmon trout. Tables are not really set up to take advantage of the view, which is wonderful by day, but somewhat lost at night. The wine list is extensive.

Moderate

Ten Li Chow at the Mill. 8 Ramban St. ☎ **02/665-956.** Reservations recommended on weekends. Appetizers NIS 9–36 ($2.70–$11); main courses NIS 22–55 ($6.60–$16.70). AE, MC, V. Sun–Thurs 12:30–10:30pm; Sat an hour after Shabbat–10:30pm. GLATT KOSHER CHINESE.

When the traditions of kosher and Chinese cuisines meet, results are not always perfect, but at Ten Li Chow, my favorite glatt kosher Chinese–Thai restaurant, you'll find vegetarian dishes in a variety of regional styles and wonderful chicken, beef, veal, and duck dishes. Ten Li Chow is spacious, and comfortable yet understated, and the Thai staff is especially skillful and hospitable. Kosher Chinese restaurants cost more than nonkosher ones, but in this case you get your money's worth. A fine pupu platter is $9 per person; the business lunch is $13. For sushi lovers, Ten Li Chow is planning Israel's first glatt kosher sushi bar; call ahead to see if it's in place.

Inexpensive

✪ **Besograyim.** 45 Ussishkin St. ☎ **02/245-353.** Appetizers NIS 14–25 ($4.20–$7.50); main courses NIS 23–44 ($7–$13.20). No credit cards. Sun–Thurs 9am–midnight; Fri 9am–3pm; Sat after Shabbat–midnight. VEGETARIAN AND FISH.

Located a few blocks from the Ben-Yehuda triangle, in a late-Victorian stone bungalow surrounded by a shady dining terrace, Besograyim is a vegetarian and dairy restaurant that has real charm and wonderful food. I recommend the marvelous soups, including Argentinean gazpacho, the very hefty, inventive salads, vegetarian pies served with salad, and the special salmon steak served in a creamy house sauce. For dessert, you can choose from a large variety of homemade cakes and pastries in the $3 range. There is often live music on Wednesday and Thursday evenings.

AGRIPPAS STREET & MAHANE YEHUDA

Walk up Agrippas Street a few blocks and you'll reach Mahane Yehuda, Jerusalem's lively fresh-produce market. You'll find yourself surrounded by no-frills restaurants and holes-in-the-walls serving generous portions of grilled meats, shashlik (chunks of meat on a skewer), and kebabs (which in Israel consist of ground meat on a skewer).

Inexpensive

Hashipudia. 6 Ha-Shikma St. ☎ **02/254-036.** Appetizers NIS 7–13 ($2–$4); main courses NIS 10–42 ($3–$13); complete lunch specials noon–5pm NIS 24 ($7.20). AE, DC, MC, V. Sun–Thurs noon–midnight; Sat after Shabbat–midnight; closed Fri. MIDDLE EASTERN.

Shipudia means "skewer," and this restaurant specializes in skewers of beef or lamb, chicken hearts and livers, chicken or goose breast, and that pièce de résistance of skewered meats, goose liver. Most of the skewers are in the $2 to $6 range, and come with your choice of two side dishes. You can put together the combination of your choice, and as an added treat, Hashipudia makes wonderful fresh Iraqi pita bread each evening in a traditional oven for its customers! A lunch special of salad or soup, main course, baklava, and tea or coffee is offered for $7.20. A full range of economically priced soups, stuffed vegetables, steaks, chops, and fish makes this one of the best restaurant choices in the Agrippas Street neighborhood.

To find it, head west on Agrippas Street; Ha-Shikma Street is a right turn after the market.

🆂 **Sammi's.** 80 Agrippas St. ☎ **02/250-985.** Appetizers NIS 7–10 ($2–$3); main courses NIS 17–36 ($5–$11). No credit cards. Sun–Thurs 11am–midnight; Fri 11am–3pm; Sat after Shabbat–midnight. MIDDLE EASTERN.

Sammi's is the newly opened challenger to Sima's, its across-the-street neighbor and longtime Agrippas Street champion in the mixed-grill category. There are partisans on both sides: Sammi's, with its polished marble floors and walls and adequate seating, has certainly elevated the mixed grill to a new standard of elegance, and because of the furious competition, you may even be allowed to order a hefty small-size mixed-grill sandwich ($5.70) and eat it at a table, although the rules of Agrippas Street eateries do not seem to permit you to receive a plate unless you order a meal (your sandwich comes in a paper bag). Steaks, kebabs, schnitzels, and salads are all excellent. Prices include pita, olives, and pickled vegetables.

Ⓢ **Sima's.** 82 Agrippas St. No listed phone. Appetizers NIS 7–10 ($2.10–$3); main courses NIS 17–36 ($5–$11). No credit cards. Sun–Thurs 9am–11pm; Fri 9am–1pm; Sat after Shabbat–midnight. MIDDLE EASTERN.

Sima's is one of the best places on the street, justly admired for its wonderfully seasoned and legendary mixed grill, which comes with chips, salad, bread, and condiments for about $10.50. Sima's is often mobbed, so the take-out mixed-grill sandwiches are a good bet. You must order a platter meal rather than a sandwich in order to qualify for table service at busy times.

NEAR THE YMCA & KING DAVID HOTEL
Expensive

Bistro. Laromme Hotel. 3 Jabotinsky St. ☎ **02/756-666.** Appetizers NIS 20–36 ($6–$10); main courses NIS 60–90 ($18–$27). AE, DC, MC, V. Dinner only Sun–Thurs 7pm–10:30pm; Sat after Shabbat. Closed Fri. CONTINENTAL.

The famous attraction here is the house specialty, meat fondue bourguignonne prepared at tableside with a variety of sauces and dressings, a pleasant way to enjoy a rich, leisurely dinner (the additional à la carte menu is good but small). Your meal might begin with a tiny plate of chef's creations, such as a poached quail egg with a jam of onion, sweet wine, and grenadine. The variety of meats offered for fondue are first quality, enough to please a real meat eater, and easily shared by two, if ordered with a salad, fresh vegetables, or a classic first course. Bistro is comfortable and dignified, with attentive, formal service, and musicians in attendance (the classical guitarist is superb); it is a standout among kosher and hotel restaurant choices.

Moderate

Le Tsriff, the Pie House Restaurant at the YMCA. 26 King David St. ☎ **02/246-521.** Reservations recommended evenings. Appetizers NIS 14–28 ($4.20–$8.30); main courses NIS 36–70 ($11–$21.30). AE, DC, MC, V. Daily 8am–midnight. CONTINENTAL.

The gracious dining room here is decorated in the Islamic art deco style of the British Mandate, with an Ottoman Turkish fireplace and French doors leading out to the terrace. The menu ranges from vegetable, meat, and shrimp pies (in the menu's lower price range) to very pricey fish and steak dinners. There is also a complete wine list. In good weather dining on the terrace is a Jerusalem tradition; there are often $10 fixed-price meals, as well as light lunch, and dessert and coffee choices served only on the outdoor terrace. There's a less expensive and less elegant branch at Hyrcanos Street.

SOUTH JERUSALEM
GERMAN COLONY & BAKA
Inexpensive

Caffit. 35 Emek Refaim St. ☎ **02/635-284.** Light meals NIS 15–25 ($4.50–$7.50); main courses NIS 25–33 ($7.50–$10). DC, MC, V. Sun–Thurs 7am–1am; Fri 7am–2pm; Sat after Shabbat. Bus: 4, 14, or 18. CAFE.

With its busy garden terrace, this is the main watering hole for the gentrified German Colony. Breakfasts are served, and the large salads with a basket of rolls and herb butter are popular. Pastas, crepes, bagels and lox, and vegetable pies round out the menu. Because people come here to sit and talk, there's a large selection of cakes, crepes, ice cream, wines, and alcoholic beverages.

Da La Thien Chinese Restaurant. 34 Derekh Bet Lehem (Baka). ☎ **02/732-432.** Appetizers NIS 10–22 ($3–$6.60); main courses NIS 22–55 ($6.60–$16.50). MC, V. Mon–Fri noon–3pm and 6:30–11pm; Sat noon–10pm. Closed Sun. Bus: 5 or 21 to first stop on Derekh Bet Lehem; then walk back two long blocks toward the town center; Da La Thien is opposite a service station. NONKOSHER CHINESE.

This bungalow, from the British Mandate period, is considered by some to house the best nonkosher Chinese restaurant in town. It is open on Shabbat, and there is a wide selection of chicken, seafood, pork, and beef dishes.

Te'enim Vegetarian Cuisine. 21 Emek Refaim St. (German Colony). ☎ **02/630-048.** Appetizers NIS 15–28 ($4.50–$8.30); main courses NIS 20–30 ($6–$9). No credit cards. Sun–Thurs 8am–11pm; Fri 8am–2pm. INTERNATIONAL VEGETARIAN.

Owner Patrick Melki, who comes from the south of France, has designed the menu of this neighborhood vegetarian restaurant with real style. Each night of the week, in addition to the standard fare, there is a special dinner from a different part of the world—for example, Monday is vegetarian sushi night; Tuesday, Indonesian gado; Thursday, pasta; Friday, couscous; and Sunday is Chinese cuisine. Salads, too, are excellent, ranging from Mediterranean classics to Chinese. Oven-baked tofu in a variety of styles, as well as marinated grilled tofu dishes, are also a house specialty. The desserts are homemade and each choice just a bit original. The carrot cake is both light and divine.

HEBRON ROAD

The magnificent hillside overlooking the Old City has developed a number of lively restaurants and cafes. To get to this neighborhood, take bus no. 5, 6, 7, 8, 21, or 48 to the railroad station, or bus no. 4, 14, or 18 and ask for the stop nearest the Cinémathèque.

Expensive

Taverna. 2 Nomi Street at the Sherover Promenade, Abu Tor. ☎ **02/719-716.** Reservations required. Appetizers NIS 25–40 ($7.50–$12); main courses NIS 75–95 ($22.50–$28.50); 13% service is added to each bill. AE, DC, MC, V. Lunch Mon–Sat noon–3pm; tea, coffee, and cake Mon–Sat noon–6pm; dinner Mon–Sat 7pm–10:30pm. Bus: 7, 8, 21, or 48 to Hebron Road and Nomi Street in Abu Tor. CONTINENTAL.

The Sherover Foundation has been responsible for the creation of the beautiful stone Tayeled, or Promenade, that winds along the hillsides and vista points south of the Old City. The Taverna is also a special project of the Sherover Foundation. At the southern terminus of the Promenade, a beautiful new glass and stone pavilion with terraces overlooking the Judean mountains has been built to house what is hoped will be a landmark among the country's restaurants. Taverna's chef is Swiss; although the heart of his menu is classic, there's also a touch of both rustic and regional Mediterranean styles. First-course choices range from a delicate vegetable carpaccio with ricotta querelle, to a robust dish of calamari grilled with garlic, tomato, and herbs; the cold vichyssoise is especially good. Main courses include rabbit stewed in red wine, Italian herbs, and served with homemade gnocchi; lamb chops Provençal grilled to perfection; and Palamida served in the spicy Moroccan style. So that visitors of all budget ranges may enjoy the beauty of the site, the Sherover Foundation has arranged for Taverna to open for afternoon tea, coffee, and cakes (around $8) from 3 to 6pm. Businesses, organizations, and tour groups are booking Taverna as the preeminent

Street Meals

Felafel & Shwarma   The best of Jerusalem's ubiquitous felafel spots are concentrated in three places. My favorite is on the corner of Agrippas Street and the wide uncovered pedestrian street of the Mahane Yehuda market (on your right as you walk up Agrippas Street from King George: It's the first broad market street past the covered market area). Here you'll find two **side-by-side felafel counters** offering well-spiced felafel fritters, and all kinds of salads, pickled vegetables, sauces, and condiments. For a bit extra, you can ask for your felafel to be wrapped inside an enormous Iraqi pita instead of a plain-pocket pita, which makes for a very filling meal. Best of all, you can carry your sandwich across Agrippas Street, and through one of the entrance portals to the old Nahalot neighborhood, where you'll find a small playground with benches. There, under the scrutiny of the local cats, you can sit down and enjoy your meal, while absorbing a feel for this picturesque part of town. (Bring your own napkins.) This park is also a good place to bring a take-out mixed-grill sandwich from **Sima's** or **Sammi's** farther down Agrippas Street. I always like to slice a few little plum or cherry tomatoes from the market into my mixed-grill takeout sandwiches.

At the corner of Agrippas and King George Streets, you'll find a large and very busy **felafel and shwarma place** with mountainous displays of chopped salads. Here you'll have to eat standing on the sidewalk, like a normal Israeli, but without the local skill of not dripping felafel sauce all over yourself and having half your sandwich land in the gutter. The felafels are average, but the spot is convenient, open until 10pm or later from Sunday to Thursday, and the turnover is fast, which usually ensures freshness. My favorite place for felafel and shwarma sandwiches in the Ben-Yehuda–King George Street area is **Moshiko's** on the Ben-Yehuda Mall. The quality is good, the portions excellent, and if you can grab an outdoor table, you can people-watch while you dine.

On the north side of Hanevi'im Street, opposite its intersection with Havatzelet Street, you'll find two places selling what many Jerusalemites consider the **best felafel in town.** See if you agree with the experts. A favorite with students, these counters offer no place to sit down, but you can shelter indoors in bad weather.

Kubbehs   Makeem at 44 Agrippas St. is famous for its Iraqi meat or hummus-stuffed kubbehs, served from its streetside window, each for less than $2. Be sure to order yours heated in the oven.

place for formal, quality meals, but it may be a while until the reputation and clientele of this new endeavor really crystalizes. Special luncheon menus range from $25 to $30. The crème brûlée is fabulous.

Inexpensive

✪ **Cacao.** At the Cinémathèque, Hebron Road. ☎ **02/710-632.** Appetizers NIS 15–30 ($4.50–$9); main courses NIS 22–40 ($6.60–$12). No credit cards. Daily 10am–after midnight. ITALIAN/MEDITERRANEAN.

With dazzling vistas of the Old City walls, Mount Zion, and the ancient City of David, the terrace of the Cinémathèque is one of the city's absolute musts for a meal or coffee and dessert from late April until November (and whenever the weather is warm enough in winter). The staff lets the freshest vegetables, the finest herbs, and wonderful breads and cheeses speak for themselves. You can feast on a range of large

Bagels   Bonkers Bagels, 41 Jaffa Rd. (☎ 244-115), right at Zion Square, sells a variety of freshly made bagels ranging from onion, garlic, and whole wheat to cheese bagels for NIS 2 (60¢) a piece. They're more breadlike than traditional American bagels, but they're tasty. Bonkers has a number of choices for sandwiches, starting with bagel and cream cheese in assorted flavors. It's open Sunday to Thursday 24 hours, on Friday until 2pm, and on Saturday after Shabbat.

Burekas   The block of shops on Hanevi'im Street opposite Havatzelet Street includes a **bakery with a sidewalk window** counter where you can order fresh-from-the-oven potato, spinach, or cheese burekas, as well as miniature cheese or fruit Danish-style pastries. You can find burekas throughout the city, but they're always more of a treat when fresh. The Mahane Yehuda market is another good place for freshly baked burekas.

Fresh Roasted Nuts   Yaavetz Street, a small pedestrian passageway running between Jaffa Road (half a block east of King George Street) and the Ben Hillel Street section of the Ben-Yehuda Mall complex, offers two shops selling absolutely the best fresh-roasted nuts in town. My favorite is the shop at the far end of the street from Jaffa Road, just at the foot of the steps leading up to the Ben-Yehuda Mall. Prices on the signs are usually quoted for 1 kilo; divide by 10, and you'll have the price for 100 grams, which is a reasonable-size bag for one person to carry around on a day's sightseeing. A delicious bag of peanuts is fortifying.

Hamburgers   Just a few steps out of Zion Square toward the Old City, **MacDavid** at 40 Jaffa Rd. (☎ 252-989), is the most visible of Israeli burger chains. A full meal costs NIS 13 ($4.20). This branch of the MacDavid chain is kosher.

Pizza   Most of what is available in Jerusalem is comparatively unimaginative and rubbery, adorned with a few pieces of olives, mushrooms, or a sprinkling of canned vegetables; choices are all vegetarian. On a Ben-Yehuda Pedestrian Mall side street, **Apple Pizza** at 13 Dorot Rishonim St. (☎ 233-888), wistfully named for the Big Apple, is one of the better choices. The kosher lemehedrin **Pizza Home at the Savion Hut,** 1 Ben Maimon Blvd., at the corner of Derekh Aza in Rehavia (☎ 618-111), is open Sunday to Thursday from 11am to 1am, on Friday from 11am to 2:30pm, and on Saturday nights after Shabbat. It also offers a lower-calorie and-cholesterol creation called pizzalite. A medium pizza is NIS 33 ($10), and Pizza Home will deliver to your hotel room; ask about delivery charges when you order.

country salads and an order of freshly baked focaccia bread (served with fresh herbs and olive oil, and highly recommended), or try the soups, elephantine bagels, home-made pastas, and excellent peasant sandwiches. Fresh salmon and trout, very moderately priced, are among the real gems of the menu. Desserts here are refined rather than hardy, and include a thick, pure chocolate cake made with no flour. Jazz players and other musicians perform on Tuesdays after 9:30pm; a full bar with a good array of wines completes the picture.

Pesto. Khan Building, Remez Street. ☎ **02/719-602.** Reservations recommended. Appetizers NIS 14–25 ($4.20–$7.50); main courses NIS 25–50 ($7.50–$15). AE, DC, MC, V. Daily noon–midnight. Bus: 4, 7, 8, 14, 18, 21, or 48 to Khan/Train Station stop. ITALIAN.

Located on the upper floor of an old stone caravanserai from Ottoman times now used as a club and for small concerts, this good, nonkosher Italian restaurant is open on the Sabbath; unlike kosher Italian restaurants, Pesto can mix milk and meat, so you can order traditional dishes like chicken parmigiana and lasagne with meat. Pastas are served with traditional sauces as well as with such house creations as a sauce of liver, cream, and vodka. In good weather, the restaurant spills out onto a broad terrace overlooking the khan's courtyard, and is a picturesque spot for a leisurely meal.

Promenade Café. Haas Promenade (Tayelet). ☎ **02/732-513.** Appetizers NIS 12–20 ($3.60–$6); main courses NIS 25–40 ($7.50–$12). No credit cards. Daily 9am–midnight. Bus: 8 or 48 from Jaffa Road. CAFETERIA.

The great overview of Jerusalem from the Haas Promenade, or Tayelet, comes with its own cafeteria–restaurant, as well as out-of-the-way spots on the grass where you can bring your own picnic. Just before twilight is an especially nice time to come as the Old City and the Judean Hills sink into a powdery mysteriousness. The Promenade Café is not up to the view, but you'll find light meals and less expensive main courses at the self-service section in the $5–$11 range and desserts and a beer or wine for under $3.

THE WESTERN EDGE OF THE CITY
MODERATE

Kohinoor. In the Holiday Inn Crown Plaza (formerly Hilton) Hotel. ☎ **02/581-367.** Reservations recommended. Appetizers NIS 10–28 ($3–$6); main courses NIS 22–55 ($6.60–$16.50); luncheon buffet NIS 45 ($13.50) plus 10% service. AE, DC, MC, V. Sun–Thurs noon–4pm and 6pm–midnight; Fri noon–4pm; Sat after Shabbat–midnight. KOSHER INDIAN.

With its black-lacquered Queen Anne chairs, decorative Southeast Asian artifacts, and attentive service, this kosher branch of Tel Aviv's famous Tandoori Restaurant creates a graceful atmosphere of Anglo-Indian elegance. Kohinoor offers a sumptuous and very affordable luncheon buffet that is a pleasure for all visitors, and a unique chance for travelers who are kosher to become acquainted with one of the world's great cuisines. For those who are not accustomed to Indian food, the staff will be happy to tone down the seasonings to moderate levels.

NORTH JERUSALEM
EXPENSIVE

Valentino's. Hyatt Regency Hotel, 32 Lehi Street. ☎ **02/331-234.** Antipasti buffet and complete pasta dinner NIS 75–90 ($22.50–$27); main courses NIS 75–90 ($22.50–$27). AE, DC, MC, V. Dinner only Sun–Thurs 7–11pm; Sat after Shabbat–11:30pm. Bus: 4. ITALIAN/MEDITERRANEAN RIM.

With the arrival of Gary Rosen, an immigrant from Australia, as executive chef here, Valentino's has skyrocketed past most other hotel competition in Jerusalem. The menu has already expanded into a touch of Asian and Pacific Rim exoticism; during the coming year, Rosen plans to move the restaurant further away from its original Italian theme. The heart of the restaurant remains the very enjoyable fixed-price dinner, which includes all you can eat from the wonderful assorted antipasti table plus your choice of up to three homemade pasta dishes, plus a choice from the dessert buffet. The antipasti buffet is always fun, with a combination of Italian, country Mediterranean, and inventive choices. Because Valentino's is kosher, there are no meat dishes, and everything depends on fresh ingredients and light preparation. Clay oven–baked fish, and grilled, exotically seasoned salmon are some of the current à la carte choices. The restaurant has flair, but the country-style menu and the buffet service make for a relaxed, easygoing atmosphere.

EAST JERUSALEM
EXPENSIVE

✪ **American Colony Hotel.** Off Nablus Road. ☎ **02/279-777.** Reservations recommended. Saturday luncheon buffet meal $28 plus VAT. AE, DC, MC, V. Sat noon–3pm. CONTINENTAL/ MIDDLE EASTERN.

In East Jerusalem, the legendary Saturday luncheon buffet at the atmospheric American Colony Hotel offers a truly marvelous feast in its Arabesque Room. The meal includes as much as you like of the soup, salads, fish, chicken, lamb, and beef dishes (as well as coffee and desserts); a whole chilled salmon, rich and beautifully prepared, is usually the masterpiece of the spread. For a touch of local flavor, a portion of the buffet is made up of Middle Eastern dishes. This is a great place to dine after spending Saturday morning in the bazaars of the Old City. The ambience, simple yet mildly exotic, harks back to the way quality was done in what we now consider the romantic days of the British Empire. For other meals, the American Colony Hotel is less exceptional. Unusually fine live music is an Arabesque Room tradition that was suspended during the Intifada; it's worth checking to see if the musicians (especially the pianist) have returned.

MODERATE

National Palace Restaurant. In the National Palace Hotel, corner of Az-Zahra and El-Masudi streets. ☎ **02/273-273.** Reservations recommended. Appetizers NIS 7–20 ($2.10–$6); main courses NIS 35–50 ($10.60–$15). AE, DC, MC, V. Daily noon–midnight. MIDDLE EASTERN.

I heartily recommend this restaurant, which has great food and a pleasant dining room decorated with Palestinian crafts on the glassed-in roof level of the hotel. It's best reached by taxi from West Jerusalem.

The menu lists all sorts of things, but in Arabic restaurants clients can depend a great deal on the waiter: Ask what's good and fresh, what he recommends, how it's prepared. For the main course, try shish kebab, grilled liver, grilled spring chicken, or grilled mutton marinated in yogurt and served over rice. For dessert, have burma (toasted shredded wheat, stuffed with pistachios and soaked in honey), or baklava, or a crème caramel (flan). Wine is about $12 a bottle, but to do it in truly Middle Eastern style, order a small bottle of arak (an anise-flavored brandy similar to pastis, ouzo, or anisette; Golden Arak is the best). Mix it with water to taste (about half and half), over ice, and sip it slowly during the meal. It's powerful, wonderful stuff!

✪ **Philadelphia Restaurant.** 9 Az-Zahra St. ☎ **02/289-770.** Reservations recommended. Appetizers NIS 6–25 ($1.80–$7.50); main courses NIS 30–55 ($9–$16.50). No credit cards. Daily noon–midnight. Az-Zahra Street is a right turn off Nablus Road coming from Damascus Gate. MIDDLE EASTERN.

This is one of the best of East Jerusalem's restaurants; its formula for success is excellent, moderately priced Arabic food served in a cozy, slightly fancy environment. Menus are printed in Arabic, English, and Hebrew. Start with a rich, savory lentil soup, go on to stuffed peppers or lamb chops, and finish up with baklava. Be aware that another unrelated restaurant has opened in West Jerusalem under the same name, so make certain you get to the right place.

5

What to See & Do in Jerusalem

Jerusalem possesses much that is striking and beautiful, but more than most great destinations, it demands a sense of vision as well as eyesight. In the Hebrew language, you do not say you will "go to Jerusalem." The idiom is to "ascend" or "go up" to the city. It is not merely the city's altitude that is alluded to in this phrase.

Jerusalem today is adorned with an enticing network of museums, concerts, and performances, as well as with the archeological treasures of its past, almost miraculously rediscovered and displayed in ways that interact with the daily life of the city. There are three main sightseeing areas in Jerusalem: inside the Old City's walls, downtown East Jerusalem, and West Jerusalem, the "New City."

SUGGESTED ITINERARIES

Day 1 Visit the Old City markets and the Jewish Quarter, the Western Wall, the Temple Mount, and the Church of the Holy Sepulcher. Catch the view from the roof of the Petra Hotel inside the Jaffa Gate.

Day 2 Spend at least a half day at the Israel Museum. Stroll through downtown West Jerusalem and ultrareligious Mea Shearim in late afternoon or early evening.

Day 3 Visit the Yad VaShem Holocaust Memorial. Spend some time exploring West Jerusalem and some of the sites in East Jerusalem.

Days 4 and 5 Your choice depends on your interests: many will want to visit nearby Bethlehem for a morning; others will want to see the archeological digs near the Temple Mount or visit Hadassah Hospital or the Hebrew University. The Old City is always worth extra time.

1 The Old City

The Old City, also called *Ir Ha-Kodesh* or the holy city, is enclosed by a 40-foot-high wall. The wall is at least 400 years old (some portions, in fact, date back more than 2,000 years), built by Suleiman the Magnificent and repaired several times since.

There are eight gates in the Old City fortress wall. Main gates into the wall are the Jaffa Gate, entered from Mamilla-Agron Street or

Jaffa Road, and the Damascus Gate, entered from Ha-Nevi'im or Nablus Road. Israelis call Damascus Gate Sha'ar Shechem; the Arabic name is Bab el Amud. The Golden Gate, traditional entrance point for the Messiah, has been walled up for centuries.

The Old City itself is divided into five sections: the Christian Quarter, the Armenian Quarter, the Muslim Quarter, the Jewish Quarter, and Temple Mount (Mount Moriah), the latter housing the Western (Wailing) Wall, the Dome of the Rock, and El Aksa Mosque.

THE JAFFA GATE

The citadel tower, beside the Jaffa Gate, is called the Tower of David, although historically, this site was only developed 800 years after David had died. Three massive towers built by Herod on the foundations of Hasmonean fortifications were originally on this spot. After the destruction of Jerusalem by the Romans, the towers guarding the Jaffa Gate were among the few structures not deliberately obliterated on orders from Rome. They were left standing to show there had once been a city that had been no pushover to subdue. Each of the subsequent rulers of Jerusalem, from Romans and Byzantines to Muslims, Crusaders, and Ottoman Turks, has rebuilt the fortifications beside Jaffa Gate, though none have come close to the scale of Herod's Towers. Today the citadel is the **Tower of David Museum of the History of Jerusalem** (☎ 02/274-111), showing well-chosen temporary exhibits and an array of permanent dioramas and multimedia presentations about Jerusalem throughout its history. Although many of the permanent exhibits look like illustrations from a junior high school textbook, they are useful teaching tools. The structure of the citadel itself, with its views of the New and Old cities, is fascinating. It's open Sunday to Thursday and Saturday from 10am to 4pm, on Friday and holiday eves from 10am to 2pm. Admission is NIS 20 ($6) per person.

A breach in the city walls beside Jaffa Gate was made for the visit of Kaiser Wilhelm II and his entourage in 1898. Here the leader of the British forces, General Allenby, liberating Palestine from Ottoman rule, entered Jerusalem in 1917. Today this breach allows automobiles to penetrate into the area of the Old City just inside the Jaffa Gate.

If you head straight into the bazaar (the suq) from the Jaffa Gate, you'll enter David Street, bustling with shops selling religious crafts and souvenirs, maps, and household items. On your left, just past the entrance to David Street, is the Petra Hotel, which in its day (more than a century ago) was Jerusalem's most elegant accommodation for tourists. The view from the roof is one of the most spectacular in Jerusalem, with the Dome of the Rock perfectly centered in front of you, and the entire Old City at your feet. Ask to visit the roof at the money-changer's desk just inside the door; the fee is NIS 2 (60¢) per person. After this overview you'll have a better idea of where things are in the maze you're about to enter.

If your first destination is the Church of the Holy Sepulcher, then take the first left off David Street, called Christian Quarter Road.

But if the Western Wall and the Temple Mount are your first goal, continue straight along David Street. It makes a quick jog to the right and then to the left in the heart of the covered bazaar, where it changes its name to Street of the Chain (Silsileh, Shalshelet). Follow the street downhill as the bazaar continues. Eventually, a right on a small side street marked Ha-Kotel leads to the Western Wall.

If you go straight, however, you arrive at the Gate of the Chain, an entrance to the Noble Enclosure (Haram es-Sharif), otherwise known as Temple Mount with the Dome of the Rock and El Aksa Mosque as its main attractions.

ARMENIAN QUARTER

As you come inside Omar Ibn el Kattab Square, you'll see a road heading off to the right, past the moat. This route leads into the Armenian Quarter, a quiet residential area of small churches that parallels the wall; the road winds around and eventually leads to the Western Wall and the Dome of the Rock.

In the Armenian Quarter are many green courtyards and ancient buildings, including the splendid **Saint James Cathedral,** the **Church of the Holy Archangels** (from the Early Medieval period), the **Gulbenkian Public Library,** the **Library of Manuscripts,** and the **Helen and Edward Mardigian Museum of Armenian Art and History** (☎ 02/282-331, open Monday to Saturday from 10am to 5pm for NIS 3 [$1]).

THE JEWISH QUARTER

Let's take a detour through the Jewish Quarter on our way to the Western Wall and Temple Mount. By doing so, you'll save an uphill walk, as the wall lies well below most of the quarter. But first, some history and information about this part of town, and its relationship to the other parts of the Old City.

The Jewish Quarter lies directly west of the Temple Mount and sits on a higher hill than the Temple Mount itself. King David (1000 B.C.) built his palace on the slope of the Ophel, south of Temple Mount. With the exception of its sacred high point on the Temple Mount, the entire original city of Jerusalem from the time of David was outside and to the south of the walls of the present Old City. Over the centuries ancient Jerusalem spread northward, up the slope. In the time of King Hezekiah, around 700 B.C., the uphill area now occupied by the Jewish Quarter had become a new addition to the city, surrounded by the Broad Wall. But the wall and its many towers were not strong enough to keep out Nebuchadnezzar of Babylon, who conquered Jerusalem and laid waste the Jewish Quarter in 586 B.C.

Jews returned to Jerusalem after the Babylonian Captivity, but it took centuries for the city to regain and surpass its former grandeur. In the late Second Temple period, the area that is now the Jewish Quarter developed into the aristocratic and priestly residential neighborhood, with many luxurious mansions overlooking the Temple Mount. The main market street of Herodian Jerusalem developed at the bottom of the Tyropoean (Cheesemaker's) Valley, which separates the heights of the Jewish Quarter from the Temple Mount. So that thousands of religious pilgrims could make their way to the Temple Mount without becoming entangled in the crush of the market, massive pedestrian overpasses were constructed. By the 1st century A.D., Herodian Jerusalem had expanded northward, beyond the present city's northern wall and Damascus Gate. A new, bustling upper market developed in this area where the present Suq Khan el Zeit market leads toward Damascus Gate. The original City of David, the oldest part of town, came to be known as the Lower City.

Jerusalem was again leveled in A.D. 70 by Roman armies (the remains of houses burnt in that conflagration have been uncovered in what is now the Jewish Quarter). Once the Jewish inhabitants were driven out, the Romans and later their Byzantine successors rebuilt the city. You can visit several recently uncovered vestiges of Byzantine times in the Jewish Quarter, including the Nea Church, and the southern end of the city's major north–south thoroughfare, the Cardo Maximus. Jews were forbidden to reside in Jerusalem during the long Byzantine period, which began in A.D. 326, and they allied themselves with the then pagan Persians, who conquered and occupied the city from A.D. 614 to A.D. 629. The Muslims were the next conquerers of Jerusalem in A.D. 638, and under their more tolerant rule, a permanent Jewish community was reestablished in the northeast quadrant of the

Old City, on the site of the present Muslim Quarter. The Crusaders conquered Jerusalem in 1099; a massacre of most of the city's Jewish population, as well as thousands of Muslims, accompanied the Crusader's triumph.

In 1267, after the Crusaders were driven from Jerusalem, a small Jewish community reestablished itself in the ruins of what is now the Jewish Quarter. This area has been the center of the Jewish community in the Old City ever since.

The Jewish Quarter's most recent destruction came during and after the 1948 war with Jordan, when all the synagogues and most other buildings in the quarter were systematically blown up. Since 1967 the quarter has been rebuilt and revitalized. Although some buildings have been carefully re-created, and many new structures were designed to blend in with them, the basic nature of the current Jewish Quarter is quite different from the impoverished, densely populated neighborhoods that existed here before 1948.

Just off the Jewish Quarter Road (Rehov Ha-Yehudim), you will come to Or Hayim Street, where you will find the **Alix de Rothschild Craft Center** at No. 4 (☎ 02/286-076). This center displays juried exhibits of contemporary Israeli crafts. The work is not usually for sale, but the staff will direct you to those craftspeople whose work you may admire. The center is open Sunday to Thursday from 10am to 4pm.

Two doors down is the **Old Yishuv Court Museum,** 6 Or Hayim St.(☎ 02/284-636). This museum belongs to the Weingarten family, whose great-great-grandfather lived here in the 18th century. The displays reflect Ashkenazi and Sephardic lifestyles from the middle of the 19th century to the end of Turkish rule in 1917. The living quarters, kitchens, and other typical elements of Jewish Quarter homes have been re-created. Admission is NIS 8 ($2.40), and it's open Sunday to Thursday from 9am to 2pm.

The **Cardo Maximus** is a recently excavated 2nd- to 6th-century street that was Roman and Byzantine Jerusalem's main market and processional thoroughfare, once bordered by stately columns and lined with shops. What you see now, some 8 feet beneath the level of the bordering Jewish Quarter Road, dates from the mid-6th century. The original street is said to have been laid out by Hadrian (A.D. 117–138) when he rebuilt the city as Aelia Capitolina after the Bar-Kokhba Revolt of A.D. 132–135. In late Byzantine times, the Cardo was extended southward and served as the route for processions between the Holy Sepulcher and the Nea, Jerusalem's two largest churches of that era.

The southern portion of the Cardo is open to the sky; the rest is beneath modern buildings of the Jewish Quarter. As you walk northward along the reconstructed Cardo, you can see some Crusader-era shops built into arches. In this restored section of the Cardo, you can look down well-like structures that reveal how far above the original level of the land the city has risen from being constantly rebuilt on the ruins of each wave of destruction. You'll also see fragments of the city's defensive walls dating from the First Temple period, about 700 B.C.

At the far side of the parking lot at the end of Jewish Quarter Road is the **Nea,** Byzantine Jerusalem's largest and second most important church (after the Holy Sepulcher). The Nea Church (or "New" in Greek) was built by Justinian in A.D. 543 and destroyed during the Persian conquest of A.D. 614. So complete was the Nea's eradication that its precise location was only rediscovered during recent excavations. Some archeologists theorize that the vast Nea's legendary marble columns may have been salvaged from the ruins of the Herodian temple, which had lain abandoned after its destruction in A.D. 70. (Procopius, a contemporary historian, reports a bit skeptically that the columns needed to build the Nea had magically appeared near

Old City Attractions

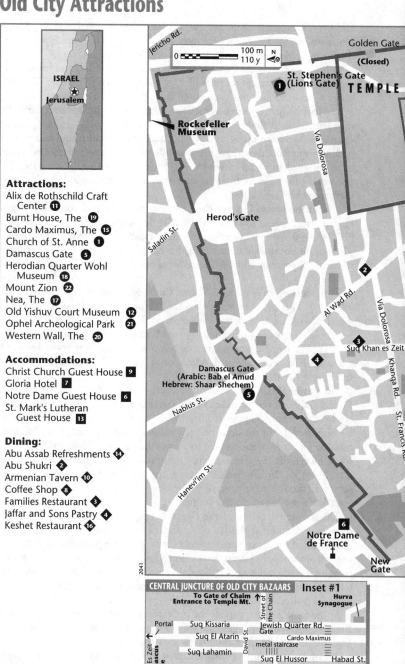

Attractions:
Alix de Rothschild Craft
  Center ⑪
Burnt House, The ⑲
Cardo Maximus, The ⑮
Church of St. Anne ①
Damascus Gate ⑤
Herodian Quarter Wohl
  Museum ⑱
Mount Zion ㉒
Nea, The ⑰
Old Yishuv Court Museum ⑫
Ophel Archeological Park ㉑
Western Wall, The ⑳

Accommodations:
Christ Church Guest House ⑨
Gloria Hotel ⑦
Notre Dame Guest House ⑥
St. Mark's Lutheran
  Guest House ⑬

Dining:
Abu Assab Refreshments ⑭
Abu Shukri ②
Armenian Tavern ⑩
Coffee Shop ⑧
Families Restaurant ③
Jaffar and Sons Pastry ④
Keshet Restaurant ⑯

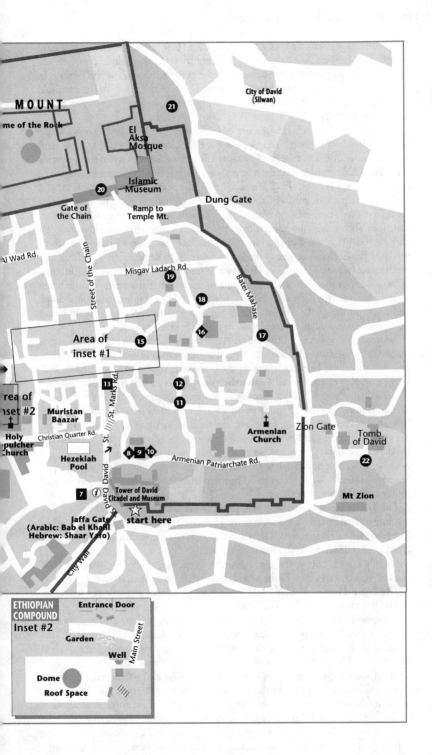

MOUNT

me of the Rock

City of David (Silwan)

(21)

El Aksa Mosque

(20)

Gate of the Chain

Islamic Museum

Ramp to Temple Mt.

Dung Gate

Al Wad Rd.

Street of the Chain

Misgav Ladach Rd.

(19)

(18)

(16)

Batei Mahase

Area of inset #1

(15)

(17)

(13)

(12)

(11)

Area of inset #2

St. ////St. Mark's Rd.

Muristan Baazar

Christian Quarter Rd.

Holy Sepulcher Church

Hezekiah Pool

(8) (9) (10)

Armenian Church

Zion Gate

Tomb of David

(22)

Armenian Patriarchate Rd.

(7)

ⓘ David St.

Tower of David Citadel and Museum

☆ **start here**

Mt Zion

Jaffa Gate (Arabic: Bab el Khalil Hebrew: Shaar Yafo)

City Wall

ETHIOPIAN COMPOUND Inset #2

Entrance Door

Garden

Well

Main Street

Dome Roof Space

the construction site as if from heaven.) Ironically, these building materials may have returned to the Temple Mount in the 7th century when the Islamic conquerers of Jerusalem reused parts of ruined Byzantine structures (destroyed by the Persians in A.D. 614) to build the El Aksa Mosque and the Dome of the Rock. To the untrained eye, unfortunately, there is not much to see, but the long-lost Nea remains one of Jerusalem's great legends.

Many Jewish Quarter buildings from other times are today recalled by only a single arch, doorway, or minaret. You can inspect the haunting arches, altar, apse, and ruined cloister from the once lost **Crusader Church of Saint Mary of the Teutonic Knights** (1128) on Misgav Ladach Street, near a small covered square known as the **Seven Arches.** In the pre-1948 Jewish Quarter, the Seven Arches was the heart of a lively market packed with vegetable vendors and customers. Rebuilt in its original form after 1967, the Seven Arches no longer host a market, and seem to perform no function. Then there's the minaret from the Sidnah Omar Mosque, and behind it a single broad, graceful arch, rebuilt from the remains of the **Hurva Synagogue,** which was once the Great Synagogue of the Jewish Quarter. Its name recalls its difficult and unfortunate history. The original Hurva was built in the 16th century with Ottoman permission, but soon destroyed by Ottoman decree; over the centuries, the name "hurva" became attached to the desolate site that had been built with so much hope and pride. In the 1850s, a new Great Synagogue was authorized and built; it was destroyed by the Jordanians soon after they captured the Jewish Quarter in 1948.

Between the minaret and the Hurva Arch is the **Ramban Synagogue** of Rabbi Moshe Ben-Nahman, who helped reconstitute the Jewish community of Jerusalem in 1267, after it had been obliterated by the Crusaders. You'll also want to take a look at the complex of **four small Sephardic synagogues** named for Rabbi Yohanan Ben-Zakkai, whose school, according to tradition, occupied this site during the Second Temple period. The four in the complex are the one named for the rabbi himself, another for Eliyahu Ha-Nevi, the Central Synagogue, and the Istanbuli Synagogue. During Muslim rule, no church or synagogue was allowed to exceed the height of the nearest mosque, so to gain headroom, the foundations of these synagogues were laid well below ground level. The Sephardic synagogues are open Sunday, Monday, Wednesday, and Thursday from 9:30am to 4pm, Tuesday and Friday from 9:30am to 12:30pm.

The **Tiferet Israel (or Yisrael) Synagogue** (Ashkenazi) was founded by Nisan Bek and inaugurated in 1865. Dedicated to the Hasidic Rabbi Israel Friedmann of Ruzhin (the synagogue's name means "Glory of Israel"), it was methodically destroyed after the War of Independence and recently restored.

Moving eastward across the Jewish Quarter in the direction of the Western Wall, you can visit two remnants of the neighborhood's elegant Herodian past.

The Burnt House (☎ 02/287-211) is a remnant of the destruction of Jerusalem by the Romans in A.D. 70. The wealthy Upper City, site of the present Jewish Quarter, held out for a despairing month after the Lower City and Temple Mount fell. From their vantage point on these heights, the inhabitants of the Upper City had stood on their roofs and watched with horror as the temple went up in flames. When the Romans finally decided to storm the Upper City, they found little resistance; much of their population was near death from disease and starvation. The Burnt House chillingly brings to light the day when the Romans burned the Upper City. In the kitchen or workroom of this building, the bones of the forearm of a young woman were found amid the debris. As archeologists continued to excavate the area of the room that lay where the arm pointed, they uncovered a wooden spear, almost as if the young woman had been reaching for this weapon when she met her death.

Most tantalizing of the household artifacts found on this site is a set of weights marked with the name "Bar Kathros," a priestly family mentioned in the Talmud (and also in an ancient folk song as one of the wealthy families that oppressed the poor). Historians know the House of Bar Kathros was responsible for the manufacture of incense for the temple. Could these be the weights for their laboratory, and have we uncovered the name of the family who once lived here? The excavated house, now preserved beneath modern buildings, is a museum with a brief slide show about the site. The entrance to the house is marked on a modern door in the Seven Arches off Misgav Ladach Road (ask if you have difficulty finding the door). The house is open Sunday to Thursday from 9am to 5pm, on Friday from 9am until noon. Admission is NIS 8 ($2.40); a combined ticket to Burnt House and Herodian Quarter can be purchased for NIS 12 ($3.60).

The Herodian Quarter Wohl Museum (☎ 02/283-448) contains archeological excavations, done in the 1970s, of the wealthy residential quarter of Herodian Jerusalem. It includes remains of a palatial mansion with painted faux marble walls, mosaic floors, an atrium pool, and ritual bath installations indicative of the standard of living and religious observance that prevailed in this affluent quarter during the Herodian period. Admission is NIS 9 ($2.70), or by combined ticket with the Burnt House. It's open Sunday to Thursday from 9am to 5pm, on Friday from 9am until noon.

THE WESTERN WALL

This is the Ha-Kotel Ha-Ma'aravi. It was formerly called the "Wailing Wall" by European observers because Jews have traditionally come here to bewail the loss of their temple. It is the holiest of Jewish sites, a remnant of the Herodian retaining wall that once enclosed and supported the Temple Mount.

For centuries the wall had stood 60 feet high and 91 feet long, towering over a narrow alley 12 feet wide that could accommodate a few hundred densely packed worshipers. The Israelis bulldozed the Moors Quarter facing the wall to create a plaza that could accommodate tens of thousands of pilgrims. They also made the wall about 6^1/$_2$ feet higher by digging down and exposing two more tiers of ashlars from the Second Temple Plaza's retaining wall that had been buried by accumulated debris for centuries. At the southern end, away from the traditional area that is still reserved for prayer and worship, archeologists since 1967 have uncovered spectacular remains from various periods.

At the prayer section of the Western Wall, grass grows out of the upper cracks. The lower cracks of the chalky, yellow-white blocks have been stuffed with bits of paper containing prayers. Orthodox Jews are always seen standing at the wall, chanting and swaying. Men who would like to go to the wall must wear a hat or take a head covering, at no cost, from a box beside the entrance to the prayer area. Women may borrow shawls and short-skirt coverings. A separate section at the extreme right of the Western Wall is reserved for women, who are not allowed into the men's section, in keeping with Orthodox Jewish tradition. Services are held here daily; no photography or smoking is permitted on the Sabbath.

The exposed portion of the Western Wall dates from the Second Temple, just before the time of Jesus. The wall built at that time to retain the western part of Temple Mount was actually much higher and longer than the portion you can see readily today. For an idea of how big the original construction was, enter the doorway located between the men's restrooms and the public telephones, on the plaza's northern side. Entry is allowed here, for free, to men and women, upon request on Sunday, Tuesday, and Wednesday from 8:30am to 3pm, on Monday and Thursday from 12:30 to 3pm, and on Friday from 8:30am to noon; closed Saturday.

Enter the dark labyrinth of vaults and chambers, pitfalls (now rendered safe by lamps, grates, and barriers), and passages. Inside, from the platform of the viewing area, the wall is clearly visible. Shafts have been sunk along the surface of the wall to show its true depth. The arches in this artificial cavern date from various periods, from the Herodian (37 B.C. to A.D. 70) to the Crusader (1100–1244) periods. The platform is behind a prayer room filled with the devout. The prayer room is off-limits to women, except in the viewing area.

A special walk into recently excavated tunnels alongside the Western Wall can be arranged by making an appointment with the Western Wall Heritage Foundation, ☎ 02/271-333. Admission is NIS 10 ($3).

TEMPLE MOUNT—DOME OF THE ROCK

Take the rising pathway to the right of the Western Wall, which leads to the Temple Mount, Mount Moriah. This is the **Haram esh-Sharif,** the Noble Enclosure of the Muslims. When David first came to Jerusalem, he purchased the flat rock on Moriah from Arunah the Jebusite, who had used it as a threshing floor. The Bible (2 Chronicles 3) relates that "Solomon began to build the house of the Lord at Jerusalem on Mount Moriah." The Second Temple (Solomon's was destroyed by Nebuchadnezzar in 586 B.C.) was first built between 525 and 515 B.C., and later enlarged and rebuilt into the most massive religious complex in the eastern Roman Empire by Herod shortly before the time of Jesus. The vast Temple Mount you see here is an artificially created flat stone-paved platform, about 30 acres in area.

There is no charge to enter the Temple Mount compound. You must not, however, wear shorts or "immodest" dress in the compound. There is an admission fee of NIS 22 ($6.60) to go inside the two mosques and the Islamic Museum. I highly recommend that you invest in the combined admission ticket, which may be purchased from a stone kiosk between El Aksa and the Dome of the Rock. Visiting hours are 8:30am to 3pm. You may remain on the Temple Mount, but cannot enter the Dome of the Rock or the El Aksa Mosque, during the midday prayers. The Temple Mount may not be visited on Friday or Muslim holidays.

El Aksa Mosque is the first shrine you'll reach. You must leave your handbags, cameras, and shoes outside, so it's best to come with a partner who can watch these things for you. After passing through the portico, you will enter a broad open hall hung with chandeliers and covered with oriental rugs. The mosque's lofty ceilings are embellished in Byzantine design. Up front, past rows of great marble pillars, is a wood-partitioned platform that had been reserved for King Hussein of Jordan when he came here to pray. A separate women's prayer chamber, in blue, is at the right.

Leave El Aksa, reclaim your shoes, and turn right. You will only be permitted to walk to the end of the building, but at the far end of the vast pavement is a corner in the city walls. Some say this is the "pinnacle of the Temple" where Satan took Jesus to tempt him (Matthew 4:5). In the distance, you can get a marvelous view of the Mount of Olives and the Kidron Valley.

A stairway leads to the so-called **Solomon's Stables,** perhaps first misidentified by the Crusaders. Today these subterranean chambers filled with pigeons are popularly believed to have been the stables for King Solomon's thousands of horses. The "stables" are actually the substructure supporting this portion of Herod's vast, artificially created ceremonial platform that is the present surface of the Temple Mount. To add to the confusion about the site, many Muslims believe the "Solomon" referred to is the Ottoman Sultan Suleiman (Solomon) the Magnificent, who rebuilt the walls that surround the present Old City and did extensive repair work on the

Dome of the Rock during his reign in the mid-1500s. (For security reasons, the area may be closed to visitors.)

Heading straight across the temple plaza, you'll pass **El-Kas,** the fountain where Muslims perform their ritual ablutions before entering the holy places. It is equipped with a circular row of pink marble seats, each of which has a faucet. The fountain is not for the use of non-Muslims.

The exterior walls of the dazzling **Dome of the Rock** are covered with a facade of Persian blue tiles. In 1994, under the auspices of Jordan's King Hussein, the great dome was completely reconstructed and regilded with 80 kg of 24-karat gold. The Dome of the Rock is reached by climbing the broad ceremonial stairs, which lead to a decorative archway and a raised center portion of the Temple Mount complex. The Dome of the Rock's interior is every bit as lavish and intricate as the outside. Plush carpets line the floor, and stained-glass windows line the upper ceiling.

Everything in this beautiful Muslim sanctuary, built in A.D. 691, centers on the rock that occupies the middle of the shrine. The rock, which is about 30 feet by 30 feet and 6 feet high, together with the nearby El Aksa Mosque, comprise the third most important religious complex in Islam, after Mecca and Medina. According to Islamic tradition, the rock is the spot from which the Prophet Muhammad ascended to heaven. Islamic tradition holds that one prayer at this rock is worth a thousand anywhere else—only at Mecca and Medina do prayers carry greater weight. Footprints of Muhammad are pointed out on the rock.

Next to the rock, a few strands of Muhammad's hair are kept in a latticework wooden cabinet. A stairway leads under the rock to a cavelike chamber; according to tradition, this is the Well of the Souls. Glass partitions have been erected to stop pilgrims from eroding the sacred rock—for centuries it has been chipped away by the faithful who wanted to bring home a memento.

Jewish tradition holds that on this rock occurred the supreme act of faith that stands at the very foundation of the Jewish religion. Genesis relates how Abraham in approximately 1800 B.C. followed God's instructions to go to Moriah and sacrifice Isaac, his beloved son. Isaac, unaware of the dreadful command, followed in his father's steps and asked, "Behold the fire and the wood, but where is the lamb for a burnt offering?" Abraham responded, "God will provide for the sacrifice," as he built the altar on the rock and prepared to bind his son. At the final moment, the voice of God intervened and ordered Abraham to lower his knife. Approximately 900 years later, in 960 B.C., the temple of Solomon was constructed either on or beside this rock. For the next millennium, the First and Second Temples were located on this site.

From the flat courtyard surrounding the two mosques you have a wonderful view. To the south are the Valley of Jehosaphat (Valley of Kidron) and the U.N. Government House (Mount of Contempt) on the hill. To the east on the lower slopes of the Mount of Olives, the Russian Magdalene Church, with its many exotic golden domes, and the Tomb of the Virgin. Midway up the Mount of Olives is a large modern white structure with many levels of arcades that seem built into the side of the slope. This is the vast Mormon Center, constructed in the 1980s, and considered to be one of the most beautiful examples of contemporary architecture in Jerusalem. On the crest of the Mount of Olives, above the Church of Mary Magdalene, you'll see the high-steepled Russian Monastery and the Dome of the Ascension, marking the place from which Jesus ascended to heaven. Farther to the right and a bit downhill is the gray, tear-shaped dome of Dominus Flevit, which commemorates the spot where Jesus wept as he saw a vision of Jerusalem in ruins. Indeed, from the time of the city's destruction in A.D. 70, until the the building of the Dome of the Rock in A.D. 691, Jews traditionally stood near this spot, and viewed the actual ruins of the Temple Mount. To the right, on the southern crest of the ridge, is the modern Seven Arches Hotel, built during Jordanian times on the ancient Jewish cemetery of the Mount of Olives.

Your combined entrance ticket also admits you to the **Islamic Museum,** in the southwest corner of the Temple Mount complex, to the right of the El Aksa Mosque. The museum is filled with architectural details, including capitals and carved stonework from earlier structures on the Temple Mount as well as ornamental details from earlier periods of the El Aksa Mosque's existence.

DUNG GATE AND SILWAN

The gate in the city wall nearby is Dung Gate. Jerusalemites claim that the name resulted from the debris from each consecutive destruction of Jerusalem that was dumped out into the valley below. Beyond Dung Gate is the Valley of Kidron and the Arab neigborhood of Silwan, where the original settlement of Jerusalem developed in prehistoric times beside the Gihon Spring. This is where the walled city of Jerusalem existed in the time of King David, and it was there that the prophets walked and the events of First Temple Jerusalem took place.

By the 2nd century B.C., the growing city of Jerusalem was expanding uphill and northward, onto the site of the present Old City. The newer, Upper City was the more affluent part of town; the older, Lower City was densely populated and poor. In the centuries after the Roman destruction of Jerusalem in A.D.70, the population of Jerusalem had so greatly decreased and the technology of warfare had progressed to such a point that the original City of David was no longer militarily defensible. It was left outside the walls of the city and by medieval times had sunk to the status of a small, sporadically settled village known as Silwan. So forgotten was the site of the original city that until the late 19th century, most European scholars and visitors believed the Jerusalem of the First Temple period had been located on the site of the present Old City. In Silwan you can visit the underground water tunnel and the collection Pool of Siloam built by King Hezekiah in 701 B.C.; this remarkable structure hid Jerusalem's water supply from the Assyrians and saved the city from destruction. At the southern end of Silwan (which takes its Arabic name from the biblical pool of Siloam), just beyond where the walls of ancient Jerusalem would have been, are ancient overgrown gardens of pomegranates and figs still watered by the Gihon Spring. These gardens, originating in prehistoric times, most likely occupy the site of the gardens of the Kings of Judah, and are probably the site of the walled gardens described in the Song of Songs. It was to a tent beside the Gihon Spring that David initially brought the Ark of the Covenant, the pivotal first step in the city's transformation into a holy city. It was here beside Silwan that the ark had rested until the Temple of Solomon was built to house it. The Bible also records that King David was buried inside this city; if so, his tomb should be somewhere in Silwan, rather than at the site on Mount Zion that has been venerated since at least medieval times. Normally, under Judaic law, burials are not permitted within the walls of a city, but an exception was apparently made for King David. Archeologists are still searching for evidence of the Davidic burial site, but the Lower City was extensively quarried for building stone in the centuries after the Roman destruction, and the true location of David's Tomb, legendary for its powers, remains one of Jerusalem's mysteries. Under current political conditions, it is best to visit Silwan with an organized tour.

OPHEL ARCHEOLOGICAL PARK

South of the Western Wall, near the Dung Gate, but not as far down into the valley as Silwan, is the entrance to the Ophel Archeological Park. Visitors are transported back 3,000 years, to the time of the Book of Kings and the prophecies of Isaiah and Micah. It was here, between the temple and the walled city below, that King David built his palace, and Solomon built his House of the Cedars of Lebanon, a palace for his many wives and concubines, and a government complex from which he ruled his empire. Here the Prophet Isaiah advised King Hezekiah; perhaps Isaiah lived in a house built on foundations recently unburied and restored. Archeologists have even found physical evidence of the kind of backsliding into pagan religions the prophets once railed about. Under the floor of a First Temple period house—within sight of the temple itself—excavators in the 1980s uncovered a hidden cache of pagan gods. The park is being expanded for the Jerusalem 3,000-year celebration. It is open Sunday through Thursday from 9am to 5pm, on Friday until 1pm; closed Saturday. Admission costs NIS 16 ($4.80), half price for children.

THE MUSLIM & CHRISTIAN QUARTERS

✪ **Church of Saint Anne.** The Lion's Gate (Saint Stephen's Gate). Admission NIS 3 ($1). Mon–Sat 8am–noon and 2–5pm (until 6pm in summer); closed Sun.

On the right, just inside the gate, is a particularly beautiful 12th-century Crusader church erected in honor of the birthplace of Anne (Hannah), the mother of Mary. It is built next to the Pool of Bethesda, the site where Jesus is believed to have healed a paralytic. As the church is just a few blocks east of the Sanctuaries of the Flagellation and the Condemnation, at the beginning of the Via Dolorosa, you might want to visit it before following the stations of the cross. Saint Anne's acoustics, designed for Gregorian chant, are so perfect that the church is virtually an instrument to be played by the human voice. Pilgrim groups come to sing in the church throughout the day, and you, too, are welcome to prepare a song of any religion—only religious songs are permitted. The church's accoustics are most amazing when activated by a soprano- or a tenor-range solo voice.

VIA DOLOROSA

This is the **Way of the Cross,** traditionally believed to be the route followed by Jesus from the Praetorium—the Roman Judgment Hall—to Calvary, which was the scene of the crucifixion. Over the centuries, millions of pilgrims have come here to walk the way that Jesus took to his death. Each Friday at 3pm priests lead a ceremony for pilgrims along Via Dolorosa (starting in the Monastery of the Flagellation at the tower of Antonia, not far from the Lion's Gate), and prayers are said at each of the 14 stations of the cross. The Via Dolorosa begins in the Muslim Quarter, in the northeast corner of the Old City, and wends its way to the Church of the Holy Sepulcher in the Christian Quarter.

You can enter the **Sanctuaries of the Flagellation and the Condemnation,** where Jesus was scourged and judged. In the sanctuaries are some of the original paving stones of the Lithostrotos. Hours are daily from 8am to noon; afternoon hours are 2 to 6pm from April through September, 1 to 5pm from October through March.

The Sanctuary of the Condemnation marks the first station of the cross. As you leave the sanctuary to follow the Via Dolorosa, keep in mind that many of the stations are not well marked. There may be only a small sign, or a number engraved in the stone lintel over a door. Paving stones on the Via Dolorosa itelf have been set in a semicircular sunburst pattern to mark those stations directly on the street. Other stations are behind closed doors; knock and a monk or nun will probably be there to open up for you. There's a restroom opposite station 3. The following is a quick guide to the stations of the cross:

Station 1: Jesus is condemned to death. Station 2: Jesus receives the cross (at the foot of the Antonia). Station 3: Jesus falls for the first time (Polish biblical–archeological museum). Station 4: Jesus meets his mother. Station 5: Simon the Cyrene helps Jesus carry the cross. Station 6: Veronica wipes Jesus's face. Station 7: Jesus falls the second time (at bazaar crossroads). Station 8: Jesus consoles the women of Jerusalem. Station 9: Jesus falls the third time (Coptic Monastery).

The five remaining stations of the cross are inside the Church of the Holy Sepulcher (see below). Station 10: Jesus is stripped of his garments. Station 11: Jesus is nailed to the cross. Station 12: Jesus dies on the cross. Station 13: Jesus is taken down from the cross and given to Mary. Station 14: Jesus is laid in the chamber of the sepulcher and from here is resurrected.

Church of the Holy Sepulcher at Golgotha.

The church is divided among six different sects: Roman Catholic, Armenian Orthodox, Greek Orthodox, Egyptian Coptic, Ethiopian, and Syrian Orthodox. Each denomination has its own space—right down to lines drawn down the middle of floors and pillars—and its own schedule of rights to be in other areas of the church at specific times. The decor, partitioned and changed every few feet, is a mixture of Byzantine and Frankish Crusader styles.

You can observe the various stations inside the church—the marble slab as you enter, the Stone of Unction where the body of Jesus was prepared for burial, the site of Calvary on the second floor, the marble tomb in the sepulcher.

After the Roman Emperor Constantine converted to Christianity and made Christianity the religion of Rome in A.D. 326, his mother, Queen Helena, made a pilgrimage to the Holy Land and located what was believed to be the tomb from which Jesus rose, and nearby, the true cross. It was over this spot that Constantine built the first church, a complex of classical structures, which was enlarged by Justinian 200 years later. Fire, earthquake, and the 7th-century Persians and 11th-century Muslims destroyed much of the church, but the Crusaders rebuilt it in the 12th century. The church has been restored many times and is currently being renovated.

If you're in Jerusalem during Easter week, you can attend many of the fascinating services, based on ancient Eastern church traditions, that are held at the church. Most notable are the Service of the Holy Fire, the dramatic pageant called the Washing of the Feet, and the midnight Ethiopian procession on the part of the church under their jurisdiction—the roof.

DAMASCUS GATE & THE BAZAARS

The Damascus Gate, largest and most magnificent of all the entrances to the Old City, is the main route into the Old City from East Jerusalem. Once you are inside the gate, cafes, shops, and market stalls line a wide-stepped entrance street going downhill; Arabs sit inside and out smoking water pipes and watching you as you watch them. The game they're playing is shesh-besh, a sort of backgammon. Music emanates from coffeehouses and shops. Whether you take **El-Wad Road** to the left, or **Suq Khan es-Zeit** to the right, the way becomes very narrow and confusing. Unlike the markets near the Jaffa Gate, which cater primarily to tourists, this part of the bazaar is an authentic market used by the people of East Jerusalem. You'll see stalls of spices and coffees, silversmiths, craft shops, pastry and bread bakeries,

Church of the Holy Sepulcher

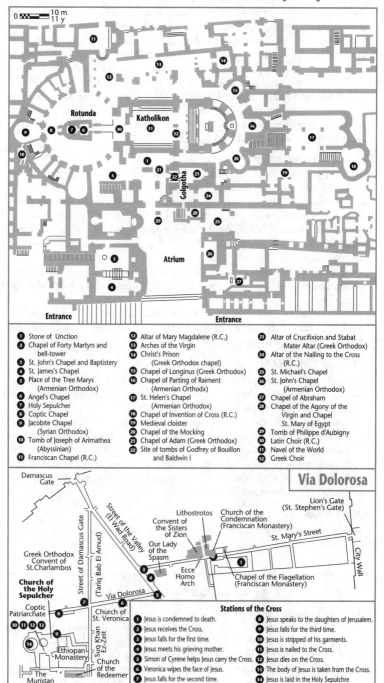

0 ▭▭▭ 10 m
      11 y

Rotunda

Katholikon

Golgotha

Atrium

Entrance   **Entrance**

1 Stone of Unction
2 Chapel of Forty Martyrs and bell-tower
3 St. John's Chapel and Baptistery
4 St. James's Chapel
5 Place of the Tree Marys (Armenian Orthodox)
6 Angel's Chapel
7 Holy Sepulcher
8 Coptic Chapel
9 Jacobite Chapel (Syrian Orthodox)
10 Tomb of Joseph of Arimathea (Abyssinian)
11 Franciscan Chapel (R.C.)

12 Altar of Mary Magdalene (R.C.)
13 Arches of the Virgin
14 Christ's Prison (Greek Orthodox chapel)
15 Chapel of Longinus (Greek Orthodox)
16 Chapel of Parting of Raiment (Armenian Orthodx)
17 St. Helen's Chapel (Armenian Orthodox)
18 Chapel of Invention of Cross (R.C.)
19 Medieval cloister
20 Chapel of the Mocking
21 Chapel of Adam (Greek Orthodox)
22 Site of tombs of Godfrey of Bouillon and Baldwin I

23 Altar of Crucifixion and Stabat Mater Altar (Greek Orthodox)
24 Altar of the Nailing to the Cross (R.C.)
25 St. Michael's Chapel
26 St. John's Chapel (Armenian Orthodox)
27 Chapel of Abraham
28 Chapel of the Agony of the Virgin and Chapel St. Mary of Egypt
29 Tomb of Philippe d'Aubigny
30 Latin Choir (R.C.)
31 Navel of the World
32 Greek Choir

Via Dolorosa

Damascus Gate

Lion's Gate (St. Stephen's Gate)

Street of the Valley (El Wad Road)

Lithostrotos

Church of the Condemnation (Franciscan Monastery)

Convent of the Sisters of Zion

St. Mary's Street

Street of Damascus Gate (Tariq Bab El Amud)

Our Lady of the Spasm

City Wall

Greek Orthodox Convent of St.Charlambos

Ecce Homo Arch

Church of the Holy Sepulcher

Chapel of the Flagellation (Franciscan Monastery)

Via Dolorosa

Coptic Patriarchate

Church of St. Veronica

Stations of the Cross

Suq Khan Ez-Zeit

Ethiopan Monastery

Church of the Redeemer

The Muristan

1 Jesus is condemned to death.
2 Jesus receives the Cross.
3 Jesus falls for the first time.
4 Jesus meets his grieving mother.
5 Simon of Cyrene helps Jesus carry the Cross.
6 Veronica wipes the face of Jesus.
7 Jesus falls for the second time.

8 Jesus speaks to the daughters of Jerusalem.
9 Jesus falls for the third time.
10 Jesus is stripped of his garments.
11 Jesus is nailed to the Cross.
12 Jesus dies on the Cross.
13 The body of Jesus is taken from the Cross.
14 Jesus is laid in the Holy Sepulchre

shops selling sneakers and children's wear, butcher stalls, tiny one-chair barber establishments, shoe stores, and fruit and vegetable stands.

Suq Khan es-Zeit becomes **Suq el Attarin,** the Street of the Spices, now mostly a clothing bazaar. In other centuries, this covered market was lined with open sacks of curry, cocoa, sesame, pepper, and all kinds of beans, dried herbs, medicines, and vegetables. Parallel and to the right of this central market street is the covered Suq El-Lahhamin (Butcher Street), its pavement often slippery with puddles of blood.

If you continue walking straight, eventually Suq El Attarin will become the renovated Cardo, which runs through the restored Jewish Quarter. The area, incidentally, is well patrolled by police officers.

The Old City Ramparts

The best place to begin your walk on the **Old City walls,** built by the Ottoman Turkish Sultan Suleiman the Magnificent in the 1500s, is Damascus Gate, although you can also enter at Zion Gate or Jaffa Gate. The views are thrilling and an entire circuit of the walls is about 2½ miles, or less than an hour's walk. Underneath the present Damascus Gate, the Roman-era gate, to the left and below, has been excavated. Within this Roman gate (which may have been extant in Jesus's time) there's a small museum worth a quick visit.

Note that it's not a good idea for anyone to walk alone on the ramparts at any time of day. The ramparts are often patrolled by groups of unruly local kids and unsavory illegal "guides."

The entry ticket costs NIS 6 ($1.80) for adults, NIS 3 ($1) for students, and is good for 2 days (3 days if you buy on Friday). The ramparts are open Saturday to Thursday from 9am to 4pm, and on Friday from 9am to 2pm.

STREET OF THE CHAIN

Perpendicular to the Suq El Attarin–Cardo market is the Street of the Chain, which runs gently downhill to the Gate of the Chain, the most important entrance to the Haram es Sharif or Temple Mount. This was the great residential street of medieval Islamic Jerusalem. It starts out as a typical market passageway, but as you get closer to the Haram, you'll begin to notice monumental, richly ornamented doorways of Mameluk period mansions and buildings decorated with carved stonework in traditional Islamic patterns. You can only surmise this area's affluent past; like much of the Old City, the neighborhood is overcrowded and has not yet benefited from programs of restoration and renovation.

MOUNT ZION

This important location can be easily spotted as you approach the walls of the Old City from the west or the south. The building with a round squat tower is the

Schindler's Grave

With the making of the film *Schindler's List,* Oscar Schindler, the German businessman who saved the lives of his Jewish slave laborers during the Holocaust, has become world famous. His final resting place is in the graveyard on Mount Zion. Exit the Zion Gate, turn immediately right, and follow the walkway alongside the Old City Wall. The second gate on the left is the entrance to the Protestant cemetery. The gate is often locked, but you can see the peaceful enclave where the often puzzling but heroic Schindler is buried.

Dormition Abbey, and near this site is **King David's Tomb** and the **Room of the Last Supper (Coenaculum)** above it. To reach King David's Tomb, walk out Zion Gate, proceed down a narrow alley bounded by high stone walls, and turn left. Although this place has been venerated as the site of David's burial, the tradition can only be traced back to early medieval times; many believe the tomb would have been located in the ancient City of David, which was south of the present Old City. The building is open daily, including the Sabbath, from 8am to 5pm, until 2pm on Friday. Cover your head when you enter the room.

Near King David's Tomb (in fact, in the same building) is a doorway and flight of stairs leading to the Coenaculum (Upper Room), where Jesus sat with his disciples to celebrate the Passover seder. Again, the room's authenticity is based on many centuries of veneration; however, some question this tradition. It is open daily from 8:30am to 4pm.

In the cellar of a building near King David's Tomb is the **Chamber of the Holocaust (71)**, an eerie room lit by candles and dedicated to the memory of the 6 million Jews slain by the Nazis. The chamber, a private memorial, is open for visits Sunday through Thursday from 9am to 4pm, and on Friday to 1pm.

Close by, the graceful **Dormition Abbey** (☎ 02/719-927) stands, according to tradition, on the spot where Mary fell into sleep before her burial and assumption bodily into heaven. Inside the church are an elaborate golden mosaic, a crypt containing particularly interesting religious artwork, and a statue of Mary, around which are chapels donated by various countries. From the tower of the church there's a good panoramic view. It is open daily from 8am to noon and 2 to 6pm.

Across the valley from Mount Zion, near the Cinémathèque, is a **peace memorial,** with a slender pillar and a tangle of metal at the bottom. The inscribed legend is Isaiah's swords-into-ploughshares prophecy. The memorial itself is a gift from Abie Nathan, Israel's celebrated flying-and-sailing "peacenik," who began making visionary solo flights into Egypt more than 20 years ago, and who, for many years, was in and out of Israel prisons for breaking the law that once forbade Israeli citizens to talk to the PLO.

2 West Jerusalem Attractions

MUSEUMS

Agricultural Museum. 13 Helena Ha-Malka St. ☎ **02/249-568.** Admission NIS 3 (90¢). Sun–Fri 8am–1pm. Bus: 5, 6, 18, or 21.

Set in the courtyard of the Society for the Protection of Nature in Israel (SPNI), this museum houses agricultural artifacts from ancient times. The building, the Sergei Hostel, was originally constructed to house Russian Orthodox pilgrims before the Bolshevik Revolution.

Ammunition Hill Memorial and Museum. ☎ **02/828-442.** Admission NIS 7 ($2). Sun–Thurs 9am–5pm; Fri 9am–1pm. Bus: 4, 9, 25, 26, or 99.

At the top of Givat Ha-Tachmoshet (Ammunition Hill), between Sheikh Jarrah and Ramot Eshkol, the site of a bloody battle in 1967, this museum is dedicated to the reunification of Jerusalem and to those who died in the Six-Day War. You can walk through bunkers and trenches, and five exhibition halls full of weapons, maps, battle plans, and more.

✪ **The Bible Lands Museum.** 25 Granot St., beside the Israel Museum. ☎ **02/611-066.** Admission NIS 18 ($5.40); discounts for students. Sun–Tues and Thurs 9:30am–5:30pm; Wed 9:30am–9:30pm; Fri 9:30am–2pm; Sat 11am–3pm.

Jerusalem Attractions

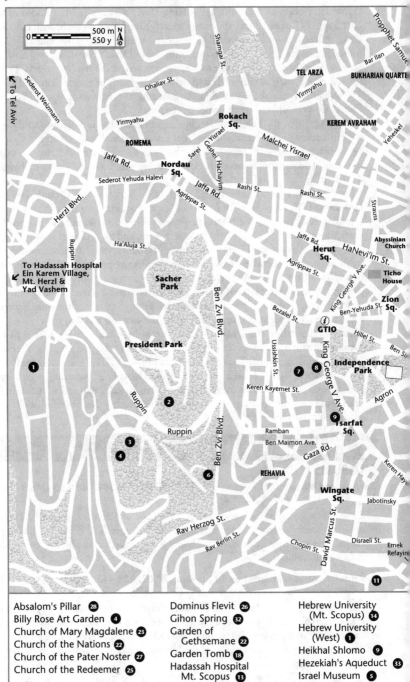

Absalom's Pillar **28**	Dominus Flevit **26**	Hebrew University
Billy Rose Art Garden **4**	Gihon Spring **32**	(Mt. Scopus) **14**
Church of Mary Magdalene **23**	Garden of	Hebrew University
Church of the Nations **22**	Gethsemane **22**	(West) **1**
Church of the Pater Noster **27**	Garden Tomb **18**	Heikhal Shlomo **9**
Church of the Redeemer **25**	Hadassah Hospital	Hezekiah's Aqueduct **33**
	Mt. Scopus **13**	Israel Museum **5**

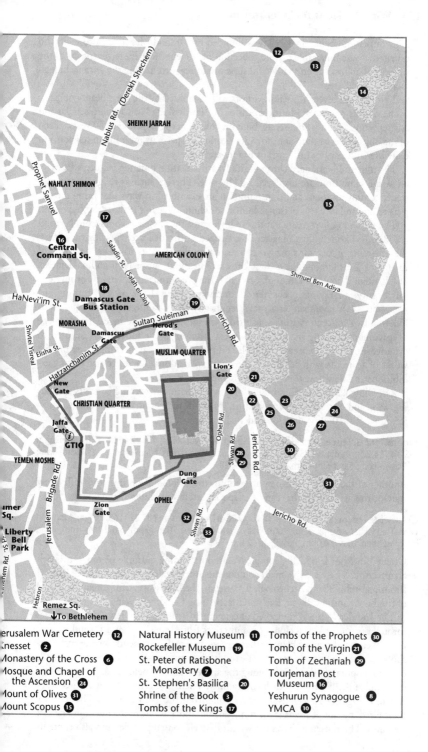

Jerusalem War Cemetery 12

Knesset 2

Monastery of the Cross 6

Mosque and Chapel of the Ascension 24

Mount of Olives 31

Mount Scopus 15

Natural History Museum 11

Rockefeller Museum 19

St. Peter of Ratisbone Monastery 7

St. Stephen's Basilica 20

Shrine of the Book 3

Tombs of the Kings 17

Tombs of the Prophets 30

Tomb of the Virgin 21

Tomb of Zechariah 29

Tourjeman Post Museum 16

Yeshurun Synagogue 8

YMCA 10

149

This museum, opened in 1992, was founded by Dr. and Mrs. Elie Borowski, who donated an incomparable private collection of ancient Near Eastern artifacts as the nucleus of an institution that would survey cultures surrounding the ancient Judeo–Israelite world.

This is an art lovers' museum: visitors will be amazed by the great beauty of many of the objects on display. In the words of Dr. Borowski, a Near Eastern scholar and adviser to museums, who carefully built his collection over a period of 40 years, "Each of the objects has its time in history, its location in space, its meaning in religion and daily life, and last but not least, its beauty and artistry."

The museum is arranged chronologically: artifacts from differing cultures that existed at the same time are displayed side by side. Themes such as religious worship, trade, communication, and transportation are examined in ways that bring the objects to life, and give us a personal, human insight into life in the times they represent.

The museum offers many impressive highlights: the Assyrian ivories from Nimrud (ca. 800 B.C.), including a masterpiece winged griffin delicately grazing on foliage; the 4th-century A.D. sarcophagus of Julia Latronilla, with its bas-relief depiction of the life of Jesus (among the earliest known representations of Jesus and of elements of Christian theology). Other objects catch the eye with charm, vitality, or mysterious beauty: an Egyptian cosmetics container in the shape of a swimming girl (ca. 1550 B.C.); a Minoan terracotta sarcophagus, freely painted in bright colors with folk motifs; a 1st-century Roman painted linen shroud with the ethereal, serene image of a woman covering its length. A special section of the museum is devoted to cylinder seals and scarabs; a remarkable computer/video program brings these minute works of art to life with detailed, fascinating explanations. There are also visiting exhibitions and new donations to the museum's collection.

The Bible Lands Museum hosts a program of Saturday evening concerts (including wine and cheese) that often features many of the country's most talented new immigrants ($10; discounts for students).

Bloomfield Science Museum. Rupin Street at Givat Ram. ☎ **02/618-128.** Admission NIS 14 ($4.20); students NIS 12 ($3.60). Mon and Wed–Thurs 10am–6pm; Tues 10am–8pm; Fri 10am–1pm; Sat 10am–3pm. Bus: 9, 24, or 28.

Another of the city's brand-new attractions, this is a hands-on museum with many state-of-the-art exhibits that can be of special interest to children and young adults.

✪ **Israel Museum.** Ruppin Street. ☎ **02/708-811.** Admission NIS 22 ($6.60). Sun–Mon and Wed–Thurs 10am–5pm; Fri, eve of holidays, and holidays 10am–2pm; Sat 10am–4pm; main building open Tues 4–10pm. Bus: 9, 17, 24, or 99.

Opened in May 1965, this complex is an outstanding example of modern Israeli architecture. There are five main components: the Bezalel Art Museum, the Samuel Bronfman Biblical and Archeological Museum, the Billy Rose Art Garden, the Shrine of the Book, and the always lively and fascinating Children's Wing.

The **Judaica Wing** is composed of ceremonial artifacts from Jewish communities throughout the world, including manuscripts from Iran, Italy, and Poland. In one room there are dozens of Hanukkah lamps, silver Torah ornaments, serving trays, and shofars; other rooms contain a vast exhibit of costumes worn by Jews in the lands of the Diaspora, all displayed among the artifacts and elements of architecture that surrounded the daily life of each community. There is a reconstructed 17th-century Italian synagogue as well as a German one from the 18th century. The recently transferred interior of a synagogue from Cochin, India, is one of the museum's newest treasures. The museum shows the work of Israeli contemporaries and also contains period rooms. The Archeology Wing contains the world's largest collection of objects found in Israel.

The **Bronfman–Bezalel complex,** in the main building and adjoining wings, houses a bookstore and gift shop in its lower level, as well as a snack bar and an auditorium. Outside, to the right of the stairs, is the museum cafeteria (moderate prices).

Three important new pavilions have been added in recent years. One contains a beautifully chosen collection of **pre-Colombian Central American art** from 2000 B.C. to A.D. 1550; another is a separate building housing ancient glass; and the third is the **Walter and Charlotte Floersheimer Pavilion for Impressionist and Post-Impressionist Art** with works by Corot, Monet, Renoir, Degas, Gauguin, Matisse, and other artists. The new **Weisbord Pavilion,** just across the walk from the museum's entrance building and gift shop, houses a small collection of Rodin as well as visiting exhibits of modern art.

Another remarkable segment of the museum is an archeological garden between the Shrine of the Book and the Youth Wing complex. It contains classical Greco-Roman sculptures, sarcophagi, and mosaics, most of which were discovered and excavated in Israel.

The **Billy Rose Art Garden,** on a 20-acre plot, has been impressively landscaped by the renowned Japanese-American artist, Isamu Noguchi. In the garden of semi-circular earth-and-stone embankments is a 100-piece sculpture collection. The out-door sculpture garden, on successive pebbled slopes, contains both classical and modern European, American, and Israeli works—Rodin, Zorach, Henry Moore, Picasso, Maillol, and Channa Orloff.

Then there's the **Shrine of the Book,** with its distinctive onion-shaped top, contoured to resemble the jar covers in which the Dead Sea Scrolls were discovered. In addition to housing the prized Dead Sea Scrolls and the Bar Kokhba letters, the underground shrine is the exhibition site for additional finds from Masada.

On Saturday or holidays, you have to buy your tickets just outside the museum, from a local ticket agent. The museum is located south of the Knesset.

✪ **L. A. Mayer Memorial Museum of Islamic Art.** 2 Ha-Palmach St. ☎ **02/661-291.** Admission NIS 12 ($3.60). Sun, Mon, Wed, Thurs 10am–5pm; Tues 4pm–8pm; Fri–Sat 10am–2pm.

This is another Jerusalem museum that is very worth visiting, with a strong permanent collection of Islamic art, and excellent visiting exhibitions. The museum also houses a large and fascinating international collection of clocks, including the famous Salomons collection of Bruquet watches from Paris dating from 1769 to1823.

Museum of Natural History. 6 Mohilever St. ☎ **02/631-116.** Admission NIS 8 ($2.40). Sun–Thurs 8:30am–1pm. Closed Aug. Bus: 4, 14, or 18.

This museum displays local flora and fauna and basic scientific exhibits.

Pontifical Biblical Institute. 3 Emil Botta St. ☎ **02/252-843.** By appointment only. Bus: 5, 6, 18, or 21.

Located near the King David Hotel, the institute houses a rich archeological collection, including an Egyptian mummy.

✪ **Sir Isaac and Lady Edith Wolfson Museum.** In Heikhal Shlomo, King George St. ☎ **02/247-112.** Admission NIS 3 (90¢). Sun–Thurs 9am–1pm. Bus: 4, 7, 8, 9, or 48.

Don't miss this outstanding collection of Judaica. Although mostly composed of an-tique objects, the collection also includes works of contemporary Judaica by craftspeople like Oded Davidson and Danny Azulai, whose shops can be visited in downtown Jerusalem.

Skirball Museum of Biblical Archeology. Hebrew Union College, 13 King David St. ☎ **02/ 203-333.** Free admission. Sun–Thurs 10am–4pm; Fri and Sat 10am–2pm.

For archeology buffs, this handsomely displayed collection is a worthwhile stop.

The Taxation Museum. 32 Agron St. ☎ **02/258-978.** Admission NIS 7 ($2.10). Sun, Tues, and Thurs 1pm–4pm; Mon, Wed, and Fri 10am–noon. Bus: 5, 18, 19, or 21.

This museum is devoted entirely to aspects of taxation and collection in ancient Israel, during the Diaspora, and in Israel today.

MEMORIALS

Mount Herzl. Free admission. Park, Apr–Oct daily 8am–6:30pm; museum, Sun–Thurs 9am– 5pm, Fri 9am–1pm; Nov–Mar both close at 5pm. Bus: 17, 17A, 18, 20, 21, 23, 24, 26, 27, 39, 40, or 99 to Herzl Boulevard.

Mount Herzl is located at the end of the Bet Ha-Kerem section. It is the memorial for Theodor Herzl, who predicted and worked for the founding of Israel until his death in 1904. A large black monolith marks Herzl's interment. Herzl's wife and his parents are buried there, too. The cemetery also contains the graves of Golda Meir, Levi Eshkol, and other important leaders.

Down the road from the Herzl cemetery, inside an entrance made of orange stone, is a military cemetery for those who have fallen in the country's many wars.

The **Herzl Museum** (☎ 02/511-108) contains a replica of Herzl's Vienna study with his own library and furniture.

✪ **Yad VaShem Memorial.** ☎ **02/751-611** for information. Sun–Thurs 9am–4:45pm; Fri 9am–1pm. Hall of Names, Sun–Thurs 10am–2pm; Fri 10am–12:30pm. Archives and Library, Sun–Thurs 9am–3pm. Closed Sat and Jewish holidays. Bus: 17, 18, 20, 21, 23, 27, or 99.

Down the road from Mount Herzl is a ridge called Har Ha-Zikron (Mount of Remembrance). The Avenue of the Righteous Among the Nations, lined with trees planted in tribute to each individual gentile who helped save Jewish lives during the Nazi era, leads into the memorial.

The heavy entrance gate to the Hall of Remembrance, designed by Bezalel Schatz and David Polombo, is an abstract tapestry of jagged, twisted steel. Inside is a huge stone room, like a crypt, where an eternal flame sheds an eerie light over the plaques on the floor: Bergen-Belsen, Auschwitz, Dachau . . .

The building to the left has a permanent exhibition of photographs and effects relating to the Holocaust. Other exhibits include a museum of works pertaining to the Holocaust, and the Hall of Names that contains more than 3 million pages of testimony, as well as the names, photographs, and personal details of as many of those who perished in the Holocaust as Yad VaShem has been able to gather. Visitors are invited to contribute information about relatives and friends in order that no victim will be forgotten.

On the crest of the western slope of the Mount of Remembrance stands a 20-foot-high monument dedicated to the 1½ million Jewish soldiers among the allied forces, partisans, and ghetto fighters. Below the monument one can see the Valley of the Destroyed Communities, commemorating the 5,000 European Jewish communities that disappeared during World War II. There is a special memorial to the Children of the Holocaust commemorating more than 1½ million murdered children.

Across the hill is an archive building that has possibly the most complete library dedicated to this topic.

⭐ **Frommer's Favorite Jerusalem Experiences**

Visiting the Old City. Wandering around the markets, archeological sites, and holy places.

An Evening at the Cinémathèque. Dinner or coffee on the terrace of the Cinémathèque Café across the Hinnom Valley from the Old City Walls. Take in a film as well. (Warm weather.)

The View from the Roof of the Petra Hotel. Bring your camera and come back at the end of the day to watch the Old City fade into twilight.

A Walking Tour with SPNI. The Society for Preservation of Nature in Israel offers the best in the country; these tours always attract interesting fellow travelers. Choose from a Ramparts Walk of the Old City, archeological tour of the City of David, or go farther afield: a late-winter hike down Wadi Kelt Canyon near Jericho when the landscape is ablaze with wildflowers, or a moonlight tour of the Judean desert.

The Concert Scene. Israel has always had a surfeit of excellent musicians. Now, with the Russian immigration, you'll find even more rare and exquisite performances, from ethnic and folk to liturgical and classical, often in dramatic venues. Check the *Jerusalem Post.*

CHURCHES & MONASTERIES

There are a number of interesting Christian sites and churches in West Jerusalem. From Zion Square, in the heart of downtown Jerusalem, cross Jaffa Road and go up the hill on Rav Kook Street. Rehov Ha-Nevi'im, "Street of the Prophets," which was the "Christian street" of 19th-century West Jerusalem, has a variety of churches and missionary societies, including the Swedish Theological Seminary at the corner of Ethiopia Street, the Christian Missionary Alliance, and the American Bible Institute.

Opposite the intersection of Ha-Rav Kook and Ethiopia streets is the entrance to the narrow, high-walled Ethiopia Street with its 19th-century stone mansions. Here you'll find the splendid **Abyssinian (Ethiopian) Church.** The elegant building with the Lion of Judah carved into the gate above the courtyard is the spiritual home of the Coptic Ethiopian clergy. The lion symbolizes the meeting of the Queen of Sheba, the Ethiopian empress, and King Solomon, from whom she traditionally received the emblem. The interior of the circular church, built at the turn of the century, is filled with a wonderful array of icons and paintings; although none are in the Ethiopian tradition, many were chosen for their charm and native beauty. The entire church enclave is surrounded by bungalows for clergy and pilgrims from Ethiopia.

In the center of the city on the corner of King George V Avenue and Gaza Road (Derekh Aza) the landmark **Terra Sancta** has had various public uses, and was the temporary quarters of the Hebrew University in the 1950s, when the original campus on Mount Scopus was cut off from West Jerusalem, and the new campus at Givat Ram had not yet been built.

Notre Dame de France is on Shivtei Israel Street at Zahal Square, just opposite New Gate in the Old City walls. This monastery was built by the Assumptionist Fathers in 1887 to serve as a pilgrim's hostel. The monumental buildings of the complex, on the old border between East and West Jerusalem, were badly damaged during heavy fighting in the 1948 war. Part of the complex, restored in the 1970s, serves as a hospital, a restaurant, hotel, and pilgrimage center.

Saint Peter of Ratisbone Monastery, next to the Yeshurun Synagogue on Shmuel Ha-Nagid Street, founded in 1874 by the Fathers of Zion order, houses a French Catholic monastery as well as a veterinary surgery and private business offices.

Saint Andrew's Church of Scotland was built by the people of Scotland in 1929 and was dedicated by General Allenby, who had liberated Jerusalem from the Ottoman Empire in 1917. This Presbyterian church is situated on a hilltop near Abu Tor and the Jerusalem railroad station.

Also at the top of Abu Tor, and built over the foundations of a medieval church, is the **Greek Orthodox Monastery,** called the "Church of Evil Counsel." It contains catacombs and crypts. The grounds contain private cottages rented to fortunate Jerusalemites, including one of the country's most talented and respected poets.

The **Russian Orthodox Holy Trinity Cathedral** is just off Jaffa Road. This multidomed edifice was originally constructed after the Crimean War for pilgrims of the Russian Orthodox faith (see "Russian Compound" above).

A number of interesting sites are located in the city's environs. The medieval **Monastery of the Cross** lies in a valley below the residential section of Rehavia. It has a beautiful garden and a medieval church with restored mosaics. Traditionally, it stands on the site where the tree was cut for the Cross.

A number of churches and sites are located in Ein Kerem, including the **Russian Church of Saint John,** with its red steeple. Also in Ein Kerem is the **Franciscan Church and Monastery of Saint John.** It is built on a 5th-century site said to be the birthplace of Saint John the Baptist. **The Church of the Visitation** marks the site of the visit of Mary to Elizabeth, mother of Saint John the Baptist. A long walk from the bus will bring you to the **Monastery of Saint John of the Desert,** another Franciscan monastery, set on a hillside 1 mile from Ein Keren, in the grotto where Saint John is believed to have spent his early years. To reach Ein Kerem, take bus 17.

There are also interesting sites in Abu Ghosh; see "Attractions Outside Jerusalem" below.

OTHER ATTRACTIONS

Hadassah Medical Center. In Kerem. ☎ **02/416-333.** Admission to Chagall windows and tours: NIS 7 ($2.10); discount for students. Bus: 19 or 27 from Jaffa Road; 19 from Jaffa Gate, Agron St., King George V Avenue, or Bezalel Street.

The largest medical center in the Middle East, the Hadassah Hebrew University Medical Center stands on a hilltop several miles from downtown Jerusalem.

This project contains a medical school, nursing school, hospital, dental and pharmacy schools, and various laboratory buildings. The hospital's synagogue contains Chagall's 12 exquisite stained-glass windows depicting the Twelve Tribes of Israel.

The Synagogue is open Sun–Thurs 8:30am–1pm and 2pm–3:45pm. Medical Center tours, including Chagall windows, leave Sun–Thurs 8:30, 9:30, 10:30, and 11:30am and 12:30pm; Fri 9:30, 10:30, and 11:30am; half-day tours of all projects by reservation at least a day in advance; synagogue tour only, Sun–Thurs 2–3:45pm. Closed holidays. Always call in advance for tour availability information.

Hebrew University. Givat Ram Campus (West Jerusalem). ☎ **02/882-819.** Free tours Sun–Thurs 10am from Visitors Center in the Sherman Building. Bus: 9, 24, or 28 to modern Givat Ram campus.

Surrounded by rolling hills, the Hebrew University is one of Israel's most dramatic accomplishments, with 14,000 students on this and the Mount Scopus campus. Built to replace the university's original Mount Scopus campus, which was cut off from

West Jerusalem from 1948 to 1967, the Givat Ram Campus now houses the university's science departments.

Take special architectural note of the Belgium House Faculty Club, La Maison de France, the Physics Building, and the huge National and University Library (partly inspired by LeCorbusier's Villa Savoye in Poissy, France) at the far end of the promenade. And don't miss the mushroom-shaped synagogue behind the library or the futuristic gym. The synagogue, with its dome supported by eight arches, was designed by Heinz Rau and David Reznik; Reznik's imprint dots the city. He also designed Jerusalem's Hyatt Regency Hotel, and co-designed the beautiful and inventive Mormon Center on Mount Scopus.

You can stop for lunch in the cafeteria of the Administration Building, or in the Jewish National and University Library.

Heikhal Shlomo. 58 King George V Ave. No phone. Free admission; Wolfson Museum: NIS 5 ($1.50). Tours Sun–Thurs 9am–1pm; Fri 9am–noon. Bus: 4, 7, 8, 9, or 48.

Facing the large main park, Gan Ha-Atzma'ut, this imposing complex includes the Great Synagogue and Seat of the Rabbinate, designed in a rather vague interpretation of what was believed to be the style of King Solomon's Temple. Square at the bottom and domed on top, the building houses the country's highest religious offices. Weekly programs—religious and folk songs, lectures, and readings—mark the end of the Sabbath and the beginning of the new week. For times of traditional religious services, check at Heikhal Shlomo, your hotel, or the tourist information office. The Wolfson collection of Judaica, one of the world's finest, can be seen on the fourth floor.

Jerusalem Artists' House and Old Bezalel Academy of Arts and Design. 12 Shmuel Ha-Nagid St. ☎ **02/253-653.** Free admission. Sun–Fri 10am–1pm and 4–7pm; Sat 10am–1pm. Bus: 4, 7, 8, 9, 19, or 48.

Many cultural activities center around exhibitions of the Jerusalem Artists' Association. Exhibitions of art, evenings of chamber music, concerts, readings, jazz, and art lectures are scheduled each year (for specifics, check with the tourist office or at the office here); there's an expensive restaurant (Cezanne) and a very good, affordable vegetarian restaurant (the Village Green) where tourists are welcome. On the main floor, paintings and sculpture of all 430 artist members are sold (if you buy, they'll ship your purchases). Upstairs and throughout the building are general exhibitions in August and the spring; special exhibitions, featuring about three artists at a time, change every 3 weeks during the rest of the year. Note the beautifully carved outside doors, the crenellated roof and dome, and the garden sculpture. The present Bezalel School is at the Hebrew University.

King David Hotel. King David St. ☎ **02/251-111.** Bus: 5, 6, 18, or 21.

This famous hotel, built in the 1930s, is a monument to the defunct British Empire. The King David, too, has suffered the trials of history. In 1946, its south wing, housing British military headquarters, was blown up by a Jewish terrorist organization in a violent demonstration against the British presence in Israel. The entire wing of the building was subsequently rebuilt, but if you look closely, you can see the difference in the stone. The outdoor patio here is a lovely place for a drink, but the lobby of the hotel (where in the 1930s, Sudanese waiters garbed in white pantaloons and red fezes once glided amongst the guests) should be experienced just for its own art deco–Egyptianesque sake. The hotel has had a long list of famous guests including Henry Kissinger and Haile Selassie of Ethiopia; normal guests may find themselves transferred to less famous lodgings to make way for a sudden emergency visit of the U.S. Secretary of State or some other diplomatic entourage (see "Where to Stay" in Chapter 3).

Model of Ancient Jerusalem. Holyland Hotel, Bayit, Vegan. ☎ **02/437-777.** Admission NIS 10 ($3). Sun–Thurs 9am–5pm; Fri 9am–1pm; summer daily 9am–8pm (Fri and Sat until 5pm). Bus: 21 or 21A from downtown.

Created by the late archeologist Michael Avi-Yonah, and constantly updated with new discoveries, this is a perfectly scaled-down model of Jerusalem as it was in the time of the Second Temple, with palaces, mammoth walls, and elegant towers.

To get there, take the road opposite Mount Herzl and follow signs pointing to Holyland Hotel. The garden is a short walk from the hotel's entrance.

Nahon Museum of Italian Jewish Art. 27 Hillel St. ☎ **02/241-610.** Admission NIS 6 ($1.80). Sun–Thurs 10am–1pm; Wed 10am–1pm and 4pm–7pm.

This museum contains the transported interior of the beautiful 18th-century synagogue of Conegliano Veneto, near Venice, which is open for services on Friday evenings and on Saturday mornings. The exhibits cover the scope of Italian Jewish life and contain ritual objects from medieval times to the present; you may be able to visit the on-site workshops of a special team of Italian and Israeli artisans working to restore and preserve these treasures of Jerusalem's Italian Jewish community. The garden and plaza in front of the complex seem to be a small piece of Italy itself.

Parliament (Knesset). Government Quarter–Kiryat Ben-Gurion, Kaplan St. ☎ **02/753-333.** Free guided tours on Sun and Thurs 8:30am–2:30pm; Knesset session Mon, Tues, or Wed 4–9pm. Closed Jewish holidays. Bus: 9, 17, 24, 28, or 99.

The most impressive of the government buildings, this is a $7-million structure of gray-colored stone. This modern landmark, West Jerusalem's "Acropolis," has a 24-foot-high Chagall mosaic in the reception hall, and contains a synagogue and exhibition rooms. The entranceway, a grillwork of hammered metal, is the work of the Israeli sculptor David Polombo, who did the dramatic doors at Yad VaShem. You must have your passport with you. Knesset sessions are usually sleep inducing, but at times erupt into heated arguments and even fistfights. Always call ahead to check current schedule.

Russian Compound. Off Jaffa Road near Zion Square. Admission NIS 3 (90¢). Sun–Tues and Thurs 9:30am–5:30pm; Wed 9:30am–9:30pm; Fri 9am–2pm. Bus: 18 or 20.

In 1965 Israel purchased this compound from Russia. Once this 19th-century series of structures that surrounds the beautiful Russian Orthodox Holy Trinity Church was the world's largest "hotel"; it could accommodate 10,000 Russian pilgrims at one time (until World War I, Russians composed the largest block of pilgrims in the Holy Land). A permanent exhibit stands in the Museum of Underground Prisoners (☎ 02/233-166), which once served as British Mandate Jerusalem's Central Prison (see the cells and execution chambers). It focuses on Jewish underground activities that occurred before 1948. Today this neglected but architecturally striking enclave serves as a municipal parking lot and an Israeli lock-up; at visiting times, families of prisoners can often be seen huddling outside the police barracades. There are plans to restore the pilgimage buildings, turn the parking lots into gardens, and turn the complex into luxury and moderate hotels—it could create an oddly romantic touch of Saint Petersburg right in the heart of Jerusalem.

As you walk along Jaffa Road from Zion Square, look up to your left (north), before the main post office, and you'll see the Russian Orthodox church.

Sanhedrian Tombs. Sanhedria. Free admission. Gardens daily 9am–4 or 5pm; tombs Sun–Fri 9am–4 or 5pm. Bus: 2 from Jaffa Gate.

Go up Shmuel Ha-Navi, off Shivtei Israel Street, to northeast Jerusalem's beautiful public gardens of Sanhedria. Here you look at the Tombs of Sanhedria or the Tombs of the Judges, where the judges of ancient Israel's "Supreme Court" (during the 1st and 2nd centuries) are buried. The three-story burial catacomb is intricately carved from rock.

Supreme Court Building. Next to Knesset. ☎ **02/759-612.** Sun–Fri 9am–3pm; free tours in English Sun–Thurs at noon. Bus: 9, 17, 24, 28, or 99.

In a country starved for good modern architecture, the new Supreme Court Building, opened in 1992, is a major hit with Israelis and tourists alike. The contemporary design of the building incorporates traditional Middle Eastern motifs of domes, arches, and passageways, all set up to create interesting interplays of shadow and light. Acoustics in trial and hearing chambers are not great, which may serve to further isolate the court's august panel of jurists.

Phone or check with Tourist Information for current schedule.

YMCA. 24 King David St. ☎ **02/252-111.** Free admission; small donations for the tower. Tours Mon–Sat 9am–3pm. Bus: 5, 6, 18, or 21.

One of the most outstanding landmarks of the city, the YMCA was built in the early 1930s with funds donated by a Montclair, New Jersey, philanthropist named James Jarvie. Designed by the architectural firm that did New York City's Empire State Building, the building is an interesting mixture of art deco, Byzantine, and Islamic styles. This is probably the most amazing YMCA in the world. On the first floor, you'll find a replica of the London room in which the YMCA was founded in 1844. The tower (open Mon–Sat from 9am to 2pm) offers one of the most dramatic panoramas of the city. Notice the six winged bas-relief seraph that ornaments the center of the tower's facade; the tower also houses the only carillon in the Middle East. Concerts played on the tower bells, especially at midnight on New Year's Eve, are among the city's little-known pleasures. Built by a combination of Christian, Jewish, and Muslim workers and artisans, the YMCA is a meeting place for all the city's communities. The complex includes a swimming pool, tennis courts, athletic fields, lecture and concert halls, a gymnasium, restaurant, and one of the best hotels in Jerusalem.

For a view of the city, take the elevator up to the top of the 152-foot tower.

3 Exploring West Jerusalem Neighborhoods

YEMIN MOSHE In the 1850s British philanthropist Sir Moses Montefiore, with the help of Judah Touro from New Orleans, built the nucleus of this residential quarter, the first outside the walls of the Old City, in an effort to bring indigent Jews from the Old City to a more healthful environment. The project included the now famous windmill for grinding flour. Despite its magnificent view and graceful architecture, the neighborhood remained poor for over a century.

Today Yemin Moshe is a picturesque, beautifully restored neighborhood—an architectural treasure and one of the most elegant addresses in town. There are no shops, but the views are spectacular. It's a fascinating place for an early evening or winter afternoon stroll; however, a noontime walk in the hot July sun is not recommended. The steep pedestrian street staircases of Yemin Moshe may make it a bit difficult for those with walking problems.

Down one of the first flights of staircases is the **Yemem Moshe Windmill,** which houses a museum dedicated to Sir Moses Montefiore. It is open Sunday through Thursday from 9am to 4pm, and until 1pm on Friday. Below the Montefiore

Windmill is the original row of **old stone buildings called Mishkanot Sha'ananim,** built by Sir Moses Montefiore in 1854. Ornamented by Victorian ironwork porches, the building is used as a residence for visiting artists and diplomats.

A replica of the Liberty Bell in Philadelphia stands in the center of Jerusalem's **Liberty Bell Garden,** not far from the windmill, and easily accessible to strollers from King David Street. The 7-acre garden has a picnic area, vine-covered trellises, and a large children's playground and an entertainment area. You may wonder why a copy of the Liberty Bell has been made into the centerpiece of a Jerusalem park. The words inscribed on the American original were spoken by the Prophet Isaiah over 2,500 years before the Declaration of Independence: "Proclaim liberty throughout the land, and to all the inhabitants thereof." It was with these words that Israel's independence was announced in 1948.

MEA SHEARIM   This area, a few blocks north of Jaffa Road, is populated by Hasidic and ultraorthodox Jews of East European origin. It is a world unto itself and a visit here is like going back in a time machine to the world of religious East European Jewry that existed before the Holocaust. Originally built in the late 19th century as a semifortified agricultural community in what was at that time open countryside about a mile beyond the walls of the Old City, the neighborhood consists of numerous courtyards designed to be defended against unruly Bedouin marauders. In the 20th century the area came to be inhabited by Hasidic rabbinical courts and followers of the many Hasidic sects that emigrated to Jerusalem from various locales in Europe. Young boys with pale white faces wear bobbing side-curls *(payot),* short black pants, and high black socks. Some married women in this area, according to strict East European Orthodox tradition, wear wigs and scarves over their shaved heads. A number of residents speak only Yiddish in conversation, as Hebrew is considered too sacred for daily use. Some don't even recognize the laws of the Israeli government, believing that no State of Israel can exist before the coming of the Messiah. There have been clashes with police in demonstrations protesting autopsies, driving on Saturday, and coed swimming pools. The neighborhood is filled with synagogues, yeshivas, small workshops and shops selling religious objects.

Architecturally, Mea Shearim has the feel of an 18th-century Polish ghetto, the more so because of the traditional dress and lifestyle of its residents. Visitors to this area are requested to dress modestly (no shorts, short skirts, uncovered arms or shoulders for women; slacks for men). Men and women are advised not to walk in close proximity (certainly not hand in hand!) and vistors are advised to stow away cameras and to be very discreet in taking photographs. No inhabitant of Mea Shearim will voluntarily pose for snapshots, and there have been incidents in which improperly dressed visitors have been spat upon or stoned.

GERMAN COLONY & BAKA   One mile south of downtown West Jerusalem, these two picturesque neighborhoods, filled with overgrown gardens, are undergoing a process of gentrification. For many years, the old cottages and mansions (built at the start of the century by German Protestants and affluent Arabic families) housed Israelis from exotic places like Kurdistan and Morocco, but more recently, members of Jerusalem's American, British, and Latin American immigrant communities have been moving in. The two charming neighborhoods offer family-run restaurants and shops that tend to reflect the area's ambience. **Emek Refaim Street** (a southern continuation of downtown Jerusalem's King David Street) is the German Colony's main artery; a walk down **Yehoshua Ben Nun Street,** which runs parallel to Emek Refaim one block to the west beginning at **Rachel Immenu Street,** gives you a better idea of the neighborhood's interesting residential architecture. Because of the area's newfound popularity, modern apartment buildings are being squeezed into every possible garden and empty lot. Much of the area might have been completely demolished and reused for housing projects had it not been for efforts spearheaded by Sara Fox Kaminiker, who came to Israel from the United States and served on the city council under the administration of Teddy Kollek (Sara Fox Kaminiker's book of Walking Tours, *Footloose in Jerusalem*, which includes this neighborhood, is highly recommended).

In Baka, the main street is **Derekh Bethlehem.** On many of the narrow side streets running off this thoroughfare, you'll find eccentric examples of Arabic mansions and 1930s bungalows. For those who like architecture, the quiet back streets of both neighborhoods are good places to meander by bicycle.

REHAVIA-TALBEYEH   A turn to the west from King George V Avenue, either at the Jewish Agency compound or at the Kings Hotel, will bring you into Jerusalem's most beautiful residential section, with its middle- and upper-class, tree-lined, quiet streets. Rehavia's glory is its collection of 1930s International Style apartment buildings and houses. Talbeyeh, just to the south, is filled with elaborate villas and mansions built mainly by families from Jerusalem's Arab Christian community in the 1920s and 1930s. Abandoned when their original owners fled in 1948, these houses are now inhabited by Israelis. Hovei Zion Street is lined with examples of these gracious homes.

Some sights in the area include the **prime minister's residence,** at the corner of Balfour and Smolenskin; the **Alfasi grotto** (also called the Tomb of Jason), on Alfasi Street, a frescoed and inscribed tomb discovered by builders while they were digging foundations (open from 10am to 4pm); and the **Monastery of the Cross,** in the Valley of the Cross outside Rehavia, built by Gregorian monks in the 11th century, and now maintained by the Greek Orthodox Church. According to tradition, the beautiful, medieval monastery is located on the spot where the tree stood from which the cross was made. If you don't want to walk down the rocky hillside from Rehavia to the monastery, take bus no. 9 or 17. At the southern edge of Rehavia, in Kiryat Shmuel, is **Bet Ha-Nassi,** the president's residence.

EIN KEREM   This ancient village, in a deep valley at the western edge of Jerusalem, is traditionally regarded as the birthplace of John the Baptist. Now incorporated into Jerusalem, you can reach it in less than a half hour by bus 17 from King George Street or Jaffa Road. The lanes and gardens of Ein Kerem (Well of the Vineyard) are lovely, the old Arabic style houses have been grabbed up and renovated by some of the city's most successful and famous inhabitants, and high above the area, on the crest of the mountains, is the vast Hadassah–Ein Kerem Medical Center (not accessible from Ein Kerem itself). Ein Kerem contains a number of 19th-century European churches, convents, and monasteries. Most important is the **Church of Saint John** in the center of town, marking John the Baptist's birthplace (open daily from 6am to noon and 2–5pm); on request you can see the grotto beneath the church with its Byzantine mosaic. On Ma'ayan Street, you'll find the **Church of the Visitation** (open daily 8am–11:45am and 2–5pm), commemorating the visit of Mary to her cousin Elizabeth, the mother of John the Baptist. Often depicted in medieval and early Renaissance paintings as a scene in which the two expectant women touch each other's stomachs, according to legend, the two infants jumped for joy inside their mothers' wombs when Mary and Elizabeth met. Below the Youth Hostel off Ma'ayan Street is a mosque and minaret marking the well from which Mary drew water; farther along the ridge is the Russian Convent, known as the **Moscobiyah,** a fascinating enclave of 40 Jerusalem stone buildings scattered among a wooded area of pines and cypresses. The nuns live in small ochre painted houses reminiscent of wooden cottages in Russia. You can make an appointment to visit by telephoning 252-565 or 412-887. Bring a snack or canteen along, or you can pick up something in the grocery at the center of town. Restaurants here look appealing, but meals are expensive and nothing special. The times for return to Jerusalem should be posted at the bus stop in the center of Ein Kerem; you may have to wait in downtown Jerusalem for up to a half hour until the infrequent bus 17 to Ein Kerem picks you up.

MAHANE YEHUDA   The Old Market Quarter—liveliest on Wednesday and Thursday—is off Jaffa Road, half a mile west of Zion Square. In a square off Mahane Yehuda and Jaffa Road, there is a war memorial commemorating the "Davidka," an improvised weapon used in the defense of Jerusalem.

4 East Jerusalem Attractions

You can probably cover the major sights of East Jerusalem in half a day. As you go along Saladin Street from the north, toward the Old City walls, you'll pass the Ministry of Justice, on the right. Farther down, across the street in a tree-shaded compound, is the famed Albright Institute of Archeological Research. Just after it, on the left, you'll find Az-Zahra Street, a modern thoroughfare of clothing and appliance stores, bookshops, restaurants, and hotels, leading to the Rockefeller Museum.

The Garden Tomb. Conrad Schick Street. ☎ **02/283-402.** Free admission (donations accepted). Mon–Sat 8am–12:15pm and 2:30–5:15pm; Protestant service in English Sun 9am. Bus: 27.

The 1st-century tomb, discovered in 1867 by Dr. Conrad Schick, is very similar to the description of the biblical one in which Jesus was interred. In 1883 General Gordon, hero of China and Khartoum, visited the tomb on his way to Egypt, and in a fit of pique over the exclusion of Protestant services from the Church of the Holy Sepulcher, had a vision that this site outside the Damascus Gate was the real tomb of Jesus. The tomb was finally excavated in 1891, and whether it is "the place" or not, it certainly meets some of the specifications: near the site of the crucifixion, outside the walls of the city, hewn from the rock, a tomb, made for a rich man and situated in a garden. As late as the early 20th century, the hill Gordon identified as Golgotha (Calvary), or according to the New Testament, "The Place of the Skull," was indeed eerily shaped like a skull—but construction has obscured this impression.

Directions: Head up Nablus Road (Derekh Shechem), opposite Damascus Gate. Look for the side street named Conrad Schick Street on the right.

Rockefeller Archeological Museum. Sultan Suleiman Street. ☎ **02/282-251.** Admission NIS 12 ($3.60). Sun–Thurs 10am–5pm; Fri–Sat and eves of holidays 10am–3pm. Bus: 23 or 27.

Located near Herod's Gate, the museum's eclectic 1930s design includes a castlelike tower and cloister gardens. The top of the castle-turret was badly shot up during the Six-Day War, but the museum's displays were barely affected, and there was no damage at all to the many Dead Sea Scrolls, kept for study in the museum at that time, under Jordanian control.

The northern and southern galleries contain one of the most extensive archeological collections in this part of the world. Much of the treasure was excavated in the areas of Acre and the Galilee by American and English archeologists in the first half of this century. Pottery, tools, and household effects are arranged by periods—Iron Age, Persian, Hellenistic, Roman, Byzantine. In the south gallery's Paleolithic section are displayed the bones of Mount Carmel Man.

Saint George's Cathedral. Nablus Road. Free admission. Daily 9am–4pm. Bus: 27.

Neogothic towers adorn this compound, which also includes an excellent travelers' guesthouse and the headquarters for the Anglican archbishopric, with jurisdiction extending as far across the Middle East as Sudan. It's a rare architectural enclave for this part of the world, recalling the courtyards of Oxford or Cambridge. Feel free to pass through the courtyard for a look. The complex also contains a religious college, a school, a small garden, and residences. There is a small exhibit of beautiful Palestinian textiles on display as well.

Directions: From Tourjeman Post, go north to intersection and turn right.

Tombs of the Kings. Saladin Street. Admission NIS 12 ($3.60). Mon–Sat 8am–12:30pm and 2–5pm. Bus: 27.

As you exit the gate from Saint George's, turn right (north) and circle around the complex to Saladin Street. You'll notice, as you circle, the gate to American Colony Hotel north of Saint George's.

Behind Saint George's, on the left side as you head down Saladin Street, is a gate marked "Tombeau des Rois." About 20 feet down a stone stairway, you'll see a hollowed-out courtyard, with several small cave openings. Inside one are four sarcophagi, covered with carvings of fruit and vines. Despite the name, the tomb is for the family of Queen Helena of the Mesopotamian province of Adiabene, who converted to Judaism in Jerusalem around A.D. 50.

Tourjeman Post Museum. Shivtei Israel/Saint George Street and Nablus Road. ☎ **02/ 281-278.** Admission NIS 8 ($2.40). Sun–Thurs 9am–5pm; Fri 9am–1pm. Bus: 1, 11, or 27.

This old Turkish house was turned into a fortress and used as an Israeli command post during the 1948 War of Independence and up until 1967. The museum is dedicated to the history of the divided Jerusalem that existed during that period.

Directions: From East Jerusalem, continue up Nablus Road; you'll pass East Jerusalem's American consulate building. Nablus Road goes to the right of the consulate. Detour left across the busy Route 1 Highway to see Tourjeman Post on the highway's western side. From West Jerusalem, it's on the edge of Mea Shearim.

Zedekiah's Cave. Near the Damascus Gate. Admission NIS 5 ($1.50). Daily 10am–4pm. Bus: 27.

Follow the Old City walls to the east of Damascus Gate and you'll soon come to a sign and the entrance leading under the walls into Zedekiah's Cave, or Solomon's Quarries, which tradition calls the source of the stones for Solomon's Temple. Because of this, the cave is of special importance to the worldwide Order of Masons, which claims spiritual descent from the original builders of the First Temple. Jewish and Muslim legends claim that tunnels in those caves extended to the Sinai Desert and Jericho. The quarries are called Zedekiah's Cave, since in 587 B.C. King Zedekiah was supposed to have fled from the Babylonians through these tunnels, to be captured subsequently near Jericho. An illuminated path leads you far back into the caves and under the Old City.

Directions: Head back down along the walls until you are just across from East Jerusalem bus station (between Herod's and Damascus gates).

MOUNT SCOPUS, MOUNT OF OLIVES & VALLEY OF KIDRON

You reach Mount of Olives Road either by driving north up Saladin Street or by taking a left turn at the wall, just past the Rockefeller Museum. For Hebrew University Mount Scopus campus, take bus no. 4A, 9, or 28 from downtown West Jerusalem.

MOUNT SCOPUS From Sheikh Jarrah (on Nablus Road), the road heads past the Mount Scopus Hotel and proceeds, gradually curving, past Shepherds Hotel. At the bend in Mount Scopus Road, to your left, you'll see the **Jerusalem War Cemetery**—the resting place for British World War I dead. You are now on Mount Scopus—Har Hatsofim, which means "Mount of Observation." It was here that the Roman armies of Titus and Vespasian camped in A.D. 70, and observed activities in the city under siege as they planned their final attack.

About 100 yards down the ridge, you will find the **Mount Scopus Hadassah Hospital** on the left. The **Hebrew University on Mount Scopus,** which opened on April 1, 1925, is now one of the largest institutions of higher learning in the Middle East. It is mostly housed in a vast fortress-like mega-complex designed by David Resnik and built over the past 20 years. The design perhaps reflects on the university's past experience. At the end of the War of Independence in 1949, the cease-fire lines found Israeli defenders still holding out at the Hebrew University and Hadassah Hospital, two important Jewish institutions deep in the heart of Jordanian-controlled East Jerusalem. For the next 19 years, these two bastions were resupplied by monthly Red Cross convoys, and a new Hadassah Hospital and Hebrew University had to be built in West Jerusalem. Since 1967, the original hospital and campus have been restored to their original functions and greatly enlarged. From the Truman Research Institute (a pink stone building) there's a sweeping view of both the New and Old cities. Tours are Sunday to Friday at 11am from the Sherman Building.

The Best Views in Jerusalem The road skirting the ridge proceeds past the high-towered Augusta Victoria Hospital—an Arab Legion bastion during the Six-Day War—as well as the Arab village of Et-Tur, the Mount of Olives, the Jewish Cemetery, and the Seven Arches Hotel. The best views of Jerusalem are from the Hebrew University on Mount Scopus, the Jewish graveyard on the Mount of Olives, and the Seven Arches Hotel. For optimum viewing and photographs, come in the morning, when the sun is behind you.

MOUNT OF OLIVES Here you'll find half a dozen churches—and one of the oldest Jewish cemeteries in the world. It was this cemetery that religious Jews had in mind when they came to die in the Holy Land. Start down the path on the right and you'll come to the **Tombs of the Prophets,** believed to be the burial place of Haggai, Malachi, and Zechariah. Many Jews have believed, and perhaps still do, that from here the route to heaven is the shortest, since God's presence is always hovering over Jerusalem; others have held that here, on the Mount of Olives, the resurrection of the dead will occur.

Farther up the road, on the southern fringe of Et-Tur, stands the **Mosque (and Chapel) of the Ascension** (ring the doorbell for admission), marking the spot where Jesus ascended to heaven. Interestingly enough, this Christian shrine is under Muslim control. Muslims revere Jesus as a prophet. However, they do not believe Jesus to be the son of God, nor do they believe that Jesus died on the cross.

Just a few steps away is the **Church of the Pater Noster,** built on the traditional spot where Jesus instructed his disciples in the Lord's Prayer. Tiles along the walls of the church are inscribed with the Lord's Prayer in 44 languages. The Carmelite Convent and Basilica of the Sacred Heart are on the adjoining hill.

From up here you can see a cluster of churches on the lower slopes of the Mount of Olives. All can be reached either from here or from the road paralleling the fortress wall, diagonally opposite Saint Stephen's Gate (Lion's Gate).

If you head down the path to the right of the Tomb of the Prophets, you'll come to **Dominus Flevit** (open daily 8am to noon and 2:30 to 5pm), which is a relatively

Princess Alice of Greece

Among the thousands of people from all times and places who have found their final resting place on the Mount of Olives, one of the most recent and unusual is Princess Alice of Greece, mother of Prince Phillip, the Duke of Edinburgh, and mother-in-law of Queen Elizabeth II. Born in Windsor Castle in 1885, the great granddaughter of Queen Victoria, Princess Alice at an early age was diagnosed as being almost totally deaf. Carefully trained in lip reading, she was fluent in both English and French; later in life she also mastered Greek.

In 1903 Princess Alice married Prince Andrew, son of King George of Greece, and devoted her life to helping others. During the 1912 Balkan War she worked as a nurse close to the battlefront, caring for sick and wounded Greek soldiers. During this time, both the princess and her father-in-law, King George, stayed in the home of the family of Haim Cohen, in the northern Greek city of Trikkala, near the war zone. Their friendship continued when Cohen later became a member of the Greek parliament. By the late 1930s, the Greek royal family was no longer in power, but Princess Alice remained in Athens, living separately from her husband and wearing the habit of a nun as she became increasingly committed to a life of religion and charitable work. In 1943, during the Nazi occupation of Greece, Princess Alice learned that the widow and children of Haim Cohen were in hiding near Athens, trying to escape deportation to the death camps in Poland. At the risk of her life and with the help of two servants, Princess Alice hid her Jewish friends on the grounds of the royal palace for 13 months, until Athens was liberated. Princess Alice died at Buckingham Palace in 1969, and in 1988, in accordance with her dying wish, was reinterred at the Church of Saint Mary Magdalene on the Mount of Olives. In 1994, Prince Phillip, accompanied by his sister, Princess Sophie, traveled to Jerusalem to receive Yad Vashem's Medal of Honor of Righteous Among the Nations, awarded to their late mother for saving the lives of the family of Haim Cohen.

contemporary church. The Franciscan church marks the spot where Jesus wept over his vision of the future destruction of Jerusalem. The **Russian Orthodox Church of Mary Magdalene** with its onion-shaped spires, built in 1888 by Czar Alexander III, is next (open Tuesday and Thursday from 10 to 11:30am). The **Roman Catholic Garden of Gethsemane** (open 8:30am to noon and from 3pm to sunset, April to October; 8:30am to noon and from 2pm to sunset in winter) adjoins the **Basilica of the Agony (Church of All Nations),** in the courtyard of which Jesus is said to have prayed the night before his arrest. The church's gold mosaic facade shows God looking down from heaven over Jesus and the peoples of the world. The church was built by people from 16 different nations in 1924. Next door, past beautifully tended gardens of ancient olive trees and bougainvillea, is the **Tomb of the Virgin,** which is a deep underground chamber housing the tombs of Mary and Joseph.

VALLEY OF KIDRON   The Valley of Kidron is between the Mount of Olives and the Old City walls. It runs south, between Mount Ophel (where David built his city) and the Mount of Contempt. Just under the wall here, roughly in front of El Aksa Mosque, are two tombs: **Absalom's Tomb** and the **Tomb of Zechariah.** At one time religious Jews would throw stones at Absalom's tomb (Kever Avshalom), in condemnation of Absalom, who rebelled against his father, King David. Scholars attribute Absalom's Tomb to Herodian times; it is Jerusalem's only relatively intact structure from before the Roman destruction in A.D. 70.

The Valley of Kidron is also known as the Valley of Jehoshaphat. The Book of Joel records that the judgments will be rendered here on resurrection day: "Let the heathen be awakened, and come up to the Valley of Jehoshaphat, for there will I sit to judge all the heathen round about." Muslims hold to a similar belief. They believe Muhammad will sit astride a pillar under the wall of the Dome of the Rock. A wire will be stretched from the pillar to the Mount of Olives, opposite, where Jesus will be seated. All humankind will walk across the wire on its way to eternity. The righteous and faithful will reach the other side safely; the rest will drop down in the Valley of Jehoshaphat and perish.

About 200 yards down the valley is the **Fountain of the Virgin,** at the Arab village of Silwan. Water from the spring—the Gihon—anointed Solomon king and served as the only water source for ancient Jerusalem. During the Assyrian and Babylonian attacks (8th century B.C.), King Hezekiah constructed an aqueduct through which the waters could be hidden inside the city. **Hezekiah's Aqueduct** is still there (underneath the church commemorating the spot where Mary once drew water to wash the clothes of Jesus). It's about 1,600 feet long, and the depth of the water is 10 to 16 inches. The walk takes about 40 minutes; take a flashlight or candles with you. You can walk through from Sunday to Thursday between 8:30am and 3pm, on Friday and holiday eves until 1pm. Entrance is free, but give the caretaker a tip. It is best to visit Silwan and Hezekiah's tunnel with a tour group.

THE CITY OF DAVID   Above the Gihon spring, but below the Dung Gate, lie the ruins of King David's city, from 1000 B.C. You can enter daily from 9am to 5pm, for free, and follow the paths along the steep hillside past the excavation site. Again, during the current political problems, it is not recommended that you wander through this area alone.

5 Attractions Outside Jerusalem

KENNEDY MEMORIAL   Seven miles from downtown Jerusalem, in the same general direction of Hadassah Medical Center, Yad Kennedy is reached by following the winding mountain roads past the Aminadav Moshav. Opened in May 1966, the 60-foot-high memorial is designed in the shape of a cut tree trunk, symbolizing a life cut short. The mountaintop memorial is encircled by 51 columns, each bearing the emblem of a state of the Union, plus the District of Columbia. The city bus no. 20 stops quite a distance away. Be prepared to take a cab and have the driver wait.

To the west is the village of Batir, site of a stronghold that witnessed the last Jewish revolt against the Romans, in A.D. 135, by Bar Kokhba. The view from the parking lot is breathtaking—a never-ending succession of mountains and valleys. The monument and adjoining picnic grounds are part of the John F. Kennedy Peace Forest.

ABU GHOSH   In the Israeli Arab town of Abu Ghosh (biblical Kiriath Jearim), 8 miles (13 kilometers) west of Jerusalem, are two sites that can be reached by bus. Abu Gosh's great treasure is the 12th-century **Crusader Church of the Resurrection,** acquired by the French in the late 19th century and now under the guardianship of the Lazarist fathers. Less heavily restored and more atmospheric than the Crusader Church of Saint Anne in Jerusalem, the Church of the Resurrection, like Saint Anne, was built to produce marvelous acoustics for Gregorian chant. It is built over an ancient cistern and well. It's open Monday through Wednesday and Friday and Saturday from 8:30 to 11:30am and 2:30 to 5:30pm The 20th-century **Church of Notre Dame of the Ark,** built on the site of a Byzantine church, marks the last place the Ark of the Covenant rested before it was brought to Jerusalem by King David. It is open daily from 8:30 to 11:30am and 2:30 to 5:30pm.

NEOT KEDUMIM BIBLICAL LANDSCAPE RESERVE   The reserve is in the Lod District between Jerusalem and Tel Aviv (☎ 08/233-840, fax 08/245-881). This is a very worthwhile excursion either from Jerusalem or Tel Aviv. Neot Kedumim is a kind of living museum of the farming, harvesting, and shepherding techniques of ancient times laid out across 625 acres of land carefully planted with flora of the biblical period. An explanatory text brings the landscape vividly to life and relates it to accounts in the Old and New Testaments and the Talmud. Guides are expert at explaining references to nature in Judeo-Christian scriptures; you'll interact with an olive press, a *sukka* (harvestors' shelter), and see how ancient ink was made from a powder composed of resin, ground pomegranates, and oak gallnuts; with advance reservation, you may be able to join a group of 15 or more for a vegetarian buffet of reconstructed ancient pastoral recipes (American food critic Mimi Sheraton found the food delicious). Admission is NIS 15 ($5), last admission 2 hours before closing. Open hours are Sunday through Thursday from 8:30am to sunset; Friday and holiday evenings from 8:30am to 1pm. Telephone for driving or bus instructions. Guided tours in English are given Friday at 9:30am; reserve ahead to arrange other times. There are also self-guided tours; trails are wheelchair accessible, and electric carts and wheelchairs are available on advance reservation.

THE SOREQ (STALACTITE) CAVES   Located 20 kilometers (12 miles) west of Jerusalem along the road out of Ein Kerem, this place is a favorite excursion for tour groups. Set in the limestone region, the caves are full of incredible formations. The scenery along the road from Ein Kerem to the moshav of Nes Harim, a mile from the caves, is by itself worth the pleasant excursion. Admission is NIS 8 ($2.40), and open hours are Sunday through Thursday from 8:30am to 4pm, Friday from 8:30am to noon. Direct service is by tour bus only. Egged will take you on a tour to the caves and nearby sights for about $17, or you can take a bus from the Central Bus Station to Nes Harim for a fraction of the cost.

6 Especially for Kids

The **Train Puppet Theater** in Liberty Bell Park offers programs (in Hebrew, but nonetheless interesting) for children and hosts an International Puppet Theater Festival each August. Call 03/618-514 for information or check the listing in Friday's *Jerusalem Post*. See "The Performing Arts" under "Jerusalem After Dark," below.

The **Israel Museum's Lively Children's Wing** has great exhibits, many of them hands-on, workshops in recycled materials, and a library of fabulous children's books you can sit and read. See "Museums" under "West Jerusalem Attractions," above.

The Tisch Family Zoological Gardens. Manahat, Jerusalem. ☎ **430-111.** Admission NIS 20 ($6) adults; NIS 14 ($4.20) children. Sun–Thurs 9am–7pm (until 5pm in winter); Fri 9am–3pm; Sat 10am–5pm. Bus: 26.

Jerusalem's Biblical Zoo has recently moved into this new, beautifully landscaped site at the western edge of the city, with a state-of-the art open design that blends into the surrounding countryside. Emphasis is on creatures mentioned in the Bible or native to Israel. Children will enjoy the friendly waterfowl and the camel encampment (camel and pony ride facilities are planned). There is a pleasant safari-style refreshment facility on the grounds. Prepare for a 10-minute walk from the bus stop.

WALKING TOUR
The Old City

Start: The Jaffa Gate
Finish: The tour has three options: the first will take you to the Jewish Quarter and the Western Wall, the second to the Islamic shrines and mosques on the Temple Mount, the third to an unusual Christian enclave on the roof of the Church of the Holy Sepulcher.
Best Times: Sunday through Wednesday from 8am to 3pm.
Worst Times: Shabbat, Muslim holidays, Friday, or after 3pm when the Dome of the Rock is closed.

This is a meandering walk that will get you to some major sites, offbeat vista points, and authentic refueling stops, but the Old City is a vast, intricate Chinese box of experiences, as unplanned and exotic as the 4,000-year history of Jerusalem itself. One way to enjoy the texture of this sublime hodgepodge is simply to plunge in and wander, chancing upon hummus parlors and holy sites, ancient bakeries and antique Bedouin embroideries. I will clue you in to a bit of Jerusalem's history and local lore as we move along.

     FROM THE JAFFA GATE TO THE CARDO   The first part of the walk takes you to the Cardo, where the walk divides into three possible options.

1. **Jaffa Gate.** Before you enter Jaffa Gate, which is the traditional entrance to the city for visitors from the West, check out the stones that make up the present Old City wall, which was erected by order of the Ottoman Turkish Sultan Suleiman the Magnificent in 1538. Some stones have been dressed with carefully cut flat borders surrounding a raised, flat central area *(the boss),* done in the style of King Herod's stone cutters, and probably dating from 2,000 years ago. You will see this style again in the monumental stones of the Western Wall, a retaining wall for the vast artificial platform that Herod constructed to surround the original Jerusalem Temple site with room for the thousands of Jews who made the pilgrimage from all over the ancient world. The stones that were used to build Suleiman the Magnificent's city wall are by no means uniform like the Herodian ashlars of the Western Wall. You will notice other kinds of stones with flat borders and rougher raised bosses, in the pre-Herodian style of the Hasmoneans (the Maccabees) who were the last Jewish rulers of Jerusalem until modern times with the exception of Bar Kokhba, who conquered the ruins of the city during the Second Jewish Revolt against Rome in A.D. 132–135. You will also see rough ashlars of the Byzantine era, as well as the virtually undressed stones of Crusader and medieval times. In each of the upper corners of the closed decorative archway to the left of the Jaffa Gate, you will notice stones carefully carved into a leaf design, which are believed to have come from a long-destroyed Crusader church. The walls of Jerusalem, like the city itself, are composed of stones used again and again, just as many of the legends and traditions of the city reappear and are reassembled by each successive civilization and religion.

2. **The Tourist Information Office**. Here you can pick up free maps, information, and tourist publications.

3. Enter the gate to the arcade of the **New Imperial Hotel,** built in the 1880s and in its time the most luxurious hotel in Jerusalem. In the 19th century, the now largely deserted arcade was a private bazaar for hotel guests, where the beggars, lepers, cripples, and "rif-raf" of Jerusalem could be neatly excluded. Slightly uphill and in the center of the arcade is a broken street lamp mounted on a

cylindrical stone that was uncovered when the foundations for the New Imperial were being dug. The Latin lettering, "LEG X" records a marker for the camp of the Tenth Legion Frentensis, which conquered and destroyed Jewish Jerusalem in A.D. 70. Flavius Josephus tells that after the temple and the buildings of Jerusalem were systematically razed and the surviving inhabitants led off to slavery, death, and exile, the Tenth Legion encamped beside the ruins of the Jaffa Gate for 62 years to guard the ruins against Jews who might try to filter back and reestablish the city. The discovery of this marker in proximity to the Jaffa Gate confirms Josephus's account of Jerusalem at this low point in its history. The once-elegant New Imperial, as it drifted into seediness, became a spot for romantic assignations during the British Mandate period. Characters played by Bogart (if not Bergman) would have felt at home.

4. **Petra Hotel.** The first modern hotel built in the Old City in the 1870s, the once elegant Petra, now undergoing restoration, is largely a backpacker's hostel. It was probably in an earlier structure on this site (the old Mediterranean Hotel) that two 19th-century American visitors to Jerusalem, Herman Melville and Mark Twain, are believed to have stayed during their visits to what was then a decrepit warren of ruins filled with lice-covered beggars and crazed religious fanatics. Neither Melville nor Twain found Jerusalem a pleasant place to stay.

Enter at the far right as you face the building and ask the person at the money-changer's booth just inside the door for permission to visit the roof (show this book). Admission is about NIS 2 (60¢) per person, although this fee may be waived if you happen to ask permission while negotiating an exchange transaction (the Petra's rates are usually a tad better than the bank rates; the Petra's hours are all day and service is quicker). As always, at money changers, be familiar with Israeli currency and count carefully.

5. **The view from the Petra Hotel's roof.** Climb three long flights of stairs, past the extra-wide second- and third-floor corridors, which were once used to accommodate the major wedding receptions, banquets, and lectures of pre–World War I Jerusalem, and emerge from the creaky wooden attic stairs onto the roof with its strange series of curved stone domes. Turn left, up a few steps and left again, and you will face one of the Old City's great panoramas—perfectly aligned, with the golden Dome of the Rock (site of the First and Second Temples) in the exact center of the vista, and with the roofline of the city spread out below you. This is where photographers come for postcard views.

As you look eastward toward the Temple Mount, you'll see the Mount of Olives across the horizon behind the Dome of the Rock. In ancient times, this now barren ridge was a natural olive grove, and its cultivation was one of the sources of ancient Jerusalem's wealth. The green area of the ridge, just behind the Dome of the Rock, is the Garden of Gethsemane (Gethsemane is the anglicized version of the Hebrew word for "olive press"), where Jesus was arrested at night after the Last Supper, the Jewish Passover feast. This is the western side of the Mount of Olives ridge. On the eastern side, out of view, is the site of the village of Bethany where Lazarus, who was raised from the dead by Jesus, and his sisters, Mary and Martha, lived. Jesus may have been making his way to their house after the Passover dinner at the time of his arrest.

The Dome of the Rock was built in A.D. 691. According to legend, the saintly warrior Omar Ibn El Khattab, who conquered Jerusalem for Islam in A.D. 638, was greeted by the Christian Archbishop Sophronius at the Jaffa Gate. Sophronius surrendered the city peacefully to Omar, and then offered to lead the new ruler on a tour of his conquest. The first thing Omar Ibn El Khattab asked to see was

Walking Tour–The Old City

1 The Jaffa Gate
2 Government Tourist Information Office (GTIO)
3 New Imperial Hotel
4 ThePetra Hotel
5 The view from the Petra Hotel roof
6 Suq El Hussor
7 Stone rooftop
8 Cardo
9 Hurva Synagogue
10 Herodian Quarter Excavations
11 Crusader Church of St. Mary
12 Western Wall
13 Archeological excavations at the southern foot of the Temple Mount
14 View from the southern wall of the Old City
15 Rothschild Centre for Contemporary Crafts
16 The Temple Mount
17 El Aksa Mosque
18 Dome of the Rock
19 Islamic Museum
20 Suq El Attarin Bazaar
21 Suq Khan Es Zeit
22 Ethiopian Compound and Monastery
23 Crafts shop
24 Large open roof space
25 Ethiopian Chapel
26 Chapel of the Archangel Michael
27 Church of the Holy Sepulcher

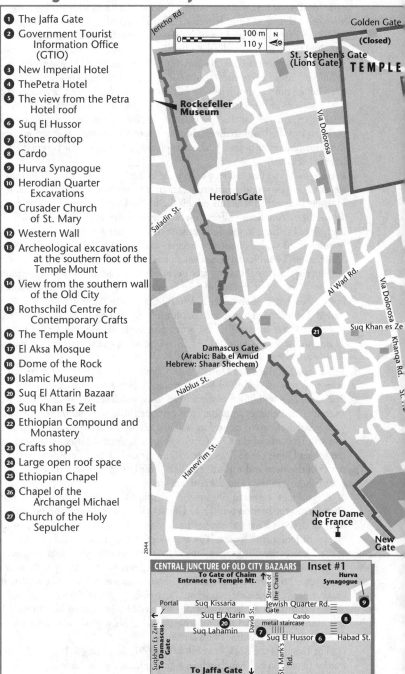

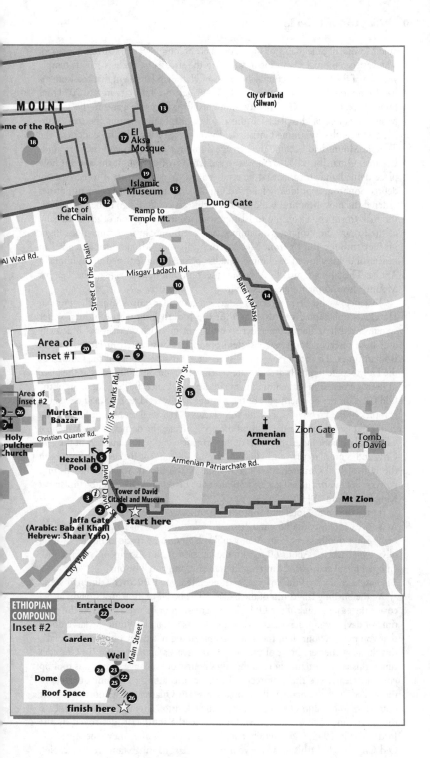

MOUNT

Dome of the Rock ⑱

⑰ El Aksa Mosque

⑬

City of David (Silwan)

⑲ Islamic Museum

⑬

Dung Gate

⑯ ⑫
Gate of the Chain

Ramp to Temple Mt.

Street of the Chain

Al Wad Rd.

Batei Mahase

⑪ †
Misgav Ladach Rd.

⑩

⑭

Area of inset #1 ⑳

⑥ — ✡ ⑨

Or-Hayim St.

⑮

② — ㉖
⑦ †

Area of inset #2

St. /////St. Marks Rd.

Muristan Baazar

Holy Sepulcher Church

Christian Quarter Rd.

Armenian Church †

Zion Gate

Tomb of David

Hezekiah Pool ⑤ ④

David St.

Armenian Patriarchate Rd.

③ ⓘ
② Tower of David Citadel and Museum
① ☆ start here

Jaffa Gate
(Arabic: Bab el Khalil
Hebrew: Shaar Yafo)

Mt Zion

City Wall

ETHIOPIAN COMPOUND
Inset #2

Entrance Door ㉒

Garden

Main Street

Well
⑳④ ㉓ ㉒

Dome
Roof Space

㉕

㉖

finish here ☆

169

"the Mosque of Suleiman," or the place where Solomon's Temple had once stood. The vast ceremonial platform surrounding the site of the ancient Jewish temple was one of the few architectural landmarks of Herodian Jerusalem that the Romans had found too difficult to eradicate when they destroyed the city in A.D. 70. Three hundred years later, as Christianity triumphed over Roman paganism, the Temple Mount was one of the places in the city left purposely in ruins (perhaps symbolically) by the Byzantine Christians. By the time of the Muslim conquest, the Temple Mount had become the garbage dump for Jerusalem and the surrounding area. Omar Ibn El Khattab was so saddened by the sight of the ancient holy place defiled and in ruins that he removed his cloak and used it to carry away debris. Sophronius prudently followed Omar's example. Later Muslim authorities ordered the most beautiful building that architects could design to be placed over the rock to which, according to Islamic scholars' interpretation of the 17th Sura of the Koran, the Prophet Muhammad had been brought in a miraculous night journey through the air from Mecca. From this spot, Muhammad ascended to heaven and was allowed to glimpse paradise before being returned to his home in Arabia. The silver-domed El Aksa Mosque, on the southern edge of the Temple Mount, also commemorates this event.

Just below the Petra's roof is a large rectangular empty area, the Pool of Hezekiah, misnamed centuries ago for the Judean king whose hidden water system saved Jerusalem from Assyrian onslaught in 701 B.C.; the pool is actually a disused reservoir for a water system originally constructed in Herodian and Roman times. To the north, you will see the great silver dome of the Church of the Holy Sepulcher, built over the site venerated for almost 2,000 years as the place of Jesus's crucifixion and entombment. In the far distance, beyond the walls of the Old City, on the northern part of the Mount of Olives ridge, the small city is the complex of the Hebrew University and Hadassah Hospital on Mount Scopus. To your right (south) inside the walls of the Old City are the domes of the Armenian Cathedral of Saint James, the roofs of the Armenian and Jewish quarters of the Old City, and 5 miles to the south, beyond the hill of Abu Tor (believed to have been the Hill of Evil Counsel as well as the site of the Blood Acre purchased for a potters' field with Judas Iscariot's 30 pieces of silver) is Bethlehem, birthplace of King David and of Jesus.

Leave the Petra Hotel and continue down David Street to the bazaar.

6. At Suq El Hussor, the now rather small basket market, turn right. (Among the many imported baskets from Asia, you'll still find some rustic examples of local olive twig baskets.) About 60 feet on the left side of Suq El Hussor, you'll notice an open metal staircase. Climb up the staircase, and you'll be on:

7. The stone rooftop of the covered markets. Here you'll discover a different world above the bustling labyrinths of the bazaars. The broad rooftop area straight ahead covers the exact center of the Old City, where the four quarters meet. At the right time of day, if you listen carefully, you will hear emanating from the large dome that you pass on your right the unmistakable sound of a game of billiards; in fact, this dome at the very heart of the Holy City covers a billiard parlor. In Crusader times, this large structure housed the city's bourse or exchange. From this rooftop you can clearly see the architectural distinctions among the four quarters of the walled city: the orange tile–roofed Christian Quarter to the northwest; the dome-roofed Muslim Quarter with its many television antennas to the northeast; the new stonework of the Jewish Quarter to the southeast, destroyed by the Jordanians in 1948, and carefully rebuilt by the Israelis after they reoccupied the Old City in 1967 (this area is devoid of antennas; its inhabitants receive cable);

and, to the southwest, the older stone buildings of the Armenian Quarter. Again, through the maze of TV antennas, you get an interesting chance to photograph the lavish Dome of the Rock.

Descend the metal staircase, and backtrack on Suq El Hussor to David Street. Turn right onto David Street. The next right on David Street leads to the:

8. Cardo, a restored and renovated section of Roman and Byzantine Jerusalem's main market street, now filled with stylish modern shops.

At this point you have three choices for the rest of your tour.

THE FIRST OPTION: THE JEWISH QUARTER   You could easily wander the streets of this beautifully reconstructed area for a number of hours. Walk south on the Jewish Quarter Road to the:

9. Hurva Synagogue (see under "The Jewish Quarter," above, for more information).

☕ **TAKE A BREAK**   A slice of kosher pizza, a felafel, a light meal, or wonderful Arabic bread fresh from the bakery oven are all available on the section of the Jewish Quarter Road beyond the Hurva Synagogue.

Walk across the square behind the synagogue and you'll see signs for the:

10. Herodian Quarter excavations in the center of the Jewish Quarter. Take Tiferet Israel Street, which runs from the northeastern corner of the big square to the end, where you will come upon the:

11. Crusader Church of Saint Mary. Turn right at the church and make a left to the great staircase, which descends down to the:

12. Western Wall. Between the Western Wall and the Dung Gate, you can enter the area of the:

13. Archeological excavations at the southern foot of the Temple Mount. From the excavations, take the road inside the City Wall uphill to the:

14. Southern wall of the Old City with its lovely view down into the valley below, which was the site of the original City of David 3,000 years ago.

You will see a parking lot inside the city walls; cross it and turn right into a pathway that becomes Habad Road. Follow Habad Road to the far end. Or Hayim Street is a left turn off Habad Road. Continue uphill to find on your left the:

15. Rothschild Centre for Contemporary Crafts, just at the point where the Jewish and Armenian quarters meet, and where our tour ends.

SECOND OPTION: THE TEMPLE MOUNT   From the Cardo, if it is not a Friday, and not after 12:30pm, continue straight onto where David Street seems to end. Turn right, then quickly take the first left, a continuation of David Street called the Street of the Chain. Continue down this road to the great green door (the Gate of the Chain) at the end, which leads directly onto the:

16. Temple Mount. The Temple Mount (in Arabic, Haram es Sharif) is open for tourists until 3pm. Give yourself ample time to walk around the ceremonial plaza and enjoy the views of the Mount of Olives. Non-Muslims must buy admission tickets (approximately $6.60; well worth the fee) from a small stone kiosk to the right of the El Aksa Mosque, which will admit you to both mosques and to the museum (you may be asked to wait outside during noonday prayers). It is permissible to take photographs outdoors on the Temple Mount, but you cannot bring a camera into mosques or shrines.

Walk diagonally to the right after entering the Gate of the Chain to the southern end of the Temple Mount to:

17. El Aksa Mosque. This is the main Islamic prayer hall on the Temple Mount. In the center of the Temple Mount is the:

18. Dome of the Rock. You can't miss its lavish exterior tiles and its golden dome. At the southwest corner is the:

19. Islamic Museum, with a collection of Islamic artifacts from earlier periods on the Temple Mount.

THIRD OPTION: THE BAZAARS & THE CHURCH OF THE HOLY SEPULCHER   This walk begins at the intersection of David Street and the Cardo. Turn left into the narrow, covered:

20. Suq El Attarin Bazaar, the Spice Market. It was roofed over in the time of the Crusaders, who perhaps could not bear the blazing summer sun of the region, and is actually an additional segment of the Cardo, once the great Roman north–south market and ceremonial street of the colonial outpost of Aelia Capitolina, built over the ruins of Herodian–Jewish Jerusalem. The Roman Cardo, originally broad and colonnaded, evolved over centuries into the present warren of narrow, parallel bazaars (including the Butcher's Bazaar, with its dangling skinned sheepheads and gutters of blood, parallel just to the left) that runs all the way north to the Damascus Gate. El Attarin is now mostly clothing and sneaker shops. Follow it until you exit from the covered portion, through a nondescript portal, and continue straight on. The next section of the street, no longer roofed over, but covered by shop awnings:

21. Suq Khan es-Zeit, the Market of the Inn of the Olive Oil. Probably since Herodian–Jewish times this area has been a major food market in Jerusalem's many reincarnations—the Frankish Crusaders called this the *Malcuisinat*, or Street of Bad Cookery, unhappy with the many Middle Eastern specialties sold here. You will notice pastry shops displaying mysteriously radiant mountains of baklava arranged on top of glowing lightbulbs and flashlights; the peanut baklava filling sometimes dyed green to approximate the more costly pistachio. There are also chewy rolled pancakes filled with nuts or sweet cheese, served in a honey syrup, shops selling dried fruits or dark globs of fruit and nut-filled nougat. There are also hibachis cooking kebabs and shashliks, and rotisseries of chickens to go. Any of these places are good bets for snacks.

☕ **TAKE A BREAK**   **Abu Assab Refreshments,** a busy Old City landmark, sells fresh orange, grapefruit, and carrot juice, and is the least expensive and best of its kind in town. A good place to stave off dehydration and fill up on vitamins, you can order these juices straight, or in any combination. You can stay downstairs for a quick break, or go upstairs where there is table service. Mike, the British-educated manager, who is often at the downstairs carrot juice counter, will translate the Arabic price list.

A short way along the same side of the street is a stone staircase. Climb the staircase to the top, turn left, and follow the lane to the end, where you will find a tall double door, usually closed or slightly ajar. Enter the doorway and you will find yourself in the enchanted:

22. Ethiopian Compound and Monastery on the sprawling segments of the roof of the Church of the Holy Sepulcher. Here on this ancient roof entire trees and gardens grow. Straight ahead, behind a low wall ornamented with a simple cross, you will see the olive trees (or offshoots of olive trees) in which Abraham found the ram he offered in sacrifice after God freed him from the commandment to sacrifice Isaac. Turn left, then right, and you will find yourself in the heart of this Ethiopian religious community. The tiny round-walled buildings offer a distinctly African feeling. For centuries, the Church of the Holy Sepulcher has been divided among the six oldest factions of Christianity, and in the most recent division, the Ethiopian Church, with roots going back to the 4th century A.D., got the roof. Both Ethiopian monks and a lay community have inhabited this location for centuries (you can often smell the wonderful spicy cooking of the communal kitchen). The church bells of this exotic community hang in the ruined gothic arches of the Crusader-era church structure to the left and above the tiny main street.

Exit through the low portal at the end of the lane, turn right, and you will pass the community's well, with a shaft running down through the Holy Sepulcher Church (running water has obviated the need for the well, but the Ethiopians still have the right to a certain amount of water from it each day).

Opposite the well is a small, sometimes open, door leading to a:

23. **Crafts shop,** where you can sometimes find Ethiopian crafts and hand-painted icons for sale. From this door continue to the:

24. Large open roof space with the protruding dome in the center. Through the windows of the dome you will be able to see the **Chapel of Saint Helena** inside the Holy Sepulcher Church below; you'll even be able to smell the church incense, and at times, hear services and prayers.

The Ethiopians use this roof area each year on the Saturday midnight eve of Easter Sunday for one of the city's most exotic religious processions. The Ethiopian Patriarch, with a great ceremonial African umbrella, circumambulates the dome, followed by monks beating ancient drums, so large that they must be carried by two men, and by chanting white-robed pilgrims. The procession then retires to a leopard skin tent (nowadays made of canvas in a leopard skin pattern) to chant and pray through the night. This very moving ceremony is open to the public, and many Jerusalemites make it a point to attend each year.

Around the corner from the craft shop is a larger ancient wooden door leading to the:

25. **Ethiopian chapel,** a structure probably built in medieval times. Here, if a monk is in attendance, you will be shown crucifix-shaped holy books written in ancient Ge'ez, and you will have time to take in the paintings, unfortunately done by European religious painters rather than by traditional Ethiopian religious artists, that depict the visit of the Queen of Sheba to King Solomon in approximately 940 B.C. Charmingly, the artist has decided to depict an anachronistic group of 18th-century Hasidic Jews among King Solomon's entourage. From the union of the queen and King Solomon, the royal Ethiopian family is believed to have descended (one of the emperor of Ethiopia's titles was "the Lion of Judah"), and in 1935, when Emperor Haile Selassie was forced to flee the Italian invasion of his country, he took up residence in Jerusalem in "the land of my fathers." There is a tray for contributions at the back of the chapel.

Continue through the rear of the chapel and down the staircase to the:

26. **Chapel of the Archangel Michael.** In this ancient chapel, with its carved and inlaid wood paneling, the community of Ethiopian monks gathers in late afternoon for prayers. It is sometimes possible for visitors to sit in the rear of the chapel and listen to the chanting, which is extremely beautiful.

The ancient wooden door of the chapel leads outside to the main entrance plaza in front of the:

27. **Church of the Holy Sepulcher.** Now that you've seen the roof, you are ready to journey through the very special interior. (See section 1 for a detailed description of the church.) After visiting the church, make your way back through the bazaars to David Street and the Jaffa Gate.

7 Organized Tours

As a general rule of thumb, if you're going to be guided—and it's not a bad idea—make certain that your mentor is officially licensed by the Ministry of Tourism. Also, on any guided tour that includes holy places, you must dress modestly. This means no shorts (men or women), no sleeveless shirts or blouses, and women should have a head covering.

BUS TOURS   The Jerusalem Circular Line Egged (☎ 248-144) bus no. 99 leaves the Jaffa Gate terminus at 10am, noon, 2pm, and 4pm Sunday through Thursday; on Friday the 4pm run is omitted. There are no Saturday buses. This bus stops at 34 of the most visited sites throughout the city, from the Mount of Olives to Yad VaShem. You can buy a single tour ticket for NIS 6 ($1.80)—a great way to get a quick rundown of what the city has to offer and where things are. You can also buy a full-day ticket, or a 2-day ticket—with these you can get off and back on the bus as many times as you like during the validity time of your ticket. It is always wise to check with the GTIO offices on King George Street or inside Jaffa Gate for the latest information on bus no. 99's timetable and route.

GUIDED WALKING TOURS   Free municipal walking tours in English are offered Saturdays at 10am from 32 Jaffa Rd.; call ☎ 258-844 for information. The Sheraton Jerusalem Plaza Hotel, 47 King George V Ave., at Agron Street (☎ 259-111), sponsors tours of various areas. Drop by the hotel to pick up a schedule, or check "Events in the Jerusalem Region," issued by the GTIO. Meet in the lobby of the hotel at 8:50am for any tour.

The **Society for the Protection of Nature in Israel (SPNI)** (☎ 244-605) sponsors excellent and fascinating walking tours within Jerusalem as well as hikes and tours of the surrounding countryside. A 1-day tour is approximately $39.

Various commercial concerns will take you on guided tours of the city that emphasize its history and archeology. For instance, **Archeological Seminars Ltd.,** 34 Habad St. in the Jewish Quarter (no phone), will guide you through the Jewish Quarter, Temple Mount, the Temple Mount excavations, the City of David (Ophel), or the Christian and Muslim quarters of the Old City. Tours run Sunday through Friday. For information, ask at the Cardo Information Center in the Jewish Quarter of the Old City.

Walking Tours Ltd. will show you the historical and archeological highlights of the Old City or the Mount of Olives. Tours depart from the Tower of David. For information, inquire at the tourist office just inside Jaffa Gate, to the left.

The **Jerusalem Rothschild Centre for Contemporary Crafts,** Or Hayim Street (☎ 286-076), in the Jewish Quarter, can at times arrange reasonably priced, interesting historical and cultural walking tours of the Old City for small groups of one to five people. Call ahead for reservations.

A WALKING PILGRIMAGE   Israelis have instituted an "Aliya le'Regel" (walking pilgrimage) to Jerusalem, which takes place each year around Passover/Easter and Sukkot time. Thousands participate, and during this 3-day excursion period you can see them walking along this road just as their ancestors did. If you are in Israel in the spring around Passover time or in the autumn during Sukkot, do catch this event. (Overseas visitors need pay no registration fee and are guests of the March Command for all meals, camp accommodations, and evening programs during the march. To register, contact the Christian Information Center inside Jaffa Gate.) And if walking up and down hills isn't your idea of fun, then be sure to pick a spot near Jaffa Gate and watch the procession as it comes into Jerusalem.

8 Sports & Outdoor Activities

BICYCLING   The Jerusalem Bicycle Club (☎ 02/816-062) is an informal group that can arrange outings and give advice to those interested in bicycling.

JOGGING   Jerusalem is not the easiest place for unplanned jogging; a very useful paperback, *Carta's Jogger's Guide to Jerusalem,* by Morton H. Seelenfreund (available at Steimatzky's Bookstores for NIS24 [$7.20]) maps out many good possibilities.

SWIMMING   You have a choice of many pools. One of the most crowded is the **Jerusalem public pool,** 43 Emek Refaim St. (☎ 02/632-092). On Saturday and holidays, Israelis pack the pools. Admission is NIS 28 ($8.30). It is open from 8am to 5pm.

The **Bet Tailor,** on Zangwil Street in Kiryat Ha-Yovel (☎ 02/414-362), is open from 8am to 4:30pm. Admission is NIS 16 ($5). Take bus no. 18.

A more convenient, although more expensive, option is to pay the visitors' rate to use a pool at one of the city's hotels. The **Laromme Hotel** (☎ 02/252-161), the **Paradise Jerusalem Hotel** (☎ 02/558-888), and the **Jerusalem (Ramada) Renaissance Hotel** (☎ 02/528-111) all have swimming facilities throughout the year. Admission policies vary according to time of year and rate of occupancy, but could be in the $16 to $20 range. In good weather, the pool at the **Mount Zion Hotel** (☎ 02/724-222), where the water is often frigid, and the pool at the **King David Hotel** (☎ 02/251-111) offer pleasant gardens and spectacular views of the Old City's walls.

9 Shopping

THE SHOPPING SCENE

Judaica and local Israeli crafts and art objects are the most interesting items for shoppers. Many shops in the Ben-Yehuda area, as well as in the Jewish Quarter of the Old City, sell reproductions of cast bronze antique wall menorahs from North Africa, medieval Italy, and Eastern Europe. The designs are authentic and decorative. There is no lack of modern menorahs, mezuzahs, dreidels, candle holders, and embroidered yarmulkes, as well as objects for Passover, Sukkot, the Sabbath, and synagogue services. There are also many outstanding individual shops that sell original art, jewelry, glass, and ceramics.

HOURS, SALES, TAX & SHIPPING

Tourist shops generally open Sunday through Thursday from 9am to 7pm, although some shops close from 1pm to 4pm for siesta. On Friday, shops are open from 9am to 2pm.

There is no sales tax; however, unless otherwise stated, the VAT tax of 17% is included in the price. Always ask about VAT exemptions when paying in foreign currency. Some expensive tourist shops will give you voucher forms, good for VAT refunds on items costing more than $50 when presented at Ben-Gurion Airport just before you leave the country. See chapter 3, "Fast Facts: Israel."

Merchants are generally cooperative about packing your purchases securely for shipping or for the plane ride home. If you decide to mail purchases home, remember to bring strong tape with you to the post office, as all packages must be inspected for security and customs before they can be sealed. You must also bring your passport to the post office for identification when you mail packages.

SHOPPING A TO Z

ART

Exodus Gallery. 22 King David St. ☎ **02/249-268.**

This nonprofit gallery is packed with the works of recent immigrant artists and craftspeople from the former Soviet Union, and Ethiopia, as well as from countries like Argentina, Canada, and France. Over 120 artists and craftspeople are represented by the gallery (only the works of a small percentage of these artists are present at any given time) and prices range from around $100 to over $2,000. All major credit cards are accepted, and the gallery will pack purchases for carrying or shipping. The gallery is open Sunday through Thursday from 10am to 9pm; Friday from 10am to 2pm; Saturday after Shabbat.

Israel Museum. Ruppin Street. ☎ **02/708-811.**

An exciting selection of posters are on sale here. Also, check out reproductions of Anna Ticho's charcoal and pen-and-ink landscapes and Shalom of Safed's vibrant primitive paintings, as well as the high-quality reproductions of Judaica and antiquities at reasonable prices.

Jerusalem Artists' House Gallery. 12 Shmuel Ha-Nagid St. ☎ **02/252-636.**

Housed in the Ottoman Turkish buildings of the original Bezalel Academy of Art and Design (the school has now moved to the Hebrew University campus), this remarkable cooperative gallery, sponsored by the Jerusalem Municipality and the Israeli government, represents more than 500 juried Israeli artists, ranging from the famous and established to the newest and most promising. Upstairs, you'll find a changing array of one-person and group exhibits. The staff of the Artists' House can put you in touch with any artist whose work interests you, and they will arrange for the shipping of your purchase. The gallery is open Sunday through Thursday from 10am to 1pm and 4 to 7pm; on Friday 10am to 1pm; Saturday 11am to 2pm.

BASKETWARE

Suq El Hussor. Old City.

This basket market has fallen victim to bamboo import items, but you can still find a few locally made, primitive olive-twig baskets, a Jerusalem tradition that is thousands of years old. Rough, almost bird's nest–like in texture, these baskets look great when filled with dried flowers, fresh fruit, yarn, or almost anything else you can think of. Don't pay more than $5 for a basket with a handle of the kind used by country women to collect fresh grapes or figs. Bigger traylike baskets are the kind women in the markets carry on their heads, and should cost $10 to $13. In New York, a stylish department store might sell such pieces for more than seven times that much. The basket market, which consists of just one or two shops, is a right turn off David Street, just before the Cardo; a shop on Christian Quarter Road also carries a small selection.

CRAFTS

Contemporary Crafts

Alix de Rothschild Craft Center. 4 Or Hayim St. ☎ **02/286-076.**

You'll find an overview of the work of Israel's best contemporary craftspeople at this craft center in the Jewish Quarter of the Old City. The constantly changing juried exhibit here is not generally for sale, but the staff of the center will be happy to put you in touch with any craftspeople whose work you admire, and can also arrange interesting, reasonably priced walking tours of the Old City, with an emphasis on crafts and cultural history. The craft center is open Sunday through Thursday from 10am to 4pm.

Cadim Gallery. 4 Yoel Salomon Mall. ☎ **02/234-869.**

This cooperative gallery displays the work of the award-winning Meira Una, as well as Mark Yudell's ceramic creatures and a range of excellent functional pottery and inventive Judaica by some of the country's best ceramists. It is open Sunday through Thursday from 9:30am to 8 or 9pm; on Friday from 9:30am to 3pm.

8 Ceramists. 11 Yoel Şalomon Mall. ☎ **02/247-250.**

For contemporary handmade ceramics, this pottery cooperative in West Jerusalem will give you a good idea of the current Israeli ceramics scene. Among the items here, look for the beautiful ceramic Hanukkah menorahs and Passover seder plates as well as functional and decorative pottery made by the cooperative's artists. The cooperative is open Sunday through Thursday from 9:30am to 8pm; on Friday from 9:30am to 3pm.

House of Quality. Hebron Road. Bus: 4, 5, 6, 7, 8, 18, 21, or 48, and walk to Hebron Road.

Across the street from and midway between the Mount Zion Hotel and the Cinémathèque, this conglomeration of craftspeople's workshops offers all sorts of delights. I especially admire the witty, unique ceramic Judaica of Gaya Smith, and the silver creations of Oded Davidson, whose studios are here, but all of the craftspeople at this center are of very high caliber. There is a central gallery downstairs. Craftspeople are in their workshops at varying hours; the gallery is open Sunday through Thursday from 10am to 12:30pm. Just around the corner, in Saint Andrew's Guest House, you can visit Craftaid, which sells traditional Palestinian embroidery.

Traditional Ceramics

The outer walls of the Dome of the Rock are covered with turquoise and cobalt blue ceramic tiles in the Persian tradition. Two Armenian pottery workshops, Jerusalem Pottery and Palestinian Pottery, listed below, were brought to Jerusalem at the start of the British Mandate in order to maintain the Dome of the Rock's lavish facade. They are internationally acknowleged masters of traditional Anatolian hand-painted ceramics. These two workshops now produce items for sale to the general public. After a quick survey of the showrooms here, you'll appreciate the difference between their hand-painted folk ceramics, tiles, and bowls, and the mass-produced work available in the bazaars; the rich colors produced by these workshops are unmatched anywhere else. Each item is unique, and prices vary, but you'll find the prices for basic items, such as hand-painted standard-size tiles, to be remarkably good at approximately $8 to $10.

Jerusalem Pottery. 15 Via Dolorosa. No phone.

Near the sixth station of the cross in the Old City, this shop, run by the renowned Karakashian family, is notable for individual plates and tiles decorated with lovely bird, animal, and floral designs, as well as for its recent interpretations of ancient Jewish and Christian motifs. I've seen this shop's magnificent and varied tiles used to face a colonial fireplace in Massachusetts and also to ornament a poolside garden wall in South Florida. The designs were equally at home in each environment. Jerusalem Pottery is open daily from 9am to noon and is closed on Sunday and full strike days. When the Old City bazaar is open all day, Jerusalem Pottery is open until 5pm.

Palestinian Pottery. 14 Nablus Rd. ☎ **02/282-826.**

This workshop's chief artist, Marie Balian, is most famous for her multi-tile ceramic panels, which are richly hand-painted visions of Persian gardens, desert oases, and Middle Eastern motifs. In 1992, the Smithsonian Museum in Washington, D.C., mounted "Views of Paradise," a special exhibit of 22 of Mrs. Balian's creations; her panels also adorn the Sukkot Patio at the home of the president of Israel. Palestian Pottery produces a steady stream of traditional plates, bowls, name and address tiles, and smaller panel compositions in floral designs that can be used as tabletops or as stunning architectural details. Be sure to ask to see the display of Palestinian Pottery's work spanning the past 70 years. The workshop is near the American consulate in East Jerusalem, and is open Monday through Saturday from 9:30am to 5pm; it is always a good idea to call ahead and check on hours. A downtown West Jerusalem branch of this workshop, called Armenian Pottery (☎ 241-592), is now open in the cellar arcade of the City Tower Building (Migdal Ha-Ir) at the corner of King George and Bezalel streets. Its hours are Sunday through Thursday from 9:30am to 7pm; Friday from 9:30am to 2pm.

Darian Armenian Ceramics. 12 Shlomzion Hamalka St. ☎ **02/258-976.**

This new shop is the creation of Arman Darian, a recent immigrant from the former Soviet Armenia where he studied traditional calligraphy and design. Here you'll find wonderful soup tureens, cups and plates, tiles and lamp bases, all hand-painted in the Armenian tradition, but with graceful designs that are uniquely Arman's. There are sometimes experiments and bargain seconds on the shelves, but you'll find beautiful first-quality pieces as well. Arman will also design to your specifications. Open Sunday through Thursday from 9:30am to 7pm and Friday from 9:30am to 2pm.

GIFTS

Chaim Peretz. 1 Rabbi Ariye St. ☎ **02/250-859.**

In this little workshop, Chaim Peretz makes attractive, very reasonably priced stained glass art and Judaica, sold for considerably higher prices at stores elsewhere in the city. The walk to his shop, in the quaint, labyrinthine Nahlaot neighborhood south of Agrippas Street near Mahane Yehuda, is always interesting (you'll inevitably have to ask the locals for directions). Once there, you'll find an array of charming menorahs, mezzuzot, Hands of Fatima, candle holders, and mirrors. If your stay in town is long enough, you can order your selection in the colors and designs you prefer. The shop, on a pedestrian lane off one of Nahlaot's neighborhood commons, is generally open Sunday through Thursday from 9:30am to 1pm, and 4 to 7pm; Friday from 9:30am to 1pm. If no one is around, ask along the street. A phone call ahead of time can be useful.

Charlotte. 4 Koresh St. ☎ **02/251-632.**

Founded in 1938, this store, on the street just behind the Central Post Office on Jaffa Road, is the oldest gift shop in West Jerusalem. The secret of its longevity is a carefully chosen mix of modern Israeli jewelry and crafts, handmade Bedouin objects, old pieces of copperware, and unusual antiquities, all at very reasonable prices. Jerusalemites have never ceased to be delighted with Charlotte's selections, and if you stop by, you'll see the difference between this place and many of the less personal tourist shops on the Ben-Yehuda Mall. It's open Sunday through Thursday from 9am to 1pm and 4 to 7pm: Friday from 9am to 1pm.

Lifeline for the Old. 14 Shivtei Israel St. ☎ **02/287-829.**

This shop sells toys, needlework, clothing, jewelry, Judaica, and crafts handmade by Jerusalem's senior citizens, and is a *mitzvah* both for craftspeople and customers. Sales and donations keep this remarkable institution afloat. The workshops, which help provide a meaningful creative outlet for Jerusalem's elderly, can be visited Sunday through Thursday from 8am to 11:30pm. The gift shop is open Sunday through Thursday from 9am to 4pm and Friday from 9am to 1pm.

Shlomo Mishaly Metal Work. 8 Yoel Salomon St. ☎ **02/257-856.**

Decades before the Yoel Salomon Mall was created as a center for trendy restaurants and craft galleries, Shlomo Mishaly had his neighborhood shop here, where he turned out handmade metal items and Judaica in designs of his own imagination. There are one-of-a-kind handwrought boxes, inexpensive Hands of Fatima, mezuzzot, lamps, and menorahs that use oil, candles, or electricity. I especially admire Mr. Mishaly's noisemakers for Purim in the shapes of fish, in the $100 price range. The shop is open Sunday through Thursday from 9am to 1pm and from 4 to 7pm, as well as on Friday from 9am to 2pm.

10 Shlomzion Hamalka St. ☎ **02/234-617.**

Jerusalem has one old-fashioned European-style shop packed full of Romanian and Hungarian embroidery, and sundry items of bric-a-brac. Run by the charming and venerable Emma Berohm, it's located just near the intersection of Jaffa Road and Shlomzion Hamalka Street, two blocks east of Zion Square. Like most good haunts for treasure hunters, its hard to see the shop's sign (Brinn and Berohm), but you'll find an eclectic, intriguing, and unplanned show window. The shop is open Sunday through Thursday from 10am to 7pm; Friday from 10am to 2pm.

GLASS

🟢 **Nekker Glass Company.** 6 Bet Israel St. ☎ **02/829-683.**

Delicate, modern interpretations of Roman glass are for sale almost everywhere in East and West Jerusalem, but it was this store, near the Mirrer Yeshiva on the northern fringe of Mea Shearim, that revived the ancient glassblowing traditions that began in this part of the world over 2,000 years ago. The Nekker family arrived in Jerusalem from Baghdad in the early 1950s and quickly set up a small glass factory employing both Arab and Jewish glassblowers. Slowly the factory began to experiment with designs and techniques from ancient times, and has even developed ways to reproduce soft, ancient patinas in a variety of colors. At Nekker's tiny workshop, you are invited to watch the glassblowers at work. Yehuda Nekkar, the patriarch and chief designer, virtually dreams in glass. The stock is on sale for a fraction of what it costs in retail shops. A special line of museum-style reproductions is higher in price. The Nekker staff will pack your purchases securely for travel. Open weekdays from 8:30am to 4pm, closing on Shabbat, and at 1pm on Friday.

JEWELRY

Ophir. 38 Jaffa Rd. ☎ **02/249-078.**

Many Jerusalemites and tourists have become fans of this shop's delicate jewelry designs that echo Victorian, Edwardian, art deco, and Middle Eastern styles, and are made by the owner, Avraham, himself. Prices are extremely reasonable, and Avraham's stock is augmented by many unusual antique and semiantique items. There's a small glass display case beside the doorway to 38 Jaffa Rd.: enter the building, and you'll find Ophir's tiny studio at the back of the ground floor. Open Sunday, Monday, Wednesday, and Thursday from 9am to 1pm and 4 to 7pm; Tuesday and Friday from 9am to 1pm only.

✪ **Sarah Einstein.** 13 Ben Shetach St., at the end of Rivlin St. ☎ **02/250-610.**

For unusual antique jewelry, visit Sarah Einstein in her studio where you'll find her taking apart vast antique Yemenite necklaces or tribal Persian headdresses and rearranging the beautifully handcrafted component pieces into smaller compositions that modern, Western women can wear with flair and elegance. Among the extraordinary creations made by Sarah Einstein and her staff, you'll find a choice of one-of-a-kind necklaces and earrings that range from delicate to dramatic and encompass every tradition in the Middle East. On the same premises is the workshop of **Hedya,** an Israeli jeweler who designs accessories such as earrings to coordinate with each of Sarah's unique pieces. Open Sunday through Thursday from 10am to 7pm and Friday from 10am to 2pm.

JUDAICA
Danny Azoulay. 5 Yoel Salomon St. ☎ **02/233-918.**

A highly skilled craftsperson who came to Israel from Morocco as a small child, Danny Azoulay specializes in porcelain and fine ceramic Judaica and his tiny shop is filled with hand-painted Hanukkah menorahs, charity boxes laced with brass or silver designs, mezuzzot, spice boxes, and dreidels. One of my favorite designs is a tiny porcelain Hanukkah lamp (too small for the strictly observant) that sells for about $120. Mr. Azoulay's creations delicately blend Florentine, Islamic, Central European, and contemporary motifs into a style that is unique. There are charming items in the $5 to $10 range, a selection of wonderful mezuzzot and dreidels well under $30, and many heirloom-quality menorahs, spice and tsadakkah boxes ranging from about $100 to several hundred dollars. At times you may be able to purchase seconds at a discount, either at this shop, or at Mr. Azoulay's studio, not far from Mahane Yehuda. A number of Danny Azoulay's pieces can be seen at the Wolfson Museum in Hekhal Shlomo. The shop also sells hand-calligraphed illuminated manuscripts and *ketubbot* (marriage contracts) by some of Israel's finest scribal artists like Amalya Nini and Arden Halter. It is open Sunday through Thursday from 9:30am to 7:30pm and on Friday from 9:30am to 2:30pm. Major credit cards are accepted.

Shulamit Noy Dunievsky. 18 Shivtei Israel St. ☎ **02/281-987.**

In her busy ceramic workshop, Shulamit Noy designs hand-built contemporary Hanukkah menorahs glazed in pastel colors, with motifs of oasis gardens, birds, starry desert nights, flowers, and pastoral creatures that ornament the back plates. A few designs are done by mold and run under $100, but Shulamit's beautiful one-of-a-kind menorahs are the real collectors' items. The elaborate openwork back-plate menorahs can run as much as $250 to $300. Interesting and very reasonably priced contemporary kiddush cups and other items of Judaica are on display in an always changing array of inventive designs. Prices for Shulamit Noy's pieces are higher at the few shops that carry them. The studio is open Sunday through Friday from 9am to 2pm.

✪ **Oded Davidson,** House of Quality. 12 Hebron Rd. ☎ **02/245-728** or 791-082.

One of the country's most interesting Judaica silversmiths, Oded Davidson combines skill and vision to create unique designs delicately engraved with personal whimsy and charm. Davidson's silver dreidels, menorahs, spice boxes, and other creations (ranging in price from several hundred to over a thousand dollars) have been bought by many collectors and museums, including the Wolfson Museum at Hekhal Shlomo. (Some items are under $100, but most original creations in silver will be more.) You may arrange to see Oded's remarkable portfolio by visiting his workshop; a small selection of his work can also be seen at the **Seven Artists Gallery,** 6 Yoel Salomon St. Oded's in-person explanations of his work are always fascinating.

Archie Granot, Papercuts. 22 Rivlin St. ☎ **02/243-956.**

Traditional Jewish papercuts began to develop as a folk art in Europe and North Africa. It seems natural that the People of the Book should have taken designs in paper to heart. In many homes it was the custom to hang a delicately cut piece of paper (called a *mizrach,* from the Hebrew word for "east") on the eastern wall of a room, to indicate the direction of Jerusalem. There are a number of excellent practitioners of this craft in Israel, but Archie Granot has raised this folk tradition to new levels of perfection and intensity. Working with multiple layers and colors, Granot creates works of amazing beauty and intricacy, ranging from *mizrachs* in traditional and contemporary styles to wedding contracts and *mezuzzot.* Prices can range from a few hundred to several thousand dollars. Granot's works are in the collections of the Israel Museum, the Victoria and Albert Museum, the Jewish Museum of New York, and the Philadelphia Museum of Judaica. To find his workshop/gallery, proceed down Yoel Salomon Street from Jaffa Road; turn left just after the last building on Yoel Salomon; look for his sign at the top of an old outdoor staircase on the left.

Gaia Smith, House of Quality. Across from the Cinémathèque on Hebron Road.

Gaia Smith takes the long tradition of using architectural motifs in the back plates of Hanukkah menorahs and goes delightfully wild. Her extraordinary hand-built menorahs and items of Judaica are designed around cottages in the Galilee with vistas of the hills, apartments on Central Park West with vistas of the Manhattan skyline, a child's toy-strewn bedroom on a wintry Hanukkah night—all filled with wit, charm, and a touch of mystery. A small selection of Gaia's ceramics are sometimes shown near Zion Square at the 8 Ceramists Gallery on Yoel Salomon St. If you like her work, you can arrange to see her studio. (You might even bring photographs of the interior and exterior of your house and commission a menorah, charity box, or mezuzzot based on the unique elements of your family's home or your special memories and favorite possessions.) Prices range from under $100 for small items to several hundred dollars and more for major menorahs and special designs. Ms. Smith's reputation among collectors, as well as her prices, are on the rise. The studio is generally open Sunday through Friday from 10am to 1pm.

Shlomo Ohana. 20 Ein Yaakov St., Mea Shearim. ☎ **02/829-996.**

Some of the best loved and most beautiful objects of Judaica have been created over the centuries by neighborhood metalsmiths working with humble materials such as tin, copper, and brass. In Shlomo Ohana's workshop, this tradition absolutely soars. You'll find amulets, *hamsas* (Hands of Fatima), and Sabbath candle holders in price ranges from less than $10 to around $50. Shlomo Ohana, who was born in Morocco, also makes the simple glass-enclosed Hanukkah lamps traditionally mounted beside doorways in Jerusalem's 19th-century neighborhoods; his *davvening* Hassidim are a popular tourist item, and more expensive at the few shops that carry his creations. The experience of visiting this workshop, deep in Mea Shearim's Ein Yaacov market, is always fascinating; in deference to Mea Shearim's ultraorthodox community, women should dress modestly, and men should avoid shorts. Shlomo Ohana is open

Sunday through Thursday from 9am to 5pm or 6pm, and on Friday from 9am to 2pm. If the shop is closed, ask one of the neighbors when it will reopen.

PALESTINIAN EMBROIDERY

You'll notice antique Palestinian embroidered robes hanging from the doors of many shops in the Old City bazaar. Red, rose, and scarlet on handwoven black cloth are the preferred colors, stemming from a tradition that goes back almost 3,000 years, to the centuries when the prophets warned against women who sewed with scarlet threads of vanity. Many of the current embroidery designs can be traced back to patterns introduced by the Crusaders almost a thousand years ago. You can find interesting scraps of embroidery, suitable for framing, for anywhere from $5 to $30. Complete caftans, especially those with long, pointed medieval sleeves, if not worn, can be hung or mounted as dramatic decorative focal points. A beautifully photographed book, *Traditional Palestinian Embroidery and Jewelry,* by **Abed Abu Omar,** is sold for approximately $20 at his Bedouin antiques and embroidery shop on the Christian Quarter Road near the Greek Patriarchate Road, or at the shop of Mr. Abu Omar's nephew (also named Abed Abu Omar) just next to the fountain in the Muristan Bazaar. The shop of **Maher Natsheh,** 10 Christian Quarter Rd., also carries a good range of antique and old textiles.

In addition to the many shops in the Old City markets selling caftans and antique or semiantique embroidery, three church-supported nonprofit shops (two in the Old City and one in West Jerusalem) offer a dazzling array of freshly made, top-quality embroideries all done by specially trained women who are working to support their families. If you're interested in buying a major piece, it would be worthwhile to visit all three shops in order to check out all the one-of-a-kind items available. Quality is assured, and prices at these shops are extremely fair.

✪ **Benevolent Arts Society of the Holyland.** Sixth Station of the Cross, Via Dolorosa, Old City. ☎ **02/284-367.**

This shop is managed by the legendary Ms. Frayda Hanna, who by teaching the skills necessary to create the best-quality traditional Palestinian crafts, has helped three generations of women to support their families. Freshly embroidered tablecloths, napkins, and traditional items are to be found here, as well as embroidered vestments and chasubles, and a selection of inexpensive gift items. The shop is open daily from 9am to 4pm.

Craftaid. Saint Andrews Hospice, King David Street and Remez Street, West Jerusalem. ☎ **02/732-401.**

This nonprofit shop sells a magnificent collection of densely embroidered divan pillowcases, wall hangings, and shawls, all alive with traditional motifs and colors, ranging in price from $30 to several hundred dollars. Many fabulous pieces are less than $100. There are also heavy woven Bedouin tent rugs, embroidered linen tablecloths and napkins, and a good selection of inexpensive handmade crafts and gift items ranging in price from about $3 to $25. The shop is run by an American (and a graduate of Mount Holyoke College) who has an excellent eye for beautiful things. It is open Monday through Saturday from 9am to noon, and Tuesday through Saturday from 4 to 6pm, as well as Sunday from 11am to 12:30pm. The location of this shop in the Saint Andrew's complex, on a hill between the train station and the Cinémathèque, offers fine vistas of the Old City.

Melia. Arab Orthodox Society Art and Training Center, Frere's Street, inside the New Gate, Old City. ☎ **02/281-377.**

The newest of the nonprofit embroidery shops, Melia offers many beautiful traditional pieces, as well as some imaginative decorative items. In addition to the classic divan pillowcases, I especially liked a dramatically embroidered mirror frame for approximately $50 as well as designer-embroidered women's jackets for several hundred dollars and embroidered T-shirts that are a bargain at $11. There is also a selection of Western-style tablecloths and embroideries. Here, as in the other shops, the pieces done using naturally dyed thread are the richest and most beautiful. Melia is open Monday through Saturday from 9am to 5pm.

THE OLD CITY MARKETS

A major attraction for tourists, the Old City markets have many shops offering such local products as olivewood chess and nativity sets, rosaries, carved camels, boxes, and (a great buy at three for a dollar) Christmas tree ornaments. You'll also find heavy, hand-blown glassware from Hebron, inlaid wooden boxes from Egypt and Syria, mother-of-pearl objects from Jordan, new and inexpensive Yemenite and Bedouin-style jewelry, and locally made leather goods.

Many shops sell suede and shearling mittens, slippers, and jackets of varying quality (the lace-up shearling baby slippers are a practical gift idea). The **leather shop of Mr. Abd El-Karim Sharabati** (no sign) at 100 Christian Quarter Rd. (on the left, three shops in from the corner of David Street), is known for the largest selection of these items, and also for well-designed sandals and women's shoes commissioned from local factories. You'll also find fair starting and final prices (although you must always comparison shop and bargain).

The Arab bazaar around the Christian Quarter Road often has a great selection of hand-embroidered Romanian peasant blouses. In the United States, the blouses would cost three or four times the going rate of $25 to $50, and you'd never find any of equal quality or variety. The shop of **Mr. Kaysi** (no sign), with a plate-glass show window and a recessed entrance on the right side of the Christian Quarter Road (just past the first pedestrian turning on the right as you come from David Street), usually has the finest selection. Mr. Kaysi, a charming man who sports a black goatee and usually dresses in a tweed jacket, often manages to obtain special items such as embroidered Romanian tablecloths and antique clothing, which he keeps folded away under the counter. His multicolored Egyptian tapestry rugs and tribal Bedouin rugs and weavings are usually the best quality in the bazaar. Prices start high, but bargain.

The shops dealing in ancient antiquities are fascinating, but judge any object you may want to purchase in terms of its decorative value rather than its alleged age or rarity.

Interesting old-looking metal trays and other metal objects abound—they're decorative, but seldom real antiques. The shop of the venerable **Abu Yussuf** (no sign), on the left side of the Street of the Chain (a continuation past the Cardo of David Street), is a cave filled with copper and brass trays and pots, as well as old door knockers and reproductions of centuries-old menorahs. Mr. Abu Yussuf loves to bargain, and good spirits can bring his initial prices down to rock bottom.

The **Ashab Ceramic Workshop** on Via Dolorosa near the first station of the cross (☎ 02/272-967) does custom-designed orders for tiles and specializes in many traditional Islamic and Armenian motifs, and is always a pleasure to visit. Open Saturday through Thursday from 9am to 5pm; closed Friday.

In the Jewish Quarter of the Old City, one of my favorite shops for old objects and Judaica is **Mansour Saidian** (no sign), opposite the Mizrachi Bank on the corner of Tiferet Israel Street. There's always a selection of 19th-century European and Iranian kiddush cups and old menorahs stashed away among the cases of newer objects and jewelry. Bargains!

Colors of Jerusalem, 43 Jewish Quarter Rd. (☎ 283-493) is a retail and consignment shop selling arts and crafts made by recent and relatively recent immigrants and ranging in price from a few dollars to several hundred dollars. You'll find items here like handmade puppets, Ethiopian basketry and ceramics, and hand-painted wooden Russian eggs.

Among the Israeli craftspeople beginning to thrive in the tiny, ancient shops of the bazaar, you'll find quality artisans like **Tamar,** who creates contemporary jewelry in her shop at 29 Jewish Quarter Rd. near David Street.

The markets are also filled with all kinds of shops selling Arabic desserts, spices, and snacks, all of which should be part of the Old City shopping experience.

BARGAINING

Under normal conditions, Middle Eastern shopping is supposed to take a good deal of time, theatrics, and diplomacy. But these days many merchants are willing to get down to the nitty gritty with fewer rituals. If you find something you like, you must bargain for it. Appear politely unsure the object is something you really want. It often helps if you're with a friend who pretends you're late for a bus or an appointment. If a merchant doesn't come down on his price, don't panic. The chance is that you'll find the same thing or something similar close by, and if not, if you leave gracefully, you can always come back and try again. If nothing else, after a few hours of browsing you'll have a new appreciation for the intricacies of the Middle East peace process.

10 Jerusalem After Dark

Although there are plenty of cinemas, cozy bars, theaters, nightclubs, and even a few discos, Jerusalemites are somehow always conscious that this is sacred ground. The variety and excitement of nighttime activities can't compare with the choices in Tel Aviv. But never fear—you'll still find enough to do here.

THE PERFORMING ARTS

You'll find the many lectures, jazz, contemporary and folk performances, concerts, dance, and theater productions listed in the Friday edition of the *Jerusalem Post*, and in the monthly *Calendar of Events,* which you can pick up free at Tourist Information Offices. Lectures, readings, and English-language theater productions are always noted.

Many concerts and productions are very small, intimate gatherings, but that's part of their charm and special feeling. Israel has long been known for the high quality of its musicians, and the recent wave of Russian immigrants has led to an even greater embarrassment of riches. Classical music lovers will discover totally new and remarkable artists performing everywhere, from concert halls and clubs to the street corners and pedestrian malls. The jazz and blues scene is truly excellent. Watch for performances of the **Rishon-le-Zion Symphony Orchestra;** this group from a suburb of Tel Aviv is filled with many remarkable musicians recently arrived in the country. Be on the lookout for **JEST (Jerusalem English Speaking Theater),** with actors and audiences drawn mainly from Israel's English-speaking immigrant community. It often does translations of topical Israeli plays and revues, which can be especially interesting to tourists. Jerusalem's own **Taverners** is a lively English-language folk group.

The following listings are the main performance venues.

Binyane Ha-Uma. Opposite Central Bus Station. ☎ **02/252-481.**

This convention center is host to performances by the renowned **Israel Philharmonic Orchestra,** which gives frequent concerts in Jerusalem.

Jerusalem Center for the Performing Arts. 20 David Marcus St. ☎ **02/667-167** for information. Bus: 15.

Located near the corner of Chopin (in the Rehavia District near the president's house), this modern complex opened its doors in 1975 and houses the Jerusalem Theater (Sherover Theater), Henry Crown Hall, and Rebecca Crown Hall. Original Israeli plays and Hebrew translations of foreign classics and modern works are performed in the theater's main hall; visiting troupes also use the main hall for performances in foreign languages. The theater's auditoriums are the home of the **Jerusalem Symphony Orchestra** and the **Israel Chamber Ensemble,** and are used for performances by the Israel Philharmonic Orchestra. Quality films are also screened here.

The Khan. 2 Remez St. ☎ **02/718-281** (bar). Bus: 4, 5, 6, 7, 8, 14, 18, 21, or 48, anywhere along King George V Avenue going south, or eastbound on Jaffa Road.

Located across from the railway station, this Ottoman Turkish caravansary was refurbished and opened in 1968 as a nightclub, catering mostly to tourists, but it has upgraded its program of performances in the past few years. Besides the Khan Club, there is a theater, the pleasant Pesto Italian restaurant on the upper terrace, and a bar for drinks, dancing, and many cultural events. Performances at the theater are usually in Hebrew, but there are often chamber music concerts and other musical events. The Khan often offers tourist programs of Israeli folksingers, traditional dances, and audience sing-alongs.

Call for information; prices vary by event.

Puppet Train Theater. Liberty Bell Park. ☎ **02/618-514.**

Jerusalem has become a center for puppetry, and delightful, inventive performances are held here throughout the year. In August, Jerusalem hosts an International Puppet Theater Festival.

Al Hakawati Palestinian National Theater. Nuzha Street, East Jerusalem. ☎ **02/280-957.**

At this theater you'll find cabaret-style productions and plays that are usually strongly political. From time to time, a specific production may be censored or unexpectedly shut down by the authorities, but both Israeli and foreign visitors are welcome, and English synopses are usually available. For those interested in the Palestinian movement, a visit here can be interesting, regardless of what is being performed. Nuzha Street runs off Saladin Street just to the south of the American Colony Hotel. Ticket prices are usually about NIS 12 ($3.60).

MORE ENTERTAINMENT

Son et Lumière. Jaffa Gate.

During the warmer months, a sound-and-light show is featured in the Citadel of David at Jaffa Gate. Performances are in English at 8:45pm, from March to mid-November, but check on times and tickets in advance. Be prepared for the chill created by the stone fortress and the night breezes. A free twice weekly outdoor concert series consisting of local music groups was begun at the Citadel during the summer of 1995; if it continues, it is a pleasant opportunity to enjoy performances ranging from ethnic to classical. Check with the Tourist Information Office for details.

Sultan's Pool. In a valley beneath the Old City walls between Jaffa Gate and Mount Zion.

This dramatic setting is great for major outdoor classical, rock, and jazz concerts in warm weather; a typical month might include concerts by Sinead O'Connor or Bob Dylan, and a performance of Carmen. Check with the Tourist Information Office for schedules.

THE DISCO/BAR/CAFE SCENE

The cafes on Ben-Yehuda Street offer outside tables where patrons come to see and be seen. Saturday nights on the Ben-Yehuda Mall are teenage mob scenes. You can also try Rivlin Street, and the neighboring Salomon Street Mall, which form the heart of the cafe/pub scene (West Jerusalem). The Russian Compound neighborhood, not far from Jaffa Road, is home to a number of pubs and bars that offer live music and dancing on various evenings.

All the large hotels have nightclubs, but with the exception of the Khan (see above) the nightclub scene barely exists outside the hotel circuit.

Arizona. 37 Jaffa Rd.

This pub/disco near Zion Square, run by travelers for travelers, aims for a younger clientele (although not too young—you must be over 18). The music is hard, the ambience brash and busy, and it's open daily from 8pm to 4am. Beer is NIS 9 ($2.70). Its neighbor, The Underground, at 1 Yoel Solomon St., is much the same. Both become frenzied during the summer student tourist season.

Arthur. 10 Hyrkanos St. Cover NIS 10 ($3) for special performers.

Also in the trendy Russian Compound, with beer going for NIS 9 ($2.70) (sometimes higher for special events), this pub/bar offers a wonderful Tuesday night program of blues singers including the African-American Hebrew Israelite community of Dimona, a Friday reggae party from 5 to 9pm featuring Routes Afriques, and an assortment of other musicians from time to time. Arthur is open daily from 6pm to 4am. A similarly mellow spot is the neighboring Mike's Place, also on Hyrkanos Street, with a Tuesday through Saturday evening program of live classic rock and blues music. Beer starts at NIS 9 ($2.70).

Fink's.   2 Ha-Histadrut St. ☎ 02/234-523.

Probably the best stocked bar in the country, this tiny, unexotic-looking bar/restaurant may also be the Middle East's most politically savvy drinking spot. Prices are reasonable, and the range of choices astonishing. It's open from Saturday to Thursday, 6pm to midnight.

Glasnost. 15 Helene Ha-Malka St. ☎ 02/256-954.

Another Russian compound watering hole, this one currently has a policy of no cover charge for tourists when there are live performers. Recorded music is hard and heavy. There is a full bar, and it is open daily from 4pm to 4am.

Pargod. 94 Bezalel St. ☎ 02/231-765.

This club features local musicians most nights, from 9:30pm to 12:30am. Wednesday and Friday afternoons are reserved for jazz (1:30 to 5:30pm). There's a cover charge of NIS 15 ($4.50); no charge on Friday afternoon (Friday night cover charge must be paid in advance).

FILMS

West Jerusalem shows the latest European and American films, almost always in the original language with Hebrew subtitles. In the eastern part of the city, the films come mostly from Arab countries and are in Arabic without subtitles.

West Jerusalem's cinemas are scattered throughout the city. The most prominent theater is the world-famous Cinémathèque (see below), which is the scene of nightly screenings of the classics, the best of the current international scene, rarely shown international films, and the experimental and the arcane. Films are usually in the original language, with Hebrew and (often) English subtitles. Members of the Cinémathèque get the first seats, but a half hour before screening time tickets go on sale to the public. Besides the movie houses, there are other places that screen films, such as the Jerusalem Theater, Binyane Ha-Uma, and the Israel Museum.

Although the *Post* carries notices of current film offerings, the notices never carry addresses or telephone numbers of the movie houses.

The **Cinémathèque** (☎ 02/724-131) or Israel Film Archive, Jerusalem, is located near the railway station. Go to the traffic intersection between the railway station and Hebron Road. Walk down the slope to the northeast, toward the Old City, and soon you'll come to the Cinémathèque, built into the hillside below the Hebron Road.

Other well-known cinemas are **G. G. Gil,** Jerusalem Mall, Malha (☎ 02/788-448); **Jerusalem Theater,** 20 Marcus St. (☎ 02/617-167); **Orion,** along an alley between Hillel and Shammai streets (☎ 02/222-914), a block south of Ben-Yehuda, and roughly parallel to it; **Rav Chen,** 1–7, Rav Meeher Building, Ha'oman Street, Talpiot (☎ 02/792-799); and **Ron,** 1 Rabbi Akiva St., off Hillel (☎ 02/234-704).

6

The West Bank

Jerusalem is the best place from which to visit the sites in this chapter, as most of them are within an hour's drive of the city. Because the West Bank is so interesting and so close to the capital, the chapter focuses on attractions rather than accommodations.

The character of this area is different from the rest of Israel. The West Bank brings the biblical scriptures to life: Jesus was born in Bethlehem; Abraham entered the land of Canaan in Samaria; the patriarchs are buried at Hebron; and Mount Gerizim at Shechem, sacred to the Samaritan sect, looks much the same as it may have when it was described by Joshua.

Just as the landscape is more biblical, the atmosphere is more bucolic. In many places you will see veiled Arab women walking by the roadside balancing great loads on their heads. Donkeys, urged on by old men or little boys, groan under their burden of olivewood twigs.

Ministry of Tourism offices have been established in Bethlehem and at the Allenby Bridge at the Jordanian border and green-and-white signposts have been set up, in English, to guide you to all the major sites. Also, you can't miss the surprising amount of new construction, both Palestinian and Israeli, that intrudes on the pristine beauty of the countryside, and the ancient stone villages.

Under present conditions, guided bus tours provide the safest method of travel. With the exception of the big main road from Jerusalem to the Dead Sea, Jericho, and the Jordan Valley, it is unwise to drive anywhere in the West Bank in a car with an Israeli license plate. Around Jericho, the "No Entry" signs are clearly posted. Past these signs, you may find yourself an unwelcome guest in a military zone beside the Jordanian border.

The State Department has advised U.S. citizens against traveling to the West Bank. For more current information, consult the American Embassy in Tel Aviv (☎ 03/517-4338), or the American Consulate General in Jerusalem (☎ 02/253-288). The safest way to visit the West Bank is on a guided tour bus. It is not advisable to drive an Israeli rental car into the West Bank at present.

What's Special About the West Bank

Major Cities and Towns
- Bethlehem, 6 miles south of Jerusalem, village of the family of King David, and birthplace of Jesus.
- Hebron, an ancient Judean city where a great Herodian period enclosure and mosque mark the burial place of the biblical patriarchs.
- Nablus, site of ancient Shechem, the largest city on the West Bank.
- Jericho, the oldest still-inhabited city on earth (from ca. 10,000 B.C.), a modern town, and some miles away the tel of ancient Jericho.

Major Attractions
- Church of the Nativity in Bethlehem, the oldest surviving church in the Holy Land.
- Mar Saba Monastery, an ancient community built into the dramatic wall of a desert canyon near Bethlehem.
- Herodion, the palace-fortress built inside a mountain near Bethlehem by King Herod.
- Wadi Kelt Canyon near Jericho.
- Countryside of ancient villages dotting the land between Ramallah and Nablus; biblical Judean desert.
- Beaches such as Ein Fesha Park, with trees and sweetwater pools beside the Dead Sea.

Special Events
- Christmas Eve concert in Bethlehem, drawing choirs from all over the world.

If you have questions or concerns while in the area, stop in any local police station. Another word of caution: It is unwise to engage in political discussions while traveling in this region.

TOURS OF THE AREA

Egged Tours, 44A Jaffa Rd. in Zion Square (☎ **02/231-604** or **224-198**), or at the Central Bus Station, offers a half-day tour of Jericho, the Dead Sea, and Qumran. The tour runs Sunday through Friday for $17 per person. Most travel agencies have similar tours; the Arab companies even run on Saturday. The **Society for Protection of Nature in Israel (SPNI),** 13 Helene Hamalka St.(☎ **02/244-605**), offers 1-day and overnight nature hikes and tours of the region.

Note: As administration of the West Bank is turned over to the Palestinian Authority, Israeli-based tour organizations and agencies may no longer be permitted to conduct tours to the area. New Palestinian agencies will open as the political situation develops.

1 From Jerusalem to Jericho and the Dead Sea

The trip from Jerusalem to Jericho and the Dead Sea is only a 45-minute ride. There are normal driving conditions from North Jerusalem on the main highway, east to the Dead Sea. From the Dead Sea you can drive south along the shore to Qumran, Ein Gedi, and Masada, or north on the main highway to Tel Jericho, Hisham's Palace, the Jordan Valley, and on up to Bet Shean and the Galilee. It is important to leave Jerusalem via North Jerusalem and not via the road through Bethany. Drivers should check with their car rental agencies about permission to drive to the West Bank and Jericho and about explicit directions for the road to the Dead Sea via North Jerusalem near French Hill.

The more direct route, which you might be able to see by tour bus, goes through Bethany. Independent travel in this area is not advised.

WHAT TO SEE EN ROUTE

INN OF THE GOOD SAMARITAN   To the right, within sight of the main road, is what is known as the Inn of the Good Samaritan, supposedly the site where Jesus' parable of the Good Samaritan took place. What is definitely known is that this site has been an important landmark since ancient times. A Roman road once passed here, as did others even before that, including an ancient caravan route. The present inn is of Turkish construction and is some 400 years old. It has a large entranceway and huge rooms leading off on either side of it. Each room has arched windows and wall niches (supposedly for fires). The entranceway opens into a huge central courtyard. In the middle of the courtyard is a large circular stone cooking area, and a well so deep that the bottom of it can't be seen. There are also stone troughs. Much of what is found in the courtyard is said to date from Roman times, when the site was a military stronghold.

WADI KELT   Back on the main road, follow the sign pointing left to the Saint George Monastery (Greek Orthodox), a place of mysterious beauty where communities of monks have lived since the 6th century A.D., perched in isolation on the side of a dramatic desert gorge near the spring of Wadi Kelt. According to tradition, it was here that the Old Testament prophet Elijah was fed by ravens. The Wadi Kelt spring once ran through the aqueducts of Herod's time (1st century A.D.) and today continues to irrigate part of Jericho. On the banks of Wadi Kelt are the remains of winter palaces of the Hasmonean and Herodian periods. A walk down Wadi Kelt toward the monastery is dramatic; the return hike involves some steep climbs that are manageable for most people in winter; in the heat of summer, it should not be attempted. The monastery, with some frescoes and architectural fragments from Byzantine times, can be visited Monday through Saturday from 8am to 4pm. Although the monks will point out the tomb of Saint George, most traditions hold that the patron saint of England is buried at the Church of Saint George in Lod, near Ben Gurion Airport. Wadi Kelt is especially lovely in winter, when it is filled with wildflowers. In past years, the SPNI has offered 1-day downhill walks through Wadi Kelt toward Jericho. The future of SPNI's programs in the West Bank is not certain at this time. *Warning:* Until the political situation is more clearly defined, no one should hike in Wadi Kelt except with a large organized group.

NEBI MUSA   From here the main road curves down more steeply, and a right turn (follow the signs) will lead you to a cluster of ancient, abandoned buildings that were used as a Jordanian encampment during the Six-Day War. According to Muslim belief, this site, called Nebi Musa, is the "Tomb of Moses" (the Bible cites Mount Nebo as Moses's burial place). Until recent years, this was also the site of an annual and much-loved Muslim pilgrimage festival.

As you continue driving, you'll descend into the Jordan Valley, from which you'll make a left off the main highway to go to Jericho. As you travel toward Jericho, you'll notice hundreds of earthen huts, once occupied by Palestinian refugees.

The West Bank

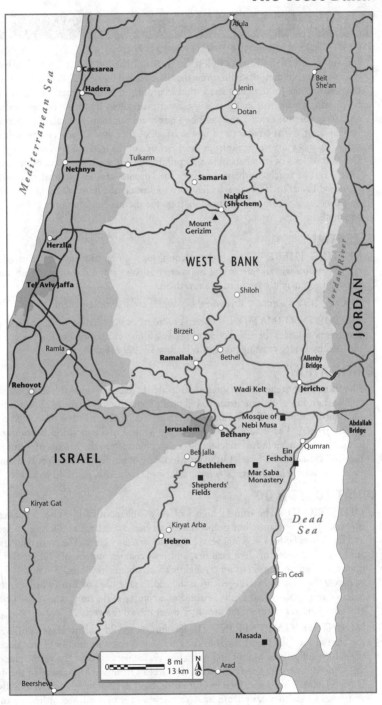

2 Jericho

35km (22 miles) E of Jerusalem; 181km (121 miles) S of Tiberias

Jericho is one of the world's oldest cities, if not the oldest. Archeologists have discovered habitations of civilizations that date back 9,000 to 12,000 years. This is the Jericho that Joshua conquered, but according to archeologists (in one of the few instances when the evidence gathered at excavations has not matched biblical accounts), the walls that came tumbling down are not from Joshua's time period. Jericho was the first city captured by the Israelites after their 40 years in the wilderness. The tribes approached it from the other side of the Jordan River, sent in spies, and to the blasts of trumpets blown by priests, the city was attacked and captured. To the east of Jericho is the place where the Israelites crossed the Jordan into the Promised Land. In 1994, this ancient city (politically the most placid in the West Bank) became administrative headquarters for the new autonomous Palestinian region of the West Bank.

ESSENTIALS

GETTING THERE   Under present conditions, group tours are recommended rather than individual travel. You must carry all your travel documents with you, although you may not be asked to show them.

By Car   It's a 35-minute drive on the main highway from Jerusalem.

VISITOR INFORMATION   There is no tourism information office in Jericho, which is now under the jurisdiction of the Palestinian Authority, but there is one at the Allenby Bridge crossing point into Jordan ☎ **02/941-038.**

ORIENTATION

The interesting archeological sites are outside the modern town. Heading north, you'll get on **Ein es-Sultan Street.** You'll finally come to a fork in the road. Just along the right-hand road is **Tel es-Sultan,** also called Tel Jericho, which is the ruined city of Old Jericho. The left fork goes behind the **Mount of Temptation Restaurant,** and after a kilometer (a half-mile) uphill, a sign points left to the **Mount of Temptation** and **Qarantal,** the Greek Orthodox Monastery of the 40 Days. **Caliph Hisham's Palace** is about 4 kilometers (2¹/₂ miles) along the right fork, past Old Jericho.

WHAT TO SEE & DO

OLD JERICHO   The artificial hillock of Tel es-Sultan, or Old Jericho, is not very interesting at first glance, but people have lived here as far back as the Bronze Age, and possibly as far back as 6,000 years before the Israelite victory. The National Parks Authority has added modern facilities, and now charges admission. Old Jericho is open from 5am to 8pm in summer, slightly shorter hours in winter.

Across the road from Old Jericho is the cool, shady oasis of **Ein es-Sultan,** the Sultan's Spring, also called Elisha's Fountain: according to the story, when Elisha cast salts into Jericho's water source the bitter water turned to sweet.

MOUNT OF TEMPTATION   The left fork near Old Jericho leads uphill. At the crest of the hill, a road heads to the left. As you come to the top of this slope, the golden cliffs of the Mount of Temptation rise before you cross the valley. Hanging precariously to the steep cliff-face is the **Greek Orthodox Monastery of the 40 Days** (Qarantal; in Arabic, Deir el-Quruntul), built in late Ottoman times (1890s) and open to visitors daily from 8am to noon and 3 to 4pm. According to the Gospels, Jesus went into the wilderness and fasted for 40 days following his baptism.

During this time he was tempted by Satan, who showed him "all the kingdoms of the world" from an "exceeding high mountain." Whether or not this particular mountain is the mountain from the Gospels, the Mount of Temptation offers a marvelous view. Unfortunately, you are only allowed to walk as far as the monastery, which is worthwhile in itself. A cave within the monastery complex is said to have been Jesus's wilderness home during the ordeal. The monastery is open to visitors Monday to Saturday.

CALIPH HISHAM'S PALACE   To reach Caliph Hisham's Palace, take the right fork at the northern end of Ein es-Sultan Street, and pass between Old Jericho and Elisha's Fountain. After 2¹/₂ kilometers (1¹/₂ miles) you'll come to a sign pointing toward the palace. Turn right, as the sign indicates, and follow the little road 1¹/₂ kilometers (1 mile) to the ruins.

The palace is a fantastic blend of Romanesque and Arabic architecture and mosaics. Be sure to see the several good groups of mosaic work: in the bathhouse and the guest hall particularly (climb the stairs behind the guest hall, which take you inside for a better view). When you get back to Jerusalem, visit the Rockefeller Museum, where you can see the best of the carved stone and stucco work from this palace, plus a model of the entire site.

Archeologists place Hisham's Palace in the Omayyad Dynasty of the 7th and 8th centuries, and inscriptions show it was built in A.D. 724 as a winter resort. Unfortunately, it was destroyed soon after by an earthquake before Hisham ever set foot inside. Still, the ruins include many well-preserved bathhouse structures, heating systems, pools, and saunalike chambers. The pillars and stone carvings are elegant, and one magnificent mosaic depicts two gazelles feeding under a pomegranate tree, while a lion feeds on a third gazelle. Drinks are available outside the palace. Hours are the same as at other national park sites: 8am to 5pm (until 4pm on Friday) in summer; closing is an hour earlier in winter. Admission is NIS 8 ($2.40).

WHERE TO DINE

There are many garden restaurants and cafes between the center of town and Old Jericho. Lunch here can be very pleasant, well away from the crush next to the Old Jericho site. The busier restaurants are more likely to have fresh supplies and a varied menu. You can also buy supplies of dates, bananas, and oranges from roadside stands.

Seven Trees Garden Restaurant. Ein es-Sultan Street. ☎ **02/922-781.** Complete meal $10; à la carte items $1.50–$12. No credit cards. Daily 8am–10pm. MIDDLE EASTERN.

Located on the main garden- and restaurant-lined road leading from downtown Jericho to the north, the Seven Trees is the town's luxury dining establishment, hosting many local weddings and celebrations (if you're lucky, you may get to look in on one). For tourists, the restaurant is interesting for its palm trees and gardens, and for the tourist menu in the self-service restaurant that features a first course of Arabic salads; a main course of kebab, hamburger, schnitzel, or traditional Palestinian oven-baked chicken; and a sampling of local Jericho fruits for dessert. With the revival of tourism at Jericho, the restaurant hopes to reestablish its past reputation for fine meals. Payment can be made in dollars, pounds, shekels, and Jordanian dinar.

EN ROUTE TO THE DEAD SEA & QUMRAN

En route, you will see in the distance a row of dark trees along the Jordan River. The building in front of them is the Abyssinian-style **Monastery of John the Baptist,** built on the spot where John the Baptist is said to have baptized Jesus. You're now in the Jordan Valley.

After turning onto the road running along the Dead Sea in the direction of Qumran, you'll see old Jordanian military encampments. As you drive by, you can't help but notice the calmness of the Dead Sea. The mountains along this stretch are sand-colored with black, fierce-looking peaks. When the mountains turn to a reddish hue, you're near the **Qumran Caves.** A side road leads up to the Qumran Village, where the Dead Sea Scrolls were found in a cave in 1947 by a Bedouin shepherd boy. These are the oldest existing copies of the Torah and other parts of the Bible, as well as previously unknown ancient Jewish writings.

3 The Dead Sea & Qumran

45km (30 miles) SE of Jerusalem

This ancient site, excavated in the 1950s by Pére Roland de Vaux, has become the subject of a major archeological controversy in recent years. Pére de Vaux initially postulated that Qumran had been inhabited since the 8th century B.C., and that by the 2nd century B.C., it had become the monastic desert retreat of the Essenes, an ascetic and mystical Jewish sect of the Second Temple period that may have influenced early Christianity. Many archeologists also theorized that the Dead Sea Scrolls, found in nearby caves, were portions of the Essene community's library, hidden from the approaching Roman armies at the time of the First Revolt Against Rome (A.D. 66–70). Structures uncovered at Qumran were interpreted in terms of the Essenes's collective religious community life as recorded by Flavius Josephus and the Roman historian, Pliny the Elder, who wrote of an Essene settlement near the Dead Sea, above Ein Gedi.

More recent interpretations of Qumran's location and structures have led some scholars to postulate that it may have been a traders' inn and military and customs outpost rather than the communal settlement of a religious sect. Qumran lies at a strategic point in an ancient trade route: Goods from Arabia and Africa were shipped up the Red Sea to Eilat, and then overland through the Arava Valley to the southern tip of the Dead Sea, where they were floated across to Qumran. At Qumran, the cargoes were unloaded and sent along the ancient Salt Road to Jerusalem. According to this theory, the otherworldly Essenes would not have chosen to settle at the crux of a major commercial route, but rather in a more remote location, perhaps in caves above Ein Gedi. If this interpretation is correct, then the previously unknown compositions found among the Dead Sea Scrolls may not be the writings of a dissident Jewish sect, but rather a more mainstream sampling of extra biblical literature from the time of the Second Temple.

ESSENTIALS

GETTING THERE   By Bus   Buses will take you to Qumran from Egged's Central Bus Station in Jerusalem. Check with Egged, as this area may come under Palestinian Authority jurisdiction.

By Car   From Jerusalem, bypass Jericho and turn right (south) onto the main road along the coast of the Dead Sea. Continue following the signs to Qumran and Ein Gedi.

WHAT TO SEE & DO

The **excavated settlement** includes trenches, pottery sheds, step-down baths, cisterns, bakery sites, and cemetery plots. You can see all the excavations from the top of the village tower. Near the ruins are the caves where the first scrolls were found. High above, in the mountains, are more caves. The **National Park at Qumran** (☎ 02/ 942-231) is open daily from 8am to 4pm and includes an air-conditioned snack-bar facility.

If you are interested in **swimming,** go to **Einot Zuqim (Ein Feshcha,** ☎ 02/ 942-355), a large park with trees, picnic table, freshwater pools, and a beach on the Dead Sea just 3 kilometers (2 miles) south of Qumran. Saturdays are packed, but fewer visitors come on the weekdays. The freshwater pools, fed by local springs, can get murky and sometimes have a fish or two swimming around, but you can always walk on the beach or go for a dip in the lifeless Dead Sea. Admission includes use of the shower facilities. Although a beach clinic is on hand to deal with problems resulting from overexposure, you can protect yourself by following these simple rules: Drink as much as you can; keep your head covered; don't stay in the sun too long; and avoid this area between noon and 3pm.

Also, if you swim in the Dead Sea, wear shoes to protect your feet from the sharp stones that cover the beach and shore; don't let the saltwater get in your eyes or touch your sunburn. If you have any scrapes, insect bites, or recently shaved areas, expect them to tingle in the salty water, but remember that it's healing rather than harmful. When you get out, hot showers are available to wash off the thin residue of minerals and oils. Many visitors to the beach here like to cover themselves with the reputedly therapeutic black mud from the Dead Sea.

The Nature Reserves Authority has outfitted the springs with dressing rooms, restrooms, and a snack bar that also sells postcards and souvenirs. Einot Zuqim is open from 8am to 4pm in the winter and until 5pm in the summer. Admission is NIS 12 ($3.60); discount for students available.

EN ROUTE TO BETHLEHEM

The direct route to Bethlehem for independent travel is 8km (5 miles) south on Hebron Road. Your tour bus, however, may take the more scenic route via Bethany.

RACHEL'S TOMB   The shrine is on the Jerusalem-to-Bethlehem road near the northen entrance to Bethlehem. It was built in 1840 by Moses Montefiore. Rachel, wife of Jacob and mother of Joseph, is revered by Muslims, Jews, and Christians. The outer room is empty; the inner room, the cupola, contains the tomb of Rachel, where dozens of women are usually praying and weeping. Men need a head covering to enter the shrine. You can visit Sunday through Thursday from 8am to 5pm (until 6pm in summer), and on Friday until 1pm.

Across the street from the tomb are several shops. Just past the tomb, you'll see an open courtyard circled by a low wall with a few olive trees and a few small houses rising behind another wall. Take a look at the latter, almost unnoticeable in this ramshackle area. The stones there are part of a water pipe made 2,000 years ago. Inside, the wall is hollow, and once conducted water from King Solomon's Pools (not far from here) to Jerusalem. Back on the road, take the left-hand fork just ahead and continue past olive groves and vineyards. Another 1¹/₂ miles and you are in Bethlehem.

4 Bethlehem

8km (5 miles) S of Jerusalem

Bethlehem is the birthplace of Jesus. Pilgrims have come here to see the traditional cave and manger of Jesus's birth for more than 16 centuries. In the Bible, Bethlehem is mentioned several times, first in connection with Rachel, who died there after giving birth to Benjamin, her second and Jacob's twelfth son. Bethlehem was also the place where Ruth, the loyal Moabite widow of an Israelite, married Boaz in one of history's most famous love stories. Joseph also visited Bethlehem. King David, a descendant of Ruth and Boaz, was born in Bethlehem and tended his sheep in the hills of Judea. From Bethlehem he went out to fight Goliath; later he was summoned from Bethlehem by Samuel to become king of Judah. To Israelis, Bethlehem is Bet Lechem, "house of bread"; to Arabs, Bet Lahm, "house of meat."

Your bus will take you to downtown Bethlehem, called Manger Square. Manger Square is not particularly attractive, filled as it is with parked cars, buses, tours, and tour groups, as well as hotels, restaurants, and shops.

Walking to Bethlehem from Jerusalem has been a tradition that pilgrims have followed for centuries, but under the present circumstances, tourists are advised to go to Bethlehem only by tour bus. The 2- to 2^1/$_2$-hour walk (best undertaken with an organized group) begins at the Jerusalem railway station at Abu Tor, continues on Derekh Hevron, the main road near the Talpiot section, past Jerusalem's industrial area to farming country. The road passes the Greek Monastery of Elias and a tall, flat-topped mountain on the left, the Herodion. Here the road takes a sharp turn, and is lined with olive trees. In the low hills beyond the trees is the Arab village of Bet Jallah (biblical Gilo), birthplace of the prophet Nathan. The road is now at the northern edge of Bethlehem. The biblical name of the road is Bethlehem Efrata.

ESSENTIALS

GETTING THERE **By Bus** You can take Arab bus no. 22 from the Damascus Gate Bus Station, or from across the road from Jaffa Gate in Jerusalem; the fare is NIS 3 ($1). Under present conditions, guided tours are the best choices for visiting Bethlehem (see below).

VISITOR INFORMATION The **Tourism Information Office,** run by the Palestinian Authority, is at the end of Manger Square opposite the Church of the Nativity (☎ **741-581** or **741-583**).

SPECIAL EVENTS There are actually three Christmases celebrated in Bethlehem: Catholics and Protestants hold their services on December 24 and 25, the Orthodox churches on January 6, and the Armenians on January 17 and 18. Tourists must have their passports with them when going to Bethlehem on Christmas Eve. Admission to the Church of the Nativity is restricted to tourists holding special tickets that can be obtained for free from the Franciscan Pilgrim's Office, Jaffa Gate, P.O. Box 186, Jerusalem 9100 (☎ **02/282-621**). There are special telephone booths for tourists to phone Christmas greetings home with the bells of Bethlehem pealing in the background. Restaurants and coffeehouses stay open all night during the season, and some banks operate until midnight. Rates in Bethlehem, Nazareth, and even some Jerusalem hotels go up during the holiday period, so be sure of your accommodations before you arrive. The weather can get very cold, and it might even snow. The tourist office will have a schedule of processions and activities. On the evening of December 24, choirs from all over the world assemble and sing in front of Saint Catherine's Church near Manger Square.

WHAT TO SEE & DO

CHURCH OF THE NATIVITY This fortress facing Manger Square is the principal shrine of Bethlehem and the oldest church in the country. The construction of the church (A.D. 326) goes back to the time of Queen Helena, the mother of the Roman Emperor Constantine the Great, who made a pilgrimage to the Holy Land in the early part of the 4th century. She searched out the grotto of Christ's birth, and ordered a church to be built over the spot. The Emperor Justinian, 200 years later, found the original church destroyed (probably by an earthquake), and built a new church on the old site. A restoration of the two previous churches was carried out by the Crusaders, which explains why the church looks like a fortress.

You'll enter through a low doorway that was, according to legend, designed to prevent the unbelievers from riding into the church on horseback. It is also probably not a coincidence that the doorway makes one pause and bow.

The basilica of the church is divided into five naves by four rows of Corinthian pillars. Every pillar bears the ancient, faded picture of an apostle. Several dozen gilded lamp fixtures hang from the oak ceiling. The floor is stone and wood, with occasional trap-door openings that reveal the original Byzantine mosaic floor beneath. Up front, beyond a magnificent silver-and-gold chandelier, is the Altar of the Nativity, equally ornate with gold-and-silver decoration. The Greek Orthodox occupy the area to the right of the altar, the Armenian denomination the area to the left. Armenian, Greek, and Franciscan priests are responsible for the preservation of the church.

On either side of the altar, narrow stone staircases lead underneath to the manger, supposedly the scene of Jesus's birth. Simply lit by hanging lights, the grotto is in the wall of the cave, marked by a silver star.

If you find your way to the grand, shiny Franciscan church on the northern edge of the Church of the Nativity, you'll see a small stairway on the right at the back of the nave. Down the stairs is a maze of rock-hewn rooms and chambers, part of which is supposedly a portion of the original stable where Jesus was born. Later used as catacombs for martyred innocents, the stable rooms here look much more "authentic" than the marble portion under Greek Orthodox control. Also down beneath the church is a cavelike chamber where Saint Jerome translated the Bible from Hebrew into Latin.

Back upstairs, exit through the courtyards of cloisters and convents. Notice the difference in dress of the various priests who administer the church—the bearded Greeks in long black robes with their long hair tied into a bun; the Armenians in purple- and cream-colored long robes; and the Franciscans in brown.

MORE ATTRACTIONS   The **Milk Grotto** is the place where Mary, in nursing the infant Jesus, is said to have dropped some milk that promptly turned the rocks of the cavern chalky white. Visits made here by nursing mothers are supposed to help their lactation, and packets of the powdered stone are sold as souvenirs. The grotto, run by the Franciscans, is open daily from 8 to 11:45am and from 2 to 5pm.

If you want to explore more of the town, walk out of Manger Square to the right of the mosque that is at the opposite end of the square from the Church of the Nativity. This is **Paul VI Street,** named after the pontiff who visited here, and Bethlehem's main drag, although it is certainly more a pedestrian street than a throughway. The street winds past cobblers' shops, a smithy, coffeehouses, hole-in-the-wall stores both ancient and modern, people buying supplies, children playing. Up the hill, you'll come to the striking **Evangelical Lutheran Christmas Church,** with a very handsome minaretlike steeple. Past the church, on Abdul Nasser Street, are a few of Bethlehem's better hotel bargains.

WHERE TO STAY

Should you decide to stay the night in Bethlehem, you've got a good, if small, collection of hotels from which to choose. The newest and best are only a short walk from Manger Square along Paul VI Street.

Al Andalus Guest House. Manger Square (P.O. Box 410), Bethlehem. ☎ **02/741-348.** Fax 02/742-280. 10 rms (all with shower). $20 single; $40 double; 25% increase at Christmas. Rates include breakfast. AE, DC, MC, V.

> Set on the south side of the square in the arcade, this hotel with a pleasant, family-style management, is probably the best place to stay on Manger Square. The centrally heated rooms are clean and cheerful, with gleaming tile showers and colorful curtains and spreads, and look out either on Manger Square or to the hills of Judea. Guests of the hotel receive a 10% discount at the Al Andalus restaurant.

Bethlehem Star Hotel. Al-Baten Street (P.O. Box 282), Bethlehem. ☎ **02/743-249.** 72 rms (all with shower or bath). $40 single; $60 double. Add 30% for Christmas and Easter seasons. Rates include breakfast and service. DC, MC, V.

> Conveniently located at the corner of Freres Street, the Bethlehem Star is quiet, friendly, and modern. The hotel has an elevator, and some triples that are perfect for families with children. A few rooms have city views.
>
> To reach the hotel, walk out of Manger Square on Paul VI Street and keep looking for Al-Baten Street at side streets on the right; the hotel is about a block away uphill.

Grand Hotel Bethlehem. Paul VI and Freres Streets (P.O. Box 18), Bethlehem. ☎ **02/741-440.** 50 rms (all with bath). A/C. $35–$40 twin. Rates include breakfast. MC, V.

> Bethlehem's most comfortable, modern hotel contains a snappy lobby, restaurant, and cocktail lounge. The bright, colorful rooms have large windows, scarlet spreads, and wall-to-wall carpeting.

Palace Hotel. Manger Square, Bethlehem. ☎ **02/742-798.** 25 rms (all with bath). TEL. $18 single; $35 double. Rates include breakfast. MC, V.

> Set in a garden to one side of Manger Square, this hotel provides good accommodations for the price. Right next to the church, and often surrounded by the sound of tolling bells, the Palace was built by the Greek Orthodox Committee. It has a large dining room, open 24 hours, with a self-service buffet featuring 12 oriental salads; a colorful sitting room with a view of the city from its bar; and attractive, centrally heated rooms, some of which have balconies and views of the Judean Hills.

WHERE TO DINE

Al Andalus Restaurant. Manger Square. ☎ **02/743-519.** Appetizers NIS 7–14 ($2–$4.20); main courses NIS 21–40 ($6.30–$12); lunch special $8. AE, DC, MC, V. Daily 8am–5pm (after 5pm with special reservations). ARABIC.

> Al Andalus caters to tourist groups with a set meal consisting of soup or grapefruit (depending on the season), salad, a main course of meat or chicken with vegetable and potatoes, and dessert. There are traditional Arabic main courses, and also hamburgers, salads, omelets, and other light fare. Service of 10% is added to the bill. Air-conditioned.

Saint George Restaurant. In the Municipality Building, Manger Square. ☎ **02/743-780.** Appetizers NIS 7–13 ($2.10–$3.90); main courses NIS 25–40 ($7.50–$12). MC, V. Daily 8am–11pm or midnight. ARABIC.

> If you want something substantial, try the Saint George, next door to the Government Tourist Information Office. Out front are umbrella tables for al fresco dining; within, the cream-colored walls are adorned with murals of Bethlehem, and tables are covered with red cloths and graced with flowers; background music further enhances the ambience. Choices are mainly well-prepared grilled chicken and meat dishes. If you're daring, try the roast pigeon stuffed with rice, meat, and almonds; or a platter of six different kinds of vegetables. Main courses include salad and potato.

EXCURSIONS

THE SHEPHERDS' FIELDS   This is where it is traditionally believed that the shepherds were told of Jesus's birth by angels. Actually, there are two Shepherds' Fields—the ones maintained by the Roman Catholic Church and others maintained by the Greek Orthodox Church. Both are east of Bet Sahur, where the road forks. The right fork leads to the Greek Orthodox fields, the left to the Roman Catholic.

By heading back toward Jerusalem for a few blocks, and taking a sharp right at the appropriate sign, you can make your way to the Shepherds' Fields along either Shepherds' Street or Bet Sahur Road. You can walk from Manger Square to either set of fields, visit for half an hour, and walk back, and the entire expedition on foot will last about 2 hours. *Warning:* Take this walk *only* in a group.

EN ROUTE TO HEBRON

Under present circumstances, check with Tourist Information in Jerusalem about tours and visits to this area of the West Bank. *Note:* Israeli rental cars may not be insured for travel to this part of the West Bank.

The distance to Hebron is only 33 kilometers (20 miles), the road wide and in good repair, and you should figure on a 30-minute drive over the twisting southward route. Beautiful villas line part of the road on the outskirts of Bethlehem; the road then dips close to the picturesque village of Bet Jalla, to the right in the nearby hills. Farther along come rich fields, more villas, and new homes. Soon you pass a big archway (on the right) spanning a road leading to the nearby villages of Husan and Nahhalin. The archway honors Saint George, depicted on horseback in the arch's center. This is the road David took from Bethlehem to carry his brother's food to the battle area in the Valley of Elah, where he subsequently met up with Goliath.

THE HERODION   Herod the Great had ambitious plans for this dry mountaintop in the barren hills of Judea. He reshaped the entire mountaintop into a perfect cone, and then built a lavish palace on top, complete with a synagogue (one of the few that can be dated to the time of the Second Temple), *mikve* (ritual bath), storerooms, and 200 marble steps leading down the mountainside. Herod even piped in water, at enormous expense.

The Herodion, finished in the 1st century B.C., was only one of Herod's grand palace-fortresses; another was atop Masada. The Herodion is cared for by the National Parks Authority, open from 8am to 5pm (closes at 4pm on Friday) every day of the week. Admission is NIS 8 ($2.40) for adults, half of that for kids.

From the Herodion, you can continue along the country road, which will eventually bring you to the main highway at the town of Halhoul. Turn left to get to Hebron, which is roughly 26 kilometers (15½ miles) from the Herodion.

SOLOMON'S POOLS   Soon you'll see signs, and a left turn takes you to Solomon's Pools. There's been some quibbling about the exact origin of the pools. Most hold that they're really the work of Herod, who brought the water here by aqueduct from springs near Hebron. Others argue that these pools were indeed built by Solomon as part of his grand scheme for supplying Jerusalem with water.

Whatever the case, it's clear that these pools were an important source of water for the Herodion, and more important, for Jerusalem, from at least the time of Herod the Great (37–4 B.C.) to the time of modern Israel. The Romans kept the pools and aqueducts in good repair, the Ottoman Turks built a fort (now in ruins) to defend them, and the British kept the system in good working order until the end of the mandate.

5 Hebron

37km (23 miles) S of Jerusalem

Of the biblical sites in the Holy Land, none is more affecting than the Tomb of the Patriarchs in the Cave of Machpelah, where Abraham and Sarah, Isaac and Rebecca, and Jacob and Leah are buried. (You can read all about it in Genesis, starting with Chapter 23). This is significant history for adherents of all three great religions, a direct link between us and the Middle Bronze Age.

Yet, sadly, Hebron is not a peaceful place. Conflict between Hebron's Arab citizens and the Israeli settlers at nearby Kiryat Arba is constant and violent. Check with the Government Tourist Information Office on the current situation before you go.

Depending on conditions, here's how you should visit Hebron: If conditions are very tense, don't! If there's been a minor flare-up of tensions, go on an organized tour. The bus tours do not run if the situation is known to be dangerous. About the worst way to visit Hebron is by rented car. With Israeli license plates, it will be assumed that the driver is an Israeli, too; rental car insurance often does not cover glass breakage.

ESSENTIALS

GETTING THERE   Under present conditions, it is best to visit Hebron in a guided tour from Jerusalem. Consult with Tourist Information about tours that will best suit your interests. *Note:* Israeli rental cars may not be insured for travel to this area of the West Bank.

VISITOR INFORMATION   The area code is 02. There is no information office in Hebron.

WHAT TO SEE & DO

Taking the main road through Hebron, you'll first pass lovely villas and a few shops and grocery stores. At one point, islands of trees, flowers, and greenery divide the highway lanes, after which the archeological **Museum of Hebron** will be on your left (nearby are several places for cool drinks).

When you see a glass factory, a pottery factory, and a woodwork factory side by side in a huge three-story building on your left, you'll be in the **shopping district** (photo shops, tailors, tiny clothing stores, shoe stores, grocery stores, etc.). In this area you'll see a roadside pillar pointing to **Abraham's Tomb;** when the road forks, bear left toward the tombs. Shortly there's another sign, a red one, pointing out the **Jewish Cemetery.** Dating back 3,700 years, this cemetery was almost entirely destroyed during the 1929 Arab massacre of Hebron's Jewish community, but people still come here to pray and stand in awe. Hereabouts the road narrows until it is just barely two lanes and leads by shops of shoemakers, carpenters, leather workers, and saddlemakers (who outfit camels and donkeys). Coming into the vegetable area, the road widens and the **Muslim Cemetery** is to the right. And now there's an open expanse and a sign guiding you left to Abraham's Tomb.

TOMB OF THE PATRIARCHS   Enclosing the Cave of Machpelah, the tomb is what gives Hebron its designation as one of the four "Holy Cities"—the others being Jerusalem, Tiberias, and Safed. To religious Jews who now can worship at the sacred Tomb of the Patriarchs, the holy experience is second only to worshiping at the Western Wall in Jerusalem. Genesis tells how Abraham bought his family burial cave from Ephron for 400 silver shekels. Tradition has it that Hebron is thus one of three places in Israel that Jews can claim by virtue of having purchased the property; the same claim is made for the Jerusalem Temple and the Tomb of Joseph.

The tombs of Abraham, Isaac, and Jacob (and their wives) are housed in a fortress built by Herod. The walls, resembling the massive walls Herod built around the Temple Mount enclosure in Jerusalem, range from 40 to 60 feet high. You may visit the tombs between 7:30 to 11:30am and 1:30 to 4 or 5pm. From 11:30am to 1:30pm devout Muslims worship inside, and no other visitors are allowed. No non-Muslim visitors are permitted on Friday, which is the Muslim Sabbath, or on Muslim holidays. *Note:* Visiting hours are determined by strict security considerations; it is best to reconfirm the hours before a visit.

Inside the walls, the Muslims built a mosque around the tombs. The square main basilica is richly decorated with inlaid wood and ornate mosaic work reminiscent of the Dome of the Rock. Inscriptions from the Koran run along the walls. In the main section you will see the tombs of Isaac and Rebecca, red-and-white stone "huts" with green roofs. Looking inside, you'll see the richly embroidered drapes covering the cenotaphs. (The real tombs are supposed to be underground, beneath the cenotaphs.) In an adjoining courtyard are the gold-embroidered tapestries covering the cenotaphs of Abraham and Sarah, behind a silver grating. Just opposite is the tomb of Jacob and Leah, with a 700-year-old stained-glass window. A shrine to Joseph is right next door, but the authentic tomb of Joseph is generally thought to be near Nablus.

6 Ramallah, Nablus (Shechem) & Samaria

We now explore the areas north of Jerusalem, biblical Samaria. This was the land of Canaan that Abraham first saw more than 4,000 years ago, the scene of great events involving Jacob, Joseph, Joshua, and the rulers of the northern kingdom of Israel. You should remember that there have been periods of unrest in these West Bank towns.

Check with the Tourist Information Office in Jerusalem on current conditions. At presstime there were no organized tours to this region.

RAMALLAH

Arabic for "the Heights of the Lord," Ramallah is a cool, high town, once the most popular summer resort in Jordan ("Switzerland of Jordan"). You will see elegant villas on hillsides green with pine groves. At 2,900 feet, Ramallah sits some 300 feet higher than Jerusalem. A Christian and Muslim town, Ramallah is quite well off, with many good restaurants, hotels, and shops.

Should you stop for a while in Ramallah, make sure to see the town's large, beautiful **park,** which contains a well-equipped children's playground. You might also want to see **King Hussein's former palace,** a pleasant but unostentatious building.

EN ROUTE TO NABLUS

Once past Ramallah, a road on your left will take you on a shortcut to Jericho (34km, or 20¹/₂ miles), via the Arab village of **Taiybah.** You'll see a large compound on your right as you continue; it was once a Jordanian hospital, and in the hills farther on is what was once a Jordanian training camp.

BETHEL Two miles farther is the Arab village of **Betin,** the biblical Bethel. Abraham passed into Canaan in Shechem to Bethel; it was to Bethel that Abraham and Lot returned from Egypt. Later, as described in Genesis, the Lord appeared to Abraham's grandson, Jacob, in a dream: ". . . and behold a ladder set up on the earth, and the top of it reached to heaven: and behold the angels of God ascending and descending it. And, behold, the Lord stood above it, and said, I am the Lord God of Abraham thy father, and the God of Isaac: the land whereon thou liest, to thee will I give it, and unto thy seed." The hill today is called **Jacob's Ladder,** but unless you have a guide to point it out, you'll never find it.

After passing through countryside of olive groves, orchards, and pastures, the next village you'll see is **Bir Zeit,** which means "the Oil Well," and from the main road, you'll see the sign for Bir Zeit University, the West Bank's most famous institution of higher learning. A bit farther along on the left is the village of **Ein Sinya,** with its cluster of old and new buildings, some dating back to Turkish times. Farther along, high in the hills, is the town of **Sinjil,** the Arab name for the settlement of the French monk Saint Giles, who lost his life here.

SHILOH   Now the road twists and turns through low hills covered by groves of olive trees. Soon you'll see a 5-foot stone pillar pointing to the ruins of ancient Shiloh on the left: Shiloh is where the Tabernacle and the Ark of the Covenant were housed in the centuries between the time of Joshua and King David. It is also the place where the men of Benjamin's tribe, short of women, carried away the daughters of Shiloh who were innocently dancing in their vineyards.

VALLEY OF DOTAN   As you pass Shiloh, note the natural Canaanite agricultural terraces still being worked in the hills. The steep winding road here was constructed originally by the British. It snakes down toward the village of **Lubban,** and the rich fields in the Valley of Dotan. Pull over before you descend and take in the magnificent view of the valley and Lubban.

As you continue on, keep an eye out for the small villages that dot the surrounding hills. The Valley of Dotan was where Joseph was sold into slavery.

NABLUS & ANCIENT SHECHEM

Just before you reach Nablus, the largest town of the West Bank, you'll want to stop on its southern outskirts for Jacob's Well, Joseph's Tomb, and biblical Schechem. At Shechem, Abraham first entered the land of Canaan. The town had been founded, according to biblical sources, by Shechem, Hamor's father, and by the period of the Patriarchs, early in the 2nd millennium B.C., it had become a major Canaanite city and cult center. Jacob sojourned nearby, built an altar, and dug a well. After the Exodus from Egypt, Joshua also built an altar at Schechem and summoned the tribes together, "half of them against Mount Gerizim and half of them over against Mount Ebal," on either side of Shechem. Joshua united the tribes in a covenant ceremony that is considered the beginning of the Israelite nation. Archeological remains of ancient Shechem show that it was a large city; some of the finds are displayed in the Rockefeller Museum in East Jerusalem. Archeologists have long puzzled over why Shechem, if it was such an important place, was situated in such a vulnerable position, in a pass between the two mountains, Ebal and Gerizim. Mount Gerizim is sacred to the Samaritans, and was the site of their ancient temple.

The origins of the **Samaritans** are complex. After the death of King Solomon in 920 B.C., his kingdom was divided into two separate nations: Judah, with its capital at Jerusalem, and the larger, more powerful Kingdom of Israel in the north, composed of the descendants of the 10 northern Israelite tribes. The division probably reflected old cultural and religious differences between the northern Israelites and the southern tribe of Judah.

The Samaritans are believed to be descended from the few Israelites who remained behind when the Assyrians carried off most of the population of the northern Kingdom of Israel in the 8th century B.C. For all practical purposes, the 10 northen tribes of Israel disappeared from history at that time; the Assyrians resettled other subject peoples on the land that had been Israel. The Jews, who are descended from the southern kingdom of Judah, survived in their homeland for another 135 years, until they were carried off into the Babylonian Captivity in 586 B.C. When the Persian king Cyrus released the Jews from the Babylonian Captivity and they returned to Judah after a 60-year absence (around 530 B.C.), the Samaritans wanted to help them to rebuild. The Jews refused their help, declaring that the Samaritans were no longer Jews; that they had intermarried with foreign peoples who had settled into the land, and had adopted pagan customs. (Despite these ancient accusations, the Samaritan tradition observes Torah regulations with great rigor.)

The factions split and remained split down through the centuries, the Samaritans claiming that they and only they have continuously inhabited Israel and kept the traditions pure. They also are the keepers of a Pentateuch (the first five books of the Old Testament), which they say came to them from Aaron, brother of Moses. The Samaritan Bible does not include the Books of the Prophets or any of the later books of the Jewish Holy Scriptures. By the second century B.C., the split between the two people had widened. The Samaritans, in the tradition of the northern Israelite tribes, maintained their Temple on Mount Gerizim beside Shechem; the Jewish Temple, following the tradition of the Davidic monarchy, remained steadfast in Jerusalem. The Samaritan Temple was destroyed by the Jewish Hasmoneans, and again during revolts against the Romans and Byzantines; however, to this day, the entire 500-strong Samaritan community gathers at Mount Gerizim on Passover. The Samaritans do not hold a seder, but together they sacrifice lambs for the Passover feast on the site of Abraham's Altar, observing, they say, the holiday as their forebears did 25 centuries ago. In ancient times, the Samaritan population numbered at least in the hundreds of thousands. Today, approximately half the present Samaritan population lives in Nablus; the rest are Israeli citizens and reside in Holon, a suburb of Tel Aviv. Despite the ancient rivalry, relations between Jews and Samaritans in modern times are cordial and cooperative.

ANCIENT SHECHEM SITES

MOUNT GERIZIM   Mount Gerizim is holy to the Samaritans, who believe it to be the true site ordained by God for the building of the temple, as well as the site of Abraham's Altar, where he prepared to sacrifice his son, Isaac. The present-day Samaritans will show it to you, between the rocks at the summit of Gerizim. The Samaritans, who celebrate many of the traditional Jewish holidays, will be glad to point out altars built by Adam and Noah on Gerizim. About 275 Samaritans live in the Nablus region these days, calling themselves the children of the tribes of Manasseh, Aaron, and Efraim, but all Samaritans gather on Mount Gerizim for their festivals and holidays, and many have built homes for holiday use on the slopes of the mountain. The right of the Samaritans to keep their holy place on Mount Gerizim has been guaranteed by agreements between the Israelis and the Palestinian Authority.

JACOB'S WELL   You'll recognize the **Convent of Jacob's Well** by its two large metal doors. Ring the electric buzzer to notify the convent's sole monk that you'd like to enter the locked gate. As the doors open, you see a beautiful cluster of well-tended small gardens. To the right is a tiny station for prayer, housing a picture of Jesus and the Woman of the Well, another name for this convent. Directly ahead are two blue pillars, mounted with ancient Roman capital stones that support a new ceramic arch leading to the shrine and the huge unfinished church. In 1912 the Russian Orthodox Church began building this enormous basilica, but work stopped with the onset of World War I. Later, this and all other Russian Orthodox holy places were turned over to the Greek Orthodox Church, which still maintains them.

The outside walls were part of a Byzantine church that once stood on this site. Inside the basilica area, with its three separate nave sections, the larger and central section is sheltered with tentlike fabrics and contains a cross atop a broken Roman pillar. Here is held the Feast of the Samaritan Woman. Two painted cement buildings, looking much like guard stations, cover and secure two 18-step passages leading down to the chapel and well. Although the small, beautiful chapel looks older, it was built in 1910 on the site of the earlier chapel, which was built in the times of Queen Helena, mother of Constantine. Rich and intimate, the chapel is hung with shining incense burners and paved with painted tiles; its walls are covered with old paintings and icons, most depicting Jesus and the Woman at the Well. In the center is **Jacob's Well,** with wrought-iron fixtures and a metal pail—a bit incongruous amid so much elegance.

NABLUS

The largest West Bank town, with houses climbing up the surrounding hillsides, Nablus is somewhat modern and businesslike compared to, say, Hebron, which has nearly the same population but looks hundreds of years older. Nablus is in fact a business center, home of the local soap-making industry and equally known for the sweet, baklava pastries and heavenly *kanaffeh* made here. The name Nablus is the Arabic contraction of the Greco-Roman city built here, Neapolis. It was founded by Titus, who named it Flavia Neapolis in honor of his father, Flavius Vespasian.

SAMARIA

The road to Samaria curves downward, and by paying attention, you'll note the many caves in the area and small houses built into the hillsides. Women sit in front of their houses near the road working with stitchery or wool and you may see a group of them working together to sift or grind grain beside the road. On the hill to the right is Samaria (in ancient times, Sebastia).

The entire region of Samaria was occupied by the tribes of Ephraim and Manasseh, the children of Joseph, in biblical times. Samaria was once the capital of the Kingdom of Israel, the northern of the two Jewish nations. Inside the village a **mosque** has been built within the ruins of an old Crusader cathedral. Beneath it, reputedly, is the **tomb of Elisha,** the prophet, and also the head of John the Baptist, brought here by Herod Antipas at the request of Salome. The hills bear witness to the Roman city that once stood here: ruins of a hippodrome, columns, towers, a theater, palace walls.

At an earlier time, however (around 876 B.C.), Omri founded the capital of the Kingdom of Israel here. His son, Ahab, married Jezebel, daughter of a Phoenician king. She brought Baal and other idolatrous pagan gods to the people of Israel. The prophets fought her, particularly Elijah, who challenged the priests of Baal in the famous cliffside battle on Mount Carmel. Samaria remained the capital under Jeru and Jeroboam, but the Old Testament recounts bad times of transgression, corruption, vice, and drunkenness. In 725 B.C. the Assyrians plundered Samaria, ending the Kingdom of Israel, and carried off 25,000 of its inhabitants.

The road from Nablus moves on past **Dotan,** traditionally the city where Joseph was sold into slavery by his brothers, to **Jenin.** Take a left at the square in the middle of this little town and follow the road north. From here you can head north to **Afula** and thence to Nazareth and Haifa, or east to the Jordan Valley and the Sea of Galilee.

Tel Aviv 7

Tel Aviv is everything Jerusalem is not. The city began with a gorgeous strip of beach along the Mediterranean and went on from there to become the bold and busy city that never sleeps. It has pizza parlors, nightclubs, samba sessions at the beach on summer evenings, and miles and miles of massive medium-rise apartment buildings. In summer, the heat and humidity can put New York to shame. Tel Aviv is the country's commercial center, and also the cultural capital; the nation's newspapers and books are published here (excepting the *Jerusalem Post*); concerts are frequent, and the Hebrew-language theater thrives. A look at the back of some of the free tourist magazines distributed throughout town, and you'll figure out that the city also hosts a thriving sex industry. To an idealistic kibbutznik, an Arab Israeli from Nazareth, or an observant Jew from Jeruslem's Mea Shearim District, the mere mention of Tel Aviv can conjure up an image of Gomorrah in its worst depravity.

1 Tel Aviv: Past & Present

TEL AVIV TODAY

At the moment, Tel Aviv is riding the wave of the country's economic boom, and it shows everywhere. In the past few years the city's hotels and stock exchange have begun to buzz with the energy of high-powered business deals from all over the world. Glass skyscrapers and new hotels dot the city's landscape; more are under construction. Optimism and signs of new prosperity abound. Many envision 21st-century Tel Aviv as the Singapore of a new Middle East.

As always, Tel Avivans love to play. In the 1980s, the city's beaches were beautifully renewed, and are now among the cleanest and most easily accessible urban beaches in the world. A dip in the sea can punctuate visits to markets like those in Old Jaffa, the Tuesday and Friday craft bazaar in Nahlat Binyamin, or even a tour of the city's museums, which are also booming. The Tel Aviv Museum of Art has just received the important Jaglom Collection of Impressionist and Post-Impressionist Art; the Diaspora Museum of Jewish History is one of the most inventive learning experiences in the world. The 1990s have seen the construction of an opera house, new performing arts centers, and the development of a rarefied luxury restaurant scene.

At the same time, Tel Avivans are thinking about the nature of their city's personality and have begun to appreciate and preserve neglected landmarks and neighborhoods that delineate the city's 85-year history. Restored Old Jaffa is a must for evening dining and strolling, loved by tourists and Israelis alike. Elsewhere in the city, you'll notice exotic Arabesque/art deco structures from the 1918–30 period and wonderful 1930s and early '40s International Style buildings that once defined Tel Aviv's ultramodern image. Many are being recycled and blended into Tel Aviv's contemporary lifestyle.

A LOOK AT TEL AVIV'S PAST

Back in 1906 the Jews of Jaffa grew tired of their cramped and noisy quarters in what was then a largely Arab city and, with a boost from the Jewish National Fund, decided to build their own city on Jaffa's northern outskirts. In 1909 they bought 32 acres and, under the leadership of Meir Dizengoff, 60 families (about 250 people) staked out their claims. A famous photograph recalls this historic moment: the 60 posed families, stuffed into their fluffy Edwardian clothes on the barren sand dunes.

Much of the pioneers' resources went into building a school, the famous Herzlia Gymnasium (Palestine's first high school), which was modeled after a scholarly conception of Solomon's Temple but emerged resembling a Turkish fortress. (This landmark was demolished to make way for an office building, but its loss helped trigger an awareness of the need for preservation.) The early settlers argued with the Arabs over their rights to the land, turned their tents into cottages, and by the time World War I began, the city's population had grown to 3,000.

During the war the Turks expelled the residents of Tel Aviv, but they returned when General Allenby's British army took control of the city. The 1917 Balfour Declaration launched a wave of immigration, and by 1921 Tel Aviv had blossomed into a separate town from Jaffa and become home to 15,000 residents. Sporadic tensions with Arab neighbors in Jaffa accompanied Tel Aviv's early development.

The city's motto, "I shall build thee and thou shalt be built," inspired many of the immigrants, who came into Israel from Jaffa port, to remain in Tel Aviv. In the early 1930s many refugee architects and designers from Germany sought shelter in Palestine. For them, the sands of Tel Aviv were a drawing board, and the housing needs of thousands of Jews fleeing Nazism provided an opportunity to create a dazzling city of the future based on the clean, functional lines of International Style. Tel Aviv burgeoned into an urban garden of ultramodern white concrete architectural wonders. The sculptured balconies and curvilinear corners of Tel Aviv's building boom were featured in architectural journals throughout the world; Tel Aviv came to symbolize 20th-century Europe's vision of social democracy and utilitarian beauty successfully transplanted to the Middle East.

Despite its architectural pizzazz, close up Tel Aviv was not the sleek, perfectly planned utopia of its legend. The personality of the pre–World War II city was a homey, slightly antique mix of Jewish culture from Eastern and Central Europe. Many of the dazzlingly photographed buildings admired by the outside world were filled with old-fashioned workshops. In summer the broad, futuristic streets (designed by architects whose hearts were still in pre-1933 Berlin) sweltered under the Palestinian sun, and blocked whatever evening breezes might blow in from the sea. By the outbreak of World War II, Tel Aviv was a small metropolis of 100,000 people, and in that capacity, the city played host to 2 million Allied soldiers who passed through during the war. Although most of Israel escaped the ravages of that war, Tel Aviv was occasionally the target of small bombing raids by Italian and Vichy French planes.

Matzoh is like Israel. . . . It may be dry and noisy, and sometimes it's hard to swallow . . . but it's ours.

—Kirschen, Dry Bones (Israeli cartoon)

After the war, Tel Aviv became a center of dissatisfaction over the British Mandate policy that prevented Jewish refugees from entering Palestine. Once, in 1946, 20,000 British soldiers placed the entire city under rigid curfew while a search was conducted for underground members. After interrogating almost the entire population of 110,000 residents, the British made two arrests. In 1948, as the British were pulling out of Israel, the Israelis launched an attack against Jaffa, from which Arab guerrillas and snipers had been firing into Tel Aviv. During the battle, much of Jaffa's Arab population fled.

After the British were gone, Tel Aviv mushroomed, first with refugee camps and temporary housing for hundreds of thousands of Jews who poured into the country; later with vast, drab housing projects. During the 1950s, Israel was overburdened with problems of defense and the absorbtion of new immigrants, and Tel Aviv, although a young city, became run-down, especially around its downtown center at Moghrabi Square. The beach, one of Tel Aviv's strong points, piled up with garbage and was neglected. The modern buildings of the 1930s and early 1940s, built of sand bricks, began to crumble; their style went unappreciated and unrepaired. The city offered little in the way of museums, hotels, or restaurants. Among tourists in the 1960s and early '70s, word was out that Tel Aviv was a hot, humid concrete heap, ungainly and uninteresting, especially when compared to larger, livelier Middle Eastern metropolises like Athens and Beirut. In the past 25 years, however, Tel Aviv has undergone a slow, carefully nurtured revolution. The beach, only a few blocks from anywhere in the city center, has made a spectacular comeback. The Diaspora Museum opened in 1980, a new concept in blending history, technology, and art; by the 1990s, the triumvirate of the inventive Tel Aviv Museum of Art, the Eretz Israel Museum and the Diaspora Museum, together with performing groups ranging from the Israel Philharmonic Orchestra and the Cameri Theater to the New Israel Opera, has put Tel Aviv on the cultural map.

Gaze upon the sweep of Tel Aviv's shoreline today from the hill of Old Jaffa: The vista shows a city that is coming of age and that actually stands on the threshold of majesty. It's an amazing achievement for a city still younger than the twentieth century.

JAFFA

Now an integrated component in the sprawling Tel Aviv–Jaffa complex, Jaffa has a long and colorful history, dating back to biblical times. It was the principal port area of Palestine prior to the British decision to create a new harbor in Haifa. Many of the earliest Zionist settlers opted for Jaffa before Tel Aviv began to emerge out of the northern sand dunes. Crusaders, pilgrims, and occasional merchants considered the city the "port of Jerusalem."

Jaffa and Tel Aviv were like two trees planted too closely together. In the beginning, Tel Aviv was under the austere shadow of the Arab enclave. Afterward, the situation reversed. Today the old section of the city has become the starlit patio of Tel Aviv, providing an exceptional view, fine restaurants, and the most beautifully restored old city in Israel. The flea market district, near the Clock Tower, is ramshackle but has real personality.

Why the name? One legend has it that Jaffa was built just after the flood by Noah's son, Japhet, and hence the city's name. Another explanation is that the name came from "Yafah," which means "beautiful." This is the port, the Bible tells us, where King Solomon's ally, the Phoenician King Hiram of Tyre, landed cedars of Lebanon for the construction of Solomon's temple; from here Jonah embarked for his fabulous adventure with the whale. The Greeks were here too, and they fostered the legend that a poor maiden named Andromeda, chained to a rock and on the verge of being sacrificed to a sea monster, was rescued by Perseus on his winged white horse. Today tourists are shown this rock, a tourist attraction since ancient times.

The Crusaders also came this way. Richard the Lion-Hearted built a citadel here, which was promptly snatched away by Saladin's brother, who slaughtered 20,000 Christians in the process. Six hundred years or so later Napoleon passed through; a few Jewish settlers came in the 1890s; and Allenby routed the Turks from the port in 1917.

Countless ships have sunk in Jaffa port, although none so tragically as the fleet of the 2nd century B.C.: Jaffa's Hebrew citizens were lured aboard ships by Jaffa's Hellenistic rulers, taken out to the high seas, and cast overboard. This incident was a major factor in the subsequent outbreak of the Maccabean Revolt in 167 B.C.

Of capsized ships, one Jewish legend notes that all the sunken treasure in the world flows toward Jaffa, and that in King Solomon's day the sea offered a rich bounty, accounting for the king's wealth. According to the legend, since Solomon's time, the treasure has once again been accumulating—to be distributed by the Messiah on the Day of the Coming "to each man according to his merits."

Today Jaffa still shows traces of its romantic and mysterious past. The city is built into a kind of amphitheater on the side of a hill. The imaginative restoration project on the top of the hill has altered Jaffa's overall face.

The streets from Tel Aviv run into Jaffa's Jerusalem Avenue and Tarshish Street where a great stone tower and the Turkish mosque, Mahmudiye (1812), reminds you of the city's continuing Arab community.

2 Orientation

ARRIVING

BY PLANE Flights arrive at Ben-Gurion International Airport, at Lod, on the outskirts of the city. To get to Tel Aviv, take the United Tours Airport Shuttle Service bus no. 222 for NIS 12 ($3.60) that departs at least once an hour, usually more frequently, between 4am and midnight (on Saturday, from noon to midnight). It leaves the airport, stops at the El Al Terminal at the Central Railway Station, the B'nei Dan Youth Hostel, then travels all along the waterfront boulevard named Ha-Yarkon Street, stopping at each cluster of hotels. The trip from the airport to your hotel should take an hour or less.

BY TRAIN The Central Railway Station (sometimes called North Railway Station because it's in the northern reaches of the city) stands at the intersection of several major arteries—Petah Tikva Road, Haifa Road, and Arlosoroff Street. From here, municipal buses will take you throughout the city.

BY BUS From the Central Bus Station into town, take no. 4 to Allenby Road, Ben-Yehuda Street; On Ben-Yehuda, you'll be parallel and a block away from

Ha-Yarkon Street, where many hotels are located. Take the no. 5 bus to Dizengoff Square.

BY CAR   Major highways connect Jerusalem, Haifa, and Ashkelon with Tel Aviv.

VISITOR INFORMATION

The Tourist Information Office (☎ 03/666-0259 or 666-0261) is at store no. 6106 on the sixth floor of the New Central Bus Station in South Tel Aviv, at the terminus of bus no. 4 and 5, and unfortunately far from the hotel and tourist areas. It is open from 9am to 6pm Sunday through Thursday; on Friday and holiday eves the hours are 8am to 1pm.

In the lobbies of many five-star hotels you may spot a small desk with a VTS sign on it. The cryptic initials stand for Voluntary Travel Service. Don't hesitate to quiz these thoughtful native Tel Avivans on anything from museum locations to theater ticket purchases.

CITY LAYOUT

Tel Aviv and Jaffa (Yafo in Hebrew) together form a large urban area. But the Tel Aviv–Jaffa you'll get to know is actually the downtown seafront section, extending east only to the thoroughfare of Ibn Gevirol Street. Granted, this is still a 6-kilometer (4-mile) strip at least 1 kilometer wide, but only certain sections are of interest to us as the commercial, cultural, and entertainment centers. The rest of the turf is residential or industrial.

MAIN ARTERIES & STREETS

Moghrabi Square is where Allenby Road meets Ben-Yehuda Street. Between Moghrabi Square and the waterfront is a short section of Allenby Road, which ends in Allenby Square at the water's edge. Here Tel Aviv's original opera house once stood (in which the very first Knesset sessions were held in 1948); it's symptomatic of Tel Aviv's short, intense existence that 6 decades provided ample time for the beachside Opera House to be built, to thrive, to decline into decrepitude, to be pulled down, to be long forgotten, and then commemorated by a luxury skyscraper and shopping mall—the Opera Tower. At the side of Allenby Square, facing the sea, the Hotel Metropole (1920s–30s) with its art-deco ground-floor arcades, hints at the waterfront Doge's Palace and Piazza San Marco in Venice. More like Venice, California, it became the crux of Tel Aviv's red light district as the neighborhood declined over the decades. Recently, it was saved from demolition and renovated.

Dizengoff Square (actually a circle) is the very heart of Tel Aviv. Its 1930s design—"the Etoile of Tel Aviv"—was altered in the 1970s when it was covered with an elevated pedestrian plaza perched above busy Dizengoff Street near the intersection of Pinsker and Zamenhoff streets. There are proposals to return Dizengoff Square to its original state.

Running north from Allenby Square along the seafront is the Herbert Samuel Esplanade, and half a block inland, parallel to the Mediterranean, is Ha-Yarkon Street. On Ha-Yarkon, overlooking the beach, you'll find Tel Aviv's oldest luxury hostelry, the Dan Hotel, and you'll also spot the big brown U.S. embassy building (the United States and most other countries have not recognized Jerusalem as Israel's capital and maintain their embassies here in Tel Aviv).

North of the Dan Hotel, the huge hotels march along the beach: the Sheraton, the Ramada, the Holiday Inn, the Radisson Moriah Plaza, the Hilton, and the under-construction Hyatt. Right next to the Radisson Moriah Plaza Hotel, where Ben-Gurion Boulevard joins Ha-Yarkon Street, is Namir, or Atarim, Square (Kikar

Namir), a modern multilevel plaza with restaurants, outdoor cafes, shops, and services.

South of Moghrabi Square, off Allenby Street, you'll find a number of interesting enclaves. At the intersection of Allenby and King George streets, the vast, outdoor Carmel Market is filled with stalls selling vegetables, fruits, and meat, interspersed with bargain clothing, pastries, and all kinds of oddities. Colorful and full of life, it's an interesting place to observe Tel Avivans on the hunt for their daily bread. Just south of the Allenby–King George Street entrance to the Carmel Market, you'll find the Nahlat Binyamin Pedestrian Mall, which hosts a wonderful outdoor crafts market on Tuesdays and Fridays. This neighborhood contains many architecturally interesting buildings from the 1920s and 1930s. Still farther south is the Neve Zedek area, Tel Aviv's oldest neighborhood, with the new Suzanne Dellal Center for Dance and the Performing Arts at its heart. This was a dilapidated, partly demolished region of cottages and workshops from Tel Aviv's first decade of existence; it is just now beginning to fill up with interesting boutiques, cafes, and shops for designer furnishings and accessories. At the inland side of the intersection of Allenby and King George streets, opposite the entrance to the Carmel Market, is Tel Aviv's archtypical Sheinkin Street: Tel Avivans love its cafes and general ambience; tourists either adore its authenticity or find it too typical to be of much interest.

All the way at the northern end of Tel Aviv, just south of the Yarkon River, is a section of small streets filled with restaurants and clubs, popular with a youngish tourist crowd as well as Tel Aviv's yuppies. Crossroads for this area is the intersection of Dizengoff and Yirmiyahu streets. The northern blocks of Dizengoff and Ben-Yehuda streets in this neighborhood are increasingly filled with top-of-the line clothing shops, and stores devoted to interior design, a concept unknown in Israel until a few years ago.

Just north of the Yarkon River, you'll find Ha-Yarkon Park, the city's major park, with walks through botanical gardens, artificial lakes and boat rental facilities, an outdoor amphitheater, and an ecology center and musuem. Further north, in the suburb of Ramat Aviv, is Tel Aviv University, with the famous Diaspora Museum (Beit Hatfutsot) on its campus.

Inland, at the center of town, is Malchei Israel Square, recently renamed Itzhak Rabin Square, where Ibn Gevirol Street, Ben-Gurion Boulevard, and Frishman Street meet. It is dominated by Tel Aviv's city hall and a great plaza. Although this is merely the Tel Aviv Municipal Government complex rather than a national center, the plaza competes with sites in Jerusalem as the focus of many national political demonstrations and marches. It was here that Prime Minister Rabin was assassinated in 1995 after addressing a peace rally. Another important inland location is Tzimoret Square, with the Ha-Bimah National Theater and Mann Auditorium (home of the Israel Philharmonic). Tzimoret Square is bounded by Dizengoff, Tarsat, Ahad Ha-Am, Rothschild, and Marmorek streets. A few blocks to the south, down Carlebach Street, is the Tel Aviv Cinémathèque. Slightly to the east, on Shaul Ha Melech Boulevard, is the Tel Aviv Art Museum complex. Finally, there's Jaffa (Yafo), actually a fairly large city, although we're interested mostly in the picturesque hilltop section known as Old Jaffa and the Felliniesque flea market district on the inland side of Yefet Street near the Clock Tower.

SURBURBAN NEIGHBORHOODS IN BRIEF

Within half an hour of Tel Aviv are some eight or so suburban residential communities, many of which were born when Tel Aviv ran out of elbow room.

Bat Yam   Meaning "Daughter of the Sea," Bat Yam is 3$^{1}/_2$ miles south of Tel Aviv, right on the beach. Popular in summer, the community is famous for fine wide beaches. See chapter 8, section 2, for more information.

Ramat Gan   Ramat Gan, or "Garden Heights," is located, gardens and all, 2 miles east of Tel Aviv. Also an industrial community, Ramat Gan is the upper-middle-class suburbia of Tel Aviv, with many private houses, flourishing gardens, and a population of 150,000.

In Ramat Gan, the "village" of Kfar Ha-Maccabia—which looks like a group of college dormitories—was built by sports enthusiasts to accommodate the international athletes who participate in the Maccabee Games. But since the games are held once every 4 years, the rooms are rented out between games, the swimming pool remains in use, and the dining room offers first-class service and kosher meals.

Also in Ramat Gan is Bar Ilan University, which emphasizes religious Judaic studies in conjunction with major academic subjects. Take bus no. 43, 45, 64, 68, 70, 164, or 400 from Tel Aviv.

B'nei Brak   This one's an Orthodox Jewish community founded in 1924, located 1 mile east of Ramat Gan. The town houses a cluster of yeshivas and other religious institutions as well as a completely furnished replica of the late Hasidic Lubavitcher rabbi's Brooklyn home. The Lubavitcher rabbi never visited Israel in his lifetime, but his followers wanted him to feel at home if he did.

Petah Tikva   Meaning "Gate of Hope," Petah Tikva was begun as a moshav in 1878, and was built with the help of Baron Benjamin Edmond de Rothschild. A stone archway commemorates Rothschild's influence on this town of 115,000. The Petah Tikva synagogue was the first to be built in a Jewish village in Israel in modern times. Seven miles east of Tel Aviv and highly industrial, Petah Tikva is surrounded by about 1,500 acres of orange groves.

Savyon   Organized by a South African group, Savyon is a posh community, 8 miles southeast of Tel Aviv. Many expensive villa-type houses are found here— also a tennis club, swimming pool, and gardens of iris, tulip, and gladioli.

3 Getting Around

BY BUS   From the new Central Bus Station into Tel Aviv, bus no. 4 goes to Allenby Road, Ben-Yehuda Street; on Ben-Yehuda, you will be running parallel to and a block inland from Ha-Yarkon Street; take bus no. 5 to go to the Mann Auditorium, Dizengoff Square, Dizengoff Street, and the IYHA youth hostel B'nei Dan. From the Central Bus Station to Jaffa, take bus no. 46, and get off near the Clock Tower on Yefet Street.

To get to Jaffa from Tel Aviv, take bus no. 10, 25, or 26 heading southward. Bus 10 runs along Ben Yehuda Street, a block inland from Ha-Yarkon Street, and takes you to Jaffa's Clock Tower on Yefet Street, close to Old Jaffa and the Flea Market. Bus 25, which you can pick up on King George Street near Dizengoff Street, runs through Jaffa on Jerusalem Street, a very long block parallel to and inland from Yefet Street. If you're walking, simply head south along the waterfront promenade, which eventually runs into Jaffa. Bus 25 running northward will get you to the Diaspora Musuem and Tel Aviv University. For intercity Egged bus information, call 177/ 022-5555. For information on Dan Bus service, which operates in the Tel Aviv/ Sharon region, call 03/561-4444.

BY TAXI/SHERUT   Seven-passenger vans run along the bus 4 and 5 lines. If a van comes along, by all means take it rather than wait for the bus. Prices are the same as bus fares, except on Shabbat, when there is a small surcharge.

When taxis are scarce, your best bet is to try at one of the major hotels. You have the right to demand that the meter (ha-sha-on) be used, but many drivers will negotiate a fixed nonmetered fare to your destination, which may or may not be to your advantage. There are legal surcharges above the metered fare on Shabbat and after 9pm. If you use the meter, ask for a receipt (cab-a-lah).

FAST FACTS: Tel Aviv

American Express   American Express International is at 112 Ha-Yarkon St. (☎ 03/524-221 or toll free 177/440-8694; fax 03/523-1030).

Area Code   The area code for Tel Aviv is 03.

Bookstores   There are eight Steimatzky branches in Tel Aviv, including those at 107 Allenby Rd. (☎ 03/529-9277), 109 Dizengoff St. (☎ 03/522-1513), 4 Tarsat Ave., near Ha-Bimah Theater (☎ 03/528-0806), and in the Diaspora Museum. There's also Quality Books, 45 Ben-Yehuda St. (☎ 03/523-4885), between Mendele and Bograshov. For used books, try Pollack's, 36 King George St. (☎ 03/523-8613), with its sidewalk browsing terrace and unusual selection inside; open Sunday through Thursday from 9am to 1:30pm and 4 to 7pm, Friday 9am to 1:30pm.

Currency Exchange   Especially convenient is Bank Ha-Poalim on Ha-Yarkon Street across from the Dan Hotel (near Mendele Street), which has a streetside ATM machine connected to Visa, Cirrus, and NYCE. Change Point, 94 Ha Yarkon St. (☎ 03/524-5505), a licensed money-changing office, offers good rates and charges no commission. It's open Sunday through Thursday from 9am to 8pm and Friday until 1pm; closed Sunday. Tel Aviv does not have Jerusalem's option of Old City money changers open every day, but it does have shady people offering to change money on the streets. Avoid them no matter what rate they quote.

Doctors and Dentists   You can get a list of English-speaking doctors and dentists from the embassy, and often from your hotel's front desk.

Drugstores   The *Jerusalem Post* lists under "General Assistance" the names and addresses of duty pharmacies that stay open nights and on the Sabbath.

Embassies/Consulates   Many countries do not accept Jerusalem as Israel's legal capital, and so their embassies remain in Tel Aviv. See "Fast Facts: Israel" in chapter 3 for a list of embassies and consulates.

Emergencies   For police, dial 100. In medical emergencies, dial 101 for Magen David Adom (Red Shield of David), Israel's emergency first-aid service. For fire, dial 102.

Gay and Lesbian Hotline   For Kav-Ha Lavan (the White Line), call **03/529-2797** on Sunday, Tuesday, and Thursday from 7:30 to 10:30pm. Two other lines offering special psychological help are 03/522-6027 and 03/292-797. You will most likely have to leave a message on a recording machine, so prepare a phone number where you can be reached. Staff at all offices will be able to respond in English.

Hospitals   For tourists with Blue Cross–Blue Shield insurance, call 03/579-0081 or 03/755-3546 for information.

Hotlines For the Rape Crisis Center, dial 03/523-4819; Emotional First Aid (especially for teenagers), dial 03/546-1111. Alcoholics Anonymous is 03/522-5255; Narcotics Anonymous 03/575-8869.

Laundry/Dry Cleaning Try 63 Ben-Yehuda St., near Bograshov, which advertises "6 hours cleaning and laundry." Hours are 7am–1:30pm and 3:30–6pm. If you want to do it yourself, 51 Ben-Yehuda St. has coin-operated machines. Figure $7.50 for washing, soap, and adequate drying.

Libraries The U.S. Information Agency Library is at 1 Ben-Yehuda St., 5th floor (☎ 03/510-6935), open Monday through Thursday from 10am to 4pm, Fri 10am to 2pm. *Note:* Because of budget cuts, the library will probably be closed during 1996.

Newspapers/Magazines See the special Tel Aviv events supplement published on Friday in the *Jerusalem Post* (available only in Tel Aviv region).

Post Office Tel Aviv's Central Post Office is at 132 Allenby Rd. General hours for all services are Sunday through Thursday from 7am to 7pm, though limited services (telephone and telegraph) are open nights and on the Sabbath. Branch post offices are on Ha-Yarkon at Trumpeldor, at 3 Mendele St., next to the Hotel Adiv between Ha-Yarkon and Ben-Yehuda, and just off Dizengoff Square on Zamenhoff Street.

Radio Israel Radio news can be heard at 576, 1170, and 1458 kHz at 7am, 1pm, 5pm, and 8pm. BBC World Service broadcasts at 1322 kHz.

Safety Israel's largest city has less crime than most cities its size, but there is still enough that you must observe the normal precautions. Don't walk in deserted areas, especially the beaches, after dark.

Telegrams/Telex See "Post Office," above.

Television There are two Israeli channels (Channel 2 is for quality programming) and one English-language channel from Lebanon specializing in American reruns. Commercial channels and cable service have arrived in Israel over the past few years, and a selection of cable channels is usually available at better hotels.

Useful Telephone Numbers For all flight arrival information, call 03/972-1122; for El Al departure information, call 03/972-2333. For train information, call 03/542-1515.

4 Where to Stay

If one word could describe Tel Aviv's hotel situation, it would be "noisy." Some 90% of these establishments are directly on the main streets—Ben-Yehuda, Allenby, and Ha-Yarkon. I once stayed in a conveniently located hotel on a busy corner, facing on the street, and soon discovered that not only was an afternoon nap impossible but the sound and fury outside the window didn't abate until well after midnight.

Therefore, more than any other commodity, make sure of the location of your Tel Aviv room. Don't take a room facing on the main street, unless of course it has air conditioning and soundproof windows. Get off the heavily trafficked streets or take a room in the back; Tel Aviv hoteliers charge the same rates for front and back rooms.

PRIVATE ROOMS & APARTMENTS The Government Tourist Information Office, New Central Bus Station, 6th Floor (☎ 03/639-5660), compiles and prints a list of agencies and individuals who rent rooms and apartments. Though they will not make a contact or reservation for you, and they cannot guarantee the quality of service or accommodations, the tourist office staff will be glad to give you a copy of the list for free.

NEAR DIZENGOFF SQUARE
MODERATE

Center Hotel. 2 Zamenhoff St. at Dizengoff Sq., Tel Aviv. ☎ **03/629-6181.** Fax 03/629-6751. 56 rms (all with bath or shower). A/C TEL. Low season: $62 single; $75 double. Regular season: $73 single; $86 double. High season: $76 single, $99 double. Rates include breakfast. AE, DC, MC, V.

Recently remodeled with a modest but spiffy '90s look for its small public areas, the Center Hotel, part of the well-managed Atlas Hotel chain, is a modern choice right at the heart of the busy Dizengoff Square area, but not close to the beach. Many of the rooms are toward the back of the building and are buffered against the neighborhood's high level of street noise. There are radios in the rooms.

ALONG BEN-YEHUDA
INEXPENSIVE

✪ **Gordon Inn.** 17 Gordon St., Tel Aviv. ☎ **03/523-8239.** Fax 03/523-7419. 25 rooms (18 with private shower). FAN. $29 single without bath, $34 single with bath; $37 double without bath, $48 double with bath. $15 per person for five or more people in a room with bath; summer surcharge. Rates include breakfast. No credit cards. Bus: 4 on Ben Yehuda Street to Gordon Street.

Opened in 1995, this newly decorated, clean and well-managed guesthouse bridges the gap between hostel and hotel. Continental breakfast is served in a pleasant dining room; small private rooms (for one or two people) have wall-to-wall carpeting, night stands, and heaters and simple but fresh decor; half have private bathrooms. There are larger group or family rooms, each equipped with wardrobes and bedside reading lamps, and a step above hostels in amenities and decor; most have private bathrooms. The location, on Gordon Street, with its many art galleries, adds a touch of class, but its spot on the corner of Ben-Yehuda Street means heavy bus and traffic noise. A popular, stylish cafe/restaurant is right on the premises. Add 15% for single and double rooms whenever high season is declared. Lockers are $2 a day extra.

ALONG HA-YARKON
EXPENSIVE

✪ **Dan Tel Aviv Hotel.** 99 Ha-Yarkon St., Tel Aviv. ☎ **03/520-2525;** in the U.S., ☎ 212/752-6120 or 800/223-7773; in the U.K., ☎ 0171/439-9893. Fax 03/524-9755. 286 rms, including 37 suites. A/C MINIBAR TEL TV. $195–$320 single; $220–$345 double. 15% service charge. Rates include breakfast. Family plans for children under 18. AE, DC, MC, V. Bus: 4 on Ben-Yehuda Street; ask for stop near Dan Hotel.

With an outstanding central location right on Gordon Beach, the Dan started out as a small hotel in the 1950s, and in an unending series of expansions and upgradings, was lovingly developed into today's modern megacomplex. Service is very strong, decor in the deluxe rooms rivals the Hilton's deluxe rooms as the best in Tel Aviv, and a new, luxurious indoor as well as an outdoor swimming pool, Jacuzzi, sauna health club with steam bath, shopping arcade, and a beautiful, efficient business center mark the hotel's latest renovations (the sparkling indoor pool, overlooking the sea, offers the best winter swimming of any hotel in town). Because the hotel was built in many sections over four decades, the layout is a bit complicated—many of the lower-category rooms (Superior) with older furniture face courtyards; upper-category rooms (Deluxe) are divided into those facing busy Ha-Yarkon Street and those facing the sea; there are no balconies. The expensive La Regence Grill Room, a solid but predictable dining choice, heads a list of three hotel restaurants; the small Bedouin-style lounge/bar is most attractive. You must walk across the road to access the beach.

Dining/Entertainment: Three restaurants, coffee shop, cocktail bar.

Services: Business center, business lounge, special services and lounge for guests in Deluxe rooms and suites.

Facilities: Indoor and outdoor swimming pools, health club, sauna, steam bath, solarium, use of golf facilities at Dan Accadia Hotel in Herzlia, 15 miles north of Tel Aviv.

Holiday Inn Crowne Plaza. 145 Ha-Yarkon St., Tel Aviv. ☎ **03/520-1111.** Fax 03/520-1122. 239 rms. A/C MINIBAR TEL TV. $230–$370 single; $255–$400 double. 15% service charge. Rates include breakfast. AE, DC, MC, V. Bus: 4 on Ben-Yehuda Street; ask for stop closest to Holiday Inn.

Currently the newest and one of the most up-to-date of the city's luxury beachfront hotels in terms of furnishings and services, the highrise Holiday Inn shares a long block just north of Gordon Street with the Radisson Moriah Plaza and Ramada Hotels, all of which offer direct access to the beach without having to cross the road. Location is convenient; other pluses include indoor and outdoor swimming pools, stylish '90s decor that has not yet worn thin, a highly praised business center, and better than average in-hotel restaurant services, including the inventive, upper-bracket Pacific Grill, serving a continental menu with interesting Pacific Rim/Asian touches. There is also an English-style pub on the premises. Nonsmoking rooms and rooms with handicap access are available; all rooms have balconies.

Dining/Entertainment: Two restaurants, pub, and lounge and poolside cafes.

Services: Business center, business lounge, Crowne Plaza Club floors with special services and snacks.

Facilities: Indoor and outdoor swimming pool facilities, health club (additional charge), sauna, massage, steam room, valet parking (fee).

✪ Radisson Moriah Plaza Tel Aviv Hotel. 155 Ha-Yarkon St., Tel Aviv 63453. ☎ **03/527-1515**; 212/541-5009 or 800/221-0203 in the U.S. 346 rms (all with bath or shower). A/C MINIBAR TEL TV. Low season: $140–$165 single; $172–$195 double. High season: $172–$195 single; $222–$250 double. Rates include breakfast. 9-day Radisson Moriah Hotels package (without breakfast): low season $86 double; high season $128 double; add 15% service charge. Children under 18 free. AE, DC, MC, V. Bus: 4 to Ben-Yehuda and Gordon streets, walk down Gordon to Ha-Yarkon Street.

With newly refurbished public areas, and a redesign of most of its private rooms by early 1996, as well as an upgraded business center with special facilities for business-women, the Radisson Moriah is putting emphasis on style and service. Located directly on the beach, not far from the heart of the Ha-Yarkon Street restaurant district, the Gordon Street neighborhood of art galleries, and a pleasant stroll to Dizengoff, the Radisson Moriah offers comfort and great value, especially if you stay here on the special package that commits you to 9 nights at your choice of Radisson Moriah Hotels in Jerusalem, Tiberias, Zichron Yaacov in the Galilee, or at the Dead Sea Plaza (the Radisson Moriah Hotel in Eilat is part of this plan according to availability). A 6-night minimum stay in Radisson Moriah Hotels is $5 per person more. Current El Al packages offer Radisson Moriah Hotels at considerably lower prices. There is free transfer service to the Radisson Moriah Plaza Hotel in Jerusalem. Clearly the best five-star hotel bargain in town.

Services: Business center, children's programs in summer.
Facilities: Outdoor pool, parking (fee).

Ramada Continental Hotel. 121 Ha-Yarkon St., Tel Aviv. ☎ **03/527-2626.** Fax 03/527-2576. 340 rms and suites. A/C TEL TV. $130–$225 single; $140–$230 double. Suites $290–$310. Breakfast $16 extra. AE, DC, MC, V.

The southernmost of three beachfront tower hotels just north of Gordon Street, the Ramada shares an excellent location with the Holiday Inn and Radisson Moriah Plaza Hotels. There is a pleasant terrace cafe overlooking the sea in good weather, and an indoor heated pool ensures the opportunity to do a bit of swimming, even in winter. Rooms are comfortable, but not exceptional; all have balconies.

Dining/Entertainment: Restaurant, two cafes, bar.
Services: Business Club.
Facilities: Indoor pool, children's pool, fitness room, sauna, Jacuzzi, parking (fee).

✪ **Tel Aviv Sheraton Hotel & Towers.** 115 Ha-Yarkon St., Tel Aviv 63573. ☎ **03/528-6222;** 201/816-0830 or 800/552-0141 in the U.S. 346 rms (all with bath). A/C MINIBAR TEL TV. $235–$290 and $270–$340 single; $270–$338 and $300–$362 double. Higher rates for Executive Tower floors. Rates include breakfast. AE, DC, MC, V. Bus: 4 to Ben-Yehuda and Gordon streets, walk down Gordon Street to Ha-Yarkon.

This is the most fun of Tel Aviv's five-star hotels: right on Gordon Beach (you must cross the road) with its interesting mix of tourists and Tel Avivans, just steps from the Ha-Yarkon Street restaurant and cafe district and the art galleries of the Gordon Street area. Unlike more isolated comparable five-star hotels farther north, the Sheraton is an easy walk to Dizengoff Square, Allenby Street, the Yemenite Quarter, and the Carmel Market. In addition, the Sheraton's dining facilities are the best of any hotel in the country; paying for the meals in dollars, as part of your general hotel bill, you avoid the 17% VAT. Rooms are comfortable and spacious, although furnishings are a bit utilitarian and lacking in style. Try for rooms with the exceptional view directly facing the Mediterranean; because of noise considerations, avoid those with adjoining doors. Personal attention in the Executive Towers is outstanding, and a full range of business facilities is available on the premises.

Dining/Entertainment: A variety of restaurants, including the acclaimed Twelve Tribes Restaurant (see "Where to Eat," below), cafes, lounge/bar, disco/nightclub.
Services: Business center, Executive Tower floors with special services and snacks.
Facilities: Outdoor pools, health club (additional charge), parking (fee).

Yamit Towers Hotel. 79 Ha-Yarkon St., Tel Aviv. ☎ **03/519-7111.** Fax 03/517-4719. 40 rms, 36 suites (all with bath). A/C MINIBAR TEL TV. $140–$160 room; $220–$250 one-bedroom suite; $335–$390 two-bedroom suite. AE, DC, MC, V.

A possible option for families who want better-quality accommodations and more privacy than a mere hotel room might offer, the modern, comfortable suites in this 5-year-old beachfront (across the road) highrise contain fully equipped kitchenettes and living areas. Facilities include a swimming pool, two restaurants, and room service. Rates include service charge and are for one to two people in the rooms, one to two people in one-bedroom suites, and one to four people in two-bedroom suites. You can add up to two additional people for $20 per person; breakfast can be arranged for an additional charge.

MODERATE

✪ **Adiv.** 5 Mendele St., Tel Aviv 63907. ☎ **03/522-9141.** Fax 03/522-9144. 71 rms (all with bath). A/C TEL TV. $57–62 single; $75–$84 double; $102 junior suites. Rates include breakfast. AE, DC, MC, V.

With gleaming, newly redesigned public areas faced with polished, rose-colored stone, and freshly spruced-up single and double rooms, the Adiv has become one of the most attractive moderately priced hotels in town. The location is excellent, on a side street half a block from Ha-Yarkon Street and the beach, convenient to many restaurants and window-shopping areas. Most rooms are toward the back of the building, where the blare of traffic is somewhat muffled. Readers' letters attest to the staff's attentiveness.

Astor Hotel. 105 Ha-Yarkon St., Tel Aviv. ☎ **03/522-3141.** Fax 03/523-7247. 120 rms (all with bath). A/C TEL TV. $80–$110 single; $115–$150 double. Rates include breakfast. AE, DC, MC, V.

Located on a busy stretch of Ha-Yarkon Street, between the Dan and Sheraton hotels, the Astor's strong point is location, just steps away from the beach, restaurants, and shopping streets. Public areas are quite small in this 30-year-old building, and rooms have not been upgraded for some time. The excellent Shangri-La Thai Restaurant is on the premises. Street noise may be a concern to some.

✪ **Basel Hotel.** 156 Ha-Yarkon St., Tel Aviv. ☎ **03/524-4161.** Fax 03/527-0005. 120 rms (all with bath). A/C TEL TV. $92–$108 single; $118–$140 double. Rates include breakfast. AE, DC, MC, V.

Located on the inland side of Ha-Yarkon Street, between Gordon Street and Atarim Square, from the outside this convenient, well-run seven-story hotel looks smaller than it really is. Given four stars under the now suspended hotel rating system, the Basel offers a functional lobby larger than that of most hotels in this class, with shops and a small bar, an outdoor swimming pool, and plain but comfortable rooms, many of which are in the depths of the building, away from street noise. Rooms have cable TV, the staff is quite good, and 24-hour room service is available. The Basel is a fabulous deal on El Al's Sunsational Package, in which a double room can run from $40 to $60 a night. Though the Basel is in the heart of the swanky beachfront hotel district, you have to detour a long block around the divided Ha-Yarkon Street underpass if you're going to the beach by foot. Parking for a fee is nearby.

Best Western Regency Suites Hotel. 80 Ha-Yarkon St., Tel Aviv 63432. ☎ **03/517-3939.** Fax 03/516-3276. 20 one-bedroom suites (all with bath). A/C KITCHENETTE TEL TV. $120–$140 single; $145–$165 double; $20 additional person. AE, DC, MC, V.

Just a few years old, with its polish not yet worn thin, this Best Western Hotel consists of up-to-date one-bedroom suites with small living room areas and fully equipped kitchenettes. It offers discounts to long-term visitors, and is ideal for families or business travelers who want to prepare some of their own meals. It is located on the inland side of Ha-Yarkon Street, across from the beach, just where the neighborhood becomes markedly better. Breakfast is not included, but can be arranged at the small in-house coffee shop.

Maxim Hotel. 86 Ha-Yarkon St., Tel Aviv 63903. ☎ **03/517-3721** or 517-3222. Fax 03/517-3726. 60 rms (52 with bath, 8 with shower). A/C TV. $49–$63 single; $78 double. Rates include breakfast. AE, DC, MC, V.

Near the corner with Bograshov, just where Ha-Yarkon Street begins to be a bit classier, the modern Maxim Hotel offers sea views from its front-facing rooms. Those rooms without tubs contain showers instead. The slightly higher rates are for the sea-view rooms.

Hotel Florida. 164 Ha-Yarkon St., Tel Aviv. ☎ **03/524-2184.** Fax 03/524-7278. 52 rms (all with bath). A/C TEL TV. $64–$70 single; $78–$82 double. Rates include breakfast. AE, DC, MC, V.

Tel Aviv Accommodations and Dining

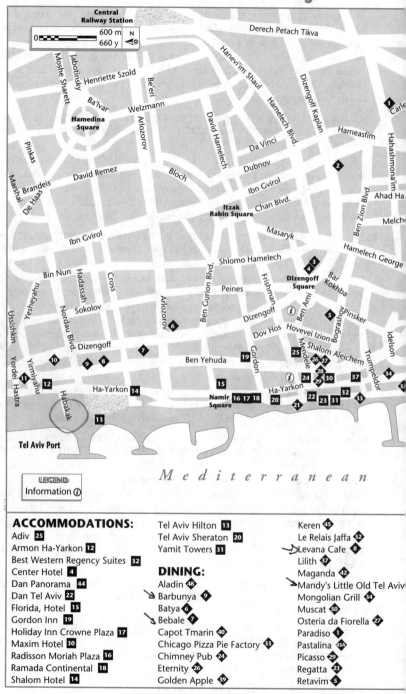

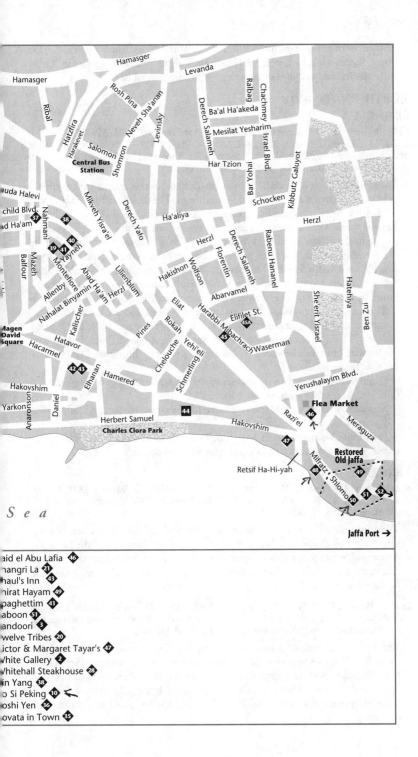

Hamasger

Hamasger

Levanda

Rosh Pina

Ribal

Hatzfira

Harakevet

Neveh Sha'anan

Shomron

Salomon

Levinsky

**Central Bus
Station**

Ralbag

Chachney

Ba'al Ha'akeda

Derech Salameh

Mesilat Yesharim

Israel Blvd.

Bar Yohai

Kibbutz Galuyot

Schocken

auda Halevi

child Blvd.

d Ha'am

Nahmani

Mazeh

Balfour

Ha'aliya

Har Tzion

Mikveh Yisra'el

Derech Yafo

Yavneh

Montefiore

Allenby

Nahalat Binyamin

Ahad Ha'am

Herzl

Lilienblum

Hakishon

Wolfson

Florentin

Herzl

Derech Salameh

Rabenu Hananel

Herzl

Abarvamel

She'erit Yisrael

Hatehiya

Ben Zui

**Magen
David
Square**

Hacarmel

Kalischer

Hatavor

Pines

Rokah

Chelouche

Yehi'eli

Eliat

Harabbi Mibachrach

Elifilet St.

Waserman

Hakovshim

Yarkon

Anaronson

Daniel

Elhanan

Hamered

Schmerling

Yerushalayim Blvd.

■ **Flea Market**

Razi'el

Meraguza

Herbert Samuel

Charles Clora Park

Hakovshim

Retsif Ha-Hi-yah

Mifratz

**Restored
Old Jaffa**

Shlomo

S e a

Jaffa Port →

219

This modern three-star-equivalent hotel is a half block south of Ben-Gurion Street. Some rooms have views of Namir Square and of the Mediterranean. Other amenities include wall-to-wall carpeting, radios, and central heat.

NORTHERN TEL AVIV
EXPENSIVE

✪ **Tel Aviv Hilton.** Independence Park, Ha-Yarkon St., Tel Aviv. ☎ **03/520-2222.** Fax 03/527-2711. 595 rms, including suites. A/C MINIBAR TEL TV. $275–$360 single; $315–$385 double; suites from $620. Breakfast included only with Executive Floor deluxe rooms. Service charge included. Breakfast buffet $20 extra. AE, DC, MC, V.

The massive Hilton is set far back from Ha-Yarkon Street in a small park overlooking a quiet, sheltered area of Tel Aviv's beachfront. The skilled staff here is probably the best in the city; restaurant facilities are good, spacious, and varied; the hotel's meeting rooms and conference facilities are always buzzing; and the business center is superb (the Hilton's kosher sushi bar and choice of a Japanese-style breakfast are indicative of its role as a focal point for business ties between Israel and Asia). The Hilton is also well atuned to tourists, with a full range of recreational facilities. Better-category rooms are decorated with tasteful accessories and classic fruitwood furniture; a variety of stylishly designed suites are offered, including one with a Jacuzzi and bathroom corner window overlooking the sea. All rooms have balconies; lower-category rooms are less elegantly furnished, but slowly being upgraded. The location is a bit of a hike to interesting streets; the waters of the Hilton Beach, less open to the sea than other nearby stretches, can at times be a trap for seaweed and garbage swept in by the tides.

Dining/Entertainment: Five restaurants, including the top-quality King Solomon Grill and the outdoor Gazebo; two bars.

Services: Business center, special service for Executive Floors and Club Room, in-house doctor, airport shuttle.

Facilities: Outdoor saltwater pool, fitness center, sauna, massage, steam bath, two tennis courts, access to marina, shopping arcade, parking (fee).

MODERATE

Hotel Armon Ha-Yarkon. 268 Ha-Yarkon St., Tel Aviv 63504. ☎ **03/605-5271.** Fax 03/605-8485. 24 rms (all with bath). A/C TEL TV. $58–$70 single; $69–$86 double. Rates include breakfast. Bus: 4 or 5. AE, DC, MC, V.

This modern hotel is across the street from the big hotel Tal. It's a small, friendly place only a block from the beach and two blocks from the action of the Little Tel Aviv nightlife area, but a walk of several long blocks to the heart of the city's tourist area to the south. Lots of good restaurants are nearby. Additional amenities include radios in every room.

Shalom Hotel. 216 Ha-Yarkon St., Tel Aviv. ☎ **03/524-3277.** Fax 03/523-5895. 48 rms (all with bath or shower). A/C TEL TV. $57–$62 single; $76–$92 double; off-season and student discounts available. Rates include breakfast. Bus: 4 or 5. AE, DC, MC, V.

The three-star-equivalent Shalom Hotel is a modern, five-story structure. All the front rooms have balconies with views of the Mediterranean and Independence Park. Decorated in understated, contemporary style, there are 36 doubles with bath and 12 singles with shower. Other amenities include central heating. In front of the hotel is the Stagecoach Restaurant and Pub with wild west decor and live music every evening.

SOUTH TEL AVIV
EXPENSIVE

Dan Panorama Hotel. 10 Kaufman St., Tel Aviv. ☎ **03/519-0190.** Fax 03/517-1777. 504 rms and suites. A/C TEL TV. $135–$200 single; $155–$230 double. Rates include breakfast. AE, DC, MC, V. Bus: 10.

Across the road from the beach in the southern part of Tel Aviv within walking distance of Old Jaffa, this modern highrise held forth by itself a mile and a half south of the main hotel district for almost 10 years. Now it has been joined by an InterContinental Hotel that will be under construction next door for part of the time span of this edition. Rooms are small, but all have balconies. There is a convention center next door, as well as a highrise textile industry center, giving the Dan Panorama a business ambience, but this may change as more hotels are built in the neighborhood. There are no nearby streets for strolling; rates here are lower than for a comparable hotel in a more central location.

Dining/Entertainment: Two restaurants, lobby bar.

Services: 24-hour room service, business center, business lounge.

Facilities: Outdoor swimming pool and sun terrace, fitness center, lobby shops, parking (fee).

5 Where to Dine

OFF AND ON HA-YARKON STREET
EXPENSIVE

✪ **Twelve Tribes.** In the Sheraton Hotel, 115 Ha-Yarkon St. ☎ **03/528-6222.** Reservations recommended. Appetizers $11.50–$16; main courses $18.50–$26; complete fixed-price dinners $30–$47. AE, DC, MC, V. Sun–Thurs 7pm–midnight. FRENCH.

The Sheraton Hotel's food preparation staff seems constantly stretching to create remarkable and ever-changing meals within the bounds of kashrut. At the Twelve Tribes, which wins my award as the most dazzling kosher as well as hotel-based restaurant in the country, the style has been an inventive, robust nouvelle called "trendy peasant," done with a light touch and a fresh elegance. The current executive chef, Hans Lelie, an immigrant from the Netherlands, plans to emphasize the natural taste and texture of the food he presents. You can choose appetizers like veal sweetmeats with mustard sauce in brioche or sliced breast of pigeon on fresh artichoke salad. Then you might go on to a cream of trout soup with almonds, and have a main course of delicately poached filet of locus with sorrel, or mullard (local hybrid duck) breast with fresh coriander, ginger, garlic, and soya smoked on a bed of parsley, or veal chop stuffed with nuts and fresh herbs served in a sauce of wild Maine blueberries and wine. For business and health-conscious travelers, a special menu of low-calorie, heathy but nonetheless fascinating dishes has been put into place. The fixed-price dinner, which includes your choice of hot or cold appetizer and soup, also allows you to choose from the lavish dessert trolley or from special creations like timbale of chocolate mango or fresh figs with lemon mousse and cassis. Service charge is included, but not VAT.

MODERATE

Mongolian Grill Bar. 62 Ha-Yarkon St. ☎ **03/517-4010.** Reservations recommended. Lunch NIS 36 ($11); Dinner NIS 60–80 ($18–$24). AE, DC, MC, V. Daily noon–1pm; lunch served noon–4pm. MONGOLIAN.

Israelis are really getting into meat, and this unusual buffet grill allows them (and you) to experiment with all kinds of possibilities. There is a large buffet table of uncooked chunks of steak, lamb, chicken, liver, and other choices as well as vegetables, spices, herbs, and oils. You gather your choices for a mixed-grill combination into a bowl and hand it to one of the cooks, who spreads it out on the restaurant's central grill. The idea of the grill is derived from the times when warriors set their shields over fires out in the open fields, and cooked up vegetables and freshly hunted meat with fiery spices and oil. You don't have to duplicate Mongolian cuisine's hot spices, but my advice is not to be shy about seasonings and vegetables; if you're hesitant, your dish will be tasteless. At dinner, you can return as often as you like with new concoctions; at the less expensive lunch price, you only get one try. The more expensive NIS 80 dinner buffet includes unusual meats such as ostrich liver, calamari, and crocodile tail. All menus come with rice and baked noodles. The place seems like an outpost in the Northeast Asian desert, especially when busy.

✪ **Picasso.** 88 Ha-Yarkon St. ☎ **03/510-2784.** Reservations recommended evenings. Appetizers NIS 12–27 ($3.60–$8.10); main courses NIS 24–45 ($7.20–$13.50). AE, DC, MC, V. Daily 7am–3am. CONTINENTAL.

Located in a yellow-and-white International Style building from the late 1930s, Picasso offers a view of the sea, stylish but affordable food, and real Tel Aviv in the '90s ambience that is hard to beat. The chef, David Prozniak, is from Paris, and it shows in his light meals, elegant but hefty salads, and fine main courses such as breast of mullard with spicy Thai sauce, or grouper filet in red wine served on a bed of forest mushrooms. A new menu of light but always intriguing creations makes Picasso a continuing yuppie enclave (you can even order sushi). Picasso also serves very well as a spot for evening drinks, or for coffee and dessert.

Regata. 87 Ha-Yarkon St. ☎ **03/527-8666.** Reservations recommended weekends. Light meals NIS 20–30 ($6–$9); main courses NIS 20–45 ($6–$22.50); pizzas NIS 30–45 ($9–$22.50). AE, DC, MC, V. Daily 10:30am–after midnight. ITALIAN/MEDITERRANEAN.

With sweeping vistas of the sea, this busy, interesting new restaurant is set in the shopping arcade of the new King David Tower, right beside the Dan Hotel. Despite its posh surroundings, Regata is not at all formal—rather it's a three-ring circus of choices. There is a daily cold antipasti bar for either $6.50 or $8.50, depending on the size of your plate (on Saturdays this popular buffet often includes two or three pastas and delicacies like salmon carpaccio). You'll also find a stone oven turning out unique pita-bread-style pizzas, a large selection of sandwiches served on freshly made breads, and interesting main courses ranging from fried calamari to chicken livers sautéed with vegetables and balsamic vinegar. Lighter meals might include a salad and a Mediterranean crab and seafood soup. Many come for dessert and for the in-house ice creams. Regata is affiliated with the more expensive Remi restaurant downstairs.

✪ **Shangri La.** In the Astor Hotel, 105 Ha-Yarkon St. ☎ **03/523-8913.** Reservations recommended for evenings. Appetizers NIS 16–33 ($4.80–$10); main courses NIS 36–63 ($10.80–$21); lunch special NIS 47 ($14). DC, MC, V. Daily 1pm–midnight. THAI.

This spacious, comfortable restaurant, adorned with columns and capitals that hint at art deco Canaanite and with vistas that overlook the Mediterranean, is the setting for a menu that is prepared with lightness and elegance. You can order your dishes mild, hot, or fiery: this is one place where mild does not mean you lose out on carefully prepared, exotic seasonings. Me krob crispy noodles with shrimp and scallions; the tam yum soup, filled with shrimps, fried mushrooms, and onions in a garlic and lemongrass seasoning; and the all-you-can-eat appetizer buffet, which is often set up for the lunch special, are real delights, as are the authentic Thai desserts.

Whitehall Steakhouse. 6 Mendele St. ☎ **03/524-9282.** Appetizers NIS 12–30 ($3.60–$9); main courses NIS 42–72 ($13.60–$22); luncheon specials with salad bar, beverage, and dessert NIS 39–60 ($12–$18). AE, DC, MC, V. Daily noon–midnight. STEAKS.

A modern, air-conditioned retreat near Ha-Yarkon Street in the heart of the tourist district, Whitehall's luncheon specials, which include salad bar, soft drink, beer or wine, bread, chips or baked potato, your choice of sauces, and coffee or tea (served Sunday through Friday noon to 6pm), are excellent value. Beyond the luncheon specials, you'll find appetizers ranging from shrimps to pâté de foie gras and shish kebabs, steaks, and prime ribs, all grilled on charcoal fires. An extra NIS 12 ($3.60) at dinner allows you to add the bottomless salad bar. There is also a dessert menu.

Yoshi Yen. 56 Herbert Samuel Promenade. ☎ **03/510-3348.** Reservations recommended. Appetizers NIS 8–50 ($2.40–$15); main courses NIS 24–55 ($7.20–$16.50); business lunch NIS 45 ($13.50). AE, DC, MC, V. Sun–Thurs 12:30–11pm; Fri 12:30–3:30pm and 7:30pm–12:30am; Sat 1–11:30pm. Just south of Mograbi Square. CHINESE.

If you get a yen for Chinese food while you're in Tel Aviv, you can get it here with a view of the Mediterranean at sunset. The restaurant is set up for the view; it also delivers a menu prepared in a wide variety of Szechuan and Cantonese styles that's a cut above most of the local competition. The shrimp soup is usually bountiful; the fresh sea fish in Szechuan sauce and chicken in ginger are recommended choices.

INEXPENSIVE

The Chicago Pizza Pie Factory. 63 Ha-Yarkon St. ☎ **03/517-7505.** Regular pizzas (for two people) NIS 30–50 ($9–$15); other selections NIS 10–25 ($3–$7.50). AE, DC, MC, V. Daily noon–1am. PIZZA.

Chicago Pizza is a smash success among Israelis, and a natural attraction for tourists and international students because of its location in the Ha-Yarkon Street hotel area near the American embassy. It's a strange mix of seafront 1930s–modern Tel Aviv cement structure adorned with a touch of neon, and an interior that is a shrine to the history of Chicago. The restaurant also sports current sports videos, 1960s music, and upmarket deep-pan pizzas that are heavy on toppings but sometimes light on the seasonings and light on the color of the tomato sauce. People come for the scene as much as the pizza. There are doggie bags, in case you're alone and can't finish a two-person pizza at one sitting. A pizza for four, fully loaded, is $18.

Chimney Pub Restaurant. 2 Mendele St. ☎ **03/523-5215.** Light meals NIS 14–22 ($4.20–$6.60); main courses NIS 25–50 ($7.50–$15). AE, DC, MC, V. Daily noon–1am. CONTINENTAL.

On the corner of Ha-Yarkon, you'll find two cozy dining rooms with fireplaces, net curtains, and an ambience that makes you think of a village cafe in the south of France. Chimney is a place for evening meetings or a light meal and drinks as well as for slightly stylish dinners. The lively crowd of Tel Avivans and tourists spills out into the table-filled, vine-covered courtyard. The bar lets you choose among 150 cocktails, wines, tropical drinks, and nonalcoholic creations. There are $10 business lunches, all-day specials for even less, and manager Albert Asseraf offers a 10% discount if you present this book.

✪ **Yotvata in Town.** 80 Herbert Samuel Promenade. ☎ **03/510-4667.** Light meals NIS 10–27 ($3–$8); main courses NIS 22–52 ($6.60–$15.60). AE, DC, MC, V. Daily 7am–4am. DAIRY/VEGETARIAN.

Thirty years ago, the kind of restaurant Israelis loved best was a little place doing simple, freshly made salads and good-quality dairy dishes. Popular Yotvata has carried this concept into the '90s and turned it into a bustling, high-powered, multi-story emporium on the beachfront where everything is made from the best-quality produce bought directly from kibbutzim and from the famous dairy kibbutz at Yotvata. For under $10 there are salads, cheese platters served with fresh herbs and vegetables, blintzes, pancakes, vegetable pies, pastas, and pizzas. At the upper end of the price range, you'll find a selection of fish dishes. The mixtures of natural fruit juices ($2.10 to $3), which you can order plain, with yogurt, with liqueur, or with milk, are famous, as are Yotvata's many ice-cream parlor dishes.

ALONG BEN-YEHUDA STREET
MODERATE

Barbunya. 192 Ben Yehuda St. ☎ **03/524-0961.** Reservations not accepted. Fixed-price meals NIS 45–NIS 54 ($13.50–$16.30). AE, DC, MC, V. Sat–Thurs noon–midnight; Fri noon–6pm. FISH.

Up near the Hilton Hotel, this small no-frills restaurant serves enormous portions of fresh, simply prepared fish, and although the sign may not be in English, at lunch and dinner time, you can often spot the place by the line of dedicated customers that extends out to the street. Once inside, you'll find paper tablecloths on the long tables, and a choice of fish (and perhaps shrimp) depending on the day's catch; there's a slightly higher price for red snapper and grouper. Fish is either grilled or fried in garlic and lemon, and comes with an array of salads and club soda. Substitutions are not possible, but you do have the option of ordering dessert for an extra charge. In its 2 years of existence, this has become a North Tel Aviv institution.

Osteria da Fiorella. 44 Ben-Yehuda. ☎ **03/528-8717.** Appetizers NIS 12–28 ($3.60–$8.60); main courses NIS 22–45 ($6.60–$13.50). AE, DC, MC, V. Sun–Fri noon–midnight; Sat after Shabbat. ITALIAN.

This tidy little nonkosher place at the corner of Bograshov advertises that it serves "vera cucina italiana" (authentic Italian cuisine) prepared by "padroni italiani" (Italian owner). You may sit at the bar inside, or outside at the small tables spread with red-and-white-checked cloths. The trattoria menu has most of the old favorite Italian dishes, and you can enjoy the plate of the day, selected by the chef, for $8 to $11, plus tax and tip. For dessert, delicious cheesecakes are baked with homemade ricotta and tiramisù is especially recommended.

INEXPENSIVE

Bebale. 177 Ben-Yehuda St. ☎ **03/546-7486.** Appetizers NIS 9–15 ($2.70–$4.50); main courses NIS 24–33 ($7.20–$10). AE, DC, MC, V. Daily noon–midnight. EUROPEAN JEWISH.

Unlike many of its decades-old competitors (such as Batya over on Dizengoff), Bebale is new to the Yiddish-cuisine-just-like-grandma-made game. Located near trendy North Tel Aviv, it has developed a discerning and devoted following of young professionals. Decor is simple, in keeping with the style of older establishments in this market, but the food is genuine and contains all the classics, with a tiny pinch of the '90s tossed in. Appetizers include pickled herrings, jellied calves' feet, and kreplach and matzoh-ball soups; on Saturdays, a Sabbath cholent of potatoes, meat, vegetable, and kishke is offered for $7.50 (half portion is $2 less). There are late-night bagel snacks on Thursdays, daily specials, and for dessert, a choice of cakes and stewed fruit. Main courses include two side dishes. The thick, fluffy, nongreasy potato-zucchini latkes ($2.30) are light, filling, and make a good minimeal or take-out snack.

✪ Eternity. 60 Ben-Yehuda St. ☎ **03/520-3151.** Main courses NIS 10–25 ($3–$7.50). No credit cards. Sun–Thurs 9am–11pm; Fri 9am–2pm; Sat after Shabbat. VEGETARIAN.

You'll be amazed by the incredibly tasty natural vegetable meals this tiny yellow-and-white no-frills restaurant offers: soya sausages, vegetarian shwarmas, wheatburgers, tofulafels, nonsteak sandwiches, soya ice creams, and carob puddings. My favorite is the barbecued twist on whole-wheat pita served with medium spicy sauce and home-made mustard. Founded by the Hebrew Israelites, an African-American religious group whose dietary laws prohibit milk or meat in any form, Eternity uses no milk or meat products; nothing is fried, there is no cholesterol, and almost no salt, yet everything tastes positively great. Among the newest creations here are tofu cheeses in assorted flavors and okra sticks that seem just like fish sticks! Drinks include juices, veggie coffee, and carob milk.

Levana Restaurant Cafe. 182 Ben Yehuda St. ☎ **03/522-2444.** Appetizers NIS 12–36 ($3.60–$11); main courses NIS 25–45 ($7.50–$13.50); cakes NIS 15 ($4.50). AE, DC, MC, V. Daily 8:30am–1am. CONTINENTAL/CAFE.

This mildly posh little place, with fruitwood paneled walls and polished stone tables, started out as an emporium of elegant desserts, and although Levana's famed cakes are still fabulous, it has expanded into a lively dining choice as well. There's good pasta, and quiche, as well as wonderful hot and cold salads; among the inventive main courses you'll find chicken breast in mango sauce stir-fried with vegetables, herbs and spaghetti, or an interesting dish of chicken livers in a wine, onion, orange, and coconut sauce. A good place for dessert, or for those staying in North Tel Aviv hotels.

ALONG ALLENBY STREET AND SOUTHWARD

This area, stretching from the beginning of Allenby Street south to the Tel Aviv–Jaffa border, is away from most tourist hotels, but it contains some of the best restaurants in the country. Some of the finest upper-price-bracket restaurants are to be found near the booming Tel Aviv stock exchange in the area between Ahad Ha-Am Street and Rothschild Boulevard. These places can be very busy at lunchtime, when there are business lunch specials; in the evening, the mood is more relaxed.

EXPENSIVE

✪ **Capot Tmarim.** 60 Ahad Ha'Am St. ☎ **03/566-3166.** Reservations required. Appetizers NIS 33–45 ($10–$13.60); main courses NIS 90–120 ($27–$36); fixed-price lunch NIS 60–90 ($18–$27); fixed-price dinner NIS 120–150 ($36–$45). AE, DC, MC, V. Lunch Sun–Thurs 12:30–3pm; dinner Mon–Sat 7:30pm–midnight. CONTININTAL/MEDITERRANEAN RIM.

Dining here is an experience that is special to Tel Aviv. Ofer Gal has carefully set his restaurant in an enclave that evokes the feel of Tel Aviv design in the 1930s—a mix of International Style touched with Arabic floor tiles, hand-painted Armenian plates, and Biedermeirer-derived chairs that might have been brought to the Middle East by refugees from Germany. The menu creations also encompass Tel Aviv's roots—sophistocated, international, but with Middle Eastern–inspired flourishes. In sum-mer you'll find refreshing watermelon soup with feta cheese and mint; in winter, look for an earthy hummus soup with baked bread crust. First courses range from deli-cate pâté of veal liver on crispy sliced potato in grape sauce, to eggplant with mild Safed goat cheese, basil, and cherry tomato in pastry, or grilled shrimp served on a refreshing, light couscous salad; the flambéed quail in salad with pâté is especially fine. Saddle of lamb in red wine sauce served with remarkable miniature stuffed eggplants is done to perfection here, the meat rare and tender, the herbed skin crisp and covered with flavor. There is a constantly changing array of fish, seafood, and poul-try choices, all prepared with a light, inventive hand (delicately smoked mullard with balsamic vinegar and meat sauce is recommended). Desserts range from figs en crêpes with hot Grand Marnier sauce to a heavenly interpretation of traditional mahalabi (thickened milk, rosewater, and cornflower) served with peanut and coconut ice cream. Typical of Ofer Gal's attention to every detail, the watermelon sorbet is flecked with chocolate seeds! The chef's suggestions, available for a surcharge on the fixed-price lunch and dinner, are worth the modest extra investment. Desserts are in the $10 range.

✪ **Golden Apple.** 40 Montefiore St. ☎ **03/566-0931** or 566-0932. Reservations required. Appetizers NIS 60–65 ($18–$19.60); main courses NIS 110–120 ($33–$36); fixed-price lunch NIS 75 ($22.50). AE, DC, MC, V. Lunch Sat–Thurs 12:30–2:30pm; dinner daily 7pm–midnight; no orders after 10:30pm. Closed Fri afternoon. FRENCH.

After making his reputation by creating the most acclaimed Far Eastern restaurants in Tel Aviv, Israel Aharoni opened this most elegant of French restaurants, complete with touches unheard of in Israeli restaurants—like Limoges china and crystal glasses. Aharoni's menu is classic, but stamped with his own personal, wide-ranging touches. Among his signature first courses are terrine of leeks with beet and balsamic vinaigrette; foie gras with caramelized apples; and thinly sliced calamari on a salad of lightly cooked beans served in a sauce of balsamic vinaigrette. The herb-encrusted saddle of lamb is superb; other choices might include shrimps in soya and ginger, served with such delights as a braised dwarf lettuce and a pastry nest filled with black mushrooms, or an enchanted plate of zucchini flowers stuffed with shrimp. You can arrange a fixed-price four- or five-course dinner, consulting in advance with Aharoni, for NIS 290 ($87); desserts are in the $10 range.

✪ **Keren.** 12 Eilat St., Jaffa. ☎ **03/518-1358.** Reservations required. Appetizers NIS 36–60 ($11–$18); main courses NIS 88–100 ($26.70–$30); fixed-price lunch NIS 75 ($23). AE, DC, MC, V. Daily 7pm–midnight and Sun–Thurs noon–4pm. FRENCH.

Perhaps the most charming of Israel's elegant dining establishments, Keren is housed in a restored antique wooden building with second-floor verandas resembling a Caribbean planter's homestead. Brought by ship from America to the sand dunes of Jaffa in the 1860s, along with an ill-fated colony of American Protestants, the building is even more incongruous today, amid the commercial and industrial neighborhood of South Tel Aviv/Jaffa that has grown up around it. Step inside, however, and you are transported to a place of vision and to a menu that is exceptional. The menu constantly changes, but among Keren's famed first courses are a seafood salad heavy with calamari; fried calves' brain in a lemony caper sauce; zucchini flower stuffed with seafood; and the red mullet and fennel salad. Your choice of main courses could include sea bass in crab sauce, steak filet with goat cheese in hot vinaigrette sauce, or carpaccio with baby lamb. Desserts (included in the prix-fixe lunch) are magnificent. The prix-fixe lunch is very good value.

Yin Yang. 60 Rothschild Blvd. ☎ **03/560-6833.** Reservations advised. Appetizers NIS 16–60 ($4.20–$18); main courses NIS 30–70 ($9–$21). AE, DC, MC, V. CHINESE.

Many consider this the best Chinese restaurant in Israel, worth the trek from the hotel district. Owner Israel Aharoni (who also created the Golden Apple, one of the country's finest French restaurants) has designed a menu more authentic than you'd usually find in a Chinese restaurant for Westerners. For a first course, sliced pork in spicy garlic sauce is recommended by Aharoni; I enjoyed the spicy cucumber salad. Duck dishes are famous here; the duck in honey garlic sauce is excellent. Among those things you usually won't find at most Israeli Chinese restaurants are calamari Szechuan style, beef in anise, and crab done in a number of interesting styles. Yin Yang is located in a 1930s Tel Aviv mansion with high-ceiling dining rooms that make a comfortable setting for a relaxed, interesting meal.

MODERATE

Lilith. 42 Mazeh St. ☎ **03/629-8772.** Reservations recommended. Lunch appetizers NIS 25–40 ($7.50–$12); lunch main courses NIS 40–75 ($12–$22.50); dinner appetizers NIS 36–50 ($11–$15); dinner main courses NIS 50–85 ($15–$25.50). AE, DC, MC, V. Sun–Thurs 10am–midnight; Fri 10am–5pm; Sat 7pm–midnight. CONTEMPORARY MEDITERRANEAN RIM.

Everything in the decor of this sleek, glass-walled restaurant was chosen for its natural textures and clean, strong shape and design. The style of the menu here matches the decor: natural elegance and artistry that enhance the textures and superb quality of everything served. Lilith's owners are perfectionists who spent years collecting the right tableware and accessories before opening their restaurant. It took 2 years to find the right supplier for their superb lamb chops; even the tiniest olive served here had to be exquisite. Karen Hendler-Kremerman, one of the owners of Lilith, is the author of *The Art of Gourmet Grilling* (Multimedia Books, 1991), and her standards of perfection and exquisite simplicity shine in light first courses like salmon carpaccio served with cucumbers and a fennel mustard sauce, or a delicate squid salad, as well as in main courses like herb-crusted New York steak, sea scallops in rice vinegar sauce, grilled goose liver with warm shallot vinaigrette, and the fabulous salmon grilled with olive oil and herbs. There are also easy, unpretentious choices here like the best grilled hamburger in the country ($11), or a hearty sandwich of avocado and marinated turkey breast, or a simple late summer fig salad. A choice of excellent desserts and carefully selected wines round out Lilith's charms.

Pastalina. 16 Elifellet St. ☎ **03/683-6401.** Reservations required. Fixed-price menu NIS 66 ($20). AE, DC, MC, V. Daily 7:30pm–midnight and Fri noon–3pm. ITALIAN.

Located in an out-of-the-way area on the Tel Aviv–Jaffa border, Pastalina, with its sleek glass-brick decor, is the trendy place to go for exquisite and exciting pasta. The fixed-price menu, which changes daily, includes antipasti, and a main-course choice of pasta, chicken, or fish. Always relaxing, worthwhile, and delicious.

INEXPENSIVE

✪ **Spaghettim.** 18 Yavne St. ☎ **03/525-1479.** Reservations recommended. Appetizers NIS 10–15 ($3–$4.50); spaghetti NIS 18–40 ($5.50–$12). AE, DC, MC, V. Daily noon–1am. ITALIAN.

This is the kind of place that can make you fall in love with spaghetti, which it offers with more than 50 kinds of interesting sauces, ranging from traditionals like carbonara and all'arrabbiata to unusual creations like an olive oil–based sauce filled with breast of tender, fresh sautéed chicken, dill, garlic, and lemon ($7), or a salmon and asparagus sauce with white wine and nutmeg ($9), or imported moules marnier ($12). Soups and salads, like the spaghetti dishes, are filled with fresh herbs and vegetables and are hefty in size. For dessert, there's a choice of panna cotta, Italian ice creams, and al dente spaghetti, this time with dark chocolate, ice cream, and brandy sauce, or poppy seeds. Delicious, filling, imaginative, and with many choices for under $6, the restaurant charges $1.50 for homestyle bread, which with these prices for main courses, is not unfair. A selection of Israeli and imported wines is also served. Excellent value!

YEMENITE QUARTER & CARMEL MARKET

Walk along Allenby Street from Moghrabi Square. At the Atara Cafe (54 Allenby), turn right and walk to the grid of little streets at its far end. This is the Yemenite Quarter, a favorite of Tel Avivans and tourists alike. Don't let the neighborhood's appearance rattle you—the people here are honest and respectable, and it's a perfectly safe area to traverse. Built in 1909, this is one of the oldest parts of the city. The tangled streets of the Yemenite Quarter harbor many restaurants; they are not especially Yemenite, but they serve some of the tastiest Middle Eastern food in the country. The following are among the best.

MODERATE

Maganda Restaurant. 26 Rabbi Meir St. ☎ **03/517-9990.** Reservations recommended. Appetizers NIS 7–16 ($2.10–$4.80); main courses NIS 18–46 ($5.40–$13.80). No credit cards. Sun–Thurs noon–midnight; Sat after Shabbat. YEMENITE/MIDDLE EASTERN.

The Maganda has recently been rebuilt, and is now airy, modern, and very attractive. The cuisine is Yemenite Middle Eastern, strictly kosher, and includes grilled meats such as lamb shashlik, kebab, and skewered duck. The menu is in English as well as Hebrew. In summer this recently remodeled restaurant offers rooftop dining.

To get there, enter the Yemenite Quarter, turn right at the end of the alley, then left onto Najara Street.

Shaul's Inn. 11 Eliashiv St. ☎ **03/517-7619.** Reservations recommended. Appetizers NIS 7–16 ($2.10–$4.80); main courses NIS 20–46 ($6–$13.80). AE, DC, MC, V. Sun–Thurs noon–midnight; Fri noon–3pm; Sat after Shabbat. MIDDLE EASTERN.

The remodeled, enlarged blockbuster of this neighborhood, with heavy wooden chairs, flagstone floors, and a large photomural of a Yemenite wedding on one wall, this kosher restaurant at the corner of Eliashiv can get packed to the street on Saturday nights. Stick to the main room on the ground floor; downstairs, where there is an intimate restaurant and bar, the prices go up by more than 100%. English is spoken here, and the waiters will help you choose from the Middle Eastern specialties. The "Specialty of the Inn" is the lamb's breast stuffed with rice and pine nuts— deliciously tasty. Have a Turkish or Greek salad, or a gorgeous stuffed eggplant, cabbage, or pepper.

To get there, go west down Ge'ulah Street off Allenby; half a block down Ge'ulah, make a diagonal left turn onto Ha-Ari Street; turn right onto Rabbi Meir Street, then left onto Kehilat Aden Street.

IN & AROUND DIZENGOFF SQUARE
MODERATE

✪ **Tandoori.** In the Dizengoff Square Hotel, 2 Zamenhoff St. ☎ **03/296-185.** Reservations recommended. Appetizers NIS 10–28 ($3–$8.30); main courses NIS 22–55 ($6.60–$16.50); all-you-can-eat lunch buffet NIS 45 ($13.50) plus 10% service charge. AE, DC, MC, V. Lunch daily 12:30–3:30pm; dinner daily 7pm–1am. INDIAN.

Right on Dizengoff Square, but a continent away from the bustle, is Tandoori. Why visit an Indian restaurant in Israel? Only for some of the best food, most relaxing but elegant ambience, and pleasant service in Tel Aviv. Decorated with Indian textiles that are framed by architectural arabesques, Tandoori is serenely presided over by Vinod Pushkarna and his wife, Reena, whose Jewish Bombay heritage helped to create the restaurant's special atmosphere.

Try the ever-changing all-you-can-eat daily luncheon buffet, one of the best values in town, or share a whole tandoori chicken for $15; with rice and side dishes, two can easily dine in the $15 per person range. Share a heaping plate of boneless tandoori chicken ($10) with side dishes and the price will be even lower. I especially like the chicken dishes served in skewered chunks, the giant prawns in ginger, and a dry sautéed vegetable dish so light and elegant it almost seems to herald an Indian nouvelle cuisine. The homemade dessert dumplings and Indian ice creams made of

Hatikvah: An Ethnic Experience

The restaurants in the Yemenite Quarter have become pricey and tourist oriented, but if you're willing to take a 15-minute bus ride to sample Tel Aviv's greatest concentration of Middle Eastern restaurants at bargain prices, then Etzel Street in the Hatikvah District of South Tel Aviv is the place to explore. Pick up bus no. 16 southbound on Allenby Street near Moghrabi Square, and ask the driver to let you off at Rehov Etzel in Hatikvah. Probably Tel Aviv's best-kept restaurant secret, Hatikvah is a vast area inhabited by Israeli families from countries like Yemen and Iraq, and the lengthy Etzel Street is virtually wall-to-wall restaurants serving skewered meats, oriental salads, and delicious Iraqi pita breads that the waiters obtain straight from the ovens of the many bakeries that also dot the street. One of the traditions of Etzel Street is that Iraqi pita more than 3 minutes old is stale. Another tradition is that you purchase your meals by the skewer, which means you can put together a skewer of beef and a skewer of turkey breast (about $2.80 each in most places) plus a salad and chips ($1.80 each), and come up with a tasty, filling meal for less than $10. Or you can be more daring and order breast of goose and chicken hearts and livers for the same price per skewer. The pièce de résistance of Etzel Street restaurants is the enormously rich but delicate goose-liver skewer, barbecued to perfection and going for $5.50 to $7. The street is like a food festival; just pick out a place that looks busy and interesting (preferably next door to a bread bakery) and grab a table. Places without English menus tend to be the cheapest, although with such competition, prices don't vary greatly. Both restaurateurs and customers provide an authentic Tel Aviv atmosphere.

thickened milk and dried fruits and nuts are very interesting. Ask about lassi, Tandoori's refreshing chilled yogurt and fruit drink. A feast here could fall into the moderately expensive range.

INEXPENSIVE

✪ **Batya.** 197 Dizengoff St. ☎ **03/527-3888.** Appetizers NIS 8–15 ($2.40–$4.50); main courses NIS 17–28 ($5.10–$8.40). AE, DC, MC, V. Daily 11am–10pm. EUROPEAN/JEWISH.

Strangely enough, trendy Tel Aviv remains Israel's center for East European Jewish cooking, and Batya (presided over by the wonderful Batya Yom Tov) is one of the oldest restaurants specializing in this tradition. You'll step into a delicious, precholesterol-conscious world of kreplachs, golden chicken soups, chopped livers, stews, duck with Polish mustard sauce, baked Sabbath puddings, tongue, and brisket with potatoes. Decor is no frills, and a good part of Batya's clientele has probably been patronizing the restaurant since it was established in 1941.

✪ **Retavim.** 39 Bograshov St. ☎ **03/528-0334.** Appetizers NIS 8–17 ($2.40–$5.20); main courses NIS 23–43 ($7–$13). AE, DC, MC, V. Daily noon–midnight. CONTINENTAL/ISRAELI.

"Retavim" means "sauces," and this inventive restaurant takes very thin slices of chicken breast escalope and sautées them in your choice of one of 49 sauces. Almost all of the sauces are amazingly delicious, although some may seem a bit bizarre. Among them are familiar creations such as a sauce of olive oil and garlic or an Italian sauce of tomatoes, garlic, and orega. The more daring and often wonderful concoctions include a sauce of juniper berries, gin, and lemon; one of grenadine syrup, sautéed onions, and butter; one of shrimps, cream, and brandy; and an interesting kind of tandoori-curry sauce. Main courses are served with rice or very thin sliced potatoes and a vegetable; vegetarians who find themselves here can make do with an appetizer such as roasted sweet peppers with goat cheese, a salad, and the vegetable side dishes of the day. At least half of the main courses are in the $7 to $10 range.

NEAR HA-BIMAH & MANN AUDITORIUM

Tel Aviv's center of culture is the area a block west of the intersection of Dizengoff and Ibn Gevirol streets. Along with the Ha-Bimah National Theater, Mann Auditorium, ZOA House, and Helena Rubinstein Pavilion, the area includes places to eat before the performance.

INEXPENSIVE

Paradiso. In the Tel Aviv Cinémathèque, 2 Sprinzak St. ☎ **03/695-0383.** Appetizers NIS 12–39 ($3.60–$12); main courses NIS 20–42 ($6–$13). DC, MC, V. Daily 9:30am–12:30am. ITALIAN VEGETARIAN.

Serving the trendy Cinémathèque crowd with quick but stylish meals, this is the kind of place where you can choose a bowl of minestrone or a serving of carpaccio di salmone as an appetizer or light meal; main courses range from simple spaghettis to hearty slices of lasagne. A lively place for wine or coffee after a performance at the Cinémathèque or the Mann Auditorium.

White Gallery. 4 Kikar Ha-Bimah. ☎ **03/561-4730.** Appetizers NIS 14–33 ($4.20–$11); main courses NIS 25–40 ($7.50–$12). MC, V. Daily 9:30am–midnight. CONTINENTAL.

This is one of the most stylish places in town, both in terms of decor and menu, and it is filled with an interesting and often elegant Tel Aviv clientele en route to and from performances. Salads, pasta dishes, and the selection of quiches are all done with somewhat special touches, and desserts (especially those in the chocolate category) are excellent, making this a good place to stop for coffee and cake. With its pleasant piano bar, this is a spot where you can get a feel for the city's vibrant, sophisticated society. It is also an atmospheric choice for drinks and quiet talk.

NORTH BY THE YARKON RIVER

The neighborhood, just south of the Yarkon River, sometimes called Little Tel Aviv, is centered on Yirmiyahu Street, a short street near the point where Ben-Yehuda and Dizengoff streets meet, a block from the bend in the Yarkon. Take a bus or a cab north on Ha-Yarkon, Ben-Yehuda, or Dizengoff all the way to Yirmiyahu.

MODERATE

Mandy's Little Old Tel Aviv. 300 Ha-Yarkon St. ☎ **03/605-1282.** Appetizers NIS 15–33 ($4.50–$10); main courses NIS 33–63 ($10–$19). MC, V. Sun–Fri noon–12:30am; Sat noon–1:30am. Bus: 4 or 5 to end of Ben-Yehuda or Dizengoff. ECLECTIC.

At Mandy's, near Ha-Sira Street, you can order practically anything: crêpes, hamburgers, calamari (squid), steaks and kebabs, ice cream, pies and cakes, boiled beef and cholent, pasta, soups and salads. The drink list is equally bewildering, containing everything from sangría to Irish coffee. Staff are friendly and efficient, and you can pick out your decor as there are a myriad of rooms, nooks, porches, and booths. Most of Mandy's is done in mod-Victorian, with exposed brick, old furniture and mirrors, period pictures, and leafy plants. Drop in just for dessert, or afternoon tea, and a slice of chocolate cream cake with a cup of coffee will set you back about NIS 22 ($6.60). In case you've heard rumors, they're true—this friendly, flamboyant place was started by Mandy Rice Davies, who was part of the events that helped bring down the goverment of Prime Minister Harold Macmillan in the early 1960s.

Yo Si Peking. 302 Dizengoff St. ☎ **03/544-3687.** Appetizers: NIS 10–22 ($3–$6.60); main courses NIS 19–46 ($5.70–$13.90). AE, DC, MC, V. Sun–Thurs noon–midnight; Fri noon–3pm; Sat after Shabbat–midnight. GLATT KOSHER CHINESE.

Although by no means a budget restaurant, this large, busy establishment usually comes in a few shekels less than the other kosher Chinese choices in town. There's an extensive selection of dishes done in a variety of styles that are tasty, if not high on either American or Chinese authenticity. Soups here are rich and filling. Chicken, vegetarian, and noodle dishes are in the $7 to $12 range; beef, duck, fish, and veal choices are at the more expensive end of the price range.

INEXPENSIVE

⑤ Pollo Campero. 281 Dizengoff St. ☎ **03/604-8233.** Appetizers NIS 10–13 ($3–$4); full meals NIS 20–25 ($6–$7.50). DC, MC, V. Daily 12:30pm–1am. CHICKEN.

The best deal in North Tel Aviv, at this restaurant you'll find chickens barbecued over red hot stones, barbecued chicken innards, chicken breast skewers grilled with fresh vegetables, chickenburgers, and many interesting salads and side orders. A whole grilled chicken, served with cabbage, salsa, french fries, dressing, and pickles, comes to $20 and easily feeds two or three people. Takeout is also available.

JAFFA

EXPENSIVE

Le Relais Jaffa. 13 Ha-Dolphin St., Jaffa. ☎ **03/681-0637.** Reservations recommended. Appetizers NIS 12–25 ($3.60–$7.50); main courses NIS 40–70 ($12–$21). AE, MC, V. Daily noon–4pm and 7pm–midnight. Bus: 10 from Tel Aviv (see below for directions). FRENCH.

Housed in a 19th-century Mediterranean mansion with beautiful gardened terraces for summer dining, this has been a landmark among Israeli restaurants for years, and is a romantic choice for that special dinner that will take you to an out-of-the-way noncommercial area of Tel Aviv–Jaffa. Once there, you'll find a treasure chest of traditional French cuisine. Among the appetizers, try the oeufs duxelles, a creation of eggs, mushroom, and shallots in béchamel sauce; or you might choose from the selection of hearty, country-style pâtés. The entrecôte bordelaise ($15) allows you to sample one of the kitchen's classic sauces at a reasonable price, but the specialties of the house, like filet of Saint Peter's fish in basil sauce stuffed with leeks ($18), are also very worthwhile. The famous charlotte au chocolate is a must for dessert. Discount offers of 10% for this restaurant often appear in tourist publications.

Ask the bus driver for the stop on Yefet Street closest to Sha'arei Nicanor Street. Turn west (toward the sea) from Yefet Street onto Sha'arei Nicanor Street, and after three blocks, right onto Ha-Dolphin Street. A taxi is advised.

Shirat Hayam. 33 Hatzorfim St. ☎ **03/681-3271.** Reservations recommended. Appetizers NIS 10–30 ($3–$9); main courses NIS 33–66 ($10–$20). MC, V. Sun–Thurs noon–midnight; Sat evening from an hour and a half after the end of Sabbath to midnight. Closed Fri. Bus: 10 to Jaffa Clock Tower. GLATT KOSHER FISH AND MEAT.

Set in an atmospheric, restored building in the gardens at the top of the hill of Old Jaffa (near the Hammam), this restaurant offers wonderful views, and fish and meat dishes all done with a special touch. Among the first courses you'll find kosher "shrimp" in sesame, and salmon pâté; excellent fresh fish that can be ordered in a number of different ways is a major attraction here, but the Shirat Hayam baked duck is also quite famous. There is a large selection of interesting desserts and parve ice creams.

⭕ **Taboon.** Inside Jaffa Port. ☎ **03/681-1176.** Reservations recommended. Appetizers NIS 16–39 ($4.80–$12); main courses NIS 48–85 ($14.50–$26). AE, DC. Daily 12:30pm–midnight. Bus: 10 from Tel Aviv. SEAFOOD.

White minimalist decor is the setting for a menu filled with seafood creations that are breathtakingly light and fresh, prepared in a special taboon oven that preserves moisture and enhances flavor. Inventive yet subtle appetizers can be ordered as small meze dishes (each for $4.50), allowing you to sample the range of the kitchen. Among the constantly changing choices, you might choose a heavenly salmon carpaccio with dill; a bonito mousse; seafood-and-mushroom ravioli in a cream sauce flavored with garlic; veal brains and shrimp served on an apple-lemon mousse; or calamari rings in a ginger-lemon vermouth sauce. Among the main courses, you'll find fresh shrimps or fish, taboon baked with fresh herbs and served in a variety of sauces (simple olive oil and balsamic vinegar is recommended); spicy seafood ragout; and excellent salmon ravioli. Two rewarding choices are goose liver and grouper slices in port wine and tarragon sauce (grouper here is excellent in all forms) and taboon-baked trout with mushroom stuffing. Meats are also available, and most main courses come with potato, green salad, and the meze of the day. There's live classical music or jazz on varying afternoons and evenings. Two appetizers and a main course that can be shared make an interesting dinner for two.

Ask the bus driver for the Old Jaffa (Yafo Atik) stop, which is just after the Clock Tower on Yefet Street. Stroll southward through Old Jaffa, exit the restored area, walk downhill, and enter the fenced Jaffa Port. Taboon is to the left along the harbor.

⭕ **Victor and Margaret Tayar's.** 4 Retsif Ha-Aliyah Shenei St. ☎ **03/682-4741.** Reservations recommended. Always call to check opening hours. Appetizers NIS 12–30 ($3.60–$9); main courses NIS 33–65 ($10–$19.50). No credit cards. Oct 1–May 31, Mon–Sat 1–7pm; June 1–Sept 30, Mon–Fri noon–4pm, 7pm–midnight, Sat noon–7pm. Closed Sun. Bus: 10 to Jaffa Clock Tower. SEAFOOD.

This fish restaurant, a landmark for Jaffa and Tel Aviv locals, has regularly made the top of the Ten Best Restaurants in Israel list put out each year by *Ma'ariv*, one of the country's largest newspapers. In the worst of winter it's a four-table affair with a fisherlike interior, but as soon as the warmer weather arrives, the restaurant expands its easygoing spirit into a large covered terrace overlooking the sea. Whatever the season, you know you are in the presence of an inspired cook who loves to see people enjoying her creations. Portions are enormous, and everything is delicious, whether you choose deep-fried filet of fish stuffed with "caviar"; rolled grape leaves filled with rice, nuts, and raisins; baked artichoke stuffed with a smooth, creamy ground lamb filling; specially seasoned whole grilled fish; or fish or meat couscous. Margaret Tayar makes everything herself each day, from the marinated North African salads and spicy fish sauces (which you might want served on the side) to the strudel filled with Middle Eastern fruits. She is always whipping up masterpiece tidbits and she'll be happy to help you put together a dinner that displays the wonders of her kitchen for $25 to $35 per person (although portions here are so large that two can easily share this kind of feast). An à la carte choice will be much less.

INEXPENSIVE

Aladin. 5 Mifratz Shlomo St. ☎ **03/682-6766.** Reservations not accepted. Appetizers NIS 10–22 ($3–$6.60); main courses NIS 25–50 ($7.50–$15). AE, MC, V. Daily 11am–1am. MIDDLE EASTERN/EUROPEAN.

You couldn't ask for a more wonderful setting in which to dine: a 600-year-old building with covered terraces overlooking the sea and a spectacular view of the Tel Aviv coastline. The building's interior (which at one point in its long history was a Turkish bath) is decorated with exotic metalwork and design touches created 30 years ago by a Moroccan immigrant to Israel. This is the place to order a selection of Middle Eastern salads with pita bread, or have a slow unhurried meal of grilled fish or meat while watching the sunset. The atmosphere is informal and congenial and there's a good selection of wines, teas, and coffees over which you can enjoy the view.

Muscat. 15 Kikar Kedumim. ☎ **03/518-1147.** Appetizers NIS 9–16 ($2.70–$5); main courses NIS 22–49 ($6.60–$15). MC, V. Daily 10am–midnight. MIDDLE EASTERN.

The indoor room at Muscat, the most affordable of Old Jaffa's restaurants, is stuccoed and atmospheric. In good weather, the tables outside, overlooking Old Jaffa's main square, are a pleasant option. Overeating here is a distinct possibility, as the food is tempting and the prices reasonable. There are spicy soups, creamy hummus, stuffed vegetable (potato filled with meat and pine nuts is delicious), tangy salads filled with cauliflower or cabbage with caraway seeds or chopped eggplant, and lots of grilled meats and fish. Beef in a sauce of plums, figs, and wine, and herbed chicken are two of the dishes that set Muscat off from neighboring Middle Eastern spots.

Ⓢ **Said el Abu Lafia and Sons Pita Bakery.** 7 Yefet St. ☎ **03/683-4958.** Baked goods $1.75–$3. Mon–Sat 8am–10pm. Bus: 10 to Clock Tower. BAKERY.

Near the Clock Tower, this bakery offers fresh-from-the-oven breads, delicious one person Palestinian pita-bread pizzas, and peasant-style, filling cheese, potato, and vegetable bourekas and stuffed breads. Everything is take-away and the parks and vista points of Old Jaffa across the street and up the hill are ideal for picnics. Don't confuse Abu Lafia's with neighboring imitations. Bring lots of napkins.

6 Attractions

THE TOP ATTRACTIONS
MUSEUMS

Plan to visit Tel Aviv University and Bet Hatfutsot on the same trip north of the Yarkon River, as both of these sights are right together in Ramat Aviv. A smart way to do it is to catch a bus that goes all the way to Bet Hatfutsot in the center of the university campus, and have lunch at any of the many school cafeterias, while getting a feel for the university's California-style campus.

Ben-Gurion House. 17 Ben-Gurion Blvd. ☎ **03/5221-1010.** Free admission. Sun, Tues, Wed, Thurs 8am–3pm; Mon 8am–5pm; Fri 8am–noon; first Sat of each month 11am–2pm. Bus: 4 or 5.

The personal items belonging to Paula and David Ben-Gurion are shown as they were when they lived here. Ben-Gurion's personal scholarship and knowledge are very impressive; his library comprises some 20,000 books. Most of the signs in the museum are only in Hebrew, but this will not detract much from your visit. In the bedroom, there is a blocked-in window that was used as a bomb shelter.

Bet Bialik Museum. 22 Bialik St. ☎ **525-4530.** Free admission. Sun–Thurs 9am–4:30pm; Sat 10am–5pm. Closed Fri. Bus: 4.

This home of the great Hebrew writer Haim Nachman Bialik remains just as it was when he died. His 94 books, with translations in 28 languages, are there, as are articles, correspondence, paintings, photographs, and an archive of hundreds of his manuscripts. If you understand Hebrew or Yiddish the guides can tell you many interesting stories about the famous writer. The house gives you a feel for the world of the cultured, European-oriented Tel Aviv of the 1920s.

Tel Aviv Attractions

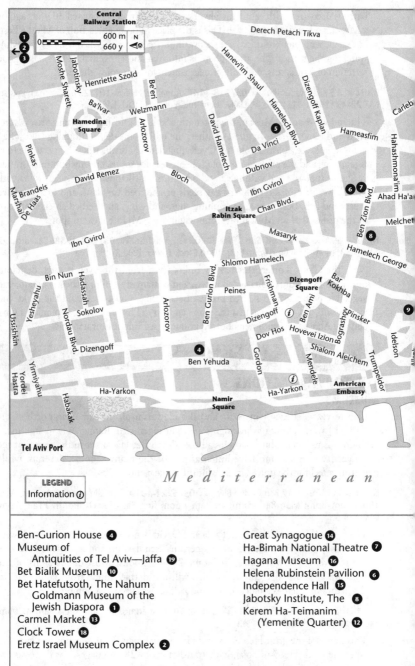

LEGEND
Information ⓘ

Ben-Gurion House ④
Museum of
    Antiquities of Tel Aviv—Jaffa ⑲
Bet Bialik Museum ⑩
Bet Hatefutsoth, The Nahum
    Goldmann Museum of the
    Jewish Diaspora ①
Carmel Market ⑬
Clock Tower ⑱
Eretz Israel Museum Complex ②

Great Synagogue ⑭
Ha-Bimah National Theatre ⑦
Hagana Museum ⑯
Helena Rubinstein Pavilion ⑥
Independence Hall ⑮
Jabotsky Institute, The ⑧
Kerem Ha-Teimanim
    (Yemenite Quarter) ⑫

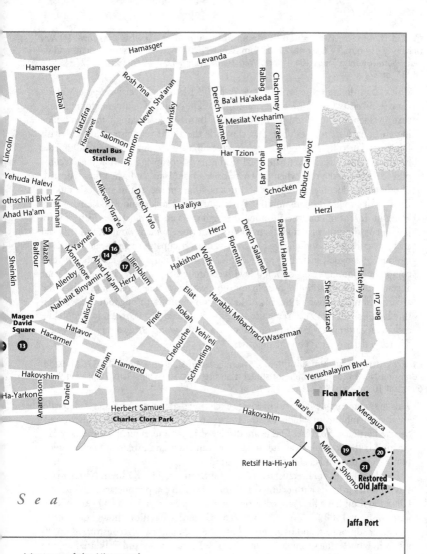

✪ **Bet Hatfutzot, the Nahum Goldmann Museum of the Jewish Diaspora**. Tel Aviv University campus. ☎ **03/646-2020.** Admission NIS 20 ($6). Discounts for students and seniors. Sun–Tues and Thurs 10am–5pm; Wed 10am–7pm; Fri 9am–2pm. Bus: 25, 27, 45, 49, 74, 86, or 274.

This extraordinary museum in Ramat Aviv, off Klausner Street inside the Matatia Gate (University Gate 2), was the brainchild of Dr. Nahum Goldmann, founder and first president of the World Jewish Congress. In the huge, strikingly modern building are countless artful exhibits that chronicle the 2,500-year history of the Jewish Diaspora. The collection contains no objects from the past, but is rather a multimedia history lesson: here is what happened to the Jewish people, and what they accomplished, between the time when they were driven from Israel and when they returned. Photographs, documents, replicas of artifacts, films, music, maps, and scale models vividly bring to life the communities, synagogues, households, and workshops of Jews living in dozens of countries. Among the highlights are a model of a 13th-century Jewish community with more than 100 tiny figurines of men, women, and children clad in period dress and engaged in their various occupations; and scale models of famous synagogues, including one in China in 1653. For a small fee you can get a computer printout on any of 3,000 Jewish communities—perhaps the home of your ancestors. Most rewarding, especially for those who have time for a return visit, is the archival film collection of dozens of Jewish communities throughout the world: a shtedl in Poland in 1912; Yemenite Jews in 1948; Salonika (Greece) in 1935. The archival recordings of Jewish music from all over the world are also very worthwhile. There's a dairy cafeteria on the premises.

✪ **Eretz Israel Museum Complex**. 2 Chaim Levanon St., Ramat Aviv. ☎ **03/641-5244.** Admission NIS 13 ($4). Discount for students and seniors. Sun–Thurs 9am–2pm; Wed 9am–6pm; Sat 10am–2pm. Bus: 24, 25, 27, 45, or 74.

This museum complex lies within a large enclosure that also encompasses **Tel Qasile,** an ancient mound in which 12 strata of past civilizations have been discovered. Selected artifacts from Tel Qasile are displayed in the museums, but especially fascinating is the archeological site, where you can enter and explore a rebuilt typical house from the pre-Israelite Canaanite period.

Besides Tel Qasile, Eretz Israel has eight attractions. The **Kadman Numismatic Pavilion** has exhibits chronicling the history of coinage and monetary systems. The **Glass Pavilion** has a fine, rare collection of glass vessels spanning 3,000 years of civilization, from 1500 B.C. to A.D. 1500. The **Ceramics Pavilion** shows how pottery was made, decorated, and used throughout the ages, and has a reconstructed dwelling from biblical times complete with pots. The **Ethnography and Folklore Pavilion** holds a wealth of Jewish ethnic art and handcrafts—household and religious items, jewelry, and costumes, set in scenes from daily life. The **Nechushtan Pavilion** is devoted to mining and metallurgy as practiced during biblical times in the Timna Valley, Arava, and Sinai. The **"Man and His Work" Center** holds displays showing how men and women have earned their daily bread in Israel since ancient times. For astronomy shows, there's the **Lasky Planetarium,** which proudly displays its collection of moon rocks and a mezuzah carried into space by the American astronaut Jeffrey Hoffman. An especially pleasant addition to the complex is a park called **Landscapes of the Holy Land,** a large expanse in which scenes once familiar in Israel will be reconstructed for modern visitors. The museum shop is well stocked with reproductions, jewelry, crafts, and other great gift choices.

Hagana Museum. 23 Rothschild Blvd. ☎ **03/560-8624.** Admission NIS 6 ($1.75). Sun–Thurs 9am–3pm; Fri 9am–noon. Bus: 1 or 4.

Established beside the home of Eliyahu Golomb, a former Hagana general, this is a fascinating place, well worth the visit. The museum records the history of the Israeli military from the time of the farm-field watchmen at the beginning of the century down through the War of Independence. Here are interesting photos, documents, uniforms, scale models, and weapons. On the third floor you see the various ways the Israelis hid arms inside farm machinery to escape British detection, and how they stealthily manufactured hand grenades and Sten guns in clandestine kibbutz workshops. There's one homemade grenade with the letters "USA" stamped on it, so that had a Hagana soldier been caught with the bomb, the British wouldn't have suspected that it had been made locally. But the joke here was that "USA" were the first letters of three Yiddish words meaning "Our piece of work." Other items relate to the Arab riots of 1937, the World War II Jewish Brigade that fought with the British throughout the Mediterranean and Middle East, and the bizarre authorization papers printed during the Exodus affair.

Almost all of the explanatory captions in this four-story museum are in Hebrew—but never fear, the museum has stationed a group of English-speaking interpreters.

Helena Rubinstein Pavilion. 6 Tarsat Blvd. ☎ **03/528-7196.** Admission NIS 14 ($4.30); includes admission to Tel Aviv Museum of Art nearby. Bus: 5, 18, or 25.

Here you'll find ever-changing exhibitions of works by Israeli and foreign artists. It's open the same hours as the Tel Aviv Museum of Art, with which it is affiliated.

Museum of Antiquities of Tel Aviv Jaffa (Jaffa Museum). 10 Mifratz Shlomo St. ☎ **03/682-5375.** Free admission. Sun–Thurs 9am–7pm; Wed 9am–6pm; Sat 10am–2pm.

The museum building was a Turkish administrative and detention center during the previous century. Displays in the five halls are of objects excavated from 30 sites within the city. They cover a time span beginning in the 5th millennium B.C. and ending with the Arab period.

To get there, at the top of the hill in Old Jaffa, walk from Kikar downhill on Mifratz Shlomo Street. The museum will be on your right.

Museum of the History of Tel Aviv Jaffa. 27 Bialik. ☎ **03/517-3052.** Free admission. Sun–Thurs 9am–2pm. Bus: 4.

This museum, housed in Tel Aviv's former City Hall, uses photographs, models, a film (in English), and documents to tell the story of the city's founding and early history. This museum may be closed for renovation in 1996–97.

✪ **Tel Aviv Museum of Art.** 27 Shaul Ha-Melekh Blvd. ☎ **03/696-1297.** Admission NIS 16 ($4.80); includes admission to Helena Rubinstein Pavilion. Discounts for students. Sun–Thurs 10am–9:30pm; Fri 10am–2pm; Sat 10am–2pm and 7–10pm.

✪ Frommer's Favorite Tel Aviv Experiences

Restored Old Jaffa. Spend a summer evening wandering this seaside casbah. Dine at one of the nearby restaurants overlooking the water.

The Beaches. My favorite is Gordon Beach, a quick dash from the many galleries in the Gordon Street area, handy to many eating spots.

Jaffa Flea Market. Magnet for some, too scuzzy for others, the market is now swamped with used jeans and Indian cotton blouses. You can still find objects from British Mandate and Early State periods plus under $10 reproductions of antique Moroccan menorahs. Bargain mercilessly.

This museum houses temporary as well as permanent exhibitions—paintings, drawings, prints, sculpture, photography of both Israeli and international artists from the 16th century to the present. The collections of modern and impressionist art are especially good and recently augmented by the addition of the Jaglom Collection of Impressionist and Post-Impressionist Art, including works by Pisarro, Matisse, Modigliani, and Chagall. Special exhibits are well chosen. Check out the mural by Roy Lichtenstein that adorns the entrance lobby.

Films, concerts, and lectures are also offered to the public. The Friday *Jerusalem Post* lists the museum's lively and well-attended events. Call for information about the museum's shuttle bus, which offers an interesting historical and architectural tour of Tel Aviv, and is included in the price of your admission ticket.

MORE ATTRACTIONS

Independence Hall. 16 Rothschild Blvd. ☎ **03/653-942.** Admission NIS 3 (90¢). Sun–Thurs 9am–2pm.

Meir Dizengoff, the first mayor of Tel Aviv, lived here, and it was in this historic house that the independence of Israel was declared in 1948.

Jabotinsky Institute. 38 King George St., Metzudat Zeev. ☎ **03/528-7320.** Free admission. Sun–Mon and Wed–Thurs 8am–3pm; Tues 8am–8pm; Fri 8am–1pm. Bus: 13, 24, 25, 26, or 61.

This historical research institute is devoted to the study of the activist trend in the Jewish Resistance Movement. Archives connected with the activities of Nili, the Jewish Legion in World War I, the right-wing Revisionist Zionist Movement, Betar, Irgun Zevai Leumi, Fighters for the Freedom of Israel (Lehi), and other organizations are preserved.

Rubin Museum. 14 Bialik St. ☎ **03/517-8961.** Admission NIS 5 ($1.50). Sun–Mon and Wed–Thurs 10am–2pm; Tues 10am–1pm and 4–8pm; Sat 11am–2pm. Closed Sat during July and August.

Israeli painter Reuven Rubin captured on canvas the spirit and the sights of Mandate Palestine. Though the holy cities of Jerusalem and Safed were among his favorite subjects, he also painted scenes of Tel Aviv, his home city. The Rubin Museum hosts temporary exhibits, usually of modern Israeli artists.

Safari Park (Zoological Center). Ramat Gan. ☎ **03/631-2181.** Admission NIS 26 ($7.80) adults, NIS 22 ($6.60) children. Sun–Thurs 9am–4pm; Fri 9am–1pm. Bus: 30 (Yona Ha-Navi Street), 35 (Central Bus Station), or 67 (Central Ramat Gan).

The park is a wide-open plain (250 acres) where African animals roam free. For obvious reasons, visitors must remain in closed vehicles while traversing the 5-mile trail, but there is a shorter walking trail as well. You will have the opportunity to see lions, elephants, rhinos, giraffes, gazelles, impalas, zebra, ostriches and storks, and many more. Across the street is the Ramat Gan National Park, with its new Man and the Living World Museum.

Simon's House. 8 Shimon Ha-Burski St. ☎ **03/683-6792.** Free admission. Daily 8–11:45am and 2–4pm (until 6:30pm in summer).

Christian tradition places the house of Simon the Tanner next to the lighthouse of the port, at the site of a small mosque. Acts 10 recalls Saint Peter's visit to Simon's house in "Joppa."

To get there, walk south through Kikar Kedumim, the main square of restored Old Jaffa. At the end of the square turn right to the steps.

Tel Aviv University. RAMAT AVIV.

It has a handsome, multifaceted campus with architecture and landscaping reminiscent of a branch of the California State University system. Thirty-five buildings house the widest spectrum of studies of any university in Israel and its enrollment of 18,000 students is the largest as well. Courses for English-speaking students are given here. You can combine a stroll around the grounds with a visit to Bet Hatfutzot (see above), which is on the university's grounds.

World of Silence Sea Aquarium. Herbert Samuel Esplanade. ☎ **03/510-6670.** Admission NIS10 ($3). Sun–Thurs 9am–6pm; Fri 9am–3pm.

Here you'll find local Mediterranean creatures as well as tanks inhabited by denizens of the Red Sea and international waters. A separate exhibit houses snakes, reptiles, scorpions, and tarantulas.

Dolphinarium. Herbert Samuel Esplanade. ☎ **03/510-4477.** Admission NIS 10 ($3). Sun–Thurs 9am–6pm; Fri 9am–3pm.

On the beach next to the World of Silence, the dolphins on display here give performing sessions throughout the day.

ESPECIALLY FOR KIDS

Eretz Israel Museum is great for kids: it has demonstrations of traditional crafts, a planetarium, a reconstructed Canaanite period house, and a nature exhibit. See "Top Attractions," above.

Bet Hatfutzot/Diaspora Museum is a real learning experience for all ages. Many exhibits are especially geared to the young. See "Top Attractions," above.

Safari Park is great for older children, who will enjoy this park where wild animals of all kinds roam free. See "More Attractions," above.

World of Silence Sea Aquarium is for children of all ages, who will enjoy the sea creatures and will be thrilled by the reptiles. See "More Attractions," above.

Shalom Meyer Tower contains Mayerland, an amusement park with rides, and the Wax Museum of events in Israeli history. See "Strolling Around Tel Aviv's Main Streets & Squares," below.

STROLLING AROUND TEL AVIV'S MAIN STREETS & SQUARES
ALLENBY STREET

This street begins at the seaside and was named after the British general who took Palestine from the Turks in 1917. It is full of furniture stores, bakeries, bookstores, kiosks, and screeching buses. In all of its hustle and bustle, Allenby is what's considered a typical Tel Avivan street.

Between Montefiore and Ahad Ha-Am streets, on Allenby, is the domed **Great Synagogue** (1926), the largest in Tel Aviv. Its extensive exterior renovations were completed in the 1970s.

Go around the corner to Ahad Ha-Am Street; one block down is the 34-story **Shalom Mayer Tower (Migdal Shalom).** It is a commercial shopping center, housing a large department store, shops, and offices. The view from the observatory can be magnificent, especially if you use the telescopes set out for that purpose. Take the glass elevator to the top where there is a cafe. For kids the Shalom Tower offers Mayerland, an amusement park with many kinds of rides, and the typical goodies such as cotton candy, ice cream, and popcorn. There is a Wax Museum (admission $3.60) that depicts events in Israeli history, personalities, and in some cases sensational news items. The amusement park, observatory, and wax museum are open Sunday through Thursday from 9am to 7pm, on Friday and holiday eves until 2pm.

CARMEL MARKET, THE YEMENITE QUARTER & NEVE TSEDEK

Going uptown, where Allenby Road approaches Magen David Square, there is a six-sided intersection, where you'll find a colorful market area, the Carmel Market (see "Shopping," below). Opposite the market, at the King George Street intersection, you'll see freelance housepainters gather, simply hanging around and waiting for a floor to scrub or a wall to paint. Tuesdays and Fridays from 10am to 5pm, there's an arts and crafts market, complete with street performers at **Nahalat Binyamin,** off Allenby Street at the edge of the Carmel Market.

Kerem Ha-Teimanim (the Yemenite Quarter) is just north of the Carmel Market, and if you are eager for a meal, you are near the source of some of the best, but slightly touristy, Middle Eastern dining (see "Where to Dine" above). Although it looks a bit shabby, Karem Ha-Teimanim is a perfectly safe network of narrow lanes and alleys. If you get a bit lost, just ask—people will be helpful. At Allenby Street near the sea you can pick up Ha-Yarkon Street, the hotel, cafe, and embassy row; and Herbert Samuel Esplanade for Tel Aviv strolling.

Just south of the Carmel Market is **Neve Tsedek,** the oldest and once the most run-down part of the city; the new **Suzanne Dellal Center for Performing Arts** is turning this area into a mildly trendy, picturesque neighborhood.

ROTHSCHILD BOULEVARD

The center of **Tel Aviv's cultural life** is at the northern end of tree-lined Rothschild Boulevard. Clustered here together are the Ha-Bimah Theater, a youth museum; the big Mann Auditorium, home of the Israel Philharmonic (IPO); and Gan Yaakov Park. (See "Tel Aviv & Jaffa After Dark," below, for details on the Ha-Bimah and the Mann Auditorium.) Farther south along Rothschild, in the center of the island at Nahalat Benyamin Street, is the impressive **Founder's Monument,** depicting the three phases of Tel Aviv's history. The bottom shows the workers of 1909 digging and planting, while snakes and animals form a lower border. The middle level shows the Herzlia Gymnasium (which was demolished in 1959); the uppermost section is modern Tel Aviv, with the Ha-Bimah Theater, Bialik's home, and many modern houses.

DIZENGOFF SQUARE

At the center of the plaza suspended above the roadway is a huge sculpture-fountain by Yaacov Agam named *Water and Fire.* Five large concentric metal rings are painted so that when the rings turn, the painted surfaces produce differing effects of light and color. At the same time, jets of water shoot upward from the rings, and at the top of the sculpture, in the midst of the shooting water, rises a jet of flame! Music accompanies the whole marvelous display in a show that lasts for 20 minutes. Agam's computerized sculpture begins to play at the beginning of each hour starting at 11am and continuing until 10pm. If you arrive a few minutes early, you may be able to get a seat on one of the benches surrounding the sculpture.

Two blocks south of the square, toward King George Street, you'll find the enormous indoor **Dizengoff Center Shopping Mall.** North of the square, Dizengoff Street is filled with fast-food stops, cafes, and restaurants.

GORDON STREET

If you'd like a look at what's happening in the Israeli art world, you'll find that Gordon Street and the cross streets, from Ha-Yarkon to Dizengoff streets, are almost wall-to-wall galleries and unusual shops. Unlike the art districts in other cities, the foot of Gordon Street offers you the chance for a pleasant dip in the Mediterranean at one of the city's best beaches when you finish making your rounds.

A STROLL AROUND OLD JAFFA

The reclamation of Old Jaffa—only a short time ago a slumlike area of war ruins and crumbling Turkish palaces—has proven to be one of the most imaginative such projects in all Israel. Atop the hill and running down in a maze of descending streets to the sea are artists' studios and galleries, outdoor cafes, fairly expensive restaurants, and gift shops, all artfully arranged among the reconstructed ruins. Climb to the top of the hill and wander through the lanes (named for the Hebrew signs of the zodiac). At the summit is **Kikar Kedumim,** the central plaza, and at one side of it, the **Franciscan Monastery of Saint Peter,** which was built above a medieval citadel. You can visit the church for prayers on Sunday. Opposite the church is an excavation area, surrounded by a fence, where you can inspect remnants of a **3rd-century** B.C. **catacomb.** Facing the catacomb is a hilltop garden, **Gan Ha-Pisgah,** atop which, surrounded by trees, is a white monument depicting scenes from the Bible: the conquest of Jericho, the near-sacrifice of Isaac, and Jacob's dream.

Past the church gardens, on the sea side of the hill, is a small and charming cafe. Wander through the elaborately decorated dome-roofed room and out onto the deck, from which the all-encompassing view of Tel Aviv and the Mediterranean coastline is superb. Incidentally, **Andromeda's Rock** is the most prominent of those blackened stones jutting up from the floor of the bay. The view is the most brilliant in the morning sunlight. At night it takes on more of a fairy-tale aura.

A short (quarter-mile) stroll south of Old Jaffa brings you to the disused port of **Jaffa Harbor,** now a fenced-in area of dockside restaurants.

ORGANIZED TOURS

The **Association for Tourism of Tel Aviv–Jaffa** leads a free walking tour of Old Jaffa on Wednesday mornings. Call the Tel Aviv Tourist Information Office (☎ 03/ 639-5660) or the Jaffa Visitors Center (☎ 03/682-6796) for current information. The new **Jaffa Visitors Center in Kikar Kedumim,** right at the center of the restored section of Old Jaffa, gives out detailed free maps of Old Jaffa accompanied by historical information that makes it easy to do a self-guided tour of the area. The helpful Visitors Center is open Sunday through Thursday from 9am to 6pm. The **Tel Aviv Municipal Tourist Information Office** (6th floor, New Central Bus Station) also gives out free Jewish municipal maps with four "Orange" self-guided walking tour routes marked on the map. Signs along the routes mark the way as you go. Some of the routes are too long to undertake on a sweltering summer day, but if you break them up into smaller units, they are a good basic itinerary of what to see in different neighborhoods.

Another good source of guided tours is the **Society for the Protection of Nature in Israel,** 4 Ha-Shfela St. (☎ 03/369-0644). These tours are for individuals or families, for a fee.

Run by former Americans, **Off the Beaten Track** (☎ 03/641-4586) offers interesting day tours of the Tel Aviv area and trips to unusual sites of natural beauty or social and historical interest throughout Israel. Groups are small and all tours originate in Tel Aviv. A schedule of Off the Beaten Track's tours is usually printed in the Tourist Information Office's monthly calendar of events. You can also telephone for information. Prices vary according to each tour. Highly recommended.

SPECIAL/FREE EVENTS

Many evenings after 8pm, in the summer, there is often free samba dancing on the Herbert Samuel Esplanade, beside the beach in South Tel Aviv. There is also music and dancing at other points along the beach on evenings throughout the week. Check with the Tourist Information Office (☎ 03/639-5660) for current information.

There are free evening outdoor concerts in the Yarkon Park and in Old Jaffa during the summer. Check the newspapers or the government tourist office for dates.

Nahalat Benyamin Pedestrian Mall, off Allenby Street, every Tuesday and Friday from 10am to 5pm, has an outdoor craft bazaar and street performers. Take bus no. 4.

7 Sports & Outdoor Activities

BEACHES Tel Aviv's seashore is within walking distance of Dizengoff Square. A promenade runs the entire length of the beach. Most beaches have free showers and facilities for changing clothes. The cleanest beaches in the city are behind the Dan and Sheraton hotels (Frishman to Gordon streets) and at the Hilton Hotel.

In a slightly more remote location, the **Bat Yam Beach,** 3 miles south of Jaffa, is wide and sandy, and gets crowded only on hot Saturdays in summer. From Ben-Yehuda Street, you can take bus no. 10, which begins its run at the City Hall.

Facing Kikar Namir and the Hilton is the **Hof Hadarim (Orange Beach),** more generally known as the Hilton Beach. Entrance and use of changing rooms are free; you can rent lockers and deck chairs. A snack bar and restaurant are also at this beach.

A word of caution: Swimming at Israeli beaches can be dangerous. Every summer the local papers report a large number of drownings. The problem is an incredibly unpredictable undertow that can be hazardous even for a strong swimmer. It's safe, however, to swim at beaches where guards are stationed. Pay attention to the safety symbols, in the form of small flags, along Israeli beaches. The color of the flag tells the story: black means absolutely no swimming in the area, red warns you to be especially cautious, and white indicates that the water's fine. Tel Aviv's city beaches are protected in many places by a system of breakwaters and are the safest in the area.

JOGGING The long beachfront promenade, running several miles, from the northern end of Jaffa to the Hilton Hotel, provides an excellent stretch for urban jogging, without the inconvenience of cross streets and traffic lights. It's busy, which adds an element of safety, and you can stop for a dip in the sea or cool off at the public showers that dot the beaches at various intervals! There is a jogging track at **Sportek, Rokach Boulevard,** at the northern entrance of Tel Aviv (☎ 03/699-0307). Admission to the track is free.

SAILING Small sailboats are availble to rent by the hour on the lake at **Yarkon Park,** near Yehoshua Gardens (☎ 03/642-0541) at the northern end of the city, daily from 9am to 6pm. At the **Tel Aviv Sea Center,** in Marina Atarim (☎ 03/522-4079), in front of Namir (Atarim) Square between the Carlton and Hilton hotels, you can rent a sailboat by the hour, with or without skipper. The marina is open from 9am to 5pm daily. An alternative is merely looking—and it's a pretty sight too, seeing those bright white and striped sails on the waves. You can also rent windsurfing equipment.

SWIMMING There's a seawater Olympic swimming pool open year-round at Gordon Street (☎ 03/527-1555), on the beach facing Namir Square. The pool is open from 4am to 5pm, until 6 or 7pm in summer.

8 Shopping

MARKETS

Carmel Market (Shuk Ha-Carmel). Magen David Square.

At this six-sided intersection you enter the throbbing open-air market where vendors hawk everything from pistachios and guavas to sunhats and memorial candles on open tables lining the many shopping streets. Many vendors have their own songs, which tell you all about the price and quality of what is being sold. Sometimes one vendor sings against another in a competitive duet. The market runs into side streets, large and small, one side favoring dry goods, and the other dried beans, fruit, nuts, and spices in all colors and fragrances, sold from sacks. The market is open Sunday through Thursday from 8am until dark and on Friday from 8am to 2pm.

Jaffa Flea Market. East of the Clock Tower at foot of Old Jaffa.

Tradition has it that you can get the best buys here early Sunday morning. If you are the first customer on the first day of the week, the seller hopes a quick sale will bring him luck through the week. You can weave your way in and out sorting through a mixed array of treasures and junk. The kinds of merchandise change from time to time, but copper, brass, and jewelry are always to be found. Bargaining is the order of the day and expected; feel free to indulge in lengthy haggling. Even if there is a little language problem, you can get a lot understood with your hands. It's great fun even if you don't buy anything.

The flea market is open Sunday through Thursday from 10am to 6pm and on Friday from 10am to 2pm. Take bus no. 10 from Ben-Yehuda Street in Tel Aviv.

CRAFTS

Cad Al Hayam. 1 Allenby St. ☎ **03/517-1423.**

A contemporary ceramics gallery on the second floor of the Opera Tower Shopping Arcade, this shop carries the work of a number of top-quality ceramists.

Contemporary Crafts. Nahlat Binyamin Pedestrian Mall.

This outdoor craft market, held every Tuesday and Friday, is filled with ceramics, jewelry, hands of Fatima, menorahs, and interesting gift items. This is one of the best weekly craft markets I've encountered, and prices are both fair and affordable. At the edge of the market, you'll often find a group of Druze women from the Galilee making delicious, freshly baked Druze-style bread.

FASHION

North Tel Aviv is the country's center for quality women's clothing and custom-designed lines. Considering that style was almost considered sinful in the early Zionist movement, there has been a revolution in Israeli attitudes, especially in the past few years. Among the many and varied places to explore are **Gideon Oberson's** stylish designer showroom at 36 Gordon St. (☎ 03/524-3822)—Oberson has moved from bathing suits to custom fashion; **Dorin Frankfurt** at 40 Ben Gurion St., near Dizengoff (☎ 03/527-9915), an acclaimed Israeli whose designs tend to natural textiles and easy, elegant lines; **Tessa**, at 278 Dizengoff (☎ 03/544-4991), carrying Paris imports from Evi Lili, Givenchy, Weill, and Ricci; **Pour Toi,** 224 Ben Yehuda St. (☎ 03/544-2444), with lines by Israeli designers Hani Yaacobson and Adi Bermann; and **Touching,** 274 Dizengoff (tel 03/544-5405), the little workshop of Irena Burstein, a Russian immigrant whose clothing is "soft, natural, a bit naughty and for those 28 to 50 something." A stroll through the upper reaches of Dizengoff and Ben-Yehuda streets will reveal many additional shops and designer showrooms.

YEMENITE JEWELRY & JUDAICA

Ben Zion David Yemenite Silver Art. 3 Mazal Dagim St. Old Jaffa. ☎ **03/681-2503.**

You can see Yemenite-style silver jewelry, with its intricate filigree patterns, at shops throughout Israel; at Ben Zion David's workshop and showroom, in the heart of the beautifully restored Old Jaffa bazaar, you'll find some of the best examples of crafts-manship and design in this tradition created by over a thousand years of Yemenite Jewish silversmiths. The many branches of the David family have been skilled silver workers for generations; perhaps because of the family's long reputation for quality and fairness, prices here are quite reasonable, despite the upmarket tourist location. There's an enormous selection of earrings, bracelets, rings, and necklaces, as well as delicate mezuzzot, candlesticks, and Hanukkah dreidels, all ornamented with fine fili-gree designs. The showroom is generally open Sunday through Thursday from noon until late in the evening, Friday from 11am to 3pm, and on Saturday evenings after Shabbat. Credit cards are accepted.

SHOPPING MALLS & DEPARTMENT STORES

Dizengoff Center Mall. Dizengoff and King George streets.

Located on the lower floors of a mega-office complex, this is a modern, jam-packed, multilevel shopping center filled with housewares, a large array of clothing, and spe-cialty shops. There are many fast-food counters, including a branch of the American Pizza Hut. It is open Sunday through Thursday from 9:30am to 9pm; Friday from 9:30am to 2pm.

Hamashbir Lazarchan. 115 Allenby St.

This department store is a part of a chain throughout the country. It offers a huge assortment of merchandise, from the basement with kitchenware, a milk bar, and a supermarket, on up through its escalated levels. Goods are serviceable (some items come from Marks and Spencer in the U.K.) but this is not Bloomingdale's. It's a good place to pick up basics you might not have brought with you. Open Sunday through Thursday from 8:30am to 7pm, Friday until 2pm.

Opera Tower. 1 Allenby St.

This brand-new luxury mall, right where Allenby Street meets the sea and a short walk from the Ha-Yarkon Street hotel district, takes its name from the municipal Opera House that was located on this site during British Mandate times. Well stocked with cafes, galleries, and shops of interest to tourists, the mall is developing into some-thing of a center for fashionable clothing. The Opera Tower is the centerpiece for the revival of a neighborhood that had been an architectural and social dazzle in the 1930s and 1940s, before sliding into a period of decline. It is open standard busi-ness hours, with some cafes remaining open later in the evening.

9 Tel Aviv & Jaffa After Dark

It doesn't matter what the season or the weather is, Tel Aviv throbs with activity after sundown. Strollers are out on the boulevards, people-watchers crowd the cafes, clubs and discos throb and crash, and restaurants are packed.

Tel Aviv's single most popular nighttime activity is strolling, sipping, and munch-ing along the seaside promenade or in the vicinity of Dizengoff Square. This diversion costs very little, is always amusing, and often exciting. For something more organized, try a cinema, concert, ballet, opera, or theater performance.

First thing to do when you plan your nighttime activities is to have a copy of the *Jerusalem Post*, preferably the Friday-morning edition, which contains the weekend magazine with all its listings of things to do and see. (If you buy your Friday *Jerusalem Post* in the Tel Aviv area, it will contain an additional, informative "In Tel Aviv" section.) Next thing to do is pick up a copy of "Events in the Tel Aviv Region" from the tourist office at 5 Shalom Aleichem St., or from a hotel lobby. Armed with these sources of information, you're ready to explore Tel Aviv by night.

THE PERFORMING ARTS

While Jerusalem has many cultural offerings, Tel Aviv is the true cultural center of Israel. Mann Auditorium is the home of the Israel Philharmonic, and there are many other musical groups. The Israel Ballet is also centered in Tel Aviv. Major ticket outlets are **Le'an,** 101 Dizengoff (☎ 03/227-7373), and **Rokoko,** 93 Dizengoff (☎ 03/522-3663).

CONCERTS, OPERA & DANCE

Bet He-Hayal (The Soldiers' House). 60 Weizmann Blvd. ☎ **03/546-4242.**

This venue has a variety of performances. The **Israel Ballet** often performs at Bet He-Hayal. Ticket prices vary, depending on the company performing.

Israel Philharmonic Orchestra. Huberman St. ☎ **03/528-9163.**

The **Mann Auditorium,** which can seat 3,000 concertgoers, is the home of this prestigious orchestra. Bronislaw Huberman founded the orchestra in 1936 by bringing together renowned European musicians who had become refugees in what was then Palestine. Some of the world's leading conductors and soloists— Arturo Toscanini, Serge Koussevitzky, Leonard Bernstein, Arthur Rubinstein, Isaac Stern, Jascha Heifetz, Yehudi Menuhin, and Zubin Mehta, now music director—have appeared with the orchestra. Yet even now that the magnificent concert hall has been built, the orchestra continues to give performances in other towns, carrying on a tradition that began during the War of Independence, when it played just behind the lines for the troops near Jerusalem and Beersheva. The orchestra is on vacation during August, September, and October until after the Jewish holidays.

New Israeli Opera. 28 Leonardo Da Vinci St. ☎ **03/692-7700.**

Housed in the **Tel Aviv Center for the Performing Arts,** a recently completed center that is both architecturally interesting and controversial, the New Israeli Opera is the country's newest cultural gem, performing a lively program of classic and modern opera. The company draws heavily on the talent of new immigrants from the former Soviet Union.

Suzanne Dellal Center for Dance and Theater. 6 Yehieli St. ☎ **03/510-5656.**

This new complex, built in postmodern style, is the venue for visiting dance groups as well as Israel's contemporary **Bat Sheva Dance Company,** and the **Inbal Dance Theater,** which often draws upon Israel's ethnic traditions for its style. The Dellal Center hosts interesting modern and experimental theater productions, as well as a wide range of concerts and music events, and has become the heart of the effort to revive and restore the old, potentially quaint Neve Tzedik neighborhood of Tel Aviv. Buses 10 and 25 pass nearby.

Tel Aviv Museum of Art. 27 Shaul Ha-Melekh Blvd. ☎ **03/696-1297.**

The museum hosts a wide range of afternoon and evening events, including music recitals, performances of chamber orchestras and ensembles, visiting choirs, theater and dance performances, and film screenings. There is a cafe on the premises for refreshments.

ZOA House. 1 Daniel Frisch St. ☎ **03/695-9341.**

The ZOA House at the corner of Ibn Gevirol, has a variety of activities, including English theater and play readings, Israeli folksinging with guest performers, lectures, concerts, art exhibitions, and celebrations in honor of Israeli and American holidays.

THEATER

Ha-Bimah National Theater. Kikar Ha-Bimah. ☎ **03/526-6666.**

Founded in Moscow in 1918 by the renowned Stanislavsky, and moved to British Mandate Palestine in 1928, the Ha-Bimah National Theater is the nation's first and best-known repertory theater. The great Russian artist inspired the group and it went on to achieve a fantastic reputation, both in Palestine and at other great theaters throughout the world. While some performances are in English, most are in Hebrew. This theater was the first to present Hebrew translations of plays by Shakespeare, Molière, Shaw, and O'Neill. Ticket prices vary, depending on the company performing.

Cameri Theater. 101 Dizengoff St. ☎ **03/523-3335.**

This theater presents both repertory classics and new Israeli plays. Tuesday evenings there are simultaneous translations in English. Orchestra and mezzanine seats generally cost about $25; balcony seats are $20. Earphone rental is an additional $1.50.

THE CLUB & MUSIC SCENE

Between them, Tel Aviv and Jaffa are the nightlife centers of Israel. Their clubs have been the breeding ground for almost all Israeli singers who have gone on to international popularity. But the real center of things—Israel's Montmartre—is located in Old Jaffa, on the side of the hill that slopes toward Tel Aviv. Here creative minds have taken wrecked Turkish baths and once grand palaces and made several different and very esoteric (and often wildly expensive) clubs.

Along with the sidewalk cafes, Tel Aviv–Jaffa is full of discos. Some are on rather tacky-looking streets, but that's no indication they'll be cheap; the atmosphere can be very different inside. Check the prices carefully before you start downing the drinks.

As for full-fledged nightclubs, they tend to be in the larger hotels, or in Old Jaffa. Many charge for cover and drinks at "international" rates. In Tel Aviv proper, a number of clubs and organizations are dependable for good evening entertainment. For current offerings, check the *Jerusalem Post* or "Events in the Tel Aviv Region."

DANCE CLUBS & DISCOS

Caravan Night Club. 10 Mifratz Shlomo, Old Jaffa. ☎ **03/6828-255.**

At the tourist-oriented Caravan, the high-arched windows offer a magnificent view of the Tel Aviv–Jaffa area. (Framed by two mosques and the tall Jaffa minaret in the foreground, and bounded by the Mediterranean breakers on the west, the Tel Aviv coastline gracefully curls northward in a busy, crowded, serpentine panorama.) At 10:30pm there is a show of international artists (including striptease). Dancing is resumed after the show. It's open Monday through Saturday from 8pm to 2am. Admission may be charged, depending on the performer.

The Cave. 14 Kikar Kedumim, Old Jaffa. ☎ **03/6829-018.** Cover NIS 20 ($6).

This popular touristy club features singers, dancers, and a folklore troupe.

Elizabeth. Inside Jaffa Port. ☎ **03/681-4752.**

A popular disco just south of the restored Old Jaffa area, Elizabeth gets moving Thursday and Friday nights after midnight, with a mainly over-22 (post–Israeli army) crowd, and on Saturday after 8pm for the younger 19-to-22 crowd. Admission is about $6, but varies according to the program. Bus 10 from Tel Aviv will bring you nearby before midnight, but after public transport stops at midnight, you'll need a cab.

Lemon. 17 Hangarim St. ☎ **03/681-3313.**

There are a variety of special nights here, including for the over-28 crowd (usually on Thursdays) and gays (often on Monday nights after midnight). Cover charges vary. It's always best to phone ahead for information.

Rendez-Vous Supper Club. 77 Ben Yehuda St. ☎ **03/524-8034.**

A favorite of the Russian community, this restaurant serves chicken kiev and other Russian dishes every night while a four-piece band and singer perform Russian and popular music, and the dance floor fills up with a mixture of Israeli Russians and tourists. Dinner and dancing is from 8pm to 2am nightly; the food is in the moderate price range ($20 per person excluding drinks).

Roxanne. 10 HaBarzel St., Ramat Aviv. ☎ **03/648-4222.**

Specializing in rock music with onstage Israeli and foreign performing groups, Roxanne, in an outlying area of the city, gets going after midnight Wednesday through Saturday. It's the biggest and most active rock disco in town, with a capacity of over 1,300. Admission is usually about $7, but can be higher, depending on what group is performing. You'll need to come and go by cab.

Soweto. 6 Frishman St. ☎ **03/524-0825.**

Conveniently located in the HaYarkon Street hotel district, Soweto is into reggae and rap and is open Monday through Saturday from 10pm until near dawn. Monday through Wednesday, the crowd is generally mid-20s or older; Thursday through Saturday, the age level drops to the upper teens. There is usually an interesting mix of Israelis, tourists, Ethiopians, and other Africans here. Entrance fee, including a beer, can be $8 on weekdays and $12 on Friday and Saturday nights, depending on performances.

Yoel Sharr's Omar Khayam. Kedumim Square, Old Jaffa. ☎ **03/682-5865.**

This very exotic club, mainly for tourists, is actually a huge room in an old Arab mansion, with lofty vaulted ceilings and stone walls. Omar Khayam abounds with atmosphere—fish netting strung about, soft candles on every table. Top Israeli singers and pianists appear nightly. The show starts at 10:45pm, but come earlier to get good seats. Open 9:30pm to 1:30am. Admission, including one drink, may be charged, depending on the performers.

Zman Amiti. 8 Eilat St., Jaffa. ☎ **03/681-0231** or 812-657.

A sometimes busy place, serving up a variety of music, Zman Amiti hosts twice monthly gay nights (usually on Thursdays—call for information) and once monthly lesbian evenings, in association with the Society for Protection of Personal Rights. Open Thursday from midnight for those over 20 and Friday from midnight for the 18-and-over crowd.

JAZZ & BLUES

Bet Lessin. 34 Weizmann. ☎ **03/695-6222.**

This club hosts jazz groups many nights as well as contemporary and folk musicians.

Logos. 14 Nahalat Benyamin St. ☎ **03/5661-176.**

Located not far from the up-and-coming Neve Tzedek neighborhood south of the Carmel Market, this bar features excellent live rock, blues, or jazz performers nightly at 11pm. Cover charges vary according to performers. Beer is $2.50; mixed drinks start at $5.

Tzavta. 30 Ibn Gevirol St. ☎ **03/695-0156.**

This club specializes in Israeli music, both folk and popular.

THE BAR SCENE

HOTEL BARS

A singer and a pianist appear nightly at the **Dan's Bar,** and the **Europa Bar** at the Ramada Continental also features nightly piano music. The Hilton offers the **Coral Piano Bar,** the Radisson Moriah Plaza has the **Marina Bar,** and the Basel has a very pleasant bar. Best of all is the **Beach Bar** at the Grand Beach, where there's dancing nightly at the pool and dining at the rooftop **Barbecue Bar.**

PUBS

Joey's Bar. 42 Allenby St. ☎ **03/517-9277.**

An American-style bar run by Americans, Joey's well-stocked bar is a haven for 30-something semi-yuppie travelers. Music is American rock from the 1960s, '70s, and '80s; beer starts at $3. Open daily from 5pm to 8am.

M.A.S.H. (More Alcohol Served Here). 275 Dizengoff St. ☎ **03/605-1007.**

Small, crowded, filled with tourists, the music is '60s and '70s, and the bar is well stocked. A local landmark. Beer costs NIS 8 ($2.40); mixed drinks begin at NIS 18 ($5.40). There's lots of pub-style food for the hungry and daytime cable TV for those who want to keep up with the news.

Terminal. Corner of Gordon and Ha-Yarkon streets. ☎ **03/544-0585.**

On the ground floor of the Gordon Youth Hostel, facing the sea, this is one of Tel Aviv's busiest pubs, crowded with conversation by late afternoon, throbbing with music, and overflowing onto the street with activity on summer nights. The music is disco, rock, and blues; the crowd is part Tel Avivan, part international, and part backpacker. Beer is NIS 7 ($2.10); other drinks NIS 7 to NIS 27 ($2.10 to $8). Snacks and pub meals range from NIS 10 to NIS 27 ($3 to $8). Open daily 9am to 4pm.

CAFE LIFE

One of the most popular forms of nighttime entertainment in Tel Aviv is to stroll around and people-watch. Two areas are traditionally popular for this pastime: Dizengoff Street and the Herbert Samuel Esplanade—Ha-Tayelet—which runs along the sandy beach. (Women take note: It's best to walk or sit in pairs in this second area, particularly at night.) Before you pick out a seat for yourself at one of the sidewalk cafes, however, make sure you understand that you will have to pay up to three times as much here for coffee as you would anywhere else. If it's hot, cool off with a coffee ice-cream soda, one of the most popular Israeli drinks, or apple cider, very refreshing and tasty.

Outdoor cafe life on Dizengoff Street starts near Dizengoff Square, and works northward. The "scene" is pretty packed most nights, but its real crescendo is reached on Saturday nights after the movies let out.

You might even take a romantic stroll to a lovely little park that juts out on a promontory 100 feet above the rolling surf. It's called Gan Ha-Atzma'ut, and it's located north of the Hilton Hotel, on upper Ha-Yarkon Street.

FILM

Tel Aviv has at least two dozen cinema houses, and they don't dub the English or American films. You can enjoy first-run shows for around NIS 20–25 ($6–$7.50). Also enjoyable is the rare experience of seeing what, to the Israeli, is a foreign film, and watching others crane their necks to read the Hebrew subtitles, while you sit back and enjoy the English soundtrack. The commercial shorts that accompany many films are fascinating.

Tel Aviv Cinémathèque. 2 Sprinzak St. ☎ **03/691-7181.**

Located not far from the Mann Auditorium, the Cinémathèque, with an ever-changing daily program, screens three or four films each day ranging from international classics to rarely seen and experimental films. The Cinémathèque also hosts an annual International Film Festival, as well as special festivals of Israeli films throughout the year.

8

The Golden Coast

Like the rest of the country, the shore strip combines the old and the new in a uniquely Israeli juxtaposition. Neon and chrome exist side by side with biblical and even prebiblical ruins. And there's much to see and do on the beaches of sand, pebbles, or rocks: Sports enthusiasts can swim, fish, dive, boat, ski, or surf.

TOURING THE AREA

It's best to see the Golden Coast in sections: the southern and central coasts are convenient to Tel Aviv and can also be visited from Jerusalem; the central and northern coasts are easily accessible from Haifa and the Galilee. The water can be almost bathtub-warm in summer and swimming is possible from April to November. In fact, in a February heat wave, some visitors from northern climes may find the Mediterranean near Tel Aviv as warm as the North Atlantic ever gets in August.

Warning: On many days undertows and whirlpools develop that not even the strongest swimmer can fight. Obey the lifeguards! Be extremely wary about swimming in unguarded areas if there is any wave activity.

1 Ashkelon

56km (36 miles) S of Tel Aviv

Ashkelon is the southernmost tourist stop along Israel's eastern Mediterranean shoreline, although the beach winds much farther south. This thriving beach town has grown up over the ruins of civilizations buried in its sands for 25 centuries. One of the five Philistine city-states (the others were Gath, Gaza, Ekron, and Ashdod, all within today's Israel), Ashkelon was an important caravan stop. This is where Delilah supposedly snipped Samson's hair and strength, where Herod was born, and where Romans and Crusaders rallied.

A LITTLE ARCHEOLOGY

Exactly what happened at Ashkelon over the last 4,000 years is a chapter of history still waiting to be written, since Ashkelon is only now being archeologically explored in depth. Only occasional excavations have been made into the sand-covered cities of antiquity that lie within its boundaries. At one point along the shore, you'll see

What's Special About the Golden Coast

Major Cities/Towns
- Akko, the labyrinthine walled city with medieval markets, minarets, and caravan-saries rising from the sea.
- Ashkelon, with fine beaches, camping grounds, and archeological sites.
- Netanya, a large beachside town, a favorite of Israeli honeymooners and retired Americans.
- Bat Yam, a suburb of Tel Aviv with the best beaches reachable by Tel Aviv municipal bus.

Best Beaches
- Aqueduct Beach, Caesarea—poster perfect; swim beside dramatic 2,000-year-old ruins.
- Ashkelon's many beaches, each with its own personality, and the longest swimming season on the coast.

Ancient Sites
- Caesarea—Roman metropolis and port, with an amphitheater beside the sea and a Crusader fortress, all dramatically excavated.
- Ashkelon, with its excavations from Philistine, Roman, Byzantine, and Crusader eras.

where a tentative longitudinal slice has been made into the cliff, revealing a network of pillars and caves several strata deep. One of the exciting objects recently uncovered is a tiny Canaanite golden calf, now on display at the Israel Museum.

Further excavations will most certainly reveal important historical treasures, because the Bible mentions Ashkelon frequently. When King Saul was killed by the Philistines, David lamented: "Tell it not in Gath, publish it not in the streets of Ashkelon, lest the daughters of the Philistines rejoice."

When the Crusaders and Muslims fought over the city, Ashkelon, like so many other Israeli locations, fell into utter ruin. Later, builders took the remains of Roman staircases, Hellenistic pillars, and Crusader stonemasonry for building materials in Jaffa and Acre.

Ashkelon is not a large town, but it's very spread out. Some Israelis think that Ashkelon has the perfect climate, blessed by cool breezes from the sea, but modified by the dryness of desert winds. Because Ashkelon is at the southern end of the coast, you have the best chance of getting in some early spring or late fall swimming here.

ESSENTIALS

GETTING THERE   By Bus   The city can be reached by Egged bus no. 300, 301, or 311 from Tel Aviv in 1 hour and 15 minutes. Your bus will come into town from the highway on Ha-Nitzahon Road. You'll pass by Migdal, the old city, on your right and end up at the Central Bus Station on Ha-Nitzahon in the newer part of town. With a hotel reservation in hand, you can start out by city bus or taxi to your chosen hotel.

By Car   There are direct main highways from Tel Aviv and Jerusalem.

VISITOR INFORMATION   The Government and Municipal Tourist Office (☎ 07/732-412) is in Afridar Center, open Sunday through Thursday from

9am to 1pm, on Friday from 9 to 11:30am. You can obtain up-to-date information on everything from picnicking and camping in the beachside national park
to seasonal events, such as the Arts and Crafts Fair in July or August.

WHAT TO SEE & DO

The part of town you must get to know is Afridar. In Afridar Commercial Center,
with its conspicuous Clock Tower, you will find the Municipal Tourist Office, banks,
shops, restaurants, cafes, a cinema, and the small Ashkelon museum. Early on during your stay in Ashkelon, check out Afridar Center.

National Antiquities Park. ☎ **07/736-444.** Admission NIS 12 ($3.60); discounts for
students. Apr–Sept, daily 8am–6:30pm; Oct–Mar, daily 8am–4pm.

As you'd expect, the highlights are archeological sites. For example, walk south along
the sea, and you'll see bits and pieces of pillar and column poking through the sand.
Toward the end of the public beach section, you'll come to a staircase leading into
a park. Walk through the park, and you'll soon come upon the sunken arena
(the "Sculpture Corner") that houses Ashkelon's handful of finds: a headless Winged
Victory supported on the shoulders of a childlike Atlas, Isis and child, and grouped
pieces of colonnade from Herod's collection of carved capitals, "Stoa of a Hundred Columns." There's also a refreshment stand here.

Painted Roman Tomb. Free admission. Daily.

Practically hidden in the sand dunes, this Roman burial cave is just north of
the Shulamit Gardens Hotel, on the beach. Romance and eternal springtime
abide in the paintings—nymphs reclining, marsh birds nesting in a stream thick
with fish. On the ceiling are nude children playing, greyhounds and gazelles,
birds and clusters of grapes. The gods Apollo and Demeter look down between
the vines, assuring the entombed man, whoever he was, that things in the after-
life are really pretty good.

THE BEACHES

Ashkelon's main attraction is the beach, and there are several public beaches. Swim
only if there is a lifeguard present or at very shallow depths, since the water tends to
have tricky currents. All beaches are free and seldom crowded. My favorite beach areas
are about a quarter of a mile north of the Antiquities Park.

WHERE TO STAY

Ashkelon charges its highest rates from mid-July to the end of August, and during
Passover and the September holidays. This all has to do with Ashkelon's weather, a
commodity that local residents discuss with fanatic possessiveness. You will probably
be offered rain insurance: for every day it rains, beginning on the second day of your
stay, you get to stay a day free—breakfast included!

An inexpensive alternative to hotels is to stay in a private home. Generally, this
costs about $17 to $20 per night per person, but can double during Jewish holidays
and high season weekends. To find out about home accommodations, contact the
tourist office, in Afridar Commercial Center (☎ 07/732-412).

Samson's Gardens (Ganei Shimshon). 38 Sonnebend (Ha-Tamar) St., Afridar, Ashkelon.
☎ **07/736-641.** Fax 07/739-615. 26 rms (all with bath or shower). A/C TEL. $39–$44
single; $50–$57 double. On Jewish holidays, add $25 to higher rates. No credit cards.

As the name suggests, this hotel is situated in a garden. Rooms are very basic, but have
terraces overlooking the garden. Guests can use the pool at a nearby hotel at reduced

The Golden Coast

LEBANON

Rosh Hanikrah

Ahkziv
Gesher Haziv

Nahariya

Akko (Acrre)

ISRAEL

Haifa

Atlit Beach Reserve

Nazareth

Nasholim

Afula

Maagan Mikhael
**Zikhron
Yaakov**

Caesarea

Jenin

Mikhmoret

Bet Yanai

Netanya

WEST BANK

Poleg

Nablus

Shfayim
Herzlia

Kfar Saba

**Tel Aviv-
Jaffa**

Bat Yam

Palmahim

Ashdod

Jerusalem

Kholot Nitzanim Reserve

ISRAEL

Ashkelon

GAZA

LEGEND

beach

253

rates. Kosher meals are available. Ha-Tamar Street is right off Darom Africa Boulevard, near the Municipal Gardens.

CAMPING

Ashkelon has a beautiful and extensive camping ground—15 acres of lawns dotted with trees and marble pillars, located inside the seaside National Antiquities Park. Trailers, tents, and simple wooden "bungalow" shelters are available for hire year-round for $15 to $18 per person in simple camp bungalows; $25 to $30 per person in caravan structures. If you bring your own tent, the fee is $6 per person. Remember, you must pay an admission fee to the National Park ($3.60) as well. There are two to four beds in each bungalow; the large caravans (trailers) can accommodate six; the smaller ones, four. The three shower and toilet areas are ample. There are a grocery store and a restaurant, or you may purchase bottled cooking gas for your own equipment. Many of your fellow campers will be Moroccan–Israeli families with fabulous food, spirit, and music!

For further information, you may write to the campsite at **Ashkelon Camping,** P.O. Box 5052 (☎ 07/736-777 or 734-027). Or contact the **Israel Camping Union,** P.O. Box 53, Nahariya (☎ 04/923-366). Members of the Israel or International Camping Union will receive a 5% to 10% discount on certain items. Take bus no. 3 or 9 to national park. Follow marked pathway to the campground.

WHERE TO DINE

Down in Migdal, the old section of town, are various lunch-counter eateries, and there's one at the Central Bus Station as well. With such limited dining possibilities, it's not difficult to see why so many visitors arrange for half or full board at their hotels.

EN ROUTE TO BAT YAM
REHOVOT & THE WEIZMANN INSTITUTE

There are two ways of heading north from Ashkelon. The easier and faster way is along the coastal road, which intentionally misses several of the population centers in the region. The inner road, however, connecting with Gedera—once the northern tip of the Negev until Israeli farmers pushed the desert back beyond Beersheva—is well worth the extra effort and time. You can reach Rehovot from Gedera, and there's also a connecting road directly off the coastal highway.

Either way, it's a short drive to Israel's foremost scientific establishment, the ✪ **Weizmann Institute of Science.** You enter through a gateway on Rehovot's main street, and as soon as you're inside the grounds you'll feel as if you've stepped into another world. This is a beautiful compound of futuristic buildings, lawns of the deepest golf-course green, lily ponds, and colorful gardens—all, apparently, for the spiritual satisfaction of the hundreds of scientists from all over the world at work here.

Dedicated in 1949 in honor of Israel's first president (himself an important chemist), the institute grew out of the Daniel Sieff Research Institute, established in 1934. Conducting both fundamental and applied research, the Weizmann Institute also has a graduate school where about 500 students work for their doctorates.

On the grounds are the **Wix Library,** where there is an exhibition on Dr. Weizmann's life, and the **Wix Auditorium,** which presents audiovisual shows on the institute's activities at 11am and 3:15pm daily (at 11am only on Friday).

Chaim Weizmann: Statesman & Scientist

Chaim Weizmann (1874–1952), biochemist, statesman, and first president of Israel, was born in a small village near Pinsk, in Russia. At the age of 11 (a decade before Herzl turned to Zionism), Weizmann wrote, "Why should we look to the kings of Europe for compassion that they should give us a resting place? In vain, all have denied . . . to Zion! Jews to Zion let us go!" A brilliant student, Weizmann gave lessons to earn his tuition at Berlin's Institute of Technology in Charlottenburg and at Fribourg University in Switzerland; in 1901 he began to teach at Geneva University. In 1903, in response to pogroms in Russia, the British foreign secretary proposed a Jewish homeland in a 5,000-square-mile area of British East Africa (Uganda). Herzl seemed willing to accept the offer; the young Weizmann sided with those who would not accept Zionism without Zion. He married Vera Chatzman, a Russian Jewish medical student, in 1906, and that year accepted a teaching position at Manchester University. In 1906, Weizmann met with Prime Minister Balfour, who wanted to interview an anti-Ugandist; Weizmann's charm and energy impressed Balfour and won him access to the highest circles of British society. He was lionized in 1916, after developing a production process for synthesizing acetone that was crucial to the British war effort. (In his professional career, Dr. Weizmann received patents for over 100 processes and inventions.) Moving to London, he continued to build support for a Jewish homeland in Palestine. At the end of 1917, the Balfour Declaration was issued.

In the 1920s and 1930s, as leader of the Zionist movement, Weizmann worked to build the infrastructure of a modern society in Palestine "house by house and dunam by dunam." Without romantic illusion and with a passion for fairness, Weizmann warned the Zionist movement to understand "the truth that 600,000 Arabs live there [in Palestine] who, before the sense of justice of the world have exactly the same right to their homes in Palestine as we have to our National Home." In 1937, addressing a Royal Commission on the Partition of Palestine, he prophetically explained the plight of European Jewry: "There are 6 million people . . . for whom the world is divided into places where they cannot live, and places which they cannot enter."

Weizmann's eloquence could not alleviate the vast tragedy that World War II brought to his people. In 1942, his own son was killed in action with the Royal Air Force over the British Channel. Struggling through the breakdown of his health and a hostile postwar British government, Weizmann's final achievement was winning American support for the incipient Jewish state in 1948. In February 1949, he was elected president of Israel, a position he held until his death. The title of Vera Weizmann's memoirs, *The Impossible Takes Longer,* summarizes the philosophy behind her husband's heavily burdened but determined optimism.

The **Weizmann House** (☎ 08/343-230) contains the personal possessions of a fascinating historical figure, and was the nation's first presidential residence. Built by Dr. and Mrs. Weizmann as their residence in the 1930s, the house is a wonderful example of International Style domestic architecture and interior design. It is a dazzling, streamlined interpretation of a Roman/Mediterranean atrium house, the masterpiece of the German refugee architect, Eric Mendelsohn, who also designed the original Hadassah Hospital and Hebrew University on Mount Scopus in Jerusalem. The interior of the house is marked by an airy, sinuous staircase set in a stair tower lit with narrow vertical windows; private living and reception wings with French doors lead to a central pool patio. Another 1930s element, round porthole windows, brings light into the house from exterior walls. The furnishings were carefully designed by Mendelsohn, who involved Dr. and Mrs. Weizmann personally in the project. The house itself (like Washington's Mount Vernon and Jefferson's Montecello) reveals much about the personality of Dr. Weizmann, the world in which he lived, and the international visitors he entertained. The Weizmann House is open Sunday through Thursday from 10am to 3pm; there are guided tours in a number of languages. To arrange a visit, call 08/343-230 or 343-328. Admission is NIS 10 ($3) and includes a tour. Near the residence is a simple tomb marking the Weizmanns' resting place and a Memorial Plaza dominated by a Holocaust Memorial depicting the Torah being snatched from flames.

A cafeteria at the institute serves light dairy/vegetarian meals.

2 Bat Yam

17km (10 miles) S of Tel Aviv

Bat Yam (Daughter of the Sea) is one of the most pleasant of the numerous public beaches between Ashdod and Tel Aviv. On the southern fringes of Tel Aviv–Jaffa, this residential area boasts an ever-growing population of more than 150,000 inhabitants. The beaches here are cleaner and more attractive than those of downtown Tel Aviv, and are easily accessible by bus.

ESSENTIALS

GETTING THERE   By Bus   In Tel Aviv–Jaffa, look for bus no. 10 or 25 headed south. Bat Yam borders on Tel Aviv–Jaffa, so the journey may take as little as 15 minutes or as long as 45, depending on your starting point and traffic conditions.

VISITOR INFORMATION   Orientation   Bat Yam is part of metropolitan Tel Aviv. Once you arrive in Bat Yam, look for Rothschild Boulevard. Your bus will probably head down Rothschild to the beachfront. The beachfront street is Ben-Gurion Boulevard (also sometimes called Ha-Nesi'im). Virtually all of the tourist hotels are arrayed along Ben-Gurion to get the benefit of the sea view, so you should start your hotel explorations at the intersection of Rothschild and Ben-Gurion, near the northern end of Bat Yam's beach. The area code is 03.

The **Municipal Tourist Information Office**, 43 Ben-Gurion (☎ 03/507-2777), is a few doors north of the Rothschild–Ben-Gurion intersection, in the same building as the Via Maris Hotel on Ben-Gurion Boulevard. The office is well organized. Hours are Monday and Thursday from 8am to 3:30pm; Tuesday and Wednesday from 8am to 2pm and 4 to 7pm; closed Friday and Saturday.

WHERE TO STAY

Armon Yam. 95 Ben-Gurion Blvd. (P.O. Box 3240), Bat Yam 59131. ☎ **03/552-2424.** Fax 03/552-2430. 66 rms (all with bath). A/C TEL. $63 single; $80 double; add $5 August and Jewish holidays. Rates include breakfast. AE, DC, MC, V. Bus: No. 10 from Tel Aviv.

One of Bat Yam's medium-class hotels is this large, modern hostelry. All rooms have tubs in the bathrooms, balconies, and the standard amenities. Prices are a bit higher than the rest of Bat Yam's hotels, which are two-star.

WHERE TO DINE

Chez Raymond. 47 Ben-Gurion. ☎ **03/687-2348.** NIS 12–NIS 40 ($3.60–$12). MC, V. Daily 10am–1am. SNACKS/LIGHT MEALS.

A few steps from the tourist office is Chez Raymond, a nice sidewalk cafe with boothlike wooden tables and benches. It specializes in such light beach fare as blintzes, pizzas, and salads. But beware! To make the cafe-sitters pay their way, Raymond's charges heavily for beer and soft drinks.

3 Herzlia

15km (10 miles) N of Tel Aviv

Herzlia is one of Israel's most famous beach resorts. It was founded in 1924 as an agricultural center, but has been changed dramatically with the unexpected growth of Tel Aviv. As that large Israeli metropolis grew northward, the beaches of Herzlia suddenly became much more accessible and desirable.

Today when you're talking about Herzlia, you're talking about luxury. The waterfront area is studded with fine hotels and restaurants abound, as do some of the country's most expensive villas. A disproportionate number of foreign diplomats reside in Herzlia; their neighbors are airline captains and other high-earners. Swimming here is better than in Tel Aviv, and many Tel Avivans, as well as tourists, come up for a day of beaching and a pleasant meal.

ESSENTIALS

GETTING THERE **By Bus** An Egged bus ride from Tel Aviv to Herzlia takes about 45 minutes; a special bus service run by United Tours connects the Herzlia hotels with downtown and north Tel Aviv. From Herzlia you take another bus to the beach. (If you tell the bus driver that you want to go to the beach, he'll let you out at the connecting bus stop near the highway, saving you a trip into town.)

By Car Herzlia is on a main highway, 20 minutes north of Tel Aviv.

VISITOR INFORMATION **Orientation** Herzlia's sprawling layout is confusing for the first-time visitor. The luxury Sharon Hotel, right on the beach, is a major landmark. Inland just a block is De Shalit Square (Kikar De Shalit), which has several inexpensive hotels and restaurants in the square or nearby. Many good restaurant choices will be found in the new industrial center.

THE BEACHES

This whole beachfront section of town is known as Herzlia Petuah, to differentiate it from the inland city, on a hill to the east. The Herzlia beach is lovely, but expensive by Israeli standards. The best beaches are the **Zebulun,** near the Daniel Hotel; the **Sharon,** next to the Sharon Hotel; and the **Accadia,** between the Dan Accadia and Daniel hotels. One additional word about the beach: A dangerous undertow exists and bathing is strictly prohibited when a lifeguard is not on duty.

WHERE TO STAY
EXPENSIVE

Dan Accadia Hotel. Herzlia on the Sea 46851. ☎ **09/556-677.** Fax 09/562-141. 187 rms (all with bath). A/C MINIBAR TEL TV. $154–$380 single; $174–$400 double. 15% service charge. Rates include breakfast. Family plan and children's rates. AE, DC, MC, V.

Located on the beach in the far southern part of town, this relatively lowrise resort hotel, built in 1956 and well maintained, is set among lawns and gardens that center on the pool area. Standard rooms are a bit small, with plain furnishings, but all have balconies; there are also deluxe chalet rooms and suites. There are activities for children on weekends and during the summer, poolside barbecues and dancing, and the management can arrange horseback riding and access to the golf course of the Dan Caesarea Hotel a half-hour drive to the north. Discounts are available on the Dan Hotels 7-day plan.

Dining/Entertainment: Two restaurants, snack bars, coffee shop, bar.

Services: 24-hour room service, massage, hairdresser.

Facilities: Outdoor pool, six tennis courts, Jacuzzi, wet and dry sauna, health club, shopping arcade, free parking.

Daniel Hotel and Spa. Herzlia on the Sea 46769. ☎ **09/544-444.** Fax 09/544-675. 165 rms (all with bath or shower). A/C TEL TV. $112–$270 single; $140–$300 double. Add 15% service charge. Rates include breakfast. AE, DC, MC, V.

A large tower complex right on the beach, and near the central part of town, the Daniel's contemporary public areas, with polished stone surfaces, curving staircases, and mezzanines, announce luxury. The strong points of this hotel are the health and beauty programs, which include whirlpools, massage therapies, saunas, inhalations, a fitness room, Dead Sea baths, mud packs, beauty treatment rooms, and a special low-calorie spa menu. Deluxe rooms on the upper floors have balconies; garden-level duplex accommodations beside the pool are spacious but can be noisy. Despite its name, this is not part of the Dan Hotel Chain.

Dining/Entertainment: Six restaurants, bar.

Services: Business services, health and beauty spas.

Facilities: Indoor and outdoor swimming pools, tennis courts, parking (fee).

MODERATE

Kibbutz Shefayim Guest House. Kibbutz Shefayim. ☎ **09-595-595.** Fax 09/595-555. 163 rms (51 with bath, 112 with shower). A/C TEL. $73–$115 single; $83–$158 double. AE, MC, V.

Right on the sea, a 10-minute drive north of Herzlia, the location of this lowrise, modern kibbutz guesthouse has put it in great demand both with Israelis and tourists. A busy water park containing a swimming pool with waves and slides, open to the public, is another attraction, especially for families with children. The grounds of the kibbutz are especially interesting, and include wild, sandy paths along the top of cliffs overlooking the sea, and a beach that's good for bathing on calm days—when the sea is even mildly rough, the presence of rocks in the water makes for hazards. Always check for the hours when lifeguards are on duty. At times, a kibbutz tractor brings guests up and down the cliff to the beach, a welcome aid on hot summer days.

It's on the main Tel Aviv–Haifa highway; look for exit sign for Shefayim.

Tadmor Hotel. 38 Basel St., Herzlia 46660. ☎ **09/572-321.** Fax 09/574-560. 58 rms (all with bath or shower). A/C TEL. Low season: $58–$69 single; $70–$85 double. Regular season: $62–$72 single; $80–$94 double. Add 15% for high season. Off-season discounts. Rates include breakfast. MC, V.

The three-star-equivalent Tadmor Hotel is an Israeli institution. Hotel staffs from all over the country train here, and chefs are assiduously cultivated and launched from the Tadmor. There is a radio in each room; large gardens, an outdoor swimming pool, and a fine park with a children's playground are additional highlights.

To find the hotel, walk three blocks east of Shalit Square. Driving from Tel Aviv, look for Basel Street to the left off the main road.

WHERE TO DINE

The best place to look for inexpensive meals is in **De Shalit Square** (Kikar De Shalit), a pleasant little plaza surrounded by snack shops, ice cream parlors, and small restaurants catering to locals and the beach crowd alike. The building complexes in

Herzlia's New Industrial Center, inland from the beach, near the Tel Aviv–Haifa highway, are increasingly home to good, inventive restaurants.

EXPENSIVE

Taverna. Dan Accadia Hotel Beach Promenade. ☎ **09/597-107.** Reservations recommended. Appetizers NIS 12–33 ($3.60–$10); main courses NIS 48–75 ($14.40–$22.50). AE, DC, MC, V. Sun–Thurs 7pm–midnight; Fri 12:30–5pm and 7pm–midnight; Sat 12:30–5pm. CONTINENTAL.

Right on the beach, with an outdoor dining terrace and a beautiful view of the sunset, this is a pricey but easygoing restaurant with an ambience of ceiling fans and sea breezes and a wide selection of seafood, fish, and meat. For appetizers, try the interesting tapas for about $3 a piece. Among the main courses, you'll find a great variety, ranging from prawns diablo in a spicy chili and cream sauce, to marinated palamida, or spinach and ricotta pie. With its fine view, this is a good place to come off-hours just for coffee and dessert.

MODERATE

✪ **Dona Flor.** 22 Ha-Galim St., New Industrial Center. ☎ **09/509-669.** Reservations recommended. Appetizers NIS 16–33 ($4.80–$10); main courses NIS 40–66 ($12–$20). AE, DC, MC, V. Sun–Thurs noon–4pm and 7pm–midnight; Fri noon–4pm. Closed Sat.

White walls, terracotta tile floors, earthenware dishes, and an open-walled kitchen all contribute to the rustic South American feel of this place. The food, too, has a light touch of exoticism: nothing is overpoweringly strange, but every dish is unusual and delicious. Among the interesting house appetizers are marinated fish in lemon, orange, and dill; phyllo pastry in pepper sauce stuffed with smoked chicken and vegetables; a fabulous dish of smoked, sliced veal brain with pecan; and a number of unusual salads. Main courses include smoked lamb chops cooked in pistachio sauce, steamed trout in lemon and mustard sauce, sea bass in vetapa (coconut-tomato-peanut) sauce, and chicken escaloppes in a vinaigrette of honey with pearl onions. Main courses come with steamed vegetable, rice or potato, or carrot french fries. The dessert list, too, is special.

✪ **Picasso.** 1 Ha-Etzel St., Herzliya Pituach. ☎ **09/566-888.** Reservations recommended. Appetizers NIS 12–27 ($3.60–$8.10); main courses NIS 24–60 ($7.20–$18). AE, DC, MC, V. Daily 8am–2am. CONTINENTAL.

This branch of Tel Aviv's most quintessential, stylish but moderate restaurant offers an exciting, intelligent menu designed by former Parisian, David Prozniak. Seafood, poultry, fish, and meat dishes, as well as enormous hot and cold salads, all presented in unusual ways, have made this a smash hit. New surprises are always being added to the menu and Prozniak plans to add a line of healthy low-calorie choices without sacrificing Picasso's much admired verve and joie de vivre. The large rooftop bar is an additional evening draw.

✪ **Tandoori.** Mercazim Building, 5 Maskit St., New Industrial Center. ☎ **09/546-702.** Reservations recommended. Appetizers NIS 10–28 ($3–$8.30); main courses NIS 22–55 ($6.60–$16.50). 10% service charge. AE, DC, MC, V. Daily 12:30–3:30pm and 7pm–1am.

Serving a very cosmopolitan clientele that includes Herzlia's international diplomatic community, this is the most opulent of the fine restaurants in the Tandoori chain, with twin curved marble staircases leading to the upper dining area, and decorative silver and enamel work imported from Jaipur. As in all the Tandoori/Kohinoor restaurants, the traditional Indian dishes you'll find here are prepared with a special lightness and elegance. I especially liked the sabzi jalfrezi, a very modestly priced dish of vegetables lightly steamed and then quickly dry-sautéed with ginger, garlic, cumin seeds, and fresh mustard. The boneless tandoori chicken dishes are my favorites, especially chicken tikka masala, but the whole range of lamb and fish choices is also superb. It's worthwhile trying the traditional Indian homestyle desserts, and you should know that the Tandoori chain is famous for its cocktails. The entire experience is one of tranquillity and elegance, yet the price is reasonable.

INEXPENSIVE

🟊 **Crocodile.** Kikar De Shalit. ☎ **03/570-762.** Reservations recommended. Appetizers NIS 12–20 ($3.60–$6); main courses NIS 38–60 ($11.70–$18); salad bar NIS 30 ($9); business lunch NIS 36 ($11). MC, V. Daily noon–midnight or later. AMERICAN/ISRAELI.

In an expensive town like Herzlia, Crocodile is an attractive oasis of good, reasonably priced food. Most notable is the luxurious salad bar, with a selection of 25 interesting fresh salads, plus four hot vegetable dishes that range from a daily Asian stir-fry to a Saturday vegetarian bean cholent, or Sabbath casserole. The bottomless salad bar is a meal in itself, but the business lunch, which includes the salad bar, soup, your choice of one of five main courses, and coffee or tea, is one of the town's great bargains. The place has a tropical feel, with style enhanced by green tablecloths, candles, and tables that offer a more private ambience. The specials bring Crocodile into the inexpensive range, but those ordering à la carte will find this restaurant more in the moderate range.

4 Netanya

34 kilometers (21 miles) N of Tel Aviv

Netanya is regarded as the capital of the Sharon Plain, the rich and fertile citrus-grove area stretching from the outskirts of Tel Aviv to Caesarea. Perched on verdant cliffs overlooking the Mediterranean, it is also the center of Israel's diamond industry.

Founded in 1929 as a citrus center, the seaside town has for many years been a popular holiday place for Israelis. Over the years tourists (especially long-term visitors and senior citizens) have been joining them, for they've discovered that Netanya is quiet and convenient, geared to service, and in easy reach of several areas, including Tel Aviv and Caesarea. It's a sizable city, with all sorts of cafes, hotels, and shops—but the real appeal remains the sunny beach and easygoing pace. (*Note:* Those with walking problems may find the stairs up and down the cliff to Netanya's beaches something of an obstacle.) Those who decide to rent an apartment and stay in Netanya for a month or more will find the local American community extremely well organized. The population of Netanya has grown by more than a fifth in recent years with an influx of new immigrants from Eastern Europe and the former Soviet Union, so Netanya may seem to have more of a European flavor than other Israeli cities.

A handsome park parallels the beach—and the coast itself has become popular with Scandinavian visitors who take dips in December and January. Most everybody else waits until April or May, when the weather is almost perfect.

ESSENTIALS

GETTING THERE   By Bus   Several express buses operate between Netanya and Jerusalem. Connections are available from Haifa, and there is regular bus service from Tel Aviv. Netanya buses (no. 601 or 605) leave Tel Aviv about every 15 minutes during the day until 7pm. The last bus to Tel Aviv departs at 11pm.

By Car   There is a main coastal highway between Tel Aviv and Haifa.

VISITOR INFORMATION   The **Tourist Information Office** (☎ **09/827-286**) is in a little modern kiosk at the southeastern corner of Independence Square. Hours are 8:30am to 6pm on Sunday through Thursday; from 9am to noon on Friday.

Winter hours may be shorter. This office is especially helpful, and will answer questions about Netanya or other places in Israel. Be sure to pick up a copy of the monthly booklet listing special events, entertainment, and services in Netanya. If you're traveling by bus, you might also want to pick up their bus timetable, which you might find clearer than the information you'll get at the station.

Netanya closes down between 1 and 4pm every day, so plan to shop or go to the bank before or after the afternoon siesta.

SOCIAL CLUBS   Many international social clubs hold regular meetings in Netanya, including Rotary, Lions, Hadassah, Freemasons, International Toastmistress, Pioneer Women, and B'nai B'rith. Ask at the tourist office, or see the listings in the free guides to Netanya for times and places. Open House for Tourists is held every Monday, Tuesday, and Wednesday from 9:30 to 11:30am, at the British **Olim Society,** 7 Ha-Matmid St., and also on Wednesday at 4pm at the **WIZO House,** 13 MacDonald St. (☎ 09/823-192). **The Association of Americans and Canadians in Israel (AACI),** at 28 Shmuel Ha-Naziv St., offers a good schedule of lectures and other social activities.

If you'd like to meet an Israeli citizen, apply 3 days in advance at the tourist office and you'll soon find yourself invited to a home for a friendly chat and a cup of coffee.

SPECIAL EVENTS   In late July, there is a 1-week art exhibit on Ha-Atzma'ut Square (Sunday through Thursday from 5:30 to 11pm; closed Friday; on Saturday from 8:30pm to midnight). The city sponsors free evening concerts and events throughout the summer. A **chess tournament** is held in Netanya yearly during May and June; every 2 years there's an international match. Games start at 3:30pm and last until 10pm. For further information, contact the tourist information office.

During Sukkot (Feast of Tabernacles), there are four free evenings of **folklore** in Ha-Atzma'ut Square, featuring the various ethnic groups living in Israel, with dance, song, and typical traditional snacks.

ORIENTATION

Netanya is a big town, but it's not really difficult to find your way around. The main coastal highway is known as the Haifa Road. Coming north on Haifa Road from Tel Aviv, you will see the exit for Netanya, which will get you onto Herzl Street, Netanya's main east–west boulevard. At the beginning of Herzl Boulevard, not far from the coastal highway, you'll pass the large Kanion (indoor shopping mall).

About six blocks down the street is the Central Bus Station, where Herzl meets Weizmann and Benyamin boulevards. Another six blocks along Herzl and you're in the great expanse of Ha-Atzma'ut Square, by the sea in the very heart of Netanya. Most of the hotels and restaurants recommended below are within a few blocks of the square.

The square, being the town's pedestrian promenade, has been enlarged in recent years, and now extends up Herzl Street all the way to Dizengoff Street.

Around this square you'll find everything you need, including eateries of many kinds, pubs, discos, cinema, hotels, the Tourist Information Office, banks, ATM machines, places to change money, a post office, and more. *Warning:* The center of Netanya was not designed for a population of almost 200,000. Parking is a serious problem and parking regulations are enforced with draconian rigor!

BEACHES, SPORTS & OTHER OUTDOOR ACTIVITIES

BEACHES   The main attraction at Netanya is, of course, the lovely beach, and you'll have perfect beach weather here more than 75% of the year. The water is great

The Anglo-Saxon Connection

Visitors to Israel from English-speaking countries are often amazed at how easy it is to get around using their native language, especially in light of the fact that Israel's two official languages, Hebrew and Arabic, don't even share alphabets that remotely resemble our own. In major cities, signs, traffic instructions, and restaurant menus are almost always in both English and Hebrew. Israeli entrepreneurs have become adept at designing shop signs and logos that blend English and Hebrew lettering (which are written in opposite directions) into interesting compositions and the chance is good that your 20-something waiter or waitress, the sales clerk where you take your film to be developed, or the elderly Palestinian owner of a grocery shop will be able to shift into fluent English at a moment's notice. Unlike many European countries, which dub English-language films and television programs, in Israel you won't have to see Katherine Hepburn, Tom Hanks, or Seinfeld bantering away in Hebrew.

Of course, the British were here from 1918 to 1948, but 30 years of the British Mandate are only one part of the formula that has made Israel so user-friendly to the English-speaking world. Immigrants to Israel from English-speaking countries, though less than 2% of the general population, have had an impact far beyond their numbers. Known locally (and to their own bemusement) as Anglo-Saxons, these Israelis have provided two of the nation's eight presidents—**Chaim Weizmann,** a British subject whose scientific discoveries were crucial to the Allied victory in World War I; and Dublin-born **Chaim Herzog,** whose father served as chief rabbi of Ireland. **Golda Meir,** a former schoolteacher from Milwaukee, held many important positions in Labor Party governments, including that of prime minister from 1969 to 1974. Prime Minister and standard bearer of the Likud Coalition, **Benjamin Netanyahu,** is also from an American family. Israel's most famous and eloquent diplomat, South African–born Cambridge-educated **Abba Eban,** served as ambassador to the United Nations and was foreign minister for many years; the American-born **Moshe Arens** was foreign minister in the Likud governments of the 1980s and early 1990s. **Henrietta Szold,** the Baltimore-born first president of Hadassah, held the social welfare portfolio of the National Council of Palestine Jewry in the 1930s and was responsible for developing many elements of the emerging nation's system of health, education, and social services. South Africans, Britons, and Americans were heavily involved in creating the Association for Civil Rights in Israel, and are in the forefront of the women's rights, religious rights, and ecology and peace movements. Americans are also strongly represented in the West Bank and Gaza Settlement movements. Despite their extraordinary contribution, Anglo–Israelis are regarded by many of their fellow countrymen as something of a people apart. As a result of the 1992 elections, for the first time since 1948, the currently sitting Knesset contained no immigrant born or raised in an English-speaking country.

for swimming—you can go out pretty far before it starts to get deep. There's a lifeguard on duty, and do swim in the approved area; it's posted not to swim beyond a certain point. In addition to sand, swimming, and sun, you can enjoy the attractions in the beach complex, with restaurants and snack shops, beach chairs, large public umbrellas, a basketball court, and a gymnastics field. You'll see people **fishing** up on the rocky breakwater. **Surfing** and **sailboarding** can be arranged at the Kontiki Club down on the Netanya beach—lessons, too—open daily from 8:30am until sunset.

Impressions

We [from English-speaking countries] have experienced democracy at first hand. We know what democracy is and should be. That can be, perhaps has been, our greatest contribution.
—Alice Shalvi, Israeli educator and founding chairwoman, Israel Women's Network

Of course it's beautiful to see the sun set into the Mediterranean, and in the high tourist season, student patrols keep watch to make sure everything is okay. The lifeguards leave the beach in the late afternoon. Still, be cautious at night here; stay where you see other people, especially if you're a woman alone. During the winter the student patrols are not around, and it's not a good idea to hang around the beach or the parks on the cliffs at night.

HORSEBACK RIDING & OTHER ACTIVITIES   Riding is available at two locations. **The Ranch** (☎ 09/663-525), near Havezelet Ha-Sharon Village, has horseback riding daily from 8am until sunset; take bus no. 17 or 29 from the Central Bus Station. There's also the **Cactus Ranch** (☎ 09/651-239), open daily from 8am until sunset.

There's a heated **swimming pool** at the **Elitzur Sports Center** (☎ 09/623-931), open Sunday through Thursday from 6am to 6pm; **squash** and **tennis** are also featured. The center is at the end of Radak Street (take bus no. 8 from the Central Bus Station), and is open daily from 6 or 8am until 5 to 10pm (call to check which hours are on what days). The **Wingate Institute** (☎ 09/639-550) also has a swimming pool, as do many Netanya hotels. **Bicycle rentals** can be arranged at the Hotel Promenade (☎ 09/626-450). **Paragliding** can be arranged through the aptly named Ariba (☎ 09/840-010).

NATURE WALKS & HIKING   The **Poleg Nature Reserve,** 8 kilometers south of Netanya, offers an interesting hike along the Poleg River, upstream from the point where it meets the sea. The riverbanks are lined with giant eucalyptus trees, planted almost a century ago to help drain the swamps that had developed throughout the plane of Sharon (eucalyptus seedlings were imported from Australia by early Jewish settlers, who valued their deep, thirsty roots and ability to withstand drought). In winter and early spring, the wildflowers flourishing along the route have made the Poleg Reserve a favorite destination for nature lovers. Unfortunately, the Poleg River has become seriously polluted, a situation not unusual in the intensively developed coastal plain. Recently, the Mediterranean beach has been closed to swimming, and the river water itself will probably be off-limits to visitors.

The **Iris Nature Reserve,** at the southern edge of Netanya, is a sanctuary for wild and cultivated irises. There is an adjacent pond that attracts seaside birds and waterfowl.

A VISIT TO A DIAMOND FACTORY

Israel is the number-one spot in the world for cutting and polishing diamonds, and Netanya is Israel's number-one diamond center, with two large factories. If you're in the market to buy, you can probably save about 20% by buying here. Even if you're not interested in buying, a visit to the **National Diamond Center,** 90 Herzl St. (☎ 09/624-770), could still be an unusual experience. Telephone for information about the center's interesting and pressure-free tours. The Tourist Information Office can direct you to additional diamond industry tours in Netanya.

WHERE TO STAY

In most cases, you needn't go far out of Ha-Atzma'ut Square to find a hotel, either cheap or expensive. Netanya is oriented toward warm-weather vacationers and prices are seasonal, and even inexpensive hotels can charge moderate to expensive rates during high season. Generally speaking, high season is from early July through the end of August, plus Jewish holidays, and low season is November through February; between these times the prices will be somewhere between the high- and low-season rates.

Be sure to check for heating and/or air conditioning, if you think you'll need them, depending on the weather and the season. In winter, days can be balmy but nights can get chilly. By the way, all of Netanya's hotel kitchens are kosher.

NORTH OF HA-ATZMA'UT SQUARE

Rehov Ha-Melekh David is the main street going north out of Ha-Atzma'ut Square, close to the beach.

Expensive

Blue Bay Hotel. 37 Hamelachim St., Netanya. ☎ **09/603-603.** Fax 09/337-475. 208 rms (all with bath or shower). A/C TEL TV. $72–$136 single; $100–$210 double. Rates include breakfast. 15% service charge. AE, DC, MC, V.

The most northern of the town's hotels, the Blue Bay offers hourly shuttle service into the center of Netanya. Away from the sometimes busy tempo of Ha-Atzma'ut Square, this Best Western hotel is one of the largest in town. Rooms are showing their age; a process of room renovation was begun in 1994, but much of the hotel will probably not be upgraded during the time span of this edition. Facilities include a swimming pool (heated in winter), a new fitness room, restaurant, disco, bar, and floodlit tennis courts.

✪ **Seasons Hotel.** Nice Boulevard, Netanya. ☎ **09/601-555;** reservations in the U.S. 201/816-0633. Fax 09/623-022. 85 rms (all with bath). A/C TEL TV. $95–$200 single; $130–$250 double; higher rates for deluxe rms and suites. Rates include breakfast and service. AE, DC, MC, V.

Until the advent of the Carmel Hotel at the southern edge of Netanya, the Seasons was the city's top hotel. Guest rooms are large, with balconies and sea view; suites are very comfortable. Much of the hotel was renovated in 1994–95. Facilities include a heated outdoor swimming pool, tennis court, three restaurants, and free parking. A refrigerator/minibar is available on request.

Moderate

Maxim Hotel. 8 King David St., Netanya 42264. ☎ **09/621-062.** Fax 09/620-190. 90 rms (all with bath). A/C TEL TV. Winter: $58 single; $82 double. High season: $65–$90 single; $88–$140 double. AE, DC, MC, V.

The Maxim Hotel is the equivalent of a four-star establishment, and has a swimming pool and bar. Since it's been put together with the former Hotel Gan Ha-Melekh next door, the hotel now has 60 suites that are roomier but more expensive than the other rooms. All come with small refrigerators, and the sea-view rooms have balconies with sliding glass doors.

Inexpensive

Hotel Ginot Yam. 9 King David St., Netanya 42264. ☎ **09/341-007.** Fax 09/615-722. 55 rms (all with bath or shower). A/C TEL TV. Winter: $35 single; $44 double. Regular season: $53 single; $67 double. High season: $86 single; $97 double. Rates include breakfast. AE, DC, MC, V.

On the left as you stroll up King David Street, this three-story building near the Bialik intersection is literally a stone's throw from the sea. Rooms have heat, wall-to-wall carpeting, and radios among other amenities, and there's a small snack bar/restaurant. You couldn't find a cleaner, better-kept place.

SOUTH OF HA-ATZMA'UT SQUARE

On the south side of Ha-Atzma'ut Square, several main streets and side streets will lead you to hotel choices that are only a short walk from the beach and from the busy square.

Expensive

La Promenade Apartment Hotel. 6 Gad Machnes St., Netanya. ☎ **09/626-450.** Fax 09/626-450. 21 apartments with bath or shower. A/C KITCHENETTE TEL TV. $100–$150 single; $130–$185 double. Up to 5 people, add $16 per person. Rates include breakfast. 15% service charge. AE, DC, MC, V.

Built in the early 1990s, this is the best of Netanya's apartment hotels. Apartments are sleek, with polished marble floors and contemporary decor; all have kitchenettes and balconies. There is an indoor swimming pool and Jacuzzi, room service, and free parking. The location is in the center of things, close to Ha-Atzma'ut Square and the beach.

Moderate

Residence Hotel. 18 Gad Machnes St., Netanya. ☎ **09/623-777.** Fax 09/623-711. 96 rms (all with bath or shower). A/C TEL TV. Winter: $52 single; $69 double. High season: $70–$108 single; $92–$140 double. Rates include breakfast. AE, DC, MC, V.

Billing itself as "Netanya's most luxurious three-star hotel," the Residence is building its clientele by offering cut-rate prices for people staying a minimum of 1 week. Most of the rooms have balconies and spectacular views of the sea. Since the hotel is eight stories tall, if you get an upper room you'll really have a bird's-eye view.

Inexpensive

Galei Ha-Sharon Hotel. 42 Ussishkin St., Netanya 42273. ☎ **09/341-946.** Fax 09/338-128. 24 rms (all with showers). A/C. Winter: $32 single; $41 double. High season: $40–$55 single; $50–$65 double. MC, V.

Those looking for a modern hotel with a decent location and reasonable prices might try this hotel at the corner of Gad Machnes. Although it's small, the Galei Ha-Sharon somehow achieves a surprising feeling of spaciousness. The rooms, while not luxurious, are adequate—all with shower in the bathroom, shuttered balcony, and wall-to-wall carpet. There's also a cozy bar beside the lobby.

Margoa. 9 Gad Machnes St., Netanya 42279. ☎ **09/624-434.** Fax 09/623-430. 64 rms (all with bath or shower.) A/C TEL TV. Summer: $60–$79 single; $72–$97 double. Winter: $56 single; $64 double. AE, MC, V.

Just a short distance from the information kiosk is the Hotel Margoa—actually two Hotel Margoas, the Margoa "A" on your left and the Margoa "B" on your right, by the sea. For either hotel, the reception, as well as the dining, are done at the Margoa A. Rooms come with heat, air conditioning, and wall-to-wall carpeting. Some of the rooms in Margoa A have balconies.

SOUTH NETANYA

Expensive

✪ **Carmel Hotel.** Jabotinsky St,. Netanya. ☎ **09/601-111;** reservations 09/601-170. Fax 09/601-166; reservations 09/601-171. 200 rms (all with bath). A/C TEL TV. $100–$235 single;

$115–$277 double; highest rates for deluxe rooms and suites; standard double in high season is $170. Rates include breakfast. 15% service charge. AE, DC, MC, V.

Built in 1994, this highrise hotel on a now quiet stretch of beach (slated to become a luxury resort center) 2 miles south of downtown Netanya, is the city's only five-star-equivalent hotel; it has set a new standard for luxury in Netanya. Public areas are busy and have a real five-star feel; rooms are fresh and attractive. Like much of Netanya, the hotel is located on a cliff above the beach—getting down to the beach can be a problem, although an elevator service is planned for sometime during 1996–98. Facilities include a large swimming pool, heated for winter, a health club, sauna, steam bath, Jacuzzi, and a variety of restaurants and pubs, including a branch of El Gaucho, a popular South American meat restaurant. There are ample parking facilities (always at a premium in Netanya); refrigerators and minibars are available on request.

PRIVATE ROOMS & APARTMENTS

One of the best ways to save money on accommodations, particularly if you plan to stay in Netanya for some time, is to rent a private room or apartment. The actual rental arrangements will generally be handled by local agents, and you'll have to pay an agent's fee, which is a flat 10% of the total rental (no extra charge if meal arrangements are made, fortunately).

Room rentals are available for at least 3 to 4 days, apartments for a week or more. Most of them are within walking distance of the sea. Rooms in private homes come with sheets and blankets, and no meals are served, though guests may use the refrigerator and stove. The cost is about $40 per person in summer; prices go up on weekends and holidays and are lower off-season.

In an apartment, you are provided with basic furniture. The place is cleaned up before you arrive, but upkeep is on you for the length of your stay. What is known as a two-room flat (living room, one bedroom, kitchen, bath, balconies) costs about $800 to well over $1,000 per couple per month. A three-room flat (two bedrooms plus) costs $900 to over $1,000 per month. A four-room flat (three bedrooms plus) would cost at least $1,100 for the same period; deluxe accommodations, of course, could be more. Bear in mind that these are summer rates, and that demand will probably drive these prices up during the lifetime of this edition. The supply of apartments may also be a problem.

Consult the **Municipal Tourist Information** desk at Ha-Atzma'ut Square (☎ 09/827-286) for listings of private room and apartment rental agents.

WHERE TO DINE

You'll want to try one of the many little sidewalk cafe-restaurants that line Ha-Atzma'ut Square. Here you can find just about anything your heart desires, and if it's not here, it's only a short walk along Herzl Street.

EXPENSIVE

Lucullus. 2 Jabotinsky St. ☎ **09/619-502.** Fixed-price lunch $16; fixed-price dinner $19. MC, V. Daily noon–3pm and 6pm–midnight. FRENCH/SEAFOOD.

This is probably the best and most stylish restaurant in town, and the place for a special meal. Tables are candlelit and decorated with fresh flowers, there's dance music on Fridays, and often a pianist at the bar in the evenings. Bernard Gabai, the owner of Lucullus, was born in Tunisia, and he has created a menu heavily colored with French tradition. First courses include choices like mousse of salmon and crevettes or pâté de foie gras; main course choices include fresh fish, calamari, shrimp, and lobster as well as filet mignon, goose liver, duck, and even chateaubriand. If you choose from the à la carte menu, a complete dinner with wine could run well over $30 per person. Lucullus is located in the southern part of town, somewhat away from Ha-Atzma'ut Square. When you call for reservations, ask about the restaurant's free taxi service policy. Lucullus has a kosher branch, Locus, at 5 Ha-Atzma'ut Square (☎ 03/617-831), with a similar French menu adapted to kashrut restrictions.

MODERATE

"Ha-Nassi" President Restaurant and Cafe Bar. 5 Herzl St. ☎ **09/617-147.** Full meal NIS 35–70 ($11–$21.50). MC, V. Sun–Thurs 11am–midnight or 2am; Fri 11am–hour before Sabbath; Sat 11am–2pm. Reserve and prepay for Sabbath meal. JEWISH.

This is a glatt kosher restaurant specializing in traditional Jewish dishes, and it's a local institution, freshly redecorated. It offers a multitude of meats from the grill or the oven. The house specialty is the Saturday meal, a traditional Sabbath feast, served from 11am to 2pm for $14, which must be paid in advance.

INEXPENSIVE

✪ **Apropo Netanya.** Gan Ha Melech. ☎ **09/624-482.** Reservations recommended for summer and holiday evenings. Appetizers NIS 13–30 ($3.90–$9); main courses NIS 22–50 ($6.60–$15). 12% service charge. AE, DC. Sun–Thurs 9am–midnight; Fri 9am–2pm; Sat after Shabbat–midnight. EUROPEAN/INTERNATIONAL.

Located in a modern, glass pavilion overlooking the sea at the far end of Ha-Atzma'ut Square, this restaurant serves the most cosmopolitan menu in town, ranging from large salads to pastas, blintzes, bagels and lox, and a list of appetizers and main courses prepared with a very tasty touch of Thai style. You can order salmon trout steamed with fine herbs, in a mildly Thai fashion, or have a genuine Thai soup, or kosher fried sesame coated faux "shrimp." A selection of lavish kosher pastries and cakes makes this a good stop for coffee and dessert.

Conditory Espresso Ugati. 1 Herzl St. ☎ **09/822-607.** Breakfast NIS 16.50 ($5); desserts and light meals NIS 15–25 ($4.50–$7.50). No credit cards. Sun–Thurs 8am–midnight; Fri 8am–3pm; Sat 6pm–midnight. CAFE.

A Central European pastry shop that is just perfect for devotees of those sinfully delicious, heavily creamy confections favored in Berlin and Vienna. Stop in for afternoon tea or after-dinner coffee—and a pastry from the refrigerator case out front. You can get espresso here, special apple pie or strudel for diabetics, and if you'd like brandy with your blintzes, they have that, too.

Pundak Ha-Yam Grill. 1 Ha-Rav Kook St. ☎ **09/615-780.** Main courses NIS 20–45 ($6–$13.50). No credit cards. Sat–Thurs noon–midnight; Fri noon–3:30pm. GRILL.

A plain, no-nonsense grill with meats sizzling, hardworking waiters, and a minimum of decor, it is nonetheless a top favorite with locals. Reasons? The grilled meats are prepared fresh, to your order, before your eyes; service is quick, portions are huge, and prices are moderate. Order shashlik, steak, heart, or liver, and you'll get a salad, french fries, a plate of spaghetti, and several rounds of flat bread, too.

Restaurant Miami. 2 Herzl St. ☎ **09/617-197.** Reservations recommended for large groups. Appetizers NIS 6–25 ($1.80–$7.50); main courses NIS 25–55 ($7.50–$16.50). No credit cards. Sun–Thurs 9am–midnight; Fri 9am–before Shabbat; Sat after Shabbat–midnight. MIDDLE EASTERN.

This popular glatt kosher restaurant is generally acknowledged to have the best shwarma in town; during the day the inexpensive shwarma is the main choice. Other

Middle Eastern delights are similarly enticing, with selections like lamb steak, veal schnitzel, the special house shashlik, or a hamburger served with rice or potato and salad. The restaurant is tiny and expands outdoors to a sheltered terrace in good weather.

✪ **Yotvata.** Ha-Atzma'ut Square ☎ **09/629-141.** Light meals NIS 10–27 ($3–$8); main courses NIS 23–54 ($6.90–$16.20). AE, DC, MC, V. Daily 8am–1am. DAIRY VEGETARIAN.

One of the best-quality dairy and vegetarian restaurants in the country, Yotvata has everything brought in fresh from the famous Yotvata Kibbutz down in the Negev. Giant servings of natural juice made from your choice of 15 different kinds of fruits are available here, as well as blintzes, vegetable pies, pasta dishes in cream sauces, cheesecakes, and great ice cream, all done with style. Saint Peter's fish rounds out the top end of the menu's price range.

NETANYA AFTER DARK

There's no problem finding plenty of things to do around Netanya after a day at the beach. Everything in Ha-Atzma'ut Square is open until around midnight or later, and the square is alive with strollers, sippers, diners, and people-watching cafe sitters on a warm evening.

Be sure to check with the Tourist Information Office and the weekly calendar in the Tel Aviv section of Friday's *Jerusalem Post* for special events, performances, and activities of all kinds. There's quite a lot going on, especially during the summer months. Each week, in the **amphitheater of Gan Ha-Melekh Park** running along the beachside cliffs just north of the square, there are community sings, screenings of free full-length feature films, and classical and light music (performed Sunday through Thursday from 5:45pm until sunset). There's entertainment in **Ha-Atzma'ut Square** by top Israeli singers and folklore groups as well as community folk dancing every Saturday, beginning at 8pm. Weekly programs for children start at 6:30pm, with magicians, clowns, and so on.

As Netanya is a resort town, with a seasonal turnover in clubs and discos, it's best to check about current choices with the well-informed tourist office at Ha-Atzma'ut Square. **Bridge** is played alternate Wednesday evenings in association with WIZO, NIS 10 ($3); for information call Juliette (☎ 09/629-233) or Anne (☎ 09/622-243). **Bingo evenings** are Sunday at 8pm at the Association of Americans and Canadians in Israel, 28 Shmuel Ha-Naziv St. (☎ 330-950). **Chess Club meetings** are every Monday from 7 to 10pm, at the Library, 30 Shmuel Ha-Naziv St.

5 Caesarea & Vicinity

40km (25 miles) N of Tel Aviv

This is one of my favorite places in Israel. From Caesarea's beautiful excavations you get a real feeling for the tide of history that has washed Israel's shores. Located about a third of the way from Tel Aviv to Haifa, behind a cluster of banana groves, Caesarea has been the scene of considerable activity and development—archeological digs, a luxury hotel, a golf course and country club.

Caesarea is the spectacular city of Herod the Great, who set out to construct a port to rival Alexandria. It later became the largest city in Judea, the chief port, the governor's residence, and the home of Pontius Pilate. Despite its splendor, within its gates hundreds of Jews and Christians were thrown to the lions following the revolt of A.D. 66.

Ancient Caesarea was a cosmopolitan city made up of diplomats, merchants, and sportsmen. Its grandeur lasted for about 300 years, but ultimately the Arabs took the town from the Byzantines in the year 640.

Some 400 years later (1107), the Crusaders conquered Caesarea, and among the treasures they recovered was a green crystal vessel reputed to be the famous Holy Grail. It was taken to Italy, where it is preserved in the Cathedral of San Lorenzo in Genoa, becoming known as the *Sacro Catino*. St. Louis (Louis IX) later built a fortress here, in 1271, and most of the Crusader ruins we see here today date from his time.

A TURBULENT PAST

The first port city here was constructed by colonists from Sidon in the 300s B.C., and named after Sharshan, king of Sidon. The name was later Hellenized to Straton, and the town called Straton's Tower.

Around 90 B.C. the town was conquered and rebuilt by Alexander Jannaeus (d. 76 B.C.), Hasmonean king of Judea. But Rome annexed all of Judea in 63 B.C., including the town of Straton's Tower. It was Herod the Great (37–4 B.C.) who enlarged and beautified the town considerably, adding a spectacular harbor, called Sebastos, and naming the city in honor of his Roman suzerain and benefactor, Augustus Caesar. By the time of Herod's death, Caesarea was developing into one of the grandest port cities of the eastern Mediterranean. During the 1st century of the Christian era, the Christian and Jewish populations of Caesarea were persecuted by their Roman overlords, and the two communities fought between themselves.

Caesarea is mentioned in the New Testament as the place where the Holy Ghost was first given to the Gentiles (Acts 10–11), a significant and controversial event in the development of Christianity. Caesarea figures prominently in the story of the apostle Paul, who was warned not to go to Jerusalem; he went anyway, returning in chains to stand trial for heresy. After his imprisonment and subsequent trial in Caesarea, he was sent to Rome, in the year A.D. 62, to stand trial again.

Caesarea was the headquarters of Roman rule in Israel, and the Jews increasingly resented the Roman militaristic domination of their land. Tensions came to a head in A.D. 60–70 when pogroms against the Jewish population began, culminating in the brutal massacre of 2,000 Jews in the Caesarea amphitheater. Many more were sent to Rome and sold into slavery. All Judea subsequently rose in revolt and the Romans destroyed Jerusalem in A.D. 70 and conquered Masada in 73.

More than 500,000 Jews died throughout the country in the rebellion of Bar Kokhba in 132. The greatest sages of the time, including Rabbi Akiva, were brought to the amphitheater of Caesarea, tortured in public, and burned alive.

Under the Byzantines, the city's history was less grisly. Caesarea was home to a succession of important church scholars, including Eusebius (264–340), who codified the rules of the church. During the 400s, Caesarea became the seat of a metropolitan bishop responsible for all the Christian communities of the eastern Mediterranean. A small but significant Jewish community thrived throughout this period. The Talmud mentions a number of judges or rabbis who lived in Caesarea, and also refers to the synagogue of Caesarea, situated near the harbor.

The Arab conquest, in A.D. 640, put an end to this time of growth. Muslim rule continued until 1101, when Baldwin I and his Crusader army landed in Caesarea and slaughtered the entire Arab population.

During the Crusader conquest, Baldwin's troops discovered what they thought to be the Holy Grail, the famous vessel from which Jesus had supposedly drunk at the Last Supper. The Crusaders began construction of a church at the spot where Saint

Paul was said to have received his condemnation, but building was interrupted when Saladin reconquered the city for Islam in 1187. Caesarea changed hands several times during the following century, even though Saint Louis of France had fortified its walls in 1252. When Muslim armies again took the town (in 1265 and 1291), they did their best to pull down the defenses, remembering that this had been Baldwin's beachhead. The pillage succeeded, and for the next 500 years Caesarea's impressive structures slowly became covered by sand.

In the 1700s Ahmed Jezzar Pasha, Ottoman governor of the province, sent his workmen to Caesarea to reclaim much of its Carrara marble, columns of decorative stone, and finely carved capitals for use in the reconstruction and beautification of his provincial capital at Acre (Akko), north of Haifa. In 1884 Muslim colonists from Bosnia arrived in Caesarea and attempted to found a fishing village. Malaria and the shifting sands convinced them to head inland and become farmers instead, but an Arab village survived here through much of our century, and was abandoned by its inhabitants during the 1948 war.

Caesarea's modern history begins in 1940, when Kibbutz Sedot Yam was founded. During the first decade of the kibbutz, its members discovered the unexpected richness of Caesarea's archeological remains. A full campaign of restoration followed, and today the city is one of Israel's most impressive archeological sites.

ESSENTIALS

GETTING THERE   By Bus   Public transportation to Caesarea is poor and very time-consuming (which makes an organized tour a good option). To get to Caesarea by bus, you must first take a bus to Hadera and transfer from there. Buses run to Hadera from Tel Aviv, Netanya, or Haifa, roughly every 30 to 45 minutes. From Hadera, bus no. 76 (NIS 6 [$1.80]) leaves six times a day for Caesarea, departing Sunday through Thursday. Check with Egged information in Haifa for current time-tables both ways. On Friday the last bus leaves Hadera at 12:40pm. Unless you plan to stay in Caesarea for the weekend, don't even consider visiting by public transport on Friday morning. No buses run on Saturday. The return bus leaves Caesarea about 20 minutes after each inbound arrival. You can also take one of the intercity Egged buses between Tel Aviv and Haifa, and ask to be let off on the main highway near the road to Caesarea. From there, it's a desolate hike of about an hour to the National Park.

By Car   There is a main coastal highway between Tel Aviv and Haifa, with the exit to Caesarea clearly marked.

VISITOR INFORMATION   Orientation   The remains of Caesarea (Qesari or Qesarya, in Hebrew) are spread along a 3-kilometer (2-mile) stretch of Mediterranean beach. North of the bungalows is the Roman theater, part of the national park, and a half kilometer (one-quarter mile) north is the entrance to the walled Crusader city. Just inland from the Crusader city entrance is a small snack restaurant and a shady parking lot. Be sure to wander behind the restaurant for a look at the ruins of a Byzantine street (described below). Finally, about a kilometer (one-half mile) north of the city, a 10- or 15-minute walk along the beach, is the impressive Roman aqueduct.

EXPLORING CAESAREA

Caesarea National Park. ☎ **06/361-358** or **228-983.** Admission (including theater and Crusader city) NIS 13 ($3.90) for adults, half price for children. Sat–Thurs 8am–4pm (Apr–Sept until 5pm); Fri 8am–3pm.

You'll arrive at either the Roman theater or the Crusader city, which are in fact right next to each other, though the entrance gates are a half kilometer (one-quarter mile) apart. You can enter the city to visit restaurants or stroll the ruins for free after hours, but special exhibits are closed.

You can get a map showing the details of all the various eras of construction at this site, both on land and in the water—the cities and harbors of Straton's Tower, of Herod, the Romans, the Byzantines, and the Crusaders. I recommend that you do this, since it will give you a much better idea of the scope of the place. The excavations you see are only a very small part of what's actually there, waiting to be discovered; new finds are constantly being unearthed. During the summer of 1995, a massive temple dedicated to Roman gods was uncovered and attributed to the great builder, King Herod; it may be open for public viewing during the time span of this edition. I'll assume you're going to see the ruins from south to north, starting with the theater.

The Roman Theater, capable of seating 5,000 spectators, was constructed in the time of Jesus and Pontius Pilate, and has been restored. You may be lucky enough to visit when a summer concert or other performance is planned, and sit on the warm, pale limestone seats with the Mediterranean as a backdrop. Test the acoustics by sitting in the stands and listening to someone on the stage speak or clap hands.

You enter the **Crusader city** on a bridge across the deep moat, then through a gatehouse with gothic vaulting. Emerging from the gatehouse, you find yourself in the large fortified town, which covered a mere fraction of the great Herodian/Roman city. Sites within the fortified town are marked by signs in Hebrew and English. Especially noteworthy are the foundations of the Crusader Church of Saint Paul (1100s), down toward the sea, near the little Turkish minaret (1800s). The citadel, next to the group of shops and restaurants, was badly damaged by an earthquake in 1837, as was most of the Crusader city.

The **Port of Sebastos,** a quay, part of the Crusader port, extends from the Crusader city into the sea, but King Herod's harbor at Caesarea, completed in 10 B.C. and named Sebastos, extended at least three times as far as what you see today. It curved around to the right, where a separate northern breakwater extended to meet it roughly where the northern Crusader fortification walls meet the sea.

The breakwater was also a wide platform, with room for large quantities of cargo, housing for sailors, a lighthouse, colossi (gigantic statues), and two large towers guarding the entrance gates to the harbor. The harbor could be closed off by a chain stretched between the two towers, preventing ships from entering; it was large and protected enough to permit ships to winter over, allowing the departure of ships laden with cargo from the East first thing in the spring, as soon as winter ended.

Herod's harbor was one of the largest harbors of the Roman world, mentioned by historian Flavius Josephus as an especially amazing feat of technology because it was a total creation—built without the usual benefit of a topographical feature such as a bay or cove. Historians did not find the harbor until 1960, when a combination of aerial photography and underwater archeological explorations revealed the ruins sunken offshore.

We don't see more evidence of this fantastic port structure because two geological fault lines are just off the coast running below the Herodian port. Historians and archeologists believe that the large harbor structure probably sank vertically downward shortly after its construction—by the 3rd century A.D. at the latest—perhaps in response to an earthquake.

The excavation of the underwater ruins is an important international project, one of the major endeavors of the Center for Maritime Studies at Haifa University.

There's a diving center at the site of the ancient harbor (☎ 06/361-441), where you can get a map of the site, complete with directions for a self-guided diving tour of the ruins, with an abbreviated version for snorkelers.

THE BYZANTINE STREET

Fifty yards east of the Crusader city entrance, behind the little snack shop, is the Byzantine Street, or Street of Statues, actually part of a forum. The statues depict an emperor and other dignitaries. Much of the stone for construction of the forum was taken from earlier buildings, as was the custom.

THE HIPPODROME

Head east from either the Byzantine Street or the theater to reach the ruined hippodrome, in the fields between the two access roads. Measuring 80 by 320 yards, the hippodrome could seat some 20,000 people. Some of the monuments in the hippodrome may have been brought from Aswan in Egypt—remember, expense was no object when Herod built for Caesar!

JEWISH QUARTER & ROMAN AQUEDUCT

Caesarea's Jewish Quarter is outside the walls of the Crusader city, near the beach directly north. The community that flourished here during Roman times was well within the boundaries, and the walls, of Herod's city.

The great aqueduct north of the Jewish Quarter is almost 9 kilometers (6 miles) in length, though most of it has been buried by the shifting sands. There was an earlier aqueduct here, but the present construction dates from the A.D. 100s. The southern part of the aqueduct is exposed to view, and you must see it.

CEASAREA'S BEACH

Swim at the white, sandy lagoons beside the romantic Roman aqueduct. Off-season (late spring, early autumn) the sea is still warmer than the North Atlantic and the Pacific ever get in the States. Some days the sea is lake-calm, but at other times, as everywhere on the coast, beware of rocks and severe undertows.

WHERE TO STAY
EXPENSIVE

Dan Caesarea. Caesarea 30600. ☎ **06/362-266.** Fax 06/362-392. 114 rms and suites (all with bath). A/C TEL TV. $78–$300 single; $100–$330 double. 15% service charge; $50 per room surcharge Thursday and Friday. Rates include breakfast. Family plan and children's rates. AE, DC, MC, V. Free parking .

Promoting itself as a golf hotel, the Dan Caesarea offers a full array of sports activities. The hotel is a lovely four-story complex set amid acres of gardens and archeological ruins. All rooms have balconies and vistas of the Mediterranean (some distance away) or the countryside. As with many of the older Dan Hotels, deluxe rooms have been beautifully renovated and contain luxurious polished stone bathrooms; furnishings in standard rooms show their age. There is a large outdoor swimming pool, and the hotel is adjacent to Israel's only 18-hole golf course, which guests can use for a fee. Horseback riding, fishing, diving, bicycling, and other country activities can be arranged, and there is a full program of in-hotel sports. The hotel is not close to many restaurant choices, and guests depend on in-house dining facilities, which are adequate, but no more than average.

Dining/Entertainment: Restaurant, snack bar/cafe, bar.

Facilities: Outdoor pool, fitness center, Jacuzzi, sauna, two day/night tennis courts, access to golf club.

INEXPENSIVE

Ilana Berner's Bed and Breakfast. 23 Harimon St., Caesarea. ☎ and Fax **06/363-936.** 4 rms (1 with private shower). A/C TEL. $55 single; $70 double; $85 triple. Rates include breakfast. No credit cards.

If you want to stay in exclusive Caesarea, close to the sea and the extensive antiquities, this large one-level villa, the home of Ilana Berner, who is a licensed tour guide, is recommended. Within walking distance to a grocery, restaurant, and synagogue, the house has a swimming pool in summer, a hot tub/Jacuzzi (available with advance notice), and offers such amenities as game boards and two bicycles for rent. Ms. Berner also has dogs and cats and maintains a no-smoking rule. Call or fax in advance. Call for instructions or pickup from Hadera (fee) or Caesarea.

WHERE TO DINE

While there are few overnight facilities in Caesarea itself, there are pleasant restaurants, especially among the ancient ruins. Few tourists realize that these places stay open after the archeological park has officially closed; you can enjoy extensive or light meals on their waterfront terraces as well as fabulous sunsets and starry nights.

Charlie's. Old Caesarea. ☎ **06/363-050.** Reservations recommended. Appetizers NIS 15–40 ($4.50–$12); main courses NIS 36–70 ($11–$21). MC, V. Daily 10:30am–1am. INTERNATIONAL.

Charlie's rambles over its site among the ruins inside the Crusader walls, offering you large and small whitewashed arched-ceiling dining areas and a covered harborside terrace. There's a really wide variety of choices here, from appetizers like avocado filled with shrimp and Moroccan cigars (edible) to main courses of shrimp, squid, fresh fish, and grilled meat. A very complete bar offers wines at $12 to $20 a bottle for long on-the-terrace evenings overlooking the sea. Friday evenings often include folklore performances and sing-alongs; large tour groups often book here, so reservations are imperative.

Herod's Palace. Old Caesarea. ☎ **06/361-103.** Reservations recommended. Appetizers NIS 12–20 ($3.60–$6); main courses NIS 33–55 ($10–$16.50). MC, V. Sun–Thurs 9:30am–1am; Fri 9:30am–before Shabbat; Sat after Shabbat. INTERNATIONAL.

This is the only kosher restaurant in Caesarea, beautifully situated in a restored building at the southern end of Crusader ruins inside the Crusader walls. It has a large upstairs terrace overlooking the sea. A romantic place to spend balmy evenings, Herod's Palace serves a selection of grilled fish, meats, and desserts. Carmel wines are NIS 36 ($11) a bottle. A 10% service charge is added to each bill.

EN ROUTE NORTH TO ACRE

ZICHRON YAAKOV

In the hills north of Caesarea, Zichron Yaakov, founded in 1882, has the distinction of being one of the first towns to be settled in Israel in modern times. Of interest here are the wine cellars (they'll give you a tour and some wine afterward) and the Rothschild Family Tomb (Ramat Ha-Nadiv), set in handsome gardens. Stop in to see the Aaronson Museum near the wine cellar; it commemorates the Aaronson family's work during World War I at an experimental farm at Athlit, from which they supplied the British with intelligence information.

Opposite Zichron Yaakov is **Kibbutz Maagan Michael**, whose beautiful carp ponds at the edge of the sea also serve as a bird sanctuary. Depending on the season, birdwatchers can find herons, cranes, and storks. This kibbutz produces plastic products, and also has a livestock center featuring in-residence Israeli cowboys and herds of Brahmin-type cows.

Where to Stay

Carmel Gardens Hotel. 1 Etzion St., Zichron Yaacov 30900. ☎ **06/300-111;** tel. 800/221-0203 or 212/541-5009 in the U.S. Fax 06/397-030. 112 rms (all with bath). A/C TEL TV. $120–$145 single; $135–$158 double. AE, DC, MC, V.

This contemporary, sprawling lowrise hotel, overlooking the countryside at the edge of Zichron Yaacov, is managed by the excellent Radisson Moriah Hotel Chain. It is comfortable and attractive, but more of a four-star property than the five-star level maintained by other Radisson Moriah Chain Hotels, and this is reflected in the rates. The hotel is a pleasant base for exploring Caesarea, Meggiddo, the artists' colony at Ein Hod, and the beaches of the Mediterranean coast. There is an outdoor swimming pool, lobby bar, restaurant, coffee bar, and children's play area.

Where to Dine

Shuni Fortress. Jabotinsky Park, Zichron Yaacov–Binyamina Road (Route 652). ☎ **06/380-227.** Reservations recommended. Appetizers $10–$20 range; main courses $15–$25 range. No credit cards. Mon–Sat lunch and dinner. Closed Sun. 1 kilometer north of Binyamina. COUNTRY FRENCH.

Set in the arched, whitewashed rooms of a renovated ancient fortress in an area that might be called Israel's wine country, this restaurant is the special creation of Chef Antoinne Taub, who has been an important force in shaping the traditional haute cuisine scene in Israel. There is no menu: everything depends on what the chef is doing on the day of your visit, but you may encounter mushrooms Provençale or goose liver pâté among the first courses, and honeyed breast of mallard or boeuf bourguinonne among the main courses. Classic preparation and sauces are the general rule, but there is a rustic feel to the menu here, with homemade breads, and wines from the area as well as from Chef Antoinne's own vineyard. In good weather, the few patio tables, with lovely vistas, are in demand and must be reserved ahead of time. Desserts are always worthwhile.

DOR

On the highway skirting the beach, road signs announce Nasholim, a kibbutz located on one of Israel's most beautiful bathing beaches, **Dor Beach.** A wide expanse of sandy beach, it is beautified by natural lagoons. Looming nearby is **Tel Dor,** a mound containing the remains of the ancient city that was inhabited since Bronze Age times by Phoenicians, Israelites, Greeks, and Romans. The ruins of a massive Greco-Roman temple dedicated to Zeus add drama to the site. Farther to the north at modern Dor is a picturesque area of caves eroded by the sea to form a natural tunnel at the water's edge.

Where to Stay

Nasholim Kibbutz Holiday Village. Carmel Beach 20815. ☎ **06/399-533.** Fax 06/397-614. 80 rms (all with shower). A/C TEL TV. $68–$84 double. July 15–Sept 1 and Jewish holidays add 50%; half board required. Winter: 10%–25% lower. Lower rate available if booked on Kibbutz Fly & Drive Plan (☎ 800/552-0141). MC, V.

This kibbutz-operated vacation village is about an hour's drive from Tel Aviv, and within easy access to Caesarea and Haifa. It's a great place to spend the day, or several days. The islets around the beach make for sheltered, warm swimming, even during the winter or storm seasons, and the recreation facilities include a children's play area and tennis courts and a video television room as well as a disco/club for younger guests. Rooms are simple, lined up like rows of cabanas with small terraces in front; they include small kitchenette units. There are antiquities around this recreation village, and it's a good base for sightseeing tours. Nasholim is justly proud of its meals, among the best in the kibbutz guest-house system, which are served in the air-conditioned dining room. The place is mobbed with Israeli families and kids in the summer school vacation program and on Jewish holidays; at other times it's more relaxed and quieter.

Note that there is no exit from the coastal highway to Nasholim. To reach Nasholim, leave the main coastal highway and use the parallel inland road between Binyamina and Faradis.

EIN HOD

Inland from the coastal highway is the artists' village of Ein Hod. Road signs will point the way for drivers, and from 10am to 5:30pm there's Egged bus service all the way up the mountainside to this famous colony. You can also take bus no. 921 to the Ein Hod roadway that intersects with the older, more inland Tel Aviv–Haifa highway, and hitchhike up the mountainside from there. (True hikers will find the half-hour uphill trek a simple one.)

Ein Hod (Well of Beauty) was built over an abandoned Arab village in 1953 by Israeli sculptors, painters, and potters, under the guidance of Marcel Janco.

The village now includes a museum of surrealist art, several workshops, and an outdoor theater. It's a picturesque place, tranquil and rugged looking, with a view of sloping olive groves and the broad Mediterranean that can inspire even the nonartistic. Crumbling archways and Moorish vaults are relics of the past. Most of Ein Hod's full-time residents are artisans, and sell their work in a large, cooperative gallery.

Cooperation is emphasized: the village members have their own council of elders; the handyman is employed by the entire community; the gallery takes a much smaller percentage on sales than do other galleries; the workshops are shared; and the proceeds from the amphitheater's shows and concerts, which range from folk and classical to hard rock (summer weekends only), are used for the welfare of the village. Call 04/984-3152 or 984-2029 for information.

The **Janco-Dada Museum** (☎ 04/984-2350) is open Sunday through Friday from 9:30am to 4pm, on Saturday until 5pm. There is a pleasant snack bar/cafe for visitors.

Shopping

The **Ein Hod Gallery** (☎ 04/984-2548) carries a good selection of the village's work—silver jewelry, lots of ceramics, lithographs, etchings, oil paintings, watercolors, tapestries and shawls, sculpture, and woodwork. The gallery staff will box your purchases and mail them to you wherever you live. Admission to the gallery is by a small donation for adults. It's open Saturday through Thursday from 9:30am to 5pm and Friday from 9:30am to 4pm; closed Jewish holidays and Israeli Independence Day.

Where to Stay Nearby

Nir Etzion Kibbutz Hotel. Carmel Beach 30808. ☎ **04/984-2541.** Fax 04/984-3344. 74 rms (all with bath or shower). A/C TEL TV. $56–$88 single; $75–$114 double. MC, V.

Continue driving along the road that runs through Ein Hod, and you'll reach the delightful resort of Nir Etzion, which is run by the kibbutz of the same name. The kibbutz offers glatt kosher meals, an on-kibbutz synagogue, in-season pool, children's playground, babysitting service, and a warm, friendly atmosphere. There is transportation to nearby Dor Beach. The kibbutz is also near Mount Carmel Forest. Jewish holidays and weekends and July 5 to September 1, you may be required to take half or full board, which adds an additional 30% to your bill. A Sabbath atmosphere is maintained on Shabbat.

6 Acre (Akko)

23km (14 miles) N of Haifa, 56km (37 miles) W of Tiberias

Acre (also Akko or Acco), with its romantic minarets, massive city seawalls, and palm trees framed against the sky, has had a long, eventful history. It was first mentioned in the chronicles of Pharaoh Thutmose III, about 3,500 years ago. It was a leading Phoenician port, and although it was allotted to the tribe of Asher, the tribe was never able to conquer it. The town is mentioned as part of David's kingdom, and was given by Solomon to Hiram, king of Tyre, in return for his help in building the temple.

Alexander the Great conquered Acre in 332 B.C., and later, in 280 B.C., it was captured by the Ptolemies, and renamed Ptolemais. Under this name it is mentioned in the New Testament as a stopping place of Saint Paul. Julius Caesar stayed here in 48 B.C.

From the time of Acre's allocation to the tribe of Asher, Jews had lived in relative peace with the other local inhabitants, but during the Bar Kokhba revolt many Jews were killed by the Romans. Still, remnants of the Jewish population continued to live here.

When the Arabs conquered Ptolemais in A.D. 636, the town reverted to the name of Acre, and it was known by that name until the Crusaders took the town in 1104 and renamed it Saint Jean d'Acre. The town became the regional seat of Crusader government, and it expanded to include an entire underground city, which you still can visit today. Except for one 4-year period, the Crusaders held Acre until the 13th century when they were defeated by the Mamelukes, who sacked the town. The fall of Acre ensured the doom of Crusader dominion in the Holy Land.

It was not until 1749, when Bedouin Sheik Daher el-Omar conquered the town, that Acre experienced a resurgence, but his plans for a serious rebuilding program came to a sudden end when he was murdered in 1775 by the notoriously cruel Ahmed El-Jezzar Pasha. Under the impetus of El-Jezzar, the town's most important rebuilding took place, including the Jezzar Pasha Mosque, the Khan El-Umdan, the Turkish bathhouse now housing the Municipal Museum, the massive stone walls, and the aqueduct to the north. These structures still stand today.

Acre's decline as a major port was sealed by the advent of the steamship and other modern naval technology, with shipping activities gradually transferred to the larger port at Haifa, across the bay, which remains Israel's primary port. On May 4, 1947, Acre was the scene of the largest prison break in history when 251 prisoners escaped from Acre Fortress with the help of Jewish underground fighters.

ESSENTIALS

GETTING THERE   By Bus   Buses no. 251 and 271 leave the Haifa bus station every 10 minutes, bound for Acre; the schedule is less frequent on Saturday.

By Car   Independence Road in Haifa port runs north out of the city past a heavily industrial area. At a crossroads called the "checkpost," bear left, following the signs, over the railroad tracks, and you'll be on the northern coastal road to Acre and Nahariya.

VISITOR INFORMATION   Directly across from the Mosque of Jezzar Pasha is the **Tourist Information Office** (☎ 04/991-1764), open from 8:30am to 4pm

Sunday through Thursday, closing early on Friday. Here—or next door, at the entrance to the Subterranean Crusader City—you can buy a large, wonderfully detailed map of the entire city of Acre for only NIS 5 ($1.50). The area code for Acre is 04.

A note for women: Medieval Acre is fascinating, but women unaccompanied by men, even in pairs or in groups, attract a lot of attention around the labyrinthine Old City.

ORIENTATION

Coming into town by car, you can simply follow the signs for the Old City. If you arrive by bus, exit from the bus station, turn left, and walk one long block to the traffic lights on Ben-Ami Street. Turn right (west) onto Ben-Ami and walk four long blocks to Haim Weizmann Street. Turn left onto Weizmann and you'll see the walls of the ancient Turkish fortress about two blocks ahead. Soon the minaret and dome of the Jezzar Pasha Mosque will come into view. There is a small parking lot on the left ($3), just inside the city walls. City buses no. 1, 2, 61, 62, 63, and 65 all make stops at the entrance to the Old City.

CITY LAYOUT   Today Acre comprises two distinct parts. There's the modern city of Acre, with about 40,000 residents, and a number of large industrial plants (including Steel City) and immigrant housing projects. Then there's the Old City, still surrounded by high, thick, stone walls on all sides, situated on the tip of land jutting out into the sea, forming the protected Bay of Acre. It's the Old City that holds the charm and interest for tourists.

EXPLORING OLD ACRE

Allow yourself a half day to wander through Old Acre's medieval streets. Unlike the restored Old City of Jaffa, which is filled with tourist shops, Old Acre is genuine, charming, and its streets teem with real life. The best place to start your tour is at the **Mosque of Ahmed Jezzar Pasha.** Right across the street from Jezzar's mosque is the marvelous **Subterranean Crusader City,** and just a few steps farther is the **Municipal Museum,** housed in Ahmed Jezzar Pasha's Turkish bath.

Next you'll wander through the pleasant and colorful streets of the **bazaar.** Be sure to see the most picturesque shop in the bazaar, Kurdy and Berit's **Coffee and Spices,** at no. 13/261 (ask around, it's deep in the market). If you make a purchase, the very hospitable owner may invite you to try a cup of thick Arabic coffee. Acre's "formal" market is **Suq El-Abiad,** but numerous streets within Old Acre serve as shopping areas. You'll pass the **El-Zeituneh Mosque** to **the Khan El-Umdan** caravansary, marked by a tall segmented tower. A caravansary was a combination warehouse, office building, banking center, stable, and factory.

The market streets, filled with delicious Arabic bakeries and hummus restaurants, are an excellent area to find snacks. Just beyond is **the port,** a good place to stop for lunch (see "Where to Dine," below). Here you can also hire a boat to take you on a **sea tour of the city walls** (about $5 per person). Don't be afraid to bargain. Many boat operators will be glad to take you on a motor or fishing boat **cruise around Old Acre.** Settle on a price in advance (about $14 to $17 for an hour is the average), and get a boat that looks comfortable. A large tourist boat, the *Princess,* takes visitors on a 20-minute ride around the Old City walls, but only when enough people are waiting to make the run profitable. The fare is NIS 10 ($3) per person.

In Venezia Square (Ha-Dayagim in Hebrew), facing the port, is the **Sinan Pasha Mosque,** and behind it the **Khan El-Faranj** caravansary. Yet another khan, named **El-Shwarda,** is a short distance to the northeast. A few steps back is the Ahmed Jezzar

Pasha Mosque. You'll also want to visit the **Museum of Heroism** and **El-Jezzar's Wall** on Ha-Hagana Street.

THE TOP ATTRACTIONS

Mosque of Armed Jezzar Pasha. Admission NIS 4 ($1.20). Open 8am–noon; 1:15–4pm and 4:45–6pm. Modest dress required. No entrance during prayers (exact times vary according to time of the year).

Ahmed Jezzar Pasha was the Ottoman Turkish governor of Acre during the late 1700s. When Napoleon invaded Egypt, the English joined the Ottomans in trying to drive him out. Jezzar Pasha, thinking Napoleon an easy enemy to defeat, set out confidently for Gaza with his forces, but Napoleon's French legions drove him right back to Acre. The French were forced ultimately to withdraw, but Jezzar Pasha's troubles were far from over. Internal unrest and the other semi-independent Ottoman governors in the region threatened the unity of Ahmed Jezzar's District. A few years later Jezzar was called upon by Constantinople (present-day Istanbul) to march into Arabia and try to put down the revolt of the ultrareligious Wahhabi movement.

The pasha died in Acre in 1804. Despite his great ability as a governor, he was branded as a stern administrator and nicknamed El-Jezzar (The Butcher).

Ahmed Jezzar's contributions to Acre included building fountains, a covered market, a Turkish bath, and the harmonious mosque complex that bears his name. Built in 1781, it is an excellent example of classic Ottoman Turkish architecture and stands among the pasha's most ambitious projects. Every great man in the empire wanted to endow a mosque in his own name, an act that not only added to his glory on earth but also made points for him in heaven. A number of charitable institutions were usually constructed around the mosque, and shops were built into the walls, the rent from the shops paying for the maintenance of the mosque. Though the greatest of these complexes were in Constantinople, the Ottoman capital, the one in Acre gives you a good idea of the exotic style of Ottoman architecture (rooted in both Byzantine and Persian traditions), and how the mosque complex worked.

As you approach the mosque area, El-Jezzar Street turns right off Weizmann Street. The mosque entrance is a few steps along El-Jezzar Street on the left. Before you mount the stairs to the mosque courtyard, notice the ornate little building to the right of the stairs. It's a sabil, or cold-drinks stand, from which pure, refreshing drinking water, sometimes mixed with fruit syrups, was distributed—another of the mosque complex's services. Note especially the fine tile fragments mounted above the little grilled windows just beneath the sebil's dome. Tile-making was an Ottoman specialty.

Up the stairs, you enter the mosque courtyard. Your ticket will enable you to explore the complex of Crusader buildings (now flooded and used as cisterns) under the mosque. Just inside the entry, mounted on a pedestal, is a marble disc bearing the tughra, or monogram, of the Ottoman sultan. It spells out the sultan's name, his father's name, and the legend "ever-victorious."

The arcade around the courtyard can be used for prayers during hot days of summer, as can the arcaded porch at the front of the mosque. The *shadirvan*, or ablutions fountain, opposite the mosque entry, is used for the ritual cleansing of face, neck, hands, and feet five times a day before prayers. You must slip off your shoes before entering the mosque proper. This is not merely a religious rule, but a hygienic one: worshipers kneel on the carpets during prayer, and want to keep them clean.

Inside, you'll notice the *mihrab*, or prayer niche, which indicates the direction of Mecca, toward which worshipers must face when they pray. The galleries to the right

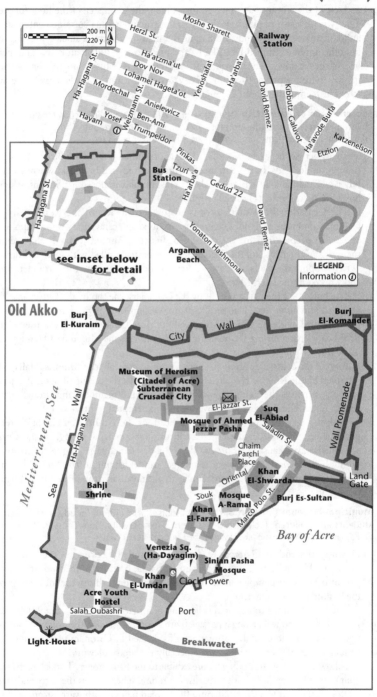

Acre (Akko)

Herzl St.
Moshe Sharett
Railway Station
Ha'atzma'ut
Dov Nov
Lohamei Hageta'ot
Mordechal
Anielewicz
Ben-Ami
Hayam
Yosef
Trumpeldor
Ha-Hagana St.
Weizmann St.
Yehoshafat
Ha'arba'a
David Remez
Kibbutz Galuyot
Ha'avode Burla
Katzenelson
Etzion
Pinkas
Tzuri
Ha'arba'a
Bus Station
Gedud 22
David Remez
Yonaton Hashmonai
Argaman Beach

see inset below for detail

0   200 m   N
     220 y

LEGEND
Information ⓘ

Old Akko

Burj El-Kuraim
Burj El-Komander
City   Wall
Wall

Museum of Heroism
(Citadel of Acre)
Subterranean
Crusader City

El-Jazzar St.
Suq El-Abiad
Saladin St.

Mosque of Ahmed Jezzar Pasha

Chaim Parchi Place

Khan El-Shwarda

Oriental

Wall Promenade

Land Gate

Mediterranean Sea

Sea

Ha-Hagana St.

Wall

Bahji Shrine

Souk
Mosque A-Ramal
Khan El-Faranj
Marco Polo St.
Burj Es-Sultan

Bay of Acre

Venezia Sq. (Ha-Dayagim)
Sinian Pasha Mosque

Khan El-Umdan
Clock Tower

Acre Youth Hostel
Salah Oubashri
Port

Light-House
Breakwater

and left of the entrance are reserved for women, the main area of the floor for men. The *minbar*, a sort of pulpit, is that separate structure with a curtained entry, stairs, and a little steeple. Around to the right is a mausoleum and a small graveyard that hold the tombs of Ahmed Jezzar Pasha and his successor, Suleiman Pasha, and members of their families. The mosque is still used by Acre's Muslim population, so when it's in service for prayer (five times a day), you must wait until the prayers are over to enter the mosque (about 20 minutes).

Subterranean Crusader City. Admission NIS 12 ($3.40) adults, reduction for students and children. Admission includes entrance to Municipal Museum. Sun–Thurs 8:30am–6pm; Fri 8:30am–2pm; Sat 9am–5pm; closings are 1 hour earlier in winter.

Virtually across the street from the Mosque of Ahmed Jezzar Pasha is the Subterranean Crusader City. In the entrance is a tourism information kiosk, where you can buy a city map and an entrance ticket. (The complex is closed for Sukkot, when it hosts the Akko Fringe Theatre Festival.)

The Crusaders built their fortress atop what was left of the Roman city. In Ottoman times the cavernous chambers were used as a caravansary until Napoleon's attack. In preparation for the defense of his city, Ahmed Jezzar Pasha ordered the walls heightened, and the Crusader rooms partially filled with sand and dirt, to better support the walls. Today you get a good look at how the Crusaders lived and worked in the late 1100s.

The bottom of the hall was built by the Crusaders, the top by the Ottomans. The next hall you enter once held an illegal (in Muslim times) wine press. Next comes the courtyard, with the 125-foot-high walls of **Acre Citadel,** which was used by the British as a prison during the mandate and now houses the Museum of Heroism (see below).

Beyond the courtyard, through a huge Ottoman gate, are the **Knights' Halls,** once occupied by the Knights Hospitalers of Saint John. In the ceiling of the hall, a patch of concrete marks the spot where Jewish underground members, imprisoned by the British in the Citadel (directly above the hall), attempted to break out.

Back through the courtyard, you now head for the **Grand Maneir,** or center of government, in the Crusader city. Past it, through a narrow passage, is the **Crypt,** so named only because of its present depth; it was actually the knights' refectory, or dining hall. Beyond the refectory is a longer tunnel leading to **the Post** (El-Posta), a series of rooms and a courtyard similar to a caravansary, the precise use of which is not known.

Municipal Museum (Turkish Bath). Admission NIS 12 ($3.40) for adults, reduction for students and children. Includes admission to Crusader City. Sun–Thurs 8:30am–6pm; Fri 8:30am–2pm; Sat 9am–5pm; closings are 1 hour earlier in winter.

Down at the end of El-Jezzar Street, just around the corner, is the Municipal Museum. The building is the Hammam El-Basha, built by Ahmed Jezzar Pasha as part of his mosque complex in the 1780s. The museum exhibits are interesting, but the building itself is fantastic.

The first few small rooms hold collections of artifacts from Acre's last 2,000 years. Beyond them you walk along a passage (with a garden through the grillwork on your right) to the folklore exhibit of mannequins dressed in Ottoman garb, arranged in various scenes of everyday life. Note especially the pretty tilework.

Follow the passage from the folklore exhibit to the bath proper. Turkish baths were built on the Roman plan, with three distinct rooms. The first was the entry and dressing room, the next was the tepidarium (its Roman name), with warm steam, and the last was the caldarium, with hot steam. The hot room was always the most ornate.

As you walk through the first two rooms, note the tiny glass skylights in the domes. The third room, the one for hot steam, is rich in marble, fancy stone, and mosaic work. In the center is a circular platform for steam bathing. The heat source was beneath it. Some Turkish baths have a small swimming pool here instead. Four private steam cubicles occupy the four points of the compass.

The exhibits here, mostly enlarged copies of drawings, lithographs, and engravings, depict Acre during the Napoleonic Wars. When you're finished with your explorations, a guard will let you out a door just off the hot-steam room.

Museum of Heroism. ☎ **04/991-8264.** Admission NIS 8 ($2.40) for adults, with reduction for children and students. Sun–Thurs 9am–5pm.

The museum is in the Citadel of Acre. This complex of buildings was used as a prison in Ottoman and British Mandate times, but is now a mental hospital. Part of the prison has been set aside in honor of the Jewish underground fighters imprisoned here by the British. With the help of Irgun forces, 251 prisoners staged a mass escape in May 1947. If you saw the movie *Exodus*, that was the breakout and this was the prison. The prison is also revered by Arab Israelis and by Palestinians, whose own national fighters were detained and, in many cases, executed here during the British Mandate.

Among the exhibits are the entrance to the escape tunnel and displays of materials showing the British repression of Zionist activity during the mandate. Not all prisoners were lucky enough to escape, however. Eight Irgun fighters were hanged here in the 10 years before Israel's independence. You can visit the death chamber, called the Hanging Room, complete with noose.

Inmates here included Zeev Jabotinsky and Dov Gruner, among other leaders of Zionism and Israel's independence movement. Before the mandate, the prison's most famous inmate was Bahaullah (1817–92), founder of the Baha'i faith (see below).

The museum can be reached by walking north from the lighthouse on Ha-Hagana Street, along the seawall. You can also come here directly from El-Jezzar Mosque. Walk down El-Jezzar Street and continue in as straight a line as possible to Ha-Hagana Street, which skirts the city's western seawalls. When you reach the sea, turn right, and soon you'll see the entrance to the museum on the right-hand side.

EL-JEZZAR'S WALL

To appreciate the elaborate system of defenses built by Ahmed Jezzar Pasha to protect against Napoleon's fleet and forces, turn right as you come out of the Museum of Heroism onto Ha-Hagana Street and walk a few steps north. You'll see the double system of walls with a moat in between. Jutting into the sea is an Ottoman defensive tower called the Burj El-Kuraim. You're now standing at the northwestern corner of the walled city. Walk east (inland) along the walls and you'll pass the Citadel, the Burj El-Hazineh (Treasury Tower), and cross Weizmann Street to the Burj El-Komander, the strongest point in the walls. The land wall system continues south from here all the way to the beach.

At the entrance to the Old City on Weizmann Street, near the Walls of El-Jezzar, is a sunken children's playground bordered by the Dahar El-Omer Walls. Dahar El-Omer (or Daher El-Amar) was the sheik who rebuilt the city walls after capturing Acre from the Mamelukes.

THE KHANS & THE PORT

Make your way south through the city, toward the port, and if you need a point of reference, ask a local to point you toward the **Khan El-Umdan.** The khan (dating from 1785) is much older than its tower, which was built as a clock tower in 1906 to celebrate the 30th year of the reign of the Ottoman Sultan Abdul Hamid II. El-Umdan means "The Pillars," and when you enter this vast colonnaded court you'll know how it got its name. Another of Ahmed Jezzar Pasha's harmonious works in the public service, this caravansary served commerce. It was built on the site of a Crusader monastery of the Dominican order.

Just to the east of Khan El-Umdan is Venezia Square (Ha-Dayagim) and the **Sinian Pasha Mosque.** The port is to the southeast and industrious fishers are still at work here. Behind the port are two more caravansaries. The **Khan El-Faranj** (Afranj), or the Inn of the Franks, is a few steps north of the Sinian Pasha Mosque. This complex began in 1729 as a Franciscan convent, but some of the building was apparently rented to French and Italian merchants.

Northeast of the Khan El-Faranj is the **Khan El-Shwarda,** right next to a tower in the city walls called **Burj Es-Sultan**. The Burj is famous because it is the only construction built by the Crusaders that remains intact. At the tower's base is one of Napoleon's cannons, cast in Liège and captured by the Ottoman and English forces.

Walk up Marco Polo Street to your next stop. Marco Polo, by the way, was one of several famous visitors to Acre in medieval times; another was King Richard the Lion-Hearted. The **Khan El-Shwarda,** at the northern end of Marco Polo Street, occupies the site of a convent of the nuns of Saint Clare that closed in 1291 when Acre fell. There's not a lot to look at today.

The **Mosque A-Ramal** (or El-Ramel), the former "Sand Mosque," on Marco Polo Street, was built in 1704–05. A Crusader inscription was found on the southeast wall of this mosque, which today forms part of the back wall of the fourth shop on the left from the mosque entrance. The Latin inscription reads, "Oh, men who pass along this street, in charity I beg you to pray for my soul—Master Ebuli Fazli, builder of the church." The mosque is now used as a scout house, and it's open daily from 4 to 6pm (admission is free).

An old **lighthouse,** still in use, stands atop the Crusader fortification of Burj Es-Sanjak, on the extreme southwest point of land at Acre. From here you get a marvelous view, both north and south. Just north of the lighthouse, you'll notice a large space in the seawall. This stretch of the wall was destroyed during the heavy earthquake of 1837, the same earthquake that leveled several cities in the mountains.

BAHJI

To Baha'is, this shrine to their prophet Bahaullah is the holiest place on earth. Baha'i followers believe that God is manifested to men and women through prophets such as Abraham, Moses, Jesus, and Muhammad, as well as the Bab (Bahaullah's predecessor) and Bahaullah himself. The Baha'i faith proclaims that all religions are one, that men and women are equal, that the world should be at peace, and that education should be universal. Baha'i followers are encouraged to live simply and to dedicate themselves to helping their fellow men and women. They look forward to a day when there will be a single world government and one world language.

The Baha'i faith grew out of the revelation of the Bab, a Persian Shiite Muslim teacher and mystic who flourished from 1844 to 1850, and was executed by the Persian shah for insurrection and radical teachings. In 1863, Mirza Husein Ali Nuri, one of the Bab's disciples, proclaimed himself Bahaullah, the Promised One, whose coming had been foretold by the Bab. Bahaullah was exiled by the Persian government, in cooperation with the Ottoman leaders, to Baghdad, Constantinople, Adrianople, and finally to Acre, where he arrived in August 1868. He and several of his followers were imprisoned for 2¹/₂ years at the Acre Citadel. The authorities later put him under house arrest, and he was eventually brought to Bahji, where he remained until his death in 1892. He is buried here in a peaceful tomb surrounded by magnificent gardens. Baha'is are still persecuted, especially in Iran, where the faith was born; the Shiite Muslims in authority today look upon them as blasphemers and heretics.

You can visit the shrine at Bahji (Delight), where Bahaullah lived, died, and is buried, on Friday, Saturday, and Sunday only, from 9am to noon. The house's beautiful gardens are open to visitors every day, from 9am to 4pm. Catch a no. 271 bus heading north toward Nahariya, and make sure it stops at Bahji.

Going north from Acre, you'll see an impressive gilded gate on the right-hand side of the road after about 2 kilometers (1 mile). This gate is not open to the public. Go past it until you are almost 3 kilometers (about 2 miles) from Acre, and you'll see a sign, Shamerat. Get off the bus, turn right here, and go another short distance to the visitors' gate. The Ottoman–Victorian house holds some memorabilia of Bahaullah, and the lush gardens are a real treat.

ARGAMAN BEACH & OTHER OUTDOOR ACTIVITIES

The favorite local spot for swimming is the Argaman Beach, just south of town by the Argaman Motel. This is one of Israel's most beautiful Mediterranean beaches, with the view of Haifa on one end of the bay, and the old seawalls of Acre on the other. Lifeguards are here in summer. Unfortunately, like other beaches along the northern coast, Argaman sometimes suffers from pollution. At times during 1995, coliform bacteria levels recorded at Akko were four times the Ministry of Health's acceptable standard; Akko presently has no sewage treatment plant.

The **Palm Beach Hotel and Country Club** (☎ 04/981-5815) on Argaman Beach has an outdoor Olympic-size swimming pool plus a heated indoor pool, tennis, volleyball, basketball, and squash courts, Ping-Pong tables, a health club, a Finnish sauna, massage by appointment (for an extra fee), a private beach with lounge chairs and shades, and so on. Although the country club is reserved for members and hotel guests, tourists are usually welcome for a day-use fee in the nonpeak seasons. Call ahead to make a reservation and ask the price.

WHERE TO STAY

If you're not up for staying in the youth hostel, which is the only choice inside the walls of the Old City, there are some fine hotel choices just a short ride from Old Acre. Listings outside the Old City are especially recommended for travelers with private cars.

Argaman Motel. Acre Beach 24101. ☎ **04/991-6691.** Fax 04/991-6690. 75 rms (all with bath). A/C TEL TV. Sun–Thurs $55 single; $78 double. 10% discount for stays over 1 week. Rates include breakfast. Fri–Sat, July–Aug, and Jewish holidays, half board may be required, $70 single; $96 double. AE, DC, MC, V.

This modern hotel consists of a group of two-story buidings set around a swimming pool and garden a mile south of Acre on the coastal highway to Haifa, at the intersection of the main northbound road and its branch into town. It has a beachfront with views of Haifa to the south and the ancient walled city of Old Acre just to the north. The Argaman is right on the beach, with spacious double rooms, all with wall-to-wall carpet, heat, and private balcony, among other amenities. The hotel has an excellent culinary reputation.

Nes Ammim Guesthouse. Mobile Post, Ashrat 25225. ☎ **04/922-566.** 48 rms (all with bath). A/C. $66–$82 single; $80–$112 double. Discount on Kibbutz Package Plan. Rates include breakfast. AE, DC, MC, V. Drive north along highway to signs pointing east to Nes Ammim and Regba; turn here and go 4km (2 miles) inland.

Another short drive from Acre, to the north and through an enchanting avocado forest, is a 200-member Christian village organized in 1963 for the purpose of bringing Jews and Christians into closer contact. While here, you can enjoy the swimming pool, bar, the wonderful greenhouse creations, the botanical gardens, and get a free tour of the community. Guest rooms are doubles. The hotel is part of the Kibbutz Guesthouse Association, and can be booked through their packages.

If you're not staying here, but are interested in the community, call ahead and arrange for a tour. The Nes Ammim community is especially interested in making the land alive again, and you will be amazed by its efforts and dedication. Coming by bus is a bit more of a challenge, but it can be arranged; call ahead and they'll tell you the best way to do it.

Palm Beach Hotel and Country Club. Acre Beach 24101. ☎ **04/981-5815.** Fax 04/991-0434. 110 rms (all with bath). A/C TEL TV. $88 single; $115 double. July–Aug and Jewish holidays $110 single; $150 double. Add 15% for non-high-season weekends. Rates include breakfast. AE, MC, V.

A luxury tower whose rooms have every convenience, the hotel is located a mile south of the Old City on the coastal road to Haifa. The greatest benefit of staying here, in addition to the wonderful beach and view, is the free use of the country club and other facilities (see "What to See and Do," above, for country club details). While there's a chance that nonguests may be able to attend the country club when it's not too busy, the only way to guarantee the privilege is to be a guest at the hotel or to become a country club member. On the premises are a swimming pool, a piano bar, a Jacuzzi, squash, basketball, and tennis courts, a beach, a discotheque, self-service restaurant, and an evening terrace cafe as well as a playground area for children. All restaurant facilities are kosher. There is a bus into town.

WHERE TO DINE

✪ **Abu Christo.** Near the Old Port. ☎ **04/991-0065.** Reservations recommended on weekends. Appetizers NIS 7–14 ($2.10–$4.20); main courses NIS 25–50 ($7.50–$15). AE, DC, MC, V. Daily 10am–midnight. SEAFOOD/MIDDLE EASTERN.

This well-known restaurant is particularly nice in good weather, when you can sit out on the terrace under reed shades and enjoy the delightful waterfront view, which often includes local daredevils diving from the ancient ruins. For appetizers, a round of Middle Eastern salads is especially good here. Most main courses are straightforward dishes like steak, grilled skewers of lamb, or grilled fish (the fresh grouper is expensive but great) all served with french fries; there are also special dishes like skewered shrimp in sesame garlic sauce cooked on an open fire. Abu Christo often features special low-price delicious treats, like tiny fresh fish fried in garlic, which you eat, bones, heads, and all! Full bar.

Oudeh Brothers Restaurant. Old City market area. ☎ **04/912-013.** Reservations recommended weekends. Appetizers NIS 7–14 ($2.10–$4.20); main courses NIS 25–50 ($7.50–$15). Higher prices for lobster. MC, V. Daily 9am–midnight. SEAFOOD/MIDDLE EASTERN.

This clean, pleasant restaurant has four large, airy dining rooms (alas, no waterfront view) and a large patio dining area beside the courtyard of the Khan El-Faranj (or Afranj), described above. It offers a wonderful 25-salad mazza, lamb shashlik with rice and salad, meat with hummus, pickles, and pita, and lots of seafood including lobster and shrimp. Turkish coffee is on the house if you've ordered a meal.

Ptolemais Restaurant. Fisherman's quay. ☎ **04/991-6112.** Appetizers NIS 7–14 ($2.10–$4.20); main courses NIS 25–50 ($7.50–$15). DC, MC, V. Summer daily 10am–1am; winter daily 10am–8pm. SEAFOOD/MIDDLE EASTERN.

This restaurant, near the Abu Christo, dishes up terrific fish main courses and meals like beef with hummus at reasonable prices. Watermelon makes a refreshing dessert. Students get a 10% reduction. Here, too, there's a full bar, and you can sit either inside or out on the waterfront patio, with the boats in the harbor bobbing up and down just a few feet away.

ACRE AFTER DARK

One of Acre's most enjoyable evening activities is strolling around through the tiny Arabian Nights streets, past the old khans and the towering minarets framed by moonlight and stars, gazing from the old port out across the bay toward the sparkling lights of Haifa and Acre's little lighthouse on duty. On a quiet night, moonlight shining in, you can stand in the courtyard of Khan El-Umdan and imagine all the people, animals, activities, and human dramas that have passed through here. Another interesting moonlight walk is around the city's seawalls. Exotic Arabic music fills the air day and night all around Old Acre, and I've rarely enjoyed a moonlight walk more.

All around Old Acre, light and music pour out into the streets from the open doors of billiard parlors, and you're welcome to come in and shoot a few games.

You can sip a beer or cocktail at one of the waterfront restaurants, at the Burj's rooftop nightclub during the warm months, or at the other Burj meeting places. But if you're ready for a real live striptease act, head for the Burj's **Han A-Sultan** restaurant and nightclub on a Friday or Saturday evening, open until 4am. Everyone is welcome.

The **discotheque** at the Palm Beach Hotel and Country Club (☎ 04/991-2892) is open to everyone every night of the week in summer months, on Friday only in winter. Music and dancing and one drink are included in the NIS 20 ($6) cover charge. Also at the Palm Beach is the outdoor **Pundak Cafe,** open in summertime only, from 8:30pm to 1am, with live music on the terrace, food, and drinks.

EN ROUTE TO NAHARIYA

Several kilometers north of Bahji is another sort of memorial: **Kibbutz Lohame Museum Ha-Geta'ot Museum (Fighters of the Ghettos),** founded by fighters and survivors of World War II ghettos in Poland, Germany, and Lithuania. Pictures and documents, models, and maps present the life and culture of Jewish communities in Europe before their destruction, and outline the suffering and resistance of ghetto dwellers. There is also an extremely moving exhibition of paintings and drawings done by the children of the ghettos. Admission to the memorial is free; donations are requested. Open Sunday through Friday from 9am to 4pm, on Saturday from 10am to 4pm. You can call 04/995-8080 for information.

Right next to the kibbutz and museum is a handsome **aqueduct** built by Ahmed Jezzar Pasha in 1780 over one the Romans left. The aqueduct originally supplied Acre with water from the Galilee's springs. Its picturesque ruins include many archways framing sabra plants.

7 Nahariya & North to the Border

Nahariya: 33km (20 miles) N of Haifa

Founded by German Jews in the mid-1930s, Nahariya is a popular summer resort with Israelis, but foreigners are catching on. On the Lag b'Omer holiday in the spring, which is the only day a Jew can marry during the 6 weeks between the Passover and Shavuot holidays, Nahariya is packed with honeymooners. Maybe there's a connection between Nahariya's honeymoon attractions and the fact that on its beach archeologists dug up a Canaanite fertility goddess. It's an interesting thought.

This holiday town has an unusual main street: A stream shaded by breezy eucalyptus trees runs down the middle of it. There is a low-key, pleasantly small-town feeling to Nahariya, which many tourists enjoy. Horsecarts will take you around town; settle on a price before you start out.

ESSENTIALS

GETTING THERE   By Bus   From Acre, take the no. 271 or 272 Haifa–Acre–Nahariya bus. The ride is less than 25 minutes.

By Car   From Acre, Nahariya is a 15-minute drive north on the coastal highway.

VISITOR INFORMATION   When you leave the Central Bus Station, turn left and walk down about half a block on Ha-Ga'aton. On the left you'll see a small square, and at the far end of the square, a seven-story edifice with flags waving in front. This is the Municipal Building, where you'll find the **Tourist Information Office** (☎ 04/929-800), open Sunday through Thursday from 9am to 1pm and 4 to 7pm, on Friday from 9am to noon; closed Saturday. If you're interested in **meeting the locals,** the staff at the Municipal Tourist Office (☎ 04/929-800) can arrange it. Local chapters of Rotary, Lions, Soroptimists, and Freemasons also extend a warm welcome to international members; contact the Tourist Information Office for meeting times and places.

ORIENTATION   It's pretty easy to find your way around this small city. The Central Bus Station and the railway station are just off the main highway on Ha-Ga'aton Boulevard, Nahariya's main road. Head down Ha-Ga'aton and you'll be going due west, to the sea. Don't worry about the weight of your bags as you only have to walk about five blocks to get to a hotel. The area code for Nahariyah is 04.

WHAT TO SEE & DO

BEACHES & OUTDOOR ACTIVITIES   The beaches of Nahariya, the town's raison d'etre from a tourist point of view, suffer from the region's lack of a sewage treatment plant and the proximity of Lebanon, where decades of chaos have led to garbage dumping in the sea; the junk often swirls into Nahariya's waters, and on the worst days, you feel as if you're swimming in a garbage soup. At times in 1995, coliform bacteria counts per 100 ml of seawater at Nahariya were four times the Israeli Health Ministry's acceptable level (although within the less strict standards of other Mediter-ranean countries). The main beach, **Galei-Galil,** just to the north of Ha-Ga'aton Boulevard, won prizes in the past for cleanliness and safety. Today it offers (in addition, of course, to the Mediterranean Sea) an Olympic-size **outdoor pool,** a heated, glass-enclosed **indoor pool** open year-round, a **children's pool,** dressing rooms, **playgrounds** for children, and restaurants. It is open daily from 8am to 6pm; end of September to June 1 until 5pm; admission is NIS 12 ($3.60); reductions for children.

At the marina breakwater you'll see people **fishing** off the rocks, and you can rent a sailboat if you like, or go skindiving. **Tennis, basketball,** and **volleyball** courts are other attractions, as is the big water slide just on the north side of the beach.

If you just want to take a dip in the Mediterranean, you can go about two blocks south to the free **Municipal Beach.** The view from both of these beaches is lovely. On a clear day—and most of them are—you can see all the way from Rosh Ha-Niqra at the Lebanese border to the north, and to Haifa in the south.

If you'd like to go horseback riding, call **Bakal's Riding School** (☎ 04/920-534) to make an appointment.

For a Saturday hike with the **Friends of Nature (Hovevei Hateva),** check with the Municipal Tourist Office (☎ 04/929-800). Hikes are offered every Saturday.

MUSEUMS & ANCIENT SITES   In the seven-story Municipal Building, on Ha-Iriya Square, is Nahariya's **Municipal Museum.** The fifth floor houses an art exhibit. The sixth floor, in addition to an interesting malacology (shell) collection, displays many artifacts and exhibits from the area around Nahariya (Israel's entire north coast), with its fascinating history dating all the way back to the Stone Age. It's definitely worth stopping in here to get a quick education about the area you're visiting. On the seventh floor is a department showing the history of the town of Nahariya, and the **Museum of German Jews,** which, in addition to cultural memorabilia, displays photographs and writings of Sigmund Freud, Alfred Adler, Erich Fromm, Albert Einstein, and Robert Oppenheimer, to name just a few. The Municipal Museum is open Sunday through Friday from 10am to noon, plus Sunday and Wednesday afternoons from 4 to 6pm. Admission is free.

Nahariya's ruin of a **Canaanite temple** was accidentally discovered on Ha-Ma'apilim Street, a few yards up from the Municipal Beach, in 1947. Experts believe it to be a temple dedicated to the Canaanite goddess of the sea, Asherah (or Astarte), dating from about 1500 B.C.

WHERE TO STAY

Most of Nahariya's hotels are located, quite logically, at the western end of Ha-Ga'aton Boulevard near Galei-Galil Beach. Walking down Ha-Ga'aton, all but one of my recommended hostelries are on side streets going right (north) off Ha-Ga'aton, so I'll start on the main street and then describe the lodging possibilities on each side street as we pass it. By the way, all the hotels except two—the Yarden and Erna House—have kosher kitchens.

Walking north along Jabotinsky, including along Ha-Ma'apilim Street, you'll spot houses with little signs out front: Rooms to Let. These house pensions may have only one or two rooms, with or without private facilities. You can check with the Municipal Tourist Office (☎ 04/929-800) for lists of what's available, or you can wander along Jabotinsky and nearby streets to see what turns up. Prices are around $20 to $30 per person, including breakfast, depending on season and facilities.

The official IYHA Youth Hostel is not right in Nahariya; it's up the coast a bit at Akhziv (see below for details).

EXPENSIVE

Carlton Hotel. 23 Ha-Ga'aton St., Nahariya. ☎ **04/992-2211.** Fax 04/982-3771. 198 rms (all with bath). A/C TEL TV. $95–$150 single; $115–$190 double. Rates include breakfast. 15% service charge. AE, MC, V.

Located on the main street in the center of town, this six-story hotel is the best and most expensive in Nahariya. Rooms are comfortable, but not really up to this price category. There isn't a real beach atmosphere at this location, but the hotel's heated outdoor pool, which is covered in winter, provides the chance for off-season swimming. In summer and weekends, the hotel is filled with activities that, together with late-night main street action, can be a bit too noisy for some. There is a sauna and Jacuzzi.

Hotel Eden. 48 Ha-Meyasdim St., Nahariya 22383. ☎ **04/992-3246.** Fax 04/982-3741. 50 rms (all with bath). A/C TEL. $70 single; $92 double. Add 10% July–Aug, 25% on Jewish holidays, discounts in winter season. AE, DC, MC, V.

This rather posh three-star hotel, at the corner of Jabotinsky and Ha-Meyasdim streets, has rooms with radio, heat, and room service, among other amenities. The swimming pool (open in warm season only) hosts diving classes; all day long, in high season, a variety of programs are offered, including aerobics, dancing, sports, nightclub entertainment, and children's programs, designed to make the hotel a minivacation center.

Hotel Frank. 4 Ha-Aliyah St. (P.O. Box 58), Nahariya 22381. ☎ **04/920-278.** Fax 04/925-535. 50 rms (all with bath or shower). A/C TEL TV. Regular season: $57–$64 single; $76–$87 double. High season: $66–$79 single; $90–$112 double, half-board required. Regular season: $57–$64 single; $76–$87 double. Passover and Sukkot, add 15% to high-season rates. MC, V.

The well-run three-star-equivalent Hotel Frank, just back from Ha-Ma'apilim two blocks north of Ha-Ga'aton, is in a quieter neighborhood, relatively close to the beach. It offers an outdoor swimming pool, recently renovated rooms, heating, and very friendly service, among other amenities. On the land side, the rooms have balconies; but on the sea side, the balcony space has been used to enlarge the rooms, making a sitting area with nice windows and views of the sea.

WHERE TO DINE

Nahariya is not exactly what you'd call a gourmet's mecca. It's small and many vacation visitors have their meals at their hotels. If you decide to go out, the first place to try is Ha-Ga'aton Boulevard, with its bistros, sidewalk cafes, and two commercial plazas, Ha-Banim Square (Kikar Ha-Banim), and Ha-Iriya Square (Kikar Ha-Iriya). The plazas are across Ha-Ga'aton from one another, at the intersection with Herzl Street, half a block west of the bus station. Each square has a cinema, lots of shops and other services, and some indoor-outdoor snack bar eateries.

Egged Bus Station Restaurant. Ha-Ga'aton Boulevard. Main courses NIS 12–20 ($3.60–$6). No credit cards. Sun–Thurs 7–10:30am, 11am–2:30pm, and 3:30–6pm; Fri 7am–1pm. CAFETERIA/SNACK BAR.

As in other cities, this eatery is recommended for low-priced fare. It's clean, pleasant, and kosher. Hot meals are served at lunchtime; by evening the pickings are slim.

El Gaucho. Ha-Ga'aton Boulevard. ☎ **04/992-8635.** NIS 28–70 ($8.20–$21). MC, V. Daily noon–midnight. ARGENTINIAN.

This restaurant specializes in Argentinian-style grilled meat—and lots of it—cooked over the coals behind the many cuts of fresh meat on display for all to see. The decor here is massive Spanish-ranch style, with lots of special touches like cowhide chairs, a South American pan flute, and horns on the walls. You can sit inside, or out in back on the palapa-covered patio. The chefs are from South America; much of the meat served here is veal. Menu items range from an inexpensive half-chicken dinner to the house specialty, a 750-gram (about 1 1/2 pounds) mixed grill, a giant repast for two (or even more) people. All meat dinners are served with bread and butter, baked potato with butter and sour cream, vegetables, salad, dessert, and the special chimichurra meat sauce that's so delicious you'll be sopping it up with the bread. For the price, the good food, and the atmosphere, you can't beat this place. In the summer you may find live, authentic South American music in the evenings.

Hollandische Konditorei. 31 Ha-Ga'aton. ☎ **04/992-2502.** Desserts NIS 13–20 ($3.90–$6); light meals NIS 14–25 ($4.20–$7.50). No credit cards. Summer: daily 6am–2 or 3am. Winter: daily 6am–10pm or midnight. PASTRIES.

A favorite among Nahariya cafe-sitters, this pleasant place has small tables out front and a few inside. Rich cakes and pastries are served as well as Neal's (of San Francisco) cookies.

Penguin Cafe. 33 Ha Ga'aton Blvd. ☎ **04/992-4241.** NIS 7–23 ($2–$7). Daily from 8am to midnight. ICE CREAM/SNACKS.

Located outside the big Penguin Restaurant complex (see below), the portions of ice cream are simply enormous, and relatively cheap (for what you get), and the menu includes such hot-weather favorites as banana splits, milkshakes, and fruit cocktail, as well as blintzes, pancakes, pastries, and beverages. You can even order pizza with a kosher "shrimp" if you want something different. There are also low-calorie frozen yogurts mixed on the spot with the fresh fruits of your choice. The Penguin, with its convenient outdoor Ha-Ga'aton location, is a local favorite. You can sit at a sidewalk table, or enjoy the old-fashioned ice-cream–parlor decor inside.

Penguin Restaurant. 21 Ha-Ga'aton Blvd. ☎ **04/992-8855.** LIGHT MEALS.

The newly renovated Penguin is the nearest thing Nahariya has to a mall, with a bookstore and many trendy shops surrounding the dining space. There are both inside and outside restaurants; it's the busiest place in town and wonderful for good, inexpensive general fare. You'll find spaghetti or lasagne, fish, or fried chicken with potato and salad, or light meals—or you can just stop in for a beer, an espresso, or a glass of fresh-squeezed juice.

Photographs on the walls remind you of the original tin-roofed Penguin and the bleak, empty landscape that was Nahariya in the 1940s.

Singapore Chinese Restaurant. Ha-Meyasdim and Jabotinsky. ☎ **04/992-4952.** Reservations recommended summer weekends. Appetizers NIS 9–30 ($2.70–$9); main courses NIS 25–50 ($7.50–$15); set combination dinner NIS 43 ($13). DC, MC, V. Lunch daily noon–3pm; dinner daily 7pm–midnight. Closed Chinese New Year and major Jewish holidays. CHINESE.

One of Nahariya's newer and better restaurants is the Singapore Chinese Restaurant, two blocks north of Ha-Ga'aton and across from the Yarden and Eden hotels. It's big, fancy, and full of atmosphere. You can get one of the fixed combination dinners from the menu, for two to six people; but if you want to enjoy a surprisingly large selection of dishes, then order from the 110-item menu. The Singapore, as you'd expect, offers a number of Singapore specialties, including lemon chicken, Shanghai fried duck with onions, a Singapore Sling cocktail, or Singapore ice cream with Chinese fruits, coconut, raisins, and a fruit garnish, for dessert.

EXCURSIONS NORTH OF NAHARIYA
AKHZIV

Heading north along the main road, after 4 kilometers (2¹/₂ miles) you'll see the road to **Akhziv Beach,** on the left (west). It's another kilometer (one-half mile) to the beach proper, where you'll find a parking lot, changing rooms, shelters and snack stands, as well as freshwater showers. It's open daily from 8am to 7pm in summer. There's a charge of NIS 8 ($2.40) per person for admission during the summer swimming season.

Heading north again, a kilometer (one-half mile) past the Akhziv Beach road, you'll pass the parking lot and entrance to **Akhziv National Park** (☎ 04/982-3263) with its sheltered beach, restaurant, picnic and changing facilities amid the ruins of a seaside Arab village.

Akhziv existed when Joshua assigned the tribes of Israel to their various territories, and is mentioned in the Bible as a Canaanite town that the tribe of Asher, to whom it was allotted, was never able to conquer. At the Nahariya Municipal Museum, you can learn about the varied history of the town through the wealth of archeological artifacts on view.

In more recent times, Akhziv was an Arab village, but the inhabitants fled in 1948 and the village remained deserted for a number of years. In 1952, Eli Avivi, one of Israel's legendary eccentrics, received government permission to settle in Akhziv, and promptly declared the "independence" of **Akhzivland,** which is just north of the park boundary. The ramshackle building that is Akhzivland's main structure houses Mr. Avivi's living quarters and his personal museum of artifacts found on and near Akhzivland. You can visit the museum for a small admission charge.

There is a NIS 12 ($3.60) summer admission to Akhziv National Park, but off-season, you can sometimes just wander through the gates and up the hill through the lovely gardens. It's a beautiful spot for a picnic; there is a guarded but somewhat rocky beach for swimming. The park is open daily from 8am to 7pm. At the far end of the parking lot is the entrance to Club Méditerranée's vacation resort.

Where to Stay

A half kilometer (about a quarter mile) north of Akhzivland brings you to **Camping Akhziv** (☎ 04/982-5054), where you'll pay about $5 per person for a camping spot with all facilities. Little bamboo bungalows are also available for rent for $65 in August, and $13 per person for the rest of the year, for up to four people. Just a bit north of Camping Akhziv, **Yad Le-Yad Hostel,** P.O. Box 169, Nahariya (☎ 04/982-3345), offers beds arranged in two-, four-, and six-bed rooms for $20 per person, plus 21 rustic beach shelter/bungalows housing four people for $14 per person.

GESHER HAZIV & THE AKHZIV BRIDGE

While the town of Akhziv has a history going back to biblical times, the name is most often remembered in connection with a tragic, heroic event that took place here on the night of June 17, 1946. Attempting to cut British rail communications with neighboring Arab states, a Hagana demolition team was destroying railroad bridges along this line. At the Akhziv bridge, however, they were spotted by a British sentry, who fired a flare in order to get a better look. The flare ignited the team's explosives. The bridge was blown, but no one survived. The 14 who perished are commemorated by a large black metal monument across the road from the youth hostel.

Where to Stay

Kibbutz Gesher Haziv Guesthouse. ☎ **04/982-5715.** Fax 04/982-5718. 48 rms (all with bath). A/C TEL. $66–$85 single; $90–$114 double. Rates include breakfast and service. AE, DC, MC, V.

Guests have access to the kibbutz seaside diving center and horseback riding stables at discount prices. There are simple but comfortable rooms, an outdoor swimming pool, and kosher dining facilities. The location is excellent, just 5 minutes from the beach, and close to Akko, and many sites in the western Galilee. Discounts are available if you book through the Kibbutz Hotel Chain 7-Day Plan.

ROSH HA-NIQRA

This dramatic site is on the border with Lebanon, astride a tall cliff overlooking the sea. On a clear day, standing atop the cliff, you can see the coastline as far as Haifa.

Beneath the cliffs are grottoes carved out by the sea, reachable via cable car. Operating from 8:30am to 5pm (until 9 or 10pm in summer), on Friday until 3pm, the cable-car ride and admission to the grottoes costs NIS 20 ($6) for adults, with a discount for children and students. You can walk into the caves and passages and see the pools of water lapping the rocks. To see the artifacts that have been recovered from these caves, visit the Municipal Museum in Nahariya.

To reach Rosh Ha-Niqra, take the bus from Nahariya, which runs several times a day; sherut service is also available, in front of the Nahariya Central Bus Station, on Ha-Ga'aton Boulevard. You can dine at a reasonably priced self-service restaurant on top of the cliff called Mitzpe Rosh Ha-Niqra. The view is terrific. Open the same hours as the cable car.

Where to Stay

Rosh Ha Niqra IYHA Youth Hostel. ☎ 04/982-5169. Fax 04/982-1330. 220 beds, family rooms available. A/C. Dorm bed $18.50; double room (when available) $23 per person. Bus: 20 from Nahariya.

Surrounded by gardens, this often heavily booked well-run hostel has pleasant dorm rooms with up to five beds, each with its own bathroom; rooms are heated as well as air-conditioned, and private or family rooms can be arranged depending on how busy the hostel is. There's a swimming pool, meals are served, and you can walk to the beach and hike to the Rosh Ha Niqra grottoes. Reception is open Sunday through Thursday from 8am to 1pm and 4 to 7pm; Friday from 8am to 1pm.

9 Haifa

Some compare Haifa, beautifully situated on a hill overlooking a broad bay, to San Francisco or Naples. Israel's third-largest metropolitan area (population 300,000) and the capital of the north, Haifa is like a triple-decker sandwich—the raucous area that comprises Israel's most important port is the lowest tier; the business district (Hadar), higher up, is the second; and the Carmel district, with its panoramic vistas, nestled even higher on the upper pine slopes, constitutes the third.

1 Haifa Past and Present

HAIFA TODAY

Very different from either Jerusalem or Tel Aviv, the city is a pleasure to visit just to get a sense of its beauty and lifestyle. In a society unlike any other in the Middle East, Jews and Arabs live and work side by side; 25% of the population is either Muslim or Christian.

Like the rest of the country, Haifa is booming. Construction of new hotels (including a Hilton down near the shore) is already under way. Planned development of the truly beautiful beaches just to the south of Haifa will change the nature of the city as a travel destination over the next few years.

Haifa is a good base for exploring this part of Israel. You won't need to rent a car if you base yourself here; many organized day tours originate in Haifa, or, since Haifa is a major transportation hub, you can just use public transportation to explore cities like Akko or even Safed on your own. In the evening, after a day of touring the area, Haifa offers a good choice of restaurants, films, and concerts, or just urban strolling to keep you busy.

A LOOK AT HAIFA'S PAST

Almost every square foot of Israel has been populated since earliest ages, and Haifa is no exception. The prophet Elijah knew this territory well—from the top of Mount Carmel he won a major victory over 450 priests of Baal during the reign of King Ahab and his notorious Phoenician wife, Jezebel. Also in biblical times, the Phoenician harbor center of Zalemona thrived here, with predominantly Greek settlers, and the Jewish agricultural village of

Sycaminos (sometimes called Shikmona) clung to the northwestern peak of Mount Carmel (3rd-century Talmudic literature mentions both towns).

The Crusaders called the area Caife, Cayphe, and sometimes Caiphas. Once a center of glass and cochineal-purple industries, Haifa was destroyed when the Arabs reconquered the area, and it virtually slept until the late 19th century when Jewish immigration helped bring about a revival.

Haifa got its first shot in the arm in 1905, when the Hiafa–Damascus Railway was built. The Balfour Declaration and British occupation boosted it some more, as did a 1919 railway link to Egypt. But the real kickoff came when the British built its modern harbor—an arduous enterprise begun in 1929 and completed in 1934. Thereupon Haifa began its transformation into the vital trading and communications center it is today, taking on major importance as a shipping base, naval center, and terminal point for oil pipelines.

In 1898, when he sailed past the spot that was to become modern Haifa, Theodor Herzl, the father of Zionism, saw a prophetic vision: "Huge liners rode at anchor . . . at the top of the mountain there were thousands of white homes and the mountain itself was crowned with imposing villas. . . . A beautiful city had been built close to the deep blue sea." Herzl recorded this experience in his book, *Altneuland* (Old New Land), and miraculously, the city developed precisely along the lines he predicted. The dream of the Zionist leader became a reality for hundreds of thousands of homeless, scarred refugees who arrived here after the Nazi Holocaust. As they crowded the rails for their first glimpse of the Promised Land, the hills of Haifa must have seemed like a sight of heaven.

On April 21, 1948, Haifa became the first major city controlled by Jews after the end of the British Mandate and the U.N. Partition decision in 1947. Although Haifa's previous growth had already spurred development of residential areas such as Bat Galim, Hadar Ha-Carmel, Neve-Shaanan, and even Herzlia, the new wave of immigration (more than 100,000) gave rise to others: Ramat Ramez, Kiryat Elizer, Neveh Yosef, and Kiryat Shprinzak. Haifa Bay, east of the port, became the backbone of the country's heavy industries, with oil refineries and associated industries, foundries, glass factories, fertilizer and chemical industries, cement works, textile manufacturing, and yards for shipbuilding and repair.

Plans are now in progress to convert the areas southwest of the port into Israel's own "Riviera." The beaches are already excellent.

2 Orientation

ARRIVING

The city's transportation center is at its northernmost tip, in the district called Bat Galim, about 2 kilometers (1 1/2 miles) northwest of the downtown port area.

BY PLANE   At Ben-Gurion Airport contact tourist information *inside* the baggage claim area about taxi, sherut, and bus service to Haifa, approximately a 2-hour trip. Service to Haifa and the north is not as well organized as service to Tel Aviv and Jerusalem.

For the return to Ben Gurion, **El Al Airlines** has an early baggage check-in service in Haifa, located at 6 Ha-Namel St. (☎ 04/677-036), open Sunday through Thursday from 5 to 9:30pm for flights departing the next day. El Al also offers a daily early-morning bus transportation to Ben-Gurion Airport (available to anyone, not only to El Al's customers). The bus leaves the Egged central bus station daily at 3:30am, stopping at many hotels along the way, with its final departure from the Dan

Carmel Hotel at 4:15am. It will pick you up anywhere along its route if you call in advance to request it. You can purchase tickets in advance from the El Al office, travel agents, or hotels (but not directly from the bus driver). For further information or to reserve a ticket, phone **El Al's office** (☎ 04/670-170). Another service to Ben-Gurion is **Kavei Ha-Galil,** 11 Berwarld St. (☎ 04/664-444, 664-445, or 664-446). El Al passengers have the option of using a special transport company, **Tisa La Tisa** (☎ 04/643-371), which will pick them up at their hotel with a shared taxi or van, and get them to Ben-Gurion Airport in time for El Al flights for NIS 20 ($6) per person.

BY TRAIN   The New Central Railway Station is in Bat Galim. In the station you'll find Olamei Hod, a cheerful air-conditioned restaurant with set-price breakfasts or lunches if you're in transit, open Sunday through Thursday from 5am to 7pm, closing early on Friday and all day Saturday. There is also the Old Railway Station in Plumer Square.

Trains to Netanya and Tel Aviv leave approximately every hour from 5:45am to 7pm, Sunday through Thursday; the last Friday train leaves at 2pm; there's no Saturday service. Less frequent service to Akko and Nahariya is available. One early-morning train departs from Jerusalem on Sunday morning. Train information can be obtained by calling **04/564-564**.

BY BUS   The Egged Bus Terminal, with intercity buses to and from all points in Israel, is next to the Central Railway Station in Bat Galim. From here, you'll have to take a city bus to either of my recommended hotel districts, in Hadar or Central Carmel. For Hadar, catch no. 10 or 12; for Central Carmel and the top of the mountain, you want no. 3, 22, or 24. Interurban bus information can be obtained by calling **04/549-555**.

Right in the Egged Bus Station in Bat Galim is the Egged Restaurant, not the most romantic place to dine, but just right for a meal before or after a long bus journey. There's a full set-price menu for lunch, and it's open Sunday through Friday from 7am to 4pm; closed Saturday.

BY CAR   Major highway networks connect Haifa with Tel Aviv, Jerusalem, and the Galilee.

BY FERRY   Your ship will dock right in the port at the Maritime Passenger Terminal. It's only a short walk to the Paris Square (Kikar Paris) station of the Carmelit subway that climbs the mountain to Hadar and Central Carmel.

VISITOR INFORMATION   The main **Municipal Tourist Office** is at 106 HaNassi Blvd. (☎ 04/374-010) in the Central Carmel neighborhood, just across the street from the Nof Hotel; there is also a downtown Tourist Office at 20 Herzl St., near the intersection with Balfour (☎ 04/666-521 or 666-522). Both are open Sunday through Thursday from 8:30am to 5pm, on Friday until 2pm; closed Saturday. Here you can obtain the monthly calendar "Events in Haifa and the Northern

---

Telephone Number Change

Most Haifa telephone numbers will be changed during the course of 1996. In most cases, phone numbers currently bearing the initial digits 2 through 7 will simply have the prefix 8 added.

Region," plus detailed free maps, directions, and any other information you might need. The Haifa Tourism Development Association puts out a monthly poster, "Special Events in Haifa," listing many events of interest; look for it in the bus station, in hotels, in all the tourist information offices, and in other places around town.

The **Israel Students Tourist Association (ISSTA)** has an office in Hadar at 2 Balfour St. (☎ **04/670-222**). It's open Sunday through Thursday from 8:30am to 1pm, plus 4 to 7pm; on Friday it is open from 8:30am to 1pm.

CITY LAYOUT

Of all its graces, Haifa is richest in panoramic views. For purposes of orientation, you might think of Haifa as a city built on three levels. Whether you come by ship, bus, or train, you will arrive on the first, or **port,** level of the city. The second level, **Hadar Ha-Carmel,** meaning "Glory of the Carmel," is referred to simply as the Hadar. This is the business section as well as the home of the Haifa Museum, and some very pleasant restaurants and budget hotels. At the top of the hills is the **Carmel** District, a patchwork of verdant residential neighborhoods with its own small but busy commercial center called **Central Carmel,** numerous hotels and pensions, restaurants, small museums, and two of Haifa's brightest cultural beacons: Haifa Auditorium and Bet Rothschild (the James de Rothschild Cultural Center).

Because Haifa is built all the way up the side of a mountain, many of its main streets are sinuous switchbacks, curving and recurving to accommodate the steep slopes of Mount Carmel. The streets are always and forever bewildering, and you will find yourself lost repeatedly. If Haifa weren't so pleasant and beautiful, this would be a chore. About the only straight road in Haifa is the one that climbs the slopes of Carmel underground: the Carmelit.

3 Getting Around

BY SUBWAY   The Carmelit is a fast and efficient means of getting up and down Haifa's various levels. Its terminal station is located on Jaffa Road, a few blocks north of the port entrance and not far from the old (Merkaz) railway station.

Pulled on a long cable up and down the steep hill, the Carmelit resembles a sort of scale-model Métro, with only 1,800 yards of tunnel. It's picturesque, yes—and it also happens to offer the fastest means of getting from the port to Hadar and Carmel. There are six stops in all. Starting from the bottom of the mountain and going up to the top, they are: (1) Paris Square (Kikar Paris, lower terminus, port area); (2) Solel Boneh (Hassan Shukri Street); (3) Ha-Nevi'im (Hadar business district, tourist office); (4) Masada (Masada Street); (5) Eliezer Golomb (Eliezer Golomb Street); (6) Gan Ha-Em (Central Carmel business district, upper terminus).

Trains run every 10 minutes. The Carmelit operates Sunday through Thursday from 6:30am to midnight, Friday from 6:30am to 3pm, and resumes service on Saturday from one-half hour after the end of Shabbat until midnight; it is closed during Sabbath. Ticket machines have English as well as Hebrew instructions. The fare is NIS 3.40 ($1.10).

BY BUS   Bus fares are charged according to destination, so you must tell the driver where you're going. Most fares to places inside Haifa itself are NIS 3.40 ($1.10). Haifa's municipal buses operate from 5am to 11:30pm Sunday through Thursday; on Friday, bus service halts around 4:30pm; there is limited Saturday service from 9am to midnight. For information on buses inside Haifa, call 04/549-131. For Inter-urban lines, call 04/549-555.

FAST FACTS: Haifa

American Express   The office is at 2 Khayat Sq. (on Ha-Atzma'ut Street in the port area (☎ 04/642-266) in a passageway beside Steimatzky's Bookstore. For lost traveler's checks, call toll free 177/440-8694.

Bookstores   There are Steimatzky branches at 82 Ha-Atzma'ut St., 16 Herzl St. in Bet Ha-Kranot, 130 Ha-Nassi Blvd., and in the Central Bus Station. For used books try Beverly's Book, 18 Herzl St., second floor.

Crime   See "Safety" below.

Currency Exchange   Banking hours are Sunday through Friday from 8:30am to 2:30pm. Afternoon hours are Sunday, Tuesday, and Thursday from 4 to 6pm.

Doctors   Call the Rambam Hospital in Bat Galim (☎ 533-111).

Drugstores   Standard hours are Sunday through Thursday from 8am to 1pm and 4 to 7pm; Friday from 8am to 2pm. According to a rotating schedule, one or two pharmacies remain on duty nights and on Shabbat; their names will be posted in any pharmacy window.

Embassies/Consulates   The U.S. consulate is at 12 Yerushalayim St., Hadar; for commercial transactions only.

Emergencies   Dial 101 for Magen David Adom first aid services, or 102 for an emergency hospital admission. For the mobile intensive care unit, call **512-233.** The National Poison Control Center (☎ **04/529-205**) is at Rambam Hospital, on call 24 hours a day.

Hospitals   The Rambam Hospital in Bat Galim (☎ **533-111**), and Carmel Hospital, 7 Michal St. (☎ **250-211**), will accommodate tourists.

Hotlines   The Rape Crisis Center telephone is 660-111, daily 24 hours. Emotional First Aid (☎ **672-222**) is open 24 hours daily.

Laundry/Dry Cleaning   Laundromats in Haifa are not easily accessible from tourist areas; ask at your hotel.

Libraries   The main library is at 50 Pevsner St. (☎ **04/667-766**). Hours are Sunday through Thursday from 9am to 8pm, Friday 9am to 2pm.

Newspapers/Magazines   The *Jerusalem Post, Jerusalem Report Magazine,* and *Eretz* (a magazine of history, nature, and travel) are readily available.

Police   See "Emergencies" above.

Post Office   Haifa's most accessible post office with the longest hours is in Hadar, at the corner of Shabtai Levi and Ha-Nevi'im streets (☎ **04/640-917**). It is open Sunday through Thursday from 8am to 7pm; Friday 8am to 2pm; closed Saturday.

Radio   English broadcasts are on Israeli radio 576kHz and 1458kHz at 7am, 1, 5, and 8pm.

Religious Services   "Events in Haifa," available at Municipal Tourist Information Offices, lists all major church, mosque, and synagogue services.

Safety   Haifa is generally a low-crime city. Extra care should be exercised near the port after dark.

Taxis   Taxi service numbers in Carmel are 04/664-444 or 382-727; in Hadar, 04/662-525; and at the port, 04/668-383.

Telegrams/Telex/Fax   Dial **171** for telegrams. You can send telegrams at the post office (see "Post Office" above). Ask at your hotel for fax services.

Television   Two Israeli channels carry many English-language programs. Channel 2 is the more highbrow; Middle East television from Lebanon specializes in American reruns.

Useful Telephone Numbers   The Israel Student Travel Association (ISSTA), 2 Balfour St., Hadar, can be reached at 670-222.

4 Accommodations

The lower and middle areas of town, the port and Hadar, have a few very reasonable hotels and pensions that put you right at the center of the business district.

Central Carmel is quieter and has trees, gardens, and views. And with the Carmelit, you're only minutes away from the other parts of the city. Up here on top of Mount Carmel, when you climb the stairs out of the Gan Ha-Em Carmelit station, you'll come above ground on busy Ha-Nassi Boulevard. Walk southwest (up the slope) and in short order you'll arrive at the main intersection of Central Carmel, Ha-Nassi, and Sea Road (Derekh Ha-Yam). If you arrive in Central Carmel by city bus no. 22, look for this same intersection to use as a reference point.

The large Gan Ha-Em Park is just west of the Carmelit station. Besides the various expensive hotels placed atop Mount Carmel for the benefit of the view, a little searching can uncover comfortable but cheaper accommodations.

HADAR
MODERATE
Haifa Tower Hotel. 63 Herzl St., Haifa. ☎ **04/677-111.** Fax 04/621-863. 96 rms (all with bath or shower). A/C TEL TV. Low, regular, and high seasons: $72, $78, $90 single; $90, $102, $109 double. Rates include breakfast. AE, DC, MC, V. Carmelit: Ha-Nevi'im.

Located in a new 17-story office building in the downtown Hadar section of Haifa, this upper-middle-ranking choice has well-decorated and -designed rooms (all with views of the harbor or the city, though not as spectacular as those from the higher Carmel neighborhood) and very pleasant public areas.

CENTRAL CARMEL
EXPENSIVE
✪ **Dan Carmel Hotel.** 85-87 Ha-Nassi Blvd., Haifa 34642. ☎ **04/306-211.** Fax 04/387-504. 219 rms (all with bath). A/C TEL TV. $150–$250 single; $170–$275 double. 15% service charge. Rates include breakfast. AE, DC, MC, V. Carmelit: Gan Ha-Em.

For 40 years, the Dan Carmel has reigned as Haifa's most luxurious hotel. The building itself is a perfectly maintained example of 1950s modernistic architecture and decor—a style just now reaching the age to be appreciated for nostalgic as well as interesting esthetic value. There are spacious public areas, overlooking beautiful gardens, a large country club outdoor swimming pool, and a top-flight staff, all of which add up to a relaxing, pleasant experience. Deluxe rooms and suites, recently renovated, are beautifully furnished and decorated, with wall panels of Chinese or classic French textile designs that add a rich, intelligent touch. Superior (standard) rooms have not yet been updated, and show their age. Deluxe and Superior rooms are divided in price between rooms with interesting views and rooms with spectacular views. The in-house **Rondo Restaurant,** perhaps the most elegant kosher choice in

Haifa, is open Saturday through Thursday evenings; its Saturday evening buffet is a worthwhile splurge at $31 (Dan Carmel guests are exempt from the VAT if the tab is charged to their room).

Dining/Entertainment: Two restaurants, lobby lounge, pub, poolside snack bar.

Services: Executive business center, 24-hour room service, hairdresser.

Facilities: Swimming pool, sauna, health club, parking (fee).

Dan Panorama. 107 Ha-nassi Blvd., Haifa 34632. ☎ **04/352-222.** Fax 04/387-504. 267 rms (all with bath). A/C TEL TV. $100–$170 single; $120–$190 double. Rates include breakfast. 15% service charge. AE, DC, MC, V. Carmelite: Gan Ha-Em.

This hotel, set in a highrise built in 1986, is less expensive and ususally has a busier pace than its sister hotel, the Dan Carmel, down the street. It's part of the up-market Panorama shopping mall complex, and a choice of clothing shops, small eateries, and snack bars is just steps away from its polished stone lobby. The pool has been fitted onto the roof of one of the building's lower wings, and is surrounded by green indoor/outdoor carpeting. Rooms are compact, of efficient, modern design (even lower-category rooms have hair dryers), and classified in price according to their views (windows in many rooms are not really big enough to take in the views). The location, a short block from the Carmelit and the Carmel shopping district, is excellent.

Dining/Entertainment: Three restaurants, piano bar lounge, Viennese cafe.

Services: Business service bureau, 24-hour room service.

Facilities: Outdoor pool, children's pool, fitness amenities, parking (fee).

MODERATE

Hotel Dvir. 124 Yefe Nof St., Haifa 34454. ☎ **04/389-131.** 30 rms (all with bath or shower). A/C TEL TV. $55–$68 single; $94 double. Rates include breakfast. AE, DC, MC, V. Bus: 21, 28, or 37. Carmelit: Gan Ha-Em.

The 10 front rooms have an incredibly beautiful view of the city, the harbor, and across Haifa Bay to Acre and the mountains beyond. Each of these rooms has an en-tire wall made of glass as well as a balcony; get one of these if you can; back rooms are cramped and confining. But as significant as the view is the service. The Dvir is run as a hotel training school for the Dan Hotel Chain, and the young people who serve you here are out to get good marks both from you and from their supervisors. Other amenities include clock radios, heat, and wall-to-wall carpeting and use of the nearby Dan Panorama Hotel swimming pool. The long flight of stairs from the street to the Dvir's front door is a minus for many visitors (call ahead if you need assistance).

From Carmelit station, cross Ha-Nassi Boulevard, and look for Shar Ha-Levanon Street; walk one block and turn right on Panorama (Yefe Nof) Road.

✪ **Nof Hotel.** 101 Ha-Nassi Blvd., Haifa 31063. ☎ **04/354-311.** Fax 04/388-810. 93 rms (all with bath). A/C TEL TV. $98–$121 single; $115–$145 double. Lower prices Dec–Feb; higher prices July 15–Aug 31 and Jewish holidays. AE, DC, MC, V.

A stay at the Nof Hotel is always an enjoyable experience and extremely good value. "Nof" means "view," and at the Nof Hotel you'll find magnificent panoramic views in all the rooms, which have large windows and decor that adds up to more dramatic accommodations than you'll find at the neighboring, more expensive Dan Panorama. The hotel dining room is good, and the in-house kosher Chinese restaurant (see "Where to Dine," below) is excellent. A drawback in summer is the lack of a swimming pool, but there are special hotel shuttles down to the beach in summer, and for a fee you can use the Dan Panorama's pool. Check about when planned construction of a new wing is scheduled before reserving. In the United States, contact Best Western for reservations.

The Nof's management has a real commitment to Haifa (it has cosponsored some of the Haifa Museum's exceptional exhibitions) and the staff will help make your stay comfortable and interesting.

INEXPENSIVE

Hotel Beth Shalom Carmel. 110 Ha-Nassi Blvd. (P.O. Box 6208), Haifa 31060. ☎ **04/ 377-481** or 377-482. Fax 04/372-443. 30 rms (all with bath). A/C TEL. $42 single; $62 double. Rates include breakfast. No credit cards. Carmelit: Gan Ha-Em.

This is a modern, efficient German Protestant guesthouse equivalent to a three-star hotel, open to all comers, with clean and airy rooms equipped with heating. Minimum stay is 3 nights. The location, just across the street from many luxury hotels and a few doors from the Municipal Tourist Office, is great; extra amenities include use of a small garden and a library.

NEAR THE PORT

St. Charles German Hospice. 105 Jaffa Rd., Haifa. ☎ **04/523-705.** $15 dorm beds; $19 single; $33 double with breakfast. No credit cards.

On one of the port area's major thoroughfares, this hospice is, surprisingly, a quiet place, set back from the street in a large, stone-walled 120-year-old complex of gardens and stone buildings. The hospice is run by the sisters of the Carmelite order, but it's open to all travelers. Rooms are simple, two or three beds to a room, with high ceilings, spare and practical furnishings, and running water in a sink in each room, with ample toilet, bath, and shower facilities down the hall, and a nice sitting room, too. You're welcome to use the kitchen to prepare meals, and to relax in the large garden. There is a 10pm curfew and 9am checkout.

5 Where to Dine

Haifa can cater to every culinary taste and pocketbook. The eateries are everywhere, escalating in price and geographic levels from the felafel stands adjacent to the port area to the Dan Carmel Grill Room overlooking the Mediterranean.

HADAR

INEXPENSIVE

Leon & Ioji Gratar Romanesc. 31 Ha-Nevi'im St. ☎ **04/675-073.** Appetizers NIS 8–12 ($2.40–$3.60); main courses NIS 22–36 ($6.60–$11). No credit cards. Sun–Thurs 8am– midnight; Fri 8am–3pm. ROMANIAN.

Leon and Ioji's is a tiny Romanian restaurant with a nationwide reputation for excellent food. A few sidewalk tables, room for only five tables inside, a bottle-stocked bar, glass cases filled with toothsome goodies—that's all there is. A real chow-down of soup or herring for an appetizer, followed by grilled meats, chicken, or fish for two, comes to a surprisingly low price.

You might start by ordering *hok* (hock, a slightly sweet Rhine-type wine), and the waiter will bring a bottle of the wine and a bottle of soda water. Mix two-thirds to three-quarters of a glass of wine with one-third to one-quarter of a glass of soda— that's the Romanian way.

✪ **U.N. Oriental Restaurant.** 10 Ha-Zionut Blvd. ☎ **04/531-046.** Appetizers NIS 4–12 ($1.20–$3.60); main courses NIS 20–40 ($6–$12); daily special full meal NIS 20 ($6). AE, DC, MC, V. Daily 8am–midnight. MIDDLE EASTERN.

Haifa Accommodations & Dining

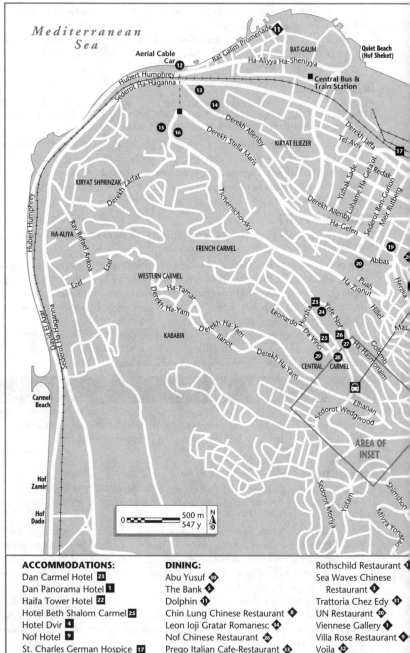

Mediterranean Sea

Quiet Beach (Hof Sheket)

BAT-GALIM

Ha-Aliyya Ha-Sheniyya

Aerial Cable Car

Hubert Humphrey

Sederot Ha-Haganna

Central Bus & Train Station

Derekh Allenby

KIRYAT ELIEZER

Derekh Stella Maris

Derekh Jaffa

Tel-Aviv

Lohame Ha-Geta'ot Redak

Yitzhak Sade

Derekh Zarfat

KIRYAT SHPRINZAK

Tschernichovsky

Derekh Allenby

Sederot Ben-Gurion

Meir Rutberg

Ha-Gefen

HA-ALIYA

Rav' Refael Ankoa

FRENCH CARMEL

Ezel

Abbas

Herzlia

Ezel

WESTERN CARMEL

Ha-Tamar

Puah

Ha-Zionut

Derekh Ha-Yam

Leonardo Da Vinci

Hordus

Yefe Nof

KABABIR

Ilanot

Derekh Ha-Yam

Ha-Hashmonaim

Hubert Humphrey

Derekh Ha-Yam

CENTRAL CARMEL

Columb

David El Azzar

Sederot Ha-Haganna

Mas.

Elhanan

Carmel Beach

Sederot Wedgwood

AREA OF INSET

Hof Zamir

Sedorot Moriya

Hof Dado

Yotam

Shimshon

Mivza Yonatan

0   500 m
     547 y

N

ACCOMMODATIONS:
Dan Carmel Hotel **23**
Dan Panorama Hotel **1**
Haifa Tower Hotel **22**
Hotel Beth Shalom Carmel **25**
Hotel Dvir **4**
Nof Hotel **9**
St. Charles German Hospice **17**

DINING:
Abu Yusuf **30**
The Bank **5**
Dolphin **11**
Chin Lung Chinese Restaurant **8**
Leon Ioji Gratar Romanesc **34**
Nof Chinese Restaurant **26**
Prego Italian Cafe-Restaurant **33**
Restaurant Abu Hani **35**
Ristorante Italiano **6**

Rothschild Restaurant **1**
Sea Waves Chinese
  Restaurant **3**
Trattoria Chez Edy **31**
UN Restaurant **20**
Viennese Gallery **1**
Villa Rose Restaurant **9**
Voila **12**
White Gallery
  Restaurant **7**

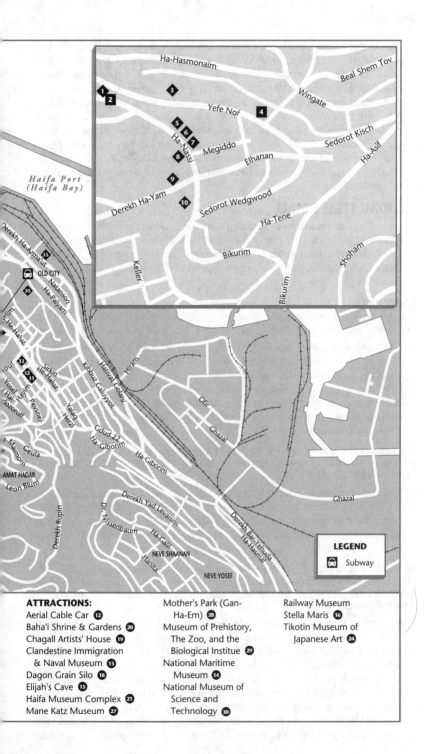

Haifa Port
(Haifa Bay)

OLD CITY

LEGEND

Subway

ATTRACTIONS:
Aerial Cable Car 12
Baha'i Shrine & Gardens 20
Chagall Artists' House 19
Clandestine Immigration
 & Naval Museum 13
Dagon Grain Silo 18
Elijah's Cave 15
Haifa Museum Complex 21
Mane Katz Museum 27

Mother's Park (Gan-
 Ha-Em) 28
Museum of Prehistory,
 The Zoo, and the
 Biological Institue 29
National Maritime
 Museum 14
National Museum of
 Science and
 Technology 30

Railway Museum
Stella Maris 16
Tikotin Museum of
 Japanese Art 24

Pronounced "Oom," this large, excellent, low-budget restaurant is filled with Jewish and Arab customers enjoying Middle Eastern food amid the functional, no-frills decor. There is an enormous salad bar filled with over 25 cold Middle Eastern dishes; for $1.70 you can take a plate and fill it with as much as you can (one trip to the salad bar per plate, but the management advises you not to be bashful). If you order a main course, the salad bar is included, and you can return as often as you like. Another great deal is the daily special buffet ($6) from which you can choose one of a selection of main courses, plus soup or the salad bar. It's always a good idea to be sure of the rules for each special. Baked lamb and fresh grilled red snapper, served with potato and salad, round out the better main courses on the menu.

NORDAU STREET MALL

After observing the success of Jerusalem's lively Ben-Yehuda Street Pedestrian Mall, Haifa decided to take the plunge and turn Nordau Street, one block above Herzl Street, into a tree-lined pedestrian area. The result has brightened the whole Hadar District, and has brought some really wonderful restaurant choices to the center of town.

MODERATE

Prego Italian Cafe-Restaurant. 20 Nordau St. ☎ **04/623-524.** Appetizers NIS 14–30 ($4.20–$9); main courses NIS 20–60 ($6–$18). AE, DC, MC, V. Daily noon–midnight. ITALIAN.

This restaurant achieves an understated elegance with its scant furnishings and decor of simple black and white. Here stylish Haifans come for salade niçoise, carpaccio, fresh pasta dishes, and elegant pizza. At the top end of the menu, choose from among salmon stuffed with ricotta cheese and herbs in a creamed wine-and-mustard sauce, or prawns in a tomato-anise sauce. Good for long, unhurried meals at prices that are not extravagant. Three-course business lunch specials are offered from noon to 4pm.

La Trattoria Chez Edy. 5 Hayim St. ☎ **04/662-520.** Reservations recommended. Appetizers NIS 15–33 ($4.50–$10); main courses NIS 33–70 ($10–$21). AE, DC, MC, V. Daily noon–midnight. FRENCH/ITALIAN/TUNISIAN.

Specializing in quality French and Italian meals and Tunisian couscous, La Trattoria is a fine place to dine. Italian pasta meals cost around $10, but the French dishes, known for their fine gourmet sauces, are more in the $20 to $30 range. Beautifully prepared couscous will cost about $18. There is also an extensive wine and dessert list.

✪ **Voila.** 21A Nordau St. ☎ **04/664-529.** Reservations recommended. Appetizers NIS 15–30 ($4.50–$9); main courses NIS 33–63 ($10–$19); fixed-price lunches NIS 50 and NIS 60 ($l5 and $18). AE, DC, MC. Sat–Thurs noon–midnight; Fri noon–4:30pm and 7:30pm–1am. SWISS/FRENCH.

A charming romantic hideaway in the Nordau Street Mall, Voila is a labor of love on the part of its owners, who have provided a secluded, intimate atmosphere with specially designed rustic French Alpine touches, both indoors and in the garden, although the restaurant is in the bustling heart of the city. The style of the kitchen is rich, but this is a worthwhile place to set aside a diet. Appetizers include mushrooms in herb butter stuffed with pâté de foie gras and stuffed shrimp. You can order a seafood fondue served with four cheeses and a basket of sliced baguette plus a salad (150 grams of shrimp, mussels, and other seafood for $33; a considerably larger portion, which two can share, is $39); a dazzling house-specialty meat fondue for two ($28) served with five sauces on a sizzling stone; or roasted mullard (hybrid of duck and goose) breast in apple cider and date sauce. A pan of Swiss rosti, a Voila specialty, or a salad, is served with each main course. Consider dividing a lavish, original dessert.

INEXPENSIVE

Kapulsky's. 6 Nordau St. ☎ **04/645-633.** Pastries NIS 10–25 ($3–$7.50); light meals NIS 19–27 ($5.70–$8.10). MC, V. Sun–Fri 9am–11pm; Sat 1pm–midnight. CAFE.

Long a Haifa landmark for lavish pastries and beautiful light meals, Kapulsky's has a busy indoor cafe and outdoor tables that are great for leisurely people-watching. In addition to its famous European-style pies and tortes, Kapulsky's serves salads, soufflés, and lasagne and other light to major meals. Another branch of Kapulsky's is at the Panorama Center in Central Carmel.

CENTRAL CARMEL

EXPENSIVE

Villa Rose. 8 Machanaim St. ☎ **04/382-212.** Reservations required. Appetizers NIS 25–50 ($7.50–$15); main courses NIS 50–95 ($15–$28.50); business lunch starting at NIS 60 ($18). AE, DC, MC, V. Mon–Sat noon–3:30pm and 7–11pm. Carmelit: Gan Ha-Em. FRENCH.

One of the few remaining villas that once dotted the crest of the Carmel Range is the setting for this new restaurant, the most luxurious in Haifa. The restaurant is divided into a series of chandelier-lit rooms, with formal window draperies and 19th-century paintings in guilded frames; beside each table is a stand for chilled wine. The decor and formal service match the menu, which is classic French with just a touch of playful invention. For a first course, you might have *carpaccio al mare* of salmon or grouper fillet. Chateaubriand for two with pepper or mustard sauce is just under $50. Fresh fish and seafood, from both the Mediterranean and Red seas, is beautifully done—I especially enjoyed prawns in ginger sauce with wild rice on a bed of marinated sweet cabbage, and a Red Sea Denis fish baked with fresh herbs. The wine list ranges from imported to Israeli choices, including a fine Golan champagne. Classic profiteroles filled with ice cream and hot chocolate and house crêpes Suzette head a rich dessert menu. Luncheon specials are excellent value.

MODERATE

Nof Chinese Restaurant. 101 Ha-Nassi Blvd. ☎ **04/354-311.** Reservations recommended. Appetizers NIS 15–50 ($5–$13.30); main courses NIS 40–NIS 55 ($13.30–$17.50); business lunch NIS 50 ($15). AE, DC, MC, V. Sun–Thurs noon–3pm and 7pm–midnight; Sat after Shabbat. Closed Fri and Sat until after Shabbat. CHINESE.

A comfortable and well-known kosher Chinese restaurant, the Nof Chinese specializes in hot-pot creations and a variety of regional styles of preparation. The view in the daytime is dramatic.

✪ Sea Waves Chinese Restaurant. 99 Yefe Nof St. ☎ **04/375-602.** Reservations recommended evenings and weekends. Appetizers NIS 15–50 ($3–$15); main courses NIS 28–60 ($8.30–$18); complete luncheon special NIS 36 ($11). AE, DC, MC, V. Lunch daily noon–3pm; dinner daily 7pm–midnight. CHINESE.

With its fabulous views, Sea Waves offers a sophisticated well-prepared menu with specialties that include skewered meats served on sizzling iron plates and hot-pot dishes. It also serves a large menu of more standard Chinese dishes at quite reasonable prices. A window table, right up against the view, especially during daylight hours, makes dining here memorable.

✪ **White Gallery.** 125 Ha Nassi Blvd. ☎ **04/375-574.** Appetizers NIS 14–33 ($3.70–$11); main courses NIS 22–54 ($6.60–$18). AE, DC, MC, V. Sun–Thurs 9am–1am; Fri 8am–3am; Sat 10am–3am. CONTINENTAL.

The Carmel Center's most stylish restaurant, both in terms of cuisine and design, this place, with sleek minimalist decor and a sidewalk terrace for people-watching, is both popular and affordable. Haifans come by for breakfast, which can be a simple coffee, a full Israeli-style meal, or a soft sesame roll (known locally as a bagel) with cream cheese and lox. For lunch and dinner, choose from inventive salads (that are meals in themselves) such as goose breast with fresh vegetables and mozzarella; the Far East salad, with chopped lettuce, chicken breast, rice noodles, and fresh vegetables in a sweet-and-sour corriander sauce; or the Hot Gallery Salad of lightly sautéed vegetables in a tasty vinaigrette. Pasta dishes are also a good choice, and include a rich lasagne filled with mushrooms, spinach, garlic, and onions. Fajitas, a variety of excellent chicken dishes, quality steaks, and a good wine list and cheese platters round out the upmarket end of the menu.

INEXPENSIVE

The Bank. 119 Ha-Nassi Blvd. ☎ **04/389-623.** Light meals NIS 12–32 ($3.60–$9.60). MC, V. Daily 10am–11pm or midnight. Carmelit: Gan Ha-Em. CAFE.

This is a bright, stylish place, with summery furnishings, where you can enjoy sitting at the sidewalk tables and watching the activity around Central Carmel. The Bank is great for light meals—pancakes, blintzes, sandwiches, salads, crêpes, cakes, and cappuccino, or many kinds of ice cream confections. The hefty Bank salad is especially recommended.

Chin Lung Chinese Restaurant. 126 Ha-Nassi Blvd. ☎ **04/381-308.** Appetizers NIS 8–17 ($2.40–$5.10); main courses NIS 18–50 ($5.40–$15). MC, V. Lunch daily noon–3pm; dinner daily 6:30pm–midnight Carmelit: Gan Ha-Em. CHINESE.

At first there seems to be no restaurant at all behind the sign and posted menu near the corner of Sea Road (Derekh Ha-Yam). But go down the adjoining steps and you'll discover a nice cellar dining room with a small-town American-style folksy Chinese decor, done in gold and crimson, with gold tablecloths and fresh flowers. The food is mostly Szechuan style, which can be spicy but needn't be if you don't like hot food. There are 50 items to choose from here. Beer, wine, and cocktails are served.

✪ **Ristorante Italiano.** 119 Ha-Nassi Blvd. ☎ **04/381-336.** Main courses NIS 24–48 ($7.20–$14.30). AE, MC, V. Sun–Thurs noon–3pm and 6–11pm; Sat noon–11pm. Closed Fri. EUROPEAN/ITALIAN.

A real favorite with Americans, this is a small, family-run restaurant where you can have a filling meal of spaghetti, cannelloni, or a truly hefty pizza with fresh toppings for less than NIS 30 ($9). Heaping salads and wonderful goulash, just like my grandmother made, are also on the menu, as are grilled meats, American homestyle hamburgers, trout, and Saint Peter's fish. A rich bowl of vegetable soup and garlic bread makes a fine inexpensive lunch. The management here is very friendly and takes good care of returning customers.

Rothschild's. 140 Ha Nassi Blvd. ☎ **04/360-070.** Appetizers NIS 11–25 ($3.30–$7.50); light meals NIS 14–23 ($4.20–$6.90); main courses NIS 22–44 ($6.60–$13.20). MC, V. Daily 9:30am–midnight. CAFE/CONTINENTAL.

Just to the far side of the Haifa Auditorium and the Cinémathèque, this stylish but reasonably priced place offers the concert crowd and film buffs an intelligent menu of large, interesting salads, soups, quiches, and desserts; specialties include salmon carpaccio with curry mustard sauce, and escallop of chicken breast served in a variety of sauces. There's a terrace for outdoor meals. Busy at performance times, this is a popular Haifa rendezvous point.

BY THE PORT
INEXPENSIVE

✪ **Abu Yusuf.** 1 Ha-Meginim St. ☎ **04/663-723.** Appetizers NIS 4–12 ($1.20–$3.60); main courses NIS 20–37 ($6–$11.30). MC, V. Sat–Thurs 9am–midnight; Fri 7am–4pm. Carmelit: Paris Square. ARABIC.

The sign is in Hebrew, English, and Arabic, and this restaurant has been loved by speakers of all three languages for decades. Newly redecorated but still basically no frills, Abu Yusuf's food tends toward the Lebanese, with kubbeh, hummus with meat, grilled heart (delicious!), and roast chicken. One trip to the wonderful salad bar of 20 Middle Eastern dishes comes with a main course, or you can order the salad bar alone and have a fine meal with fresh pita bread and a shot ("jot") of anise-flavored arak brandy, and two people will pay about $7 each. A meal with a large main course would be $10 to $15. Abu Yusuf offers fresh fish and grilled lamb dishes and has won awards several years in a row. Very good value.

IN THE MARKET

Restaurant Abu Hani. Eliyahu Ha-Navi Street. No phone. Light meals NIS 7–25 ($2.10–$7.50). Daily 8am–4pm. Closed Sat. Carmelit: Paris Square. ARABIC.

If you're here around lunchtime (or anytime, actually), you're likely to find Abu Hani, on the corner of the little passageway leading into the market, packed with people, and since it's a small place with only a few chairs inside, many of the munchers will be standing around inside or out on the sidewalk. The attraction here again is delicious food at a good price. Choices include grilled shashlik on pita, felafel, and hummus.

BAT GALIM

Bat Galim means "Daughter of the Waves" in Hebrew, and you'll know how it got its name when you stroll along its beachfront promenade. If you take a ride on the aerial cable car between the beach and Mount Carmel, at the lower terminal you'll be right at the end of Bat Galim. The restaurants I'll mention are all within about a 5-minute walk from there.

If you're not coming from the cable-car terminal, you can easily walk over from the main bus or train stations—Bat Galim is located behind the stations. If you're at the Central Station, go through the underground tunnel that connects it to the train station; when you come out of the train station, you'll be in Bat Galim. You can also take bus no. 40, 41, 42, or 44, which go from the bus station to the cable-car terminal; or if you're driving, come across at Hel Ha-Yam, the main boulevard running just east of the bus station.

MODERATE

✪ **Dolphin.** 13 Bat Galim Ave. ☎ **04/523-837.** Reservations recommended evenings. Appetizers NIS 10–33 ($3–$10); main courses NIS 40–66 ($12–$20). AE, DC, MC, V. Daily noon–4pm and 7pm–midnight. Bus: No. 40, 41, or 42. SEAFOOD.

À la carte prices are higher than in other neighborhood choices, but the reputation of the restaurant is very good. A typical dinner might include the excellent house fish soup, tomato-based and richly herbed; shrimp cocktail or fried calamari; followed by a main course of fresh fish. It's one block inland from Bat Galim Promenade.

CAFES
CENTRAL CARMEL

On the loft balcony above the dairy self-service Cafe Carmel in the vast Panorama Center is the **Viennese Gallery** (☎ 04/352-222). The view is incredible from up here, and the distinctive architecture does everything to maximize the view, with a curved, two-story, 100% window wall. The Viennese Gallery serves mostly desserts and coffees; but there is also a selection of quiches, salads, omelets, soups, and cold platters, as well Saint Peter's fish or "Dakar" fish served with white wine and caviar ($14.50). Although the surroundings are fancy, prices really are quite reasonable. You can get a gorgeous Viennese pastry with a whole pot of freshly brewed tea or coffee for $6, or for $5, the "Viennese Fantasy," a combination of as many flavors of ice cream and as many toppings as you like—you select the combinations. You'll find it open from 10am to 11pm daily (until midnight Friday and Saturday nights). If you're not a guest at the Panorama Hotel and unable to put the tab on your VAT-free bill, you will pay an extra 17% above the dollar prices.

PORT AREA & HADAR

Exodus Conditoria, 31 Ha-Atzma'ut Rd., is just the place for a light breakfast, afternoon tea, or dessert after lunch. The glass cases are crammed with delicious croissants, chocolate cakes, pastries, strudels, cream cakes, and the like. Coffee and tea are served, prices are fatteningly low (that is, you're tempted to go for another serving), and hours are 8am to 7pm, except Friday when they close at 2pm, and Saturday when they're closed all day. Coffee and pastry won't cost more than $3. The Exodus is down the street from the American Consular Agency, on Ha-Atzma'ut near the intersection with Eliyahu Ha-Navi Street (that's the vegetable-and-fruit market street).

Another good bakery in the downtown area is **Hershko Melekh,** which, although the address is 21 Asfor St. (no phone), can be found by walking down Ha-Meginim Street until you're directly across from the Italian church; by this time you will smell the bread baking, and you can just follow your nose to find it (the sign outside is in Hebrew only). This is not so much a sweets shop as it is a bakery for bagels, rolls, pretzels with onions and spices, or pizza. Prices here are good, and you stand an excellent chance of walking in to find something coming piping hot out of the oven—couldn't be any fresher than that. Another plus is that, no matter when you come, you're sure to find it open—it's baking away 24 hours a day. This, too, is a popular place with locals in the know.

Pinat Hatzaut (no phone), on the corner of Ha-Nevi'im and Hehalutz streets, specializes in those Turkish pastries dripping with honey and nuts, and whatever variety is your special favorite, you'll probably find it here, with extra-large sizes of all kinds priced at only NIS 2 (60¢). There are also doughnuts, bagels, huge pretzels, and other treats. Open Sunday through Thursday from 4am to midnight, closing Friday afternoon and all day Saturday.

Over on Herzl Street, near the corner of Shemaryahu Levin Street, look for **Contidory Ha'uga,** 14 Herzl St. (☎ 04/665-288), a bakery doing a lively business in every kind of baked goods, from simple rolls, bread, doughnuts, and cookies, up to the most artistic refrigerated confections of chocolate and whipped cream. You can get a cup of cappuccino here too, and enjoy it with a sweet, but you'll have to stand up along the coffee counter—the place is so busy, they've taken out the chairs to make room for all the customers. Hours are Sunday through Thursday from 8am to 8pm, on Friday until 3pm; closed Saturday.

6 Attractions

Before setting out, check with the Haifa Municipal Information Office's "What's on in Haifa," which tells you what's doing during the month that you're in town.

SUGGESTED ITINERARY

Day 1   Visit the Baha'i Gardens, enjoy the panorama, and take in the Haifa Museum while checking out central Haifa.

Day 2   Spend at least half the day at one of Haifa's fine municipal beaches if the weather's good. Hof Carmel or Hof Dado, south of the city, are best. Choose from among Haifa's other fine museums, such as Clandestine Immigration, Mané Katz, or the Japanese Tikotin Museum for the rest of your day.

Day 3   Take an excursion to Mount Carmel, the Carmelite monastery at Mukraqa (with its sweeping view, the site of Elijah's contest with the prophets of Baal), and the Druze villages (see section 10); or to the artists' village at Ein Hod (see chapter 8, section 5); or to Old Akko (see chapter 8, section 6).

THE TOP ATTRACTIONS
IN HADAR

✪ **Baha'i Shrine & Gardens.** Free admission. Modest dress required. Shrine daily 9am–noon; gardens daily 9am–5pm. Bus: 22 from the port, 23 or 25 from Hadar.

Haifa's most impressive sightseeing attraction is the splendid Baha'i Shrine and Gardens, reached from Zionism (Ha-Zionut) Avenue. The immaculate, majestic Baha'i gardens—with their stone peacocks and eagles, and delicately manicured cypress trees—are a restful, esthetic memorial to the founders of the Baha'i faith. Haifa is the international headquarters for the Baha'i faith, which began in Persia in the mid-19th century in a bloodbath of persecution.

Baha'is believe in the unity of all religions and see all religious leaders—Christ, Buddha, Muhammad, Moses—as messengers of God, sent at different times in history with doctrines varying to fit changing social needs, but bringing substantially the same message. The most recent of these heavenly teachers, according to Baha'is, was Bahaullah. He was exiled by the Turkish authorities to Acre, wrote his doctrines there, and died a peaceful death in Bahji House just north of Acre. (See chapter 8 under "Acre (Akko)" for more information.)

In the Haifa gardens, the huge domed **shrine** entombs the remains of the Bab, the Bahaullah's herald. The tomb is a sight to see, with ornamental goldwork and flowers in almost every nook and cranny. The Bab's remains, incidentally, were hidden for years after he died a martyr's death in front of a firing squad. Eventually, however, his followers secretly carried his remains to the Holy Land.

On a higher hilltop stands the Corinthian-style **Baha'i International Archives** building, modeled after the Parthenon, and the **Universal House of Justice,** with 58 marble columns and hanging gardens behind. These are business buildings, not open to tourists. They, and the shrine of the tomb of the Bab, all face toward Acre, the burial place of Bahaullah.

The beautiful grounds were planned by Shoghi Effendi, the late Guardian of the Faith. In addition to curious tourists, you'll see pilgrims who have come from all parts of the world to pay homage to the first leaders of this universal faith. (Incidentally, at the entrance to the shrine, where you must remove your shoes, you will be given a pamphlet providing further details on Baha'i history and doctrine.)

Note: The Baha'i gardens are currently undergoing a massive redesign that will make them into one of the horticultural wonders of the world. You may be able to see part of the hanging-garden concept of the design as it is completed, but much will be under construction during the time span of this edition.

✪ **Haifa Museum Complex.** 26 Shabtai Levi St. ☎ **04/523-255.** Admission NIS 9 ($2.70), NIS 7 ($2.10) students. Sun–Fri 10am–1pm; also Tues–Thurs 5–8pm; Sat 10am–3pm. Bus: 12, 22, or 41. Carmelit: Ha-Nevi'im station in Hadar.

This complex contains several museums of interest. The **Museum of Modern Art** has a collection of paintings and sculpture by Israeli artists as well as prints by Israeli and foreign artists. The library and slide collection is open to the public where lectures, art films, and slide presentations are held in the evenings.

Mané Katz Museum. 89 Yefe Nof (Panorama Rd.). ☎ **04/383-482.** Admission donation. Sun–Mon and Wed–Thurs 10am–4pm; Tues 2–6pm; Fri 10am–1pm; Sat 10am–2pm. Bus: 22, 23, or 31. Carmelit: Central Carmel.

This building, near the Dan Hotel in Central Carmel, was once a rustic mountaintop villa in which the French artist Mané Katz lived (the neighborhood has certainly changed). The museum now houses Mané Katz's own work and personal art collection—drawings, aquarelles, gouaches, oil paintings, sculpture, and Judaica—as well as visiting exhibits of contemporary art.

Mitzpoor Ha-Shalom (Peace View Park). Zionism Avenue.

The grounds of the Baha'i gardens are split by Zionism Avenue. Farther up the hill is the lovely Mitzpoor Ha-Shalom (Peace View Park), also called the Ursula Malbin Sculpture Garden, at the corner of Shnayim Be-November Street. Amid trees, flowers, and sloping lawns are 18 bronze sculptures by Ursula Malbin of men, women, children, and animals at play. The view from here is magnificent—you can see all of Haifa's port area, Haifa Bay, Acre, Nahariya, and up to Rosh Ha-Niqra at the Lebanese border, plus the mountains all around.

IN CARMEL

Mount Carmel National Park. Bus: 37.

Israel's largest national park has 25,000 acres of pine, eucalyptus, and cypress forest. It encompasses a large area of the Carmel mountain range, and contains many points of interest that are well marked and easily reachable. And, of course, it also has picnic areas, playgrounds, a restaurant, and restrooms.

Technion City. Free admission. Visitor center, Sun–Thurs 8am–2pm. Cafeteria, Sun–Thurs 8am–2pm; Fri 8am–noon. Closed Sat. Bus: 17 from Central Bus Station, 31 from Central Carmel, 19 from Hadar at Daniel Street, next to the Armon Cinema on Ha-Nevi'im Street, just down from Masaryk Square.

Technion, the Israel Institute of Technology, is Israel's version of MIT. Begun in 1954, its 300-acre campus now consists of 50 buildings, including 12 dormitories, a wind-tunnel laboratory, and the Churchill Auditorium. It's a most impressive university complex with its view of the city, the bay, the coastline clear to Lebanon, and the snow-topped Syrian mountains. Most important, the reputation of the school has grown so rapidly that it attracts students from many foreign countries.

Because so many people come to see the Technion, the **Coler-California Visitor Center** (☎ 04/320-664) has been established to introduce the campus to visitors. You'll be greeted by a real working robot when you come in. There's also a free 25-minute video showing the different kinds of modern technology being practiced, researched, and taught here. You'll also receive a pamphlet and map of the campus, which you can use to take your own **self-guided tour.** The student-priced **cafeteria** downstairs is highly recommended for a good budget lunch.

Many **entertainment activities** are held every evening (except Monday) at Bet Student, the Technion's Student House (☎ **04/234-148**). Call during the daytime for info on folk, disco, and '60s dancing, films, and other activities. You can also stop in at Bet Student's pub, cafeteria, or restaurant for a meal at student prices.

University of Haifa. ☎ **04/240-003,** 240-007, or 240-097 for tour reservations. Campus tours Sun–Thurs 10am. Bus: 24 or 37.

On the road from Haifa to the nearby Druze village of Daliat-el-Carmel you'll see the buildings and tower of the University of Haifa. The campus center, designed by the Brazilian architect Oscar Niemeyer, was never fully executed according to his plans. The university began operation in 1963, under the joint auspices of the City of Haifa and the Hebrew University. At that time, the students numbered 650, now 9,000 (regular and extension), and today the university offers bachelor of arts programs in some 31 departments as well as graduate programs.

The campus covers 200 acres and has a magnificent view. From the 30th (top) observatory floor of the **Eshkol Tower,** which you can visit Sunday through Thursday from 8am to 4pm (admission free), you get an incredible view of practically the entire north of Israel. All the university's public spaces were designed by the Department of Fine Arts and there's a surprising amount of art everywhere you look around the campus. The large murals located in the university lobby are especially notable.

The campus has several impressive art galleries. The **Oscar Ghez Gallery,** on the tower's 30th floor, houses a moving memorial collection of works by artists who perished in the Holocaust, compiled by Mr. Ghez over a 30-year period. The **University of Haifa Gallery** and the **Regina Helm Sculpture Gallery,** in the main part of the university, display important works by Israeli and foreign artists. The **Reuben and Edith Hecht Museum of the Archeology of the Land of Israel** has a large number of exhibits, complete with interesting and informative explanations, on all aspects of Israel's archeological heritage. The art galleries and the museum are open Sunday through Thursday from 10am to 4pm, Friday from 10am to 1pm, Saturday from 10am to 5pm. Admission is free. To take a free **guided tour** of the campus, you must call in advance to reserve a spot (see above).

The Haifa University Students Association sponsors many activities throughout the week, including movies, disco, folk dancing, and more. Call the **Students Association** (☎ **04/240-513** or **240-519**) for information on these and other activities. Regular bus and sherut service connects the university with many parts of Haifa; from downtown, take bus 24 or 37.

Stella Maris. Stella Maris Road. ☎ **04/337-758.** English masses Mon–Sat 6:30am; Sun 7 and 9am. Modest dress required. Church open daily 8:30am–1:30pm and 3–6pm. Bus: 25, 26, or 31.

From Ha-Nassi Boulevard and Tchernichovsky Street go northwest to the Stella Maris French Carmelite church, monastery, and hospice (P.O. Box 9047). Construction of the present complex was begun in 1836. Situated across the street from the Old Lighthouse, with a magnificent view of the sea, this monastery served as a hospital for Napoleon's soldiers during his unsuccessful siege of Acre in 1799. The pyramid in front of the church entryway stands as a memorial to these soldiers, bearing the inscription "How are the mighty fallen in battle," from King David's lamentation over Saul and Jonathan.

The **church** is a beautiful structure, with Italian marble so brightly and vividly patterned that visitors sometimes mistakenly think the walls have been painted. Colorful paintings on the dome, done by Brother Luigi Poggi (1924–28), depict episodes from the Old Testament, the most dramatic being the scene of Elijah swept up in a chariot of fire; but the statue of the Virgin Mary, carved from cedar of Lebanon, is also notable. The **cave** situated below the altar, which you can walk down into, is believed to have been inhabited by Elijah.

Be sure to visit the rooms to the right of the entryway, where you'll find a charming nativity scene, a **museum** with artifacts from the Byzantine church occupying this same spot before the Carmelites built here, and a small **souvenir shop.** One of the monks will gladly give you a free pamphlet with information about the history of this site, and the Carmelite order, dating back to the arrival of the Crusaders on this mountain in the late 12th century. They will answer any questions you may have, and guide you to the various interesting details of the church, such as the many little votive candles burning on the alter above the cave, each representing a Carmelite community in another country (the United States has its candle up on the left).

IN THE PORT

Clandestine Immigration and Naval Museum. 204 Allenby Rd. ☎ **04/536-249.** Admission NIS 6 ($1.80) adults, NIS 3 (90¢) students. Mon and Wed–Thurs 8:30am–3pm; Sun and Tues 8:30am–4pm; Fri and holiday eves 9am–1pm. Closed Sat. Bus: 3, 5, 43, or 44.

The vessel *Af-Al-Pi (Nevertheless)* is now a part of the Clandestine Immigration and Naval Museum. It is a memorial commemorating all the ships that defied the British blockade to smuggle immigrants into Palestine. This clandestine immigration movement—called "Aliya Beth"—is one of the most harrowing phases of Israeli history. Refugees from the Nazis and escapees from DP camps were packed onto these illegal ships; many succeeded in making it undetected past British ships guarding Palestine's Mediterranean coastline; others were not so fortunate. The *Struma,* in 1941–42, waited for months at sea for some country to accept the 765 refugees aboard until at last it sank. All on board perished. Others, like the *Patria,* went down in Haifa harbor, with hundreds killed; still others, like the *Exodus,* ran the British blockade only to have its passengers shipped to a Cyprus detention camp, or, pathetically enough, returned to a detention camp in Germany. Farther along Jaffa Road, past the bus and train stations, west in the direction of Tel Aviv, the road changes names, becoming Sederot Ha-Hagana (Hagana Boulevard). The *Af-Al-Pi* is on the left-hand side of the road.

Aerial Cable Car. ☎ **04/335-970.** Round-trip NIS 12 ($3.60), one-way NIS 8 ($2.40) adults. Sat–Thurs 10am–6pm; Fri 10am–2pm. Bus: 26, 28, or 31 to the top terminal, or bus 40, 41, or 42 to the bottom terminal.

Directly across the road from the *Af-Al-Pi* is the lower terminal of the Haifa Aerial Cable Car, on your right-hand side beside the sea. It rides through the air from the beach at the western end of Bat Galim up to the tip of Mount Carmel, the site of the Old Lighthouse and Stella Maris. The round aerial cars, imported from Austria, are equipped with recorded messages about what you're seeing as you go up and down (flip the switch to choose English or Hebrew). Both the top and bottom terminals have restaurants and bars, and in the bottom terminal's downstairs hall, an exhibit of a featured artist's work is held every Saturday.

⊛ **Frommer's Favorite Haifa Experiences**

Promenading. The view of Haifa from the promenade in Central Carmel makes you keep coming back for more. By day or night, it's always lovely. Combine it with a meal that gives you a table right by the edge, or coffee and an elysian vista with dessert (see "Cafes," above).

Beachcombing. Haifa's great beaches are to the south of the city, reachable by municipal bus or, in summer, special shuttle from the big Central Carmel hotels, as well as sheruts. At Hof Ha-Carmel (Carmel Beach) or the quieter Hof Dado just to the south, you can combine a dip in the warm gentle waves with shish kebab or felafel from one of the many beachside stands. Stay late and you'll see the sunset over the Mediterranean. For Haifans, such paradisical luxuries are routine!

A Day Trip to Old Akko. It's amazing to think that two such different cities could be located on opposite ends of Haifa's sweeping bay: modern Haifa with its panoramas, and medieval Akko, with its labyrinth of bazaars, caravansaries, and mosques. A short bus ride gets you the 14 miles up the coast where you can explore this largely unrestored architectural treasure, have lunch or dinner in true Mediterranean style at an outdoor harborside cafe, and even take a boat ride around the Old City walls.

Elijah's Cave. 230 Allenby Rd. ☎ **04/527-430.** Free admission, but donations are accepted. Summer: Sun–Thurs 8am–6pm; Fri 8am–1pm. Winter: Sun–Thurs 8am–5pm; Fri 8am–1pm. Closed Sat and holidays. Bus: 3, 5, 44, or 45 will let you off at the highway nearby.

From the *Af-Al-Pi*, it's just a short walk up to Elijah's Cave, nestled at the base of steep Cape Carmel, below the Stella Maris lighthouse and the Carmelite Monastery. Tradition has it that Elijah hid here when fleeing the wrath of King Ahab and his wife, Jezebel. It's also the site where Elijah established his school upon his return from exile, thus earning the name "School of the Prophets," where Elijah, among others, studied. The cave is also said to be a place where the Holy Family found shelter for a night on their return from Egypt.

The cave is sacred to Jews, Christians, Muslims, and Druze, all of whom venerate the prophet Elijah. Pilgrimages and huge dramatic ceremonies are held at this cave many times each year. Head coverings are available at the entrance to the cave.

MORE ATTRACTIONS

The **Rothschild Community House** (Bet Rothschild) in Central Carmel near Haifa Auditorium at 142 Ha-Nassi Blvd. (☎ **04/382-749**) often has something of interest for tourists. Call to see what's up. Interesting, too, are the changing art exhibits and folklore programs at **Bet Ha-Gefen** (☎ **04/525-252**), the Arab-Jewish Community Center, on Ha-Gefen Street opposite the Chagall Artists' House.

Railway Museum. 40 Hativat Golani Ave. ☎ **04/564-293.** Admission NIS 5 ($1.50). Sun, Tues, and Thurs 9am–noon. Bus: 17, 42, or 193.

Two 1950s-vintage diesel locomotives, several cabooses, a club car built in 1922, and a passenger coach dating from 1893 are the major exhibits, but there are also displays of photographs, timetables, tickets, and other memorabilia going all the way back to the railroad's construction in Ottoman times (1882). This museum is in the old Haifa East railway station near Feisal Square.

Tikotin Museum of Japanese Art. 89 Ha-Nassi Blvd. ☎ **04/383-554.** Admission NIS 10 ($3), free Sat and holidays. *Note:* The museum is currently closed for renovation. Bus: 22 or 23. Carmelit: Gan Ha-Em station.

The Tikotin has examples of almost all kinds of Japanese art and crafts, along with a library of 2,000 books. It's located just north of the commercial district in Central Carmel.

Museum of Prehistory, the Zoo, and the Biological Institute. 124 Ha-Tishbi St. ☎ **04/371-833** for the museum, **371-886** for the zoo. Admission NIS 20 ($6), NIS 15 ($4.50) students. Museum and Institute: Sun–Thurs 8am–3pm; Fri 8am–1pm; Sat 10am–2pm. Zoo: Sept–June Sun–Thurs 8am–4pm, Fri 8am–1pm, Sat 9am–4pm; July–Aug Sun–Thurs 8am–6pm. Bus: 22, 31, or 37. Carmelit: Central Carmel.

The first of these maintains a permanent exhibit of fossils and artifacts from the Carmel region. Each of the others, in its own way, features the animal life of the country, with particular attention to the fish indigenous to Israel's waters and the fauna of the Carmel region.

National Maritime Museum. 198 Allenby Rd. ☎ **04/536-622.** Admission NIS 8 ($2.40); free Sat and holidays. Sun–Thurs 10am–4pm; Sat and holidays 10am–1pm. Bus: 3, 5, 43, 44, or 45.

This museum just up the street from the *Af-Al-Pi*, near Bat Galim, encompasses 5,000 years of seafaring in the Mediterranean and the Red Sea. The **Museum of Ancient Art**, recently relocated here from the central Haifa Museum Complex, displays archeological collections of Mediterranean cultures from the beginning of history until the Islamic conquest in the 7th century. There are outstanding collections of Greco-Roman culture, Coptic art, painted portraits from Fayyum, coins of Caesarea and Acre, terracottas of all periods, and finds from the Haifa area. The artifacts obtained through underwater archeology are particularly impressive.

Israel Edible Oil Museum. In the Sherman Oil Factory. ☎ **04/670-491.** Admission NIS 5 ($1.50). Sun–Thurs 9am–2pm. Bus: 2.

Many interesting items connected with the cooking oil industry in Israel, from over 2,000 years ago up to the present, are housed in the original old stone factory building.

Chagall Artists' House. 24 Ha-Zionut Ave. ☎ **04/522-355.** Free Admission. Sun–Thurs 9am–1pm and 4–7pm; Sat 10am–1pm. Bus: 10, 12, or 41.

This gallery exhibits the works of contemporary Israeli artists.

Dagon Grain Silo. Kikar Plumer. ☎ **04/664-221.** Free admission. Tours Sun–Fri 10:30am; call for reservations. The museum is only open to the public for the guided tours. Bus: 10, 12, or 22.

Next to the old Merkaz railroad station, at the entrance facing Kikar Plumer, you'll find the fascinating **Archeological Museum of Grain Handling in Israel.** On display are earthen storage jars, striking mosaic murals, and various exhibits showing the development of one of humankind's oldest industries—the cultivation, handling, storage, and distribution of grain. There are even some grains of wheat here that are more than 4,000 years old—as well as fertility statues and flint grain sickles. The exhibit traces the course of history in this land from 12,000 B.C. to the modern day. Every visitor receives a table of the archeological periods of history, a handy little reference that's especially valuable when you go poking around some of the ancient sites in Galilee and the Negev. The public is admitted only for scheduled tours, or by appointment.

National Museum of Science and Technology. Old Technion Campus, Balfour St. ☎ **04/ 628-111.** Admission NIS 14 ($4.20) adults; discounts for students. Mon and Wed–Thurs 9am–5pm; Tues 9am–7pm; Fri 9am–1pm; Sat 10am–2pm. Bus: 18, 19, 21, 28, 37, 42, and 50 come nearby.

The old campus is being developed as a museum site, home of the Technoda—the National Museum of Science and Technology. The exhibits here are working models, designed to stimulate the curiosity of young people in particular, but actually of interest to all ages. Exhibits include such common devices as the car, elevator, toilet, solar water heater, and airplane, showing how all these things do what they do. Exhibits also include demonstrations of laser technology and mathematical principles. Plans are in the works for a space gallery, including a planetarium, and you may find more attractions when you arrive. Turn right on Balfour, walk up the hill more or less behind the tourist office, and you'll find the entrance to the Old Technion campus, on the right.

ORGANIZED TOURS

For a free 2¹/₂-hour **guided walking tour** of Central Carmel (atop the mountain), be at the signposted meeting point by 10am any Saturday morning. The meeting point, marked by a sign, is on Panorama Road (Yefe Nof) at the intersection with Shar Ha-Levanon; Ha-Levanon is the little street that meets Ha-Nassi right behind the Gan Ha-Em Carmelit station. Ha-Nassi curves and heads northwest behind the Carmelit station. Don't curve with it; keep going straight—that's Shar Ha-Levanon, and Panorama Road (Yefe Nof) is a short block down. To come by bus, you can take bus no. 23 from Ha-Nevi'im Street, or bus no. 21 from Herzl Street, both in Hadar; they run on Saturday (note that the Carmelit does not).

The following companies have all sorts of tour plans for your consideration: **Egged Tours,** 4 Nordau St. (☎ **04/623-131**); **United Tours,** 5 Nordau St. (☎ **04/ 665-656**); and **Mitzpa Tours,** 1 Nordau St. (☎ **04/674-341**).

The **Society for Protection of Nature in Israel (SPNI),** 8 Menachem St. (☎ **04/ 664-135**), does excellent urban and nature trail tours.

7 Sports, Outdoor & Other Activities

Ha-Peol and **Maccabi** are two sports leagues in Israel. By contacting either of the leagues—or the Haifa Municipality—you can get the latest data on where to go to play tennis, to exercise or work out in a gym, or take in sports events as a spectator.

BEACHES   Carmel Beach (Hof Ha-Carmel) can be reached by bus no. 3 or 45 from Shapiro Street. In winter, at least one restaurant pavilion remains open until 7pm; in summer until 8:30pm. Never more than $10, and usually less, dinner at the beach in summer, with the sunset over the Mediterranean at the end of an afternoon swimming in the warm turquoise sea, is one of the most memorable dining experiences Haifa has to offer.

Hof Shaket (Quiet Beach), with an entrance fee of NIS 4 ($1.20), in the harbor area of Bat Galim, is open with a lifeguard year-round. It can be reached via bus no. 40, 41, or 42. The Bat Galim sea beach is on the opposite side of the small Bat Galim promontory.

There is also an adjoining beach, a sandy stretch known as the **Municipal Beach,** and this—budgeteers note—is free to all comers. These in-city beaches are often crowded and not as clean as the more distant strands of Hof Carmel or Hof Dado. There's also a public beach at **Kiryat Haim,** a Haifa suburb; take bus no. 51. South of town, heading toward Tel Aviv, are a number of other good public beaches, including **Hof Zamir** and **Hof Dado.**

FOLK DANCING   Israeli **folk dancing classes** meet Monday at 8:30pm at Haifa University and Thursday at 9:30pm at Bet Ha-Student at the Technion. **International Folk Dancers** meet Thursday at 8:30pm at Bet Rothschild, to the side of the Haifa Auditorium on Ha-Nassi Boulevard.

HORSEBACK RIDING   Located 20 minutes to the south of Haifa, the **Carmel Riding Center,** Ein Hod (☎ 04/841-828), offers horseback riding excursions with a magnificent view of Carmel National Park and the sea.

SWIMMING   In the Central Carmel section you'll find the **Maccabi swimming pool** on Bikkurim Street (☎ 04/388-341), heated in winter, and serviced by bus no. 21, 22, or 23 and by the Carmelit. Admission is NIS 13 ($3.90), but the fee doubles in winter. Don't forget the **pool at the Dan Carmel Hotel,** for a whole day's worth of pool, shower, and sporting privileges.

TENNIS & SQUASH   A 15-minute ride south of downtown Haifa, in the Kefar Zamir suburb, are the **Haifa Tennis Center** (☎ 04/522-721 or 532-014) and the **Haifa Squash Center** (☎ 04/539-160). Both have regular hours, and you're welcome to come and play—but you must call in advance to reserve a court. Take bus no. 43, 45, or 3A.

8 Shopping

Haifa has a number of modern indoor shopping malls, including the **Panorama Center** in Central Carmel, **Migdal Haneve'im** in the Hadar District, and the **Chorev Center** on Chorev Street at the intersection of Pica Street. **Herzl and Nordau streets** make for a pleasant window-shopping stroll.

The street behind Ha-Atzma'ut Road, running roughly parallel to it, is **Jaffa Road** (Derekh Yafo), where you can buy many of your souvenirs at prices considerably cheaper than elsewhere. This is an unusually inexpensive semi–flea market area, off the tourist path, where you'll see the residents of the lower town doing their shopping. The finjan coffee sets and brass trays, as well as the Middle Eastern–style earrings available here, undercut by several shekels the going prices in the fancier shops.

The best place for interesting gifts is the WIZO (Women's International Zionist Organization) Shop, 9 Nordau St. (☎ 04/667-028), with a good selection of crafts, Judaica, jewelry, silver, and hand-embroidered baby and children's clothing.

If you take an excursion to the artists' village of Ein Hod, you can shop for silver, enamel, and gold jewelry, hand-blown glass, pottery, and other crafts at the village's official gallery. See chapter 7, section 6.

9 Haifa After Dark

Haifa does not have as much nightlife as Tel Aviv, or even Jerusalem, but there are some nighttime activities. Check in the *Jerusalem Post,* which despite its name is a national paper covering events, cultural offerings, and movies throughout Israel. The Friday-morning edition includes the indispensable weekly calendar of happenings, some of which are in Haifa. Better yet, call the 24-hour telephone hotline for **"What's On in Haifa"** (☎ 04/374-253), and check with any of the tourist information offices, to find out about special events happening around town.

The student associations at the Technion and at the University of Haifa have entertainment of one kind or another going on almost every night. Check the universities for details.

THE PERFORMING ARTS

Haifa Auditorium. 138 Ha-Nassi Blvd. ☎ **04/380-013.**

This is Haifa's largest concert hall, where you can find symphony, opera, the Israel Philharmonic, dance concerts, and many other cultural events and big happenings; there's also usually an interesting art display in the lobby, which you can see anytime for free, from 4 to 7pm (except Friday). Haifa Auditorium is just a short distance south of the Central Carmel commercial district, where Ha-Nassi Boulevard becomes Moriah Avenue. Ticket prices vary with performance.

Haifa Municipal Theater. At the intersection of Pevsner, Yehoshua, and Trumpeldor. ☎ **04/670-956.**

Lots of shows are offered at this theater where the play performances are sometimes in Hebrew, sometimes in English, and sometimes both, in simultaneous translation. Ticket prices vary with performance.

James de Rothschild Cultural and Community Center. Bet Rothschild, 142 Ha-Nassi Blvd. ☎ **04/382-749.**

Next to Haifa Auditorium, this community center always has something going on: a dance, exhibit, or concert. Also inside the community center is the Haifa Cinémathèque (see below).

THE CLUB & MUSIC SCENE

Looking for a club, a place to hang out, listen to music, have a drink, and dance? The **Haifa Tourism Development Association,** 106 Ha-Nassi Blvd. in Central Carmel, across the street from the Nof Hotel (☎ **04/374-010**), has compiled a list of recommendable spots; stop by for information.

Martef Esser (Cellar Ten). 140 Ha-Nassi Blvd. on far side of Rothschild Center.

Once a Rothschild wine cellar, this is now a nightspot run by and for students, with live music of many kinds (jazz, classical, and more), and a nice wicker coffeehouse/bar atmosphere. There is a cover charge on Friday.

Fever. Gan Ha-Em Promenade. No phone.

This disco is a favorite with teenagers. Summer weekend evenings are busiest.

THE BAR SCENE

Many of Haifa's restaurants have bars with entertainment. Both the upper and lower terminals of the Aerial Cable Car, too, are enjoyable places to stop on an evening out, with restaurants, bars, and dancing; you can ride the cable car until 11pm; most of the year, until midnight.

Panass Boded. Bat Galim Promenade. ☎ **04/534-978.** Daily in summer 8pm–4am.

Walking along the promenade toward the cable-car terminal, you'll pass a black-and-white pub/piano bar with an archway over the door. Though the sign is in Hebrew, you'll know it's Panass Boded by the entertainment listings posted out front. (If you're walking by in the daytime, though, you'll find it closed;

this is a nightspot.) Inside you'll find Israeli Maccabee beer for NIS 7 ($2.10) and a network of rock videos for decor.

FILMS

Haifa's Cinémathèque. 142 Ha-Nassi Blvd. ☎ **04/383-424.** Tickets NIS 18 ($5.40).

Housed in the James de Rothschild Cultural and Community Center, this theater shows a wide variety of international films (up to three different movies every day, many in English, most with English subtitles), including special-interest art film screenings. The Cinémathèque hosts the Haifa Film Festival each fall at the time of Sukkot. Call for information about what's going on.

10 Easy Excursions

DALIAT-EL-CARMEL & ISFIYA

These Druze villages are located 15 minutes from the Ahuza section of Carmel. If you're driving, just ask for the road to Daliat-el-Carmel. Isfiya is the first village you'll reach from Haifa; Daliat-el-Carmel is a very short ride farther. The trip takes about half an hour, and it's a splendid drive along the uppermost rim of Carmel. The Mediterranean is way down below you, and so is the entire city, the port, and the industrial area. Bring your camera.

Architecturally, the villages are no longer the quaint enclaves of 30 or 40 years ago; instead, they've become part of the urban sprawl at the outer edge of the city. Haifans visit the villages for the many homestyle Middle Eastern restaurants that have sprung up, and for bargain shopping (see below).

The Druze are Arabic-speaking people who are, however, not Muslims. Theirs is a rather secretive religion; they draw heavily on the Bible and venerate such personages as Jethro (a Midianite priest and the non-Israelite father-in-law of Moses). The Druze were loyal to Israel during the 1948 war, and several of their brigades are highly respected detachments in the Israeli army.

They are an industrious people; you'll see their terraced hillsides, meticulously cared for and, as a result, very fertile. Many houses are new, and also square and boxlike in the Arabic style. Outside their own villages, Druze find employment on kibbutzim as electricians, builders, carpenters, and mechanics. Their hospitality is legendary.

In both villages, you can buy quite unusual souvenirs and handcrafted items, such as new or antique baskets and trays in the Druze style at moderate prices, but bargaining is necessary. (Markets will be closed on Friday, the Druze Sabbath day.) There are several pleasant cafes in both villages. You'll see older men in flowing gowns and headdresses, often wearing big mustaches, while the younger men wear Western-style clothes.

You can reach the villages on bus no. 192, which leaves infrequently from the Central Bus Station; but bus service back to Haifa seems to vanish by 3pm. Various tours also go to these villages (check with the Tourist Information Office for details). There's a sherut service that leaves Haifa during the evening from 6pm to 6am, departing from Hadar at the corner of Shemaryahu Levin and Herzl streets. Between 6am and 6pm, the sherut service from the port area is at the corner of Ha-Atzma'ut Road and Eliyahu Ha-Navi Street, near Kikar Paris. The sherut takes 25 minutes to reach Daliat-el-Carmel and the fare is the same as by bus.

WHERE TO STAY

Stella Carmel Hospice. Isfiya (P.O. Box 7045), Haifa 31070. ☎ **04/391-692.** Dormitory and private rooms. $20–$30 single; $50 double; $10 per person dormitory. Rates include breakfast. No credit cards. Bus: 192 from Haifa bus station.

Operated by the Anglican Church, this is an atmospheric place in the style of an old-fashioned Middle Eastern country inn. Public areas are filled with crafts; private rooms are plain but adequate. Only married couples may share double rooms. Lunch and dinner, as well as breakfast, are available here.

WHERE TO DINE

The Druze villages are lined with eating establishments geared to the weekend crowd.

Ganei Daliyah. Isfiya–Daliat-el-Carmel Road. ☎ **04/395-367.** Reservations recommended on weekends. Appetizers NIS 8–25 ($2.40–$7.50); main courses NIS 25–45 ($7.50–$13.50). AE, DC, MC, V. Daily noon–11pm. MIDDLE EASTERN.

This place has a pleasant garden filled with the sound of its fountain, a covered dining terrace, and a colorful proprietor, Mr. Toufik Halaby. Standard Middle Eastern dishes are a cut above normal, and there are a few well-prepared unusual offerings. The pidgeon stuffed with onion, pine nuts, and sumac, grilled on an open fire, is earthy and excellent, as is the homemade Druze bread, and the oven-baked sweetbreads. This is a good choice for a leisurely roadside repast. Arabic and Hebrew are spoken.

Coming from Haifa, look for the restaurant with its front garden and sign on the right as you leave Isfiya, and before you enter Daliat-el-Carmel.

MUHRAKA

Half a mile south of Daliat-el-Carmel, the road to Muhraka forks off to the left side of the main road. Its destination is not posted, but it meanders and climbs through scrub oak and pine woods to the monastery at Muhraka, the place where Elijah defeated the prophets of Baal. You'll see a dramatic stone **statue of Elijah,** sword raised to heaven, and a lovely **Carmelite monastery,** open Monday through Saturday from 8am to 1pm and again from 2:30 to 5pm (on Friday until noon only). The view from the roof of the monastery (NIS 1 admission) is unsurpassed; you can see halfway across Israel to Migdal Ha-Emek and the mountains near Nazareth. There are tables for picnics on the grounds outside the monastery. The name "Muhraka," or "place of burning," refers to a time when this extraordinary vista point was a sacred high place for burnt offerings and sacrifices in Canaanite and early Israelite times. Interurban bus 192 or sheruts from downtown Haifa will take you to the fork in the road that leads to Muhraka for NIS 9 ($2.70). From there it's a half-hour uphill climb; returning buses are few, and seem to stop by 3pm. The Druze–Muhraka area is most easily visited by car, or as a day-long bicycle excursion from Haifa.

ORGANIZED TOURS

A 3-hour tour to **Ein Hod** leaves Haifa most weekdays at 9:30am. It includes a drive through the Carmel mountain range, visits to University of Haifa and the Druze market of Daliat-el-Carmel, and stops at art galleries, artists' studios, and other points of interest. Check with the tourist office for current schedules. The **Society for Protection of Nature (SPNI)** at 8 Menachem St. (☎ **04/664-135**) sells excellent hiking and walking maps of the Carmel range.

10 | Galilee

Roughly speaking, everything to the north and east of Haifa is known as "the Galilee" (Ha-Galil)—Israel's lushest region. In February and March, the residents of Haifa pour out into Galilee to enjoy the ocean of wildflowers and blossoming trees that cover the valleys and slopes, and to marvel at the perseverance of the original settlers of Galilee communities (kibbutzim) who lived in tents, risked malaria, and fought off Arabs to cultivate the land.

Beginning in March a vast blanket of green covers Galilee and its watchtowers, settlements, and stone Arab villages. The land is a carefully designed texture of orange groves, rich vegetation, vineyards, and fruit orchards.

In Herodian times, according to Josephus, 204 towns in these hills supported about 15,000 residents each, giving Galilee a population of 3 million. This estimate is regarded by most historians as high, but there is no doubt that the ancient Galilee supported a population unsurpassed until modern times. Today this fertile countryside is the site of most of Israel's collective farms, and it is also home to most of Israel's Arab citizens, who maintain a traditional way of life closely tied to the land.

It was only natural that this fertile region should have been the first area to have been redeveloped early in this century. Initially it was to the shores of the Sea of Galilee, in the Jordan Valley and around the Emek Yizreel (Valley of Jezreel, usually just called the Emek) that the early Zionist pioneers came with their dreams of a socialistic utopia, founded on principles of agricultural toil. Then, in the '20s and '30s, they brought their communal settlements to the western plains and to the mountains of the north of Galilee. They established Israel's front line of defense, sweating out malaria attacks and returning the fire of Arab snipers. Babies born in these settlements grew into hardy young farmers, their playgrounds not the ghettos of Russia and Poland that their parents had known, but rather the meadows and fruit fields of their settlements. During the War of Independence in 1948 several Galilee settlements fought and farmed at the same time. War memorials throughout the region are a testament to these times.

TOURING THE REGION

Aside from the Galilee–Jerusalem road skirting the Jordan River, there are two good central routes for entering Galilee: One is from

Haifa to Acre and east to Safed, then down to the Sea of Galilee. The other is due east from Haifa to Nazareth and straight across to Tiberias. The third route we will follow is an offshoot of the Haifa–Nazareth road that detours down through the Jordan Valley and lands us south of the Sea of Galilee. In summer, the Jordan Valley, which is far below sea level, can be oppressively hot. Give yourself time to enjoy the beaches of the Sea of Galilee, which can be paradisical.

The Galilee is filled with so many places of natural and historical beauty that it's worth it to rent a car, at least for a few days of travel.

1 Nazareth & the Yizreel Valley

Nazareth: 40km (26 miles) SE of Haifa

The largest and most fertile valley in Israel, the Yizreel Valley, or the Emek, lies between the Galilee mountains to the north and the Samaria range to the south. Nazareth, the town where Jesus grew up, was only a tiny hamlet in biblical times, scarcely recorded on maps or mentioned in historical works. Today Nazareth is a bustling city, filled with industry and new construction.

ESSENTIALS

GETTING THERE   By Bus   Bus service is available to Nazareth from all major cities.

By Car   Nazareth is on the main road from Haifa to Tiberias and Tel Aviv to Tiberias, less than an hour from Haifa. Leave the port city via Ha-Atzma'ut Road and head inland over the four-lane highway that runs along the foot of the Carmel range. Nazareth is also connected by main roads to the Jordan Valley.

VISITOR INFORMATION   The **Tourist Information Office** (☎ 06/573-003) is on Casa Nova Street, open Monday through Friday from 8am to 5pm, Saturday from 8am to 2pm.

NAZARETH

This ancient part of town clings to the inside of a vast bowl, its mud and limestone houses tiered like the seats of an amphitheater. Today the city houses Israel's largest Arab community outside Jerusalem—more than 80,000—half Christian, half Muslim. With Jerusalem, it is also the headquarters of the Christian mission movement in Israel, with more than 40 churches, convents, monasteries, orphanages, and private parochial schools. Nazareth's very name is used by Arabs and Israelis to designate Christians, just as Jesus was also known as the Nazarene. In Arabic, Christians are called Nasara, and in Hebrew Notzrim.

To see what the increasingly modern Nazareth would have been like 40 years ago, turn into the narrow alleys that wind up and back into the terraced limestone ridges, and wander through the narrow cobbled streets of the Arab Market. Keep in mind that Nazareth is completely closed on Sunday and in full swing on Saturday.

ORIENTATION

ARRIVING   As you approach Nazareth from Haifa, the road is a series of hairpin turns up through the King George V Forest, planted by Keren Kayemet (the Jewish National Fund) more than 40 years ago.

After the trip from Haifa, you come over the hill and enter Nazareth on Paul VI Street, the town's main stem. Nazareth has a "bypass," a road that circles the town, which explains the confusing signs that point in opposite directions for the same destination. One of these destinations is **Nazareth Elit** (or Nazorat Ilit), the new, modern, mostly Jewish suburb to the north, built on land commandeered from the city of Nazareth, which is actually a separate municipality. You'll pass by it on your way to Tiberias.

CITY LAYOUT   Down Paul VI Street and into the center of Nazareth, you follow the signs to the Basilica of the Annunciation, Nazareth's principal religious monument off Paul VI Street on Casa Nova Street. Use the basilica's huge cupola, topped by a beacon, as your landmark—everything you'll need is within sight of the basilica. There are very few street signs and building numbers are often in Arabic. Remember that it's downhill to the basilica and the center of town from most points in the city.

Casa Nova Street is the approach to the basilica, and on it you'll find restaurants, cafes, hotels, and hospices.

The Central Bus Station in Nazareth is off Paul VI Street just east of Casa Nova Street, a few steps from the Basilica of the Annunciation.

WHAT TO SEE & DO

There are three occupations for tourists in Nazareth: shopping in the market, visiting the holy Christian shrines, and taking a glance at the new Jewish quarter.

CHRISTIAN SHRINES   The **Basilica of the Annunciation** is located on Casa Nova Street, on the spot where, according to Christian tradition, the angel Gabriel appeared before Mary, saying: "Behold, thou shalt conceive in thy womb, and bring forth a son, and shall call his name Jesus." The present Basilica of the Annunciation, a beautiful monument completed in 1966, was built over earlier structures dating from 1730 to 1877.

The earliest church was built over the grotto in which Mary sat when Gabriel spoke to her. As you enter the basilica, you'll be on the ground (or grotto) level, which is in fact the church's crypt. After you've toured the crypt, walk back to the entrance and you'll see steps up to the nave.

Unlike most Christian shrines in Israel, this basilica has a bold, modern design. Around the nave, on the walls, are murals that were created by artists from around the world. Note the Japanese mural of the Madonna and Child on the left (north) wall—Mary's robe is made entirely of Japanese seed pearls. The mural from the United States, on the right (south) wall, at first seems discordant and excessive, but it works when viewed from the basilica's north-side door.

Summer hours are daily from 8 to 11:45am and from 2 to 5:45pm; in winter it's open daily from 9 to 11:45am and from 2 to 4:45pm. (Many of the churches in Nazareth observe these same hours, closing for the "noontime siesta" during the middle of the day.) Walk out the north side door to reach the other religious sites.

The **Church of Saint Joseph** is 100 yards away, constructed on the site thought to have been occupied by Joseph's carpentry workshop. From the sanctuary, stairways on either side go down to another floor below, where you can see old stone construction, an ancient water cistern, and a mosaic floor dating from the Byzantine period. Hours are the same as at the Basilica of the Annunciation, above.

On the main street in the bazaar is the **Greek Catholic Synagogue Church** that Jesus frequented: "And He came to Nazareth, where He had been brought up; and, as His custom was, He went into the synagogue on the Sabbath day, and stood up for to read" (Luke 4:16). Farther along the road is the **Franciscan Mensa Christi Church,** believed to occupy the spot where Christ dined with his disciples after the resurrection.

What's Special About the Galilee & Jordan Valley

Major Towns/Cities

- Tiberias, a resort town on the Sea of Galilee.
- Nazareth, the village of Jesus and his family. The region's major Arabic community.
- Safed, a hilltop town with an Artists' Quarter and an ultrareligious neighborhood that was a center for Jewish scholarship and mysticism in the 16th century.
- Metulla, the northernmost Israeli town and a center for regional vacationing.
- Bet Shean, a modern development town offering vast archeological discoveries to public view.

Ancient Sites

- Megiddo (Armaggedon)—with more than a dozen levels of habitation uncovered in Israel's archetypical dig.
- Gamla, the dramatic Golan mountaintop where an entire Jewish town committed mass suicide rather than surrender to Rome in A.D. 67.
- Capernaum and the north shore of the Sea of Galilee, with churches and ancient synagogues at sites of Jesus's ministry.
- Baram, best preserved of synagogues from the late Roman period.
- Chorazim, the ruins of a Jewish town from the Roman–Byzantine era (including classical synagogue) overlooking the Sea of Galilee.
- Hazor, the northern Canaanite–Early Israelite city.

Major Attractions

- The Sea of Galilee, the mysterious, lovely freshwater lake, its shoreline filled with farms, olive and banana groves, beaches, and many historic sites.
- The Golan Heights—wild mountain plateau above the Sea of Galilee, with rushing streams in winter, prehistoric monoliths and dolmens, and an excellent local museum in Qasrin. Mount Hermon, near the Lebanese border, offers skiing in winter.
- Nature reserves at Hurshat Tal/Tel Dan, with luxurious forests, groves, ice-cold natural streams, pools, wildlife areas, birdwatching, archeological sites, camping areas, and kibbutz guesthouses in the northernmost part of Israel.

Special Events

- Ein Gev Music Festival, held each year in the Passover season.
- Karmiel, Israeli Folkdance Festival, attracting Jewish folk dance and ethnic groups from around the world and Israel. Mid-July.
- Kefar Blum Days of Chamber Music, offering 5 days of concerts and rehearsals open to the public. End of July/early August.
- Safed Klezmer Festival, featuring East European and Hasidic music. End of July.
- Hurshat Tal, Jacob's Ladder Country, Folk and Blues Festival, scheduled for early July.

Mary's Well, with its source inside the **Greek Orthodox Church of the Annunciation,** is another Christian holy site. The church was built at the end of the 17th century over the remains of three former churches. At the church entrance, on the archway above the stone staircase leading down to the well, there is a colorful mural showing the angel Gabriel coming to Mary and announcing in six languages, "Hail, thou that are highly favored, the Lord is with thee: blessed art thou among women." The ceiling is covered with brightly colored murals depicting scenes from the Bible. Proceed through the archway before you and you'll come to the well—a small spring and a round stone well.

The **Basilica of Jesus the Adolescent,** maintained by the French Salesian order, is one of the most beautiful churches in Nazareth. Built in 1918, the gothic church contains pillars composed of clusters of slender columns that support the vaulted roof. There's a lovely marble statue of Jesus the Adolescent by the sculptor Bognio. It is a climb to get to the top of the hill north of the center of town, but it is worth the effort. Go down Casa Nova Street to Paul VI Street, turn left, go up two blocks, and go down the street to the left of the public fountain; the church is one short block up this street, straight ahead. It's open year-round daily from 8am to 5pm.

Our Lady of Fright Chapel, sometimes called the Tremore, is built on a wooded hill south of the center opposite the Galilee Hotel. It is on the spot where Mary watched while the people of Nazareth attempted to throw Jesus over a cliff—the Precipice, or Lord's Leap rock, a quarter of a mile away.

Nazareth, which is half Muslim, also has some lovely Muslim structures. Built between 1960 and 1965, the beautiful and modern **Al-Salam Mosque** is in the eastern quarter of town, a block away from Paul VI Street. In the southern part of the city is the new **Al-Huda Mosque.**

A NEARBY ATTRACTION   **Mount Tabor** (at 1,800 feet above sea level, the tallest of the Lower Galilee Mountains) is a little more than 6 miles southeast of Nazareth. At the summit stands the **Basilica of the Transfiguration,** which marks where Jesus was transfigured in the presence of three of his disciples. Also on the mount is the **Church of Elias,** built in 1911 by the Greek Orthodox community. On a clear day, you can see the Sea of Galilee, Mount Hermon, the Mediterranean Sea, and the Emek from here. Mount Tabor is accessible from Nazareth by Egged bus or taxi.

SHOPPING IN THE MARKET   The market streets, entered via Casa Nova, are narrow, crowded, and highly exotic. Remember that the deeper you get into the market, the smaller the shops become and the lower the prices. One of the first things to note is the trench running dead center of the street, and one of the first precautions is to stay out of it as much as possible—it's the donkey trail. Snaking upward, the narrow roadway is lined with tin-roofed shops in which you'll see everything from plows and ram's horns to cakes, leather goods, chandeliers, plastic buckets, and fine jewelry. Daily necessities are displayed side by side with antiques from Turkish times that sell for thousands of shekels. You can buy a *finjan* coffee set here or a *kefiya*, which is the Arab headdress. One shop, deep in the market, carries *narghilis* (bubble pipes). One reliable shop is the **Mazzawi Bazaar.** If you're a coin collector, try the tiny **shop of Amin,** where you'll find a variety of coins and prices. Whatever you buy, be sure to shop around, and whatever you do, bargain over everything.

WHERE TO STAY

Prices for accommodations in Nazareth remain the same year-round.

Hotel Galilee. Paul VI Street, Nazareth. ☎ **06/571-311.** Fax 06/556-627. 93 rms (29 with bath, 64 with shower). A/C TEL. $45 single; $72 double. Rates include continental breakfast. No credit cards.

This modern, pleasant three-star establishment is a 5-minute walk south of the basilica. The entire hotel has recently been renovated, and in 1994, a new 30-room wing was added. The hotel has a bar and coffee shop, as well as heated rooms.

WHERE TO DINE

Astoria Restaurant. Casa Nova Street ☎ **06/573-497.** Appetizers, felafel, and shwarma sandwiches NIS 7–10 ($2.10–$3); main courses NIS 15–33 ($4.50–$10). No credit cards. Daily 8am–10pm. MIDDLE EASTERN.

Located at the intersection with Paul VI Street, one block from Basilica of the Annunciation, this clean, airy restaurant offers reasonably priced Middle Eastern dishes. The incongruous decor includes full-wall photomurals of the Rhine Valley. The menu includes two dozen lamb and chicken dishes and a fine selection of salads.

Middle Eastern Desserts

On the left-hand side of Casa Nova Street, just before it meets the basilica, is **Abu-Diab Mahroum's Sweets** (☎ 06/571-802 or 576-022). There are several stores named Mahroum's Sweets—make sure you go to the original near the Basilica of the Annunciation. The shop windows are filled with baklava, Turkish delight (maajoun) with nuts, Esh el-Bulbul ("Hummingbird's Nest," a shredded-wheat bird's nest filled with nuts and laced with honey), or burma (a roll of shredded wheat stuffed with pistachios and soaked in honey or syrup). Dessert and Turkish coffee costs about NIS 10 ($3) or less. Mahroum's is open daily from 7am to 9pm.

THE YIZREEL VALLEY

The Yizreel Valley houses some of Israel's oldest and best-known settlements— **Mishmar Ha-Emek, Hazorea, Givat Oz, Ginegar,** and the giant moshav, **Nahalal.** The rich, dark soil is crisscrossed in checkerboard patterns of fruit trees, vineyards, and green vegetable fields. It is a breathtaking quilt of colors, some blocks golden with wheat, some black with heavy cultivation, others orange with brilliant flowers.

About 70 years ago, however, this lush area was a breeding swamp of malaria. In the early 1920s the Keren Kayemet (Jewish National Fund) launched its biggest land reclamation project; over a period of time, the swampland was drained and every mosquito was killed. Russian, German, and Polish settlers filled the new settlements. The cultivation of the Emek became legendary, rhapsodized in dozens of romantic songs in which the tilling of soil and the smell of roses are common lyrics.

But as you look at this splendid fertility, remember also that this was one of the bloodiest battlefields in history. Here the Egyptians shed blood 4,000 years ago, as did the Canaanites, the Mongols, the Greeks, the Romans, and the Crusaders in later centuries. From Mount Tabor, overlooking the Emek's northeast corner, the prophetess Deborah launched her famous attack against the Canaanite armies. And several years later, Gideon's forces came from Mount Gilboa on the Midianites and slaughtered the plundering Bedouin tribe.

But it was also on this fertile plain that the Israelite tribe suffered one of its most calamitous national defeats—when King Saul and his sons, including Jonathan, died during a clash with the Philistines. It is with regard to this battle that the book of Samuel records David's immortal lament.

How the mighty are fallen!
Tell it not in Gath,
Publish it not in the streets of Ashkelon
Lest the daughters of the Philistines rejoice . . .
Saul and Jonathan were lovely and pleasant in their lives,
And in their deaths they were not divided . . .
Lo, how the mighty are fallen,
And the weapons of war perished.

Later, the Turks fought here, as did Napoleon. In 1918 General Allenby defeated the Turkish forces on the Emek, and Israel's armies in 1948 overwhelmed the Arabs. It is ironic that the Emek region, which has been so ravaged, today flourishes in such splendor.

WHAT TO SEE & DO

As you travel from Haifa to Nazareth, you pass farm settlements, the most important of which are **Yagur** and **Allonim.** Yagur is one of the country's oldest kibbutzim, founded in 1922. About 30 or 40 minutes out of Haifa be sure to stop at the observation signpost on your right, after climbing into the foothills of Lower Galilee—the view of the Yizreel Valley spread out below is one of the loveliest in Israel.

Zippori (Sepphoris) National Park. 6.5km (4 miles) northwest of Nazareth. ☎ **06/568 372.** Admission NIS 13 ($3.90). Sat–Thurs 8am–5pm; Fri 8am–3pm. No public transportation.

Sepphoris dates from the era of the Maccabees in the 2nd century B.C. An enormous period of expansion and building, starting in the 1st century A.D., turned the city into "the ornament of the Galilee," according to Flavius Josephus. With its worldly, mixed population of Hellenistic pagans and Jews, it is interesting to speculate about the influence of Zippori on Jesus, who grew up in what was then the small village of Nazareth, a mere 4 miles away. As the traditional birthplace of Mary, and as a city requiring the services of many skilled carpenters and builders, cosmopolitan Zippori may have been a place often visited by Jesus; the landscapes and vistas around Zippori, unlike those of modern, urbanized Nazareth, may still resemble the countryside Jesus knew.

The Jewish community in Zippori grew rapidly after the Bar Kochba revolt of A.D. 135, when thousands of refugees from Judea migrated into the Galilee. By the late 2nd century, Zippori was the seat of the Sanhedrin and the home of many great rabbinical sages, including Yehuda Ha-Nassi, who codified the Mishnah. During the Talmudic era, the city contained numerous synagogues; in 1993, archeologists uncovered a mosaic synagogue floor from the 5th century A.D., decorated with an elaborate zodiac design and inscriptions in Hebrew, Aramaic, and Greek. Most impressive are the ruins of a 4,000-seat Roman amphitheater, and a late Roman-era Dionysian mosaic floor of a villa that includes the "Mona Lisa of the Galilee," a hauntingly beautiful young woman that is one of the greatest examples of ancient mosaic portraiture ever discovered. There is also an intricate mosaic depiction of Nile landscapes, including the famous Nilometer. In other parts of the site, you'll find a Crusader fortress and church.

Bet Shearim Burial Caves. 20 km (12 miles) from Haifa. ☎ **06/831-643.** Admission NIS 13 ($3.90). Apr–Sept, Sat–Thurs 8am–5pm, Fri until 3pm; Oct–Mar, Sat–Thurs 8am–4pm, Fri until 3pm. Bus: 301 bus from Haifa.

Somewhat reminiscent of the Sanhedrin Tombs in Jerusalem, the burial caves are located on the main road from Haifa that heads toward Afula (which is the principal town of the Jordan Valley).

In the 2nd century, Bet Shearim was the home of the Supreme Religious Council, the Sanhedrin, as well as headquarters of the famous Rabbi Yehuda Ha-Nassi, the compiler of the Mishnah. Many learned and famous Jews were laid to rest in the town's cemetery, a tranquil grove of cypress and olive trees. Over the centuries, however, the tombs were destroyed and the caves looted. Earth and rock covered the catacombs as if they had never existed. But finally they were unearthed, first in 1936, and then fully explored after the War of Independence.

Enter the burial chambers through an opening in the rock or a stone door. Inside are sarcophagi carved with rams' horns and lions' heads, and a menorah. So far, catacomb 20 is the most interesting, with its legible inscriptions, carvings, and interesting relics. Archeologists claim that only a fraction of the original effects remain, that robbers have looted the almost 200 sarcophagi.

The entire site here is particularly well tended, with a parking lot, visitors' facilities, and outdoor cafe. The bus from Haifa runs every half hour. Ask the driver to let you off at the archeological site.

MEGIDDO (ARMAGEDDON)

Megiddo (☎ 06/420-312) is about 35 kilometers (22 miles) southeast of Haifa. On the road, you pass Hazorea and Mishmar Ha-Emek, two old and large kibbutzim, before you come to Megiddo (Armageddon). This has always been the primary fortress overlooking the Emek, which due to its strategic position on the major route leading from Egypt to Syria and Mesopotamia, has always been coveted and attacked. Archeologists have uncovered the remains of cities of fully 20 distinct historical periods here on this tel, dating from 4000 to 400 B.C. It is mentioned frequently in biblical and other ancient texts.

In the Old Testament, you'll find it appears in a number of places, mostly in relation to war. In the New Testament, the book of Revelation names Armageddon (a corruption of the Hebrew *Har Megiddo*—Mount Megiddo) as the place where the last great battle will be fought when the forces of good triumph over the forces of evil.

Megiddo has been a place of battle continuing right down into our own century. General Allenby launched his attack against the Turks from the Megiddo Pass in 1917, and in 1948 the Israeli forces used the fortress site as a base of operations against the entrenched Arab armies. As you enter Megiddo today, now a national park, there is a **museum** with detailed information about the excavation, the artifacts found there, the biblical and historical references relating to its past, and a model of the site as it now exists. Many more artifacts discovered here have been removed, and may now be found in the Jerusalem Antiquities Museum and the Rockefeller Museum.

You can walk among the ruins, including a **palace** from the time of King Solomon, and **King Ahab's "Chariot City"** and **stables** with a capacity of almost 500 horses. There is also a large **grain silo** from the reign of Jeroboam Ben Joash, king of Israel in the 8th century B.C., and a building from the time of King David (1006–970 B.C.). On strata way down below the later buildings, you can see excavated ruins of temples 5,000 and 6,000 years old, constructed during the Chalcolithic period.

Perhaps most amazing of all is the **water tunnel** dating from the reign of King Ahab in the 9th century B.C. You enter it by walking 183 steps (120 feet) down into a large pit in the earth, whereupon you can walk along the tunnel extending 215 feet to a spring located outside the city, which was camouflaged by a wall covered with earth, designed to assure a constant supply of fresh water to the city even when it was under siege.

You can see remnants from Megiddo's imposing city walls, gates, and entranceways, some of which were built during the time of King Solomon. The observation points offer a spectacular view of the huge valley below.

To get to Megiddo by bus, take bus no. 302 from Haifa, which leaves Haifa's Central Bus Station several times in the morning and returns from Megiddo several times in the afternoon. The **Visitors Center** at Megiddo and the **archeological park** are open daily from 8am to 4pm, except for the water tunnel, which closes at 3:30pm. Admission is NIS 13 ($3.90) for adults and NIS 8 ($2.40) for children.

2 Tiberias

From Haifa the favorite road to Tiberias is the one from Nazareth, if only for that dip in the road and that sudden unfolding of the mountains when the Kinneret, the Sea of Galilee, is suddenly spread down below you. It happens best on a clear day, about 5 miles from Tiberias. Arab villages are sprawled on the hillsides, and sabra cacti, with their dangerous spiked arms and little orange fruits, line the road's edge. Then you round a bend and there it is—an incredibly beautiful azure lake set like a jewel in a pastoral valley.

Tiberias is the year-round tourist center for the Galilee and Golan regions, making an excellent base for explorations of these nearby areas as well as Lake Kinneret. Although the waterfront at Tiberias has large, modern hotels and the area is filled with beaches, Tiberias also offers a scattering of old, charming houses and the arabesque domes of Ottoman Turkish mineral water bathhouses as well as a scattering of archeological digs, and the tombs of the great rabbinical sages. Two blocks inland from the lakefront, Ha Galil Street, with its black native basalt buildings filled with shops, brings to mind an old-fashioned, small-town American main street. The pubs and restaurants along the Waterfront Promenade pound with disco and heavy metal on summer evenings. Little of the town's splendid history is immediately visible. The climate is mild in the fall, winter, and spring, but brutally hot when Tiberias is busiest in July and August. In the winter visitors are able to snow ski on Mount Hermon (1^1/$_2$ hours' drive, 9,000 feet above sea level) in the morning, and (on warm days) waterski on Lake Kinneret (700 feet below sea level) in the afternoon. In the evening, you can eat a $2 felafel at the pedestrian mall or a $25 supper at one of Israel's most acclaimed restaurants, and go dancing or sailing afterward. In less than an hour you can drive from Tiberias to the Golan Heights, the Lebanese border, Safed, Nazareth, the Yizreel Valley, or down through the Jordan Valley to the south, as well as to any place on the Sea of Galilee.

The ancient town of Tiberias, built in A.D. 18 by Herod Antipas (son of Herod the Great) in honor of the Roman emperor Tiberias, with its hot springs and mild climate, became one of the most elegant winter resorts in this part of the ancient world.

After the Temple of Jerusalem was destroyed, Tiberias became the great Jewish center. It was here that the Mishnah was completed in A.D. 200 at the direction of Rabbi Yehuda Ha-Nassi, "Judah the Prince." Here the Jerusalem Talmud was compiled in A.D. 400, and the vowel and punctuation grammar was introduced into the Hebrew language by the learned men of Tiberias. Mystics, academicians, and men believed to have magic powers have been drawn to Tiberias throughout its history.

Both the town and the towering scholarship declined after the 5th century A.D., due to the many wars fought here by the Persians, Arabs, Crusaders, and Turks. A medieval Arab historian named Al MuQadassi recorded that the residents of the town led a life of decadence—dancing, feasting, playing the flute, running around naked, and swatting flies.

Tiberias lies on one of the earth's major geological fault lines, the Syrian/African Rift, and in 1837 Tiberias was virtually destroyed by an earthquake. A few portions of the city's black basalt medieval walls survived that catastrophe, but almost nothing else of medieval or ancient Tiberias can be seen today outside of the archeological sites open to the public.

The entire area, geologically speaking, is known as the "Valley of the Rift." The fault line begins in southern Turkey and northern Syria, extends southward through

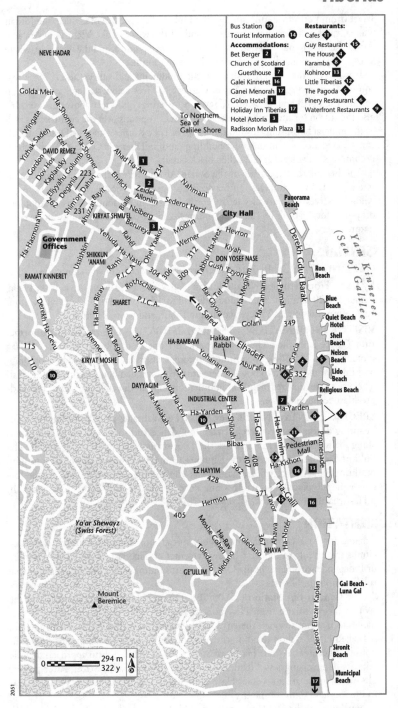

Tiberias

Bus Station ⑩
Tourist Information ⑭
Accommodations:
Bet Berger ②
Church of Scotland Guesthouse ⑦
Galei Kinneret ⑯
Ganei Menorah ⑰
Golon Hotel ①
Holiday Inn Tiberias ⑰
Hotel Astoria ③
Radisson Moriah Plaza ⑬

Restaurants:
Cafes ⑪
Guy Restaurant ⑮
The House ④
Karamba ⑧
Kohinoor ⑬
Little Tiberias ⑫
The Pagoda ⑤
Pinery Restaurant ⑥
Waterfront Restaurants ⑨

NEVE HADAR

Golda Meir

Wingate
Ha-Shomer
Yizhak Sadeh
DAVID REMEZ
Gordon
Dov Hos
Kaplansky
Eliyyahu Columb
262
Degania
231
Shim'on Dahan
223
Ezel
Mino
Ha-Shomer
Ahad Ha-Am
234
Nahmani
Ahuzzat Bayit
KIRYAT SHMU'EL
Ehrlich
Zeidel
Allonim
Bialik
Neiberg
Berureya
Rahel
Sederot Herzl
Modi'in
Werner
Yehuda Ha-Nassi
Ohel Yaakov
312
Ha-Hasmona'im
Ussishkin
Rashi
304 306
309
City Hall
Hevron
Kiyah
DON YOSEF NASE
Gush 'Ezyon
Bar Giora
Golani
To Northern Sea of Galilee Shore

Government Offices

RAMAT KINNERET

Ha-Rav Birav
Brenner
Aliza Begin
P.I.C.A.
Rothschild
P.I.C.A.
SHARET
to Safed
300
HA-RAMBAM
Hakkam Rabbi
Elhadeff
Yohanan Ben Zakai
Abul'afia
Dona Gracia
Tajar
352
338
335
Yehuda Ha-Levi
DAYYAGIM
Ha-Melakah
INDUSTRIAL CENTER
Ha-Yarden
411
Ha-Shiloah
Bibas
408
407
362
'EZ HAYYIM
428
Hermon
405
Moshe Cohen
Ha-Rav
Toledano
Toledano
Tavor
371
367
AHAVA
Ahawa
Ha-Galil
Ha-Bannim
Ha-Kishon
Ha-Galil
Ha-Note'
GE'ULLIM

Derekh Ha-Cevu
115
110
KIRYAT MOSHE

Ya'ar Shewayz
(Swiss Forest)

Mount Beremice

0   294 m
     322 y

Derekh Gdud Barak
Ha-Palmah
Ha-Zanhanim
349
Ron Beach
Blue Beach
Quiet Beach Hotel
Shell Beach
Nelson Beach
Lido Beach
Religious Beach
Promenade
Pedestrian Mall
Ha-Yarden

Panorama Beach

Yam Kinneret
(Sea of Galilee)

Sederot Eli'ezer Kaplan

Gai Beach - Luna Gai

Sironit Beach

Municipal Beach

2051

Israel (from north to south, through the Hula Valley, the Sea of Galilee, the Jordan Valley, the Dead Sea, down to Eilat), and all the way to Lake Victoria in Malawi, Africa. Relative to one another, the east side is moving north, and the west side (where you are if you're standing by the lake) is moving south.

It is this rift that has given shape to the mountains and valleys, and it is the reason why you can stand at the Sea of Galilee, 700 feet below sea level, and look up toward the north and see Mount Hermon towering 9,000 feet above sea level. It's also the reason for the earthquakes and volcanic eruptions over the centuries, as well as the mineral hot springs around the shores of Lake Kinneret and the Dead Sea. You can see evidence of it in the older buildings and in Tiberias's Old City Wall, which is composed of volcanic rock, called black basalt.

Another interesting feature of the Syrian/African Rift is that it forms an incredible highway for bird migration between Europe and Africa. Two of Israel's major wildlife reserves—Hula Valley in the north, Hai Bar in the south—serve as stopping-off points for the birds on their long journey, and are popular with birdwatchers and nature lovers.

ESSENTIALS

GETTING THERE   By Bus   There is direct service from all major cities.

By Car   From Jerusalem via the Jordan Valley, it's a $2^{1}/_{2}$-hour drive; from Haifa, 1 hour and 20 minutes. Four main roads lead to Tiberias and the Sea of Galilee: from Safed, from the Jordan Valley, via Mount Tabor, and from Nazareth.

VISITOR INFORMATION   The area code is 06. The **Tiberias Tourist Information Office** is in the archeological park in front of the Radisson Moriah Plaza Hotel (☎ 06/725-666), open Sunday through Thursday from 8:30am to 3:30pm, on Friday from 8:30am to noon. There are often extended hours in July and August. The office gives out free maps and information and can direct you to lists of bed-and-breakfast accommodations.

SPECIAL EVENTS   The **Ein Gev Music Festival** takes place at Kibbutz Ein Gev in spring during Passover week. Israeli folk dance and song festivals are organized along the waterfront in summer; ask the Tourist Information Office for details. The **Sukkot Swimathon** is across the Kinneret (3 miles). Everyone is welcome to join, but bring a medical certificate stating that you are in good health. Contact the Jordan Valley Regional Council, Mobile Post, or the Ha-Poel Sports Organization, 8 Ha-Arba'ah St., Tel Aviv (☎ 03/260-181).

ORIENTATION

Tiberias (or Teverya; population 45,000) spreads out along the Kinneret shore and climbs the hillside to the west. The very center of Tiberias is **Kikar Ha-Atzma'ut,** or Independence Square, in the Old City. Surrounding Ha-Atzma'ut Square is what is left of historic Tiberias.

The **Central Bus Station** (☎ 06/791-080 or 791-081), on Ha-Yarden Street, is two blocks inland from Ha-Atzma'ut Square. Tiberias's main street changes names as it winds through the city. As it descends from the mountains to the lake it's called Ha-Nitzahon Road; in the residential district of Kiryat Shmuel up on the hillside it becomes Yehuda Ha-Nassi Street, and as it descends to approach the Old City its name changes to Elhadeff (or El-Hadeff or Alhadif) Street. After passing Ha-Atzma'ut Square it becomes Ha-Banim Street, and this name serves it all the way to the southern limits of the city.

Northwest of the Old City, up on the hill that overlooks downtown, is the large residential district of **Kiryat Shmuel,** which has many moderately priced hotels.

South of the Old City about 1¹/₂ kilometers (1 mile) is the section called **Hammat,** or **Tiberias Hot Springs.** Ruins of an ancient synagogue and town, a national park, a museum, and the Tomb of Rabbi Meir Baal Haness are located near the springs.

North of the Old City, Gdud Barak Road skirts the water's edge and several beaches on its way to Magdala (where Mary Magdalene came from), Tabgha (where the miracle of the loaves and fishes took place), Mount of Beatitudes (where Jesus preached the Sermon on the Mount), and Capernaum (Kefar Nahum).

FAST FACTS: TIBERIAS

Banks   Bank Mizrachi at the corner of the Pedestrian Mall and Ha Banim Street has an outdoor ATM machine that is connected to Visa, Mastercard, and CIRRUS and NYCE systems.

Bookstores   Steimatzky's is located at 3 Ha Galil St., 06/791-288, open Sunday through Thursday from 8am to 1pm and 4:30 to 7pm; Friday 8am to 2pm; closed Tuesday afternoon and Saturday.

Emergencies   Magen David Adom (☎ 100 or 06/790-111), at the corner of Ha-Banim and Ha-Kishon streets across from the Jordan River Hotel, is open 24 hours.

Police   Telephone 100 or 06/792-444.

GETTING AROUND

You can rent a **bicycle** at Hostel Aviv (☎ 06/720-007), at the southern end of Ha-Galil Street, starting at NIS 25 ($7.50) for standard bikes, NIS 33 ($10) for mountain bikes for 24 hours, with hourly and half-day rates available. It is open daily. You can also rent bicycles at comparable rates at the Lake Castle Hostel and Nahum Hostel (see "Where to Stay," below). You can rent a car at any of five different major rent-a-car companies with offices in Tiberias, many of them found in the block of Elhadeff Street north of Ha-Yarden Street, where the tourist information office is located. In alphabetical order, here's a listing of their telephone numbers: **Avis** (☎ 06/722-766), **Eldan** (☎ 06/720-385), **Europcar** (☎ 206/724-191), **Hertz** (☎ 06/723-939 or 721-804), and **Reliable** (☎ 06/723-464).

WHAT TO SEE & DO

Tiberias is a small town, but it offers a great number of sights and activities. Special activities are organized for groups and include lectures and slide shows on the geographical, historical, and archeological aspects of the region. These shows are given, usually upon request, by the Ministry of Tourism regional director.

Ha Galil Street, the main shopping street, runs outside the old wall. Here you can see the ruins of the **rampart** that enclosed the city, as well as the **remains of mosques** at the wall's edge. Walk along the street running perpendicular to Ha Galil Street down toward the sea; on your left is a small war memorial, and on your right the Bank Leumi, with a sculptured frieze on its outer wall.

The **Waterfront Promenade** has a magnificent view across the lake. One hundred yards to the left are the remains of a **Crusader fort** (now the Castle Inn), jutting up in basalt stone from the water. Directly across the lake is Kibbutz Ein Gev and other settlements. To the left is Mount Hermon. It is from these foothills that the sources of the Jordan River are formed. The mountains in the distance, opposite you, are part of the Golan Heights (see section 4 at the end of this chapter for a description of a Golan trip).

The **Galilee Experience** (☎ 06/723-620) is a multimedia exhibition depicting the history and heritage of the region. The entrance fee is $6, and what you get is a 30-minute state-of-the-art multi-slide show that highlights Jesus and the rise of Christianity, and 20th-century Zionism. (Some visitors to the Galilee Experience are not prepared for the exhibit's attention to the area's most famous inhabitant, Jesus.) Strangely, no mention is made of Israel's large Arabic community, which makes up half the population of the Galilee. Located on the Waterfront Promenade, the Galilee Experience is open Saturday through Thursday, from 8am to 10pm, and Friday from 8am to 4pm.

Located off Yohanen Ben-Zakkai Street is **Rambam's (Maimonides's) Tomb.** Rabbi Moses Ben-Maimon, known as Maimonides, or Rambam, was the greatest Jewish theologian of the Middle Ages. A Sephardic Jew, born in Cordova, Spain, but who lived most of his life in Morocco and Egypt, he was an Aristotelian philosopher, a humanistic physician, and a leading scientist and astronomer. His principal work was *The Guide for the Perplexed.* The famous philosopher, who died in 1204, is now honored by a newly restored and beautified mausoleum and gardens. Nearby is the **tomb of Rabbi Yochanon Ben-Zakkai,** founder of the Yavne Academy in the years following the destruction of Jerusalem in A.D. 70, and on a hillside just west of town is the **memorial to Rabbi Akiva.** This great sage compiled the commentaries of the Mishnah before the Romans tortured him to death at Caesarea in A.D. 135 for his role in aiding the Bar Kokhba revolt.

The tomb of the 2nd-century A.D. **Rabbi Meir Baal Haness,** located on the hill above the hot springs, is considered one of Israel's holiest sites; pilgrims visit in hope of medical cures and help with personal problems. Rabbi Meir, called the "Miracle-Worker" and the "Light-Giver," is remembered in a white building that has two tombs. The Sephardic tomb, with the shallow dome, was built around 1873 and contains the actual grave, close to the interior western wall of the synagogue; the building with the steeper dome is the Ashkenazi synagogue, erected about 1900. Huge bonfires are lit at his tomb by the Orthodox 4 days before the Lag b'Omer holiday in the spring. All the tombs are open daily between 8am and 4pm (possibly later in summer); there is a 2pm closing on Fridays.

Down on Tiberias's lakeside promenade, squeezed in among the fish restaurants and inconspicuously set back from the shore, stands **Terra Sancta.** The church and monastery are run by the Franciscans. Another name for the church is Saint Peter's Parish Church. The first church was constructed here by the Crusaders around A.D. 1100. After the Muslims conquered Tiberias in 1187, the church was converted to a mosque; around the middle of the 17th century, the Franciscans began coming each year from Nazareth to celebrate the Feast of Saint Peter, paying the Muslims for the use of the site. Later on in the same century the Franciscans obtained the site for themselves.

The present church still contains part of the original Crusader church, but only a part of the apse (altar), which, on the outside, is shaped like the bow of a boat. The rest was built by the Franciscans in 1848, except for the facade, which dates from 1870. The church's facade is identical to that of the Franciscan church in Assisi where the order began, with red stone imported from Assisi. In the courtyard facing the church is a white stone monument built by the Polish in 1945, dedicated to Our Lady of Czestochowa, and a bronze statue of Saint Peter, a copy of the statue in Saint Peter's Basilica in Rome. You can visit the church daily from 8 to 11:45am and from 3 to 5:30pm. Masses are weekdays at 7am, and on Sunday and holidays at 8:30 and 11am. See "Where to Stay," below, for information about the adjoining hospice.

While you're here, you can also visit the historic **Greek Orthodox Church** located along the waterfront, a block or two south from Terra Sancta, or the **Church of Scotland,** which is a block or two to the north.

The **art gallery district** is located between Elhadeff and Dona Gracia streets, extending northward from Ha-Yarden Street. You'll find one gallery in the medieval castle on Dona Gracia Street, and many others nearby.

ORGANIZED TOURS

Every Sunday and Monday morning at 9am, and Thursday evening at 6pm, a free 2-hour walking tour of Old Tiberias leaves from the **Tourist Information Center** across from the Radisson Moriah Plaza Hotel; Saturday mornings at 10pm, a free walking tour leaves from the lobby of the **Radisson Moriah Plaza Hotel,** under the hotel's sponsorship. These walks are a real pleasure, led by interesting guides; reconfirm all times with the Tourist Information Office. With Tiberias as a starting point, you can take guided tours of both the Golan Heights and the Sea of Galilee. Check the sections on those areas, below, for details.

In addition to the large tour companies, you may want to hire **private tour guides** to take you by sherut or taxi. Inquire at your hotel or youth hostel, at the major hotels, or at the Tourist Information Office. These tours can be reasonably priced and a welcome change of pace from the bus tours.

CRUISES & FERRIES

The **Kinneret Sailing Company,** on the Waterfront Promenade (☎ 06/721-831), runs ferry service between Tiberias on the west side of the Kinneret and Kibbutz Ein Gev on the east side, departing daily from the Tiberias Waterfront Promenade and arriving at Ein Gev 45 minutes later. After spending an hour at Ein Gev, it departs for Tiberias. Schedules vary according to season, with three or four lake crossings in summer. The round-trip costs NIS 30 ($9). The **Lido Kinneret Sailing Company** (☎ 06/721-538 or 720-226) does ferry runs between Lido Beach in the northern part of town, and Kibbutz Ginnosar, toward the northeastern corner of the lake, for NIS 18 ($5.40); bicycles are free and there is no reduction if you only travel one way. Departures often depend on a minimum number of passengers.

Many people take this opportunity of crossing the lake by ferry to try out the excellent restaurant at Kibbutz Ein Gev, or just to stroll around the kibbutz. You can also plan to take the ferry one way, and take bus no. 18 or 21 back to Tiberias. Buses go between Tiberias and Ein Gev about every 2 hours.

The Lido Kinneret Sailing Company also operates a daily ferry between Tiberias and Capernaum; call for details on this, as well as on waterskiing and sailboard rental.

Both of the above sailing companies offer evening cruises, some of which have dancing on board; call for information or ask at the Tourist Information Office.

SPORTS & OUTDOOR ACTIVITIES

Water sports are offered on and around the lake, including waterskiing, water parachuting, sailboarding, giant water slides, kayak trips, and more. Call the Tourist Information Office for information.

BEACHES   The **Blue Beach** charges $5 for the use of its lake facilities and a beach-chair rental.

The **Quiet Beach**'s $3.50 fee includes all the swimming facilities, and is open from 8am to 6 or 7pm.

The **Ganei Hammat Swimming Beach,** opposite the Ganei Hammat Hotel, near the Tiberias Hot Springs, is open daily from 9am to 5pm. It offers deck chairs, showers, and a snack kiosk. Admission is $3.

The **Gai Beach** near the Galei Kinneret Hotel has a fine waterfront and all the requisite facilities. There's also a nearby Wimpy and the Valley Beach Restaurant. There's a charge for entrance and use of facilities May through September; the rest of the year it's free.

Sironit Beach is open from 8am to 5pm, April through October. There's also a **municipal beach** ($3 fee) south of Sironit Beach, open from 9am to 5pm.

HORSEBACK RIDING   In the countryside around the lake, you can join groups for trail riding in the Galilee; call **Vered Ha-Galil** (☎ 06/935-785; see below in section 3) or **Kefar Hittim Horse and Pony Ranch** (☎ 06/795-921 or 06/795-922).

WHERE TO STAY

Tiberias has everything from youth hostels to five-star hotels, with a few religious guesthouses as well. You should note that most hotels here have kosher kitchens and several are Orthodox.

DOWNTOWN TIBERIAS

Expensive

✪ **Galei Kinneret Hotel.** 1 Kaplan St., Tiberias. ☎ **06/792-331.** Fax 06/790-260. 120 rms (all with bath). A/C MINIBAR TEL TV. $150–$235 single; $165–$255 double. Rates include breakfast. 15% service charge. AE, DC, MC, V.

Located a long block south of the landmark Radisson Moriah Plaza (but not on the Waterfront Promenade), the Galei Kinneret, hidden from the main road by gardens, is the oldest of the quality hotels in town (it was a favorite of Ben-Gurion). The original building from the early 1940s is a rather severe white International-Style design to which a number of new wings have been added. The general atmosphere is relaxing; unlike other downtown hotels, the Galei Kinneret has shaded lawns and a beach directly on the lake. Service is careful; public areas and guest rooms are comfortable but not spectacular. The hotel's prestigious in-house restaurant, Au Bord du Lac (open Saturday through Thursday, dinner only), is the only French restaurant in Tiberias.

Dining/Entertainment: Three restaurants, lounge/bar, often live entertaiment.

Facilities: Heated swimming pool, fitness center, floodlit tennis court, sauna, hot tub, water-sports rentals.

✪ **Radisson Moriah Plaza Tiberias.** Ha-Banim Street, Tiberias. ☎ **06-792-233;** reservations in the U.S. 800/221-0203 or 212/541-5009. Fax 06/792-320. 272 rms (all with bath). A/C TEL TV. $175–$225 single; $190–$250 double. Rates include breakfast. 15% service charge. Discounts on Radisson Moriah 7- and 9-day packages. AE, DC, MC, V.

A modern 14-story highrise with a pretty and convenient location at the southern end of the Waterfront Promenade, the Radisson Moriah Plaza's public areas and lightly elegant guest rooms are the most stylish in town. There is ongoing room redecoration; ask for an upgraded room, and one with a view toward the lake. The pool area is pleasantly sheltered from the Promenade; dining facilities are above average, with theme buffets at the main in-house restaurant; service is attentive; and in season and on weekends there is live entertainment.

Dining/Entertainment: Three restaurants, lobby bar, cafes.

Facilities: Outdoor swimming pool, health club, sauna, Jacuzzi, massage, hairdresser, video games, shops.

✪ **Church of Scotland Center Guest House.** P.O. Box 104, Tiberias 14100. ☎ **06/723-769.** Fax 06/790-145. All rms with bath. A/C. $38 single; $65–$70 double (both include breakfast). No credit cards.

A hidden enclave centrally located behind the Meyouhas Youth Hostel, this well-run guesthouse is surrounded by beautiful walled gardens and has stone terraces and balconies with sweeping vistas of the lake. Built 100 years ago as a Scottish missionary hospital, the ensemble of buildings is constructed of the black basalt stone native to the Galilee. All rooms have recently been renovated; they are simple but comfortable, and double-glazed windows keep out the noise from Tiberias's summer disco scene; a gate through the garden wall leads to the Guest House's private beach.

Yoseph Meyouhas Youth Hostel. P.O. Box 81, Tiberias. ☎ **06/721-775** or 06/790-350. Fax 06/720-372. 240 beds. A/C. Dorm bed $18.50; $17 for IYHA members; $23 per person double. Rates include breakfast.

Housed in a large 19th-century building constructed of local black basalt stone, and located close to the Waterfront Promenade and the town's supermarket, this top recommendation is clean, well run, and noted for its good food. It's a popular place, so reserve in advance or check in early during peak seasons. All rooms are air-conditioned. The building is closed up tight from 9am to 3:30pm in winter, and from 10am to 1pm in summer (that means everybody out, office closed), but you can check in anytime after 4pm. Curfew is at midnight or 1am.

Dinner here is a good deal—for $8 you get soup, salad, cooked vegetables, meat, rice or potatoes, bread and butter, and beverages.

The hostel is on the corner of Ha-Yarden and Ha-Banim streets, one block from the lake.

SOUTH OF DOWNTOWN TIBERIAS
Expensive
Holiday Inn Tiberias. Route 90, Tiberias. ☎ **06/792-890.** Fax 06/724-443. 246 rms (all with bath). A/C TEL TV. $136–$200 single; $177–$245 double. Rates include breakfast. 15% service charge. AE, DC, MC, V.

Located 2 miles south of downtown Tiberias, next to the Tiberias Hot Springs, the Holiday Inn is a 20-year-old highrise surrounded by lawns and gardens that was heavily renovated in 1993. Rooms are spacious; minibars can be requested. There is no pool, but the hotel has access to a lakefront beach. Sports facilities include two tennis courts, and rental of kayak and water equipment at the beach.

Inexpensive
Ganei Menora/Days Inn Hotel. P.O. Box 99, Tiberias. ☎ **06/792-770.** Fax 06/790-101. 71 rms (all with bath or shower). A/C TEL. $46–$67 single; $69–$78 double. Rates 25% higher during Jewish holidays. MC, V.

Located 2 miles south of the center, on the main lakefront road not far past the hot springs, Ganei Menora compensates for its distance from town. It is one of the few moderately priced hotels on the beachfront, and it offers a quiet, country club–like setting, with trees and flowers, and a variety of guest rooms. There are a main building (with kosher dining room), bungalows, and motel-type rooms. Some of the rooms in the main building have balconies and wonderful views of the lake; all come with radio and other amenities. The Ganei Menora often has many retired guests.

KIRYAT SHMUEL
Kiryat Shmuel is a residential and hotel district on the hill overlooking Tiberias and the Sea of Galilee. Unless otherwise mentioned, all of the following hotels have the equivalent of three-star facilities, private bathroom, air-conditioning, and heat. All these hotels have kosher dining rooms. Most have good views.

You may want to take a taxi to get up to Kiryat Shmuel if you're arriving in Tiberias by bus—it's a half kilometer (one-quarter mile) away from downtown, and that half kilometer is all uphill.

Moderate

Golan Hotel. 14 Ahad Ha-Am St. (P.O. Box 555), Tiberias 14222. ☎ **06/791-901** or 791-904. Fax 06/721-905. 99 rms (all with bath). A/C TEL TV. $58–$92 single; $81–$115 double. AE, DC, MC, V.

This fancy four-star establishment offers magnificent views and a swimming pool. It's quite a nice place, with an outdoor cafeteria and garden, and an intimate bar with dancing. In winter or at slow times, the lower rates can be obtained.

Hotel Astoria. 13 Ohel Yaakov St., Tiberias. ☎ **06/722-351** or 06/722-352. Fax 06/725-108. 65 rms (all with bath). A/C TEL TV. $63–$90 single; $80–$107 double. MC, V.

This hotel is another fine choice. All rooms have three-star-equivalent amenities and some rooms have balconies. There are facilities for children, a video TV room, and, in season, a swimming pool.

Inexpensive

Bet Berger. 25 Neiberg St., Tiberias. ☎ **06/720-850.** Fax 06/791-514. 45 rms (15 with bath, 30 with shower). A/C TEL. $30–$45 single; $40–$55 double. MC, V.

This constantly expanding, well-run place has an excellent reputation in the budget category. Rooms are simple but clean, and have refrigerators, which helps cut down on your restaurant expenses; some of the rooms have terraces. There is a video television room on the premises.

WHERE TO DINE

In addition to the choices in Tiberias, many travelers who have use of a car will enjoy dining at some of the delightful restaurants in the countryside and on the shore around Kinneret; see "Country Dining Around the Sea of Galilee" below.

ON THE WATERFRONT

The specialty in Tiberias is Saint Peter's fish, so called because it is the very fish that swam in the Sea of Galilee when Jesus called Peter away from his nets to become a "fisher of men." It's a white fish that is indigenous to the Sea of Galilee and its taste resembles that of bass.

The best place to search out a good portion of Saint Peter's fish, or even shish kebab for that matter, is along the Waterfront Promenade in the Old City. You can get there by walking down Ha-Yarden Street until you reach the lake. Or just look for the minaret of the Great Mosque and pass by the mosque, heading for the shore. This is Old Tiberias, a municipal redevelopment project in which ancient crumbling buildings have been restored and new amenities, such as the popular waterfront promenade, have been added.

Three of the attractive waterfront restaurants have the same management, the same menu, the same prices, and the same delicious food. These are the **Nof Kinneret** (☎ 06/720-310), the **Galei Gil** (☎ 06/720-699), and the **Roast on Fire** (☎ 06/720-310). The indoor decor is different in each restaurant, although outdoor dining on the boardwalk is virtually the same, so stroll along and see which you like the best; but if the weather is good, you'll likely want to eat by the water. Plan to spend about NIS 45 ($13.60) for a large (more than a pound) serving of Saint Peter's fish, french fries, salad, and pita bread; if you add wine, coffee, and dessert besides, it could come to about NIS 66 ($20). All three restaurants offer the fish fried, charcoal grilled, or in a special sauce. Hours are daily from 8:30am to midnight; in summer, they may be open 24 hours.

Moderate

✪ **Karamba Restaurant/Bar.** Waterfront Promenade. ☎ **06/791-546.** Reservations necessary on weekends and in summer. Appetizers and light meals NIS 12–27 ($3.60–$8); main courses NIS 27–55 ($8–$16.60). AE, MC, V. Daily 11am–after midnight. SEAFOOD/ VEGETARIAN.

This more unusual, attractive place along the waterfront has a tropical decor and a tree-shaded patio. It offers hearty dishes such as vegetable pie topped with cheese, inventive hot and cold soups, light meals, fruit dishes, and salads that are meals in themselves—the Karamba special house salad has assorted vegetables, cheese, nuts, raisins, and yogurt dressing. Karamba's fish, served with a choice of sauces, is probably the best and most inventive on the waterfront. Most of Karamba's tables are on its patio, but you can reserve one of the restaurant's few tables right on the water's edge if you call ahead. There is also a tropical bar and after-hours spot, with nice music, open in summer from 11am to 2am, in winter from 5pm to 2am.

✪ **Kohinoor.** In the Radisson Moriah Plaza Hotel. ☎ **06/724-939.** Reservations recommended. Appetizers NIS 10–28 ($3–$8.30); main courses NIS 22–55 ($6.60–$16.50); fixed-price lunch NIS 42 ($12.70); fixed-price dinner NIS 65 ($19.70); 15% service charge. AE, DC, MC, V. Sun–Thurs noon–3pm and 6:30pm–midnight; Fri noon–3pm; Sat after Shabbat– midnight. KOSHER INDIAN.

This beautiful, spacious restaurant is probably the most elegant place to dine in Tiberias. This kosher branch of Tel Aviv's excellent Tandoori Restaurant turns out absolute miracles, wonderful by any standards; it is also an unusual chance for everyone, including kosher visitors, to sample very light, elegant renditions of classic Indian dishes. You might want to start your meal with zafrani lassi, a refreshing, chilled parve yogurt and fruit drink. The boneless tandoori chicken dishes are a favorite main course, succulent and flavored by the traditional tandoor oven. I was amazed by the fine nawabi korma, a boneless chicken dish prepared in lightly creamed and seasoned saffron sauce based on soya instead of milk in order to conform to kashrut regulations. In the evenings, Indian musicians and a classical dancer perform. A 10% service charge, very well deserved, is added to the bill.

NEAR THE MOSQUE

This historic edifice is now incongruously surrounded by a modern commercial center. Head for the mosque; walk around the many shops, restaurants, cafes, and pubs. Almost every place has outdoor tables.

For espresso, cappuccino, and excellent baked goods and pastries, try the **Contidoria Yatsek and Kapulsky,** which are right next to each other. At either place, a pastry and cappuccino at a sidewalk table will cost about $6. Both also sell baked goods to go. They're open daily from 8am to 10pm.

Pizza Pinate. Mosque Mall. ☎ **06/792-204.** Pizza NIS 20–30 ($6–$9). No credit cards. Daily 8am–midnight; 24 hours in July–Aug. PIZZA.

The pizza at this stand is tasty, good-sized, and well priced: the most expensive pizza is the full combination for approximately $9.

DOWNTOWN

A bit away from the crush of the Waterfront Promenade, around Ha-Galil and Ha-Banim streets, you'll find less tourist-oriented restaurants, although you must remember that tourism is Tiberias's major industry. Ha-Yarden Street next to Shimon Park is "Felafel Row." The lineup starts right outside Ha-Atzma'ut Square and stretches up toward the bus station. Quality and fixings can vary, but the cost should be about NIS 6 ($1.80). Many say the felafel here is the best in Israel.

✪ **Guy Restaurant.** Ha-Galil. ☎ **06/721-973.** Appetizers NIS 7–15 ($2.10–$4.50); main courses NIS 20–40 ($6–$12). No credit cards. Sun–Thurs noon–midnight; Fri noon–1pm; Sat after Shabbat. Closed during Shabbat. SEPHARDIC HOMESTYLE.

This friendly kosher, family-style Middle Eastern restaurant is one block south of Ha-Yarden at the southern end of Ha-Galil Street, in a small white building. Delicious house specialties include eggplant, artichokes, tomatoes, or other vegetables stuffed with rice or rice with meat, and pastry stuffed with nuts. Main meat courses, with french fries and salad, pita bread, and pickles, are also served. Prices are very reasonable.

✪ **Little Tiberias Pub Restaurant.** Ha-Kishon Street. ☎ **06/792-806.** Reservations useful. Appetizers NIS 8–20 ($2.40–$6); main courses NIS 25–60 ($7.50–$18). AE, DC, MC, V. Daily noon–1am. CONTINENTAL.

To my experience, this is the best of the downtown restaurants: relaxed, unpretentious, and serving wonderful food. Everthing comes out of the kitchen a bit more special than at other restaurants—even that Israeli standby, chicken schnitzel, is a pleasant surprise here. There are hefty salads that are meals in themselves, and good spaghetti and lasagne at the lower end of the main-course menu. In the upper price range, I strongly recommend the steaks and fresh fish; shrimp and calamari are also available. You can have a very good meal here, away from the hustle of the Waterfront Promenade, for somewhere in the $10–$13 range.

NORTH OF DOWNTOWN

Tiberias has three Asian restaurants that are about a 10-minute walk from downtown. They have great atmosphere, nice decor, and delicious food.

Moderate

✪ **The House.** Gdud Barak St. ☎ **06/725-513.** Reservations recommended. Appetizers NIS 11–33 ($3.30–$10); main courses NIS 24–58 ($7.20–$17.30). MC, V. Lunch Mon–Fri 1–3pm; dinner 6pm–midnight; Sat 1pm–midnight. Closed Sun. CHINESE/THAI.

The House is the most famous restaurant in Tiberias, serving a wide array of exotic, expertly prepared, Chinese–Thai dishes. My favorite is a duck-and-eggplant dish in spicy honey sauce. While it's not cheap, this may be one of the best restaurants for the price anywhere in Israel. The lovely decor includes a waterfall and fountain as well as a fireplace in the bar/lounge. The House is sometimes open only on Friday and Saturday. When it is closed, visit its kosher affiliate, the Pagoda, across the road. To find them from downtown, go north on Gdud Barak, heading out of town toward Safed; after a few minutes' walk, The House is on the left.

✪ **The Pagoda.** Gdud Barak Street. ☎ **06/725-513.** Reservations required. Appetizers NIS 11–33 ($3.30–$10); main courses NIS 24–58 ($7.20–$17.30). MC, V. Lunch Sun–Thurs 12:30–3pm; dinner Sun–Thurs 6pm–midnight. KOSHER CHINESE/THAI.

The Pagoda, with a kosher menu but under the ownership and supervision of the excellent nonkosher House (see above) across the road, maintains the reputation of its affiliate, and even enlarges upon it. The building itself is an airy, newly built lakeside pavilion designed by Chinese architects to take advantage of the site. The pagoda-style roof, with its traditional Chinese beaming and joinery, is one of Israel's most unusual contemporary structures. The entire menu, prepared by chefs trained in Bangkok's finest hotel, is filled with unexpected pleasures. The lamb spare ribs are meaty, succulent, and presented in a mild but fascinating sauce. The noodle soup overflows with chunks of tender stir-fried chicken, doughy homemade noodles, and crisp slices of fresh cucumber; the spicy Thai chicken coconut soup is an exotic light meal in itself. For light, healthy food, the Thai-style steamed dishes, including fresh fish, are excellent choices.

COUNTRY DINING AROUND THE SEA OF GALILEE

Tiberias can become very hectic in the evening, especially during the summer. If you have a car, a drive out into the countryside for dinner can be very pleasant.

✪ A Good Spot in the Middle. Tiberias-Degania Road. ☎ **06/752-074.** Appetizers NIS 7–24 ($2–$7.20); main courses NIS 25–50 ($7.50–$15); beer NIS 7–10 ($2–$3). MC, V. Summer daily 11am–4am; winter daily 11am–1am. GRILL/PUB.

Away from the rush of downtown Tiberias restaurants, this is a roadhouse restaurant/bar with a broad picnic table–covered porch overlooking the road and the lake across the street. Its always friendly spirit shifts in style according to the hour—it's a good choice for a hefty or light meal as you drive around the lake, but after dinner, A Good Spot in the Middle spends its summer evenings slowly building into a night-long party as regulars and visitors filter in from the countryside. The restaurant is proud of its fried cheese, salads, and oven-smoked grilled pork steaks, pork filet, and filet mignon. The traditional stuffed vegetables, especially the eggplant, were the best I've had in this part of the country. Owners Mati and Pamela Abutbol offer a 10% discount to readers of this book. The restaurant is located 4 miles south of Tiberias on the right side of the road.

✪ Kibbutz Ein Gev Fish Restaurant. Kibbutz Ein Gev. ☎ **06/758-035.** Reservations recommended. Appetizers NIS 8–15 ($2.40–$4.50); main courses NIS 39–45 ($11.70–$13.50). MC, V. Daily 10am–4pm; July–Aug daily 10am–10pm. SAINT PETER'S FISH.

For great freshly caught fish served indoors, or on covered and open terraces overlooking the lake, this is the place to come, either by excursion boat from Tiberias, or as you meander around the Sea of Galilee by car, bus, or bicycle. The fame of the fish here has spread; the restaurant is enormous, and constantly expanding. It is often filled with tour groups; nevertheless, this is a pleasant place for a meal. You can order your fish in two sizes: medium and slightly larger—it will come with chips and salad on the side. You get a half-price discount admission ($2.50) to the kibbutz beach with your meal.

✪ Vered Ha-Galil Restaurant. Vered Ha-Galil Guest Farm, Korazim Road. ☎ **06/935-785.** Reservations recommended Fri–Sat. Appetizers NIS 10–15 ($3–$4.50); main courses NIS 25–50 ($7.50–$15); light meals NIS 10–30 ($3–$9); desserts NIS 14 ($4.20). MC, V. Daily 8am–9:30pm for meals; 8am–11pm for dessert. Follow Korazim Road a few miles north of the Sea of Galilee. AMERICAN.

This famous country lodge offers hearty American-style food in a lovely garden setting in the hills above the Sea of Galilee. You can choose hamburgers, chicken in a basket with all the fixings, smoked trout fresh from the Dan River, as well as baked or grilled fish or a selection of less expensive light meals. Many just stop by for coffee and homemade pie (apple, pecan, or boysenberry), or to talk over a bottle of wine. The scene is mellow and the clientele is largely into nature.

TIBERIAS AFTER DARK

There are summer shows and performances at the **Samakh Amphitheater** on the southern tip of the Sea of Galilee by local and foreign entertainers.

Folklore events are often scheduled at the hotels, where everyone is welcome to attend. For full details, contact the tourist information office at the end of the Ha-Banim Street Pedestrian Mall.

There are also many late-night pubs, cafes, bars, and restaurants. Good places for a quiet drink, with live music, include the **Radisson Moriah Plaza** and the **Jordan River** hotels, at the southern end of the Old City.

There are plenty of opportunities to go dancing, as well. The most unusual, I'm sure, is the summer **disco dancing** on the boat operated by the Kinneret Sailing Company on the Sea of Galilee; call 06/721-831, or stop by its office at the Waterfront Promenade, for information. An evening **disco cruise** also leaves from the Lido Kinneret Beach at varying times, depending on demand. Be there before 8pm.

For a lively pub and dancing crowd, but still right down beside the water, there's the **Petra Pub** (☎ 06/721-175) at the Lake Castle Hostel, near the southern end of the lakeside promenade. There's a NIS 20 ($6) entrance fee, less for Castle Youth Hostel guests. You'll find it open every night in summer from 9pm to 2am; on Friday and Saturday only during the winter.

Many, in fact most, of the hotels (and even the youth hostels) around town have nice bars and pubs where you can relax in the evening and enjoy a drink and conversation with fellow travelers.

EASY EXCURSIONS

Hot Springs of Tiberias. ☎ **06/791-967.** Admission to all the pools NIS 35 ($10.60) for adults; bathing suit and bathrobe rental NIS 7 ($2.10) extra. For pools in the old building and for the physiotherapy treatments in the new building: Sun–Fri 7am–1pm. Thermal pools at the Young Tiberias Hot Springs (the large indoor/outdoor swimming pool): Sun–Tues, Thurs, and Sat 8am–11pm; Wed 8am–8pm; Fri 8am–4pm. Egged bus: 2 or 5. Free transportation is available at some hotels.

Located a mile south of Tiberias, the thermal baths have been famous for their curative powers for more than 3,000 years, and have continued to have a following to this day. Pharmacies in Israel keep well-stocked supplies of mineral salts from these Tiberias springs.

All the springs at the seafront are operated by Tiberias Hot Springs Company Ltd., which offers baths and treatments in both old and new buildings. There's an inexpensive restaurant on the premises.

The hot waters contain high amounts of sulfuric, muriatic, and calcium salts, and over the centuries they've reportedly cured such ailments as rheumatism, arthritis, and gynecological disorders. They are probably the earliest-known thermal baths in the world, noted by Josephus, Pliny, church historians, and many Arabic writers. Some biblical commentators have surmised that Jesus cured the sick here, and others place their origin at the time of Noah, when the insides of the earth were supposedly disrupted by the flood. In Israel, there's a legend that Solomon entered into a conspiracy with demons to heal his kingdom's ailing people at this site, tricking them into perpetually stoking the fires in the earth below to heat up the water.

Several medical treatments are available, including physiotherapy, therapeutic massage, inhalation, mudbaths, and so on.

To gain a better understanding of the waters, check out the **Lehman Museum** next to the springs. While visiting the springs, you can plan to spend some time exploring the ancient ruins of Hammat. See "Hammat Gader" in the next section.

Hammat Tiberias National Park. ☎ **06/725-287.** Admission NIS 7 ($2.10). Daily 8am–4pm. Egged bus: 2 or 5.

The **ancient ruins of Hammat,** a spa and city 2 miles south of Tiberias, existed well before the founding of Tiberias in the 1st century A.D. Hammat and Tiberias existed side by side for hundreds of years as "twin cities." Hammat is now a national park.

This ancient town contains some of Israel's most magnificent mosaic work: on the floor of the synagogue (4th century A.D.) are colorful mosaic depictions of the zodiac circle, four women representing the seasons of the year, the sun god Helios riding on a chariot through the heavens, plus various Jewish symbols, including the Ark of the Covenant. The famous naive zodiac floor of the Bet Alpha synagogue (which served a Byzantine-era farming village in the Jordan Valley) may have drawn on this sophisticated mosaic for inspiration.

Entrance to the ruins is through the **Ernest Lehman Museum,** which inventories information on regional history and the curative powers of the hot springs. Beware that the open water flowing through the ruins comes directly from the hot springs and will scald you should you decide to do something foolish, like test it with your toe! Up the hill from the baths is the **Tomb of Rabbi Meir Baal Haness,** a disciple of Rabbi Akiva, and one of the great sages who helped to compile the Mishnah in the 2nd century A.D.

2 The Sea of Galilee

The Arabic and Aramaic poets called it the Bride, the Handmaiden of the Hills, and the Silver Woman. The ancient Hebrews called it the Lute in honor of the soothing harplike sounds of its waves, and because it roughly resembles the shape of a lute. Today, Israelis still call the Sea of Galilee "lute"—in Hebrew "Kinnor," or Kinneret, as it is popularly known. According to one lexicographer, an ancient sage has written: "God created the seven seas, but the Kinneret is His pride and joy."

Some 700 feet below sea level, the Sea of Galilee is 13 miles long, from the place where the Jordan flows in at the north to where it empties out in the south.

It was here that Jesus preached to the crowds and fed them by multiplying the bread and fishes; it is also where he restored the sick and maimed. Today, parts of the sea are filled with speedboats and waterskiers; other parts are as tranquil and mysterious as in ancient times.

Kinneret's waters are a vast reservoir of sardine, mullet, catfish, and the unusual combfish. They are the same fish once caught by the disciples, and they are caught in the same manner today, though some of the kibbutzim have developed careful methods of farming fish.

ESSENTIALS

GETTING THERE From Tiberias, buses no. 18 and 21 go south around the lake to Ein Gev, leaving every 2 hours or so. For Capernaum and other sites to the north, take bus no. 841, leaving Tiberias every 40 minutes. In summer, there is boat service from Lido Beach to Capernaum.

If you'd like to cruise up to the Christian sites on the northwest shore of the lake, **Lido Kinneret Sailing Company** (☎ 06/721-538) operates an 8:30am ferry to Capernaum, returning at 11:30am and 12:30pm. Their fare is NIS 23 ($6.90) one way or round-trip. Bicycles are free. The **Kinneret Sailing Company** (☎ 06/ 721-831) leaves for Ein Gev on the eastern shore of the lake at 10:30am, with returns at 12:15 and 1:15pm.

TOURING THE AREA

To tour the Sea of Galilee, we'll head north, starting a circle that will bring us back to Tiberias before heading into the Upper Galilee region. As of this writing there is no regular bus route that completely circles the lake, so you'll have to depend on tour bus, rental car, bicycle, or boat.

Galilee

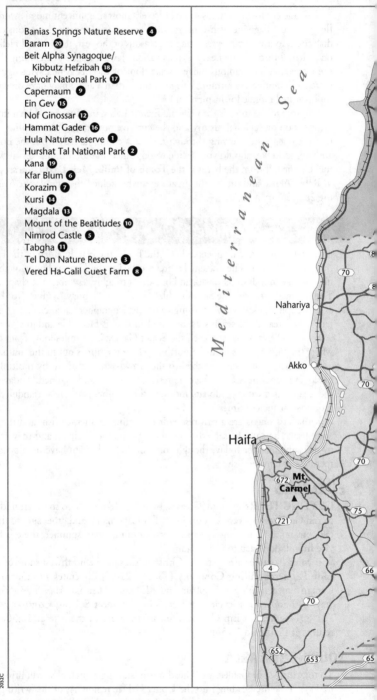

Banias Springs Nature Reserve ❹
Baram ⓴
Beit Alpha Synagoque/
   Kibbutz Hefzibah ⓲
Belvoir National Park ⓱
Capernaum ❾
Ein Gev ⓯
Nof Ginossar ⓬
Hammat Gader ⓰
Hula Nature Reserve ❶
Hurshat Tal National Park ❷
Kana ⓳
Kfar Blum ❻
Korazim ❼
Kursi ⓮
Magdala ⓭
Mount of the Beatitudes ❿
Nimrod Castle ❺
Tabgha ⓫
Tel Dan Nature Reserve ❸
Vered Ha-Galil Guest Farm ❽

Mediterranean Sea

Nahariya

Akko

Haifa

Mt.
Carmel
672

2052C

340

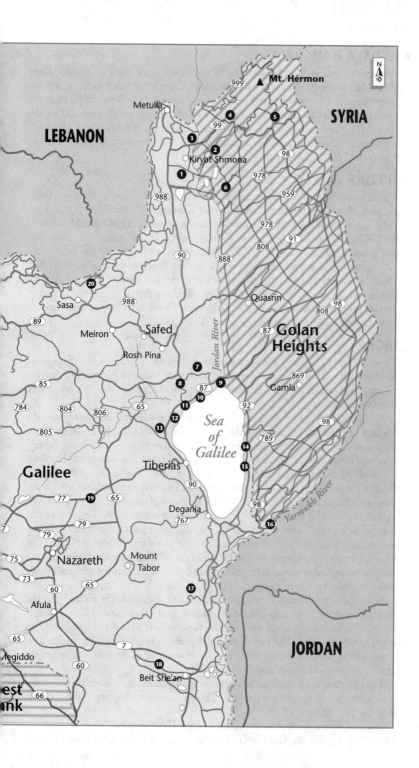

MAGDALA & MIGDAL

Two miles north of Tiberias along the lakeside road, you'll come to the old village of Magdala, the birthplace of Mary Magdalene. There's not much to see, except for lovely scenery. The town was right down by the water's edge. On the hill just to the south of old Magdala, along the far (west) side of the highway, you can still see the sarcophagi (stone coffins) carved out of the rocks, in the place that was Magdala's cemetery. The modern town of Migdal, founded in this century, is about 1 mile to the north of the site of ancient Magdala.

GINOSSAR VALLEY

A little farther on, you'll find yourself in a lush valley with many banana trees. These are part of the agriculture of **Kibbutz Nof Ginossar** (☎ 06/792-161), and the valley is the Ginossar Valley. The excellent new multimedia **Yigal Alon Museum of the Galilee** (☎ 06/722-905), more a learning experience than a museum, offers only one genuine antiquity, a Galilee fishing boat, from approximately the 1st century A.D., preserved in the muddy sediment of the lake floor and revealed in the 1980s when, because of drought, the lake receded to record low levels. The wooden frame of the boat is preserved in a climate-controlled boathouse structure. It's open Sunday through Thursday from 8am to 5pm, on Friday from 8am to 1pm, and on Saturday from 9am to 5pm; admission is NIS 16.50 ($5).

TABGHA

To reach Tabgha, where Jesus miraculously multiplied the loaves and fish, proceed northward along the shoreline from Migdal, passing Minya, a 7th-century Arabian palace that is one of the most ancient and holy Muslim prayer sites. It's open daily from 8am to 4pm.

At Tabgha, you'll find the beautifully restored **Benedictine monastery** and the **Church of the Multiplication of the Loaves and Fishes** (☎ 06/721-061). When the ancient church ruins, hidden for 1,300 years, were excavated, the mosaic basilica floor of a Byzantine-era church that once stood on this site was discovered. The floor is one of the most beautiful and best-preserved in Israel. The section of the floor in front of the ancient altar is starkly unadorned and interesting mainly for what it depicts: two fish and a humble basket filled with loaves of bread. The main section of mosaic is a colorful tapestry of all the birds that once thrived in this area: swans, cranes, ducks, wild geese, and storks. The mosaic artist has captured the liveliness, humor, and grace of these creatures with a style rarely seen in this art form. The Nilometer, used to measure the flood levels of the Nile and famous throughout the ancient world, is also represented, leading some to speculate that the unusual mosaic designer might have been Egyptian.

Be sure to read the history of this church posted just inside the entrance, in the church's courtyard. The early Judeo-Christians of nearby Capernaum (Kefar Nahum) venerated a large rock, upon which Jesus is said to have placed the bread and fish when he fed the 5,000. The rock, a natural **dolmen,** is believed by historians to have been a sacred place since prehistoric times, and was used as the altar in a Byzantine church erected over the spot in about A.D. 350.

The church is open daily from 8:30am to 5pm; modest dress is required. Admission is free, but donations are accepted. There's also a good bookstore and souvenir shop on the premises.

Just east of the Multiplication Church is the **Heptapegon** ("Seven Springs" in Greek), also called the Church of the Primacy of Saint Peter, or Mensa Christi

(☎ 06/724-767). To reach it, you must leave the Multiplication Church, return to the highway, turn right, and climb the hill to a separate entrance. This Greek Orthodox church is open daily from 8am to 5pm; modest dress is required, and admission is free.

It was here on the shores of Galilee that Jesus is believed to have appeared to his disciples after his crucifixion and resurrection. Peter and the others were in a boat on the lake, fishing, but with no luck. When Jesus appeared, he told them to cast their nets again. They did, and couldn't haul in the nets because they were so full of fish. As the disciples sat with their master having dinner, Jesus is said to have conferred the leadership of the movement on Peter, as first among the disciples. The theory of Peter's primacy, and the tradition of that primacy's being passed from one generation of disciples to the next, is the basis for the legitimacy of the Roman pontiff as leader of Christendom.

The black basalt church rests on the foundations of earlier churches. Within is a flat rock called **Mensa Christi,** "Christ's Table," where Jesus dined that evening with his disciples. Outside the church, you can still see the stone steps said to be the place where Jesus stood when he appeared, calling out to the disciples; on the beach are seven large stones, which may once have supported a little fishing wharf. If it's not too hot, you can easily walk to nearby Capernaum (3km, or about 2 miles) and even to the Mount of Beatitudes.

MOUNT OF THE BEATITUDES

Just beyond Tabgha, on a high hill, is the famous Mount of the Beatitudes, now the site of an Italian convent. Here Jesus preached the Sermon on the Mount. There are many good views of the Sea of Galilee and its surroundings, but the vista from here is among the most magnificent. One odd fact about this church is the inscription on the sanctuary, which informs you that the entire project was built by Mussolini in 1937. The church is open daily from 8:30am to noon and 2:30 to 5pm. Admission is free. Take bus no. 459, 541, or 963 from Tiberias. Ask the driver to let you off at the closest stop, which is 1 kilometer (half a mile) from the church.

CAPERNAUM (KEFAR NAHUM)

This site marks the prosperous lakeside town where Jesus preached, and his disciples, Peter and Andrew, made their homes. Today you'll find a modern Franciscan monastery, which was built on the abandoned site in 1894, as well as ancient excavations spanning six centuries. Among the most impressive are the ruins of a 3rd- or 4th-century synagogue built on the site of an even earlier synagogue. Nearby are several houses of the period and a 5th-century octagonal church built over the ruins of the traditional site of Saint Peter's house. Byzantine architects frequently built domed octagonal structures over places of special veneration (the octagonal Dome of the Rock in Jerusalem, built by early Muslim rulers in A.D. 691, but designed by Byzantine architects, is an example of this type of structure). Other finds include an ancient olive press, and a 2nd-century marble milestone on the Via Maris (Coastal Road), the Roman route that stretched from Egypt to Lebanon (an inland extension to the Via Maris passed through this district).

Capernaum was the home of perhaps four of Jesus's other original followers; it was the place where Jesus began to gather his disciples around him, saying, "Follow me, and I will make you fishers of men."

Capernaum's splendid synagogue was built of imported white limestone rather than native black basalt. The ruins include tall columns, marble steps, shattered statuary, a doorway facing south to Jerusalem, and many ancient symbols: carved seven-branched menorahs, stars of David, palm branches, and rams' horns. It's not the actual synagogue in which Jesus taught, since it dates from around the 3rd or 4th century A.D., but it may stand on the same site. It is interesting to speculate on what the proximity of Saint Peter's house to the synagogue might tell us about the position of his family in the community. The excavations of basalt stone in the garden lead toward the sea, where you can still glimpse the remains of a small-boat basin with steps leading to the water. Admission is NIS 3 (90¢); the site is open daily from 8:30am to 4:15pm.

KORAZIM

Four kilometers north of the lake, on a rise of land, are the ruins of Korazim (Chorazin), a flourishing Jewish town in Roman times. According to the New Testament, Korazim was one of the towns chastised by Jesus. A large 2nd- or 3rd-century synagogue of black basalt has been excavated, as well as streets, houses, and ritual baths attached to the synagogue, which was apparently destroyed either by earthquake or during civil unrest in the 4th century. This is a hauntingly evocative site, with sweeping views of the lake. The national park office here (☎ 06/934-982) is open from 5am to 4pm; admission to the site is NIS 9 ($2.70).

At the Korazim–Almagor crossroad between Tiberias and Rosh Pinna is the beautiful guest farm and dude ranch, Vered Ha-Galil (see "Where to Stay Around the Sea of Galilee," below).

LUNA GAL WATER AMUSEMENT PARK

Coming around the northern end of the lake, you reach a junction from which Highway 87 heads into the Golan Heights to its new capital, the town of Qasrin (see "The Golan Heights" in the next section). Where the Jordan River enters the lake, we come to Luna Gal (☎ 06/731-750), on the eastern shore, one of the largest water-amusement parks in Israel. It offers a variety of activities including waterskiing, pedalboats, kayak tours of the Jordan River, sailboarding, water parachuting, and more. There is a substantial entrance fee of NIS 33 ($10), but especially for kids it's worth it. Luna Gal is open Saturday through Thursday from 9:30am to midnight, Friday 9:30am to 5pm, April to October. From Tiberias, you can take bus no. 22.

KURSI

Kursi is on the eastern shore; according to the Gospels, it is the "country of the Gergesenes" (or Gadarenes), where Jesus cast the demons out of two men and into a herd of swine, which then plunged into the lake and drowned.

For many years, speculation existed about the location of Kursi (also called Gergasa) and its church, but after the Six-Day War, a bulldozer clearing the way for a new road happened to uncover the ruins of a Byzantine church complex, complete with a monastery, dating from the 5th to 7th centuries. Most remarkable among the discoveries was the underground crypt where more than 30 skeletons were found, all of middle-aged men, except for one child. The national park at Kursi is open daily from 8am to 4pm; admission is NIS 6 ($1.80).

EIN GEV

About two-thirds of the way south along the lake's eastern shore brings you to **Kibbutz Ein Gev,** one of the loveliest places in Israel. Nestled between the hills of Golan and the lakefront, Ein Gev was founded in 1937 by German, Austrian, and Czechoslovakian refugees. (It was Jerusalem mayor Teddy Kollek's kibbutz.) These days Ein

Gev has a 5,000-seat auditorium, which has presented some of the world's greatest musicians at its annual music festival. On the hillsides are tiers of vineyards, and elsewhere on the grounds are a banana plantation and date groves. Fishing is another big industry here. The kibbutz offers accommodations at Ein Gev Holiday Village (see "Where to Stay Around the Sea of Galilee," below).

Not far from the auditorium, in a garden, is a bronze statue by the Israeli sculptress, Hanna Orloff, depicting a woman holding a child aloft, in memory of a young mother-to-be from the kibbutz who was killed in the 1948 battle for Ein Gev. This settlement bore the brunt of heavy attacks in the 1948 war, and its position at the foot of the Golan Heights, below heavy Syrian military emplacements, made it a perennial target. From 1949 to 1967, Ein Gev kibbutz members depended on an endless maze of slit trenches throughout the grounds, as well as concrete, underground shelters.

It's easy to get to Ein Gev from Tiberias, by bus no. 22, or ferry. Farther south along the lake is a campsite, at **Kibbutz Ha-On** (☎ 06/751-144); continue south along the shoreline and you'll come to **Ma'agan,** with its **Holiday Village.** Ma'agan is very near the junction for the road to the hot-spring resort of Hammat Gader. (Ask at the tourism information office in Tiberias for information on other campsites around the lake and in the vicinity.)

HAMMAT GADER

The **hot springs of Hammat Gader** (☎ 06/751-039), east of the southern tip of the Sea of Galilee, are a favorite Israeli spa and vacation spot. Nestled in the valley of the Yarmuk River, this dramatic site has been occupied for almost 4,500 years.

The springs can be reached by bus no. 24 from Tiberias. Bus schedules vary according to season, so check with the bus station for a morning departure and afternoon returns. Hammat Gader is 21 kilometers ($12^{1}/_{2}$ miles) southeast of the city. If you're driving, it's $8^{1}/_{2}$ kilometers (about 5 miles) east of the junction with the highway that rings the lake. As you wind down the steep road into the Yarmuk Valley, you'll pass several sentry and guard posts. The steep hillside on the other side of the valley is Jordan; you are also close to the Syrian border.

The Roman city here was first constructed in the 3rd century A.D., restored and beautified in the 7th century, and destroyed by an earthquake around 900. The ruins of the Roman spa city are extensive and significant, and several important parts (the baths, the theater) have been excavated and beautifully restored. The still-apparent elegance of the Oval Hall, the Hall of Fountains, and the Hall of Pillars in the Spring Area point to the magnificence of this rustic resort in ancient times. Don't miss the wonderful lions of the mosaic synagogue floor (5th century A.D.). The

---

The Grand Old Man of the Lake

Ein Gev's patriarch fisherman, **Mendl Nun,** an expert on Lake Kinneret's nature, archeology, and fishing traditions, has recently founded the **Anchor Museum,** a museum of the lake's nautical history, at Ein Gev. Those interested in the ethereal Sea of Galilee, both in modern and ancient times, should pick up his book, *The Sea of Galilee and Its Fisherman in New Testament Times.* Mr. Nun's writing is filled with real feeling for the place he has made his home for over half a century. This and his other books about the Sea of Galilee are available at Kibbutz Ein Gev's gift shop beside the Ein Gev Restaurant in Kibbutz Ein Gev.

ruins are set up as a **self-guiding tour** (ask the park office about guided tours of the park).

The spa was known as El-Hamma to the Arabs and Turks, and the site is dominated by the minaret of a mosque that has fallen into disuse and been disfigured by graffiti.

There are swimming pools, hot sulfur springs, and baths for medical therapy and beauty treatments; there is an alligator farm in a jungle setting with elevated walkways. For the kids, the park has trampolines and water slides. You will also find showers, changing rooms, a bar, and a restaurant. Admission costs NIS 30 ($9). Bring your own towel. Sit in the far end of the warm-water pool and feel the mineral water crash down onto your back from the waterfall.

You'll find Hammat Gader open daily from 8am to 4pm, except for Friday and holiday eves, when it closes at 1pm. From November through February it closes at 3:30pm (still 1pm on Friday). These are the hours for the closing of the ticket offices; you may remain on the site 1 hour beyond these times. Saturday can be very crowded.

From Hammat Gader, as you're climbing back up out of the valley toward the lake, look at the park from above and you'll see still more ponds that are used for raising shrimp. On the lakeshore road once again, turn and head west. You'll pass the entrance to Ma'agan on your right, then the junction with the highway heading south to Bet Shean and the Jordan Valley. Just after the junction, the road turns northward, heading for Tiberias, right by Kibbutz Degania.

DEGANIA

On the lakeshore road once again, turn and head west. You'll pass the entrance to Ma'agan on your right, then the junction with the highway heading south to Bet Shean and the Jordan Valley. Just after the junction, the road turns northward right by **Kibbutz Degania.** Degania is the country's very first kibbutz, founded in 1909 by Russian pioneers. Without any real experience in farming, this handful of self-made peasants left city jobs to fight malarial swamps and Arab bands. Much of the philosophical basis of kibbutz life was first formulated in this Jordan Valley settlement by its leader, A. D. Gordon. Gordon believed that a return to the soil and the honesty of manual work were the necessary ingredients for creating a new spirit in people. Although never a member of the kibbutz, he farmed until his death at age 74. On Degania's grounds a natural history museum, **Bet Gordon** (☎ 06/750-040), contains a library and exhibition of the area's archeology, flora, and fauna.

Degania grew so quickly that its citizens soon branched out to other settlements. The father of Moshe Dayan, the famous commander with the eyepatch of the Sinai Campaign, left Degania to help establish Nahalal, Israel's largest moshav settlement. Eventually, too, some of the younger Degania settlers established their own kibbutz right next door, and called it simply Degania B.

If you get confused as to which is which, Degania A has the older, yellow stucco buildings and a tank at the front gate—a reminder of the battle the settlers waged against Syrian tanks in 1948 (the members fought them off with Molotov cocktails). Degania A and B have about 450 settlers each, and both settlements are prosperous.

HOF ZEMACH WATER AMUSEMENT PARK

Near Kibbutz Degania, there's another water amusement park called Hof Zemach (☎ 06/752-440). The carnival atmosphere includes a beach, sunbathing areas, grassy picnic grounds, a buffet, and water-sports equipment rentals. Like Luna Gal, Hof

Zemach is open only in season; check with the tourism office in Tiberias for current information.

RIVER JORDAN BAPTISMAL SPOT

Kibbutz Kinneret, just west of Degania, has established a spot where Christian pilgrims can immerse themselves in the waters of Jordan in safety and tranquillity. The Baptismal Spot, called **Yardenit** (☎ 06/759-486), is 200 yards west of the lakeshore highway (follow the signs). The river seems to flow peacefully, but its currents can be dangerous, so no swimming is allowed. The area set aside for baptisms is sheltered and there are guide railings leading into the water. Snack and souvenir stands provide refreshment and sustenance (no charge for the baptismal dip). A special lift has been installed to enable those with disabilities to enter the water with a minimum amount of difficulty.

WHERE TO STAY AROUND THE SEA OF GALILEE

Ein Gev Resort Village. ☎ **06/758-027.** 144 bungalows and doubles (all with shower). A/C. $45–$73 single, $66–$100 double (without breakfast; higher on weekends and holidays); $53 single, $64 double plus 50% during high season on Kibbutz 7-Day Package (including breakfast). MC, V. The Village is 1 mile south of Ein Gev Kibbutz.

Set in a date palm grove and a eucalyptus grove beside the lake, the Holiday Village offers basic rooms in five-person bungalows (higher priced) and caravans (lower priced, but with the same floor plan and facilities) that include a bedroom-kitchenette with dining nook and a small bunk-bed room off the main room. There are also standard double rooms in motel-style buildings overlooking the lake but a bit away from the beach. Some plans here include breakfast or half board, and there is a minimarket for groceries. Ein Gev Kibbutz, down the road, has an excellent lakeside restaurant (see section 2 under "Country Dining Around the Sea of Galilee," above) with free transportation and discounts for Holiday Village guests. The Ein Gev Resort Village beach is the loveliest on the lake, but there are few special activities for children.

Call or write for reservations; at busy times you may have to pay for four beds minimum in the bungalows or caravans. If so, plan to come with family or friends. Discounts under Kibbutz Hotel Chain 7-Day Plan.

Kibbutz Lavi Guesthouse. Kibbutz Lavi, Lower Galilee Post 15267. ☎ **06/799-450.** Fax 06/799-399. 124 rms (all with bath or shower). A/C TEL TV. $56–$95 single; $70–$130 double. Rates include breakfast. MC, V.

This beautifully gardened religious kibbutz offers a heated indoor swimming pool and comfortable accommodations plus lectures on kibbutz life. There is a synagogue on the kibbutz. Buses travel to Lavi direct from Tiberias, and the ride takes only 15 minutes. There is a minimum weekend rate of one full board plus one half board, and holy-day prices are considerably higher. Discounts under Kibbutz Hotel Chain 7-Day Plan.

Kibbutz Ma'agan Holiday Village. Kibbutz Ma'agan, Sea of Galilee. ☎ **06/753-753.** Fax 06/753-707. 132 rooms and suites (all with bath or shower). A/C TEL TV. $70–$80 single; $80–$120 double. Breakfast $6 per person extra. Kibbutz 7-Day Package (including breakfast), $64 double; 25% more for high season. MC, V.

Located on the southeastern shore of the Sea of Galilee, with a beautiful guarded beach and vistas, Ma'agan sports freshly built minisuite units, arranged in subtle tiers so that each suite has a water view. There is a living room/kitchenette with a couch that converts into a bed, and a separate bedroom in most units; many guests do their own cooking. The holiday village is geared toward families, with an outdoor swimming pool and a children's playground. Discounts available on Kibbutz 7-Day Package.

Kibbutz Nof Ginossar Guesthouse. Kibbutz Ginossar 14980. ☎ **06/792-L6L** or 792-L64. Fax 06/792-170. 170 rms (all with bath or shower). A/C TEL TV. $80–$102 single; $100–$130 double. Rates include breakfast. 15% increase for Jewish holidays. MC,V.

This beautiful but rather expensive kibbutz guesthouse is on the kibbutz nearest to Tiberias—only a 10-minute ride from downtown. There is regular bus service, but it's a better choice for someone with a rented car. The kibbutz is next to the lake and offers very comfortable rooms; it has its own museum, tennis courts, gardens, and beach, with kayaks, sailboards, sailboats, and fishing poles for rent. The second-floor dining room (kosher) has a view of the Sea of Galilee; readers' feedback on the food has been mixed. Rooms include central heating, among other amenities. The guesthouse conducts a regular series of kibbutz tours and lectures with slides of kibbutz life. The **Yigal Alon Museum of the Galilee** (Admission $3.60), an interesting media exhibit, is on the grounds of the kibbutz (see above, under "Gnossar Valley"). Discounts are available on the Kibbutz Hotel Chain 7-Day Plan.

Poria Taiber Youth Hostel. P.O. Box 232, Tiberias. ☎ **06/750-050.** Fax 06/751-621. 140 beds. A/C. $17 IYHA member; $18.50 nonmember; $23 per person double. Rates include breakfast. No credit cards.

Located at Poria, in the hills overlooking the Sea of Galilee 4 kilometers (2 1/2 miles) to the south of Tiberias, this rustic hostel can arrange for family rooms, kitchen facilities, clean sheets, and hot water, and is open all day long. Because it is so high above the lake, it's a bit cooler on summer nights than Tiberias itself, which is below sea level. This is a good inexpensive base for travelers with cars; there is no public bus, and it's often reserved for large groups who come with their own bus. Call for current information.

۞ Vered Ha-Galil Guest Farm, Restaurant, and Horseback Riding Facility. ☎ **06/935-785.** Fax 06/934-964. 20 units: luxury suites, superior studios, moderate cabins, bunkhouse. Single $35–$100; double $47–$135. Rates include breakfast and service charge. Midweek rates lower; Jewish holidays supplement. AE, MC, V. Directions: 3 1/2km (2 1/4 miles) past the turnoff to the Mount of Beatitudes; the ranch is at the Korazim–Almagor crossroad.

This very personal place is the creation of Yehuda Avni, originally from Chicago (who immigrated to Israel in the late 1940s) and his wife, Yonah (fantastic cook), who created a paradisical enclave with gardens, a pool, buildings that fit in with nature where there had once only been acres of impassable thistles. Now their children and grandchildren, as well as a carefully chosen young staff, contribute to the attentive but informal spirit of Vered Ha-Galil. The Guest Farm and its facilities are ideal for those who want to ride and to intimately explore the Galilee countryside. It is also a beautiful retreat and a fine base for travelers who want to explore the region by car.

There are four kinds of accommodations: two simple bunkhouse rooms, each sharing bathroom facilities and available for from two to six people; rustic, 1960s northern California–style one-room cabins, each with private bath, double beds, and shaded porches overlooking the countryside; new studios with roomy living areas, kitchenettes, private bathrooms, and terraces; and country apartments with cathedral ceilings, 1 1/2 baths, a spacious living room, separate bedroom, and private garden. A family or group of four or five can easily share these accommodations. Backpackers are welcome to sleep on the lawn or in the hayshed for free, so long as they pick up their litter.

Yehuda offers trail rides by the hour, day, or week, into the hills or down toward the Sea of Galilee. Other planned tours last several days, exploring places such as

Nazareth, and combining Arab meals with camping or hotel overnights to Gilboa, Mount Tabor, around the Sea of Galilee, and into the Golan Heights.

Horseback rides cost $20 an hour, $30 for 2 hours, $45 for half a day on the trail, $80 for an entire day with lunch, and $100 for an overnight "Bonanza." There are also 2- to 5-day all-inclusive trips for $140 a day. All rides are accompanied by guides. A riding tour to Amman in Jordan is also being planned.

In addition to the stables, Vered Ha-Galil has an outdoor swimming pool, rooms for changing and showers, an outdoor grill, picnic tables, a restaurant (see below), and a bar and grill.

BED & BREAKFAST CHOICES IN THE GALILEE

There is a good range of bed-and-breakfast establishments in the region, including accommodations in private homes and in moshav and kibbutz facilities that are somewhat less expensive than those in the official Kibbutz Hotel and Guest House Chain. Most tourist information offices in major cities (including those in Tiberias, Haifa, and Safed) now are equipped with computers that let you access the current lists of bed-and-breakfast facilities available throughout the Galilee. You can telephone for reservations ahead of time, or play things by ear when you arrive.

The **Kibbutz Country Lodging Bed and Breakfast** network rents simple but pleasant rooms in various kibbutzim throughout the Galilee. Rooms are a bit less fancy than in the Kibbutz Guest House Chain, but they're adequate, sometimes in beautiful locations, and give you a closer look at kibbutz life than the more insulated guesthouses. At some kibbutzim, the rooms are in special guest buildings; in others, you get an empty kibbutz member's room or apartment that has been especially set up for visitors. Rates are $40–$44 for a double most of the year. In North America, you can book a 1-week or more intinerary of Kibbutz Bed and Breakfasts as well as a package with a rental car through the **Israel Hotel Reservations Center** (☎ 201/ 816-0830; 800/552-0141 in the U.S.; 800/526-5343 in Canada). There is a $35 booking fee. Ask for a brochure of the bed-and-breakfasts so that you can plan which kibbutzim you'd prefer. You can book kibbutz bed-and-breakfast accommodations in Israel through the **Kibbutz Hotels Chain Office,** 90 Ben Yehuda St., Tel Aviv (☎ 03/524-6161; fax 03/527-8088).

Among some of the recommended private families offering guest facilities are: **Mary and Sasson Soffer,** M. P. Maale HaGalil 25167, Israel (☎ 04/966-060), offering charming rooms and fabulous breakfasts in a contemporary Israeli dream house with wonderful vistas. The house has three guest rooms, one with private shower, and is located at Tal El north of Highway 85 between Akko and Karmiel; about $30–$35 per person with facilities and discount for children. **Buki and Rochelle Cohen,** M. P. Maale HaGalil 25129, Israel (☎ 04/802-471), have four pleasant rooms in Har Chalutz, a community founded by Americans from the Reform Jewish Movement. Located in the Tefen Mountain Range of north central Galilee, the rates are about $30 per person. At the completely vegetarian **Moshav Amirim, Bella Shuldebrand** (☎ 06/989-788) and **Yael Goldman** (☎ 06/989-232) offer rooms in their beautiful chalet-style homes with lovely vistas; write to either c/o Amirim, M. P. Karmiel, 20115, Israel. All of the above families can prepare superb meals for you with advance notice. Bed-and-breakfast arrangements in private homes are not generally recommended for families traveling with children.

Another interesting choice is **Bed-and-Breakfast in a Galilee Arab Village,** which you can arrange by calling **Ruthi Avidor** (☎ 04/901-555; fax 04/800-554). Rates are in the $25 to $30 per person range. This program offers a unique opportunity to meet members of the Galilee's large Arabic community, and to experience the traditional hospitality of an Israeli Arab home. Accommodations are either in a family house or in a nearby apartment, to which the hosts will bring breakfast. You can specify whether you would like accommodations in which you have more personal contact with your host family. Rooms are comfortable, clean, and usually filled with little personal touches that the women of the house have planned for their guests' comfort. Most guests in this program so far have been Jewish Israelis, but the host families look forward to having foreign guests, and hope that the visits will help create greater understanding. Roads in these communities are hard to follow; be certain your hosts make a map, and note the way to the main road from your lodgings.

At Horashim, on Mount Meron in the northern Galilee, **Ami Efroni** (☎ 04/802-555) has built four small, isolated country cabins, each with a kitchen, living room, bedroom, and sleeping loft. You're on your own here, supplying your own food, and operating the wood-burning stove, but the heavily wooded countryside has a wild beauty, and the price of $50 to $60 for a couple is very reasonable. Children over 10 are an additional $15 per night. There is a grocery shop in the Arab village of Beit Jann, several kilometers away, and a restaurant in the nearby town of Peki'in, once so isolated that its Jewish community was able to remain in continuous residence from ancient times until the early 20th century, undisturbed by wars, expulsions, and invading armies. Safed, Rosh Pina, and Tiberias are also in comparatively easy driving distance. For reservations, write to **Ami Efroni,** Horashim 24954, Israel.

Readers' comments on especially good or bad experiences at bed-and-breakfast establishments are welcome.

4 Safed (Zefat)

36km (24 miles) NW of Tiberias, 74km (46 miles) E of Haifa

From Tiberias and the Sea of Galilee, our next destination is the ancient and mystical city of Safed (Zefat, Zfat, Tsfat, Tzfat, etc.), an hour due north of Tiberias and less than 2 hours due east of Nahariya. Once Israel's major mountain resort, Safed is now more religiously oriented.

Skirting the Yermak mountain range (3,000 feet), you finally climb up into Safed (pronounced with one syllable—"Tsfaht"—in Hebrew), which at 2,790 feet, is Israel's highest town. This quiet city is built on three slopes and looks down onto a beautiful panorama of villages and tiered hillsides. Safed's name comes from a Hebrew root word, *tsafeh,* meaning to scan, or look—in other words, a lookout.

Safed's history began in A.D. 66, during the time of the Second Temple, when Flavius Josephus started building atop the Citadel mountaintop. In 1140, the Crusaders built a fortress on this peak, the ruins of which can be seen today.

During the 16th century the Ottoman Turks chose Safed for the provincial capital, and it became the primary government, economic, and spiritual center for the entire Galilee region. It was during this period that the Sephardic Jews from Spain came here. Having escaped the horrors of Spain under the Inquisition, these Jewish intellectuals launched into a complex and mystical interpretation of the Hebrew scriptures called Cabala (Cabbalah, Kabala, Kabbalah). The town became a great center of learning, with a score of synagogues and religious schools. The first printing press in the East was introduced during this period of intellectual mysticism, and in 1578 the first Hebrew book—a commentary on the scroll of Esther—was printed. During this Golden Age of Safed, Askenazi Jews were also attracted to Safed, and the entire community and its rabbinical scholars became renowned and revered throughout the Jewish world. The Jewish community numbered about 10,000, but by the 18th century, Safed was in serious decline.

In 1837 the entire town was leveled by a powerful earthquake after which both the Jewish and Muslim communities of Safed struggled on in increasing poverty. The wave of anti-Jewish rioting that swept British Mandate Palestine in 1929 was particularly severe in Safed, where the Jewish population was mainly elderly and religious. During the 1948 war, control of the strategic heights of Safed was crucial to control of the Galilee. Although outnumbered, Israeli forces held the town, and the large Arab population of Safed fled. Since then, the center of Safed (population 18,000) has had three parts to its personality—a resort town, an artists' colony in the abandoned Arab neighborhoods of the city, and the long-established religious community. As Israelis have become more international in their vacation habits, Safed's tourism industry has withered; and the once vibrant Artists' Quarter is now relatively quiet. All the better for those who decide to explore the town. Although large apartment complexes have been built on the periphery, and Jerusalem Street is an architectural hodge-podge, the back streets of Safed, winding, cobbled, and resounding with the chant of prayers, are still medieval. July and August are the most popular months because of Safed's cool climate. In the winter it can be windy and as much as 20 degrees cooler than Tiberias. Year-round, especially at night, Safed is usually the coldest town in the country.

ESSENTIALS

GETTING THERE   By Bus   Buses run between Safed and Tiberias, Tel Aviv, and Jerusalem.

By Car   Follow the main but winding roads from Tiberias, Haifa, and Akko.

GETTING AROUND   Most city buses, such as no. 1, 1/3, 1/4, or 3, go from the center to the hotels on Mount Canaan.

VISITOR INFORMATION   The **Safed Tourist Information Office** is in the Municipality Building, 50 Jerusalem St. (☎ 06/920-961), open Sunday through Thursday from 8am to 1pm and 4 to 6pm, and until noon on Friday.

ORIENTATION

CITY LAYOUT   Safed is built on hilltops. The main part of town is compactly clustered atop one hill, while South Safed occupies another hilltop to the south, and Canaan perches on a hillside across the valley to the east. Although you may find occasion to go to Mount Canaan (a few hotels are there), you'll spend most of your time in the center of Safed. Jerusalem Street (Rehov Yerushalayim) is a circular street that girdles the hill, passing through the commercial street, the Artists' Quarter, and residential sections, before beginning its circle again. Walking the circle should take only 15 minutes, and it is a good way to see most of Safed.

The **Egged Bus Station** (☎ 06/921-122) is at the lowest point on Jerusalem Street's circle through town, where it intersects with Derekh Jabotinsky. Walk up to Jerusalem Street from the bus station and go right, and after 400 yards you will come to the Tourist Information Office. But if you come up from the bus station and go left, you'll be headed toward the commercial district. In any case, once you find Jerusalem Street you can't get lost in Safed.

WHAT TO SEE & DO

While there is much to see in Safed, a traveler unfamiliar with the city's crooked streets and unimpressive doorways may pass some of the city's best sites. I'll do my best to help you uncover the secrets of Safed, starting with its fascinating synagogues. But first, consider getting some local help by taking a guided tour. For $7 you can arrange for an informative 2-hour walking tour of Old Safed with **Aviva Minoff,** an excellent licensed tour guide. Tours generally leave from the Rimon

Inn, Monday through Thursday at 10am and Friday at 10:30am. For information, call 06/920-901. Note that modest dress is required when touring the religious quarter of Safed.

THE SYNAGOGUES

During Safed's Golden Age in the 16th century, the synagogues here were devoted to the study of the Cabala, a system in which every single symbol in holy writ has deep significance: each letter, number, and even accent in the holy books actually says a lot more than it appears to say. In addition, the names of God have mystical powers in themselves, and can be used to ward off evil and to perform miracles.

Cabalists believed that the system originated with Abraham and was handed down by word of mouth from ancient times. Historians of religion dispute this, however, saying that Cabalism arose only in the 600s; it continued to be a thriving belief until the 1700s. Cabalism was, in a way, a reaction to the heavy formalism of rabbinical Judaism. It allowed for more latitude in the interpretation of holy writ and gained great popularity in the 1100s. The most significant Cabalist text is the *Zohar*, a mystical commentary on the Pentateuch (the first five books of the Hebrew scriptures). For an interesting fictionalized interpretation of what Safed was like at the height of its glory as a Jewish religious center, I recommend the chapter, "The Saintly Men of Safed," in James Michener's novel, *The Source.*

It's not easy to describe exactly where these Cabalist synagogues are—the religious quarter has few street names, and is really a collection of alleyways and courtyards. Ask for "kiryat batei knesset," the synagogue section.

Among the most famous old synagogues here is the one named for the scholarly 16th-century **Rabbi Joseph Caro,** author of the *Shulchan Aruckh (The Set Table),* which is the standard guide for Jewish prayer and daily life today. Nearby is another named in honor of **Rabbi Moses Alsheikh.** Just a few steps away is the synagogue of **Rabbi Isaac Abuhav,** a sage of the 1400s; it contains an ancient Torah scroll said to have been written by the rabbi himself. Nearby is another, dedicated to **Rabbi Yosef Bena'a,** also called Ha-Lavan (The White).

The synagogue quarter has two houses of worship dedicated to the greatest of the Cabalist scholars, **Rabbi Isaac Luria** (known as Ha'Ari, or "the Lion," an acronym for Adoneinu Rabbeinu Itzak, "Our Master Teacher Isaac"). Although Luria lived, studied, and taught in Safed for only 2 ^{1}/$_2$ years at the end of his life (he died here at the age of 38), his work changed the face of Judaism forever. The fortresslike Sephardic synagogue, graced by fine carved-wood doors, is built where the rabbi studied and prayed, at the edge of the cemetery. The **Ashkenazi Ha'Ari Synagogue** is closer to Jerusalem Street, at a spot where the rabbi is said to have come to welcome the Sabbath with his followers. Rabbi Luria was the author of the *Kabbalat Shabbat, (Receiving the Sabbath),* the liturgical arrangement of prayers recited at the start of the Sabbath in normative Judaism.

The original building, constructed after Rabbi Luria's death, was destroyed by an earthquake in 1852 and later restored. Its ark, done in the 1800s, is especially notable. If you come with an official guide, you will get a better sense of how every nook and cranny has a story and sometimes a supernatural occurrence connected with it.

At the end of the synagogue area is a **cemetery** containing the sky-blue tombs of many famous religious leaders; they're the ones with rocks placed upon them as symbols of love, respect, and remembrance. There is also a military cemetery containing the resting places of soldiers who fell in all the wars, and nearby is a third cemetery containing the graves of Israelis who served with the underground Stern Gang and Irgun forces. Buried here are those executed by the British in Acre prison, including Dov Gruner, who is one of the best known of the outlawed fighters.

Another holy site is the **Cave of Shem and Eber** (or Ever), the son and grandson of Noah. This cave, located just off Ha-Palmach Street near where the Ha-Palmach stone overpass crosses Jerusalem Street, is said to be the place where Shem and Eber lived, studied, and were buried. Legend also has it that Jacob spent 14 years here studying before he went to the house of Laban, and that here he immersed himself in a ritual purifying bath before he wrestled with the angel. Today there is a synagogue opposite the cave; if the cave is locked, you can ask the caretaker of the synagogue to open it for you.

20TH-CENTURY MEMORIALS

Going down the hill from Jerusalem Street, in the area between the synagogues and the Artists' Quarter, is a straight stairway: **Oleh Ha-Gardom.** Stand at the top of this stairway, where it intersects with Jerusalem Street, and you're within sight of a lot of Safed's 20th-century historical landmarks.

Oleh Ha-Gardom was the dividing line between Safed's Jewish and Arab quarters until 1948; that's why all the synagogues are clustered on the right-hand side, as you're facing down the stairway. The present Artists' Quarter is in what used to be the Arab section. Look up toward the Citadel and you'll see a small opening in the fortress from which a direct line of machine-gun fire could be sent straight down the stairway, a British attempt to keep an uneasy peace between the two communities. The same day the British withdrew, the Arab and Jewish factions went to war. Look at the walls of the old police station and you'll see it's pocked with bullet holes from the fighting.

Down Jerusalem Street from this intersection you can also see a war memorial, with a tablet describing how the fighting favored first the Arabs, then the Jews. Poised on a stone mount is a Davidka (little David), one of those homemade Jewish mortars that, though not too accurate or damaging, made a terrific noise and gave the impression of being much more dangerous than it actually was.

At the top of the hill, in the beautiful hilltop park, are the ruins of a Crusader fortress (unfortunately not well maintained at present) from which you can enjoy a fine view of Mount Meiron, Mount Tabor, the Sea of Galilee, and a scattering of tiny hill villages and settlements. This site, the highest in Safed, was once the scene of a 1st-century Galilean stronghold and later a 12th-century Crusaders' lookout post. A war memorial commemorates the Israelis who were killed pushing the Arabs back from the heights.

MUSEUMS & EXHIBITIONS

The **Artists' Quarter** is the area down the hill from Jerusalem Street between the Oleh Ha-Gardom stairway facing the police station and the stone overpass that crosses Jerusalem Street. Here you will find picturesque houses, tiny streets, manicured gardens, and outdoor art displays. Many artists have galleries in their homes, and the homes themselves are often so charming and atmospheric that some owners charge a small admission. This is a good place to think about acquiring good, inexpensive gifts and souvenirs. Many of the exhibitions sell reproductions of the artists' work. Prices vary, but many are fairly inexpensive.

General Exhibition. Old Mosque, Artists' Quarter. ☎ **06/920-087.** Sun–Thurs 9am–6pm; Fri 9am–2pm; Sat 10am–2pm. Directions: Downhill from the intersection of Jerusalem and Arlosoroff streets.

While many of the houses in the artists' colony may be closed in winter, the General Exhibition is open year-round. The galleries display everything from paintings to ceramics to silk.

Habad (Or Chabad) House. ☎ **06/921-414.** Free admission. Sun–Thurs 9am–4pm.

Located between Ha-Maginim Street between Maginim Square (Kikar Maginim) and the Oleh Ha-Gardom steps, this is a Jewish history museum, with special exhibitions for children.

Hameiri House. Old City. ☎ **06/971-307.** Admission NIS 7 ($2.10). Sun–Fri 9am–2pm.

Located down the hill, in south Safed, Hameiri House is the **Museum and Institute for the Heritage of Safed.** It's housed in a historic 16th-century edifice, the restoration of which was done over a 27-year period, completed in 1985. Artifacts and documents portray the history of Safed's Jewish community. The museum can open on Saturday for groups, with advance notice.

Israel Bible Museum. ☎ **06/973-472.** Free Admission. Mar–Sept, Sun–Thurs 10am–6pm, Fri–Sat 10am–2pm; Dec–Feb, Sun–Fri 10am–2pm.

Dedicated in 1985, this museum (previously the home of the Turkish governor in Safed) is full of inspirational, dramatic art pieces by contemporary artist Phillip Ratner. The building is lovely, with dramatic vistas, and well worth the climb up the staircase at the north end of the Town Park. Or you can enter from the other side, walking down from Derekh Hativat Yiftah, which is the road that circles the Citadel.

Museum of Printing Art. Corner of Arieh Merzer and Arieh Alwail streets. ☎ **06/920-947.** Free Admission. Sun–Thurs 10am–noon and 4–6pm; Fri–Sat 10am–noon.

Safed was the site of the first Hebrew press in Israel, which was set up in 1576 and published Israel's first Hebrew book a year later. Here you can see a copy of the first newspaper printed in Israel (1863); a copy of the *Palestine Post* of May 16, 1948, announcing the birth of the State of Israel; a centuries-old Cabalistic text printed in Safed; examples of modern Israeli graphics; and many other things.

Ora Gallery. Artists' Quarter. ☎ **06/974-910.** Summer, Sun–Thurs 9am–6:30pm, Fri 9am–1pm; winter, Sun–Thurs 9am–4pm in good weather, or 1pm in bad weather, Fri 9am–1pm.

This unique gallery specializes in Hasidic art and mystical calligraphy. You'll find unusual pieces here, mostly paintings, with symbolism based on the Cabala.

PLANT A TREE

Just outside the highway entrance to Safed is a **Keren Kayemet Le-Israel (Jewish National Fund) Tree Planting Center.** At this site, Joseph Caro wrote in the 16th century, and here during the British Mandate, Palmach soldiers built a fortress, which the British destroyed, only to have it built again. The **restored fortress** was opened to the public in 1971, with an exhibition of documents, press cuttings, and photographs relating to the site.

Here the Jewish National Fund has established the **Biriya Forest,** where you are welcome to plant a tree with your own hands. It costs about $10. Hours are Sunday through Thursday from 8am to 2pm, on Friday until 12:30pm. For further information you can ask at the tourist information office.

SPORTS & OUTDOOR ACTIVITIES

SWIMMING   As you turn into town, in a hollow to the right of the road, near the Central Bus Station, is **Emek Hatchelet Swimming Pool** (☎ 06/920-217), which has been around since 1959. The area is beautifully landscaped, and has lounge chairs, tables, and big umbrellas. Admission is NIS 14 ($4.20), half price for children. There are two pools (one for children), game tables, a playground, plus a minigolf course. Aside from showers and dressing rooms, facilities include a restaurant serving everything from ice cream to a full steak-and-chips meal. It's open daily from June through part of September, from 9am to 5pm. Several days a week the afternoon hours are reserved for men-only or women-only swims.

A heated **swimming pool** in the Industrial Zone (☎ 06/974-294) is open all year. In summer, hours are Sunday through Thursday from 10am to 10pm, on Friday until 5pm, on Saturday until 6pm. In winter it's open Sunday through Thursday from noon to 10pm, on Friday from 10am to 3pm, and on Saturday from 10am to 4pm. Take bus no. 6 to the industrial part of Safed. Admission fees are the same as at the outdoor pool.

TENNIS   Ask at the tourist information office for details about the new **Sports Center,** with tennis and basketball courts and more, and a capacity of 600 people. It's covered, and heated in winter. For more information about tennis courts, also call 06/971-222.

WHERE TO STAY
MODERATE
✪ **Rimon Inn.** Artists' Quarter (P.O. Box 1011), Safed 13110. ☎ **06/920-665** or 920-666. 36 rms (all with bath or shower). A/C TEL TV. Summer: $92–$120 single; $103–$130 double. Winter: $76 single; $96 double. AE, DC, MC, V.

This four-star place in the Artists' Quarter, just a 5-minute walk from the center of town, is my favorite inn in Safed, a lovely place. Part of the main building derives from the 17th-century Turkish period, when it served as a khan (inn) and a post office. The dining room was originally the stable, and you still can see where the horses were tied. In addition to the usual luxuries, you'll find acres of gardens and wooded areas, a swimming pool, over half the rooms with large balconies, beautiful views, extra touches like a guitarist in the bar on weekends, and some interesting history as well.

INEXPENSIVE
Bet Benjamin (Bet Benyamin). 1 Lohamei Ha-Getaot St. (P.O. Box 1139), Safed. ☎ **06/921-086.** Fax 06/973-514. 128 beds. $17 member; $18.50 nonmember. Rates include breakfast. No credit cards. Bus: 6 or 7 from the Central Bus Station in Safed.

This modern hostel is located in south Safed on the corner of Ha-Nassi and Lohamei Ha-Getaot streets, not far from the intersection of Ha-Nassi and Weizmann. While you're here, be sure to see the statue in the park adjoining the hostel. Rooms are heated and there are hot showers.

Hotel Hadar. Ridbaz Street, Safed. ☎ **06/920-068.** 20 rms (all with shower). Summer: $33 single; $46 double. Spring and fall: $30 single; $40 double. Winter: $20 single; $25 double. Rates include breakfast and service. Aug, $15 per person extra for required half board. No credit cards.

This is a quiet hotel with serviceable, basic rooms. Room rates may be negotiable. To find it, turn left onto Ridbaz Street (a small passageway) near 24 Jerusalem St.

WHERE TO DINE
The first thing you'll notice about Safed is its multitude of sandwich, snack, and felafel shops along Jerusalem Street, open day and night, except for the Sabbath, when the whole town is closed up tight.

By the time you read this, there will likely be a big new commercial center across Jerusalem Street from the Restaurant Ha-Mifgash, with a large cafeteria, various restaurants, a cinema, and more.

Ha-Mifgash. 75 Jerusalem St. ☎ **06/930-510.** Appetizers NIS 7–12 ($2.10–$3.60); main courses NIS 15–33 ($4.50–$10). AE, MC, V. Thurs–Sun 9am–11pm (until midnight in summer); Fri 9am–4pm; Sat 10am–3pm and after the Sabbath. ISRAELI.

Located on the main street in the center of town, this restaurant, which means "meeting place" in Hebrew, has four different parts. The first thing you'll see is the self-service felafel counter in front. Inside, there's the main dining room, and to the left side is another room, which was a large water cistern in the 19th century. Service is not great, but this is one of the few kosher choices where you can sit down to a really full meal.

✪ **Restaurant Pinati.** 81 Jerusalem St. ☎ **06/920-855.** Appetizers NIS 7–12 ($2.10–$3.60); main courses NIS 15–40 ($4.50–$12). DC, MC, V. Daily 9am–11pm. ISRAELI.

Just a few steps down the hill from Ha-Mifgash, this plain but clean and friendly family-run restaurant offers excellent full meals of grilled, baked, or goulash meats with salad, potatoes, rice, and cooked vegetables. If you're feeling adventurous, you might try the unusual lung goulash. As amazing as the variety of dishes served is the decor, which is a monument to Elvis Presley!

SAFED AFTER DARK

Summer is the time for most of Safed's musical events. About eight chamber music concerts are held throughout the year, mostly in the summer, as well as a summer musical workshop. The **Klezmer Festival of East European Jewish Music** is the highlight of the summer programs. Check with the tourist office for the weekly scene. For piano concerts, check out **Hemdat Yamim** (☎ 06/989-085) on the Acre-Safed highway, which usually has concerts every Monday and Saturday evening during the summer.

The new **Yigal Alon Cultural Center and Theatre** on Jerusalem Street (☎ 06/971-990) has everything from Shakespeare to ballet and popular folk dancing. It's named for the man who led the forces that liberated Safed in the 1948 war.

EASY EXCURSIONS
MEIRON

Five miles west of Safed is the town of Meiron, a holy place for religious Jews for 1,700 years. Meiron has had a continuously Jewish population for nearly 18 centuries. When Jerusalem fell to the Romans in the 2nd century, the Israeli tribes took to the high grounds near here. One early Meiron inhabitant, a 2nd-century Talmudist named Shimon Bar Yochai, was ultimately forced to hide in a cave in Peqiin, outside Meiron. There, according to legend, he wrote the *Zohar,* or *Book of Splendor,* which is central to the Cabalist belief.

Meiron is the scene of considerable pageantry during the holiday of **Lag b'Omer,** which occurs in the spring just 3¹/₂ weeks after Passover. Thousands of Orthodox Jews pour into Safed and there follows a torchlight parade to Meiron, with singing and dancing. There they burn candles on top of Rabbi Shimon's tomb and light a great bonfire into which some, overcome by emotion, throw their clothes. In the morning, after the all-night festivities, 3-year-old boys are given their first haircuts, and the cut hair is thrown into the fire.

There still exists a **ruined ancient synagogue** from the 3rd century A.D., as well as **Rabbi Shimon's tomb,** and a rock called the **Messiah's Chair.** Reputedly, on the day the Messiah arrives, he will sit right here while Elijah blows the trumpet to announce his coming.

SASA & THE BAR'AM SYNAGOGUE

Kibbutz Sasa is on the northern foothills of Mount Meiron. In 1949 American and Canadian settlers built atop a 3,000-foot-high hill and persevered despite many problems, including a polio epidemic. The thriving kibbutz is now the center of an area of forest reservations.

Just 2 miles away, the 3rd-century A.D. **Bar'am Synagogue** is probably the best preserved and most beautiful of all the ancient synagogues in Israel. There is evidence that the synagogue may have been in use through early medieval times. The **National Park at Bar'am** (☎ 06/989-301) is open daily from 8am to 4pm and admission is NIS 9 ($2.70).

The ruins of the Christian Arab village of **Birim** surrounded the cleared areas around the synagogue. As noncombatants during the 1948 War of Independence, the residents of Birim had quartered Israeli troops in their homes. Late in the war, the people of Birim were told by the Israeli army to evacuate their town for what was promised would be a short time during a possible enemy offensive. They were never allowed to return. Since then, the former inhabitants of Birim, who all possess Israeli citizenship and are now scattered throughout the Galilee, have maintained a decades-long legal struggle to reclaim their homes.

Past the synagogue, you can follow a path to the left and uphill to the **Church of Birim,** still maintained by the people of the village for weddings and funerals. The view from the roof is very beautiful. An inscription (now in the Louvre) from the lintel of a vanished Roman-period smaller synagogue was discovered in 1861; it reads: "May there be peace in this place and in all the places of Israel. . . . "

5 Upper Galilee & the Golan Heights

TOURING THE REGION

From Tiberias or Safed, the main highway heads north toward Kiryat Shmona and Metulla. North of Kiryat Shmona, roads head west and south along the Lebanese border back toward Safed, and east to Hurshat Tal National Park, Baniyas Waterfall, and the Mount Hermon Ski Center in the Golan Heights.

GUIDED TOURS   I highly recommend a 1-day guided tour. Several are available from Tiberias. A 1-day tour of the Golan Heights will cost you $22 to $32, depending on which tour you choose. The two major touring companies in Tiberias, Egged and Galilee, each offer Golan tours for the same prices, going to about the same places. The Egged tours go at 8:30am on Tuesday, Thursday, and Saturday, leaving from the Tiberias Central Bus Station; you can also arrange to be picked up at your hotel for no extra charge. You should reserve in advance; contact the **Egged Tours** office in the Central Bus Station (☎ 06/720-474). The Galilee tours leave at 9am on Tuesday; contact the **Galilee Tours** office, 10 Ha-Yarden St. (☎ 06/720-330), to reserve.

A third option, especially popular with younger travelers, is to see the Golan with various **local taxi drivers,** who pick up tourists from all the Tiberias youth hostels every morning in summer season (call in advance to reserve your space through any hostel). The price, $22, is a bit less than many official bus-company tours, and it must be noted that these are not official government-licensed tour guides. However, the tours are lively and personal. Many readers have been disappointed with standard tours, and this is a colorful alternative.

Yet another option is to check with Tiberias's major hotels, many of which will have information about private guided tours. If you want to start out from somewhere other than Tiberias, Egged and Galilee offer tours leaving from Haifa, Tel Aviv, and Jerusalem; check their information booklets, or call, for details.

A NOTE ON ACCOMMODATIONS   You won't find many hotels in Upper Galilee and Golan. There is one four-star hotel in Kiryat Shmona, a youth hostel in nearby Tel Hai, and another youth hostel in Rosh Pinna. Kiryat Shmona is the hub of this area, and thus a desirable place to stay, if you're traveling by bus. Metulla, a prettier town on the Lebanese border, has several good moderately priced hotels, and a sports center and small shopping mall. There is one accommodation near the Mount Hermon Ski Center.

Then there are bed-and-breakfast accommodations in a growing network of private homes and homes in moshavim and kibbutzim. In addition, there are many kibbutz guesthouses in the Kibbutz Hotel Chain. East of Kiryat Shmona, Ha-Gosherim and Sha'ar Yashuv guesthouses are conveniently located next to the Hurshat Tal Park, on the road to Baniyas and the Mount Hermon Ski Center. Kefar Giladi is between Kiryat Shmona and Metulla. Kefar Blum is southwest of Kiryat Shmona. Ayelet Ha-Shahar is the farthest south of these, closer to Rosh Pinna, on the main road north to Kiryat Shmona.

Try to make arrangements in advance. If you don't phone ahead, travel early from Tiberias or Safed and pin down a place to stay as soon as possible.

UPPER GALILEE

From Tiberias, you can catch buses going northward as far as Metulla, Israel's most northerly town—and you'll find that the ride passes fascinating sights (depending on the season, you might have to change buses at Kiryat Shmona).

The trip begins along the western shore of the lake, goes through the valley of Ginossar and past Capernaum. Alongside the names of Kinneret, Galilee, and Tiberias, Ginossar must also take its place as a biblical name for the Sea of Galilee.

ROSH PINNA

Look for the turnoff to this pleasant small town (its name means "corner stone" in Hebrew), founded in 1882 by Romanian Jewish immigrants; it is the oldest modern town in all of Galilee and is even doing a bit of historical restoration. Just outside Rosh Pinna is the only memorial in the country to the underground extremist army member, Shmuel Ben Josef, the first Jew hanged by the British in Palestine. This simple but striking monument looks from a distance like an arm thrust upward at the sky, its fist shaking in defiance at the heavens.

FROM MISHMAR HA-YARDEN TO AYELET HA-SHAHAR

Farther along the main road is the turnoff to Mishmar Ha-Yarden, Galilee's oldest moshav, established around the turn of the century, and one of the few Jewish communities overrun and destroyed during the 1948 war. Beyond the moshav, crossing the Jordan into Golan, is the bridge called **Benot Yaakov (Daughters of Jacob),** believed to be the place where Jacob crossed the river on his return from Mesopotamia. The bridge is also on the ancient caravan route from Damascus to Egypt, which is part of the Via Maris.

On the left (west) side of the road is **Tel Hazor,** a prehistoric mound that serves as yet another reminder of this land's history. For 2,000 years Hazor was one of the region's most important cities. Artifacts from the area are exhibited at the **Hazor Museum** (☎ 06/934-855), at the entrance to Kibbutz Ayelet Ha-Shahar. Displays are from 21 different archeological strata spanning 2,500 years, from the early Bronze Age to the Hellenistic period in the 2nd century B.C. The excavation of Hazor is recorded in the extensively photographed book, *Hazor*, by Yigael Yadin, whose writing makes archeology truly accessible and exciting for all readers. Admission to the national park at Hazor and museum at Hazor is NIS 13 ($3.90). It is open daily from 8am to 4pm.

Where to Stay

Kibbutz Ayelet Ha-Shahar. Upper Galilee 12200. ☎ **06/932-611.** Fax 06/934-777. 136 rms (all with bath). A/C TEL. $74–$85 single; $88–$100 double. Rates include breakfast. 5% off-season discounts available; add 15% in high season. AE, DC, MC, V.

A short distance past Tel Hazor, on the east side of the road, this almost luxurious guesthouse is one of the most beautiful hotel choices for Upper Galilee travelers. Set among magnificent gardens, rooms have radios, central heat, and glorious views. Facilities include an outdoor pool, tennis courts, a playground for children, and a TV/video room.

THE HULA VALLEY

The best view of this beautiful reclaimed swampland is from the **Nebi Yusha fortress** just off the main road, on the Hill of the 28. A memorial in front of the British Taggart Fort recalls the time when these Hagana soldiers climbed the hill from Hula in the dead of night and fought to gain this strategic point. The odds were against them as they weathered a rain of machine-gun fire and grenades from the windows of the fort. When efforts to dynamite the building failed, the group's commander strapped the dynamite to his back, ignited it, and threw himself at a weak point in the wall. In all, 28 fighters died in taking this hilltop strongpoint, and today, birds make nests in the many shell holes on the walls of the fort.

Beyond the memorial plaques is an observation point with a magnificent view of the valley below. This breathtaking area, which stretches in both directions as far as the eye can see, was once a vast marshland teeming with wildlife. It was the smallest of the three lakes fed by the Jordan—the Sea of Galilee and the Dead Sea are the other two. To Israelis who remember the marshland, the Hula was a lovely place—a home for water buffalo, wild boar, exotic birds, and wildflowers. Species of cranes and storks would migrate here, coming and going from as far away as Russia, Scandinavia, and India. To those who knew its thickets of papyrus, its dragonflies and kingfishers, and its tropical water lilies (some claim it looked a little like the shores of the Nile), the Hula was a bit of paradise. The Arabs had legends about the Hula's charms, where spirits walked in the evening mist luring young people into the mysterious marsh.

After years of wrangling with neighboring governments—as well as with the French and British—the Israelis finally drained the marshes after they achieved independence. Because the country needed every drop of water and every square foot of fertile land, only one small section of the valley was left as a wildlife preserve. Control over the Hula's waters was also a necessary phase of the Lowdermilk and other Jordan River diversion plans, which bring water to the barren southern reaches of Israel.

However, the project upset the ecosystem and harmed the region's natural aquifer. In 1970 a reconstruction project to re-create the marshes was launched, and the Hula Nature Reserve was created.

Hula Nature Reserve. ☎ **06/937-069.** Admission NIS 12 ($3.60) adults, NIS 6 ($1.80) children. Sat–Thurs 8am–4pm; Fri 8am–3pm.

The reserve today is once again alive with gray herons, cormorants, ducks, wild boar, jamoos (water buffalo), and other former inhabitants that had died or went elsewhere when the swamps were drained. At the visitors' center, free films about the reserve are shown. The reserve is located 15 kilometers (9 miles) south of Kiryat Shmona and 3 kilometers (1¹/₂ miles) east of the highway. A combined ticket with the nature reserves at Baniyas, Dan, Gamla, and Ayun costs NIS 30 ($9).

Where to Stay

Kibbutz Kfar Blum Guest House. Upper Galilee 12150. ☎ **06/943-666.** Fax 06/948-555. 89 rms (all with bath or shower). A/C TEL. $65–$75 single; $75–$105 double. Rates include breakfast. 15% increase for Jewish holidays. Discounts are available on the Kibbutz Hotel Chain 7-Day Plan. AE, MC, V.

This three-star guesthouse offers heated rooms and a swimming pool. Fishing, birdwatching, and jogging are prime kibbutz activities. In summer, there is a short Chamber Music Festival. The guesthouse has a kosher dining room and synagogue. As you head north from the Hula Nature Reserve, you'll pass the turnoff to the guesthouse (to the right, east) toward Kefar Blum.

KIRYAT SHMONA

This is the "big town" in Upper Galilee (population 18,000), with a wide main boulevard, carefully laid-out residential districts, a busy bus station, and a fascinating monument to the turbulent past: three old army tanks, painted in bright basic colors, next to a gas station on the left side of the road as you enter from the south.

Kiryat Shmona was founded in memory of Joseph Trumpeldor. The name of the community, which means "Town of the Eight," refers to Trumpeldor's group of six men and two women who died at nearby Tel Hai defending their settlement from Arab attackers in 1920. Trumpeldor is the Israeli model of courage and heroism; he was born in Russia in 1880, served in the czar's army, lost an arm, and was decorated for gallantry by the tsarina of Russia. The Zionist leader came to Palestine in 1912, and with his self-styled Zion Mule Corps, fought with the British in Gallipoli. After the war he became a leader of Palestine's pioneer agricultural youth movement and settled at the Tel Hai kibbutz. Trumpeldor defended the settlement against marauding Arabs, until one day, when a particularly heavy attack came, and he refused to leave the kibbutz grounds. In a last-ditch stand, he and seven comrades were killed. His memorial, a few miles north at Tel Hai, is a statue of a lion at the edge of a cliff, head thrown back and mouth open, bellowing at the skies.

Today Kiryat Shmona is a development town, largely populated by Israelis of Middle Eastern descent, with a smattering of new immigrants from the former Soviet Union. In the tradition of the early settlements of the region, Kiryat Shmona at times comes under attack by katushya rockets fired from Lebanon.

Where to Stay

Kibbutz Kfar Giladi. Upper Galilee 12210. ☎ **06/941-414.** 155 rms (all with bath). A/C TEL. $65–$75 single; $75–$105 double. Rates include breakfast. 15% increase for Jewish holidays. Discounts are available through the Kibbutz Hotel Chain 7-Day Plan. AE, MC, V.

If you don't mind staying out of town, you can head halfway to Medulla to this guesthouse. The kibbutz offers tidy rooms, a pool, tennis courts, a playground, and kosher dining facilities.

EN ROUTE TO METULLA

From Kiryat Shmona, you can head north past Kefar Giladi and Tel Hai to Metulla, then backtrack to Kiryat Shmona before heading east, to Golan.

Situated along the Lebanese border, Metulla is as far north as you can go in Israel proper. Founded in 1896 by a Rothschild grant, Metulla is a pretty, pine-scented oasis where residents farm and cultivate bees. During the rainy season you can see a waterfall cascading from the Tanur Pass into the Iyon River. Because of its proximity to the border, the town has many soldiers and has experienced a considerable amount of military action.

Metulla became a bustling place during the Israeli invasion of Lebanon, but now that the troops are withdrawn it has settled back into its picturesque serenity. With its limestone buildings accented by dark wood, cypress, and evergreen trees, Metulla is reminiscent of a Swiss mountain village, tidy and tranquil.

Metulla has a tiny museum, and the Nahal Ayoun Picnic Ground is by the Lebanese border, shaded by tall eucalyptus trees and furnished with picnic tables and campgrounds. Past the picnic ground, a rough road skirts the Lebanese border, heading east and south to the **Nahal Ayoun (or Ha-Tanur) Nature Reserve** (☎ 06/ 951-519) that runs along the entire east side of Metulla, along the Ayoun Stream, between Metulla and the Lebanese border. You can drive or walk into the reserve from here; admission is NIS 13 ($3.90) for adults, half price for children. It's open daily from 8am to 4pm, and until 3pm on Friday.

Ha-Tanur, the Tanur Waterfall, is in the Ayoun Nature Reserve, 2 kilometers (1¼ miles) south of Metulla. To get to the waterfall, you can come down through the nature reserve, or you can take any bus, or walk downhill out of town toward Kiryat Shmona, and after 2 kilometers (1 mile) turn left (east) and walk down into the valley another 400 yards. After the 20-minute walk, you'll find the waterfalls, one of Israel's loveliest spots. In all but the driest months, the falls tumble into tempting, shaded pools.

About a kilometer (half mile) west of Metulla you can visit the **Good Fence,** the border crossing between Israel and Lebanon. The fence got its name in 1976 when a Lebanese child was brought across into Israel to receive medical care, and the name stuck. Today Lebanese cross the border daily to work in Israel.

If you have a car, or if you don't mind a bit of a hike, go to **Lookout Mountain,** the peak about 1 kilometer (half mile) west of Metulla, for a bird's-eye view of the area.

Where to Stay

Ha-Mavri Hotel. Metulla. ☎ **06/940-150.** 24 rms (all with bath or shower). $40–$56 single; $56–$69 double. Rates include breakfast. 20% increase for Jewish holidays. No credit cards.

This simple, two-star hotel is a few doors down from the Arazim. Rooms have radios and some rooms have a balcony and view of Lebanon, which can also be seen from the airy dining room. Guests receive discounts for the Canada Center.

Hotel-Pension Arazim. Metulla 10292. ☎ **06/997-144** or 997-145. Fax 06/997-666. 34 rms (all with bath). A/C TEL TV. $64–$80 single; $80–$100 double. Rates include breakfast. 10% student discount during July and August and 20% in winter. AE, MC, V.

This comfortable hotel in the center of town has an old-world attention to service and quality. It has a bar, gift shop, swimming pool, and tennis courts. The food is kosher and there is central heating. The hotel serves as a communications center for journalists when things get hot on this portion of the Lebanese border. Guests receive discounts for the Canada Center.

Where to Dine

Allegro. Canada Center. ☎ **06/950-112.** Appetizers and light meals NIS 10–20 ($3–$6); main courses NIS 20–39 ($6–$11.70). No credit cards. Daily 10am–9pm. ITALIAN/ INTERNATIONAL.

If you want a major meal in Metulla, this is the town's main choice, overlooking the Canada Sports Center Swimming Pool. There's a cafeteria area for light meals, soups, and salads, and a section for full meals. Although advertised as an Italian restaurant, choices go beyond pasta and traditional Italian fare to include a wide variety of dishes.

Metulla Restaurant. No phone. Appetizers NIS 7–13 ($2.10–$3.90); main courses NIS 15–33 ($4.50–$10). No credit cards. Daily 11am–midnight. LEBANESE/EUROPEAN.

Located on the second floor of the large white building across from Ha-Mavri Hotel, this friendly and comfortable glass-enclosed restaurant is literally over-hanging the Lebanese border. There is an outdoor terrace and a wood-burning stove.

EN ROUTE TO MOUNT HERMON & THE GOLAN HEIGHTS

East from Kiryat Shmona, along the road to Mount Hermon—that snowcapped peak you've probably already noticed—is a beautiful national park, hot springs, a Crusader fortress, and a ski center.

Hurshat Tal National Park. ☎ **06/942-360** or 940-400. Admission NIS 15 ($4.50), half price under 18. Apr–Sept, daily 8am–5pm; Oct–Mar, daily 8am–4pm. Bus: 26, 27, or 36 from Kiryat Shmona stop close to the park entrance.

You can swim, picnic, and camp (in season) just 5 kilometers (3 miles) from Kiryat Shmona. The national park is famous for its ancient oak trees, some of which may date from the time of Jesus and the Second Temple. The Dan River, a tributary of the Jordan, passes down this valley, collecting in a series of artificial lakes and ponds. The freezing (or refreshing) pool in the park is also fed by these streams.

Where to Stay

Kibbutz Ha-Goshrim Guest House. Kibbutz Ha-Goshrim. ☎ **06/956-231.** Fax 06/956-234. 120 rms (all with bath). A/C TEL TV. $65–$75 single; $75–$105 double. Rates include break-fast. 15% increase for Jewish holidays. Discounts are available through the Kibbutz Hotel Chain 7-Day Plan. MC, V.

Located next door to the beautiful Hurshat Tal National Park, this very popular kib-butz guesthouse is a good base for exploring Upper Galilee and the Golan. Founded by Turkish Jews in 1948, it has a kosher dining room, swimming pool, children's playground, tennis courts, and a video/TV room.

Where to Dine

Pub Gosh. Kibbutz Hagoshrim, Upper Galilee. ☎ **06/945-343.** Appetizers/light meals NIS 20–25 ($6–$7.50); main courses NIS 25–48 ($7.50–$14.30). MC, V. Daily noon–10pm or later. KOSHER VEGETARIAN/FISH.

For those seeking a good kosher restaurant in this part of the countryside, Pub Gosh, run by Kibbutz Hagoshrim, is kosher, despite the fact that it's open 7 days a week (food is brought from a traveler's guesthouse, which has a kashrut certificate and op-erates on Shabbat). In a rustic wooden building set in a forest beside a stream, it's a good choice for any visitor to the area. The menu includes hefty portions of soups, salads, pasta dishes, pizzas, and the restaurant's star attraction, excellent local trout prepared in a number of ways. Soups, a meal in themselves, are served inside a small loaf of country bread (quite a stylish presentation for a kibbutz-run place), but as at many restaurants, the stock seems powder-based. In good weather, there are outdoor tables along the side of the stream; the building is blessedly heated and air-conditioned.

TEL DAN

The prehistoric settlement at Tel Dan, 9 kilometers (5¹⁄₂ miles) east of Kiryat Shmona and then 3 kilometers (1¹⁄₂ miles) north, was a thriving Canaanite community when

Joshua led the conquering Israelites here more than 3,000 years ago. In fact, Dan was the northern limit of the Promised Land (the southern limit was Beersheva).

Tel Dan Nature Reserve. ☎ **06/951-579.** Admission NIS 13 ($3.90) adults, half price children. Sat–Thurs 8am–4pm; Fri 8am–3pm.

Cold-water springs gush right up from the ground here, forming the Dan River, which is one of the three principal sources of the Jordan River. The dense vegetation around the site is lovely, but swimming is not permitted. Excavations in the reserve, which include a pre-Israelite cult center, are ongoing. In 1993, an inscription bearing what may be a reference to the "House of David" was found here, an exciting discovery as it would be the first extra-biblical mention of King David's royal family to be discovered.

There is also a 700-year-old Arabic stone flour mill. Reconstructed by the National Parks Authority, it is run by water power, and is near a 2,000-year-old pistachio tree, walking trails, and picnic areas.

If you come by bus, it's a 30-minute walk from Kibbutz Dan. Buses run between Kibbutz Dan and Kiryat Shmona about every 2 hours. You can buy a combination ticket for all nature reserves in the area for $9.

In nearby Kibbutz Dan is a nature museum, Bet Ussishkin (☎ 06/941-704), with exhibits covering the flora, fauna, geology, topography, and history of the region. Bet Ussishkin also contains a Society for Protection of Nature in Israel (SPNI) station where you can get information about hiking safely in the Golan. You must check in at an SPNI station before hiking independently through the Golan Heights. You can also pick up information about seasonal birdwatching in the area here. Hours are Sunday through Thursday from 8:30am to 3:30pm, and on Friday until 2pm. There's a nominal admission fee for adults, reduced for children. Keep your receipt: the admission fee here gets you a discount at the National Park.

Where to Dine
Dan Eden Trout Restaurant. Tel Dan Nature Reserve. ☎ **06/953-826.** Full meals NIS 43–60 ($13–$18). No credit cards. Daily, winter 8am–4 or 5pm; summer 8am–5 or 6pm. FRESH FISH.

This rustic spot on the banks of the Dan River can get absolutely frantic on weekends and in the summer, when it's often more of an obstacle course than a restaurant, but the kibbutz farm-raised trout and salmon (which are the only meals offered here) are excellent. You can have your straight-from-the-pond choice prepared in one of three ways: fresh grilled, smoked (served hot or cold), or rapid-boiled in a seasoned fish stock and served with either a hollandaise or a butter sauce. Weekdays out of season, the place is not usually too overrun unless a group is passing through. If weather permits, a bucolic option is to ask for your order served on a tray, and to escape the crowds by picnicking on the banks of the river. Wonderful fish by any standards, this is probably the most delicious restaurant meal available in the Upper Galilee. A policy that deducts your admission fee to the nature reserve may be in effect.

THE GOLAN HEIGHTS
The wild plateau, with its vistas of the Galilee below, is especially worthy of a visit. Occupied since 1967 by Israel, which annexed the Golan for security reasons in 1981, the heights are lightly populated with Druze villages and Jewish towns constructed by the Israeli government specifically for security purposes. Unlike the occupation of Gaza and the West Bank, the period of Israeli control in the Golan has been marked by economic development, prosperity, and tranquil relations between the Druze and the Israeli settlers, who do not share the sometimes fanatic ideologies of settlers in

the West Bank. The future of the Golan is not clear at press time. Prime Minister Rabin was quoted as stating that in exchange for a genuine peace with Syria, most of the Heights may be returned to that country. Meanwhile, the Golan affords visitors the pleasure of flowing winter springs and waterfalls, and a variety of ancient sites ranging from prehistoric dolmens to the ruins of 1,900-year-old synagogues, as well as Israel's only ski resort and one of its best wineries. The region's most spectacular site is the ruins of Gamla, a Jewish town destroyed in A.D. 67 during the First Revolt against Rome, located on an especially beautiful and dramatic mountain ridge. The Golan is one of the areas where a rental car is most useful. In summer, the plateau is blazing hot; in winter it can be bitterly cold and windy.

Warning: When touring the Golan area, do not go exploring for shell fragments or souvenirs in the hills near the bunkers. As many as 100,000 to a million Syrian mines have been planted in this area over the last two decades, and it may be 10 or 20 years before the Israeli army finishes minesweeping the area. It must be done inch by inch, and since many of the mines are plastic—not detectable by metal-seeking devices—laboriously slow probes and earth-turning machines must be used. En route you will see a couple of places where the tour buses stop to give visitors a look at the bunkers. Two million visitors (mostly Israeli) have been there before you—so you can be sure it's safe. The barbed-wire fences that line much of the road, and the triangular yellow-and-red Hebrew signs on them, all mean the same thing: minefield.

Hiking in the Golan Heights must be arranged in advance through an SPNI field school or information station. SPNI can be contacted in Qasrin (☎ 06/752-340) and in the Upper Galilee at Kibbutz Dan (☎ 06/941-704).

BANIAS (NAHAL HERMON) AND THE CRUSADER CASTLE

For thousands of years, Banias has been a holy place to a dozen peoples and half-a-dozen religions. Banias figures in the New Testament as the place where Jesus designated Peter as "the rock" on which the church would be built. In ancient times the Canaanites, and later the Greeks, built shrines and temples here. The Greek name Paneas (after Pan, the god of fertility) was modified in Arabic to Banias as Arabic has no "p" sound. Though an earthquake collapsed the impressive grotto of the Greeks, you can still see little shrines, most of which date from the Hellenistic period. Under the Romans, the settlement was named Caesarea Philippi after Philip, son of Herod, who followed in the ancients' ways and also built a temple.

The Crusaders fortified the nearby hilltop with what is now Nimrod Castle. Christians built a chapel to Saint George on the hillside, which Muslims later converted into a shrine dedicated to El-Khader (the prophet Elijah). A steep path still leads up to the shrine. While the shrine is usually closed, you should still go up for the view.

WHAT TO SEE & DO
Banias Waterfall

The beautiful and legendary Banias Waterfall is less than a mile inside the Golan, some 15 kilometers (9¹/₂ miles) from Kiryat Shmona, and less than 1 kilometer (half mile) off the main road. Banias is one of the principal sources of the Jordan River. Head down to the stream for a look at the waters that begin several hundred feet higher on the Hermon slopes. From here the destination, after dropping into the Jordan River, is the Sea of Galilee. Jordan (Yared-Dan) means "descending from Dan," and the river, whose origins are right here, picks up again south of the Sea of Galilee for a twisting, turning run of 70 miles before emptying into the Dead Sea and becoming a stagnant, oily mixture.

Banias Springs (Nahal Hermon) Nature Reserve. Admission NIS 13 ($3.90) adult, half price children. Sat–Thurs 8am–4pm; Fri 8am–2pm.

One kilometer (half mile) east of the falls, turn left, then left again into the parking lot of the nature reserve. The prime attractions at Banias are the pure, ice-cold springs that burst from the earth beneath a sheer rock wall and rush downward to Banias Waterfall and into the Jordan. The waters originate on the slopes of Mount Hermon. This ancient site has been landscaped by the Nature Reserves Authority. You can go swimming, if you can stand the icy waters.

You can buy a combination ticket to the Banias, Hula Tel Dan, Nahal Ayoun, and Gamla nature reserves for NIS 30 ($9).

Nimrod Castle. Admission NIS 10 ($3). Sat–Thurs 8am–4pm; Fri 8am–2pm.

Nimrod Castle, now a national park, is one of the biggest and best-preserved Crusader ruins in the area, and has a spectacular view. It can be brutally hot and shadeless in summer, but at cooler seasons, the 1 1/2- to 2-hour hike is well worth the effort.

As you come under the wall of the castle you'll see the narrow vertical slits where archers were once stationed. Inside, see many deep water-filled cisterns, some 30 feet deep.

As you can see from up here, whoever controlled Nimrod in bygone days controlled the traffic from Lebanon to Tiberias and the Jordan Valley. To the left is the zigzagging cleft of Banias rift. In a lush, green pocket farther on, you see Tel Dan kibbutz, then a series of carp ponds, Kiryat Shmona on the hills beyond, and the rectangles of brown and green of the Hula Valley extending southward for miles and miles. Behind the castle to the north sits Mount Hermon, rising to 6,500 feet.

To get to Nimrod Castle, follow the signs to Kalaat Namrud. It is approximately 1 1/2km (1 mile) northeast and uphill from Banias.

THE DRUZE VILLAGES

The Druze villages on the slopes of Mount Hermon are inhabited by the fiercely independent people whose religion is still something of a mystery to outsiders. They are farmers for the most part, and don't mind tilling the steep, rocky ground so long as they are left in peace. For the past 1,000 years, the Druze have had considerable autonomy. It just wasn't worth the time and expense to conquer them.

The Druze religion is an offshoot of Islam, but very different from either of the major branches, Sunni and Shiite. It all starts with the Fatimids, an Islamic dynasty that grew powerful in the 900s. The Fatimids conquered most of North Africa and parts of the Mediterranean, even taking Genoa for a time. Among their caliphs (leaders with both religious and secular powers) was Hakim (996–1021), the sixth of the Fatimid line, who in the year 1020 proclaimed himself to be the reincarnation of God. Many people disagreed with his assertions, and he was assassinated within a year. But he was believed in Syria and Lebanon, especially among the people who would come to be called Druze. Thus, the foundation of the Druze faith is that Hakim was and is an incarnation of God, that he did not die (because God can't die), but rather is in hiding and will reappear to rule the world when the time is ripe. The Druze also revere Jethro, the Midianite father-in-law of Moses.

The Druze believe in loyalty to the countries in which they reside, and Israeli Druze have served with distinction in the Israeli army. The Druze of the Golan, however, though they admit they have had a tranquil and prosperous existence since the Israeli occupation began in 1967, also feel they must uphold their commitment to Syria, and many support a return of the Golan Heights to Syrian control.

Between the two villages is the small lake of **Birkhet Ram,** now used as a reservoir. Although its round shape hints at a volcanic origin, Birkhet Ram was actually formed by the action of underground springs. Visit the **Birkhet Ram Restaurant** if you're hungry, because you won't find many restaurants in Golan, and it offers the best view of the lake from its balcony. It's open from 8am to 6pm. There's a felafel stand and snack shop here as well.

EN ROUTE TO QASRIN

After the slow, bouncing ride back from Hermon to the main road, the road becomes well paved. Heading toward Kuneitra, you pass houses of the black basalt rock of this region. Where the roofs are tiled red on these black homes, the villages are Circassian ("Cheerkhasi" in Hebrew). The Circassians reached this part of the world via southern Russia, the Caucasus, and Iran. A new road circumvents Kuneitra. There's a mound though, near the United Nations base, which is worth visiting. You can look out into the ruined city and across, into the wide, barren plain that leads to Damascus.

Kuneitra (or Quneitra, now in Syria) was the chief Syrian city in Golan before the war. Now, largely deserted, it is just one of many ghost towns created by politics and war.

Nearby is **Kibbutz Merom Ha-Golan,** a commune of settlers from all over the world. It is worth visiting this kibbutz or similar settlements throughout the heights.

QASRIN

Situated in the center of Golan, the new (1977) Israeli "capital" of Golan, Qasrin (Kazrin, Katzirin, etc.), was founded on the site of a 2nd- to 3rd-century Jewish town of the same name. Qasrin is the region's administrative hub, with new apartments, offices, schools, factories, and a few shops. It is a good place to stop for groceries or snacks and emergency services. And there are many interesting sights nearby. Bus service is from Kiryat Shmona (take no. 55).

A few unlikely contrasts serve as strong reminders of the town's strategic locale: a pleasant suburban town surrounded by barbed wire, bomb shelters encircled by rose gardens, and bomb shelters that house recreation centers, clubhouses, and music halls. Qasrin is known for its sweet, natural mineral water, which is bottled and exported to the rest of the country.

What to See & Do

Golan Archeological Museum and Park/Jewish Heritage Doll Museum/Golan Winery. P.O. Box 30, Qasrin, Golan Heights 12900. ☎ **06/961-350.** Admission to all venues: NIS 10 ($3) adults, NIS 4 ($1.20) children.

This complex is made up of several museums. A small **museum of regional history** that is modern, light, and well planned is the heart of the complex. Here you can also see an exhibit and short film about the Golan stronghold of Gamla, destroyed by the Romans in A.D. 67, during the First Revolt against Rome. The museum is open Sunday through Thursday from 8am to 4pm, Friday until 1pm, and Saturday from 10am to 4pm. A combined ticket is sold for all venues.

The **Ancient Archeological Park** is just outside Qasrin to the southeast along the main road. Here you'll find the partially restored ancient synagogue of Qasrin, dating from the Byzantine and Early Arab periods. You'll also find two reconstructed houses from the Talmudic era, complete with reproductions of furnishings and implements from those times. This reconstruction helps give a revealing picture of what daily life in the early Jewish communities of the Golan and Galilee would have been like.

The **Doll Museum** on the Main Plaza of Qasrin, opposite the Golan Archeological Museum, opened in 1994, and has quickly become one of the country's special, although little-known, attractions. The creation of Leonardo Nisemblatt and Shalom Kahila, who worked on this project for many years, 80 often poetic, wonderfully detailed, and charmingly human dioramas depict the entire history of the Jewish people, starting with the Garden of Eden, and continuing through Abraham's abandonment of Hagar and Ishmael, the parting of the Red Sea, the revolts against Rome, the Diaspora, the Inquisition, the Dreyfus Affair, and the resettlement of Israel. As if this were not tour de force enough, additional dioramas portray the Jewish holidays and storybook fantasies. Truly wonderful for everyone from children to history buffs and even those who normally hate dolls and dioramas, the museum is open Sunday through Thursday from 9am to 4pm, Friday from 9am to 1pm, and Saturday from 10am to 4pm. You can also visit the nearby Golan Winery for a tour and a bit of wine sampling.

YA'AR YEHUDIYA NATURE RESERVE

The reserve stretches from Qasrin to the shores of the Sea of Galilee, and is famous for its ancient oaks, forested valleys, and waterfalls. Within the reserve are several waterfalls (especially at Mapal Gamla) and rivers.

Berekhat Ha-Meshushim, a pool amid natural hexagonal shaped columns, is also worth seeing. The columns were formed when mineral-rich molten rock cooled slowly, taking on the crystalline structure. Also in Ya'ar Yehudiya are several ancient dolmens, the use and provenance of which is still something of a mystery. The dolmens are not far from Gamla (see below).

GAMLA

Gamla, where Jewish residents battled Roman legionnaires in A.D. 67, is a dramatic historical as well as nature site, 12km (7 miles) southeast, near Zomet Daliyot. Gamla was one of the early Jewish strongholds recaptured by Rome during the First Revolt against Rome (A.D. 66–70). At the end of this war, Jerusalem and the Second Temple were destroyed (A.D. 70), and the Zealots of Masada committed mass suicide rather than fall into Roman hands (A.D. 73). The story of the battle at Gamla is chillingly similar to that of Masada, but the number of dead was many times higher.

The well-fortified town of Gamla was first conquered by Jewish forces under Alexander Yannai in 90 B.C. Its name came from the site: a hill that looks like the hump of a camel (gamal). Shortly after the Revolt against Rome broke out in A.D. 66, Gamla filled with Jewish refugees fleeing Roman control. The inhabitants at first held out against a Rome siege army, but in the end (according to the Roman Jewish historian, Josephus), when the Romans breached Gamla's defenses, 9,000 people flung themselves from the cliff—choosing death before subjugation.

There is a shorter trail to the ruins as well as a longer nature hike. Both routes are marked; the longer hike from the road to the site of Gamla, though an arduous 1 to 1 1/2 hours, is especially beautiful amid the waterfalls and wildflowers of late winter and the spring. The dramatically located synagogue, one of the very few that can be dated from the time of the Second Temple, is memorable. Bring drinking water in warm weather.

MOUNT HERMON SKI CENTER

The moshav of Neve Ativ has developed the Mount Hermon Ski Center (☎ 06/ 981-337), high on the slopes of Mount Hermon. The ski center caters to skiers and nonskiers alike. There's even a lift that is exclusively for nonskiers that goes the 1 mile to the 6,630-foot summit, where there's an observation point and cafeteria. The snow season usually begins in December or January and lasts until about mid-April.

Roads up to the site are subject to blockage by heavy snow, so check on conditions in advance by telephone, radio report, or newspaper. On Saturday in ski season, the hotels in this region, the roads, and the parking lot fill up early. Also, on Saturday and holidays a special traffic pattern is in effect for the narrow roads in this region: You must approach the resort via Masada and Majdal Shams only; you exit via Neve Ativ. Those driving should just follow the flow of Saturday traffic. Or take the bus from Kiryat Shmona.

The parking lot is below the ski center. You'll be stopped on the road to pay an entrance fee of NIS 30 ($9) to the site. From the parking lot, shuttle buses run you up to the base station.

As for the slopes, there are four runs from the upper station, the longest of which is about 1^1/$_2$ miles, for average to good skiers. Beginners can use the short chairlift, which is a 1,300-foot trip to a height of 885 feet above the base station. Gentle slopes at the bottom of the hill are good for first runs and for children.

Other facilities include picnic tables and a snack bar at the base, a ski school, and an equipment rental shop. Most Israelis rent equipment, which is yet another reason why you should arrive early if you plan to ski on Saturday. Cost for ski rental is about NIS 66 ($20). Plan on spending about $50 per person for a day on the slopes: admission and lift fees, equipment rental, and a snack for lunch.

The ski center is open daily from 8:30am to 3:30pm, weather and security conditions permitting.

6 South of Galilee: The Jordan Valley

Although the River Jordan is little more than a desert stream, its waters, which come from the Sea of Galilee, are crucial to the agriculture of the area. It has brought fertile silt down from the Sea of Galilee for so many centuries that its valley is one of the most bounteous farming regions in the country.

If you're coming along the lakeshore from Tiberias, see that section for a description of the lake entrance to the valley and the first major town, Degania.

THE APPROACH TO THE VALLEY: AFULA TO BET SHEAN

The road to Afula follows a historic route, although road signs announce only communal settlements. Throughout history, pilgrims have traveled along this path to reach the waters of the River Jordan.

Southeast of Afula, you'll pass **Kibbutz Yizreel.** The road then skirts the slopes of **Mount Gilboa,** where the tragedy of Saul occurred. There is a farm collective and a road running right to the top of the mountain, where there is a view of everything—the Galilee mountains, the Emek, the Mediterranean, Jordan.

On the left is a string of communal settlements—**Ein Harod, Tel Yosef, Bet Ha-Shita.** A large, well-developed settlement, founded in 1921, Ein Harod has a population of nearly 2,000 settlers. It has a hostel, an amphitheater, a culture hall, an archeological and natural history museum, and an art gallery that has exhibited works by Chagall, Hanna Orloff, Milich, and the American artist Selma Gubin.

Just after Ein Harod, the road sign points to Heftziba and Bet Alpha, both communal settlements. **Kibbutz Bet Alpha** was one of the early Jordan Valley settlements, founded in 1922 by pioneers from Poland and Galicia who cleared the swamps. During one of their swamp-draining operations, a remnant of a 6th-century rural synagogue was uncovered. Financed by Temple Emmanu-El of New York City, excavation produced what is one of the most famous ancient synagogues uncovered in Israel.

The ❂ **Bet Alpha Synagogue** (☎ 06/531-400) in Kibbutz Heftziba has a highly ornamental and charmingly naive 5th-century A.D. mosaic floor (probably the most famous in Israel) that is divided into three panels, including a depiction of Abraham's near sacrifice of Isaac, a depiction of the sun pulled by a star chariot surrounded by the signs of the zodiac, and a tableau of religious ornaments. Protected by a modern enclosure, the Bet Alpha Synagogue is open daily from 8am to 4pm. Admission is NIS 9 ($2.70).

Sachne (☎ 06/586-219), Israel's largest natural swimming pool, lies in **Gan Ha-Shlosha Park,** just beyond Bet Alpha kibbutz. With its waterfall, tall trees, and distant mountains, it is a favorite Israeli picnic and swimming site. It is open daily from 8am to 4pm; in summer from Saturday to Thursday until 6pm, with a 4pm closing on Friday. Admission to the park is NIS 17 ($5).

Nearby in Gan Ha-Shlosha Park is the **Museum of Regional and Mediterranean Archeology** (☎ 06/480-445), an interesting exhibition that attempts to place ancient Palestine within the framework of Mediterranean civilization. There are displays of locally collected statuary, pottery, metalwork, jewelry, and coins dating from the Neolithic to the Mameluke eras, as well as objects from more distant places. Open Sunday through Friday from 8am to 2pm, and admission is NIS 8 ($2.40).

BET SHEAN

As you approach the pass at Bet Shean, the temperature increases as the altitude plummets to 300 feet below sea level. Despite the burnt-orange rocky hillsides and the low rainfall of 12 inches annually, this is a highly fertile area. Springs and streams from Mount Gilboa have been directed toward the Jordan Valley's fields, and the fertile soil here supports thousands of acres of wheat, vegetables, banana groves, and cotton fields.

Bet Shean, now an agricultural center and a quiet development town, is another ancient city that, due to its position on the great caravan route from Damascus to Egypt, has had a long succession of foreign rulers.

At ❂ **Tel Bet Shean,** archeologists have cut into layer upon layer of civilization. They uncovered five separate strata of Canaanite and Egyptian civilizations, with altars and ruins of the Ramses II period, and early Israelite ceramics dating from the time King Saul's body was hung by the Philistines on the Bet Shean wall. Later strata revealed a Scythian period (the Greeks named the town Scythopolis), and in a higher stratum the layers of dirt and rock revealed fragments from Roman times. Some 70 feet into the "tel" (Hebrew for an archeological mound or hill), the dig uncovered a 6th-century Byzantine town with mosaics and delicate columns. Closer to the top they uncovered the remains of Crusader castles from the Middle Ages, and still higher up, the jugs and farm tools of the Arab and Turkish settlers of the last 5 centuries.

Elsewhere at Bet Shean you'll see the best-preserved **Roman theater** in Israel. This 8,000-person playhouse has 15 tiers of white limestone in nearly perfect condition, and several more tiers of crumbling black basalt. Broken columns and statue fragments are scattered on the floor. Outside the archeological park to the north, at the edge of modern-day Bet Shean, is the late-Byzantine **Monastery of the Noble Lady Mary,** with an extremely beautiful and complicated series of mosaic floors. Information about the many sites in the vast archeological area, which is in the process of being developed for the public, is best obtained at **Bet Shean National Park**

Visitors Center (☎ 06/585-200). Admission is NIS 13 ($3.90). The park is open daily from 8am to 4pm.

THE JORDAN VALLEY

Once you head south from Bet Shean, you are in the abundantly fertile Jordan Valley. You'll see emerald-green splashes of farm settlements in the distance, and soon you'll come to the straight rows of beautiful fruit trees. The vegetation is particularly apparent in the Bet Shean Valley, at the entrance to the Jordan Valley. One ancient sage has written: "If Israel is Paradise, then the Bet Shean Valley is the gate to Paradise."

You are now in subtropical country—notice the profusion of date palm trees, banana groves, pomegranate and grapefruit orchards, and mango trees as well as the neat blue rectangles of carp-breeding ponds. It's hard to imagine the heavy toll this land took on the lives of early settlers.

The river Jordan often dwindles to a mere trickling stream, and rarely looks like it's supposed to—lush and green, with myrtle and reeds.

BELVOIR (KOCHAV HA'YARDEN) NATIONAL PARK

The park, in the Jordan Valley between Beit Shean and the southern tip of the Sea of Galilee, near Kibbutz Gesher, contains the most spectacular Crusader castle ruins in the region. Constructed by the Knights Hospitalers in 1140, this fortress, with dramatic views of the Jordan Valley, was conquered by Saladin in 1189, and dismantled to prevent a Crusader reoccupation in 1218. Especially interesting are carved basalt stones that can be seen in secondary use at various places in the Crusader ruins. Some of this stonework, bearing the menorah and other Jewish motifs, has been identified as having originally been part of a synagogue, and testifies to the ravaging of the land by the Crusaders. A car is necessary if you wish to visit the site on your own.

The park is open daily from 8am to 4pm (5pm in summer). Admission is NIS 9 ($2.70). Call 06/587-000 for more information.

The Dead Sea & the Negev

11

If you have the usual preconception of what a desert is like—nothing but sand—you're in for a surprise. The Negev is not a desert in that sense at all. In fact, the Hebrew word for this southern region is *midbar,* meaning wilderness. There are stretches of sand in the Arava region just north of Eilat, but for the most part the Negev is a great triangular swath of boulders, pebbles, wind-sculpted mountains, eroded landscape, Bedouin encampments, and brave, lonely settlements. The people of the region are different—they have to be. The Negev could easily be regarded as a sort of Israeli Siberia; instead, the taming of the desert is the prime challenge of the idealistic, and perhaps the greatest single achievement of the people of Israel.

Just a few decades ago the Negev reached north and lapped at the settlements of Rishon-le-Zion and Gedera. But today, the desert has been pushed back beyond Beersheva. Where vultures and scorpions once reigned, winter crops and early vegetables are grown. Inch by inch a dead land is being reclaimed, and if there is ever peace in the region, the most arid of lands will be taught to bloom again.

It is a pity that so many tourists overlook the Negev in favor of the more conventional sites. The historical artifacts of the wilderness are as intrinsic to Jewish history as the more settled regions in the far north. Flying over the area on the way to Eilat will give you a general appreciation of the region, but to really understand what Israel is about you have to smell the desert, wipe the sand out of your eyes, and tread the paths of the Hebrew nomads.

TOURING THE REGION

Because of the sometimes extraordinary desert heat, it's best to see it by rented car, if at all possible. If you are traveling by bus, choose one or two places to see intensively, rather than scurrying from site to site in the heat. Dehydration occurs very quickly. Keep emergency water with you at all times. It's a good idea to bring along salt pills and insect repellent.

1 South to Beersheva

83km (52 miles) S of Jerusalem, 113km (70 miles) SE of Tel Aviv

A few years ago, this town of 130,000 was the "Dodge City" of Israel—only the adventurous came here to work and live. Today,

What's Special About the Dead Sea & the Negev

Major Cities
- Eilat, the Red Sea resort with great beaches, snorkeling, dining, and night-clubbing.
- Beersheva, a development town, center for the northern Negev.

Ace Attractions
- The Dead Sea, the beautiful, unearthly salt lake where sinking is impossible.
- Ein Gedi Nature Reserve, an enchanted canyon oasis where David hid from King Saul 3,000 years ago.
- Ramon Crater, one of the largest in the world, a geological and ecological dazzle.
- Hai Bar and Timna nature reserves, noted for desert wildlife and countryside.
- Red Sea Beach and Coral Reef at Eilat, teeming with exotic fish and international tourists.

Historic Sites
- Masada, the legendary desert fortress where Jewish resistance to Rome ended in mass suicide.
- Avdat, with ruins of a Nabatean and early Christian desert city.

Kibbutzim
- Sde Boker—Ben-Gurion retired here; a lavish green vision of the Negev's possible future. Perhaps Israel's most inspiring place.

Special Events
- Arad Hebrew Song Festival, with performances by popular Israeli singers and groups. Late July.
- Eilat Red Sea Jazz Festival, featuring performances by Israeli and international musicians in mid- to late summer.

Beersheva is the capital of the Negev, and that old spirit is dwindling, as housing developments and municipal buildings go up in the new part of town.

Still, as you travel from Tel Aviv to Beersheva, the face of the countryside changes; hills disappear and green fields turn dustier; housing projects give way to occasional black tents; the metal of the car burns you as you rest your arm on the window.

Beersheva is another of the ancient cities of Judah. The book of Genesis contains two versions of the story of the town's origin. The first tells of a covenant made between Abraham and Abimelech over a well that Abraham had dug in the desert here. The second story also involves a well, dug by the servants of Isaac, who gave the well and the town its name: "And he called it Shebah: therefore the name of the city is Beer-sheba unto this day." The phrase "from Dan to Beersheva" appears repeatedly throughout the Bible. Dan is at the northern boundary of the Israelites' territory; Beersheva at the southern end.

Beersheva has been a watering place and trading post for thousands of years, due to its locale on the northern fringe of the Negev. But as a town, its history dates only from its founding as an outpost of the Ottoman Turkish Empire in 1907.

Increasingly, tourists use this ancient biblical town as their base of operations for excursions into the desert. From here it's only an hour to Sodom and the Dead Sea and 3¹/₂ hours by bus to Eilat.

ESSENTIALS

GETTING THERE   By Bus   From Jerusalem or Tel Aviv, several buses make the 1¹/₂-hour ride every hour. There is no bus service in Shabbat.

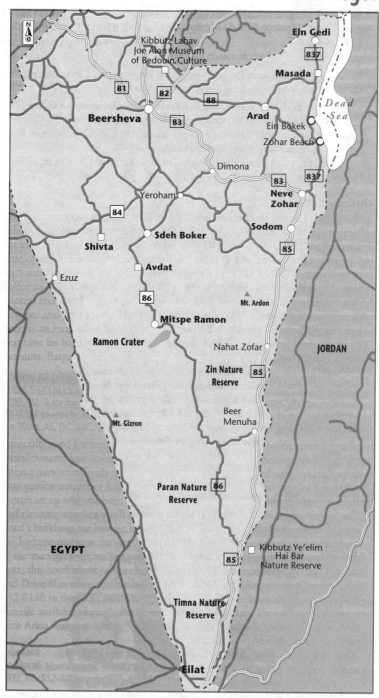

The Negev

By Sherut   Contact **Yael Daroma,** whose terminals are at 32 Rothschild Blvd., Tel Aviv (☎ 03/566-0222), 12 Shamai St., Jerusalem (☎ 02/257-366), and 195 K. K. Le-Israel St., Beersheva (☎ 07/281-144). Sheruts usually operate (very sporadically) on Saturdays.

By Car   From Jerusalem I strongly advise the long route via Kiryat Gat, which circumvents the West Bank; from Tel Aviv, via Kiryat Gat.

VISITOR INFORMATION   The **Beersheva Tourist Information Office** (☎ 07/ 236-001) is at 6A Ben-Zvi St., located directly across the street from the Central Bus Station, in the Ein Gedi Building. It's open Sunday through Thursday from 8:30am to 5pm, on Friday until noon (closed Saturday).

All the shops and businesses in Beersheva close between 1 and 4pm, reopening from 4 to 7pm.

ORIENTATION

Beersheba's **Central Bus Station** is located on Eilat Street, across from the modern Canion Ha-Negev Shopping Center. To the left of the entrance to the bus station are stops for local buses to the Old City, where most of the hotels and restaurants listed below are located. A new railway station has been constructed nearby, but at present there is limited rail service to Beersheva. Other trains may be added, however, if a planned railway heading south to Eilat is put into operation.

West of the bus station, you'll find a Muslim cemetery, and beyond that, a small, densely packed business section of Beersheva. The **Old Town,** or the original Turkish and British Mandate–era town, is laid out as a grid. It is the commercial "downtown" of Beersheva, where you will find the shops and budget and moderately priced hotels and restaurants.

Herzl Street is the major downtown north–south thoroughfare. Main streets east and west are **Ha-Atzma'ut (Independence) Street** and **Keren Kayemet Le-Israel,** which has been made into a pedestrian mall. Right where Herzl and Ha-Atzma'ut intersect is the old Turkish city hall, the Allenby Garden; and behind the Turkish city hall is the Great Mosque, now the Negev Museum.

The rest of modern, apartment-complex Beersheva sprawls northward from the old downtown section.

WHAT TO SEE & DO
THE BEDOUIN MARKET

The famous Bedouin market is next to the municipal market, on the southeastern edge of downtown. Although the Thursday morning market, when the Bedouin tribes come in from the desert to buy and sell in the colorful marketplace, is no longer the exotic event it once was, you can still see Bedouins in long gowns, bartering over sacks of flour and coffee, and holding conferences on the dollar rate of exchange for hand-woven rugs and baskets. Most of the marketeering goes on between 5 and 7:30am.

While you watch the Bedouins, you can also pick up some (sometimes questionable) bargains yourself. Although most of the beautiful tribal crafts have vanished, you can find spices, sheared wool in sacks, copper and brass coffee sets with decorated trays, long knives, wood carvings, fancy Arabian saddles, bubble pipes, and rugs and baskets. You can also climb aboard a camel and be photographed (don't be perturbed by his protesting spits and snorts).

Plans are now in the works for the construction of several permanent shops at the market site, so that the arts and crafts can be displayed all the time. A motel is in the planning stages here as well; you can ask at the Municipal Tourist Information Office for current details.

MUSEUMS

Negev Museum Complex. 60 Ha-Atzma'ut St. ☎ **07/239-105.** Admission NIS 6 ($1.80) adults, NIS 3 (90¢) children. Sun 10am–6pm; Mon–Thurs 10am–4:30pm; Fri 10am–12:30pm; Sat 10am–1pm.

This museum, on the corner of Ha-Atzma'ut and Herzl streets, is housed in a turn-of-the-century Turkish mosque, in a pleasant little park in the center of the Old City. As you approach the mosque, note the graceful *tughra* (the Ottoman sultan's mono-gram) in a medallion over the main door. Old photographs of pashas, provincial gov-ernors, staff officers in ancient motorcars, and early settlers provide a fascinating glimpse into Beersheva's early days as a municipality.

You'll find several displays of excavations here; a model of Tel Beer Sheva from the Chalcolithic period (3500 B.C.) shows how the people lived, in underground cities and houses. Sixth-century mosaics from the church of Kissufim in the western Negev depict colorful desert scenes with inscriptions in Greek. Next to the part of the mu-seum housed in the renovated mosque is the former Turkish governor's mansion, where you'll find a collection of contemporary art; your ticket admits you to this part of the museum as well.

Museum of Bedouin Culture. Kibbutz Lahav. ☎ **07/918-597** or 913-322. Admission NIS 10 ($3). Sun–Thurs 9am–4pm; Fri 9am–2pm.

This museum, located several miles outside of town, is well worth a visit. Displays illustrate the way of life for Bedouin tribes in the Negev and the Sinai, and also the Jbaliyya (Jebaliya) tribe that has been associated for centuries with the Santa Katerina Monastery on Mount Sinai. There are folklore guides, and there is a traditional Bedouin tent where you can stop for spiced dessert tea or coffee.

To get there, drive north from Beersheva on the road to Tel Aviv; after 24 kilo-meters (14½ miles) you'll see a sign for Lahav, or Kibbutz Lahav, and the Joe Alon Center. Turn right here; go another 7 kilometers (4 miles) until you see the sign directing you uphill to the **Joe Alon Regional and Folklore Center;** the Bedouin Museum is part of this center. As you go uphill, you'll go through part of the Jew-ish National Fund forest, a shady place to stop for a picnic. There is no bus service.

MORE ATTRACTIONS

Abraham's Well is located at the southern end of Keren Kayemet Le-Israel Street, at the intersection of Derekh Hevron, down by the riverbed. Two large round stone walls, one open, the other covered by an arched stone roof, are surrounded by a stone courtyard, some desert date palm trees, and a wooden water wheel for drawing up the water. The wells are no longer in use, but you can still see the water far down below.

It may have been here that Abraham watered his large flocks almost 4,000 years ago, and settled a dispute with Abimelech over rights to the water. Scholars still can-not decide whether "Beer-Sheva" means "Well of the Covenant" or "Well of the Seven" for the seven ewe lambs that Abraham gave Abimelech as a peace offering. Behind Abraham's Well, look for signs to the **Ethiopian Jewish Handicrafts Exhibit,** which opened here in 1994. Its future at this location is not certain.

The pride of Beersheva is the **Ben-Gurion University of the Negev,** whose faculties include the humanities, the sciences, and a medical school. Many of the more than two dozen departments emphasize the development of the Negev. The imagi-native architecture combines awareness of climatic conditions with practical needs of the students and teachers. Tours can be arranged in advance through the **Guest Relations Department** (☎ 461-111). Visiting students might want to try the **Gimmel Disco,** open nightly except Friday when the action moves to the Library Building on the new campus. Foreign students can also take an *ulpan* (Hebrew-language course) here for credit.

The **old railway station** on Tuviyahu Street is worth a look. It was along the Beersheva line that ran to Egypt that Lawrence of Arabia played his train-blowing tricks.

ATTRACTIONS IN TEL BEER SHEVA

Of all Israel's war memorials, the **Monument to the Negev Fighters Brigade,** completed in 1969, is possibly the most original, certainly the most evocative. It is the work of Dani Caravan, one of Israel's most famous artists. It's on the northeastern edge of the city, just off the road that leads to Hebron, and commemorates the Palmach brigade that captured the Negev during the 1948 War of Independence.

The memorial, consisting of 18 symbolic sections, flows like a fantastic cement garden over the summit of raw windy hill. Here the entire Negev campaign has been reduced to its essentials: a concrete tent wall, a bunker, a hill crisscrossed by communications trenches, a pipeline, nine war maps engraved in the floor of the square. You can climb all over these structures and to the top of the tall cement tower (representing the watch and water towers that were shelled on the Negev settlements); you can file singly through the inclined walls of the pass that lead into the Memorial Dome, and enter the symbolic Bunker. Sadly, this memorial to those who fell in the battle for the Negev has not been well maintained and has been vandalized with graffiti.

The monument can be reached by taking bus no. 55, going to Tel Beer Sheva several times a day. Ask the driver to let you off near Andarta; it's about a 15-minute, half-mile walk up the hill.

The digs of many seasons have unearthed an ancient Israelite city at Tel Beer Sheva that can be seen at the new **archeological park.** The city walls and gates have been uncovered, and a dominant feature of the city, a circular street with rows of buildings on both sides. A deep well was found right outside the city gates and the city's central canalization project was discovered. A huge ashlar four-horned altar was found and reconstructed and is now in the Negev Museum, mentioned above.

A village of homes has been constructed in Tel Beer Sheva for the usually nomadic Bedouin (some keep tents nearby, perhaps in case four walls become a bit too much). A **Bedouin tent–restaurant** (☎ 07/273-308) has been set up, with an interesting exhibit called "Man in the Desert." There's also a **gift shop** carrying local Bedouin handcrafts, and even a camel, in case you want a ride. This is a tourist enterprise, and prices must be judged in this context.

To reach the area, take bus no. 55, running several times each day from the Central Bus Station.

OUTDOOR ACTIVITIES & PARKS

In Beersheva's hot, dry climate, there are several beautiful parks full of trees, playgrounds, and picnic facilities. **Pa'Amon Ha-Cherut Park** is located just across the riverbed from Abraham's Well, at the south side of the Old City. A much larger park, **Lon Grove,** is on the western outskirts of the city; go out Tuviyahu Boulevard, the road heading to Ashkelon and Gaza, and you'll see it on your left as you're almost out of town. Yet another park is **Gan Moshe,** located between City Hall and the Beersheva Theater, across Shazar Street from the Zohar Hotel. All of these are very pleasant places; take a look at the map and you'll see several more parks, large and small, dotted around town.

SWIMMING   Beside the parks, the four-star **Desert Inn** (☎ 07/424-922), located out the same way but just before Lon Grove, also on the left, has a pool; you will have to pay a nonguest fee. In the Old City, **Bet Yatziv Youth Hostel** and **Bet Sadot Valev Guesthouse** (☎ 07/277-444) have a large swimming pool behind the hostel. You'll find them at 79 Ha-Atzma'ut St., about three blocks northwest of Herzl Street, past the Turkish mosque. Admission is NIS 12 ($3.60) with a discount for guests of the hostel. It's open Sunday through Friday from 8:30am to 5pm, Saturday from 8:30am to 4pm.

ORGANIZED TOURS

It is possible, while in Beersheva, to join a group tour for a visit to a **Bedouin encampment and a Bedouin-style dinner.** Ask at the Tourist Office across from the Central Bus Station. The cost will be anywhere from $12 for the "short visit," which consists of a chat with the sheik over coffee or tea, camel ride, and Bedouin music, to about $25 or $30 for the full "sunset visit" with Bedouin dinner, which includes the above as well as a typical rice, mutton, and fruit meal, eaten with the fingers or in pita. Prices include transportation, and can be higher if there are fewer than 25 people in the group. It is a good idea to phone ahead before reaching Beersheva to find out when the next group is going out.

WHERE TO STAY

Desert Inn (Neot Midbar). Shderot Tuviahu, Beersheva. ☎ **07/424-922.** Fax 07/412-772. 164 rms (all with bath). A/C TEL. $60–$80 single; $80–$110. Rates include breakfast. 15% service charge. AE, DC, MC, V.

Built in the 1960s and located away from the center of town, this is the only hotel in Beersheva above the rock-bottom level. It's utilitarian, rather than stylish, but comfortable, with a heated outdoor swimming pool, a children's pool, three tennis courts, basketball courts, a sauna and hot tub. There are also three in-house restaurants.

WHERE TO DINE

Beersheva has never had a stunning culinary reputation, but the dining situation is starting to improve. For an inexpensive meal, there are many quick-service counter restaurants in the pedestrian mall on Keren Kayemet Le-Israel Street. The air-conditioned Kanion Shopping Mall across from the Central Bus Station has Pizza Hut, Burger Ranch, China Town, and a number of other places to grab a bite for $4 to $6. Also, the omnipresent shashlik and french fries aren't bad.

INEXPENSIVE

✪ **Apropo.** 32 Herzl St. ☎ **07-236-711.** Reservations recommended. Appetizers NIS 13–30; main courses NIS 22–50. 12% service charge. AE DC. Sun–Thurs 9am–midnight; Fri 9am–2pm; Sat after Shabbat–midnight. EUROPEAN/INTERNATIONAL.

The most stylish restaurant in town, both in terms of food and decor, Apropo offers a large variety of menu items, ranging from salads and omelets to genuine Thai dishes, and inventive dishes with a touch of Asian or Thai flavor. You can even order kosher faux "shrimp" in a number of styles, or fish steamed in the Thai manner but seasoned with Mediterranean-style herbs. With its kosher dessert list, this is also a good choice for a leisurely coffee and cake. Service is usually excellent; the service charge is obligatory.

⑤ Bet Ha-Fuul. In Gan Ha-Nassi Park. No phone. Light meals NIS 10–22 ($3–$6.60). No credit cards. Sun–Fri 7am–midnight. HUMMUS/FELAFEL.

Located near Ilie Restaurant, between Herzl, Ha-Histadrut, Ha-Avot, and Smilansky streets, this place is not much in terms of decor, but it's popular with the locals for its good food. A hearty lunch might include hummus or Egyptian fool beans with sauce and a boiled egg, assorted salads, and fresh, thick pita bread. The outside felafel counter is open daily until 8 or 10pm, and serves a fine felafel.

Ilie Steak Restaurant. 21 Herzl St. ☎ **07/278-685.** Reservations recommended weekends. Appetizers NIS 8–20 ($2.40–$6); main courses NIS 33–48 ($10–$14.60). No credit cards. Sun–Thurs noon–midnight; Fri noon–3pm. STEAK.

What this place lacks in decor it makes up for in good, fresh food. Set a little farther down Herzl Street than Ha-Mirpesset, this restaurant is not fancy, despite its wall-size photograph of camels, and a meat-and-fish display. House specialties include Romanian kebab and sirloin filet steak, grilled over charcoal.

BEERSHEVA AFTER DARK
PERFORMING ARTS

Beersheva is justifiably proud of its **Israel Sinfonietta** (☎ 07/231-616), which performs throughout the country. Tickets are by subscription, but you may be able to buy a ticket before the performance at the box office. The concerts start promptly at 8:30pm. Concerts are also given at the S. Rubin Music Conservatory (☎ 07/231-616). The **Beersheva Theater** performs at Bet Ha-Am, in the Hever Community Center, the large white building in Gan Moshe Park. Performances are usually in Hebrew only. Check with the Tourism Information Office (6A Ben-Zvi St., ☎ 07/236-001) for current programs.

PUBS & CAFES

Beersheva has a number of cozy pubs, especially on the southern side of Old Town. Stroll around, listen to the music, and see the lights flood the streets from the open doors. At 18 Ha-Avot St. (☎ 07/276-670), there's **Trombone,** housed in a charming, whitewashed Turkish limestone building. Open daily from 9pm to 2am.

The most spirited of these pubs is the **Simta Coffee Theater,** 16 Trumpeldor St., which sometimes features wild, participatory nights of Israeli folk songs, jazz, or country music. It's open daily from 8pm to 2am. Other pubs, with a touch of desert delirium, are tucked away on Shloshet Bnei Ha-Od Street between Ha-Avot and Smilansky streets. Several of the places I mentioned as restaurants have nice bars and pubs, too.

FOLK DANCING

There are several places to go for folk dancing. Saturday nights, starting at 8pm, there's dancing at **Ben-Gurion University;** on Thursday, dancing is held at **Makiv Gimel High School,** on Mitvza Yoav Street in the Shechuna Bet District (take bus no. 12). Tuesday evenings, there's dancing at **Skateland** (☎ 07/235-186). Skateland is found in the southern part of the city; go out Keren Kayemet Le-Israel Street, past Abraham's Well and the riverbed, and go about 1 kilometer (half mile); you'll see Skateland on the left, across from Montana (a good place for an ice cream).

EN ROUTE FROM BEERSHEVA TO ARAD

As soon as you leave Beersheva, you'll see clusters of Bedouin tents and flocks—and also houses, for today the Bedouin are being encouraged by the government of Israel to settle down.

At the first major intersection not far from Beersheva take the right turn for Arad and the Dead Sea. A bit farther on you'll begin to see Bedouin villages—the Abu-Rabiya tribe has four such settlements between Beersheva and Arad, all fairly close together. The villages consist largely of huts and some planned housing projects. At times it may be possible to see a few traditional black goat-hair tents, which are amazingly cool in summer and warm in winter. Some villages may be quite large; others may be nothing more than three houses and five tents. Another thing to note is that the Bedouin here do a lot of farming, growing mostly wheat, but also other grains, and fruits and vegetables, most of which they sell in the Beersheva markets. A great deal of experimental agricultural work is being done along this road: sisal is grown without irrigation; tamarisk, eucalyptus, and other trees are planted in small areas, where their growth is watched carefully by scientists who are planning to cultivate even more of Israel's desert.

When the road starts snaking around tight curves, you'll know you're approaching Arad.

2 Arad, Neve Zohar/Ein Bokek & Sodom

Arad: 60 km (80 miles) E of Beersheva

ARAD

The modern desert city of Arad is not a mirage, but rather a well-planned town located on the site of an ancient Israelite settlement—a concrete testimonial to the continuity of Jewish history. Located about 30 miles east of Beersheva, it is regularly served by buses and sheruts. Arad is the logical place to stay if you're coming east from Beersheva, or if the youth hostel at Masada is full up, which often happens. Although there are several hotels at Neve Zohar/Ein Bokek, and more being built, they cater to those coming to take the curative waters.

It is interesting to note that Arad is a planned Western-style city, begun in 1961, and mapped out to efficiently meet the rigid desert restrictions in the most comfortable manner. Unfortunately, some now believe a city plan more rooted in desert tradition, with narrow, shaded, labyrinthine streets, might have been more successful. The cityscape is bleak here, and even more so in some of the other planned settlement communities in the Negev, such as Yeroham and Dimona. However, people are working to make these places succeed—Israel's future is here, and the way these desert cities eventually develop will shape the country's direction.

Arad is some 2,000 feet above sea level and its ultradry climate is considered a blessing to sufferers of asthma and similar troubles. Each year it grows more popular as a vacation place for singles, couples, and families; by staying here, you are at the doorstep of the powerful, charismatic desert.

ESSENTIALS

GETTING THERE   By Bus   There is regular bus service from Jerusalem, Tel Aviv, and Beersheva.

By Car   Main highways run east from Beersheva and west from the Jordan Valley at the southern end of the Dead Sea.

VISITOR INFORMATION   The post office is at the corner of Hebron and Ben-Yair. The **Tourist Information Office** is in the **Arad Visitors Center** at 28 Ben-Yair St. (☎ 07/954-409). Follow the signs to find the office in the commercial center of the town, opposite the Community Center. It's open Sunday through Thursday from 9am to 5pm and on Friday from 9am to noon; closed Saturday. There are publications of the Society for Protection of Nature in Israel (SPNI) here (some free, some for sale), including information about the area (including a video presentation), books, maps, and desert hiking gear. The Visitors Center can also give you advice about hotels and rooms in the area, and book you onto tours, treks, and other desert activities.

ORIENTATION

Driving into Arad is like entering almost any small modern city—there are wide highways with overhanging lights, highrise apartments everywhere, a sleepy commercial center, and an air-conditioned shopping mall *(merkaz)*. As Arad is a town of only some 15,000 souls (but growing), finding your way around it is simplicity itself. You will probably come into town from the main highway **via Hebron Street.** The third cross street is **El'azar Ben-Yair** (named for the leader of the stronghold at Masada in A.D. 73). The corner of Hebron and Ben-Yair is the town's principal commercial center.

Once you've reached the **commercial center** you've just about got Arad figured out. Go east on Ben-Yair for a kilometer or two; the street's name will change to Moav Street, and you'll be in the hotel area. Go only three blocks east from the post office on Ben-Yair, turn right (south) on Ha-Palmach Street, and you'll be headed for the youth hostel.

WHAT TO SEE & DO

Most people come to Arad's high, dry location for relief of asthma rather than for sightseeing. However, you should make the effort to see the spare landscape from the far eastern end of Ben-Yair/Moav Street near the Hotel Masada. At the road's end, a path begins, heading out to a modern sculpture on the promontory.

Most everything can be found at the commercial center, including food, clothing, cosmetics, stationery, banks, a hairdresser, pharmacy, and a photography store.

Many activities take place at the **Matnas Cultural Center** opposite the Tourist Information Office. Youngsters meet on Friday night, and local activities like the **Chess Club** and **Melave Malka,** the **Bridge Club,** and the **folk dancing group** meet once a week. You can obtain a schedule of events from the Tourist Information Office.

For the past decade, in mid-July, a **Hebrew Song Festival** (mostly rock music) has turned Arad into a desert mecca for teenagers and students, but in the summer of 1995, a stampede at the festival resulted in a number of deaths and injuries and left the country in a state of shock; the future of this event is now in doubt.

Arad is such a friendly place that it's a good spot to **Meet the Israelis.** Ask at the tourist office.

Four miles west of Arad is Tel Arad, a partially reconstructed 5,000-year-old Canaanite town with a 3,000-year-old Israelite fort. It's open October through March, Sunday to Thursday, from 8am to 4pm; until 5pm the rest of the year, closing an hour earlier, respectively, on Friday and holiday eves. The entrance fee is NIS 8 ($2.40).

WHERE TO STAY & DINE

In Arad, you can stay in the hotel area, in a smaller, modest hotel downtown, or in the youth hostel. It is also possible to rent a room in a private home. Check with the tourist office. However, you can ask shopkeepers or most anyone on the street, and if they can't help you, they'll probably have a friend who will. Arad has few restaurants, but snack places can be found in the commercial center.

Arad Hotel. 6 Ha-Palmach St., Arad 80750. ☎ **07/957-040.** Fax 07/957-272. 48 rms (all with shower). A/C. $41 single; $67 double. No credit cards.

The two-star-equivalent Arad, between Yehuda and Atad streets, is the only real downtown hotel. It has a garden full of roses and cacti, and is decorated with a 6-foot driftwood sculpture. The clean and comfortable rooms sleep up to five people, and all are heated. Students do not pay the 15% service charge.

Margoa Arad Hotel. Moav Street, Arad 80750. ☎ **07/957-014.** Fax 07/957-778. 146 rms (all with bath). A/C TEL TV. $73–$83 single; $100–$114 double. AE, DC, MC, V.

This excellent semiluxury choice offers hotel rooms and cottages as well as a pleasant restaurant/dining room. The large swimming pool is open from the spring (Passover) to the late fall (Sukkot). Entertainment is sometimes available. The Margoa also offers a clinic for asthma sufferers.

Nof Arad Hotel. Moav Street, Arad 80750. ☎ **07/957-056** or 957-057. Fax 07/954-053. 117 rms (all with bath or shower). A/C TEL. $55–$63 single; $74–$92 double. Rates include breakfast. MC, V.

Across the street from the Margoa, this three-star establishment has cabins and hotel rooms. Rooms in the hotel's new (1984) wing are more luxuriously furnished and cost about $5 per person more. The hotel features a swimming pool and offers self-service breakfasts.

EN ROUTE TO NEVE ZOHAR & SODOM

If you're traveling during Israel's 7 dry months, be sure to get an early start; by noon a weird kind of languid breathless heat settles over the entire area.

The ride from Arad to the Dead Sea (just 45 minutes) is almost all downhill—the word *steep* is hardly adequate. From Arad's heights, where the land is a chalky sandy color, the wilderness to the west turns increasingly darker, changing to tans and then deeper shades of brown. During the 28½-kilometer (17-mile) trip, the scenery will doubtless hold your attention. You'll pass through the **Rosh Zohar** fields of large underground reservoirs of natural gas. Don't miss an observation point to the left, called **Mezad Zohar.** For the best view, be sure to lean against the rail of the sunshelter and look out and down. Here are remains of a **Roman fortress,** in the valley that once served as the major roadway from the Dead Sea. (These desert valleys, or wadis, were carved out over the centuries by fierce and sudden rains.) A second observation point is a bit farther down; there is a huge map to help you identify what you're looking at. Then the road swings down to reveal a vista of the Dead Sea and part of the Judean wilderness beyond it.

If you come directly from Beersheva (by bus, sherut, or private car), you'll drive just over an hour, and you can take the road through another of those desert development towns, **Dimona.** The most famous of Israel's hastily constructed boomtowns, Dimona was the subject of considerable controversy, because at one time many thought it was inhuman and impossible to expect people to live and work in such a climate. However, the handful of tents that started the town in 1955 soon became a community of 22,500 people living in cement housing complexes—a town complete with movie theaters, cultural centers, textile and phosphate plants, and even an atomic reactor.

Three miles farther, on the right, is a deserted stone blockhouse—a former police station on a high hill that stands on the site of **Mamshit,** an ancient Byzantine town. Nearby, in a deep gorge, are three **ancient dams,** in which 6th-century A.D. engineers were able to store enough water to sustain the residents. Mamshit is one of the many old desert cities under close scrutiny by Israel's modern scientists, who are convinced that many of the inventive methods of water collection and desert living devised by these ancient cities are still applicable in the Negev.

Beyond a Roman fort called **Tamar** (20km, or 12 miles, farther on), the road descends rapidly. Abruptly, around a turn, you are confronted with one of Israel's most amazing sights—and certainly the most bizarre. Surrounded by the Moab and Edom mountains, the Dead Sea is 3,000 feet below, in a heavy haze.

Soon you pass the sea-level sign, as you descend through the Arava plain, passing potash and bromide factories along the way. Signs commemorate the workers who were ambushed constructing this road in 1951, and the actual opening of the road to Sodom in 1953. Suddenly, you are at the edge of the **Dead Sea,** the lowest point on earth, 1,300 feet below sea level. (Death Valley in California, America's lowest point, is only 282 feet below sea level.)

Half of the 48-mile Dead Sea is in Israel's territory (about 100 square miles of it), but even working with that little area the technicians find that they can scarcely deal fast enough with the vast reservoir of chemicals being constantly removed from the sea. This water is 25% solids, of which 7% is salt—six times as salty as the ocean. Each day, tons of chlorides, bromides, and sulfides are removed for processing and export. No fish can live in these miles of mineral-rich liquid.

NEVE ZOHAR/EIN BOKEK & THE DEAD SEA

It is a 45-minute ride from Arad to the Dead Sea. The main highway intersects a road paralleling the coast. Turn right for Sodom and the Dead Sea Works, and for the highway to Eilat. Take the left turn to Ein Bokek, Masada, and Ein Gedi (this road goes all the way to Jerusalem).

Just before the intersection, there is a gas station on your left; from here you can also see the **Neve Zohar Camping Site.** Just across the road from the camping site is an excellent place to take your dip in the Dead Sea. But a few words of caution: Wear sandals and a hat—the sandals protect your feet from sharp stones, and the hat prevents your head from sizzling. And be sure to keep the water out of your eyes— it burns! The water has a very bitter, oily taste should you accidentally get a mouthful, but it's almost impossible to go under accidentally; you float on the Dead Sea even if you don't know how to float. Afterward you may opt to rinse off with a shower or leave the mineral residue on your body until bedtime, as some Israelis do. They say it's healthy and good for the skin. In fact, many physicians recommend soaks in the Dead Sea. Israelis also take the black mud from the sea bed and smear it on their bodies. It is especially good for anything that stings, and muscle and joint ailments.

ZOHAR SPRINGS

Unlike the waters of Ein Gedi's spa, those at Zohar Springs (Hamei Zohar) (☎ 07/584-201) can be very helpful for skin diseases like psoriasis. These were Cleopatra's favorite waters for her beauty needs, and today the waters are said to be cleansing for skin and scalp, improving skin texture, and even smoothing wrinkles.

Experts came out here in the 1960s, had the waters analyzed by Hadassah experts, and found that they contained the highest mineral content of any waters in the world: 300 grams per liter. People with doctors' notes can take advantage of a weight-loss program devised by the local medical team—but the current management prefers to emphasize the strictly curative powers of Zohar Springs. "In the baths here," they explain," you take 10% to 14% more oxygen than in any other water in the world, which is helpful for people with respiratory problems and heart disease. In addition, tired and nervous people come here for a week and it changes their lives. . . ." The experts here will tailor the treatment baths to your specific ailment. If you want the whole spa treatment, though, you'll have to have a medical okay. You can be examined by a resident physician, but a doctor's note certifying that your blood pressure can stand the stimulation of the waters will suffice. In order to really get any benefit from the Dead Sea spas, you must stay here for at least 1 or 2 weeks. You can do this economically by staying at the hostels at Masada, Ein Gedi, and Arad and commuting. The four- and five-star hotels at Ein Bokek, though expensive, are the only way to really do an intesive, relaxing program of spa treatments.

The spa is quite a luxurious place. It is equipped with a central air-conditioning system, excellent facilities in the sulfur baths and pools, mudbaths, vibration and electrogalvanic baths, underwater massages, and cosmetic treatments. The baths are open every day of the week from 7am to 3pm. It's advisable to check your valuables.

WHERE TO STAY

All hotels in this community offer health and beauty programs, but these should not be your only reason for staying at a hotel in Neve Zohar or Ein Bokek; they also provide a very comfortable base for exploring the desert and enjoying the Dead Sea. Both Hilton Hotels and Hyatt Hotels will be building luxurious new properties at Ein Bokek/Neve Zohar during 1996–98. The Hyatt Hotel alone will account for 600 new rooms in the area.

Expensive

Radisson Moriah Plaza Dead Sea Spa Hotel. Dead Sea. ☎ **07/584-221;** 800/221-0203 or 212/541-5009 in the U.S. or Canada. Fax 07/584-238. 220 rms (all with bath). A/C TEL TV. $165–$200 single; $205–$255 double. Discounts on Radisson Moriah 7- and 9-Day Packages; special long-term and spa treatment rates. Rates include breakfast. 15% service charge. AE, DC, MC, V.

With an inspiring private beach and perhaps the most extensive programs of therapeutic and beauty treatments at its spa, the Radisson Moriah Plaza is at the top of the list of the Dead Sea's best hotels. This is a comfortable base for exploring the desert and Dead Sea region as well as for the various spa treatments. Rooms are spacious, with balconies overlooking the sea; minibars are availble on request. Facilities include indoor and outdoor swimming pools (heated) including one indoor Dead Sea water pool, natural sulfur pools, sauna, Jacuzzi, mudpack treatments, massage, solarium, and psoriasis treatment center. In addition to the main dining room, there is an Italian dairy restaurant, piano bar, pool cafe, and lobby lounge. Radisson Moriah Hotels packages make staying here possible at rates much lower than at less desirable hotels. The less expensive, nearby Radisson Moriah Dead Sea Gardens Hotel offers special long-term psoriasis programs and long-term stay discounts.

Nirvana Resort and Spa Hotel. Ein Bokek. ☎ **07/584-626.** Fax 07/584-345. 220 rms (all with bath). A/C MINIBAR TEL TV. $170–$190 single; $220–$250 double. Rates include breakfast. 15% service charge. AE, DC, MC, V.

The spirit here is a bit livelier and more innovative than at neighboring hotels, where many guests are in residence for therapeutic programs. The hotel has a convenient private beach, freshwater, saltwater, and mineral pools, complete health and beauty packages at its spa, three restaurants, bar and disco, fitness center with sauna and hot tub, and an in-house synagogue. Readers report the dining facilities as superior. Public areas and guest rooms are also among the most stylish in the area.

WHERE TO DINE

Kapulsky. Ein Bokek, Dead Sea. ☎ **07/584-382.** Main courses NIS 21–48 ($6.30–$14.30); cakes and desserts NIS 9–15 ($2.70–$4.50). MC, V. Daily 8am–midnight. CAFE/LIGHT MEALS.

For passers-through as well as guests at local hotels, this is one of the better choices, with a glassed-in terrace overlooking the Dead Sea. Kapulsky's is a national chain, famous for rich desserts and pleasant light meals. At this branch, the selection is often limited (depending on demand and what's been shipped into this remote location), and prices are somewhat higher than elsewhere in the country. When supplies are in you can order fish, pasta dishes, salads, and sandwiches.

SODOM

Retrace your drive along the shore, back to whichever highway (Arad or Beersheva) brought you to the sea-hugging road. Don't turn there; just keep going and you'll reach Sodom in 10 kilometers (6 miles). The wicked city of Sodom, lowest inhabited place on earth, is no more. The famous citadel of degeneracy is now a potash concession, not a real town as such. Here the road that runs along the Dead Sea shore is bordered on the left by a wall of solid salt. Reportedly, one of the pillars along the bordering wall is Lot's wife. According to the biblical story of the destruction of Sodom and Gomorrah, angels intended to save Lot, nephew of Abraham, and his family; in telling them to run for it, they also admonished them not to look back. Lot's wife, however, turned back in curiosity and was mummified in perpetuity as the pillar of salt. The legendary pillar—which does suggest such a shape—stands above the entrance to the Sodom cave (now closed).

The fire and brimstone that hit Sodom and Gomorrah was probably a Tertiary-era volcano that shattered this area, according to scientific evidence. A proposal to construct a gambling casino here drew a wrathful protest from religious leaders. Their objection? The city was destroyed once for its wickedness; don't tempt history to repeat itself.

The calm, oily sea is on one side; bizarre, agonizing mountain slopes on the other. Clumps of white foam, a solid brine, cling to the dried shrubs and clumps of whitened stone. There is a noxious smell of sulfur in the air, and some of the trees next to the sea are petrified and laced with gypsum and bitumen crystals. Nearby, however, is Moshav Neot Ha-Kikar—proof that even the most arid and desolate desert land can be reclaimed.

3 Ein Gedi & Masada

Ein Gedi: 50km (30 miles) S of Jericho, 15km (10 miles) S of Ein Gedi

Your adventure into the Negev can start from Jerusalem eastward through the Judean desert to the outskirts of Jericho, and then south along the dramatic Dead Sea road via Ein Gedi and Masada. The route from Jerusalem south through Bethlehem and Hebron to Beersheva is not recommended at this time. Don't fail to see Masada, and to take a dip in the Dead Sea at Ein Gedi. The road from Jerusalem along the Dead Sea coast passes the ruins of Qumran, near the caves where the first Dead Sea Scrolls were found in 1947. In addition to the Scrolls, hidden at the time of the First Jewish Revolt against Rome in A.D. 70, archeological excavations of caves in this region during the early 1960s uncovered mysterious and beautiful copper ritual objects, used 5,000 to 6,000 thousand years ago by members of a prehistoric civilization, as well as artifacts and personal documents and letters hidden by refugees from the Second Jewish Revolt against Rome in A.D. 135. Other caves in the area, their openings or interior reaches sealed by rockfalls over the centuries, may conceal still more treasures.

ESSENTIALS

GETTING THERE   By Bus   There is service from Tel Aviv via Jerusalem and from Eilat four times daily.

By Car   There are main roads to Eilat and Beersheva via Arad, and from Jerusalem via the Jordan Valley and the Dead Sea.

EIN GEDI

Ein Gedi has been an oasis in the desert for thousands of years. The Song of Solomon rhapsodized it thus: "My beloved is unto me as a cluster of camphire from the vineyards of Ein Gedi." After more than a thousand years of desolation, the region was resettled in 1949 by a group of pioneers who planted it with cotton, grapes, vegetables, and flowers. Beginning with nothing but fertile land, the settlers created a beautiful kibbutz with stunning views of the wild, unearthly area, including the desert cascade of Ein David Gorge, where the water drops from a height of nearly 300 feet.

WHAT TO SEE & DO

The spectacular waterfalls are within the **Ein Gedi Nahal David Nature Reserve** (☎ 07/584-285). Follow the trail and the signposts, winding through tall pines and palm trees up and into the desert hills. You proceed between slits in the rock formations, under canopies of papyrus reeds, and, after about 10 minutes of steady climbing, you'll hear the wonderful sound of rushing water. In another 5 minutes, your appetite whetted, you arrive at what is surely one of the wonders of the Judean desert—the Nahal David–Ein Gedi waterfalls, hidden in an oasis of vegetation that hangs in a canyon wall. In this miraculous place, the Bible records that the youthful David took refuge from King Saul 3,000 years ago. A second trail involving a 30-minute climb takes you to the **Shulamit Spring** and then to the **Dodim Cave** at the top of the falls. A 20–30-minute walk to the left brings you to the fenced-in ruins of a **Chalcolithic sanctuary** dating from about 4000 B.C. The mysterious copper wands and crowns on display in the antiquities section of the Israel Museum (found in caves above the Dead Sea during archeological searches for Jewish scrolls from the period A.D. 70–135) are thought to be the sacred vessels of this site. The reserve is open from 8am to 4pm. No food or cigarettes are allowed on the grounds. Admission is NIS 13 ($3.90). There is a snack kiosk at the entrance.

Near Ein Gedi are the ruins of **ancient Ein Gedi,** one of Israel's most important archeological sites. Ein Gedi was renowned throughout the ancient world for its exotic spices. A mosaic synagogue floor from the 3rd century has been excavated, as well as a later Byzantine synagogue superimposed on the original site. The extraordinary personal papers, letters, and possessions found in the Dead Sea caves and dated to the Second Jewish Revolt against Rome (A.D. 135) belonged to Jewish inhabitants of Ein Gedi who attempted to escape the Roman armies by hiding in the region's almost inaccessible caves. Yigal Yadin's book, *Bar Kokhba,* details these dramatic finds.

Across the Dead Sea to the far left are the **Moab Mountains,** where Moses was buried, and where Gad, Reuben, and half the Manasseh tribe settled after helping Joshua claim the rest of the Promised Land. To the right it seems the sea ends, but it's actually the **Ha-Loshon** (The Tongue)—a strip of peninsula from the Jordanian side, at about the middle of the Dead Sea. The water here is more than 1,000 feet deep, but from the other side of the peninsula to Sodom it's only about 15 feet deep.

About 5 kilometers (3 miles) south of Ein Gedi, **Hamme Mazor,** or the Ein Gedi Sulfur Springs (☎ 07/584-813), are housed in a modern building. Here you can take the mineral-rich spring waters on the shores of the Dead Sea, or have a meal. Admission to the spa costs NIS 40 ($12) for adults. Facilities include a total of six single-sex and coed indoor warm and hot mineral pools. There's a fish and dairy restaurant downstairs that serves lunch for $10 to $12. The spa has its own Dead Sea swimming beach and plenty of the famous Dead Sea black mud to smear on your skin. Come and take the waters any day of the week from 7am to 5pm. Any bus to Ein Gedi will drop you here; try bus no. 486 or 487 from Jerusalem.

WHERE TO STAY

Ein Gedi is not a full-fledged resort with hotels, but Kibbutz Ein Gedi has a popular and dramatically sited guesthouse; the youth hostel is good, and the Ein Gedi Holiday Village rents caravan bunglows on the shore of the Dead Sea. Make sure to reserve in advance. Beds are scarce and in great demand.

Moderate

Ein Gedi Guesthouse. Kibbutz Ein Gedi, Mobile Post, Dead Sea 86980. ☎ **07/594-222.** Fax 07/584-328. 120 rms (all with shower). A/C TEL TV. $78–$106 single; $124–$160 double. Discount available on Kibbutz Chain 7-Night Package. AE, DC, MC, V.

A beautiful place, with comfortable rooms, a swimming pool, gardens, tennis courts, and stunning vistas of the Dead Sea in the distance, this lowrise complex, set around a swimming pool, has the feel of a desert resort. The price for most stays here includes use of the Ein Gedi Spa, daily transportation to and from the sulfur springs and the beach, movies, slides, and lectures, as well as breakfast and one additional meal (there are few other dining options). As in many kibbutz hotels, however, guests clean their own rooms. The office is open from 8am to 8pm, and the kiosk for supplies opens twice daily. Full board is usually $12 per person additional. Lowest rates here are for January, February, and July. Reserve well in advance. Buses arrive from all cities on regular schedules.

Inexpensive

Ein Gedi Camping Village. Kibbutz Ein Gedi, Mobile Post, Dead Sea 86980. ☎ **07/584-342.** 65 caravans and 23 rms (all with shower). A/C. $58–$66 single; $75–$80 double. $18 per person for third or fourth person. $8 per person for camping. Sabbath surcharge. Rates include service. DC MC V.

This practical but not very beautiful official camping village has both caravans and motel-style rooms, all close to the beach. Twenty-five of the units are recently built and quite pleasant; four of the caravans are deluxe. The caravans can accommodate five people. Minimum occupancy of four people on Jewish holidays, weekends, and whenever else the place may be busy (usually March 15 to June 15 and September 15 to November 15); Friday night to Saturday night add 50%. There's also a nearby self-service restaurant at the beach called **Pundak Ein Gedi.** Guests staying at the village get a 15% discount. The air-conditioned restaurant seats 140 people and serves breakfast, lunch, and "tea" (until 4:30pm). Main courses are NIS 18 to NIS 30 ($5.40 to $9). Guests also get discounts for the Ein Gedi Spa restaurant and for the Ein Gedi Nature Reserve.

MASADA

It is a national tradition to have made the ascent at least once—for Masada is the scene of what many believe is one of the most heroic and tragic incidents in Jewish history. Few non-Jews outside Israel had heard of Masada until the events were dramatized in a book and a subsequent television miniseries in 1981. The story of a small garrison that defied the Roman army, as the historian Flavius Josephus recorded and perhaps embellished it, is worth retelling.

King Herod had built a magnificent palace complex and fortress atop this nearly inaccessible desert plateau mountain around 30 B.C. Underground cisterns assured the fortress of an adequate water supply. Most impressive was Herod's personal winter villa, the extraordinary hanging palace on the northern tip of Masada, calculated to catch the breathtaking vistas of the lake as well as the refreshing breezes from the north. He furnished the luxurious place with every comfort as well as storehouses of food and arms, protecting the entire establishment with impregnable fortifications. The audaciousness of such an undertaking tells much about Herod's personality. After Herod's death, a small Roman garrison occupied the mount. However, during the Jewish revolt against the Romans in A.D. 66, a small band of beyond-the-mainstream Jewish zealots attacked and overtook the almost unattended fortress. They lived off the vast storehouses of food and had more than enough arms with which to defend themselves. The weapons were even put to use in raids on the surrounding countryside.

Finally, in A.D. 73, three years after the fall of Jerusalem and the end of the First Jewish Revolt, the Romans became so incensed with the Masada situation that they decided to put an end to this last pocket of Jewish resistance. After a lengthy attack using siege engines, flaming torches, rock bombardments, and battering rams, the Masada fortress was still in Jewish hands. But with 10,000 Roman troops camped on the hillside and daily bombardments smashing at the walls, it became only a question of time until the 900 defenders would succumb.

One brutal night attack spelled the end: flaming torches thrown at the fort's wall were whipped by a wind into the midst of the defenders, and the garrison's gates caught fire. The Romans, seeing that Masada was practically defenseless now, decided to wait until dawn and take it over in their own good time.

During that final night, the 900 men, women, and children who inhabited Masada held a strange meeting. Their leader, Eliezer Ben-Yair, in a lengthy and dramatic speech, as reported by Flavius Josephus (who, of course, was not actually present), persuaded his followers to accept death bravely, on their own terms. In the darkness at Masada nearly 2,000 years ago, one of history's greatest mass suicides occurred. Ten men were chosen by lot as executioners. Members of families lay side by side and bared their throats. After the rest had been killed, one man killed the other nine and ran himself through on his own sword. Two women and five children survived, hiding in one of the caves on the plateau. The Romans, who had expected to fight their way in, were doubly astonished at the lack of resistance and at the "calm courage of their resolution . . . and utter contempt of death." So, Flavius Josephus wrote, ended the Jewish resistance against Rome. Like almost everything in Israel, the meaning of Masada has become a matter of controversy, with many contending that the current glorification of a political stand that resulted in mass suicide is not good for the national psyche.

CLIMBING THE ASCENT

From the parking lot at the foot of **Masada National Park** (☎ 07/584-207), you've got two choices—climb on foot or ride the cable car that carries you almost to the summit. If you climb, especially in the summer months, be sure to start literally at the crack of dawn. The heat is murderous by the middle of the day. Climbers are frantically urged by the National Parks Authority to wear hats and drink as much as possible before starting up.

Climbers have two choices: the route from the Dead Sea side, or the one from the mountain side, facing in the direction of Arad. The route from the Dead Sea side requires from a half hour to an hour; it is called the **Snake Path** because of the steep, hairpin curves. Snake Path opens at 7:30am and closes at 3:30pm, and you must start down by then just to get to the bottom before dark. The same hours apply to the path up the other side. The mountainside path is called the **Battery,** after a battery the Romans built there. Getting to the top via that route takes only 15 to 30 minutes.

Admission to Masada is NIS 12 ($3.60); the cable car is NIS 12 ($3.60) for a one-way ticket, NIS 24 ($7.20) round-trip. Round-trip cable car fare plus admission is sold in a special package for NIS 36 ($11). Students and children get a third reduction. Cable cars operate Sunday through Thursday from 8am to 4pm, on Friday and eves of holidays (including Saturday) from 8am to 2pm. The cable car will deposit you about 75 very steep steps from the fortress top.

THE RUINS OF MASADA

Masada excavations have unearthed perhaps the most exciting ruins in the entire country in terms of physical drama and historical mystique. Masada remains a symbol of courage, and has long moved scholars, laypeople, and soldiers to make the ascent. Yigael Yadin's beautifully photographed book, *Masada,* carefully recounts the archeological expedition that uncovered the original palace, walls, houses, straw bags, plaits of hair, pottery shards, stone vessels, cosmetic items, cooking utensils, synagogue, and important scroll fragments. Among the most intriguing finds are the ways the palace was adapted for use as a stronghold for guerrilla fighters and their families. Evidence from this period includes ritual baths *(mikvehs)* built by the observant defenders, and the ostraca marked with Hebrew names that might have been the very lots cast by the defenders in their final moments as they decided who among them would be chosen to kill the others rather than die at the hands of the Romans. You can also see the ruins of the Roman siege encampments, which provide an amazingly preserved visual lesson in Roman military field strategy. A later Byzantine chapel with a mosaic floor was built on Masada, and there are signs of Byzantine-era habitation in the ruined buildings of the palace.

WHERE TO STAY

Isaac H. Taylor Youth Hostel. Mobile Post, Dead Sea 86935. ☎ **07/584-349.** Fax 07/584-650. 140 beds. A/C. $17 with IYHA card; $18.50 nonmembers; $23 per person double room. Rates include breakfast.

The youth hostel at Masada offers dormitory-style beds and kitchen privileges. Each six- to eight-bed room now has its own shower and can be easily converted into a family or private accommodation. Meals are available from $6 to $8. Reserve in advance—the closest accommodation is 42 kilometers (25 miles) away in Arad.

4 Into the Negev

The Talmudic scholars say that Negev means "dry," and Old Testament experts claim it means "south." Both are correct—in literal terms. A vast wasteland of almost 4,000 square miles, this desert is Israel's future—for population expansion, for chemical industries, and for farming. In fact, studies show that one-fifth of the desert can be used for some form of agriculture.

This region is a constantly varying landscape of red, black, and yellow, accented by valleys, deep craters, and burnt-brown mountains. Craggy limestone walls, mounds of sandstone, red and green dunes of sand are everywhere strewn with great blocks of black volcanic silex. Sawtoothed mountain ridges, abruptly hollowed out by the wild gorges left from the Great Middle Eastern Earthquake, starkly point back to the day when these mountains just fell down and this desert opened its granite jaws to everything living on top of it. In this petrified desert world, temperatures can range from 125°F during the day to 40°F in a winter dawn.

There are two possible routes into the Negev. The faster route is to head toward the Jordanian border and take the highway from Sodom to Eilat, but the scenery is stark. Or you can go to Beersheva and take the older and slower but more interesting route through the heart of the Negev to the port of Eilat on the Red Sea. If you choose the latter, there are several major points of interest along this bleak but fascinating road. If you're going by sherut or driving yourself, stop the car at some uninhabited spot and listen to the almost frightening stillness. Equally mysterious are the secondary roads—cryptic paths winding their way into the flatlands and beyond the dunes, toward agricultural collectives. The port of Eilat on the Red Sea is at the end of the road. Be sure to bring extra water when you drive this road, both for yourself and your car.

You will see black-tented Bedouin camps, though these will grow sparser as you proceed farther south—all natural growth is in the northern part of the Negev, so even the perennial wanderers do most of their wandering in the northern desert regions.

Roughly 32,000 Bedouin roam Israel's deserts and hills—an estimated 27,000 in the Negev, 5,000 in the Galilee mountains. Until recently they haven't respected border lines very much, but Israel has been campaigning to entice them with benefits: clinics and hospitals give their babies free service, the government has provided them with land, and some have settled down to become nonmigratory workers.

SHIVTA

Shivta is an impressive site, but it's in the middle of nowhere and has no facilities. If you have a car or plan to go on a tour, this can be a very worthwhile, atmospheric excursion; otherwise spend your time at Avdat.

Shivta is about 50 kilometers (30 miles) southwest of Beersheva, in the military zone about 5 miles off the Nizzana road. It's important not to get lost in the military zone, so here are explicit directions: From the highway, the Shivta road is two lanes and paved for the first $2^1/_2$ kilometers ($1^1/_2$–2 miles). It then narrows, and after another kilometer you pass a road, on the left, to the military installation. After passing this road, it's another 5 kilometers (3 miles) over a rough, curvy one-lane road to Shivta. There are few signs. Officially Shivta is a national park, but there is no office or telephone at this deserted location. Admission, if anyone is around to collect it, is NIS 5 ($1.50); half price for children under 18.

The Nabateans built a way station here in the 1st century B.C., but Shivta (or Subeita) became rich and famous during the time of Justinian the Great (500s), when Byzantine wealth and power were at their height. Caravans laden with pilgrims and merchandise made their way between Egypt and Anatolia, the Red Sea and the Mediterranean, and many stopped at Shivta. Besides this commercial wealth, Shivta's ingenious citizens built an elaborate irrigation system that allowed them to farm the barren soil.

But Shivta's location on major trade routes proved its undoing; the easily accessible city was overrun by Arab armies, the trade routes slowly changed, and, though Shivta survived as an Arab outpost many centuries, by the 1100s it was a ghost town.

The ruins of Shivta remained in fairly good condition throughout the centuries because they were too far away from newer building sites to make pillage economical. As a result, the city, which dates from the 500s, is still intact. Restoration work began in 1958, and restored buildings include three churches, a mosque, a caravansary, and houses. Signs identify and discuss the principal buildings.

SDE BOKER

About 50 kilometers (30 miles) due south of Beersheva, surrounded by sand and parched mountains, you suddenly come to a farm settlement—the famous Ben-Gurion kibbutz, Sde Boker. The settlement was begun in May 1952, at the prime minister's instigation, when the country was first encouraging settlers to populate the Negev. Ben-Gurion became a member of this kibbutz in 1953; he lived and worked here until his death in 1973, at the age of 87. He and his wife, Paula, are buried here, and many of his books and papers may be seen in the **Paula and David Ben-Gurion Hut** (☎ 07/560-320). Visiting hours are Sunday through Thursday from 8:30am to 3:30pm, on Friday, Saturday, holidays, and holiday eves from 9am to 1pm. Groups are asked to phone in advance. Bus no. 60 from Beersheva runs to the kibbutz every hour from 8:30am to 2:30pm. The stop for the Ben-Gurion house is the first after the kibbutz.

Over the years Sde Boker began to thrive, as did several other young settlements in the Negev. A campus of the Ben-Gurion University of the Negev has been established at Sde Boker. A modern library, housing the **Ben-Gurion Institute and Archives,** and containing 750,000 documents associated with Israel's first chief of state, is located here. The institute also serves as a center for the study of desert areas.

Ten kilometers (6 miles) south of the Paula and David Ben-Gurion Hut is the national parks archeological site of **Avdat** (☎ 07/550-954). This was a city of the Nabateans, the same desert people who built a magnificent city at Petra, in Jordan, which was their capital.

Besides the Nabatean ruins, you can see Roman and Byzantine construction. Most impressive is the north church, with still-standing columns, and apse. A booklet, on sale at the site, explains it all.

In addition to the ruins, Avdat offers a commanding view of the desert. Avdat, restored with U.S. government funds, is administered by the national parks department. Admission is NIS 13 ($3.90); half price for those under 18. It is open from 8am to 5pm, but if no one is on duty during these hours, just enter.

MITZPE RAMON

Mitzpe Ramon, 139 kilometers (84 miles) south of Beersheva, appears to be a typical Negev development community if you approach it from the north. What you don't immediately see is the town's location right at the edge of the spectacular **Ramon Crater,** a vast, breathtakingly beautiful geologic depression formed by erosion that has exposed a virtual encyclopedia of fossils and geologic structures. Founded in 1954 as a clay-mining town and way station on the long road being built in the 1950s through the desert to the then-isolated outpost of Eilat, Mitzpe Ramon was bypassed by the new, more direct road to Eilat built through the Arava Valley after the 1967 war.

Mitzpe Ramon struggled to survive as a viable economic community during the 1970s and 1980s. The Ramon Crater (which had not been picked up by aerial surveys during British Mandate times, and which was only discovered after the 1948 War of Independence) had not yet captured the imagination of travelers. It has only been since 1990, with the establishment of the Ramon Inn to accommodate middle- and upper-range visitors, that a tourism industry has begun to develop here.

The community has a great public spirit, and gives you an opportunity to get a feel for day-to-day life in the kind of Negev community that Ben-Gurion envisioned as an important part of Israel's future. You can also feel the isolation and mystery of the Negev plateau. Sunsets and twilights at the edge of the crater usually bring out an extraordinary vista of changing colors, as the landscape slowly sinks into darkness.

WHAT TO SEE & DO

The **Mitzpe Ramon Visitors Center** (☎ 07/588-620) at the edge of the crater, housed in a large modern structure designed to resemble the spiral-shaped sea fossils embedded in the local rocks, is manned by staff trained by the Society for Protection of Nature in Israel (SPNI), and the bookstore/gift shop is a good place to pick up background and hiking information as well as topographical maps. There are slide and film shows, and a museum exhibit of the area's geology, flora, and fauna. Admission is NIS 9 ($2.70). It is open Sunday through Thursday and Saturday from 9am to 4:30pm, Friday 9am to 3pm.

The Ramon Crater is perhaps at its most accessible in the spring or fall, when it's not too hot or too bitterly cold. Whenever you happen to visit, it is worthwhile to invest in a professional tour or guide. **Desert Shade** (☎ 07/586-229), a tour company with offices in Mitzpe Ramon and Eilat (☎ 07/335-377), offers a range of activities including Jeep tours that leave Mitzpe Ramon at 8am, noon, and 4:30pm and cost $24 for adults, $15 for children. Desert Shade also arranges 2- and 3-day desert expeditions, including accommodations in Bedouin-style tents, camel tours, mountain-bike rentals, rappelling, escorted hikes, and Bedouin evenings, complete with dinner. **SPNI** offers excellent nature hikes, but you must book in advance. SPNI's office in Jerusalem is at 13 Helena Ha-Malka St. (☎ 02/244-605); in Mitzpe Ramon, contact the SPNI field school at 07/581-516. Guided bus tours to the crater (minimum of 20 people generally required) run about $4.50 per person.

For an overview of the Ramon Crater, turn left as you exit the Visitors Center, and follow the 1-kilometer (six-tenths of a mile) promenade alongside the crater's rim. Sunset is a good time for walking; with luck, you'll spot an ibex in the distance, or an eagle aloft on the evening wind. In the opposite direction, you'll find the wonderful **Desert Sculpture Park,** with the sky and the crater as the backdrop for works by a number of international and Israeli artists. To get there, drive out of the Visitors Center, make a left onto the main road, and past the gas station on the right, make a right turn at the sign for Ma'ale Noah.

The **Alpaca Farm** (☎ 07/588-047) is 3 kilometers (1.8 miles) outside of town. Founded in 1987, this establishment raises both alpacas and llamas, and produces fine alpaca and llama wool. The alpacas have a charm of their own, and after the Ramon Crater, they have become the town's most memorable tourist attraction. Adorable, gentle, and fluffy, they quickly bond with anyone carrying a small paper bag of feed sold on the premises for NIS 4 ($1.20). At times they may spit (they are distantly related to camels), but they mean nothing personal. You can also visit the llama herd, but the llamas are not as whimsical. Guided **llama treks** through the Ramon Crater can be arranged through the Alpaca Farm, with gentle, intelligent llamas carrying your packs and serving as mounts for small children. The Alpaca Farm has an open-air snack bar with light meals costing $3 to $5. Admission is NIS 8 ($2.40); children pay NIS 6 ($1.80). The farm is open daily 8:30am to 6:30pm.

WHERE TO STAY
Moderate

✪ **Ramon Inn.** 1 Aqev St., Mitzpe Ramon. ☎ **07/588-822,** or 800/552-0140 in the U.S., 800/526-5343 in Canada. Fax 07/588-151. 96 rms (all with bath). A/C TEL TV. Suites for two to six persons, low, regular, high seasons: $75–$260; $95–$280; $108–$300. Rates include breakfast. Half board $20; full board $45. Substantial discounts on Isrotel and Kibbutz Hotel Chain plans. AE, DC, MC, V.

With its comfortable accommodations, the Ramon Inn has made the beautiful countryside around the Ramon Crater accessible to the kind of traveler who was unwilling to stay in the youth hostel or the field school. The inn has also brought hope of a genuine tourist industry to the economically depressed community, and the entire town is helping to make the project a success. An apartment block was totally renovated to create the inn: the very comfortable, tastefully decorated living room/bedroom suites with kitchenettes were once small apartments. Public areas are sleek but friendly, and the lobby sports a freestanding fireplace for chilly desert nights. The spirit of the staff is wonderful, but perhaps best of all are the inn's fabulous buffet meals (see below). There is no swimming pool yet, but the community pool is just across the road. Although this is not a kibbutz, you can include the Ramon Inn on the Kibbutz Hotels Chain Guest House Plan and get a considerable discount.

Inexpensive

Bet Noam Youth Hostel. Mitzpe Ramon. ☎ **07/588-443.** 160 beds. $18.50 dorm; $23 per person double room. $1.50 discount for IYHF members. Rates include breakfast. No credit cards.

The lowest budget option in town is the modern, IYHF youth hostel, with 160 beds, family accommodations with private bathrooms, hot showers, cooking facilities, and a cafe and supply store. Unfortunately, there is no air conditioning. The hostel, which is close to the Visitors Center and the edge of the Ramon Crater, serves a hefty breakfast, as well as kosher lunches and dinners, for $6 to $8.

✪ **Succah in the Desert.** P.O. Box 272, Mitzpe Ramon 80600. ☎ **07/586-280.** 6 succot (desert shelters made of natural materials). $60–$70 single for 3 nights; $90–$100 double for 3 nights; two vegetarian meals per day, $15 per person per day extra. No credit cards.

Succah in the Desert, 7¹/₂ kilometers (4¹/₂ miles) outside of Mitzpe Ramon, is the vision of Rachel Bat Adam, who has created a place to experience the desert's immense silence, its calculation of time, the wind and stars; she hopes it is a place to live on the earth as a guest and not as a settler. Six *succot* or simple shelters dot the landscape around the central succah, which serves as the place for meals and as a central place for guests to meet. Each succah is different, but all are made with walls of sheltering rocks, roofs of natural materials, and have areas open to the air. There are carpets covering earthen floors, tribal objects and objects formed in nature for decoration, comfortable mattresses, blankets and bed linens, an enormous clay jar in which water is kept miraculously cool, copper vessels for washing, and ecologically correct solar-powered lamps. In winter, there are solar heaters. For those who do not wish to blend totally into nature, there is a nonpolluting toilet and a solar shower near the main succah. The staff of this encampment has an agenda of meditation and spiritual renewal, but you are free to come and go as you like as long as you do not intrude on the quiet of others. Only vegetarian meals are served. Tourists and passersby can stay overnight in a succah in a sleeping bag (if there are vacancies) for NIS 115 ($35) per night for one to three people. Breakfast for 1-night guests is extra. If you have no car, call from Mitzpe Ramon for transportation or hiking instructions. For students, prices may be a bit negotiable.

Staying in a Bedouin-Style Tent

For a less expensive desert experience, **Desert Shade Tours** (☎ 07/586-229; fax 07/588-074) rents space in Bedouin-style tourist tents in the crater. Bed and breakfast is $16; other meals are $10. Call ahead for reservations. In-season only.

WHERE TO DINE

✪ **Ramon Inn Restaurant.** In the Ramon Inn. ☎ **07/588-822.** Full meal $20. AE, DC, MC, V. Dinner 7–9pm. INTERNATIONAL.

Like the Ramon Inn hotel, the restaurant is an effort that involves many residents from the town of Mitzpe Ramon. The menu here is composed of family recipes prepared by the best local cooks and served in an all-you-can-eat buffet that varies from night to night; when it's good it is one of the best meals you'll find in Israel. The choices change each night, but represent traditions that range from Morocco and Yemen to Russia and Hungary, and I strongly urge you to sample everything! Then zero in on a dish with herbs, seasonings, or sauce that catches your fancy. Dessert, sometimes exotic, sometimes rather average, is included, as are coffee, tea, and other beverages. The restaurant also serves a buffet breakfast and lunch, with many special homemade jams, salads, and other unusual items. If you are a guest at the Ramon Inn and charge your meal to your room, the 17% VAT should be deducted from the price if you pay your bill in foreign currency.

KADESH-BARNEA

Scholars have three different versions of the route they believe Moses took as he led the Jewish people out of Egypt and into the Promised Land. But all three versions converge at Kadesh-Barnea, located about 40 kilometers (24 miles) to the east of Mitspe Ramon.

Kadesh-Barnea served as a center for the confederation of tribes that wandered in the Negev and the Sinai during the time of Abraham; it was also called Enmishpat at that time. But most of the biblical references to it are connected with the time of the Israelites' sojourn in the desert under Moses. It was from Kadesh that Moses sent 12 men to spy out the land of Canaan, at Kadesh that he smote the rock and got water, and here that his sister, Miriam, died and was buried.

There has been a longstanding controversy over the location of the biblical Kadesh; early in this century, a general consensus emerged, identifying the site with **Tel el-Qudeirat,** located in the fertile valley watered by the spring of Ain el-Qudeirat. Excavation has unearthed three fortresses built one atop the other, the earliest dating from the early 10th century B.C., the latest existing up until the time of the destruction of the First Temple (586 A.D.). Numerous examples of pottery and *ostraca* (tablet writings) have also been found here, but no traces of the followers of Moses, a fact not inconsistent with the nomadic character of that society. But although we see no evidence of their passing, it is very moving to stand here and look around at the scenes where the great biblical stories took place. Kadesh-Barnea is well represented at the Negev Museum in Beersheva, and also in the Rockefeller Museum in Jerusalem.

5 Eilat

243km (151 miles) S of Beersheva, 356km (221 miles) SE of Tel Aviv

This city at the southern tip of the Negev is the country's leading winter tourist resort. Eilat's chief claims to fame for the tourist are fine beaches, coral reefs filled with exotic fish, and year-round sunshine. At the moment, the once easygoing, relaxed desert and Red Sea resort town is undergoing a construction revolution, with gargantuan four- and five-star hotels being put up wherever possible. The architectural style of Eilat's hotels and shopping malls has been agreed upon—new buildings are all of white concrete with straight, crisp geometric lines; older hotels are being redesigned to conform to the light, airy look. There is a unity to the new Eilat, but from the outside, most hotels seem to vary only in size and shape. Planners have not emphasized the desert and Beduoin traditions of the region—instead they've aimed for the generic look of a gleaming white international resort, like Cancun, Mexico. If you're hoping for a touch of regional color in your hotel, you'll have to try the Sinai or the new five-star establishments in Petra (Jordan).

Eilat is also a combination military outpost and shipping port—you'll see ample evidence of this all along the shoreline. The city's present first-class hotel area is less than a mile from the Jordanian border and you can see the Jordanian port city of Aqaba, with a population of 20,000 across the bay, dazzling in a haze of desert sand, ringed by date palms. For almost 50 years, until Israel and Jordan signed a peace treaty in 1994, Aqaba seemed as unattainable as a mirage. There is now a border crossing for tourists just north of Eilat, and you can also book excursions to Jordan's fabulous Petra from Eilat. At present you cannot go across merely to check out Aqaba for a few hours; to enter Jordan you have to have a valid visa and stay at least overnight. For some time, Egypt, Israel, and Jordan have quietly been planning a regional coordinating committee and international park that will protect the ecosystem of this end of the Red Sea, in anticipation of the regional peace agreement. Meanwhile the area remains the most peaceful of Israel's borders. A few years ago, before the peace agreement, when one of King Hussein's prize race horses bolted and swam from Aqaba to Eilat, he was returned as if such incidents were an everyday occurrence. Saudi Arabia is 20 kilometers (12 miles) south of Aqaba; to the west are the mountains of Sinai.

It was from the port of Eilat that King Solomon sent and received his ships from the land of Ophir, laden with gold, wood, and ivory, dominating this exotic trade route with Hiram of Tyre, Solomon's famous naval ally (Hiram was king of the Phoenician trading city of Tyre on the Mediterranean coast north of Israel). It is even thought by some that the Queen of Sheba landed at Eilat when she came to Jerusalem to see Solomon and "commune with him all that was in her heart." From 1000 to 600 B.C., Phoenician shipping from Eilat plied the shores of East Africa and at times developed trade with the coasts of India and even Southeast Asia. There is evidence that on occasion, Phoenecian vessels circumnavigated the African continent. Today the port is again bustling.

Eilat has a youthful, adventurous spirit that seems to move the entire population. Israelis who had begun to find the north too confining and cramped have moved down here for the challenge; so, too, have a few who practice yoga, pluck guitar strings, and who, in general, were displeased with "the people up north." This is an individualist's town, and it's also a town for making money.

During summer, the outdoor afternoon heat in Eilat can exceed 110°F, or 45°C; it's best to stay in the shade between noon and 3pm, to avoid sun poisoning. In winter, the thick dusty heat is gone, the air is cool and dry, yet the water is warm enough for swimming.

ESSENTIALS

GETTING THERE   By Plane   Several daily Arkia flights (☎ 07/371-311 or 371-828) arrive from points north. The downtown airport can receive only small aircraft; larger planes land at Ouvda airport, 60 kilometers (37 miles) north of Eilat. One-way flights from Tel Aviv or Jerusalem are approximately $80; if you fly both ways, you'll miss the Negev Desert close up, but there are good flight/hotel packages offered by Arkia. El Al passengers can also purchase an add-on to Eilat with their flight ticket to Israel. The bus ride from Ouvda to town can take an hour.

Eilat

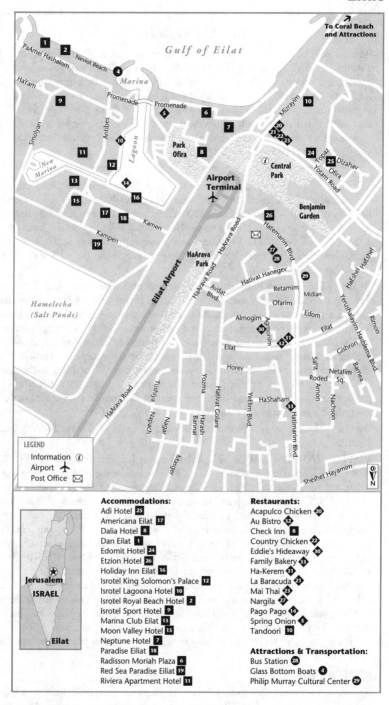

Gulf of Eilat

To Coral Beach
and Attractions

LEGEND
Information ⓘ
Airport ✈
Post Office ✉

Accommodations:
Adi Hotel 25
Americana Eilat 17
Dalia Hotel 8
Dan Eilat 1
Edomit Hotel 24
Etzion Hotel 26
Holiday Inn Eilat 16
Isrotel King Solomon's Palace 12
Isrotel Lagoona Hotel 10
Isrotel Royal Beach Hotel 2
Isrotel Sport Hotel 9
Marina Club Eilat 13
Moon Valley Hotel 15
Neptune Hotel 7
Paradise Eiliat 18
Radisson Moriah Plaza 6
Red Sea Paradise Eiliat 19
Riviera Apartment Hotel 11

Restaurants:
Acapulco Chicken 20
Au Bistro 12
Check Inn 8
Country Chicken 22
Eddie's Hideaway 30
Family Bakery 33
Ha-Kerem 31
La Baracuda 21
Mai Thai 23
Nargila 27
Pago Pago 14
Spring Onion 5
Tandoori 10

Attractions & Transportation:
Bus Station 28
Glass Bottom Boats 4
Philip Murray Cultural Center 29

From Eilat to Jordan

Bus service is now available from Eilat to Aqaba, Jordan, at the United Tours Terminal in Eilat. Fares are NIS 4.80 ($1.50) each way. Buses stop at the hotel district, the airport, and the New Commercial Center in Eilat before continuing on to Aqaba via the Arava Crossing north of Eilat. Passengers must have a Jordanian entry visa and must pay a crossing fee of NIS 48 ($15) from Israel into Jordan. For those coming from Aqaba to Eilat, the crossing fee is $6. As regulations are constantly being revised, check with the Eilat Tourist Information Center for the latest information.

If you arrive at Eilat's little downtown airport, you will be right at the bottom of the hill, where Hatmarim Boulevard meets Ha-Arava Road (the road north to Beersheva). It will be a 10-minute walk to almost any of our Hatmarim Boulevard hotels and hostels, or to the hotels on the North Beach. All the local city buses (no. 1, 2, or 15) run every 20 to 30 minutes or so, from early morning until about 7 or 8pm. They run daily except Saturday, stopping early on Friday (about 3 or 4pm) in observation of the Sabbath.

By Bus   There are a number of daily buses (except on Shabbat) from Jerusalem and Tel Aviv to Eilat. The trip takes about 4$^{1}/_{2}$ hours. If you arrive by bus, you will be planted in the center of town on the main street—Hatmarim (or Ha-Temarim) Boulevard. From there, hostel row, just around the corner on Ha-Negev Street, is within walking distance; local city buses no. 1 and 2 go from the Central Bus Station to the North Beach area, around the lagoon, and down as far as the Jordanian border. You must take a taxi, or city bus no. 15, if you're heading out to Coral Beach. You can also leave your luggage at the bus station. It is best not to even think about carrying luggage even short distances in Eilat's hot weather. For your return bus ride out of Eilat, the Egged information phone number is ☎ 07/375-161.

By Car   The trip takes approximately 4 hours by direct road from Tel Aviv and Jerusalem.

VISITOR INFORMATION   The **Eilat Tourist Information Center** (☎ 07/372-111) is located in a new white building set back from the road at the corner of Arava and Yotam roads. Pick up a free English-language map and a copy of "Events in Eilat." You can also get help and advice on hotel and hostel accommodations, bus schedules, discount coupons, and schedules of events in the region. The staff here, headed by Karen Peer, was the most efficient and best informed I've encountered in the country, especially attuned to the problems of budget travelers. In the same building, you'll find the **E. T. I. Attractions Office** (☎ 07/370-380; fax 07/370-434), which shares a shop with a small branch of Steimatzky's Bookstore. At E. T. I. you can book tours of the Eilat region, diving cruises, and excursions to Sinai (see below) with the highly respected **Neot Ha-Kikar,** as well as package tours to Petra and to Egypt. Hours for the Tourist Information Center are Sunday through Thursday from 9am to 9pm; Friday, Saturday, and eves of holidays from 8am to 3pm.

Eilat has no VAT tax, but since many supplies have to be shipped in, prices tend to be higher.

ORIENTATION

There are three easily distinguishable areas in Eilat: the town itself, built atop hills that roll toward the sea; Coral Beach, with its great snorkeling, about 6 kilometers (3$^{1}/_{2}$ miles) south of town on the western shore of the harbor; and North Beach, a

10-minute walk from the center of town on the eastern shore of the harbor. North Beach is the most central and busiest public beach, and where you'll find the most restaurants, bars, and better-quality accommodations. It is also the site of an elaborate marina system that started with the building of an artificial lagoon, cutting several hundred yards inland in back of the "hotel row" section. Around this lagoon are hotels, restaurants, and a promenade filled with pubs, discos, shops, and street vendors. Here tourists can enjoy the sun, the red-tinted green waters, the calm, the dusty hills, and the cool desert breezes of night.

SPORTS & OUTDOOR ACTIVITIES

BEACHES   Although the waters around Eilat are safe, always take the elementary precaution of not going out too far alone, keeping in mind that depth is deceptive and that the numerous sharks are not particularly hungry for you; spiny sea urchins are the major danger.

North Beach is a sandy beach in front of the Radisson Moriah Hotel that extends as far eastward as the Dan Hotel; because it's free of coral and sea urchins, this is a good beach for ordinary swimming. Waterskis and boats can be rented, but make sure you know where you're going, because you don't have to ski very far to get into both Jordanian—and hot—water.

Coral Beach, which is a short drive or bus ride around the curve of the bay, is the better beach for snorkeling and diving. It's inundated with coral and fish, and snorkeling equipment can be rented. Much of Coral Beach is now a nature preserve, perfect for both first-time and intermediate snorkeling and scuba diving. *Warning:* Spiny sea urchins and sharp, burning corals are always to be avoided here; footware or flippers are advisable when swimming at this beach. Never put your feet down on the floor of the sea unless you can see that you will be standing on a clear, urchin-free space.

The Dolphin Reef is a new attraction and certainly the prettiest beach in Eilat, dotted with palm trees and thatched-roof palapa structures for shade. Once in the water, you'll find the area designated for humans, with its sandy floor, is also the best in Eilat for swimming. The dolphins are an added attraction. As you swim and sun, you can watch them frolicking and being fed just beyond the roped-off human zone; you can also walk out to a wooden observation pier in the dolphins' free-swimming area for a closer look. Or, for about $44 per person, you can join a guided group of snorkelers for a 20-minute swim among the dolphins. (Advance reservations are recommended.) Sometimes, especially when the dolphins are ready for a meal, this can be an expedition of wonderful close encounters; at other times, the free-swimming dolphins (who are under no obligation to perform) keep their distance. You must be a good swimmer. There are no guarantees, refunds, or rainchecks. For $21, you can sit right on the float while the dolphins come up to the trainers for snack and trick sessions. The Dolphin Reef also hosts a program of scientific studies, as well as a program in which people with medical or emotional problems may visit and interact with the dolphins as part of their therapy. From time to time you may notice participants in these programs on a raft in the dolphins' free-swim zone. The reef's institute believes in informal, personal relationships between humans and dolphins, and has even had plans for the dolphins to witness a human underwater birth.

There is a reasonably priced cafeteria serving hot and cold drinks, snacks, and full meals on the premises, as well as a pub and a program of films on dolphins. The whole feel of the beach is friendly, easygoing, and interesting. Many evenings and nights, when admission to the beach is free, there is live or disco music and dancing. All in all, this is one of the best places in Eilat to spend a day or an evening.

Dolphin Reef is on Southern Beach (P.O. Box 104, Eilat; ☎ 07/371-846) and is open daily from 9am to 5pm. Admission is NIS 25 ($7.50), NIS 20 ($6) for children, from 9am to 5pm, with no admission fee after 5pm, when the restaurant and beach continue to be open, but when the dolphin sessions finish for the day.

BOATING   You can hire boats 24 hours a day at the North Beach marina and lagoon—boats for waterskiing and water parachuting, sailboats, fishing boats, paddleboats, motor sea-cycles, sailboards, and kayaks are all available.

GLASS-BOTTOM BOATS   Boats leave from the jetty just north of Coral Beach, or from North Beach near the Neptune Hotel. These boats offer a wonderful view of a fairy-tale marine world, with mounds of coral and clusters of rainbow-colored fish. **Israel Yam** (☎ 07/375-528) operates daily 1 1/2-hour glass-bottom boat trips, leaving North Beach several times during the day for about $10 per person. For a trip down by the Coral Beach Nature Reserve and the underwater observatory/aquarium, a newer state-of-the-art vessel that offers underwater vistas is the ***Jules Verne Explorer*** (☎ 07/334-668). The price is $17 per person. Mornings, when the sea is calm, usually provide the clearest water for viewing. A 50-minute dive in the ***Yellow Submarine*** (☎ 07/376-666) runs about $55 for adults, $30 for children, including entrance to the Coral World Observatory. A child in the company of two adults goes for free.

SAILBOAT CRUISES   Several yacht and sailboat cruises will take you on a full-day (10am to 5pm) excursion to **Taba,** on the Egyptian border, or to **Coral Island and the Fjord**—two points of interest along the Egyptian Sinai coast south of Eilat. If you go to the Egyptian coast, you can't land (you won't have a visa, and there's no Customs post on the beach!), but you can swim from the boat, snorkel, scuba dive, relax in the sun on board, and have a lunch that is included in the cost of the cruise. For a bit more money, you can also waterski or go sailboarding for a full or half day. Cost for all day is about $25 to $35, lunch included (several of the boats have kosher kitchens); prices start at around $7 for a simple sail. Special diving cruises can, of course, go above the $50 range. Walk along the marina in front of the North Beach lagoon and see which boat or itinerary appeals to you; you can reserve in advance at most travel agencies, at the marina, or at large hotel desks.

SNORKELING & SCUBA DIVING   The best-equipped firm for snorkeling and scuba diving is **Aqua Sport,** also called the International Red Sea Diving Center (P.O. Box 300, Eilat; ☎ 07/334-404). Right across the highway from the Red Sea Sports Club Hotel on Coral Beach, the Aqua Sport center can fulfill your needs for mask, fins, and snorkel ($8 per day for the complete ensemble), wet suits, weight belts, depth gauges, buoyancy compensators, cylinders, etc. Diving lessons (in English), diving tours (half or full day), and even 3-day camping/diving or snorkeling safaris are on the program. A 6-day diving course ($235) leads to internationally recognized two-star diver certification; with 6 days' bed-and-breakfast at the divers' hostel, the cost comes to $345. Many other programs are offered as well, including rental and lessons in sailboarding. Bed-and-breakfast at the Aqua Sport hostel is $16 per day in double or quadruple rooms. Aqua Sport also has a program of week-long summer camps for kids ages 10 to 15 during July and August; parents can leave the kids and go off for a week, and the kids are exposed to a world of underwater and maritime activities and fun. Also operating through Aqua Sport is the School of Underwater Photography, with half-day to 14-day programs on underwater video and still photography. In the evening, there's a pub, underwater video films, and occasional live entertainment, dancing, etc. Aqua Sport is open every day from 8:30am to 2:30am.

Write directly to Aqua Sport for information on prices, programs, and to arrange for courses and trips.

Red Sea Sport Club, located at the Red Sea Sport Hotel (☎ 078/373-145), is another highly recommended diving center at the Coral Beach. It offers facilities similar to those at Aqua Sport, plus other activities including sailing, windsurfing, and boating, deep-sea fishing, night cruises, organized diving trips to Sinai, desert safaris, horseback riding, camel treks, canoes and paddleboats, waterskiing, and bicycle rental, in addition to its diving and sailboarding programs. There is even a special sauna facility for divers. It's open daily from 8:30am to 4:30pm in winter, until 6pm in summer.

Both of the above places offer introductory dives for people who have never done diving before and want to try it out. It costs about $44 for an hour-long, one-to-one session with a diving instructor, who spends about half an hour giving you the instruction you need to go down and another half hour with you 18 to 20 feet below the water, out in the Red Sea coral reefs. This is a great way to get a short introduction to diving before committing yourself to a full 6-day program.

OTHER OUTDOOR ACTIVITIES
BIRDWATCHING

Eilat is one of the best places on earth for birdwatching, due to its prime location on the Jordan Valley–Red Sea–Great African Rift Valley migration path between Europe and Africa. Migration times are twice a year: from September through November the birds head south to Africa, and from March through May they head back north to Europe.

Eilat's **International Birdwatching Center** on Hatmarim Boulevard (☎ 07/374-276), in the small City Centre Shopping Mall, is a storehouse for information and activities relating to birdwatching around Eilat. It conducts guided birdwatching tours daily between February 15 and May 30, from 8 to 10am, for a fee of $5; for a minimal fee, you can rent a pair of binoculars to use on the hike. Between February 15 and May 15 a general spring census of birds is conducted, in which you may participate. The center will also offer advice on birding throughout the country. The International Birdwatching Center is open Sunday through Thursday from 9am to 1pm and 5 to 7pm, on Friday from 9am to 1pm. Also visit the bird-banding station during the morning hours on most days of the week. Similar activities take place again in the fall. Lectures, nature films, literature, and background material are also offered.

If you would like to be in Eilat at the best time for birdwatching, you should know that each year in March, the center hosts an **International Birdwatchers' Festival** of growing renown. Write to the International Birdwatching Center, P.O. Box 774, Eilat 88106, for information about the many special programs and discounts on accommodations at the time of the festival. Throughout the year, the center currently can help arrange discount car rental programs.

✪ **Coral Beach Nature Reserve.** ☎ **07/376-829.** NIS 14 ($4.20) adults, NIS 7 ($2.10) for children ages 5 to 18. Daily 8am–5pm. Closed Yom Kippur. Bus: 15.

The reserve is just down the coast south of Eilat, a beautiful place, developed and set aside by the Israel Nature Reserves Authority for its wonderful natural coral reefs teeming with colorful, exotic sea fishes of every description. Illustrated books about the reserve are for sale at the snack bar/gift shop.

You get a flyer pointing out a number of underwater trails. For NIS 23 ($7) you can rent a snorkel, mask, and fins, or you can bring your own, or your diving gear.

Wings Over Israel

After the Second Revolt against Rome in A.D. 135, Judea was left so desolate that olives, the ancient staple of the region, were not harvested again for over a century, and according to tradition, even birds avoided the once verdant hills. The loss of the birds must have been especially noticeable. Today in Israel are found 91 resident species, 121 regularly migrating species, and over 200 winter or summer residents—an amazing number and variety for so small an area. In ancient times, the variety and number of birds must have been even larger. Israel is located on the main migration route of the birds of Europe and Western Asia to and from Africa. For millions of years migrating birds have followed the line of the below-sea Jordan Valley to the Great Rift Valley because they need warm air thermals to help them cover the distance between Europe and Africa. At times in the migration season—an amazing spectacle that includes overflights of 500 million birds—Israel hosts an estimated 85% of the world's stork population! Birds stop for several days' rest in the Galilee among the thriving kibbutz fishponds and farms along the Jordan River before continuing south across the Negev to Eilat.

The flight over the desert can be so difficult that exhausted birds commonly drop dead out of the sky, in the Western Negev and Sinai, sometimes only a short distance from a watering hole on the fringe of Israeli agricultural land. Some migrants, including a dozen families of storks, have become so habituated to the lush agricultural scene developed in Israel over the past decades that they have begun to breed in Israel rather than their traditional European nesting areas. During migration season the skies can be so thick with birds that they are a major hazard to military and commercial flights in the area. With the new peace agreements between Israel, Egypt, and Jordan, the governments of those countries have begun plans to build a network of migrating bird radar-tracking stations throughout the area in an effort to save the lives of both human passengers and the birds themselves. Over the next several years, this network will also be put to use for the benefit of worldwide bird enthusiasts who visit the region. Meanwhile, the first station of the network, the **Inter-University Institute for Research of Bird Migration,** is under construction at Latrun, in the foothills of the Judean Mountains not far from Jerusalem. It is scheduled to open in 1997, in cooperation with the Hebrew University of Jerusalem, Tel Aviv University, and Haifa's Technion, and will include a research center, a museum, and an auditorium for screening films. The institute will join Eilat's International Birdwatching Center, the Society for Protection of Nature in Israel, the Zipari Bird Park in Tel Aviv, and the Nature Reserve Center at northern Israel's Beit Ussishkin in Kibbutz Dan as a major resource for birdwatching enthusiasts traveling in Israel.

The nature reserve also operates a scuba program for novices in which you can dive tethered to an oxygen tank on a floating dingy—the safest, easiest way to dive! It costs $30 for 1¹/₂ hours, including instruction. There are showers and changing areas. *An important warning:* Be very sure to wear some sort of foot covering every time you enter the water here.

City bus no. 15 from downtown Eilat runs half-hourly, and takes you to Coral Beach in about 15 or 20 minutes.

✪ **Coral World** Underwater Observatory and Aquarium. ☎ **07/376-666.** Admission NIS 36 ($11) adult, NIS 25 ($7.50) children ages 5 to 16. Sat–Thurs 8:30am–4:30pm; Fri 8:30am–3pm. Bus: 15.

Located just south of Coral Beach is this fascinating complex. The complex consists of three one-story buildings on the beach with distinctive rounded roofs, and two underwater observatories, which are 100 yards out to sea in what is called the Japanese Gardens. A pier binds the observatories to the coast. In addition to the underwater observatories, you'll also find the **Maritime Museum and the Aquarium.** The aquarium is built so that you stand in the middle and the fish swim around you in a huge circular tank. The third building is a pleasant snack bar/cafe. There are also large outdoor observation pools—one for big sharks, and another for sea turtles and rays. The tower of the observatory rises out of the sea to a height of 20 feet; inside, a spiral staircase of 42 steps leads down to the observatory itself. Since the water in the gulf is generally crystal clear, observation of the magnificent fish and coral life is unparalleled.

The best time to visit the observatory is between 10am and 3pm. The Eilat local city bus no. 15 comes this way every half hour.

WHERE TO STAY

If there is a low season here, it is from May to June. Europeans tend to come from October to April; Israelis come from July to August. In the past, winter was Eilat's high season, but with the prevalence of air conditioning, and the development of the town for tourism, it's become a popular year-round spot.

Since the change is a gradual one, many hotels have developed their own systems for determining when to charge high- and low-season rates. High-season rates are usually charged during July, August, and the Jewish and Christian holidays; many places also charge high-season rates during the October-to-April period.

We'll start with hotels on the main centers of downtown Eilat (such downtown as exists), Hatmarim Boulevard and the New Tourist Center. Then we'll look at hotels in the bustling North Beach area, with many restaurants, nightclubs, and discos, both attached to and separate from hotels. This area is within walkable distance of downtown Eilat, especially in the relative cool of the evenings. A third hotel area is the Coral Beach, several miles south of town. For those into exploring the reefs, this is a good choice, since North Beach is basically coral-free. In the streets west of the Bus Station are numerous private hostels; the Tourist Information Center is the place to check on which are currently up to standard. You can also gather information there about rooms in private homes and rental apartments.

HATMARIN BOULEVARD
Moderate
Etzion Hotel. Hatmarim Boulevard (P.O. Box 979), Eilat 88000. ☎ **07/370-003.** Fax 07/370-002. 97 rms (all with bath). A/C TEL TV. $70–$95 single; $90–$120 double. 10% student discount. Rates include breakfast. AE, DC, MC, V.

Located right in the center of town, this three-star-equivalent hotel has a large dining room, sauna, swimming pool, snack bar, nightclub, and video movies. Ask about special discount prices.

NEAR THE NEW TOURIST CENTER
The New Tourist Center, right across (west of) the main highway from North Beach at the corner of Derekh Ha-Arava and Derekh Yotam, is a useful landmark and a prime nightlife area for Eilat's younger crowd.

Moderate
Edomit Hotel. New Tourist Center, Eilat. ☎ **07/379-511.** Fax 07/379-738. 85 rms (all with bath). A/C TEL TV. $80–$100 single; $114–$130 double. Rates include breakfast. DC, MC, V.

This three-star-equivalent, eight-story hotel, located to the rear of the New Tourist Center, has a swimming pool and offers rooms with heat, radio, and a sea view. A dairy dinner is available for $12. The Edomit also can arrange triple or quadruple rooms, and family plans, too.

Inexpensive

Adi Hotel. P.O. Box 4100, Eilat. ☎ **07/376-151** or **376-153**. Fax 07/376-154. 32 rms (all with bath). A/C T. $48–$58 single; $62–$74 double. AE, MC, V.

This modern, two-star hotel is set behind the New Tourist Center, up the hill and off Yotam Boulevard. Although hidden away, the quiet hotel is within walking distance to North Beach. Housed in a small, stucco building with a front patio, it has some rooms with balconies and a partial, distant view of the Red Sea. Go 50 yards west uphill behind the New Tourist Center in the Zofit (or Tzofit) Tahtit section of town; look for the red-and-white ADI sign.

Readers of this book get special reductions of 10%, except for Jewish and Christian holidays, when rates rise by 10%. These prices are for people arriving at the hotel; rates may be higher if you're reserving in advance, so be sure to clarify the price at the time you reserve your room.

NORTH BEACH

This is the main hotel district, covering the area from the northern shore of the Red Sea inland to the local Eilat Airport. An artificial lagoon has been created in the heart of this neighborhood, but it's not for swimming. A few hotels are right on the beach, but most hotels (including some of the most expensive) are anywhere from one to four blocks inland.

Very Expensive

Dan Eilat Hotel. North Beach, Eilat. For reservations, ☎ **800/223-773** in the U.S.; 0171/439-9893 in the U.K. Fax Dan Hotels, Tel Aviv, 03/527-1431. 378 rms (all with bath). A/C MINIBAR TEL TV. $165–$320 single; $215–$400 double; rates include breakfast. Jewish holiday increase. 15% service charge. AE, DC, MC, V.

Opened at the end of 1995, this five-star blockbuster is the newest of the well-managed Dan Hotels. Its location, right on a palm-dotted piece of North Beach just next door to Isrotel's Royal Beach Hotel, is excellent (and especially good for swimming); the hotel itself is glistening new and impressive. Rooms come in three categories: superior (standard), deluxe, and family (with additional sleeping alcove); designers were daring and decorated with bold desert colors. There's a Polynesian outdoor restaurant, a Mexican restaurant, a jazz cellar, and a nightclub, as well as a virtual reality laser arena.

Dining/Entertainment: 10 restaurants, bars and cafes, nightclub, jazz cellar.

Services: Concierge, secretarial services, 24-hour room service, children's programs.

Facilities: Two pools, fitness gym, Turkish bath, sauna, massage, Jacuzzi, squash courts.

✪ Isrotel Royal Beach Hotel. North Beach, Eilat. ☎ **07/368-888**; 800/552-0140 in the U.S.; 800/526-5343 in Canada. Fax 07/368-811. 363 rms. A/C MINIBAR TEL TV. $240–$480 single; $310–$565 double. Rates include breakfast. 15% service charge. AE, DC, MC, V.

Opened in 1994, this is the lavish new star of the Isrotel Chain, with a palm-shaded beach, airy, sparkling, beautifully furnished public areas, and a swimming pool landscaped around natural rocks and artificial waterfalls. Architecturally, this is one of the best hotel buildings in the country, with glass upper-story corridors that look out onto wonderful vistas of Eilat and the desert mountains. Rooms are graceful, decorated with well-chosen artwork and noninstitutional touches like wooden moldings around the ceilings; every room faces directly onto the Red Sea. There are standard, deluxe, and family rooms (which include a sleeping alcove for two children) as well as a variety of suites. Electric kettles with a supply of teas and coffees in each room are a convenient extra touch. The hotel offers a wide variety of ethnic and theme restaurants; among the most successful is the American-style Ranch House serving prime ribs, barbecue beef spare ribs, and charcoal-grilled steaks. Packages can make the Royal Beach available at lower rates.

Dining/Entertainment: 10 restaurants, cocktail lounge, English pub, disco, entertainment lounge, piano and terrace lounge.

Services: 24-hour room service.

Facilities: Swimming pool, paddling pool, sauna, steam bath, fitness room, gym, shops, free parking.

Expensive

Holiday Inn Eilat. North Beach, Eilat. ☎ **07/367-777**; 800/HOLIDAY for reservations in the U.S. and Canada. Fax 07/330-821. 266 rms (all with bath). A/C TEL TV. $161–$258 single; $207–$328 double; highest prices are for suites. Rates include breakfast. 15% service charge. AE, DC, MC, V.

On the Lagoon Waterfront Promenade, but a few blocks inland from the beach, the new (1994) nine-story Holiday Inn is a beautiful structure, but can seem a bit jumbled at busy times, with activities in its Carnival Lobby and Pub. Guest rooms are attractively decorated; an entire floor is reserved for nonsmokers. Facilities include a pool, heated in season, a health club, and a sauna.

✪ Isrotel King Solomon's Palace. North Beach, Eilat. ☎ **07/334-111**; 800/552-0140 in the U.S.; 800/526-5343 in Canada. Fax 07/334-189. 419 rms (all with bath or shower). A/C MINIBAR TEL TV. Low, regular, high seasons: $190, $210, $237 single; $214, $227, $292 double; less on packages. Rates include breakfast. AE, DC, MC, V.

If you decide to experience Eilat in its new incarnation as a luxury resort, this hotel, built in the early 1980s and the first of the city's five-star blockbusters, is a worthy choice. Located right in the center of things on the Lagoon Promenade (but, like many downtown hotels, a walk to the beach), the King Solomon is luxurious, with freshly redecorated rooms, and has perfected an amazing program of daytime and evening activities for kids, teens, and under and over 25ers. The pool is gracefully shaped around an island and is heated in winter; you can join the daily poolside aerobics there, or enjoy the open-air tropical snack bar. There's tennis, a health club, sauna, and Jacuzzi. For kids, in addition to daytime activities, there's a well-organized Snoopy Disco from 5 to 9:45pm. Adult entertainment is from 10:30pm on, and the downstairs Sheba Disco, with its laser sound-and-light system, is the acknowledged high-powered nightspot in town. The hotel's many restaurants are among the best in Eilat for quality kosher dining. Five-person suites with large terraces and private Jacuzzis can be a viable choice if you're with a family or group.

Reservations and package information can be obtained through the Israel Hotel Reservation Center (☎ 800/552-0140 in the U.S.; 800/526-5343 in Canada).

Isrotel Lagoona Hotel. North Beach, Eilat. ☎ **07/366-666**; 800/552-0140 in the U.S.; 800/ 526-5343 in Canada. Fax 07/366-699. 256 rms (all with bath). A/C MINIBAR TEL TV. $145–$205 single; $195–$275 double. Rates include breakfast. 15% service charge. AE, DC, MC, V.

Located on the lagoon, just beside the Isrotel King Solomon's Palace, the Lagoona is smaller and quieter than its more lavish neighbor, but certainly comfortable. There are many returnees among its clientele, and this branch of the Isrotel Chain often may have fewer children than the other branches. An atmospheric Bedouin Tent restaurant, with excellent food, a heated pool, and direct access to the Lagoon Promenade, are the strong features of this comfortable hotel. The highly recommended Tandoori restaurant is in the Lagoona's waterfront promenade.

Isrotel Sport Hotel. North Beach, Eilat. ☎ **07/333-333**; 800/552-0140 in the U.S.; 800/ 526-5343 in Canada. Fax 07/332-766. 327 rms (all with bath or shower). A/C MINIBAR TEL TV. $145–$205 single; $195–$275 double. Rates include breakfast. 15% service charge. AE, DC, MC, V.

As its name indicates, this Isrotel medium-rise property, just across the road from the palm-studded beach at the Royal Beach Hotel, offers a real emphasis on sports activities. Facilities (for which there is an extra fee) include tennis, basketball, squash, and raquetball courts, an excellent fitness center, heated pool for year-round swimming, massage programs, a sauna and hot tub. The hotel is very comfortable throughout, but less fancy than the nearby Isrotel King Solomon's Palace.

✪ Radisson Moriah Plaza Eilat. North Beach, Eilat. ☎ **07/361-111**; 800/221-0203 or 212/ 541-5009 in the U.S. Fax 07/334-389. 330 rms (all with bath). A/C MINIBAR TEL TV. $200–$260 single; $240–$300 double. 15% service charge. Rates include breakfast. AE, DC, MC, V.

The glistening, elegantly designed Radisson Moriah Plaza ranks just below the Royal Beach and the Dan as one of the three most luxurious hotels on North Beach. The entire hotel was rebuilt in 1992. Polished stone public areas lead out to meandering, natural-form swimming pools laid out amid rocks and small cascades. Staff and dining facilities are strong; the in-house Trattoria Italian restaurant is even a favorite among Eilat residents and features a special low-budget pasta menu in summer. Light, attractive style marks the guest rooms, most of which have balconies and water views. As the jewel in the Radisson Moriah Hotels Chain, this hotel is not always available in the Radisson Moriah Package plans, but it is excellent value when it is included. The location, on the beach and in walking distance to town, is a plus.

Dining/Entertainment: Two restaurants, pub.

Services: 24-hour room service, concierge, business center, hairdresser.

Facilities: Three swimming pools, including a water jet and a children's pool, health club, shopping arcade.

Neptune Hotel. North Beach, Eilat. ☎ **07/334-333.** Fax 07/334-389. 278 rms (all with bath). A/C MINIBAR TEL TV. $120–$230 single; $160–$270 double. Rates include breakfast. 15% service charge. AE, DC, MC, V.

Well located on the Lagoon Promenade close to the beach, the 20-year-old Neptune has a reputation for excellent service and good restaurant facilities. Totally renovated in 1994, the hotel offers a tastefully designed ambience at prices below what the other top-flight Eilat hotels charge. The swimming pool (heated in winter) is large and especially pleasant because its landscaping has had time to develop. Facilities include three restaurants, a disco, cafe, bar, fitness center, hot tub, message services, and shops.

Paradise Eilat Hotel. North Beach, Eilat. ☎ **07/335-050.** Fax 07/332-348. 247 rms (all with bath). A/C MINIBAR TEL TV. $140–$180 single; $172–230 double. Rates include breakfast. 15% service charge. AE, DC, MC, V.

Built in 1991, this is one of two lowrise Paradise/Koor Chain hotels in North Beach. The guest rooms surround a pleasant central pool area, which is the heart of the hotel; there's a large reception area (good for receiving groups) but a rather jumbled lounge/ lobby. Guest rooms are adequate, but motel-like. The location is a few blocks inland from the actual beach. Rooms at the Paradise Hotels are often available at a discount in packages.

Red Sea Paradise Hotel. North Beach, Eilat. ☎ **07/363-636.** Fax 07/363-630. 282 rms (all with bath). A/C MINIBAR TEL TV. $140–$180 single; $172–$230 double. Rates include breakfast. 15% service charge. AE, DC, MC, V.

This new, sprawling three-story complex is a choice in the lower part of the expensive price range. Architecturally, the hotel consists of a series of large atriums and courtyards connected by shaded outdoor passageways. Guests resemble those in a standard American motel; most surround a vast central swimming pool. The hotel's design is among the best in Eilat, but the location, in the part of North Beach most distant from the actual beach, can be difficult for those without rental cars. There are adult and children's pools, as well as a fitness center, Jacuzzi, sauna, tennis court, entertainment lounge, and dance floor.

Moderate

Marina Club Eilat. North Beach, Eilat 88141. ☎ **07/334-191.** Fax 07/334-206. 131 convertible suites (all with bath and kitchenette). A/C TEL TV. $110–$215 four-person suite; $163–$268 six-person suite. AE, DC, MC, V.

Eilat's newest and most luxurious apartment hotel has two- and three-room suites that are ideal for families or small groups. Suites vary according to number of rooms and type of view, which determine the rate (pool view is $20–$30 extra per suite), but each suite has its own kitchenette equipped with basics for producing anything from coffee to a full meal. The hotel surrounds a magnificent gardened pool (heated in winter) and all services are provided. The high end of the price range is during July, August, and Jewish holidays and Israeli school vacations, but at other times the hotel is an excellent deal for three- to six-person groups. Sunday to Thursday is the best time for bargaining a bit or finding a "special" rate. Weekends, prices go up $30 per suite. Bargain in off-seasons or if you are only two people.

⑤ Riviera Apartment Hotel. North Beach, Eilat. ☎ **07/333-944;** 800/552-0141 in the U.S.; 800/526-5343 in Canada. Fax 07/333-939. 172 rms (all with bath or shower and kitchenette). A/C TEL TV. Suite for two to four persons $115–$265 low season; $115–$300 regular season; $172–$367 Jewish holidays and Christmas. Substantial discounts on Isrotel or Kibbutz Hotel Chain Plans. AE, DC, MC, V.

Especially good for families or people traveling in small groups, this busy, brand-new establishment, just across the street from the luxury King Solomon's Palace Hotel, offers a number of kinds of pleasantly furnished and decorated suites (many with their own garden terraces or balconies), a vast swimming pool, and state-of-the-art kitchenettes set up with the basic equipment (including, in some suites, a microwave oven) and cleaning supplies you'll need to prepare your own meals during your stay. The hotel's buildings are lowrise, set around the pool, and the feel is less formal than the big highrise places in the area. Readers report a number of nice touches on the part of the management, such as packages of herbal teas. Although not located on a kibbutz, this hotel is one of the choices available at a discount rate on the Kibbutz Fly and Drive Plan when you book through the Israel Hotel Reservation Center (☎ 800/552-0140 in the U.S., 800/526-5343 in Canada). Check with the center about any specials available through the Riviera's parent company, Isrotel, or in conjunction with Arkia Airlines.

Moderate

Dalia Hotel. North Beach. ☎ **07/334-004.** Fax 07/334-072. 52 rms (all with bath or shower). A/C TEL TV. $52–$75 single; $75–$112 double. MC, V.

At the beginning of North Beach, just in from the intersection of Durban Road and Arava Road, this well-located hotel, built in the early 1970s, has no view and offers plain, utilitarian rooms, but it is one of the most affordable choices in town. Pluses are a pleasant swimming pool and the Check Inn Chicken restaurant on the premises, where you can dine well on the $9 all-you-can-eat buffet.

Moon Valley Hotel. North Beach, Eilat. ☎ **07/361-111.** Fax 07/334-110. 182 rms (all with bath). A/C TEL TV. $74–$96 single; $96–$126 double. Rates include breakfast. AE, DC, MC, V.

Another lowrise hotel, about two decades old, with units opening to outdoor walkways or overlooking the large pool, the Moon Valley has recently been completely renovated. Its lobby and guest rooms now sport light, pleasantly tropical furnishings and decor. Rooms are small but efficient. Much of the clientele is 20 to 30-something. Despite the careful update of the hotel, service is average. Low season is May, June, September, and October except for Jewish holidays. High season includes Christmas.

Inexpensive

Ⓢ **Americana Eilat Hotel.** North Beach (P.O. Box 27), Eilat. ☎ **07/333-777.** Fax 07/334-174. 140 rms (all with bath and shower). A/C TEL TV. $60–$80 single; $80–$100 double. Add $8 per person for Jewish holidays and high season. AE, DC, MC, V.

This busy three-star-equivalent hotel, built in the 1970s, has a young, festive atmosphere, and a reputation for good service. The rooms are situated around a large swimming pool/terrace with one huge pool and another children's pool; 40 rooms have private balconies, 26 have private kitchenettes, and all come with wall-to-wall carpet, heat, and radio; 34 sparkling rooms in the newly completed (1996) wing will be $10 per person extra. Films are shown daily in the TV room; water-sports bookings, billiards, and table tennis are all available. If you book 7 nights or more, the management will offer a 10% reduction. May, June, and September (except for Jewish holidays) are considered low season here. From this hotel, and from its neighbor, the Moon Valley (see below), it's a hike of a few blocks to the beach, which can be a problem on a 100° day.

CORAL BEACH & SOUTH TO THE BORDER

Very Expensive

❸ **Eilat Princess Hotel.** Eilat. ☎ **07/365-555.** Fax 07/376-333. 418 rms and suites. A/C MINIBAR TEL TV. $235–$460 single; $265–$480 double. Rates include breakfast. 15% service charge. AE, DC, MC, V. Bus: 15.

Built in 1992, the Eilat Princess has set a new standard for hotel design and room decor in Israel. Deluxe rooms offer a variety of design themes, ranging from European to Chinese and Philippine (there are no genuine Negev and Bedouin motifs); suites develop design themes even further. As the southernmost of Eilat's hotels, 2 miles south of the Coral Beach, the Princess is somewhat isloated unless you have a car, but it's a self-contained resort, with soaring, light-filled public areas, swimming pools designed around artificial cascades, continental, Cajun, and Asian restaurants, as well as the standard range of hotel cafes and lounge/piano bars. There is also a fitness club and spa with therapeutic and beauty programs. The beach, along a strip of water containing some reefs, is just across the highway; at present it's narrow and bare, but there are plans for upgrading.

Dining/Entertainment: Six restaurants and cafes, disco, piano bar, live entertainment.

Services: 24-hour room service, desert and diving bookings, shuttle into Eilat.

Facilities: Two swimming pools, heated in season, two tennis courts sports facilities, fitness room, health and beauty spa, parking.

Expensive

Orchid Hotel and Resort. Coral Beach, Eilat. ☎ **07/360-360**. 136 private bungalow units (all with bath). A/C TEL TV. $200–$240 single; $220–$310 double. Rates include breakfast. 15% service charge. AE, DC, MC, V. Bus: 15.

Designed to suggest a Thai village, with a beautifully authentic wooden Thai pavilion serving as both a centerpiece and Thai/Asian restaurant, the Orchid is one of Eilat's most architecturally interesting hotels, especially if you can conceive of a Thai community transported to the barren, rocky desertscape of the Negev (a fire destroyed the hotel's tropical landscaping, but new plantings are slowly being installed). Located half a mile south of the Coral Beach, on the inland side of the road leading along the coast to Taba, the Orchid has graceful public areas surrounding a large, often busy pool, and further uphill, wooden A-frame guest units with a double room and bath on the ground floor, and a sleeping loft reached by ladder/steps. A golf cart shuttle carries guests up to their accommodations, which are decorated with non-Thai print curtains and bedspreads. There is an in-house restaurant serving a daily buffet, piano bar, disco in high season, and programs of entertainment for children and adults, usually in Hebrew. Off-season, the Orchid can have a tranquil charm; during school vacations it's packed with Israeli families, which means lots of children.

Moderate

Club Inn Villa Resort. Coral Beach, Eilat. ☎ **07/334-555**. Fax 07/334-519. 165 two-room units (137 with shower, 28 with bath). A/C KITCHENETTE TEL TV. $120–$240 per villa 4-person occupancy. 15% service charge. Breakfast $9 per person extra. AE, DC, MC, V. Bus: 15.

Built around a very pleasant, gardened swimming pool, the Club Inn is a lowrise complex of units built in the late 1970s and completely renovated in 1994. Each unit, with simple, clean, practical decor, contains two bedrooms and a kitchenette (there are minimarkets on the premises, and just outside the property). You can easily walk to the Coral Beach Nature Preserve from here, but it can be a hot 10-minute walk in the summer sun. Quieter rooms face away from the pool. The swimming pool is heated in winter; other facilities include a fitness room, two floodlit tennis courts, children's programs, bar, disco, and restaurant.

Red Sea Sports Club Hotel. Coral Beach, Eilat. ☎ **07/373-145** or 373-146. Fax 07/374-241. 250 rms by summer 1997. A/C TEL TV. $72–$92 single; $96–$132 double. AE, DC MC, V. Bus: 15 along Hatmarim Boulevard or Ha-Arava Road to Coral Beach.

Perfect for those who want to spend their time exploring Eilat's reefs, this comfortable, relaxed place is just a 4-minute walk across the road from the Coral Beach Nature Preserve, with its wonderful snorkeling and diving. For years, this was a small whitewashed beachside hotel; then in 1993, the original buildings were torn down, and a new construction project was begun, leaving only the hotel's landmark thatch-roofed bar, diving instruction pool, and easygoing ways. Rooms now are spanking new, all with balconies or private terraces overlooking a vast central swimming pool and terrace. There is a well-equipped diving center and school on the premises, offering excellent lessons and rental equipment. The staff will arrange for desert safaris, bicycling, horseback riding, and other Eilat regional activities. About 100 rooms are now complete, but there may be ongoing construction to deal with during 1996.

JUST ACROSS THE BORDER: TABA

Just across the Israeli–Egyptian frontier at the southern edge of Eilat, Taba came under Israeli occupation, along with the rest of Sinai, at the end of the 1967 Six-Day

War. When Israel returned the Sinai Peninsula to Egypt as part of the Camp David peace accord in the early 1980s, Taba remained in dispute. International arbitration in the late 1980s decided in favor of Egypt, but by then it had become a very valuable few acres, encompassing the site of the Taba Hilton, which visitors and residents alike had come to think of as a southern precinct of Eilat. Today travelers from Eilat can pass across the border to the Taba Hilton for a few hours without problem, but to venture into Sinai beyond Taba requires a special visa. Guests at the Taba Hilton may and frequently do taxi into Eilat; however, Egyptian rental cars may not currently be taken across the border, nor can Israeli rental cars be taken out of Israel.

Taba Hilton Hotel. Taba Beach, Sinai, Egypt. ☎ **20/02/578-3620** via Egypt; 07/379-222 via Israel; 800/HILTONS in the U.S. and Canada. Fax (via Egypt) 20/02/578-7044. 326 rms and suites. A/C MINIBAR TEL TV. $165–$250 single; $215–$260 double. Breakfast $9 per person; tax and service extra. AE, DC, MC, V.

One of the most comfortable hotels in the Eilat area, built before Israel returned Taba to Egypt, the Hilton is a comparatively good bargain because it is priced according to Egyptian standards. Everything here is equal to the best hotels in Eilat, the Egyptian staff is very professional and attentive, the private beach is lovely, and the hotel's gardens and palm trees have had time to gracefully mature. Among unique attractions here are the casino (visited by travelers from Eilat) and a saltwater swimming pool. The Hilton's restaurants are above the level of those at most Eilat hotels.

   Dining/Entertainment: Four restaurants, four bars, casino.
   Services: Travel and cruise bookings, 24-hour room service.
   Facilities: Outdoor pool, five floodlit tennis courts, diving and water-sports center, children's club.

CAMPING

🟉 **Caroline Camping** at Coral Beach (☎ 07/375-063 or 371-911) offers wooden A-frame tent/cabins with electricity for one or two people for NIS 60 ($18); or bungalows for five people for NIS 140 ($42). There are central toilet and shower buildings. The cost is NIS 15 ($4.50) per person if you bring your own tent.

PRIVATE ROOMS & APARTMENTS

Ask at the **Tourist Information Center** (☎ 07/732-111) at the corner of Yotam and Arava roads. It's best to use the Tourist Office for referral, since there have been complaints from people using other sources. Prices for a two-bedroom apartment (for four people or more) are about $60 per day during most of the year, and $80 to $100 or more per day during high season (July, August, and holidays). Especially for a group, this is one of the best ways to economize in Eilat.

WHERE TO DINE
NEAR HATMARIN BOULEVARD
Expensive

✪ **Au Bistro.** Eilot St. ☎ **07/374-333.** Reservations required. Appetizers NIS 14–40 ($4.20–$12); main courses NIS 40–75 ($12–$22.50); lobster and chateaubriand for two $44–$50. AE, DC, MC, V. Dinner daily 5:30–11:30pm. FRENCH.

At this small gem of a restaurant, chef Michel Tourjeman turns out a nightly menu of dishes in the Belgian/French tradition. Among first courses, a house specialty is a flawlessly presented goose liver in Cassis sauce, its richness enhanced by the subtle cakelike toast on which it is served, and the taste variations of almonds and peeled grapes in the sauce. Fish and seafood are exquisitely fresh, turned into small masterpieces like grouper fillet with shrimp in an exotic sauce served on a bed of seafood

---

Eilat's Street Food

A local favorite is the **Family Bakery,** 133 Hatmarim Blvd. (☎ 07/335-846), a partly open-air stand where you can get all kinds of delicious breads, rolls, and minipizzas (sold by weight) for about NIS 1.50 to NIS 3 (45¢ to 90¢) per piece. There are also lots of fresh-from-the-oven pastries. It's open Sunday through Thursday 24 hours, on Friday until 4pm, and Saturday after Shabbat.

Also, you should know about Eilat's small **Indian and Natural Foods** shop (☎ 07/375-266) in a small shopping courtyard on Hatmarim Boulevard across the street from the bus station. Soya milk and natural fruit juices sold here are nourishing and a good defense against dehydration. It's open normal business hours; closed for Shabbat.

Just south of the New Tourist Center, facing the road to Coral Beach and Taba, you'll find **Alcapulco Chicken** (☎ 07/376-222) where you can get a fresh (not frozen) rotisserie-style chicken with a unique flavor. They'll deliver to your hotel. The intersection of Ha-Arava Road (the north–south highway) and Yotam Road, at the western limits of North Beach, is the place for beach snacks and light fare.

---

mousse, or the house seafood bisque, rich with shrimp, calamari, and fresh fish. Everything is perfectly executed, and although the understated decor and service are in the formal style, the staff is knowledgeable and helpful, and the atmosphere relaxed. Prices are very reasonable and very good value; the list of French and Israeli wines is superb, with the more exceptional choices at $150 a bottle. Nothing in Eilat's hotel restaurants comes close to a meal here.

Moderate

✪ **Eddie's Hideaway.** 68 Almogim St. ☎ **07/371-137.** Reservations required. Appetizers NIS 14–30 ($4.20–$9); main courses NIS 30–60 ($9–$18). D, MC, V. Daily 6pm–midnight. CONTINENTAL.

One of Eilat's very best restaurants, this quality establishment serves an enormous menu in a variety of inventive styles, yet manages to keep its prices reasonable and its customers very happy. Main courses, designed by Eddie himself, include personal creations such as Nairobi shrimp cooked in butter and hot paprika with onion, fresh mushrooms, and a touch of pineapple, or moist, delicate Shanghai fish, smothered in a spicy soybean paste. I'm also a fan of the homemade lasagne, the steaks, and the honey barbecued ribs. Salad, vegetable, and potato are included with most main courses. A 10% service charge, which covers the tip, is added to the bill.

Eddie's is aptly named, as it's not directly on Almogim Street, and once you locate the building you must enter from around back. To find it, go up Hatmarim Street past the bus station, turn right on Almogim Street, and turn left at Peace Cafe.

Inexpensive

❺ **Ha-Kerem Restaurant.** Eilat Street, corner of Hatmarim. ☎ **07/374-577.** Light meals NIS 8–17 ($2.40–$5.10); full meals NIS 25–39 ($7.50–$12). No credit cards. Lunch Sun–Fri noon–3pm; dinner Sun–Thurs 6–9:30pm; Sat after Shabbat. YEMENITE.

At this kosher homestyle Yemenite restaurant, service is friendly though often in limited English. The decor is basic, except for a few family photographs in traditional Yemenite costumes, but the food is delicious and reasonably priced. Melawach, the traditional flaky Yemenite pancake, starts at NIS 6.5 ($2), depending on what you have on it. A full selection of Middle Eastern appetizers is available, and meat dishes are served with rice, salad, or chips. A glass of arak (anise brandy) costs $2. A 10% service charge is added.

❸ Nargila. Central Bus Station. ☎ **07/376-101.** Appetizers and light meals NIS 9–NIS 17 ($2.70–$5.10); main courses NIS 18–28 ($5.40–$8.40) DC, MC, V. Daily noon–11pm. MIDDLE EASTERN/YEMENITE.

This is a very good choice for anyone interested in tasty, unusual, low-priced food. The ambience is akin to a fast-food place; the menu is filled with modern interpretations of homestyle Yemenite Israeli dishes that are delicious and different from what you'd find in standard Middle Eastern restaurants. You can order hummus with sautéed mushrooms and onions, fried *mellawach*, or phyllo pancakes; my favorite is the Ziva, a rolled *mellawach* stuffed with melted cheese. You can also order sweet *mellawachs*. There are hearty hot dishes like Yemenite calf's foot soup, and at the top of the very reasonable price range you'll find grilled meats.

NEW TOURIST CENTER
Moderate

La Barracuda. In front of the Sonesta/Sun Suites Hotel. ☎ **07/376-222**, ext. 457. Reservations recommended. Appetizers NIS 16–33 ($4.80–$10); main courses NIS 55–80 ($16.50–$24); lobster $50. AE, DC, MC, V. Daily 1–3:30 pm and 6:30pm–midnight. FRENCH SEAFOOD.

Excellent fresh fish from the Red Sea, shrimps, crabs, calimari, and lobster are the heart of the menu here, grilled, fried, or served in a variety of sauces, but you'll also find choices like veal or chicken cordon bleu, and steak if you're not up for fish. There is an excellent house soup filled with fruits of the sea; good wines and desserts round out this very comfortable, enjoyable place.

Inexpensive

❸ Country Chicken. 6 New Tourist Center. ☎ **07/371-312.** Appetizers NIS 10–20 ($3–$6); main courses NIS 22–48 ($6.60–$14.40). MC, V. Sun–Thurs 9am–midnight; Fri 9am–3pm; Sat after Shabbat–midnight. ISRAELI/AMERICAN.

Tucked away in a corner of the New Tourist Center, you might not notice this restaurant, but it's where many Eilat residents go when they want good value and hefty portions without the touristy glitz. There are lots of surprises once you step inside. First, the place is quite large, though no-frills in decor. Second, chicken is not really the main thing here; the menu includes excellent goulash, kebab, schnitzel, and liver (all less than $7 and served with chips or rice and salad), as well as very upmarket lamb chops and even fresh Red Sea fish in wine and garlic sauce (priced according to weight) as good as you'd get in the fanciest restaurant, and much cheaper. Third, if you strike up a conversation with the very hospitable family running the place, you'll find they are Israelis from Karachi, Pakistan; and although the menu offers nothing Pakistani, you'll be delighted with the nice little Israeli extras that are served when you order a full meal. Finally, ask if they're at the end of a batch of their "Kentucky Fried Chicken" (which, despite its name, is not like the American franchise recipe); it's best when really fresh. Homestyle soups and appetizers are a good choice for a light meal.

✪ Mai Thai. New Tourist Center. ☎ **07/370-104.** Reservations recommended. Appetizers NIS 9–30 ($2.70–$9); main courses NIS 20–39 ($6–$12); business lunch NIS 30 ($9). AE, DC, MC, V. Lunch daily 11:30–3pm; dinner daily 6–11:30pm. THAI/CHINESE.

Housed in a glassed-in upper-story pavilion with a virtual garden of paper parasols and bamboo basket lampshades hanging from the ceiling, Mai Thai serves a menu that is 75% Thai, 25% Chinese, and entirely excellent. There are *patai* noodle dishes, both vegetarian and with meat; classic Thai dishes like *omm olai* (chicken in a coconut, chili, and mint sauce); or heavenly Beef Chang My Style, all of which the management will adeptly tone down in case you're not yet used to Thai seasonings. Excellent for Thai food fans, and a great place to learn a new cuisine. It's located at the edge of the New Tourist Center facing Yotam Road.

NEAR NORTH BEACH

Expensive

Pago Pago. Eilat Laguna. ☎ **07/376-660.** Reservations recommended evenings. Appetizers NIS 15–36 ($4.50–$11); main courses NIS 38–75 ($11.40–$22.50). AE, DC, MC, V. Daily 1pm–3am. SEAFOOD/FRENCH.

Moored in the North Beach Lagoon near the King Solomon Hotel, this floating restaurant, club, and bar offers a South Seas tropical ambience, and a menu of exotic seafood, fresh fish, and meats prepared and served with flair. You might try gratinée of shrimps and calamari in cream sauce or royal platter catch-of-the-day for two (NIS 130, or $40) served in a giant ruffled clam shell, as well as tropical drinks and mellow desserts served with chocolate liqueur coffee. A 10% service charge is added to the bill.

Moderate

⬥ **Tandoori.** In the Laguna Hotel. ☎ **07/333-879** or **333-666.** Reservations recommended. Appetizers NIS 10–28 ($3–$8.30); main courses NIS 22–55 ($6.60–$16.60); 15% service charge. AE, DC, MC, V. Lunch daily 12–3pm; dinner daily 6:30pm–midnight. INDIAN.

Located in the Laguna Hotel on King's Wharf, this is one of Eilat's most special restaurants. Beautifully decorated with Indian artifacts, the restaurant serves a variety of Indian dishes, although specializing in tandoori cooking. The Tandoori's kitchen does everything with a light, elegant touch. All traditional styles are spectacular, and house creations, such as giant prawns in ginger marinade, are very much worth trying. Look into the reasonably priced luncheon specials, which include soup, breads, four choices for your main meal plus vegetable curry, basmati rice, dessert, tea or coffee, wine or soft drink. As if this weren't enough, Tandoori also provides live traditional instrumental music, with performances by a classical or regional Indian dancer every evening. If you are wondering why an Indian restaurant has become such a landmark in Eilat, remember that the Red Sea has been the West's gateway to India since ancient times. The homemade desserts are both exotic and delicious, and lassi, a yogurt-based tropical drink, is a cool antidote to Eilat's torrid temperatures.

Inexpensive

Check Inn. In the Dalia Hotel. ☎ **07/330-389.** Self-service buffet NIS 30 ($9); main courses NIS 22–36 ($6.60–$11). AE, MC, V. Daily noon–11pm. EUROPEAN/MIDDLE EASTERN.

The self-service buffet is the great deal here, including a salad bar with lots of fresh ingredients and Middle Eastern appetizers. From there you go on to the hot counter, where there's a daily selection of fish, meat, chicken, vegetables, and rice and potatoes. The food is solid, but generally good, and you're sure to find things you especially like. Some of the dishes, like chicken or pot roast, will be safe, Western-style choices; others like spicy Moroccan fish will have a bit of local style to them. You can come back for more. The restaurant's food is kosher; because of its affiliation with the Dalia Hotel, Check Inn is open on the Sabbath.

Spring Onion Restaurant Cafe. North Beach Promenade near the bridge. Appetizers and light meals NIS 12–28 ($3.60–$8.40); main courses NIS 22–48 ($6.60–$14.40). MC, V. Daily 8am–after midnight. VEGETARIAN/FISH.

A favorite of Eilat vegetarians, with fresh, nicely prepared food, this small modern place expands to a large outdoor terrace after the sun goes down, and is a good spot for watching promenaders as you dine. Salads are excellent and enormous here, and can easily be shared by two people. Pastas and fresh fish fill out the main courses, and there's also an assortment of rich cakes for dessert. The sign is in English, but if you're asking directions from locals, the Hebrew name actually translates as "Green Onion."

SOUTH OF TOWN & THE CORAL BEACH
Moderate

Last Refuge. Coral Beach. ☎ **07/373-627.** Reservations recommended. Appetizers NIS 16–45 ($4.80–$13.50); main courses NIS 35–66 ($10.60–$20). AE, DC, MC, V. Daily 1–4:30pm and 6–11:30pm. SEAFOOD.

Right across the street from the Fisherman's House, this rather expensive but good fish restaurant has weather-beaten nautical decor (not unlike something you'd find on Cape Cod or Long Island), tables inside or out on the seaside terrace, and generous portions of seafood. Simple, very fresh grilled fish is an excellent choice here. A 10% service charge is added to each bill.

Mandy's Chinese Restaurant. Coral Beach. ☎ **07/372-238.** Reservations recommended. Appetizers NIS 9–55 ($2.70–$16.50); vegetarian courses NIS 20–25 ($6–$7.50); main courses NIS 29–63 ($8.60–$19). AE, DC, MC, V. Sun–Fri noon–3pm and 6:30pm–midnight; Sat noon–midnight. SZECHUAN/CANTONESE.

A pretty place overlooking the water, with tropical Asian decor, Mandy's serves Szechuan and Cantonese specialties. Egg rolls, sweet-and-sour pork or fish, seafood, spareribs, and a number of Southeast Asian dishes (chicken with lemon and mint, for instance) are on the 108-item menu. À la carte noodle and vegetarian selections are available and less expensive.

Inexpensive

Dolphin Reef Seafood Restaurant. Dolphin Reef. ☎ **07/374-293.** Reservations useful. Appetizers and light meals NIS 10–25 ($3–$7.50); main courses NIS 30–45 ($9–$13.50). MC, V. Daily 11am–after midnight. SEAFOOD/PUB.

This thatched-roof, tropical pavilion at the easygoing Dolphin Reef is a good place for lunch, should you have paid admission to the Dolphin Reef's private beach for the day; it's also a congenial place to hang out in the evening, when admission to the Dolphin Reef is free, and when the management often provides live entertainment and dancing on the sand. The floor is sand, the bar is lively in the evening, and the menu choices range from cold yogurt and Greek salad to grilled whole fish or hamburgers. There's also a cafeteria on the premises of the Dolphin Reef beach.

Fisherman's House. Coral Beach. ☎ **07/379-830.** Reservations not accepted. All-you-can-eat buffet NIS 32 ($9.70). No credit cards. Daily noon–midnight. Bus: 15 to Coral Beach. SEAFOOD.

I enjoy this place immensely. It is a large, very informal self-service, all-you-can-eat restaurant with long indoor and outdoor tables—a great place for a casual meal. Choose from a selection of six kinds of fish cooked in different ways, savory rice, baked potatoes, cooked vegetables, and several kinds of spicy Middle Eastern salads. Children up to age 10 eat for half price. Or, for the same price, you can order meat or chicken from the grill (one big serving) and still get all you can eat of everything else. Some of the fish offered may be rather fatty or greasy, but don't be afraid to try all the offerings until you find something you like. Desserts and drinks cost extra.

EILAT AFTER DARK

In this sun-and-fun resort the crowds move from beach to bar, disco, or club after the sun goes down. The Government Tourist Information Office's weekly bulletin, "Events in Eilat," available for free at the tourist office, will let you know what's happening where.

Several of the major hotels have **nightclubs, piano bars,** and **discos.** These are some of the liveliest places in town, patronized by international tourists, Israelis, and native Eilatis alike. Of the discos, **Sheba,** in the **King Solomon's Palace Hotel,** is the most popular, with spectacular laser and sound effects; **Ha-Nesiha,** at the **Princess Hotel** just before the Taba border, runs a close second. Best of all for easygoing beach atmosphere and spirit is the **Dolfin Reef,** with its thatched-roof restaurant/bar: there's dancing on the beach Monday and Thursday nights, and Friday afternoon/evening. The **New Tourist Center** also has a lot going on in the evening, with several pubs and indoor/outdoor cafes humming with activity. **Yatoosh Baroosh Disco Bar** (☎ 07/334-223 or 742-23), a local landmark currently under reconstruction near the North Beach Carousel, and **Kermit Pub,** 1 Hativat Golrni (☎ 07/332-642), near the police station, are popular with younger travelers. **The Yacht Pub** (☎ 07/334-111), near the King Solomon Wharf, has large indoor and outdoor bars that offer live entertainment almost nightly, ranging from Israeli folk groups to European rock.

Various Israeli **folklore evenings** are sponsored by the big hotels, usually beginning about 9:30pm several nights a week. Music for dancing, or a disco, often follows the performance. The fee (usually about $5 to $7) includes first drink, or perhaps wine and cheese.

The **Cinémathèque Club** screens films in English at the **Philip Murray Cultural Center** (☎ 07/332-257), at the corner of Hatmarim Boulevard and Hativat Ha-Negev. Regular starting time seems to be around 9pm; admission is charged. The major hotels show films and videos about excursion in the Eilat area as well. Check the tourist office's bulletin "Events in Eilat" for details.

EASY EXCURSIONS

Timna Valley National Park. 27 kilometers (17 miles) north of Eilat. ☎ 07/356-215 for information. Admission NIS 13 ($3.90) adults, half price for children. Daily 8am–4pm. Tour buses daily 8am .

If you're driving, head north, pass the Timna Mines (on your left, to the west), and after a few kilometers you'll see a sign for Timna. Turn left onto the road indicated, and head west toward the striking, jagged black hills. Not far in from the highway is the main gate; follow the road 3¹/₂ kilometers (2 miles) to a right turn for the **ancient Egyptian copper mines,** another kilometer along. The mines consist of sandstone arches, underground mining shafts, and galleries. About 3 kilometers (2 miles) from the mines, along another side road, is a parking area from which you make the short walk to see a **wall face carved with figures in chariots.** All these twists and turns are marked clearly by signs.

Along the roads you will have noticed **"The Mushroom,"** a curious rock formation with a huge boulder resting on a column of sandstone, the result of erosion. But the most striking formation in the preserve is undoubtedly **Solomon's Pillars.** Go back to the main road of the preserve and head east for several kilometers. The pillars, a series of sandstone fins jutting out of a rock face, are at the end of the road. Climb into the fins along a path with steps to see some **Egyptian rock carvings,** and then down the steps on the other side to the remains of a **small temple** dedicated to the Egyptian goddess Hathor.

The spare, clean air of the desert, the hot sun, the quiet of the preserve are sure to make a lasting impression. You can get information on **hiking trails** from the staff at the main gate. The development of Timna Valley National Park has become a major project of the Jewish National Fund of America. An artificial recreational lake and architecturally stunning **Visitors Center** have been built in the **Nechushtan Recreation Area** not far from Solomon's Pillars and the Sphinx. The lake provides facilities for swimming, boating, and fishing. The Visitors Center pavilion includes a cafeteria and a shop for traveling supplies.

Hai Bar National Biblical Wildlife Reserve. 40km (24 miles) north of Eilat. Admission NIS 20 ($6.60) for adults, NIS 13 ($4) for children. Daily 8:30am–1:30pm.

If you have no car, you can take a guided tour from town, which takes about 2 hours. The purpose of the 8,000-acre reserve is to save rare and endangered desert animals mentioned in the Bible, as well as other rare desert animals of western Asia and northern Africa, breeding them for eventual release into the wild. Among the 450 kinds of animals found here are the Nubian ibex, the Dorcas gazelle, the Persian onager, the scimitar-horned oryx, the addax antelope, and the Arabian gazelle, as well as wolves, hyenas, foxes, desert cats, leopards, cheetahs, wild donkeys, lots of ostriches, and many species of snakes, lizards, and even predatory birds. Many of these animals are nocturnal, due to the blistering desert heat, but a special dark room makes it possible to observe these creatures during your daylight visit. You can ride around the reserve in special coaches (closed vehicles only) and observe the animals at close range.

You'll notice that the Hai Bar Reserve has many trees, signifying that water is lying below the arid desert. This area is known as the Yotvata Oasis, and it is believed that it was one of the places where Moses stopped as he brought the Children of Israel up out of Egypt.

6 On to Sinai

The Sinai is a place of fateful, haunting crossings. If the human race originated in Africa, it was through the trials of this harsh, unrelenting land bridge connecting Africa to Asia that the ancestors of much of the human race had to pass as they moved toward their destinies to the far corners of the earth. The Sinai Peninsula, mountainous and awe-inspiring, is the unearthly triangle of wilderness in which the Israelites wandered after the Exodus from Egypt. It was here that the Torah was given to them; after the journey through this vast crucible of monotheistic faith, the Israelites were transformed, and the journey of human civilization was set onto new pathways. Even if you were unaware of its history, the primordial splendor of Sinai can be an overwhelming personal experience.

Mount Sinai and the ancient Byzantine monastery of Santa Katerina on its slope have been a destination for pilgrims for 15 centuries, almost mirage-like in their sanctity. The coast of the Gulf of Aqaba is a diver's and snorkeler's paradise, with some of the most beautiful and unusual coral reef systems in the world.

Since the Sinai was restored to Egypt in 1982, after a 15-year Israeli occupation, the area has been developed as never before in its isolated history. The few simple beach hut accommodations, with their accompanying restaurants and dive shops that were the sum total of Nuweiba, Dahab, and Sharm-el-Sheik in the late 1960s, are as forgotten now as a lost civilization, while Hiltons, Inter-Continental Hotels, and other international chains dot the coastline for miles, and new vacation complexes continue to rise. There are also literally hundreds of beach bungalow hotels and encampments along the Gulf of Aqaba, with discos throbbing under the starry desert

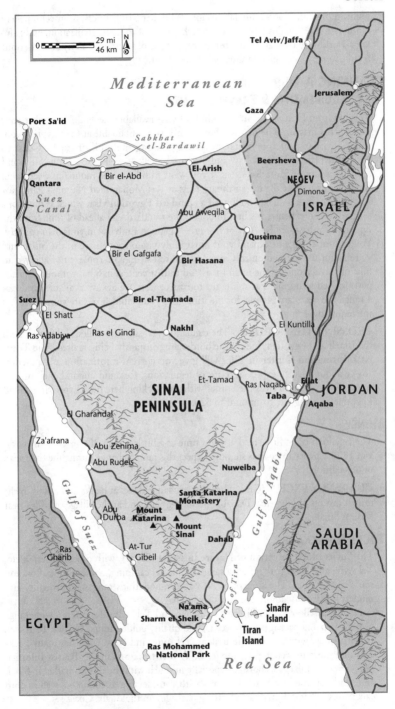

Sinai

Tel Aviv/Jaffa

Mediterranean
Sea

Port Sa'id

Jerusalem

*Sabkhat
el-Bardawil*

Gaza

Qantara

Bir el-Abd

El-Arish

Beersheva

NEGEV

*Suez
Canal*

Abu Aweqila

Dimona

ISRAEL

Suez

Bir el Gafgafa

Bir Hasana

Quseima

El Shatt

Ras Adabiya

Ras el Gindi

Bir el-Thamada

Nakhl

El Kuntilla

SINAI
PENINSULA

Et-Tamad

Ras Naqab

Eilat

JORDAN

Taba

El Gharandal

Aqaba

Za'afrana

Abu Zenima

Abu Rudeis

Nuweiba

Gulf of Aqaba

Santa Katarina
Monastery

Abu
Durba

Mount
Katarina

Mount
Sinai

SAUDI
ARABIA

Dahab

Gulf of Suez

At-Tur
Gibeil

Ras
Gharib

Strait of Tira

EGYPT

Na'ama

Sinafir
Island

Sharm el-Sheik

Tiran
Island

Ras Mohammed
National Park

Red Sea

0   29 mi
     46 km

N

415

night, rudimentary accommodations for well under $10 per person (insect repellent is a must). The Sinai is now on the superhighway of touristic civilization, and gaining a worldwide reputation as a fun place, but the old austere majesty and mystique is still close by, accessible to those who seek it out.

PLANNING A TRIP

VISA REQUIREMENTS & TRAVEL PERMITS

Coming from Israel, there are two kinds of visas available, depending on what your travel plans may be. The first is a **Sinai Only visa,** obtainable at the Egyptian consulate in Eilat, which permits you to travel along the Gulf of Aqaba Coast to Nuweiba, Dahab, Na'ama Bay, and Sharm-el-Sheik as well as to Mount Sinai and the Monastery of Santa Katarina. If you want to hike in the mounains near Santa Katarina, or to visit the extraordinary reefs at Ras Mohammed National Park, just south of Sharm-el-Sheik, you'll need a **standard Egyptian visa,** which is more of a procedure and expense. It's best to obtain the standard visa ahead of time from the Egyptian Embassy in Tel Aviv or from the Egyptian Embassy in your own country. You cannot change or expand your Sinai Only visa once you are in the Sinai, and you cannot use it to go on to Cairo and the rest of Egypt. You are not allowed to hike or travel alone off the main roads and tourist centers in Sinai without a special permit. Bedouin guides at the main tourist centers are always available, and can arrange the necessary permits for the itineraries you plan. Make sure your guide has the required permits.

CROSSING THE BORDER The regulations, crossing schedules, and fees on both the Israeli and Egyptian sides of the border are constantly being revised. The **Tourist Information Center in Eilat** will give you current information and practical advice about what to expect in terms of regulations, fees, and ongoing bus connections. Do not plan to cross the border without checking here first. Expect Israeli and Egyptian crossing fees to amount to $20.

MONEY

The Egyptian pound is valued at press time at a bit less than 30¢ in U.S. currency, and 18 new pence in pounds sterling. Expect this rate to change during the time span of this edition.

CURRENCY EXCHANGE There are exchange desks at banks and hotels in the tourist centers of Nuweiba, Dahab, Sharm-el-Sheik, and at the village of Milga near Mount Sinai.

TOURS & PACKAGES

The **Society for Protection of Nature in Israel (SPNI),** with offices in Jerusalem, Tel Aviv, and New York, offers a range of hiking, camping, and nature exploration tours to the Sinai. The scale of SPNI's accommodations ranges from quality and modest hotels to Bedouin tent and sleeping bag.

Neot Ha-Kikar, with offices in Jerusalem and Tel Aviv, also offers a wide range of well-prepared packages for travelers, and quality guided tours. **Galilee Tours,** an Israeli agency, with offices in Jerusalem, Tel Aviv, and New York, has many packages in a more moderate price range. **E. T. I. Attractions** in the Tourist Information Center at Eilat (see above) is especially in touch with the tourist market in Sinai, and can book you into hotels (at times with considerable discounts) as well as onto excursions to Santa Katarina and diving packages on the Aqaba Coast.

GETTING THERE

BY PLANE   From Eilat, you can fly to Santa Katerina and Sharm-el-Sheik on Air Sinai, either as an independent passenger, or on package trips and guided tours.

BY BUS   Egyptian buses leave from the Egyptian side of the Israeli–Egyptian border at Taba, near Eilat, a number of times a day on routes southward to Nuweiba, Dahab, and Sharm-el-Sheik. Buses will either let you off at your hotel in any of these centers, or you can take a shared taxi from the bus station to your hotel. There are also buses from Taba and Nuweiba to Santa Katarina and to Cairo. Schedules are unpredictable. It is always wise to reserve a seat if possible, and arrive at the bus station more than an hour ahead of time. The Tourist Information Center in Eilat can give you advice about current schedules and prices. The trip from Taaba to Sharm-el-Sheik should be no more than $10–$12, including local taxi.

BY CAR   You cannot take an Israeli rental car across the border from Eilat into Sinai; if you want to rent a car, you must make arrangements at Taba, on the Egyptian side of the border, where most international car rental agencies have offices. If you decide to rent a car, you always get a better deal by making your reservations from overseas, or with a prepaid package. Driving can be unnerving, if not downright dangerous, in Sinai, with massive long-haul trucks charging around curves on the wrong side of narrow two-lane highways with small concern for a rented Fiat coming from the other direction.

MOUNT SINAI & SANTA KATERINA

Located in the rugged interior of the peninsula, this is not the isolated pilgrimage site it once was; nevertheless it is a charismatic and powerful place. Nestled on the lower slopes of Mount Sinai (Gabal Mussa, or the Mountain of Moses in Arabic), is the **Monastery of Santa Katerina,** with origins reaching back to the times of the cave-dwelling monks of the 2nd century A.D. Much of the monastery is over 1,500 years old; its library includes what is probably the most important collection of rare and ancient manuscripts outside of the Vatican. The unrestored Byzantine mosaics of the Chapel of the Burning Bush and a vast collection of ancient icons are among the dramatic monastery's other treasures.

The climb up steep pathways and staircases to the top of Mount Sinai is arduous. Most people do it in the cool (or cold) of night and enjoy the incredible sunrise. The hike can take from 2 to 4 hours, depending on your strength. It's by no means an easy ascent—you may want to consider taking a Bedouin guide and renting a camel at a cost of $12 for the climb. The view from the summit (if you can get away from tour groups) is transcendent.

Six kilometers to the south is **Gabal Katarina** (Mount Catherine), the highest in Egypt. The path to the summit of this mountain is more beautiful and less trafficked by hordes of tourists than Mount Sinai; from the village of Milga the climb can take 6 hours. Although the tradition of identifying Mount Sinai as the place where the Ten Commandments were given to Moses is very strong, there are other traditions and theories attached to other mountains, and Gabal Katarina could possibly be the genuine place. There is a chapel and a source of water at the very top of the mountain.

The village of **Milga,** a kilometer from the monastery, has banking facilities, groceries, and a bread bakery, and inexpensive restaurants where you can take a meal for $3 to $8. Those with Egyptian visas can ask in Milga about hiring a Bedouin guide for hiking in the surrounding countryside. Guided hikes start at around $20 for a guide and permit.

WHERE TO STAY

One of the most atmospheric and economical choices is the **Santa Katarina Monastery Hostel** (☎ 62/770-945), on the left side of the monastey complex. Rooms are hot and airless in summer, and rather cramped with seven or eight beds to a chamber, but they are clean, and you'll find interesting fellow travelers. Dorm beds are $12 a night; beds in rooms with three to four beds and a private bathroom are $17. Check-in is from 8:30am to 2pm and from 5 to 7pm. You cannot enter the monastery after 9:30pm.

The **El Salaam Hotel** (☎ 62/771-409) at the Santa Katarina Airport, 10 kilometers from Mount Sinai, offers simple double rooms with baths and has a restaurant and cafeteria. Prices are moderate and depend on whether you come as an individual or book in through a tour. You must take a taxi to Mount Sinai.

The **Danielle Village** (☎ 62/771-379) is more expensive and comfortable, with 52 air-conditioned rooms, all with private baths. It is located 2 miles from the monastery and includes a restaurant and shopping facilities.

NUWEIBA

This beach resort is a mixture of sprawling camps and beach-hut hotels, especially to the north at **Tarabin,** where you can easily find a place in the $4–$10 per person a night range. There are also many recently built upmarket Holiday Villages and pleasant, lowrise hotels.

The modest but solid **El Sayadin Village Hotel** (☎ 62/520-341) offers air-conditioned rooms, restaurant facilities, and a private beach. Doubles are in the $30 range.

One of Sinai's best is the beautiful new **Nuweiba Hilton Coral Resort** (☎ 62/520-320; fax 62/520-327). It has romantic doubles for $140, from which you can watch the sunrise over the Red Sea; at times, a good travel discounter in Eilat can book you in here for $70 for a double room, including breakfast. Rooms are air-conditioned, and have TVs, phones, and refrigerators; facilities include a swimming pool, diving and water-sports center, restaurants, and a private beach.

DAHAB

Once the flower child of the Aqaba Coast during the years of Israeli occupation, Dahab has not grown old gracefully and is now distinctly seedy. Diving opportunities and dive schools, however, are superior to those at Nuweiba.

As at Nuweiba, hutlike accommodations abound. The **Dahab Holiday Village** (☎ and fax 62/640-301) is a good moderate choice, with 141 air-conditioned lowrise rooms and bungalows with baths, a wide beach, an assortment of restaurants, and its own water-sports and diving center. Doubles are in the $100–$120 range, but can be much less through a good travel agent or package when business is slow.

SHARM-EL-SHEIK

At the southernmost point of the Sinai Peninsula, Sharm-el-Sheik itself is a sprawling center for commercial and industrial action as well as a mecca for divers.

The best diving and snorkeling, perhaps in the world, is just south of Sharm-el-Sheik, at the **National Park at Ras Mohammed**. You must have the standard, rather than Sinai Only, visa in order to enter this most elysian of the earth's coral reefs. Admission to the National Park is $5. Many divers arrange to get to Ras Mohammed by chartering a boat and diving or snorkeling from the boat. Diving and snorkeling areas are carefully marked. It is forbidden to damage the reefs or to remove sea shells.

WHERE TO STAY

The area is filled with international hotel chains. Top-rated hotels in the Na'ama Bay area, just to the north of Sharm-el-Sheik itself, offer very good value. In Na'ama Bay there are good beaches, diving and snorkeling reefs, a good selection of moderate and expensive accommodations, and more of a holiday atmosphere. However, prices are on the rise, and demand is very great: more than 3,000 new hotel rooms are planned for Na'ama Bay in the next few years. If you plan to stay in one of the better complexes, book way in advance, as diving groups and tours fill the most desirable (as well as the less desirable) places as much as 6 months or more in advance.

Expensive

✪ **Movenpick Sharm-el-Sheik Beach Resort**. Na'ama Bay, Sharm-el-Sheik. ☎ **62/600-100**. Fax 62/600-111. 337 rms (all with bath). A/C TEL TV. $95–$125 single; $120–$185 double; including service and tax. Breakfast $8.50 per person extra. AE, MC, V.

This large, lowrise outpost of the Swiss Movenpick Hotel Chain is a complete vacation enclave in itself, catering mainly to travelers who come to Sharm for the diving. Covered outdoor passageways and open-air pavilions provide an architectural theme and connect the white, contemporary desert structures of the complex. Deluxe rooms are in the front section, along the beach; less expensive rooms are across the street, near the sports facilities. Special facilities include fresh- and saltwater swimming pools, a complete diving center, tennis courts, a casino, and a bookstore stocked with material about the area. President Clinton stayed here during the 1996 Sharm-el-Sheik Conference.

Dining/Entertainment: Two restaurants, plus cafes and pubs and casino.

Services: Shuttle to Sharm-el-Sheik Airport, desert excursion bookings.

Facilities: Two swimming pools, diving center, fitness room, health and massage spa, shops and hairdresser.

Sonesta Beach Resort. Na'ama Bay, Sharm-el-Sheik. ☎ **62/600-725**; 800/766-3782 in the U.S. Fax 62/600-0733. 228 rms. A/C MINIBAR TEL TV. $120–$160 single; $150–$195 double. Add 20% for service and tax. Breakfast included; children under 12 in room free. MC, V.

Another lowrise, whitewashed self-contained vacation and diving center, the rooms at the Sonesta are marked by pleasant Arabesque touches to their structure, such as terraces, as well as practical amenities like hairdryers in every room. There's a swim-up bar in one of the three pools, a rooftop cafe for sunsets, a health club with sauna and Jacuzzi, and, of course, a diving center.

Dining/Entertainment: 12 restaurants, cafes and bars, offering everything from felafel to continental cuisine.

Services: Desert and diving excursion bookings; complimentary shuttle to airport.

Moderate

The **Sanafir Tourist Village** (☎ 62/600-197; fax 62/600-195) is located on Na'ama Bay, with good reefs for snorkeling. There are moderately priced rooms with private baths and air conditioning as well as cheaper reed bungalows (huts) with fans.

The moderate **Marina Sharm Hotel** (☎ 62/600-170), also on Na'ama Bay, has 105 rooms with private bathrooms, air conditioning, and televisions as well as a swimming pool; it is located close to good diving reefs.

12 Excursions to Jordan

The Hashemite Kingdom of Jordan offers a new horizon for travelers to the Middle East. It contains dazzling, unspoiled desertscapes and countryside and legendary lost cities from ancient times, but it's also an orderly country with a modern infrastructure and a population that has a long tradition of natural hospitality and courtesy. Since 1994, when Jordan and Israel signed a peace agreement ending a 46-year-long state of war, the Kingdom of Jordan has been host to a wave of international and Israeli tourists. The word is out that sights are magnificent, roads are excellent, and prices for lodgings and restaurants are far, far lower than in Israel.

In terms of history, as well as logic, the lands east and west of the Jordan have always been a continuous entity. Ruth, the Moabite ancestor of King David, came from what is now a central region of Jordan; Herod the Great, an Ideumean, came from what is now the southern part of the country; Jesus was baptized by John the Baptist in Jordan; and the Crusaders, who swept in from Akko, Jerusalem, and the Galilee, built the most formidable of their mountaintop castles at Kerak. An excursion to the Nabatean canyon city of Petra, one of the wonders of the world, should be a highlight of any visit to the Middle East. For the first time, visitors to Israel can include in their itineraries the wonders of Wadi Rum (backdrop for the filming of *Lawrence of Arabia*); the sweeping views from Mount Nebo, reputed to be the place where Moses died; the vast Byzantine mosaics at Medaba; the Red Sea coral reefs at Aqaba; and the Hellenistic/Roman ruined city of Jerash (ancient Gerasa), which hosts a world-famous festival of Western and Middle Eastern performing arts each July.

Although the barriers to travel between Israel and Jordan have fallen, an excursion to Jordan still involves some amount of hassle. Border-crossing regulations and procedures (as well as fees) are still in the process of evolving: the rules constantly change. The country is at times overwhelmed by the numbers of international tourists and Israeli visitors. The touristic and ecological capacity of Petra, the most dazzling of Jordan's attractions, is being mightily taxed. Admission to Petra may have to be limited to 1,000 visitors a day or less.

Under these circumstances, many tourists find it best to book onto a tour of Petra that will guarantee admission, or book a guided

Jordan

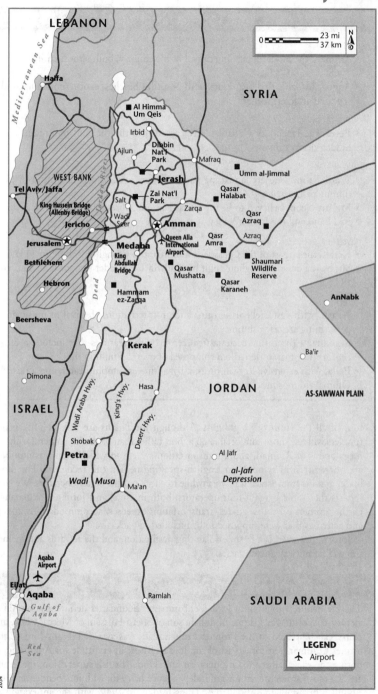

What's Special About Jordan

Cities
- **Amman,** the modern, bustling capital of the country, built almost entirely since 1948.
- **Aqaba,** Jordan's Red Sea resort, with beautiful beaches, exotic snorkeling, and spectacular desert scenery.

Ace Attraction
- **Petra,** the legendary Nabatean city carved into the rocks of mountains and hidden desert canyons.

Great Vistas
- **Wadi Rum,** a desert landscape par exellence, used as a background in the filming of *Lawrence of Arabia.*
- **Mount Nebo,** believed to be the burial place of Moses, overlooking the Promised Land and the Jordan Valley.

Crusader Castles
- **Kerak,** the largest of the Crusader's mountaintop strongholds, built in 1132.
- **Shobak,** a desert stronghold built by Baldwin I, Crusader king of Jerusalem, in 1115.

Ancient Sites
- **Jerash,** with vast Hellenistic ruins and an international festival of music and performing arts each summer.
- **Madaba,** a Byzantine ecclesiastical center with treasures that include a 6th-century A.D. map of Jerusalem composed of over 2.3 million tiles.
- **Pella,** with extensive Roman ruins, a Byzantine-era amphitheater, and a ruined Ommayyid mosque.

tour of all the country's highlights. Although Jordanians are very helpful, many travelers will feel more comfortable on a tour, rather than having to contend with the megalopolis of Amman, and a transportation system in which even bus numbers are not written in symbols an English-speaking person can recognize. For those booking tours from Israel, it is worthwhile to check out the better operators. We have reports that some bargain-tour operators, both in Israel and Jordan, are blatantly cutting corners on tours, guides, transportation expenses, accommodations, meals, and activities that were supposed to be included in packages.

Jordan, however, is a fresh, exhilarating destination, and the rewards and memories will far outway any obstacles.

1 A Look at Jordan's Past

The Hashemite Kingdom of Jordan encompasses boundaries defined by the Allied victors of World War I. Emir Abdullah, son of Sherif Hussein of Mecca, whose ancestry can be traced to the Prophet Muhammad, was awarded Trans-Jordan, the former Ottoman territories east of the Jordan River, in gratitude for Arab support during the war against the Ottoman Empire. Under British supervision, the Emirate of Trans-Jordan moved toward independence in 1946; with independence, Emir Abdullah became King Abdullah of Trans-Jordan. In 1949, with the annexation of the West Bank, the name of the country was changed to the Kingdom of Jordan.

In 1951, King Abdullah was assassinated in front of the El Aksa Mosque in Jerusalem by forces who felt the king was working for reconciliation with the new state of Israel. Abdullah's 14-year-old grandson, the future King Hussein, was at his side when he was struck down. Hussein has ruled since 1953, bringing his country through more than four decades of wars and crises, walking a delicate tightrope between the larger powers in the Middle East. In the process, Jordan has absorbed and given citizenship to well over a million refugees from the 1948 and 1967 wars, as well as to more than 300,000 Palestinians expelled from Kuwait and other Gulf states in the wake of the 1991 Gulf War.

In a land devoid of oil and with few natural resources, Jordan has created one of the most progressive and energetic societies in the Middle East, but the burden of absorbing so many refugees, largely without help from the outside world, has taken its toll on the nation's economy. The annual per capita income, approximately $2,000 in 1990, fell to less than $1,400 in subsequent years. The opportunities afforded by peace may turn this trend around. If it does, tourism will be an important element in Jordan's economic revival.

2 Planning a Trip to Jordan

VISITOR INFORMATION & ENTRY REQUIREMENTS

VISITOR INFORMATION

Jordan Tourist Information Offices in the United States are at 2319 Wyoming Ave. NW, Washington, DC 20008 (☎ 202/265-1606, fax 202/667-0777). In the U.K., 11/12 Buckingham Gate, London SW1E 6LB (☎ 0171/630-92-77, fax 0171/233-75-20). In the past, these offices were equipped only with nicely photographed brochures, but with the tourist boom, they may offer more detailed information and services. At press time there is no Jordan Tourist Information Office in Israel.

ENTRY REQUIREMENTS

You must have a valid passport, preferably one that does not have an expiration date within 6 months of your planned visit. American, British, and Canadian citizens are issued visas upon arrival at Queen Alia Airport in Amman. Travelers plannning to enter Jordan over land must have a visa stamp, obtainable in person or by mail at Jordanian embassies and consulates upon completing the necessary forms; a recent photograph is required. The fee is $26 for U.S. citizens. Those applying for visas at the Jordanian Embassy in Tel Aviv should allow a minimum of 2 days for visa application processing.

Most visas are issued for 1 month, renewable at local police stations. Good travel agents, abroad as well as in Israel, and reputable tour companies can generally handle the arrangements for their clients' visas. Visa fees are not included in most package tour prices, but there should be no charge for the service of obtaining the visa.

The Jordanian Embassy in the United States is at 3504 International Drive N.W., Washington, D.C. 20008 (☎ 202/966-2664); in Canada, 100 Bronson Ave., Number 701, Ottawa, Ont. KIR 6G8 (☎ 613/238-8090); and in the U.K., 6 Upper Philimore Gardens, London W8 7HB (☎ 0171/937-36-85). In Israel the embassy is at the Dan Hotel, Ha-Yarkon Street, Tel Aviv (☎ 03/520-2525).

MONEY

The Jordanian dinar is valued at approximately 1.40 U.S. dollars, 0.84 pounds sterling, or 4.2 Israeli shekels. The Jordanian dinar (JD) is divided into 1,000 fils: 10 fils are 1 piaster; 500 fils are generally referred to as 50 piasters. Paper currency comes in denominations of JD 1, 5, 10, 20, and 500 fils; there are silver coins for 25 fils, 50 fils, 100 fils, and 250 fils; copper coins are 5 and 10 fils.

GETTING THERE

LAND TRANSPORTATION FROM ISRAEL   Most visitors from Israel enter Jordan from Jerusalem via the Allenby/King Hussein Bridge at the Jordan River near Jericho, or from Eilat via the new Arava Crossing just north of Eilat (initially opened for non-Israeli visitors in 1994). Many tours originating in Jerusalem are routed into Jordan via a new Jordan River Crossing Point in the northern Jordan Valley, near the Israeli city of Beit Shean. From there, tours continue on to Jerash, north of Amman, and then proceed to Amman for the night.

Independent travelers from Jerusalem are advised to make arrangements with an East Jerusalem travel agency for sherut service to the Allenby Bridge. You must disembark, carry your baggage across the border checkpoints, and connect with ongoing Jordanian service sheruts or air-conditioned **Jordanian Express Tourist Transport (JETT)** buses to Amman; the cost is JD 7 ($10).

From Eilat, you can cross into Aqaba, where a number of JETT buses (equipped with air conditioning, hostess service, sandwich service, and Arabic videos) as well as minibuses and private taxis leave for Amman each day.

BY PLANE   Royal Jordanian Airlines has service between Ben-Gurion Airport and Amman Tuesday through Friday and on Sunday in the evening. Call 212/949-0050 or 800/RJ-JORDAN in the U.S. for information. El Al plans to begin a similar service in 1996.

ORGANIZED TOURS

Royal Jordanian Airlines (☎ 800/RJ-TOURS-8 in the U.S.) offers a range of well-tested land packages and tours for its passengers and has a reciprocal arrangement with El Al and Tower Air in which passengers may fly from North America to Amman, and return home on Tower Air or El Al from Ben-Gurion Airport in Israel, or fly first to Israel on Tower and El Al, and return on Royal Jordanian via Amman.

El Al (☎ 800/EL AL SUN in the U.S.) and **Tower Air** (☎ 800/34-TOWER in the U.S.) also offer Jordanian land-package tours and accommodations for their passengers.

TOUR ORGANIZERS IN ISRAEL   Travel agencies in Eilat can arrange package tours of Jordan that originate in Eilat. **E. T. I. Attractions** in the Eilat Tourist Information Center, Arava/Yotam Junction (☎ 07/372-111; fax 07/376-763), is recommended.

In Jerusalem, tours are offered by **Galilee Tours** (☎ 800/874-4445 in the U.S.), 3 Hillel St. (☎ 02/258-866); **B. T. C. Tours,** 2 Ha-Soreg St. (☎ 02/233-990); and **Mazada Tours,** 4 King Solomon St. (☎ 02/235-777).

There has been mixed reader feedback on the performance of almost all tour companies, partly due to the fact that travel to Jordan has undergone a sometimes unmanageable boom in the first year of the Israeli–Jordanian peace agreement. The budget-range Mazada Tours has evoked the greatest number of readers' complaints.

TOUR ORGANIZERS IN AMMAN   **International Traders,** Shemaysani District (☎ 06/607-014; fax 06/669-905), is the representative of American Express in Jordan. Their arrangements will be top quality and very dependable. They also manage the beautiful and atmospheric Taybet Zeman hotel in Petra.

3 Amman

The sprawling capital of Jordan undulates over seven hills, and is home to more than a million people, making it larger than any of Israel's cities. In biblical times, it was Rabbath-Ammon, the capital of the Ammonite people; in the Hellenistic/ Roman period, this was the formidable city of Philadelphia, a member of the league of cities known as the Decapolis—impressive ruins from those times still blend into the structure of modern Amman. During the early 1920s, when Trans-Jordan was carved out of the wreckage of the Ottoman Empire, centrally located Amman (at that time little more than a village), rather than the larger town of Salt to the north, was chosen as Emir Abdullah's administrative center. Until 1948, Amman remained essentially a small town with a population of less than 12,000. Palestinian refugees from the 1948 war swelled the city's population; like the rest of the country, more than half the inhabitants of Amman are of Palestinian origin.

The city is an interesting, lively base for exploring northern and central Jordan. Independent travelers will, of necessity, spend time here making touring arrangements. There are interesting local craft cooperatives and shops to visit.

ESSENTIALS

VISITOR INFORMATION   Ministry of Tourism Building, near Zahran Street, off the Third Circle (☎ 06/642-311; fax 06/648-465), is open Saturday through Thursday from 8am to 2pm. Here you can pick up free maps, brochures, and lists of hotels. The country code for Jordan is 962; the city telephone code for Amman is 06.

GETTING AROUND   Taxis are the best option for first-time tourists. Most taxi rides in the central city come to 450–600 fils (70¢ or less).

ORIENTATION
CITY LAYOUT

There are no addresses in Amman, and street signs in any language are rare. Neighborhoods are known in relationship to landmarks and to the eight traffic circles that are stretched across the hills and valleys of the city. For this reason, it is best to take taxis, which are inexpensive and generally fair to foreigners. Very seldom will a taxi fare across the city come to more than JD 2 ($2.80); most taxi rides will be in the $1 range. Because the city is built on hills and around ravines, it is difficult to judge walking distances or accessibility from maps. The good thing is that people are very friendly about giving directions (basic English is widely spoken) and the vistas from high points throughout Amman have become part of the city's charm. You orient yourself by the direction of the landmark hills of the city.

King Feisal Street running toward the Al Husseini Mosque, surrounded by the city's seven hills, is at the heart of **Al Balad,** the downtown center of Amman. The main market area lies several blocks southwest of the Al Husseini Mosque; the ancient **Roman Amphitheater,** another landmark, is to the northeast. The hill of **Jabal Amman** is the upper-class hotel and government district; the well-to-do foreign community makes its presence felt here. Beyond Jabal Amman is the outlying district of **Shemaysani,** with more expensive hotels, cafes, and the Petra Center, which houses an American Pizza Hut and a Kentucky Fried Chicken. The American Express representative (see below) is located in this area, across the street from the Ambassador Hotel.

FAST FACTS: AMMAN

American Express   The representative is **International Traders,** Shemaysani (☎ 06/607-014). You can book tours here, and American Express card holders can receive mail.

Embassies   The U.S. Embassy (☎ 06/820-101) is in Abdoun near the Fifth Circle; the Canadian Embassy (☎ 06/666-124) is in Shemaysani, near the Petra Bank; the U.K. Embassy (☎ 06/823-100) is also in Abdoun, near the Fifth Circle and the Orthodox Club.

Newspapers & Publications   Most helpful is *Your Guide to Amman*, a free tourist publication put out each month and available at major hotels and many travel agencies. The weekly *Jerusalem Star* lists Amman performances and cultural events; the *Jordan Times* has interesting English-language reporting of Middle Eastern news as well as practical information such as current government price guidelines for fruits and vegetables. The *International Herald Tribune* generally arrives in Amman late in the second day after its publication. *Time* and *Newseek* are also available.

WHAT TO SEE & DO

The **Roman Theater,** on Jabal al-Qala'a, near the center of downtown Amman, built in the 2nd century A.D., is the most famous and easily accesssible of the city's ancient sites. It was restored in the late 1950s and can accommodate 6,000 spectators. The theater is used for special events and performances. It is open from Wednesday to Monday from 9am to 5pm; there is no admission fee, but you may be thronged by potential "guides." Their going rate is JD 2. The **Museum of Folklore, Costume, and Jewelry**, filled with spectacular examples of Jordanian embroidery and regional costumes, is part of the restored theater complex. The museum is open the same hours as the theater; admission is JD 1.50 ($2.10).

A colonnaded Roman Square that was once part of the city's forum lies in front of the theater. To the east, at the far end of the ancient forum, is the **Odeon,** a smaller 2nd-century theater used for music performances. The ancient buildings have been woven into the main flow of city life with a busy, newly built piazza.

Jabal al-Qala'a (the Citadel Hill), is a steep walk up from the Roman Theater complex. This was the site of the acropolis and fortress of ancient Rabbath-Ammon. The views from the top of the hill are beautiful, encompassing all of the modern, hill-strewn city. The Citadel Hill includes Byzantine and early Islamic ruins, and the **Archeological Museum,** containing finds from all over Jordan.

Walk down the hill to the landmark **al-Husseini Mosque,** the bustling center of modern downtown Amman. In the triangle between the Citadel Hill, the al-Husseini Mosque, and the post office, you'll find the streets of the **Gold Market,** open Saturday through Thursday from 9am to 9pm, and on Friday until about 1pm. Very few shops in the maze sell old Bedouin and tribal silver.

WHERE TO STAY
EXPENSIVE

Amman Marriott Hotel. Shemaysani, Amman. ☎ **06/607-607;** reservations in North America and U.K. through Marriott Hotels International. Fax 06/670-100. 296 rms (all with bath). A/C MINIBAR TEL TV. $180–$200 double; suites at higher rates. Rates include breakfast. 10% service charge and 10% tax. AE, DC, MC, V.

Along with the Forte Grand and the InterContinental, this is one of the three best hotels in Amman, well located, with indoor and outdoor swimming pools and the best and most extensive health club and sports facilities of the major hotels. There

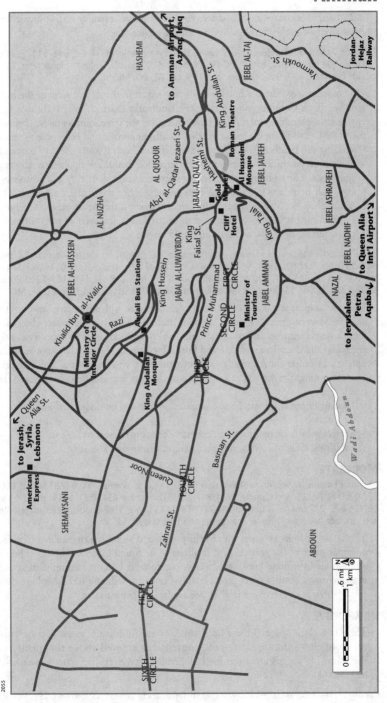

HASHEMI

to Amman Airport, Azraq, Iraq

JEBEL AL-TAJ

Yarmouth St.

Jordan-Hejaz Railway

AL QUSOUR

King Abdullah St.

King Abdullah St.

Abd al-Qadar Jezaeri St.

AL NUZHA

JABAL AL QALA'A

Hashemi St.

Gold Market

Roman Theatre

Al Hussein Mosque

JEBEL JAUFEH

JEBEL ASHRAFIEH

JEBEL AL-HUSSEIN

JABAL AL-LUWAYBIDA

King Faisal St.

Cliff Hotel

King Talal

JEBEL NADHIF

to Queen Alia Int'l Airport ↗

Khalid Ibn al-Walid

Abdali Bus Station

King Hussein

Prince Muhammad

FIRST CIRCLE

SECOND CIRCLE

JABAL AMMAN

Ministry of Tourism

NAZAL

Razi

Ministry of Interior Circle

THIRD CIRCLE

King Abdallah Mosque

to Jerusalem, Petra, Aqaba ↓

to Jerash, Syria, Lebanon ←

Queen Alia St.

American Express

SHEMAYSANI

Basman St.

Wadi Abdoun

Queen Noor

FOURTH CIRCLE

Zahran St.

FIFTH CIRCLE

ABDOUN

SIXTH CIRCLE

N

0   .6 mi
0   1 km

2055

is 24-hour room service, a good selection of in-house restaurants, live music and entertainment in the evenings, and a business service office.

✪**Forte Grand Hotel.** Queen Noor Street, Shemaysani, Amman. ☎ **06/696-511.** Fax 06/674-261. 303 rms (all with bath). A/C TEL TV. $180–$200 double. Suites at higher rates. Rates include breakfast. 10% service charge and 10% tax. AE, DC, MC, V.

This modern, comfortable hotel, one of the newest in the city, is next to the busy Housing Bank Complex, one of the city's landmarks in which over 100 shops and businesses are located. Not quite as high powered as the InterContinental (see below), the Forte Grand is known for its excellent staff; diplomatic and economic missions (including the Israeli mission) have headquartered here. Rooms are very spacious, with welcome amenities such as extra thick terry cloth bathrobes; doubles contain two double beds. The in-house restaurants are above average in quality and reasonably priced, with attendants in traditional dress bringing coffee and Jordanian desserts. The Al Dalal Shop, with excellent Bedouin embroideries, is on the premises. The hotel has a swimming pool, fitness room, tennis courts, sauna, live evening entertainment, a large selection of shops, and 24-hour room service.

Hotel InterContinental Jordan. Jabal Amman, near the Third Circle, Amman. ☎ **06/641-361;** 800/327-0200 in U.S. and Canada; 0181/847-2277 (London) or 0345/581-444 in the U.K. Fax 06/645-217. 400 rms (all with bath). A/C MINIBAR TEL TV. $185–$210 single; $200–$230 double; $345 suite. Rates include breakfast. 10% service and 10% tax. AE, MC, V.

Perhaps the most fast-paced of Amman's deluxe hotels, with a Reuter's News service at its business center, this massive, modern landmark is a very comfortable choice for both business travelers and tourists. Club-level rooms and suites have been recently renovated and decorated with graceful furnishings; standard rooms have not yet been updated. A center for Amman's social life, there are wedding parties and banquets here almost nightly; the goings and comings add extra interest and excitement to the hotel.

Dining/Entertainment: Two restaurants, indoor and outdoor cafes, English pub, bar, nightclub.

Services: 24-hour room service, executive business floor, travel agency.

Facilities: Outdoor swimming pool, shops, hairdresser.

MODERATE

⑨**Amra Forum Hotel.** Amra Street, near the Sixth Circle, Amman. ☎ **06/815-071;** 800/327-0200 in the U.S. and Canada; 0181/847-2277 (London) or 0345/581-444 in the U.K. Fax 06/814-072. 277 rms (all with bath). A/C TEL TV. $115 single; $145 double; $230 junior suite. Rates include breakfast. 10% service charge and 10% tax. AE, MC V.

This attractive four-star hotel with recently renovated rooms has an excellent staff and provides most of the services and facilities to be found in deluxe hotels. There's an outdoor swimming pool, terrace cafe, comfortable hotel restaurant, fitness and massage room, tennis courts, and a business center as well as a travel booking desk and 24-hour room service. Minibars are available in some rooms.

INEXPENSIVE

There is no lack of inexpensive hotels in Amman. At discount rates, package trips can book you into moderate-range hotels that are well above the quality of the following suggestions, but for independent travelers, these are some of the best bets.

Canary Hotel. Jabal al-Luwaybida, across from Terra Sancta College. ☎ **06/654-353.** Fax 06/638-353. 21 rms (all with bath). JD 18 ($25) single; JD 28 ($39) double. AE, V.

Comfortable rooms with radios in a building overlooking one of Amman's older neighborhoods, plus a pleasant garden and a very helpful management, make this an extremely popular choice for budget travelers.

Commodore Hotel. Shemaysani, around the corner from Safeway. ☎ **06/607-185.** Fax 06/668-187. 96 rms (all with bath or shower). JD 30 ($41) single; JD 35 ($49) double. AE, MC, V.

The building is contemporary Middle Eastern nondescript, but the location in upmarket Shemaysani is good, close to the Safeway complex with a variety of moderate and fast-food eating choices. Extra perks include use of the nearby Middle East Hotel's outdoor in-season swimming pool.

American Center for Oriental Research (ACOR). Northwest Amman, behind Amman International Hotel (near Jordan University). ☎ **06/846-117.** Fax 06/844-181. Dorm beds, three to a room. $26 per person; students $21.

This is a center for archeologists and academicians, and it's likely to be packed in the summer. If you can get in, the staff is knowledgeable, rooms are clean, the atmosphere is congenial and well informed. There is a good library, a dining hall serving three meals a day, a laundry, and private shower rooms. The drawback is that it is a bit out of the way. Reservations are necessary. Special long-term rates are available.

WHERE TO DINE
EXPENSIVE

L'Olivier Restaurant. Abdoun, Amman. ☎ **06/819-564.** Reservations required. Complete meals $25–$40. MC, V. Daily 12:30–3:30pm and 7:30pm–midnight. Best visited by taxi. FRENCH.

This is one of the most elegant and expensive restaurants in the city, offering a menu of classic French cuisine. You can be confident of a relaxed, gracious atmosphere here, and a good selection of standard dishes and desserts as well as one of the best wine lists in the country. The building also contains the Arabian Nights Garden Restaurant, and Le Cavalier Pub on the first floor, all under the same management.

MODERATE

Very reasonably priced restaurants with delicious food are one of the pleasures of the Amman scene. You'll find them everywhere; those in the Middle Eastern style are usually the best bets. The following are two especially pleasant suggestions that offer extra style and quality at modest prices.

Al-Bustan. Jordan University Road near the Jerusalem Hotel. ☎ **06/661-555.** Meals $8–$15. MC, V. Daily 12:30–11:30pm. MIDDLE EASTERN.

Al-Bustan (the Garden) is generally acknowledged to turn out the best Arabic-style food in Amman, yet despite its reputation, prices are quite reasonable by most travelers' standards. The restaurant is comfortable, with pleasant service and a wide choice of traditional appetizers, baked dishes, grilled meats, and desserts. Breads are freshly baked. In summer, there is terrace dining.

✪ **Kan Zeman Restaurant.** Yadudda, 7 miles south of Amman off the Desert Highway. ☎ **06/736-449.** Reservations recommended. Middle Eastern buffet $14. AE, MC, V. Daily noon–midnight. A $4 taxi ride from the center of town. MIDDLE EASTERN.

The name of this restaurant means "once upon a time," and the old, atmospheric buidings have been renovated and turned into a complex of workshops and craft stores as well as an establishment serving traditional Middle Eastern food. Although this is an enjoyable spot on the tourist circuit, Jordanians love it as well, and there's an interesting mix of tour groups and locals. You can enjoy a very fine buffet for a relatively modest price, watch bread being made, and stroll around the excellent shops. There is often live music. A must for every visitor to Amman.

INEXPENSIVE

The overwhelming majority of restaurants in Amman, many of them quite good, are in the lower price range. Most budget Middle Eastern–style restaurants do not serve alcoholic drinks; unless they are listed in the menu, it is a good idea not to ask for them, especially during Ramadan.

Abu Ahmed's New Orient Restaurant. 10 Orient St., near the Third Circle. ☎ **06/641-879.** Meals JD 4–JD 10 ($5.60–$14). No credit cards; traveler's checks accepted. Daily noon–midnight. MIDDLE EASTERN.

In summer, this well-known, centrally located place offers garden dining. There are fresh breads, and the standard array of appetizers and grilled main courses, all served with style by a courteous staff. Abu Ahmed's is an Amman institution; another branch of Abu Ahmed's, with good food but less decor, is on Basman Street (☎ 06/636-069). These restaurants are known for the fine quality of their main courses, but appetizers are merely average.

El Maida. In front of the Roman Terrace. ☎ **06/648-445.** Light meals JD 3 ($4.20). No credit cards. Daily 11am–10pm or later. MIDDLE EASTERN.

Perfectly located in a place almost every traveler visits, this informal restaurant serves absolutely delicious Greek-style souvlaki, Indian chicken tikka, Middle Eastern shwarma (your choice of chicken or meat) and shish kebab, and it even ventures into the realms of pizza and sandwiches. The fresh fruit juices are especially welcome. An instant favorite with everyone who tries it.

El Quds (Jerusalem) Restaurant. King Hussein Street near the First Circle. ☎ **06/630-168.** Meals JD 3 ($4.20) and under. No credit cards. Daily 7am–11pm. MIDDLE EASTERN.

The window is filled with Arabic pastries, but inside this busy establishment, you'll find all kinds of traditional Middle Eastern appetizers and dishes. *Mensaf*, a rice, meat, and yogurt dish served *on'aish tanoor* (freshly baked, extra thin pitalike bread) is one of the specialties here; you can also get *mahalabiya*, a traditional thin custard dessert with pistachios. Less daring are the very good grilled meats.

4 Petra

Three and a half to five hours by public transport south of Amman, this is the jewel in the crown of Jordan's attractions, and the main objective of travelers to the country. The canyon city of Petra is vast, mysterious, and really demands a 1- or 2-night stay and 2 full days of exploring to get a feel for the atmosphere, to say nothing of the contents of the ruins.

ESSENTIALS

GETTING THERE   **JETT** offers day excursions from Amman, leaving at 6:30am; the price is JD 35, including lunch, a guide, and a horse; $14 busfare and the admission to Petra are extra. You must reserve well in advance, especially in the fall and spring.

VISITOR INFORMATION   The **Visitors Center** at the entrance to Petra (☎ 03/336-060) is open Saturday through Thursday from 7am to 5pm. Admission to Petra is JD 25 ($35). At the Visitors Center, independent travelers can hire guides for $12 to $80 per trip, depending on how long and how extensive you want your tour to be. Rental of a horse begins at $11. The park is open daily from 6am to 6pm, but guards usually let visitors stay later. A flashlight is necessary if you plan to explore after dark. It's a good idea to bring your own supply of water, but the Bedouin, who until recently inhabited the site, sell refreshments and food inside Petra.

EXPLORING PETRA

You enter Petra through the *siq*, a narrow crevass-canyon lined with niches that once held statues of gods and spirits that protected the city. The incredible siq winds its way through the rocks for a mile before opening to Petra's wonders of rock and light. Traditionally, visitors entered on horseback, or in special carts (these days, with horse manure covering the passageway, walking is not a pleasant alternative). Most visitors now enter on horses that are available for rent near the entrance to the *siq*. As you proceed through the *siq*, you feel as if you are in the shadowy prologue to a mysterious adventure. Indeed, Petra was chosen as the location for the climatic sequence of the film *Indiana Jones and the Last Crusade*.

The Nabataeans, who carved the elaborate palaces, temples, tombs, storerooms, and stables of their city into the solid rock of the cliffs, dominated the Trans-Jordan area in pre-Roman times. They commanded the trade route from Damascus to Arabia; through here the great caravans passed, carrying spice, silk, and slaves. Eventually, Nabataean civilization died, and Petra was virtually forgotten for more than 1,000 years. It was rediscovered by the West in 1812, and was only fully uncovered after 1958. The fabulous facades carved into the rose sandstone cliffs of Petra are exotically Hellenistic rather than classical Greek or even Roman, and reflect the mixture of Western and Eastern, Semitic and European influences in which Nabatean civilization developed.

A guide (or a good guidebook) is necessary as you wander among the hidden canyon's monumental cliff edifices and sites ranging from prehistoric to Crusader times. But also give yourself time to just respond to the romantic mystery and beauty of the place.

WHERE TO STAY

EXPENSIVE

Petra Movenpick Hotel. Petra. ☎ **06/655-345;** 800/344-6835 in the U.S. Fax 06/655-363. 183 rms (all with bath). A/C TEL TV. $160 single; $200 double. Rates include buffet breakfast, service charge, and tax. AE, MC, V.

This sparkling new (opened in 1996) top-quality hotel, right at the entrance to the *siq*, is an extraordinary base for exploring Petra. An interesting lowrise design built of the local rose sandstone, and touched with architectural motifs that echo the facades of Petra itself, the hotel contains spacious guest rooms with terraces and polished stone bathrooms. Included in the complex are an outdoor swimming pool that is covered and heated in winter, a fitness center, sauna, and steam bath, and a wood paneled library with reading material about Petra and Jordan. There are a number of restaurants and cafes, including one in the roof garden, three bars, a shopping arcade with arts and crafts galleries, a local pastry shop, and a Movenpick bakery.

✪ Taybet Zeman Village. Petra. Reservations through International Traders–American Express in Amman, ☎ **06/607-014.** Fax 06/669-905. Bungalow suites and rooms with baths. A/C MINIBAR TEL TV. $160 double, including breakfast. AE, MC, V.

Taybet Zeman is the most beautiful and unusual hostelry in Jordan. The rustic buildings of an abandoned 19th- to early-20th-century village, 5 miles from Petra, have been renovated and decorated in a Bedouin-style chic that could easily grace the pages of *Architectural Digest*. (Indeed, Taybet Zeman has been featured in a number of interior design and architecture publications.) Everything has been carefully done. The rooms have hidden heating and air conditioning, and such modern amenities as minibars are blended into the hotel's design. The complex, with its beautiful tribal crafts for sale in rustic shops and galleries, reminds one of Santa Fe. There is a swimming pool, a fitness center, an attentive staff, and spectacular vistas of the countryside. A traditional bakery and a variety of restaurants are offered. A full range of tourist and guide services for Petra and the vicinity are available. Totally delightful, Taybet Zeman is a memorable addition to the Petra experience.

MODERATE

Petra Forum. Wadi Musa, Petra. ☎ **03/336-266.** Fax 03/336-977. 146 rms (all with bath). A/C MINIBAR TEL TV. $112 single; $126 double; $211 suite. Breakfast additional. 10% service charge and 10% tax. AE, MC, V.

Located on a hill above the entrance to Petra, until recently this modern, very professional hotel was the most expensive and luxurious lodging in the Petra area. The hotel has a swimming pool, a number of restaurants (including one maintained inside Petra), comfortable rooms, and an experienced staff. You can obtain good touring information here and the hotel will even send you off on your explorations with a picnic box.

INEXPENSIVE

Petra Rest House. ☎ **03/336-011.** $35 single; $42 double.

The best choice in the budget range is this well-located place, right at the entrance to the *siq* of Petra. The rooms are clean and simple, though not air-conditioned, and all rooms have private baths. The building is somewhat bland but the restaurant has been built into an ancient Nabatean tomb, and travelers you meet here tend to be interesting people.

5 Other Excursions

Travel agencies in Amman can arrange private or group tours to other important sites.

An interesting excursion is to the Hellenistic/Roman ruined city of **Jerash,** north of Amman. This beautifully preserved city was discovered in 1806; excavations began in the 1920s and are still going on today.

The Byzantine city of **Madaba** has a vast collection of surviving mosaic floors, including one that contains a map of the entire eastern Mediterranean, with a detailed depiction of Jerusalem at its center, showing the Church of the Holy Sepulcher. Medaba can easily be combined with a trip to the nearby **Mount Nebo,** where according to tradition, Moses died and was buried. The views from Mount Nebo are dramatic, and on clear days include the towers of Jerusalem, crowning the mountains far beyond the Dead Sea.

Excursions also include a visit to **Kerak,** the most massive and best preserved of the Crusader castles. If you go to Kerak, you're in a good position to travel on to Petra for the night, rather than return to Amman.

Appendix

A Hebrew Terms & Expressions

The Hebrew alphabet is, of course, entirely unlike our Latin ABCs. Fortunately for us, however, Israelis use the same numerals that we use: 1, 2, 3, 4, etc.

Hebrew has a number of sounds that we don't use in English. They're difficult to communicate in writing, and until you hear them spoken correctly, you may not get the flavor of them. The first is the "ch" or "kh" sound—which you'll find repeatedly in many words throughout the vocabulary. This is not the sound of "ch" in either "change" or "champagne." We don't use this sound in English, and the closest to it are the "ch" sounds in the German exclamation "ach," and in the Yiddish-Hebrew toast "le-chaim." It's a raspy, hacking sound that comes from the back of the mouth.

Another difficult sound, and also very common in Hebrew words, is the "o" sound. The best advice for practicing this sound is to say the word "oh" and halfway through saying the word suddenly cut your voice off. That's what many call a short "o." You get an approximation with the "o" sound in the word "on" and the German word "von," although they're not exactly it either. You just have to cut the "o" short, so when you say the Hebrew word "boker," meaning "morning," you don't "bowker."

USEFUL WORDS

hello **sha-*lom***	good morning ***bo*-ku tov**
good-bye **sha-*lom***	good evening **erev tov**
good night ***lie*-la-tov**	I speak English **ah-*nee* m'dah-*behr* ang-*leet***
I **ah-*nee***	
you **ah-*tah***	I don't speak Hebrew **ah-*nee* lo m'dah-*behr* ee-*vreet***
he **hoo**	
she **hee**	today **hah-*yom***
we **an-*nach*-noo**	tomorrow **ma-char**
where is? ***eye*-fo?**	yesterday **et-*mohl***
there is **yesh**	right (correct) **na-*chon***
there isn't **ain**	too much **yo-*tair* mee-*die***
little **m'*aat***	patience ***sav*-la-*noot***
much **har-*beh***	hands off ***blee* yah-*die*-im**
very **m'*od***	what? **mah?**

so-so *kac*-ha-*ka*-cha
good **tov**
hot **ch*aa*m**
bad **rah**
see you later **le-hit-rah-*ott***
friend **cha-*vare***
excuse me **slee-*cha***
yes **ken**
no **lo**
please **be-var-kah-*sha***
thank you **to-*dah* rah-*bah***
you're welcome **al low da-*vaar***

why? *la*-ma?
how? **aych?**
when? **mah-tiee?**
how long? **kama-zman?**
pleasant **nah-*im***
excellent **met-soo-*yan***
wow, far out **shiga-on**
crazy **me-shugga**
healthy **ba-*ree***
sick cho-*leh*
doctor **row-*feh***
dentist **row-*feh* shin-*eye*-yim**

POST OFFICE

post office **dough-are**
letter **mich-tav**
stamp **bool (pl. bool-im)**
envelopes **ma-ata-*foth***

postcard **gloo-yah**
telegram **miv-rock**
airmail **dough-are ah-*veer***

SHOPPING & STORES

how much is it? *ka*-mah zeh oh-*leh*?
store **cha-*noot***
pharmacy **bait mer-kay-*chat***
barber, hairdresser **mahs-peh-*rah***
shampoo **ha-fee-*fah***

manicure *mah*-nee-koor
appointment **p'gee-*shah***
expensive **ya-*kar***
cheap **zol**

THE COUNTRYSIDE

sea *yaam*
sand **chol**
desert **mid-*bar***
forest **yah-*are***
cold **car**
village **k'far**
road *der*-ech
mountain **har**

hill **giv-*ah***
house **bay-yit**
synagogue **bait k-*ness*-et**
school **bait say-*fer***
newspaper **ee-*tahn***
spring, well **ayn, ma-ay-in, ay-in**
farm *mesh*-ekh
valley *eh*-mek

HOTEL TALK

hotel **meh-*lon***
room *che*-der
water **my-im**
toilet **bait key-*say*, no-chi yoot, she-roo-*teem***
money *kes*-sef
bank **bank**
do you speak English? **ah-*tah* m'dah-*behr* ang-*leet*?**

dining room *che*-der *oh*-chel
bill *chesh*-bon
Mr. (sir) **ah-don-ee**
Mrs. (madam) **g'ver-et**
where is? **ay-fo?**
key **maf-*tay*-ach**
manager **min-ah-*hel***
accommodations **ma-*kom***
balcony **meer-*pes*-eth**

LOCAL TRAVELING

station **ta-cha-nah**
railroad **rah-*keh*-vet**
airport **sde t'u-*fah***

west **m'ar-*av***
north **tsa-*fon***
near **ka-*rov***

bus **auto-boos**
taxi **taxi**
taxi (sherut) **shay-*root***
straight ahead **ya-*shar***
street **re-*chov***
to the right **yeh-*mean*-ah**
to the left **smol-*ah***
south **da-*rom***
east **miz-*rach***

far **rah-*chok***
central **meer-ka-*zith***
bus stop **ta-cha-*naht* ha-auto-boos**
which bus goes to . . .? **eh-zeh auto-boos**
  no-*say*-ah le . . .?
stop here **ah-*tsor* kahn**
to **le**
wait **reg-gah**
trip **tee-*yule***

RESTAURANT & MENU TERMS

to eat **le-eh-*chol***
to drink **lish-toth**
restaurant ***miss*-ah-dah**
food **o-chel**
cafe **ca-*fe***
menu **taf-*root***
breakfast **ah-roo-chat *bo*-ker**
lunch **ah-roo-*chat* tsa-ha-*rye*-im**
dinner **ah-roo-*chat* erev**
waiter **mel-*tsar***
ice cream **glee-*dah***
wine ***yah*-yin**
milk **cha-*lav***
ice **ker-*ach***
veal **e-*gel***
chicken **tar-ne-*gol*-et**
fish **dag**
tea **tay**
coffee **cafe**
vegetables **yeh-rah-*koht***
salad **sal-*at***
fruit **pay-*rote***

apple **ta-*poo*-ach**
orange **tapooz**
tomatoes ***ag*-von-ee-*oat***
butter **chem-*ah***
cheese **g'-vee-nah**
egg ***bayt*-sa**
hard-boiled egg **bay-*tsa* rah-*sha***
soft-boiled egg **bay-*tsa* rah-*kah***
scrambled eggs **bay-*tsim* m-bull-*bell*-et**
fried egg **bay-*tsee*-ah**
soup **ma-*rock***
meat **bah-sahr**
cucumber **mah-la-fe-*fon***
pepper **pil-*pel***
salt **me-*lach***
sugar **sue-*car***
omelet **cha-vi-*tah***
sour **cha-*muts***
sweet **mah-*tok***
bread ***lech*-hem**
satisfy ***save*'a**
hungry **ra'*ev***

DAYS & TIME

Sunday ***yom* ree-*shon***
Monday ***yom* shay-*nee***
Tuesday ***yom* shlee-*shee***
Wednesday ***yom* reh-vee-ee**
Thursday ***yom* cha-mee *shee***
Friday ***yom* shee-*shee***
Saturday ***sha*-baht**
what time? ***ma* ha-sha-*ah*?**

minute **da-*kah***
hour **sha-*ah***
seven o'clock **ha-sha-*ah shay*-va**
day **yom**
week **sha-voo-*ah***
month ***cho*-desh**
year **sha-*nah***

NUMBERS

1	eh-*had*		20	ess-*reem*
2	*sht*a-yim		21	ess-*reem* v'eh-*had*
3	sha-*losh*		30	shlo-*sheem*
4	*ar*-bah		50	cha-mee-*sheem*
5	cha-*maysh*		100	*may*-ah
6	shaysh		200	mah-tah-*yeem*

7	*shev*-vah	300	shlosh may-*oat*
8	sh-*mo*-neh	500	cha-*maysh* may-*oat*
9	*tay*-shah	1,000	elef
10	*ess*-er	3,000	shlosh-*et* elef-*eem*
11	eh-*had* ess-ray	5,000	cha-maysh-*et* elef-*eem*
12	*shtaym*-ess-ray		

B Arabic Terms & Expressions

USEFUL TERMS

please **min fadlak**

thank you **shoo-khraan**

hello **a-halan, mahr-haba**

good-bye **salaam aleikum, ma-ah-salameh**

how are you? **kee falak?**

in the hand of Allah (**reply to "how are you?"**) **'hahm du'allah**

do you speak English? **te-kee Ingleesi?**

what is your name? **shoo ismak?**

my name is . . . **ismay . . .**

how much is this? **ah-desh ha dah?**

yes **ay-wah**

no **la**

good, okay **tay-eeb**

where is? **wain?**

right **yemina**

left **she-mal**

straight **doo-ree**

today **il-yaum**

tomorrow **boo-kra**

pardon **sa-mekh-nee**

coffee **kah-wah**

market, bazaar **suk**

MEASURES & NUMBERS

one kilo **wahad kilo**

half kilo (500 grams) **noos kilo**

100 grams **mia gram**

1 **wa-had**

2 **ti-neen**

3 **talatay**

4 **ar-bah**

5 **ham-seh**

6 **sitteh**

7 **sabah**

8 **tamanyeh**

9 **tay-sa**

10 **a-sha-rah**

50 **ham-seen**

100 **mia**

Index

FROMMER'S COMPLETE TRAVEL GUIDES

(Comprehensive guides to sightseeing, dining, and accommodations, with selections in all price ranges from deluxe to budget)

Acapulco/Ixtapa/Taxco, 2nd Ed.
Alaska, 4th Ed.
Arizona '96
Australia, 4th Ed.
Austria, 6th Ed.
Bahamas '96
Belgium/Holland/Luxembourg, 4th Ed.
Bermuda '96
Budapest & the Best of Hungary, 1st Ed.
California '96
Canada, 9th Ed.
Caribbean '96
Carolinas/Georgia, 3rd Ed.
Colorado, 3rd Ed.
Costa Rica, 1st Ed.
Cruises '95-'96
Delaware/Maryland, 2nd Ed.
England '96
Florida '96
France '96
Germany '96
Greece, 1st Ed.
Honolulu/Waikiki/Oahu, 4th Ed.
Ireland, 1st Ed.
Italy '96
Jamaica/Barbados, 2nd Ed.
Japan, 3rd Ed.

Maui, 1st Ed.
Mexico '96
Montana/Wyoming, 1st Ed.
Nepal, 3rd Ed.
New England '96
New Mexico, 3rd Ed.
New York State '94-'95
Nova Scotia/New Brunswick/Prince
    Edward Island, 1st Ed.
Portugal, 14th Ed.
Prague & the Best of the Czech Republic,
    1st Ed.
Puerto Rico '95-'96
Puerto Vallarta/Manzanillo/Guadalajara,
    3rd Ed.
Scandinavia, 16th Ed.
Scotland, 3rd Ed.
South Pacific, 5th Ed.
Spain, 16th Ed.
Switzerland, 7th Ed.
Thailand, 2nd Ed.
U.S.A., 4th Ed.
Utah, 1st Ed.
Virgin Islands, 3rd Ed.
Virginia, 3rd Ed.
Washington/Oregon, 6th Ed.
Yucatan '95-'96

FROMMER'S FRUGAL TRAVELER'S GUIDES

(Dream vacations at down-to-earth prices)

Australia on $45 '95-'96
Berlin from $50, 3rd Ed.
Caribbean from $60, 1st Ed.
Costa Rica/Guatemala/Belize on $35, 3rd Ed.
Eastern Europe on $30, 5th Ed.
England from $50, 21st Ed.
Europe from $50 '96
Greece from $45, 6th Ed.
Hawaii from $60, 30th Ed.

Ireland from $45, 16th Ed.
Israel from $45, 16th Ed.
London from $60 '96
Mexico from $35 '96
New York on $70 '94-'95
New Zealand from $45, 6th Ed.
Paris from $65 '96
South America on $40, 16th Ed.
Washington, D.C. from $50 '96

FROMMER'S COMPLETE CITY GUIDES

(Comprehensive guides to sightseeing, dining, and accommodations in all price ranges)

Amsterdam, 8th Ed.
Athens, 10th Ed.
Atlanta & the Summer Olympic Games '96

Bangkok, 2nd Ed.
Berlin, 3rd Ed.
Boston '96

Chicago '96
Denver/Boulder/Colorado Springs, 2nd Ed.
Disney World/Orlando '96
Dublin, 2nd Ed.
Hong Kong, 4th Ed.
Las Vegas '96
London '96
Los Angeles '96
Madrid/Costa del Sol, 2nd Ed.
Mexico City, 1st Ed.
Miami '95-'96
Minneapolis/St. Paul, 4th Ed.
Montreal/Quebec City, 8th Ed.
Nashville/Memphis, 2nd Ed.
New Orleans '96
New York City '96

Paris '96
Philadelphia, 8th Ed.
Rome, 10th Ed.
St. Louis/Kansas City, 2nd Ed.
San Antonio/Austin, 1st Ed.
San Diego, 4th Ed.
San Francisco '96
Santa Fe/Taos/Albuquerque '96
Seattle/Portland, 4th Ed.
Sydney, 4th Ed.
Tampa/St. Petersburg, 3rd Ed.
Tokyo, 4th Ed.
Toronto, 3rd Ed.
Vancouver/Victoria, 3rd Ed.
Washington, D.C. '96

FROMMER'S FAMILY GUIDES

(Guides to family-friendly hotels, restaurants, activities, and attractions)

California with Kids
Los Angeles with Kids
New York City with Kids

San Francisco with Kids
Washington, D.C. with Kids

FROMMER'S WALKING TOURS

(Memorable strolls through colorful and historic neighborhoods, accompanied by detailed directions and maps)

Berlin
Chicago
England's Favorite Cities
London, 2nd Ed.
Montreal/Quebec City
New York, 2nd Ed.

Paris, 2nd Ed.
San Francisco, 2nd Ed.
Spain's Favorite Cities
Tokyo
Venice
Washington, D.C., 2nd Ed.

FROMMER'S AMERICA ON WHEELS

(Guides for travelers who are exploring the USA by car, featuring a brand-new rating system for accommodations and full-color road maps)

Arizona and New Mexico
California and Nevada

Florida
Mid-Atlantic

FROMMER'S SPECIAL-INTEREST TITLES

Arthur Frommer's Branson!
Arthur Frommer's New World of Travel, 5th Ed.
Frommer's America's 100 Best-Loved State Parks
Frommer's Caribbean Hideaways, 7th Ed.
Frommer's Complete Hostel Vacation Guide to England, Scotland & Wales

Frommer's National Park Guide, 29th Ed.
USA Sports Traveler's and TV Viewer's Golf Tournament Guide
USA Sports Minor League Baseball Book
USA Today Golf Atlas

FROMMER'S BEST BEACH VACATIONS

(The top places to sun, stroll, shop, stay, play, party, and swim, with each beach rated for beauty, swimming, sand, and amenities)

California
Carolinas/Georgia
Florida
Hawaii

Mid-Atlantic from New York to
Washington, D.C.
New England

FROMMER'S BED & BREAKFAST GUIDES

(Selective guides with four-color photos and full description of the best inns in each region)

California
Caribbean
Great American Cities
Hawaii
Mid-Atlantic

New England
Pacific Northwest
Rockies
Southeast States
Southwest

FROMMER'S IRREVERENT GUIDES

(Wickedly honest guides for sophisticated travelers and those who want to be)

Amsterdam
Chicago
London

Manhattan
New Orleans
San Francisco

FROMMER'S DRIVING TOURS

(Four-color photos and detailed maps outlining spectacular scenic driving routes)

Australia
Austria
Britain
Florida
France
Germany
Ireland

Italy
Scandinavia
Scotland
Spain
Switzerland
U.S.A.

FROMMER'S BORN TO SHOP

(The ultimate travel guides for discriminating shoppers from cut-rate to couture)

Great Britain
Hong Kong

London
New York

FROMMER'S FOOD LOVER'S COMPANIONS

(Lavishly illustrated guides to regional specialties, restaurants, gourmet shops, markets, local wines, and more)

France
Italy